*where art leaves its own field and becomes visible as part of something else*

**visible**
where art leaves its own field and becomes
visible as part of something else

a project by Cittadellarte–Fondazione Pistoletto and Fondazione Zegna
a book edited by Angelika Burtscher and Judith Wielander
Publisher: Sternberg Press


ISBN 978-1-934105-09-2

Translation: Hu Fang, "New Species of Spaces" translated from the Chinese by Hsiao Hwei Yu,
and from Italian to English by Simon Turner
Copy editing: Courtney Johnson
Graphic design: Studio Lupo & Burtscher, Bolzano, Italy
Printing and binding: Agit Mariogros s.r.l., Turin, Italy

Acknowledgements:
Special thanks to the authors, artists, and curators who have contributed to *visible*.
Thanks are also due to Luigi Coppola and Daniele Lupo.

Cittadellarte–Fondazione Pistoletto
via Serralunga 27, I-13900 Biella
www.cittadellarte.it

Fondazione Zegna
via Marconi 23, I-13835 Trivero
www.fondazionezegna.org

Sternberg Press
Caroline Schneider
Karl-Marx-Allee 78, D-10243 Berlin
1182 Broadway #1602, New York, NY 10001
www.sternberg-press.com

# visible
# where art leaves its own field and becomes visible as part of something else

a project by
Cittadellarte–Fondazione Pistoletto
and Fondazione Zegna

edited by
Angelika Burtscher and Judith Wielander

*Sternberg Press*

# visible
## where art leaves its own field and becomes visible as part of something else

Introduction by the editors
Angelika Burtscher and Judith Wielander

The research project and publication, *visible—where art leaves its own field and becomes visible as part of something else,* is the first visible step in a sweeping project undertaken by Cittadellarte– Fondazione Pistoletto in collaboration with Fondazione Zegna.

*visible* examines the spatial relationships within which different players, from different cultural backgrounds and with different temperaments, generate meaning and form alliances. The content that emerges brings into discussion the regime of the visible so that it can then work toward the establishment of a new order. The alliance between actors and spectators brings to life the space of action and of cultural and social relationships.
This first *visible* project brings to light and gives strength to artistic actions which have a true capacity to experiment with and produce visions that can have real impacts on the social and cultural imagination of our contemporary world.

The publishing project, which took shape between the spring of 2009 and 2010, has involved nine curators. They each present recent artistic productions, all of which contain a critical observation of the social, cultural, and political landscapes of which they are part and from which they draw inspiration.

*visible* is based on an idea put forward by Michelangelo Pistoletto, which he originally expressed in 1994 through his *Progetto Arte Manifesto*: "Art is the most sensitive and complete expression of thought and it is time for artists to take upon themselves the responsibility of ensuring communication between all other human activities, from the economy to politics, to science and religion, through to education and behaviour. In other words, all aspects of the social fabric." This vision introduces a substantial and formal repositioning of contemporary art, which is a movement that is now underway on a planetary level, bringing forward innovative ideas of analysis and intervention directed by the artist, and focusing on the geographical, political, and social environment.

The scope and complexity of the phenomena that *visible* places in the spotlight have triggered a whole system of involvement, aperture, and debate. Nine international curators, each with their own methodological and formal approaches and disciplinary backgrounds, share a common awareness that artistic production should be seen as an active force within contemporary society, and as a critical and future-oriented process. In the introductory essays, the curators describe the characteristics of their own research, putting their choices of artists and collectives into context and highlighting the relationships and links that constitute the fundamental models that underpin this publication. Each curator focuses on a particular theme in order to describe the visible and invisible complexities of our everyday world, thus helping put a number of viewpoints into focus. This book contains dialogues on imaginary developments and worlds which reflect on history, examining the public sphere as a field of social and political action, and reflecting on the state and potential of the public realm. *visible* analyzes particular cultural and geographical contexts, clearly expressing their different forms of perception. It points to struggles in social power as a fundamental indicator for the development of society. And it sets in motion discussions about the art system, institutional mechanisms, and the complexity of relationships between power systems. The actions and approaches of *visible* work on the consciousness of the present and of possible changes in contemporary society.

The result of this process is a reconnaissance tour of forty-one artistic positions involved in building or rebuilding the imagination of the present. The interdisciplinary ideas published in this volume consign to art the potential for acting and deciphering commonly acknowledged codes of the world, reinterpreting the events of history, and thus guiding their influence on our future. The positions adopted by *visible* show how we are part of a much broader history, not just from the point of view of art, but also from that of a wider, overarching culture. What are the angles from which events and facts are observed, and how are the conditions of life modified when these perspectives are radically reversed? What is the "we" that to which we refer when we say "we"? The artistic approaches we see in this publication show how it is possible to demolish economic and political strategies and transform invisible processes into both potential and real areas of action. Conflict zones are thus perceived as places where dialogue and debate can be initiated, and thus lead to change.

Even though it began with a selections of curators by area of origin, the research carried out by *visible* doesn't intend to give rise to processes of geographical recognition of particular formal characteristics. On this matter, Boris Groys[1] states that while in the past it was possible to distinguish the various national schools of art and international movements by means of their clear and recognizable signs, artists today are using the same forms and processes around the world, even though they are using them in different cultural and political contexts. The context in which the work is produced is often an intrinsic dimension of the work itself. Works of art do not simply tell us about themselves, for they also allude to the context in which they were made and they can immediately be perceived as signs and symbols, and as information that tells the spectator about the particular conditions that exist in the area of the world they come from.

The forty-one artistic processes described in this publication are ideal

for building up hybrid, transversal, and open narratives. What we find are artistic approaches that, first and foremost, question their own autonomous abilities to act as conduits—with the capacity to connect up different "worlds," often through networks and alliances with territories, artists, thinkers, and public and private institutions. The areas of action and thought that are opened up by these approaches bring today's economic and political decision-making models into serious question. The benefits are not those of self-referential actions in art-based contexts, for the target is the creation of alternative models of public action. Most of the artistic processes we are showing here are detached from institutions and from the normal places of art, for they interact with the public realm or attempt to take over new and carefully targeted scenarios for the creation of culture.
*visible* consequently does not present isolated processes but rather defines a common field of action, a relational space—a public "space of appearance," as Hannah Arendt puts it—in which a form of political action closely linked to circumstance and to the unexpected takes place, submitting itself to a variety of visions and perspectives. This "space of appearance" seeks out and sparks off new reactions, and understands them and puts them on stage, promoting the creation of interactive links.

This publishing project is thus an accumulator of potential energy, which is transformed by a series of concrete actions into available energy. It is a platform on which a number of interrelated modus operandi models are shown. They are brought together in such a way as to give rise to potential new relationships and meanings. Processes in certain in-between areas thus come to light, bringing into question our perception of the visible and, as Jacques Rancière[2] says, combining them with invisible elements and significance: "Artists are those whose strategies aim to change the frames, speeds and scales according to which we perceive the visible, and combine it with a specific invisible element and a specific meaning. Such strategies are intended to make the visible invisible or to question the self-evidence of the visible; to rupture given relationships between things and meanings and, inversely, to invent novel relationships between things and meanings that were previously unrelated."

**Notes**

1 Boris Groys, *Back From the Future in 2000 + Arteast Collection*, (Bolzano/Vienna: Folio Verlag, Bolzano/Vienna, 2000)

2 Jacques Rancière, *Dissensus On Politics and Aesthetics*, (London: Continuum, 2010)

# visible
# An Interview With Michelangelo Pistoletto

by Judith Wielander

***Judith Wielander*** — Michelangelo, I'd like to start this interview by attempting to understand the historical, political, and social scenario that brought about the need to start up the *visible* project.

***Michelangelo Pistoletto*** — In the first part of the twentieth century, an unprecedented level of autonomy of art was achieved in society throughout the Western world. A form of *orthodoxy* was imposed, and this led personal and subjective expression to its extreme consequences. The 1960s, however, introduced a different approach, which acknowledged that the acquisition of this independence had been of fundamental importance, but that led the artistic avant-garde to abandon its subjective position and to orient itself toward a new understanding of *objectivity*. The concept of objectivity led to widespread recognition of the artistic message, and art came back into contact with the world and reestablished direct links with society. Artists thus went beyond subjectivity, but they maintained the value of autonomy, and they incorporated this autonomy in their process of objectification. A number of movements in the 1960s moved in this direction, and they ranged from Neo Dada to Pop Art and Arte Povera, and to actions that started out from performance and from relational and process art. They later tended toward an artistic approach that was increasingly detached from the object-based nature of the work and from market logic, thereby creating the premises for what I refer as *heterodox* art. This artistic approach brings the intellect and creativity into direct contact with all spheres of society—toward what, taking up an idea from Marx, Paolo Virno has referred to as *general intellect*. In post-Fordist society, what matters is thought and movement, rather than the object itself. While on the one hand artistic *orthodoxy* is increasingly closed within its own self-referentialism, the *heterodox* paradigm makes art integrate into society as a whole. What is being opened up now is a third paradigm, which I would call *interodox*. It is what comes "in between"—in other words, between the two previous paradigms. Acting as a bridge between them, the *interodox* movement injects new lifeblood both into the self-centered world of art and into a form of art that extends into the most diverse areas of the social fabric. *visible* puts the spotlight precisely on this *interodox* artistic ferment. An art that does not just create the object, but that also creates a place for it. Art as an event that transforms places. Art as a force that transforms both society and art itself. It is only like this that art can preserve its own autonomy, which would otherwise run the risk of being swallowed up by systems of (especially economic) power, as occurred previously at the hands of religion and of the aristocracy. Today's economic aristocracy is attempting to represent its own liberalism through art. Art, which closes in on itself, lives in the illusion that it is autonomous, whereas it is actually becoming increasingly representative of a space that is not its own. A space in which it is used as an economic symbol, and thus in which it is intellectually transformed. I believe that there is always a profound and poetic intimacy in art—an invisible space that can be drawn upon, but if it does not have an autonomous area of its own outside of an economically and politically subjugated art system, its poetic creativity ends up by betraying its basic freedom, or by altering its integrity. If it then attempts to isolate itself, it ends up hiding deep in its burrow, without really taking part in the world. *visible* starts as an inevitable necessity to bring to the light those aspects of art that escape the spotlight of the economy, which is mainly interested in action through the *orthodox* phenomenon. *visible* attempts to broaden the beam of light, or rather focus it on the *interdox* practices that are emerging. All too often these practices remain in the shadows because they do not satisfy the demands of a glamorous media-based economy.

***Judith Wielander*** — How have these opinions formed through your work?

***Michelangelo Pistoletto*** — The works I made in the early 1960s, such as *Quadri specchianti* ("Mirror Paintings") and my *Oggetti in meno* ("Minus Objects"), expanded my view of the world. Indeed, when society, with all its complexity, entered the mirror, it acquired a dominant role in my works and dragged me out of the painting and into the places of everyday life. And this is how street performances first came about in the second half of the 1960s: they were a creative encounter with artists who worked with different art forms in an attempt to develop artistic activities that were increasingly integrated into the mechanisms of everyday life. Creative joint ventures continued into the following decades until the creation of Cittadellarte, a non-state-controlled institution, in the 1990s. Cittadellarte actually arises from the artist, and thus from art itself, developing autonomously by interacting directly with all sectors of society. In this fertile creative ground, it is not only artistic languages that come together but also the mechanisms of politics and of the economy, communication, production, education, religion, and so on.

***Judith Wielander*** — The system of orthodox art has created a neutral space in which objects can be presented, and artists are giving a clear signal that this system has broken down. In your opinion, what are the mechanisms and roles that artists, curators, and the institutions can expect, and how should they change and reinvent themselves to respond to the new needs you are talking about?

***Michelangelo Pistoletto*** — I think that curators and artists need to work together. Like in the 1950s and 1960s, when gallery owners were artists' accomplices, we now need to bring about new forms of synergy. The institutions shouldn't decide in advance, seeking out curators who strictly adhere to pre established decisions. Both artists and curators need to realize that they are prime movers and that they are aesthetically and ethically involved in these changes. Right now, they need to identify within the social context the fundamental elements required for the creation of the artistic product. The institutions too can benefit by making sure that those curators who are truly committed to a new artistic ethic start shouldering responsibility. If this is achieved, it will be possible to purify an art system that is jeopardized by an economy which overshadows the power of art. These artists and critics, whom I would refer to as "artivators," will be of enormous use to society, for they will allow museums to become proactive, and not just places of preservation. The new task facing art institutions is to place *art at the center of a responsible form of social transformation.* This is what we are attempting to do at Cittadellarte.

***Judith Wielander*** — We can see a renewed interest in this regeneration of art and of its institutions on a number of fronts. For example, there is renewed interest in bringing art out of the institutions, and in the global south and in areas of conflict and crisis, this is partly because the institutions themselves are lacking. Do you see links between this and the impetus you felt in the 1960s and 1970s?

***Michelangelo Pistoletto*** — In those days we went out into the streets because it seemed to us that the institutions were like closed cages, for they didn't give us the dynamism we needed in order to work on interaction with society. On the other hand, we can now see that institutions simply don't exist in many countries. Here too, with a lack of institutions on the one hand and an excess of institutionalization on the other, what is emerging is an unprecedented situation, something *in between*, which is leading art to act in very new and different spheres. This situation is not exclusive to the world of art, but it is much more generalized. Fierce criticism about the present socio-economic system and a recognition of the need for change is spreading everywhere. The creation of new organizations capable of changing the art system is a response to far broader social, political, and economic needs. These needs are emerging all together, extending into the global network and finding areas of implementation through interaction. During the Futurist period in the early years of the last century, progress was seen as a vast territory to be conquered, and the artistic avant-garde was also linked to models for the development of production, which shaped the popular imagination. Progress has now reached saturation point and there is a need for cooperation between art and public life, in order to guide society toward a different destiny.

***Judith Wielander*** — Looking back to the historical processes in our Western world, it would seem that the one that started up in the 1960s and 1970s has not been consistent through to the present day. There have been abrupt fractures and changes of direction. A series of historical processes in the 1980s and 1990s interrupted this transformation and possibly even took it backwards. Artists, curators, and cultural practitioners are currently seeking links with those experiences—here I have in mind this renewed interest in participative and community practices, as well as the work that is being carried out on historical memory and identity.

*Michelangelo Pistoletto* — A penalty for the previously excessive impetuousness and aggressiveness was paid in the 1980s and 1990s, when the dream of 1968 turned into a nightmare, because the slogan "Power to Art" was applied with heedless political violence. In general terms, another key historic moment came with the fall of the Berlin Wall, which transformed the previous territorial, political, and economic order. The interesting hiatus that was briefly created was then absorbed by a globalizing system that was consumerist in nature. Art was gradually relegated to a system of its own, which reflected the general trend of society. In those years, the power of the art market expanded in the West with the discovery of artists in developing countries, such as China and India, and Africa as well. But it was a superficial interest based only on an itching for novelty which could be forced onto the market. It was only in the late 1990s that the economic growth of emerging countries upset the world order. Many artists realized that the situation needed to be taken from the beginning and they once again started looking at the way things had been in the late 1970s.

*Judith Wielander* — Your own artistic progress does not, however, appear to have been interrupted in this way.

*Michelangelo Pistoletto* — As far as I'm concerned, I have always been moving in the same direction. In those in-between periods I embarked on an even more profound reflection on the processes that I had been working on. I continued looking at society in the mirror to understand how to return to society itself in an even more focused manner. And this led, for example, to Creative Collaborations in the late 1970s, and this experience has extended all the way through to the present day Cittadellarte. These operations worked on the artistic mechanisms that, like the Zoo, had started up in the second half of the 1960s. In 1979, for example, it gave rise to a huge workshop that involved many public sectors and spaces in Atlanta, Georgia. I was invited to the city by the first black mayor in the United States—whose election was a significant step toward the election of a black American president.

*Judith Wielander* — Other important experiences that reveal your wish to open up and hand on to the younger generations and, at the same time, to work toward the creation of an art that is committed to social change include those of teaching at the academy in Vienna, setting up Cittadellarte in Biella, and running the Biennale Arte Giovane in Turin.

*Michelangelo Pistoletto* — Throughout the 1990s, the works we created with the young people at the academy in Vienna were not focused solely on the art object, however intimist, sensitive, or inventive it might have been, but especially on the relationship between art and the world. With my students I was attempting to open up new vistas toward society. The idea was to change the *habit,* the *habitus,* and the *habitat*. At the same time, I was starting up Cittadellarte in Biella, working on those very principles. It is no coincidence that the first project that took real shape in this institution was exactly the *Università delle Idee—UNIDEE*: young people from all over the world who came together for four months to experiment with new forms of artistic action, creating social change through art. In 2002 I was asked to direct the Biennale Internazionale Giovani in Turin, which I entitled *Big Social Game*—a game to change society. The Biennale took place in the open spaces in the city and in the surrounding areas of Piemont.

*Judith Wielander* — For the Biennale, you asked the artists to live in the city with a residency programme and to detect and react to the needs that emerged from the social fabric.

*Michelangelo Pistoletto* — The main aim was to establish direct contact with the real situation in the city, rather than just presenting art in a "white cube." Many of the artists invited, such as Lara Almarcegui, etoy, Dominik Hislop & Erhardt Miklós, Andreja Kuluncic, Superflex, Jerôme Bel, n55, Rene Gabri and e-Xplo, Christoph Schäfer, Marcelo Expósito, Michael Blum, Anri Sala, Leopold Kessler, Maja Bajevic, Yto Barrada, Xavier Le Roy, Sislej Xhafa, and many others continued along these lines and acquired visibility. And there were also artists who wanted to carry out violent political actions—pure protest: with them, we attempted to reach some form of mediation and to beat the aggressiveness that unfortunately some still aren't able to overcome, even now. While on the one hand we need to react proactively to the passiveness of the institutions, and on the other hand we should never indulge in forms of aggressive intolerance. It's always necessary to move forward with restraint. It's more interesting to work *in between*, discovering the power and energy that emerges from the polarization of conflicting forces.

*Judith Wielander* — Coming back to the idea of *visible*, a good deal of the practices reported by the nine curators are in no way connected to the logic of the market: they do not create objects, but rather relationships, considerations, revelations, and proposals. How do you think these can be received by art institutions that are mainly focused on the idea of the commercialization of art? How can these practices find their own form of support?

*Michelangelo Pistoletto* — I think that the problem of support can be solved *in between*. When I was teaching in Vienna, I was dealing with very young people from Eastern countries, and who thought of art as a projection into the future: for them it was a vital choice. Almost all of them used to work in the evenings as waiters, and they would experiment with art during the day. Art was a mission for them, a way of overcoming the state of coercion they'd experienced in countries behind the Iron Curtain. When the Berlin Wall fell, it created the most wonderful void—the void we need to create in order to change our sphere of action. This is what I mean when I talk about creating a "space for the object," because I think that otherwise one tends to work in a cushy dimension that might just as well be communist as consumerist. It's also possible to change our way of earning, and this can be a creative act. We must however be aware that we are floating on a consumerist system based on two factors: hyper-production on the one hand, and the idea of the uniqueness of a brand on the other. And the media have become at once a means and an end. The frantic striving to appear in the media is the ephemeral transmutation of self into light and image. It gives concrete form to what Andy Warhol suggested, in his American vision, that we can all have our brief moment of glory. Burning our lives in order to be light and image for a few seconds. It's like the attraction, the fatal attraction of the mosquito to the lamp. There may be something very ancient in this idea: it's probably linked to a timeless need for ritual. Rites have always involved people in a process of liberation from the burdens of everyday life. But only the priests drew economic benefit from their rites. What rites do the high priests of art think they can live on today? According to what aesthetic and what ethic? Artists can also be like worker-priests, though not priests of religion—only of art and of life. Art needn't be afraid to find its way through all these phenomena—indeed, acting within this incredible complexity can open up the most extraordinary horizons. This also concentrates the most poetic talent of the artist: that of giving tangible form to the invisible. The direction is the opposite of that of religious sublimation, which attempts to evaporate the tangible. Making visible also means giving human form to what religion attempts to have us see as celestial or diabolical.

*Judith Wielander* — From the studies that have been selected we can see that the artist, like others who work on the tangible, is a creator of knowledge—a transversal knowledge that augments the ability of criticism to reveal complex and invisible systems in order to make way for new propositions and possibilities.

*Michelangelo Pistoletto* — The knowledge of the artist needs to be combined with other forms of knowledge. It can't be considered as absolute and unique, for his autonomy needs to help penetrate all other forms and spheres. The artist must know how to make best use of other forms of knowledge.

*Judith Wielander* — Categories of knowledge, such as history, science, and economics, often move within rigid and clearly established confines. As Jacques Rancière says, enacting art actually means "displacing the borders of art and questioning its limits and powers."

*Michelangelo Pistoletto* — That's true: many categories of knowledge are well aware of their own limits. The artist, however, has this ability to be "in between"—between the various territories—and thus to open up possible new confines and to link together these areas of knowledge.

*Judith Wielander* — Another line of research that can be perceived in the artistic practices which have been selected is that of history, identity, and the need to generate a new political and social order which can include and grant representation to those who are excluded from it.

*Michelangelo Pistoletto* — Acquiring or reacquiring an identity is fundamental. It is personal or collective positioning that allows us to act within the public domain. Identity is acquired through knowledge and understanding. The language of the Net is an incredibly powerful instrument at our disposal: it enormously speeds up knowledge as it makes it shareable by all.

*Judith Wielander* — How do you think the relationship between local and global is changing as a result of the development of the language of the Net?

*Michelangelo Pistoletto* — The Net is representative of the potential for each individual, and for each node, to play a fundamental role. Even small cultural and territorial families, which are concealed by the dynamics of traditional capitalist mechanisms, feed into and are fed by the Net. We need to look for these small fires and make them visible, stoke them up and not devour them, for they are what will allow a new global society to take shape. But if an oasis is not constantly supplied with water, it dies and is taken over by the desert. The artist can be the ideal custodian of these small paradises: in an etymological sense, a "paradise" is a fenced, protected place, in the midst of a barren desert. Preserving oases cannot be achieved without daily commitment—great daily commitment. Much of what we save today will be the knowledge of tomorrow.

# Nomadic Territories and Times

a text contribution by
Saskia Sassen

The curators have brought together artwork that has the potential to make legible critical aspects of the current moment.[1] I want to single out a few aspects that are bubbling in the discussions but that somehow remain slippery. I want to grab this slippery intimation of something that is part of the transformation we are living, even as it remains opaque. But I do this not as an art critic or historian. Mine is a very different language, and I can only hope for a dialogical intersection with the vocabularies of art.

There are rumblings in these artworks that signal that there is much happening beneath the surface of our modernity. I see these rumblings in the tension between a generic modernity that can be globally present and the thick, situated making of a range of dimensions present in some of these artworks—the making of place, of events, of the political. In much of the work, this thick, situated making becomes part of artistic practice, and, I think, a heuristic in that it allows us to see something that gets lost in the visual order of our modernity, one marked by generalities and the generic. Artists can detect, and see, in ways that those of us shaped or confined by prose cannot.

This work illuminates some of the issues I am grappling with in prose. For many readers—perhaps most—my prose may seem completely unconnected to these works of art. All I can hope for is the possibility of a dialogic that transcends the one-to-one equivalence that is a zone of comfort. The fact of a generic modernity beneath which lies the possibility/necessity of thick, situated making is, in my reading, one version of what I see as a defining dynamic or systemic logic at work today. It is, also one that gets easily lost in accounts that only take in the generic, the standardized, the "globalized." Here, then, are some thoughts offered as a way of disentangling some issues about globalization, the national, and the interactions between globality as a generic standardization and globality as a kind of thick making that can take place anywhere.

At its deepest level, today's emergent realities and possibilities are a sort of unshackling of foundational categories of social existence (time, subjectivity, territory, authority, rights) from their national encasing. We lack the language with which to capture the thousands of operations that are worming themselves into the established national cages for these foundational elements. These are the cages produced by the project of building the nation-state and the work of rendering all building blocks of social existence as national, albeit never fully achieved.[2]

Today, territory and time, subjectivity and identity, are beginning to seep out of these national cages. This easily gets experienced as disorder and crisis, because this nation-state-building project standardizes, bureaucratizes, and nationalizes time, territory, and identity. Although it never completely succeeded, the nation-state-building project constituted the organizational formats, the notions of justice and ethics, and the subjectivities of belonging and identity that have dominated during the last century. A synthetic way of saying this is that when the national state is the dominant format, the overarching dynamic is centripetal: the center grasps most of what there is to be had. And what happened outside the borders of territorial states—whether in the impoverished terrains of former empires or at the earth's poles—was written out of history.

Elsewhere I have developed the notion of denationalization as a category for analysis that aims at capturing a specific set of components in today's major global transformations, for which the typical terms in use—globalization, postnationalism, and transnationalism—are inadequate. These three terms all point to locations for change that lie outside the nation-state. The effort behind developing a fourth category—denationalization—arises out of an as yet small but growing body of research showing that critical components of today's major transformations actually take place inside the nation-state. The processes that constitute the transformation in this case have the effect of denationalizing that which has historically been constructed as national. These processes are partial, often highly specialized, and obscure. Further, they frequently continue to be coded, represented, and experienced in the vocabulary of the national, and hence can remain unrecognized and undetected. Thus, this new category for analysis opens up a vast research and theorization agenda connected to global trends but focused on the nation-state.

Today's catastrophic conditions—the melting of the glaciers, the radicalness of today's poverty, the violence of extreme economic inequality, the genocidal character of more and more wars—are often seen as part of major "negative" change, of our decay. But it seems to me that they are not new, but rather that they are just becoming visible today in novel ways. They have been there all along, and they are part of our deep past. They are part of that putative no-man's-land that absorbed the costs of the making of nation-states and capitalism over the last few centuries. They are floating signifiers, speech acts that narrate the current condition in a far more encompassing manner than standard narratives about nation-states and globalization. While these conditions have existed for a long time, today they are crossing new thresholds and, crucially, they become legible as the cages of the national begin to fall apart and reveal the landscapes of devastation on which they were built. "Our over-cantilevered bridge cannot cope with the warming waters below."[3]

We are seeing a proliferation of partial, often highly specialized assemblages of bits of territory, authority, and rights once firmly ensconced in national institutional frames which today begin to escape the cages of the national. These assemblages cut across the binary of national versus global. They are well beyond this binary, which is the usual way of attempting to understand what is new today. These emergent assemblages inhabit both national and global institutional and territorial settings. They can be localized, and in that localness have the (powerful) effect of denationalizing bits of national territory. Or, they can span the globe in the form of translocal geographies connecting multiple, often thick subnational spaces—institutional, territorial, subjective. One aspect that matters here is that these thick, subnational settings are building blocks for new global geographies. They do not run through supranational institutions that take out that thickness and generalize across differences. Globalization has brought with it an incipient unbundling of the exclusive authority over territory, people, and identity that we have long associated directly and indirectly with the national state. One way of conceptualizing this unbundling is to posit that it entails a dynamic of denationalizing what had been constructed as the "national" over the last century and more. This construction of the national was in many, though not all, parts of the world a political, economic, legal, and culturally thick process. Thus, current dynamics of globalization need to be understood in the context of this thickly constituted national.

These thick, sub-national settings are building blocks for new global geographies. They do not run through supranational institutions that take out that thickness and generalize across differences. Today's transformation does not simply refer to that which transcends the national, as is commonly asserted. It names a far more complex and ambiguous negotiation that happens largely inside multiple instances of the national. Such a conceptualization relocates the analytic task from the macro level of interdependencies and cross-border flows to microsites that may well remain coded as national. It is an analytic inversion of the usual strategy used to address or study or represent transnationalism and also globalization.

There are sites where these dynamics of denationalization take on thick and consequential forms. Among these sites are, from the perspective of my own research experience, global cities. The global city is a border zone where the old spatialities and temporalities of the national and the new ones of the global digital age become engaged in complex, multi-sited, and multilevel ways. Out of this juxtaposition comes the possibility of a whole series of new economic and cultural projects. Conceivably there are other sites, including microsites, where the juxtapositions of different spatialities and temporalities are likely to be thick and charged. The centrality of place in a context of global processes engenders a transnational economic, subjective, and political opening in the formation of new claims and hence in the constitution of entitlements, notably of rights to place, and, at the limit, in the constitution of "citizenship" as a more urbanized and less formalized condition. The denationalizing of urban space and the formation of new claims centered in transnational actors and involving contestation raise the question: Whose city is it?

If this lens is used to look at some current, often minor and barely visible, developments, it opens up some interesting vistas.[4] For instance, this way of narrating the current period allows us to reposition immobility, at a time when the focus is on mobility as an indicator of globality. If globalities are constituted inside the national, then the immobile can be global actors, if they care to—their bodies do not cross the borders of national states, but that does not preclude their being part of global subjectivities and politics. And while the immobile are likely to be among the disadvantaged, the condition is less absolute and less oppressive than the emphasis on mobility suggests. Their powerlessness can become complex and thereby contain the possibility of politics, of making the political. Localized struggles by actors who are not globally mobile are nonetheless critical for the organizational infrastructure of a globally networked politics: it is precisely the combination of localized practices and global networks that makes possible a new type of power for actors who would be seen as powerless in terms of conventional variables. While geographically immobile, these localized actors and their practices are also inflected by their participation and constitutive role in global civil society. Even if contained within an administrative unit of a national state, they are not simply local.

The dominant narrative or mainstream account of globalization is a narrative of eviction. Key concepts in the dominant account of globalization suggest that place no longer matters. It is an account that privileges the capability for global transmission over the concentrations of built infrastructure that make transmission possible; that privileges information outputs over the workers producing those outputs, from specialists to secretaries; and that privileges the new transnational corporate culture over the multiplicity of cultural environments, including reterritorialized immigrant cultures, within which many of the "other" jobs of the global information economy take place. The focus is on the upper circuits of capital and with global power and powerful new capabilities.

The importance of accounts, such as these works of art, that make visible that which remains obscured and opaque in mainstream narratives is that they signal that powerlessness can be complex in that it can make history, and it can make the political. And this is so even if the actors are immobile and the work is place-centered. The partial unbundling of the national through the insertion of the global in that national produces a rescaling of old hierarchies—running from the local, regional, and national, on to the global. Going to the next scale in terms of size is no longer how integration is achieved. The local now transacts directly with the global: the global installs itself in locals and the global is itself constituted through a multiplicity of locals. The distinction between the global and the local—notably in the assumption about the necessity of proximity in the constitution of the "local"—needs to be rethought. Ultimately, much of the artwork in question is disassembling the national as the dominant encasement for membership, security, subjectivity, legitimacy, and politics. In this process it points to new, possibly already emergent, assemblages of these critical dimensions.

**Notes**

1 *visible—where art leaves its own field and becomes visible as part of something else*, ed. Angelika Burtscher and Judith Wielander (Berlin: Sternberg Press, 2010).

2 For a full development of these issues see Saskia Sassen, *Territory, Authority, Rights: From Medieval to Global Assemblages*, (Princeton: Princeton University Press, 2006).

3 Hilary Koob-Sassen, Serpentine Gallery Manifesto Marathon, *Faith in Infrastructure*, Serpentine Gallery, London, October 18, 2008. See: www.TheErrorists.com

4 See here also Roland Kapferer, "Interview. Women on the Move," *Frieze Magazine*, no. 105 (March 2007).

**Angelika Burtscher** was born in Austria, lives in Bolzano, Italy, and works as a designer and curator since 2002. She is a partner in the design studio Lupo & Burtscher, and in 2003 founded the project and exhibition platform Lungomare with designer Daniele Lupo. Lungomare opened as an experimental and project–related platform to rethink and give space to the interdisciplinary aspects among design, architecture, urban planning, art, and theory. The studio develops a wide range of design projects, and is above all interested—in exchange with Lungomare—in the multidisciplinary approach to design. Lupo & Burtscher develops communication campaigns, book designs, corporate identities, and communication projects in public space, and works in direct contact with artists and curators to realize exhibition designs and catalogues. In 2009 she co-authored, with Daniele Lupo, Alvise Mattozzi, and Paolo Volontè, the book *Biografie di oggetti / Storie di cose* (Bruno Mondadori) and in 2008, with Manuela Demattio and Roberto Gigliotti she wrote *Dream City Us —Exercises for Urban Perception* (Studienverlag, Innsbruck). She was appointed to a research position in the design department at the Jan Van Eyck Akademie in Maastricht in 2009.

> www.lupoburtscher.it

> www.lungomare.org

**Saskia Sassen** is the Lynd Professor of Sociology and Member, The Committee on Global Thought, Columbia University (www.saskiasassen.com). Her recent books are *Territory, Authority, Rights: From Medieval to Global Assemblages* (Princeton University Press, 2008), *A Sociology of Globalization* (W. W. Norton, 2007), the third fully updated *Cities in a World Economy* (Sage, 2006), the edited *Deciphering the Global* (Routledge, 2007), and the co-edited *Digital Formations: New Architectures for Global Order* (Princeton University Press, 2005). Her books are translated into twenty-one languages. She serves on several editorial boards and is an advisor to several international bodies.

**Michelangelo Pistoletto** was born in Biella in 1933. He began to exhibit his work in 1955, and in 1960 he had his first solo show at Galleria Galatea in Turin. An inquiry into self-portraiture characterizes his early work. In the two-year period 1961–1962, he made the first *Mirror Paintings*, which directly include the viewer and real time in the work, and open up perspective, reversing the Renaissance perspective that had been closed by the twentieth-century avant-gardes. These works quickly brought Pistoletto international acclaim, leading, in the 1960s, to one-man shows in important galleries and museums in Europe and the United States. The *Mirror Paintings* are the foundation of his subsequent artistic output and theoretical thought. In 1965 and 1966, he produced a set of works entitled *Minus Objects*, considered fundamental to the birth of Arte Povera, an art movement of which Pistoletto was an animating force and a protagonist. In 1967 he began to work outside traditional exhibition spaces, with the first instances of that "creative collaboration" he developed over the following decades by bringing together artists from different disciplines and diverse sectors of society. In 1975–1976 he presented a cycle of twelve consecutive exhibitions, *Le Stanze*, at Galleria Stein in Turin. This was the first of a series of complex, year-long works called *time continents*. Others are *White Year* (1989) and *Happy Turtle* (1992). In 1978, in a show at Galleria Persano in Turin, Pistoletto defined two main directions his future artwork would take: Division and Multiplication of the Mirror and Art Takes On Religion. In the early eighties he made a series of sculptures in rigid polyurethane, translated into marble for his solo show in 1984 at Forte di Belvedere in Florence. From 1985 to 1989 he created the series of "dark" volumes called *Art of Squalor*. During the nineties, with *Project Art* and with the creation in Biella of Cittadellarte–Fondazione Pistoletto and the University of Ideas, he brought art into active relation with diverse spheres of society with the aim of inspiring and producing responsible social change. In 2003 he won the Venice Biennale's Golden Lion for Lifelong Achievement. In 2004 the University of Turin awarded him a *laurea honoris causa* in Political Science. On that occasion the artist announced what has become the most recent phase of his work, *Third Paradise*. In 2007, in Jerusalem, he received the Wolf Foundation Prize in the Arts. In 2008, Pistoletto—Cittadellarte was awarded the Special Prize City of Sasso Marconi, for innovative languages of communication. Preparing for 2010 the retrospective at the Contemporary Art Museum, Philadelphia. Recently Michelangelo Pistoletto was nominated artistic director of the second edition of the Bordeaux Urban Art Biennale, Evento 2011.

> www.cittadellarte.it

**Judith Wielander** is a curator of contemporary art projects focusing on public art and cultural activation. She currently works at the Art Office of Cittadellarte—Fondazione Pistoletto where she curated and co-curated exhibitions and conferences such as *Contemporary Myths, Place Beyond Borders, Turning-point Literature—Writing the Transformation* and *Michelangelo Pistoletto & Cittadellarte* at MUHKA Antwerp. She has collaborated with numerous museums and centers of contemporary art, including the Biennial Big Social Game in Turin, Museion, Arge Kunst–Galleria Museo and Gokart in Bolzano. She is a founding member of Agenzia n-2, a locally grounded cultural activation project, and co-curator of the project *Atti Democrati*.

Raimundas Malašauskas
Pedro Reyes
Patrick Bernier + Olive Martin
Francisco Camacho
Darius Mikšys
Judi Werthein

Gabi Ngcobo & Elvira Dyangani Ose
Wanda Raimundi-Ortíz
Nástio Mosquito
Mlu Zondi
Frente 3 de Fevereiro
Fadaiat: Observatorio Tecnológico del Estrecho
Gugulective

Emiliano Gandolfi
Goddy Leye
Teddy Cruz
Jeanne van Heeswijk
Santiago Cirugeda (Recetas Urbanas)
Bert Theis

Hu Fang
Zheng Guogu
Xu Tan
Ming Wong
Sou Fujimoto Architects
Cao Fei

Anna Colin
Neil Cummings and Marysia Lewandowska
Goldin+Senneby
CAMP
Ana Laura López de la Torre
Maria Thereza Alves

Cecilia Canziani
Alterazioni Video
Anna Scalfi
Progetto Diogene
Aspra.mente
Publink

Julietta Gonzáles
Jesús Bubu Negrón
Paul Ramírez Jonas
Javier Téllez
Anna Best
Tercerunquinto

Mihnea Mircan
Ciprian Mureşan
Jill Magid
Jonas Staal
Alon Levin
Offer & Exchange

**Raimundas Malašauskas** is a writer who was until recently a curator-at-large of Artists Space, New York; from 2007–2008, a Visiting Curator at California College of Arts, San Francisco; from 1995–2006, a curator at CAC Vilnius and CAC TV (also known as *Every program is a pilot, every program is the final episode*); and in 2007, co-wrote the libretto of *Cellador*, the opera in Paris. His works evolve around contemporary phenomena, persons, biographies, and stories, addressing the parallel worlds of science, media, film, literature, and mass culture.
> www.rye.tw

**Pedro Reyes** was born 1972 in Mexico City, and lives and works in Mexico City. The work of Pedro Reyes addresses the interplay between physical and social space, making tangible the invisible geometry of our personal relationships. His expanded notion of sculpture examines the cognitive contradictions of modern life, and the possibility of overcoming our particular crises by increasing our individual and collective degree of agency. His work has been shown at South London Gallery; Museum of Contemporary Art, Chicago; the Aspen Art Museum, Colorado; the Reina Sofia, Madrid; Yvon Lambert Gallery, NewYork; the Jumex Collection, Mexico City; P.S.1, New York; Kunstwerke, Berlin; Museo-estudio Luis Barragan, Mexico City; the Kunsthalle Wien, Vienna; the Witte de With, Rotterdam; the Shanghai Bienniale; the Seattle Art Museum; the Venice Biennale; and the Carpenter Center for Visual Arts at Harvard University.
> www.pedroreyes.net

**Patrick Bernier** was born in 1971 in Paris and selectively participates in group exhibitions in France and abroad, and gives accounts of the projects deployed on these occasions by the intermediary of a collaboration with Carlos Ouedraogo, a storyteller from Burkina Faso. He was also an activist for an association for solidarity with immigrant workers in Nantes, giving legal and writing assistance. He is engaged in the struggle for equal rights between Europeans and foreigners, notably in terms of freedom of movement and settlement.

**Olive Martin** was born in 1972 in Liège, Belgium and works in a way that questions the notion of identity, its travesties, and its tendencies and pursues the idea of an "ordinary singularity" in her photos and films. She produced books in collaboration with the American writer April Durham, titled *Common Objects* (published at Joca Seria in France and Beyond Baroque books in the US), and *Américains d'Amériques* (self produced).

**Patrick Bernier and Olive Martin** first met at the Ecole des Beaux Arts in Paris. They have worked together for several years and developed a varied body of work combining writing, photography, installation, film and performance.
> www.plaidoiriepourunejurisprudence.net

**Francisco Camacho** was born in 1979 in Bogota Colombia, studied Visual arts at the Universidad Nacional de Colombia, ERSEP Tourcoing in France and was a Researcher Fellow at Rijksakademie van Beeldenden Kunst in Amsterdam (2008–2009). His works analyze social strategies of organization and the ways in which these strategies generates images to the community. Recent projects include *Group Marriage Initiative* for the Spinoza Manifestation in Amsterdam and the Video Documentary *Truth or Consequences* on how the community of Hot Springs, New Mexico voted to change the name of the town after a TV and radio show during the 1950's.

**Darius Mikšys** was born 1969 in Kaunas, Lithuania, and lives and works in Vilnius. He participated in many projects, among them *PR 04* in Puerto Rico, the 16th Biennale of Sydney, and the 9th Lyon Biennial. His projects vary from a video documentation of a visit to the Parapsychology Fair at the Vilnius Sport's Palace to organizing of artists' parents meetings, selling an empty bottle of perfume on e-bay, a procrastinating lecture *On Procrastinating*, proposing an ABBA museum in a Qantas plane for the Tempelhof airport in Berlin, and establishing the Vilnius Cricket Club.
> www.dariusmiksys.com

**Judi Werthein** was born 1967 in Buenos Aires, Argentina, and is an artist that works across media. She received an MA in Architecture and Urbanism from the Universidad de Buenos Aires. She now lives and works in Buenos Aires and New York. In her work, Werthein relishes relinquishing control, moving art from the gallery into the world, where its power and effectiveness can be questioned. "Recognizing the individual subjective power of the audience," Werthein writes, "I attempt to provide an opportunity to recast the limitations that structure our existence." Her work has been included in exhibitions at the Tate Modern, London, UK; De Appel, Amsterdam, The Netherlands; The Aldrich Museum of Contemporary Art, Ridgefield, Connecticut; The Bronx Museum for the Arts, New York; and the Center for Contemporary Art, Vilnius, Lithuania. Werthein has also participated in Manifesta 7, Bolzano, Italy; InSite_05, San Diego/Tijuana; the Bienal de Pontevedra, Galicia; and the 7th Bienal de La Habana, Havana, Cuba, among others.

# A Few Notes on Being Invisible and Visible at the Same Time

An old truism states that artists make invisible things visible. They give form to unexpressed feelings, social undercurrents, and things ranging from connections of interplanetary movements to the growth of plants. They analyze corporate power structures and their relations to governments, articulating them in elaborate diagrams. They employ data visualization tools from visual communication laboratories and help us to understand complexities of contemporary economics through easy-to-digest images. It is like the Vulgata explaining the Bible through images to the illiterate in the Middle Ages. Even if one needs a higher degree of education to be able read data, visualization images manifest vulgarity best. Numbers are never enough to convince the mind of existence of something—one needs forms, shrouds, and apparitions.

On the other side of this equation is the magician who makes things disappear, or makes them temporarily invisible. The magician is elegant and flawless; he or she lifts weightless things and blows heavy rings of smoke in between. There is always a time for standing ovations. However, often we forget to look at whether things that have disappeared under a movement of his magic were there in place prior to that. The magician convinces us that there was something before, and that he made it disappear. "And now it is back!" he says, and pulls a white rabbit out of his sleeve. "But it was black before!" I remember, but don't throw myself at it: my memory might be lying too. This is how magic works. Things disappear before they appear, or they reappear different, but we are convinced that they are the same.

One of the best unrealized projects of disappearance is what Loris Gréaud proposed in 2007 for Palais de Tokyo in Paris: to invite David Copperfield and ask him to make the whole building of the Palais vanish. Just imagine if he had not been able to put it back—we would have to have fully trusted him then.

The roles of con artist, magician, and alchemist are eagerly appropriated by the art world, as they demonstrate the mechanisms of production of value out of nothing with the highest degree of sophistication. There is also a glamour of conceptual virtuosity that hints at the business of banks and their graphic collapse. I am almost sure that a trend of exhibitions of invisible works of art consolidated with the height of the credit bubble. We were not able to see how those banks were producing credits, yet we were most empirically faced with its consequences. Visibility always comes later, as graphic proof, as familiar as an old dog in front of the door as opposed to a rabbit from a sleeve.

Invisibility comes as rhetorical tool of power because whenever we are faced with higher complexities or things that we simply don't understand, we assume that what we see is just "a tip of an iceberg" of something. (See the cartoon that appeared in *The New Yorker* in 1998 about this subject.)[1] Therefore, someone claiming to orchestrate invisible forces (or at least the signs of invisibility) comes as an agent of a power much higher than we could see, literally. Seeing power is gaining power over what you see. It is about making things transparent, too.[2]

1

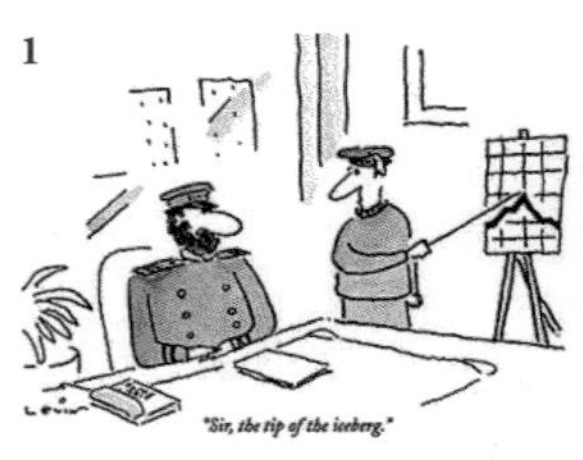

"Sir, the tip of the iceberg."

2 Here we turn to the second aspect of the concept, or to transparency as a specific way of knowing. Transparency is about something empirical, which can be seen; it refers to optics and rationality. It is not about obscure principles or ideologies, but rather concerns empirical reality and practices. Transparency is more about what is being done than about what is being said. Furthermore, transparent practices are those that can easily be detected and that can easily be understood. Consequently, to be commonly seen and understood, these practices must cohere with the dominant norms in a given society, for, if they do not, exposure would threaten to undermine them and cause disruption, just like the effect of the light cast on Count Dracula. Transparency, as a norm, is usually used in two ways: to refer to the moral dimension, and for efficiency of performance. The interconnection of the two dimensions is best revealed in the genesis of auditing and accountability.
Egle Rindzeviciute, "The Powers of Transparency." *The Weird But True Book.* (Vilnius: CAC, 2005)

That is why being visible at what you do is the fastest way of being codified and over-identified.

When someone happens to be seen at his work, no mysteries about how that work is done remain: we see how many eggs a cook puts in an omelet and which buttons an elevator boy pushes. Yet in the realm of artistic production, often the work is a secret that stays at the core of the identity of an individual practice. This secret is what makes one artist different from another, and is reflected in the prices of works of art. Since the art industry is a rather totemic and obscure business, to protect your value often means to guard your secret. When the secret is occasionally revealed, it may suddenly appear invisible. And here is another link of art with magic: the biggest secret is that there is no secret.

No lesser degree of magic is involved in the practice of making invisible things visible, though. In order to authorize a specific method of making things visible, one has to prove that those things have not existed before. Here is where the myth of chronological superiority comes in—one has to have proof of having done something before anyone else has done it. But this is already another subject. Let us stick to visibility as a metaphor. Is there a sensitive way to combine the modes of being visible and invisible things at the same time? A way of working without falling into a posture of shaman and not betraying the discretion of an individual process either? Or another level, it also involves a reluctance to display signs of visibility as proof of something that one has done because maybe that something is purely mental or is not intended to be exposed. "Visible" is too often meant to speak to foundations or magazines and thus to gain further visibility. "Invisible" cultivates the aura of esoterics and enchantment. Being more visible as an artist helps to promote an invisible work of art, while being visible as artwork work of art allows the figure of an artist to remain farther in the shadow. "Don't close your eyes completely, yet don't open them fully too," adds a sentence from the manual of some meditation practice.

Despite all of what has been said, I am interested in a certain invisibility that someone's practice acquires as soon as it goes beyond the borders of the art world into other domains. A twist comes in precisely here, where art leaves its own field and becomes invisible as art, but visible as part of something else. Or art that retains all the potential of a magic object combined with rules of law, like in a case of **Patrick Bernier and Olive Martin**, who weaved their story masterfully in the voice of "undocumented" citizens to be deported so that their expulsion is halted. A gift of collective storytelling becomes a burden for prosecutors—they cannot deport someone that claims an authorship of a collectively authored work of art. A rather different thing happens when something starts as an art project and then becomes a reality of its own. When **Darius Mikšys** went to London to play cricket in a local club, everybody took it as an artistic project. However, when he came back and founded *Abdul Aziz Holiday Club* in Vilnius, Lithuania, it became a continuous gathering of expats living and working far away from their countries, notably India and the United Kingdon. Only honorable members of the club abroad may see it as an art project (yet it is an art project too!). **Francisco Camacho** recently started a legal campaign to legalize polyamorous relationships in Holland. In the beginning, he saw it as a painting, yet lately this "painting" has been receiving more coverage in Dutch media than probably any of the paintings of a Colombian artist has thus far in Holland. Several years ago, **Judi Werthein** made a project in the Bronx Museum: images of works from the collection of the institution were offered as images for the fingernails of local women. Micro-apparitions of the works left the museum and entered temporary manual routines. I do not think this work had enough visibility yet despite being produced a few years ago. Its existence somewhere between the annals of the museum and long-removed fingernails allows for the readjustment of another tool belonging to the field of optics: a focus. A focus is something that is supposed to pull things in the realm of resolution even if they are far away or too close. The *Baby Marx Cartoon* by **Pedro Reyes** has not received enough visibility yet since this tale of economic and social theories has not yet been fully produced and distributed—it is in progress. It is introduced here along with an excerpt of a not-yet-published interview with Antanas Mockus, the former mayor of Bogotà, who, according to some experts, applied artistic methods to city governing.

Counterfactual history attempts to answer "what if" questions. It seeks to explore historical incidents that did not happen or that had outcomes which were different from those which did in fact occur. One step further is to imagine the encounter of historical figures who didn't have the chance to meet but who we would like to bring together in a hypothetical debate.

In similar fashion, *Baby Marx* brings together the main philosophers who have advocated either for socialism or capitalism as primers on the main politico-economic ideas that have shaped the world in the past two centuries. In this TV project, each character (in its incarnation as a puppet) holds a different view and wishes to persuade the other of his own.

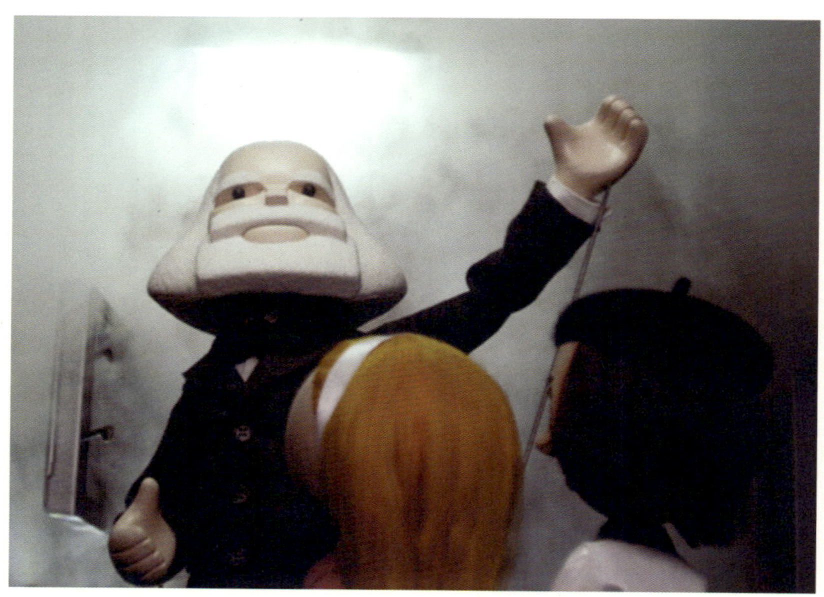

# Pedro Reyes

■■
***Baby Marx***, 2010, stills from the first episode of an experimental telvision comedy

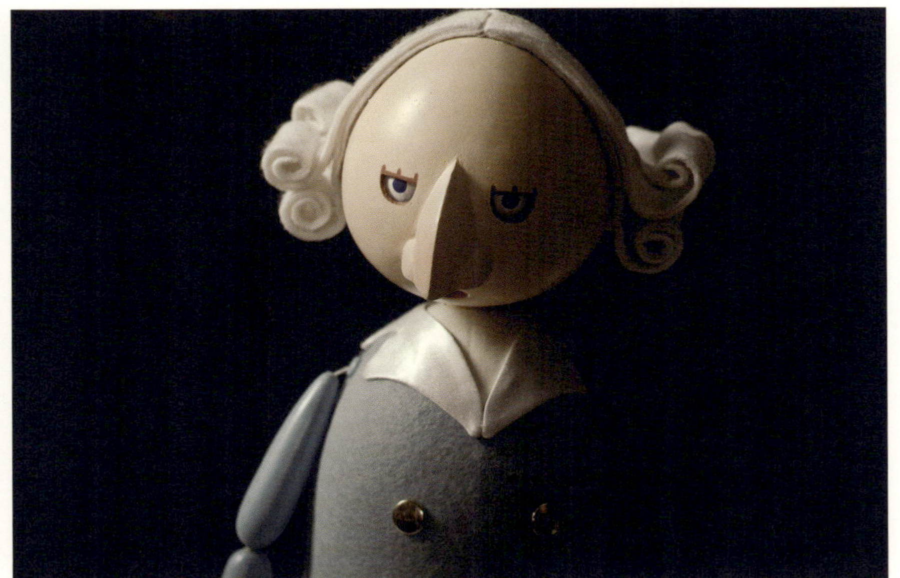

- - - - - - - - - - - - - - - - - - - - - - - - -

## ANNEX: PEDRO REYES IN DIALOGUE WITH ANTANAS MOCKUS [1]

**Pedro Reyes:** Could we broaden this stance to imagine the role of the artist as a social agent?

**Antanas Mockus:** I think one could very convincingly put forward: "Commit art, not terrorism." Art is capable of producing commotions on par with a terrorist act, of installing itself in the people's memory and imagination. In *Les Misérables*, Victor Hugo expresses how injustice pains him. Art is a route—more laborious, but a route nonetheless. First message: "Substitute art for terrorism." Second message: "Combat terrorism with art." Gianni Vattimo, an Italian philosopher who fights to rid philosophy of the pretensions Marxism had, and who strives for modesty, declared that the West should bombard Iraq, but with condoms and pornography. To culturally infuriate. Exacerbate the feedback loop created by polarization. They would have surely been much more enraged than by physical bombings; the stakes would have been clearer. Behind terrorism lie genuine emotions. There are cold calculations and reasoning, but there are also feelings, emotions. And art is a way to share, transform, and elaborate emotions as well as to connect them with reasons.

One of Elster's central ideas concerning art is how strange a thing it is: art produces emotions, but then reassures us. "Relax, it's just art..." You don't need to go out and march, or donate to charity, or take up arms and fight. It is practically emotion for emotion's sake. In everyday life, emotion serves as a trigger—even etymologically-for action. With fear, for example, the ceiling comes crashing down: it's fight or flight. One doesn't just stand still. The artist, on the other hand, moves our ceiling, but then comforts us: "Relax, no need to get worked up..."

**Pedro Reyes:** Can citizenship be a creative act?

**Antanas Mockus:** The heart of the question lies in what being a citizen means and how a citizen takes into account the rights of others. Keep others in mind but without categorizing them. We forbade inaugurations during my first term; during the second we celebrated and honored public service.

**Pedro Reyes:** Why prohibit inaugurations?

**Antanas Mockus:** Because they usurp authority in a way. That is, a mayor executes policy that is formulated collectively. However, most mayors tend to take the resulting credit and resources.

**Pedro Reyes:** This idea of citizenship had not taken hold yet.

**Antanas Mockus:** An unusual source for talk of the rights of men *and* citizens during the French Revolution. A Marx text on citizens and the bourgeois also drew my attention; in it, he sarcastically describes a type of person who as a bourgeois is incredibly selfish but who becomes altruistic as a citizen. Marx saw this as schizophrenic, a con, a false ideology, and a moral subterfuge.

I read it rather as an interesting device: in certain situations, you are authorized to act purely out of self-interest, but in other contexts, or perhaps even to limit the previous tendency, you are invited to function as a citizen, to adopt the city's criteria, to think of others.

**Pedro Reyes:** It seems to me that this contradiction does not spring from hypocrisy. After all, you are not lying to others, just to yourself: it's self-deception.

**Antanas Mockus:** I spoke of a culture of citizenship, of citizens as producers and reproducers. The citizen as a producer is an economic subject and is capable of occupying public spaces, but as a reproducer, as a family man or woman, as a person striving for a certain quality of life, he does not want those spaces invaded. There is a contradiction at play, like the prostitute who would rather her daughter grow up in a neighborhood free of prostitution. There is a tension between accepting prostitution on the one hand

and wanting to avoid it on the other. In a way, this reformulates constitutional privacy and property rights. (...)

**Pedro Reyes:** One of the biggest reasons for people choosing self-regulation over admiration for the law is that self-regulation includes all possibilities. Self-regulation practically aspires toward ultimate human potential. Law, on the other hand, limits the self with a greater good in mind. A sort of tension develops between the greater good and a personal cosmic good with greater room for individualism.

**Antanas Mockus:** But utopia—the original anarchist utopia of "neither God nor law" and government only through conscience—would require a deep and permanent pedagogy to correct small details, to give someone a timely warning or signal. Some individuals would still need to regulate. If someone goes mad and causes too much destruction, what do we do? Do we react spontaneously or have rules in place to deal with transgressors? Basic rules are always needed to address security, sovereignty, and property rights for both tangible and intangible assets.

**Pedro Reyes:** Anarchy would require at the very least a law that decreed, "No more laws."

**Antanas Mockus:** If we were all equally sensitive to each other, equally self-conscious of consequences, of each act's implications, there would be no need for cultural or legal regulations. Obviously, this is almost a model of individualist hubris, perhaps very attractive in our highly individualistic age. But if one looks back, we are almost always such string individualists due to the influence of individualist mentors or parents. Our debt to culture is always immense and the regulation of certain areas such as property and, above all, the freedom from violence requires the famous Leviathan, that imperfect earthly mortal god that is the State and that guarantees basic rules. Now, thanks to those rules, more options can blossom. Art provides the best schooling in this. Following rules does not represent a disaster: the artist normally imposes on herself more rules than fashion dictates. The trick even consists of saying, "I will violate a rule, but to do so I will adopt five or six others." Art transgresses as well.

[1] Pedro Reyes in dialogue with Antanas Mockus, an excerpt from *Ad Usum: To Be Used,* ed. by Pedro Reyes and José Luis Falconi (Cambridge: Harvard Univeristy Press, 2008)

- - - - - - - - - - - - - - - - - - - - - - - -

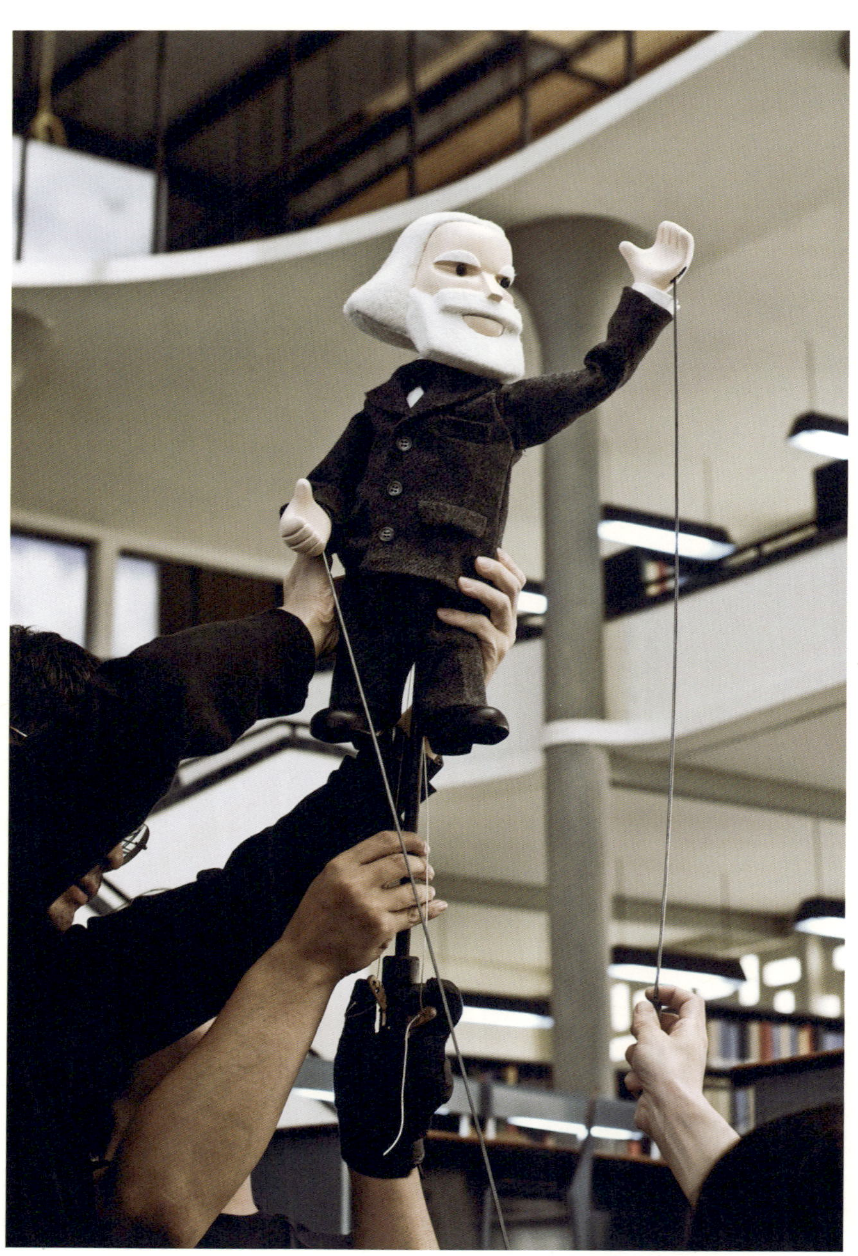

*Baby Marx*, 2010, stills from the first episode of an experimental telvision comedy; all images courtesy of Pedro Reyes and Detalle Films

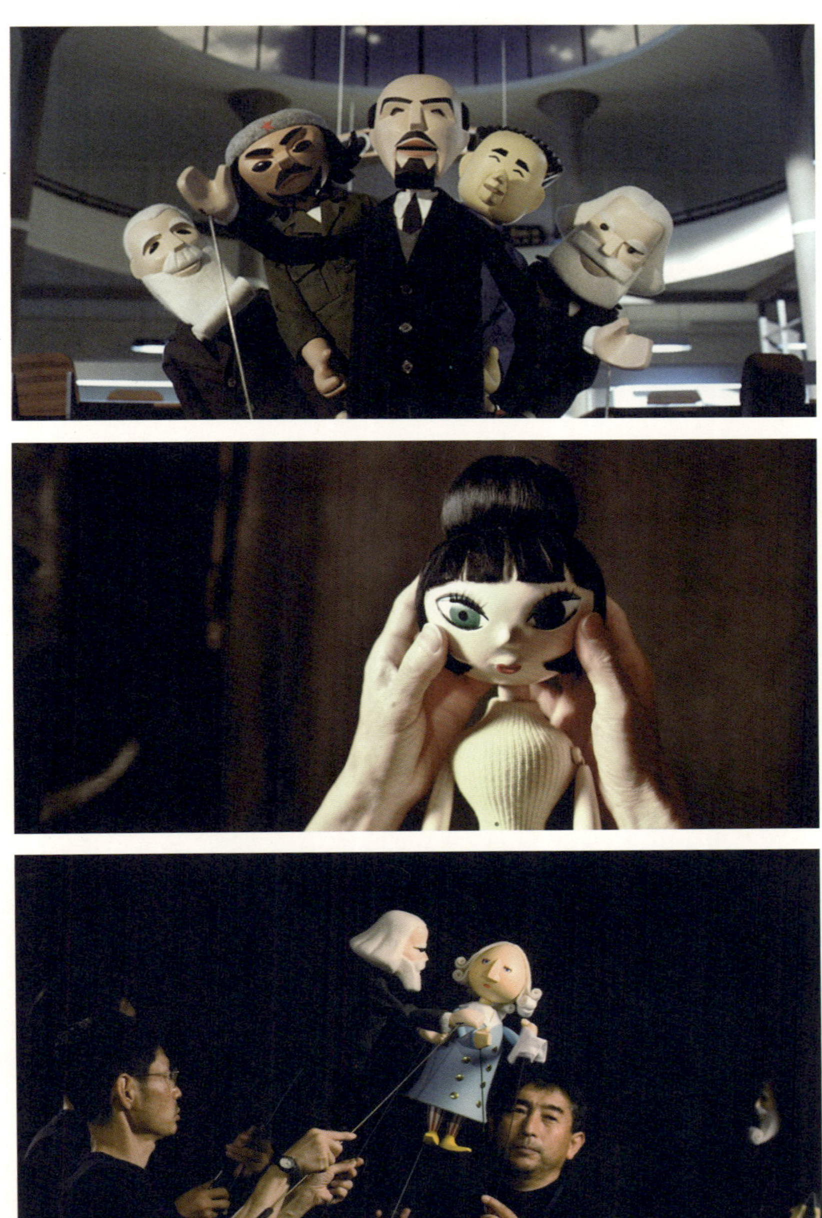

A combination of exceptions of law, powers of fiction, and paradoxes of art create the magic of protecting the rights of people who are unprotected in their newly adopted countries. Adoption of an artwork, even a conceptual one, empowers a person carrying it in a precarious situation of survival with a set of civil rights that would not be manifested if the same artwork had been presented in the art world. However paradoxical it sounds, one needs to leave the art world to test the power of artwork.

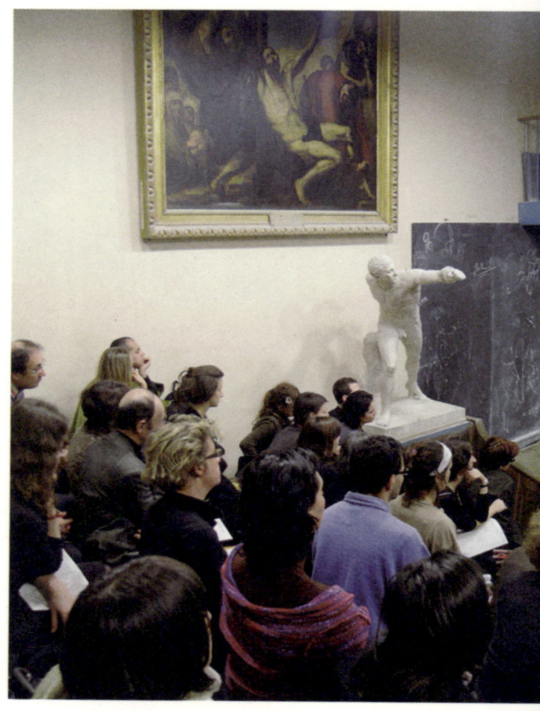

# Patrick Bernier + Olive Martin

***X. c/ Préfet de…, Plaidoirie pour une jurisprudence*** ("X and Y v. France: The Case for a Legal Precedent"), 2007–ongoing, project performed in Paris at the Ecole des Beaux-Arts, 2007, color image (photo by Cédric Schönwald)

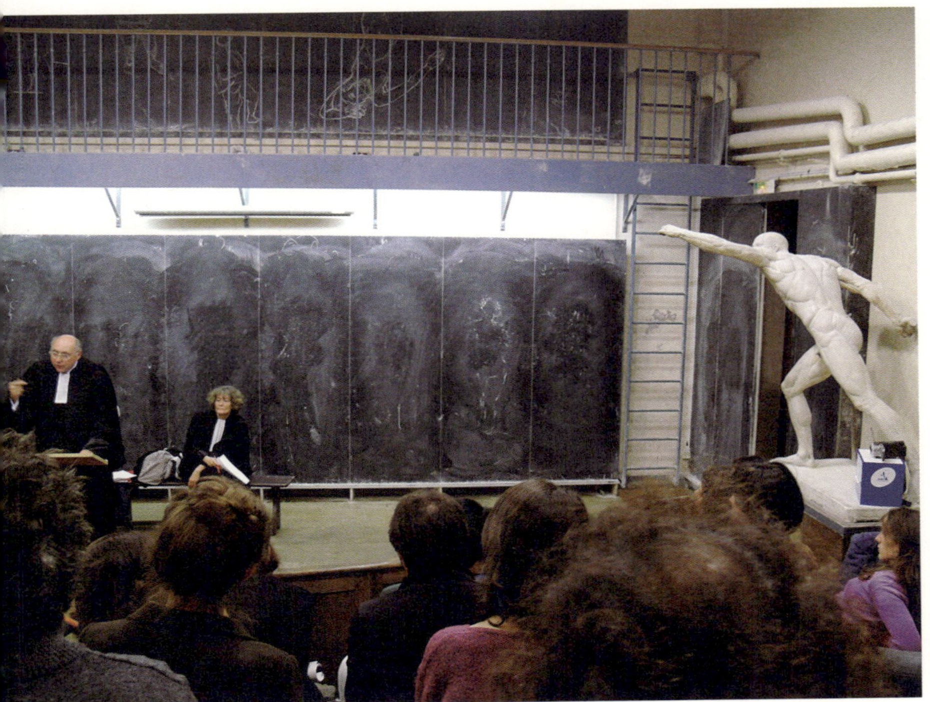

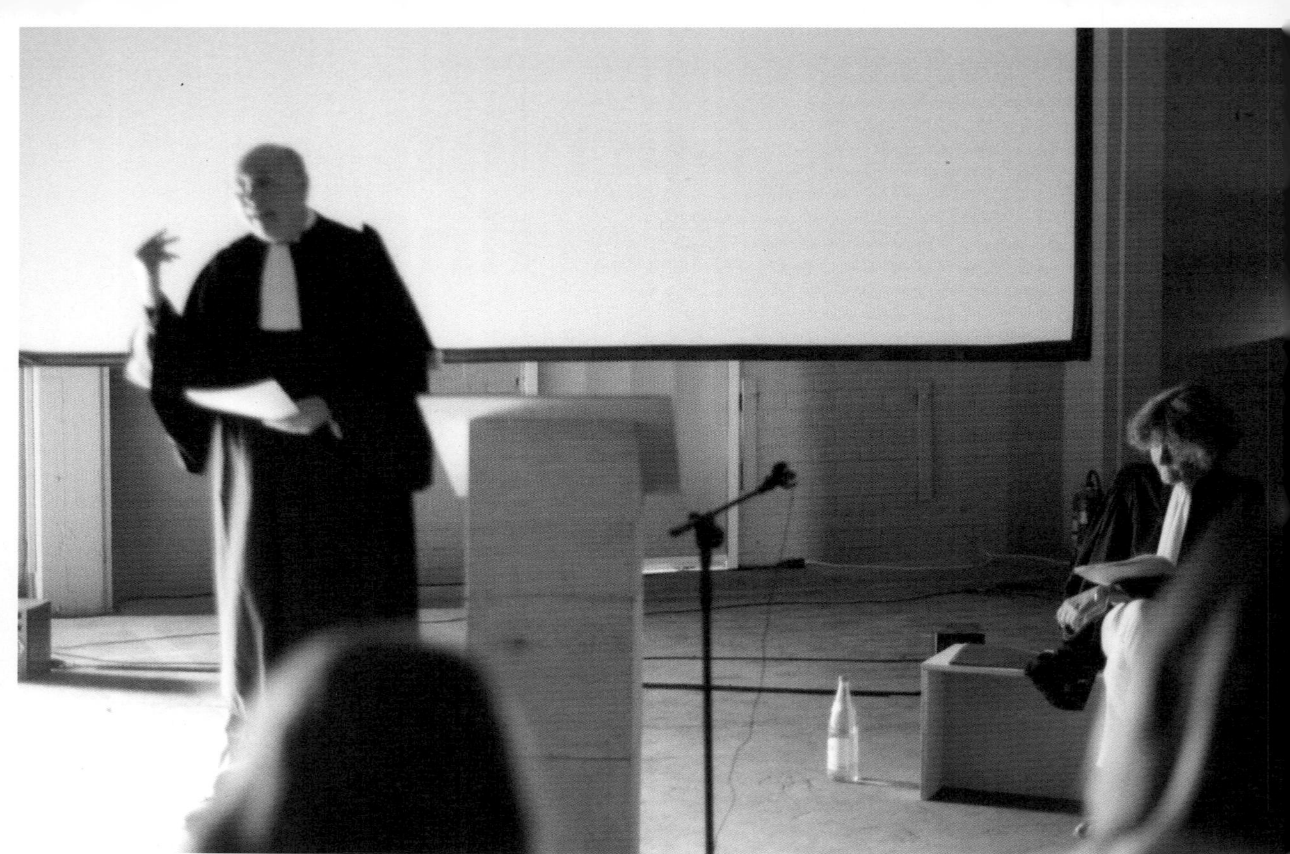

***X. c/ Préfet de…, Plaidoirie pour une jurisprudence*** ("X and Y v. France: The Case for a Legal Precedent"), 2007—ongoing, project performed in Antwerp at Extra-City, 2008 (photo by Olive Martin)

- - - - - - - - - - - - - - - - - - - - - -

**A TALE FOR A LEGAL PRECEDENT**

short story written by P.B., 2004

*At the Administrative Court of N., on the morning of 20th September, a foreign woman whose situation is irregular, and to whom the prefect has served a deportation order, rises to address her final appeal to the judge.*

Your Honour,

I appear before your Court to contest the deportation order that the Prefecture of N. has served on me. If you uphold this order, I will be deported to the country that I managed to escape from only at the cost of painful sacrifices and at considerable risk. The Asylum and Immigration Tribunal of your country did not believe the reasons that forced me to leave and refused me asylum. Today, returning would represent an infringement of my private life and a danger to my life itself which seems inadmissible. Regardless of my esteem for you, I have no hope that you will be susceptible to my arguments, given the political and economic relationship that your country is currently cementing with my country of origin: everything is fine there now, your Honour, everything is fine there! However, before you give the green light to my deportation, let me warn you that I will not be the only one to leave the territory, because I carry with me an artwork conceived in collaboration with P., an artist from your country. Don't bother lowering your eyes to my belly, you won't learn anything: I am not pregnant. I am not expecting a child whose birth would give me the right to remain in this country. My relationship with P. is merely friendly and artistic. He has confided his part of the artwork to my memory; I am its guardian and interpreter, the co-author insofar as my memory effects it. This artwork is a story: the story of an artistic project and its effects. Please listen to it as I tell it today; I will tell it differently tomorrow. Some time ago, an exhibition curator of international renown invited P. to participate in a shared curatorial experiment. He invited him to select ten works by different artists who would be exhibited along with others in a wellknown London gallery. A few days later, P. read in the press that a 28-year-old Iraqi had died at the entrance to the Channel Tunnel, crushed under the truck he was trying to hang on to in order to reach England. This fatal attempt struck him as being like a photographic negative of the curator's proposition. The invitation to present works across the Channel was superimposed on the impossibility for some people to cross this little stretch of water. Henceforth, when invited to send artworks, how could one send people instead? Now, P. had recently begun working with a storyteller to whom he confided his artistic experiments in order to publicly transmit them, the storyteller modifying them according to his know-how and his own memory. Thus was formed the idea of creating collaborations between wellknown artists and people in transit; conceiving works that would not take the form of an object, a piece of writing, or any other tangible form but would retain an immaterial aspect so that it fell to their guardians to reconstitute them by employing their own faculties such as storytelling, playing an instrument, dancing, singing, or giving instructions! The presentation of these works of art in London would necessitate the crossing of the Channel by the co-authors and exclusive interpreters of these original artworks. These works would thus confer on stowaways the status of couriers. He contacted artists, researchers, choreographers, film directors, and composers whose research and approaches seemed to correspond to this proposition. It seemed important to him to go beyond mere sponsorship; it should be a real collaboration which would enrich everybody. Artists responded and the collaborations with "undocumented people" started with the help of refugee support groups. A choreographer showed a sequence of movements that he had observed in the recent history of contemporary dance to a young Kurd who then performed it and completed it with new gestures. A composer created a piece of music for an instrument that an Afghan had constructed during his journey. A conceptual artist evoked a sculpture in a few words for a Nigerian woman to subsequently sculpt using other words that were tinged with nostalgia. The carriers of artworks wrote to the French and British authorities to obtain the right to enter Britain and honor the invitation to present the work of which they were the co-authors, guardians, and interpreters. They received no reply. The artists then wrote to obtain passage for the people carrying their works so that they could be presented in London. The prefect replied that, given the irregular situation of the people in question, it would not be possible to comply with their request and reminded them that any help with entry or residence extended to a person in irregular circumstances constituted an offence. P. wrote, as assistant curator of the exhibition, to request permission for the passage of the ten people carrying the works that he had selected. He received the same reply with the reminder that the penalties for the afore mentioned offence are at least doubled when committed by an organized group. The main curator wrote that the refusal of transit of the ten persons concerned would eliminate important works from his exhibition. He received a letter from the British authorities explaining that it was not possible to comply with his request because of bilateral agreements signed between the French Interior Ministry and the British Home Office. The director of the gallery did not write because he was afraid of the reaction of his state sponsors. None of the couriers were authorized to enter Britain. On the day of the opening in London, the public found ten title cards for the absent works next to the works selected by the other assistant curators. The titles of the artworks were displayed along with the names of the co authors accompanied by a text explaining that the French and British authorities had refused to grant passage to the author-interpreters of these works and that the organizers regretted not being able to present them. Visitors were invited to send a letter of complaint to the authorities. Many did so but none received a response. Some of the artists who had collaborated with the couriers were present. They were put under pressure to present their works themselves but refused, speaking instead of their experiences. The story circulated. A boycott was organized that united the disgruntled artists unhappy at seeing their works enriching those they would rather denounce. Musicians who wished to free themselves from the major multinationals, authors avoiding publishing (because it is mostly in the hands of arms dealers) and artists disgusted with feeding a speculative market, all decided to no longer publish, exhibit, or represent things. They remembered that, in order to allow forbidden works to continue to circulate, men and women from a literary resistance movement each committed a work to memory and recited it to anyone who wished to hear it. Ready to return the favour, now that it was no longer a case of books circulating hidden under coats but rather men hidden under trucks, our artists were prepared to entrust their latest creations to the memory of those without documents and without rights whose very existence was denied. They banned any tangible form of their artworks (whether books, films, or discs) that might lead to the circulation of the works without the guardians. The works were necessarily collaborative, the guardians adapting the works to his or her memory and enriching them with his or her own history and knowledge. The guardians reconstituted the works as he or she wished, in a more or less whole, fragmented, hybrid, or original manner. At first, the illegal situation of the carriers of artworks obliged presentations to take place during clandestine meetings. One day a woman was arrested. Her situation was irregular as she was an "undocumented person," but she was also the guardian of an artwork. The court did not consider that the fact of containing a piece of intangible national cultural heritage constituted an obstacle to deportation and upheld the deportation order despite the protestations of the artist co author who happened to be present and who appealed, a bit inconsequentially, to the inalienable rights of authorship. During her detention prior to deportation, a number of enthusiasts requested visiting rights in order to hear the work. The detention center switchboard was saturated with calls from people asking for information about visiting times, making the place resound like a performance venue. The number of collaborations increased. It was no longer just artists who entrusted their creations to the memories of "undocumented people": scientists confided their discoveries, the venerable their memoirs, and chefs their recipes. The very memory of the country was gradually exiled at the same pace as the deportations. Their fame crossed borders, despite the absence of artworks and individuals. Artists of all countries put pressure on their authorities to allow entry to foreign carriers of works of art. Refusal by the authorities gave rise to a feeling among local artists that they were out of touch, new things only arriving in bits and pieces reported by travelers who may have heard the work in another country. Often the story was second hand or transmitted via several people and thus by various memories. They became fabulous, combining embellishments encountered in various exhibitions or conferences. The art world started to desert the closed countries. The artistic buzz crossed frontiers. Transit camps of foreigners mutated into art center, while artistic institutions in closed countries withered away. So, to avoid collections being hit with obsolescence and museums with lethargy, consultants from these countries softened up and made exceptions for the passage of people carrying artworks. But they are still waiting for a judge, who could be an aesthete, to break the deportation order issued against one of them.

You've been warned, my thanks and greetings.

Judgement under deliberation.

NB: The exhibition "I Am A Curator" was conceived by Per Hüttner for the Chisenhale Gallery in London in November 2003. The project as described was not accepted by the gallery and has remained in the planning stage.

*Written in french by Patrick Bernier in 2004, translated by Simon Welch, published in* Untitled, *n°43, Autumn 2007.*

*> www.plaidoiriepourunejurisprudence.net*

\- - - - - - - - - - - - - - - - - - - - -

---

**Press Release: Group Marriage**
July 31, 2009

A Group Marriage in the courtyard of SKOR on July 31, 2009 in Amsterdam, The Netherlands.

Francisco Camacho, artist and initiator of the Group Marriage project, will marry two people. You are cordially invited to the courtyard of SKOR to celebrate this special moment.

Camacho and his two spouses will sign a "Living together" contract validated by a notary in Borne, The Netherlands on Friday, July 31, 2009. That evening at 5 p.m. we will celebrate the wedding with a formal reception at SKOR in Amsterdam. Later the newlyweds will honeymoon at the Lloyd Hotel in the "cumunal bed" made by artist Joep van Lieshout.

The contract will reveal that a group marriage is not permitted the same rights as a conventional monogamous relationship. After signing the contract, the members of this group marriage hope to litigate to obtain the same rights as a married couple. Francisco Camacho hopes that this project will begin a discussion on the limits of state power related to the freedom to love.

# Francisco Camacho

*Group Marriage*, Amsterdam, 2009

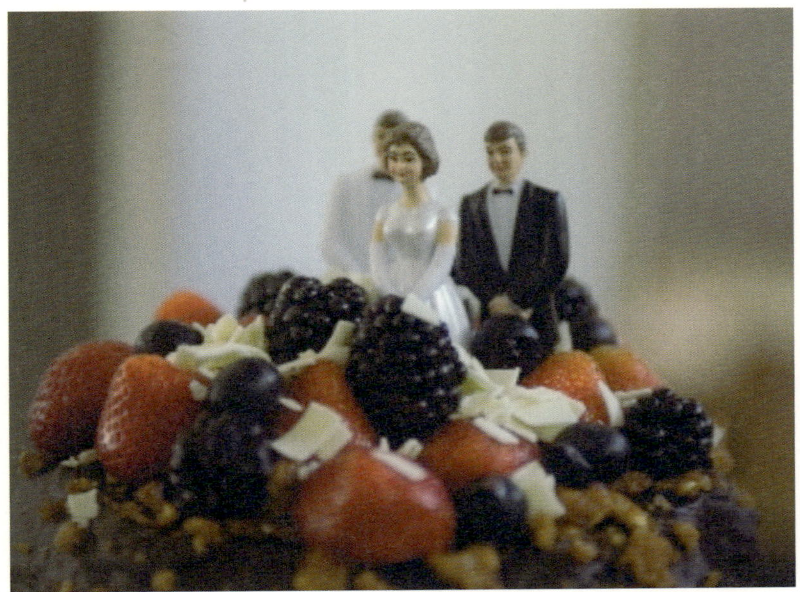

"Why can't people marry several partners and live happy, fully developed lives?" thought Francisco Camacho one day and started his campaign in Holland to promote multi-partner marriage regardless of one's sex, ethnicity, and religion. Holland has been known for many years as a country of highly organized biopolitical life, but if it accepts multi-partner marriage, at least it may become even more populated than it is now.

***Group Marriage***, Amsterdam, 2009, Poster

SPIN MY NAME IS ZA

# JA wij willen!

teken de petitie

www.groepshuwelijken.nl

ontwerp: mannschaft.org

Publicatie : Echo Amsterdam Westerpark
Datum : 29/07/2009 Oplage : 27,700 Advertentiewaarde : € 84.77
Pagina : 24 Frequentie : wekelijks Regio : Amsterdam

# Trouwen met zijn tweeën

**STAD – Niet iedereen vindt dat het huwelijk iets is tussen een man en een vrouw. Francisco Camacho, kunstenaar en initiatiefnemer van het Groepshuwelijkenproject, gaat vrijdag op de binnenplaats van SKOR aan de Ruysdealkade met twee mensen trouwen.**

Camacho en zijn twee echtelieden gaan die dag een samenlevingscontract ondertekenen, bekrachtigd door een notaris in Borne. De kunstenaar wil met het contract duidelijk maken dat een groepshuwelijk niet over dezelfde rechten beschikt als een klassieke monogame relatie of een geregistreerd partnerschap. Na de ondertekening van het contract hopen de leden van het groepshuwelijk een rechtszaak te starten om dezelfde rechten te verkrijgen als een getrouwd koppel of geregistreerde partners. Camacho hoopt dat dit project een discussie op gang brengt over de grenzen van de macht van de staat met betrekking tot de vrijheid van liefde.

Het Groepshuwelijken Initiatief is onderdeel van de kunstmanifestatie My name is Spinoza.

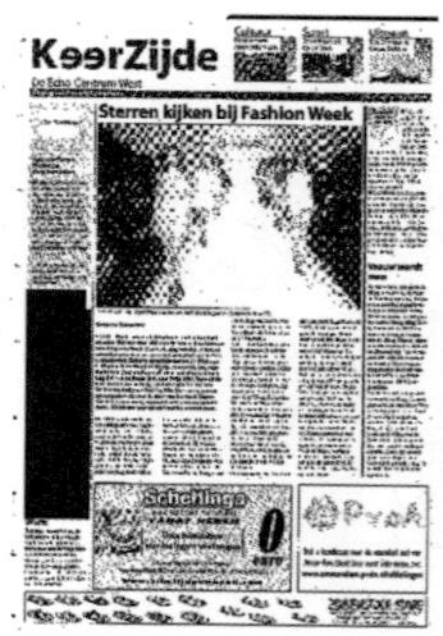

*Group Marriage*, Amsterdam, 2009

Francisco Camacho interviews Samira Al-Quadusi, VPRO Netherlands 2 Channel; all images courtesy of: Francisco Camacho, Spinoza Foundation Center, and SKOR Amsterdam

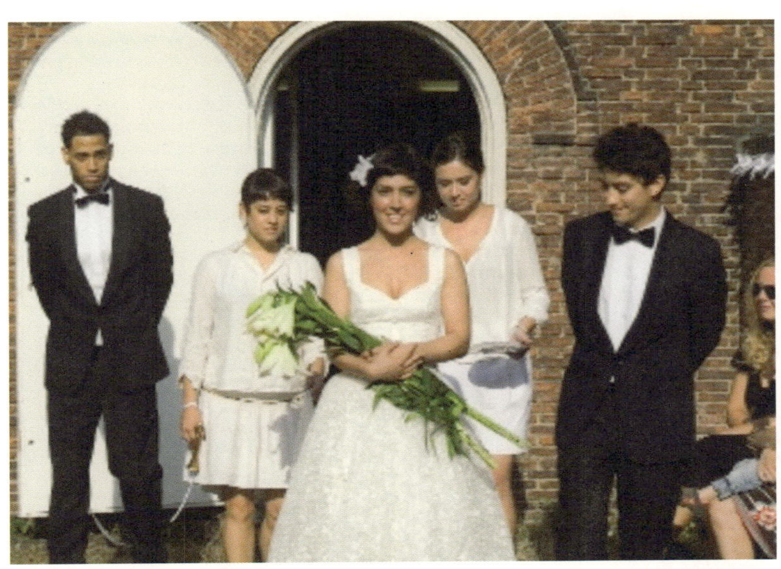

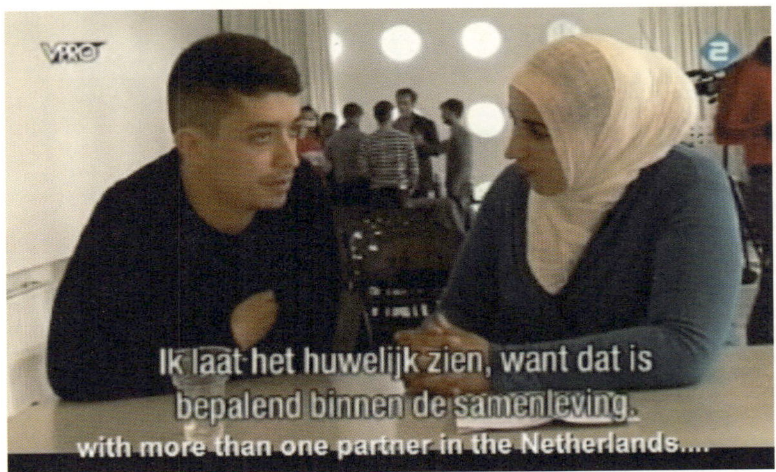

Publicatie : Parool
Datum : 30/04/2009
Pagina : 16
Oplage : 87,230
Frequentie : dagelijks
Advertentiewaarde : € 10316.00
Regio : landelijk

# Trouwen voor twee, dat is beperkt

LOES DE FAUWE

**AMSTERDAM – Waarom zou je eigenlijk niét kunnen trouwen met meerdere partners? Met twee of, doe wild, met vier of vijf? Die vraag stelt de Colombiaanse kunstenaar Francisco Camacho (1979).**

Het stellen van deze vraag en het daaruit volgende in initiatief om handtekeningen te verzamelen voor de openstelling van het burgerlijk huwelijk voor groepen, is geen stunt. Een debat over het huwelijk is een eerbetoon aan de zeventiende-eeuwse Nederlandse filosoof en vrijdenker Spinoza, zegt hij.

Eigenlijk gaat het om kunst, betoogt de *artist in residence* van de Rijksacademie, die zijn atelier heeft in de Sarphatistraat.

Dat we niet denken dat hij zelf zo achter de wijven aanzit, verzekert hij – hij grijnst: "Nee, ik ben homo, geen vaste vriend" – want die indruk zou kunnen ontstaan bij het zien van de 'Ja, wij willen'-pamfletten waarmee hij zijn actie begeleidt. "Een vrij burger moet in staat zijn te kunnen beslissen met hoeveel mensen hij of zij het leven wil delen."

Het is ook de petitie waarmee Camacho met zijn team, ook vandaag op de Elandsgracht, handtekeningen verzamelt. Als het aan hem ligt, komt er nu een beweging op gang. Die gaat er voor zorgen dat in september in Den Haag veertigduizend handtekeningen liggen waardoor het onderwerp in de Tweede Kamer op de agenda moet worden gezet.

En hoe kwam Spinoza tot Camacho? De stichting Kunst en Openbare Ruimte en de Amsterdamse Spinozakring houden de manifestatie *My name is Spinoza*. Je kunt geen kunstvorm bedenken die er niet aan mee doet.

Camacho vindt dat de wijsgeer straks niet alleen moet voortbestaan als beeld op het Waterlooplein, maar dat het juist gaat om zijn gedachtegoed. Liberalisering van de Nederlandse huwelijkswetgeving zou daarvan een mooi staaltje zijn, meent hij. Het was een proces van denken, maar via polygame migranten en moslims kwam hij uit bij het groepshuwelijk: "In oude culturen hadden die vrouwen geen rechten, ze moeten zeker dezelfde rechten hebben als mannen. Maar waarom zou het huwelijk zelf beperkt moeten blijven tot twee partners? Dat debat is Spinoza waardig."

Het staat er nu deftiger dan Camacho het kan zeggen, zijn Engels is niet vloeiend, maar het is mooi hoe een Colombiaan te gast in Nederland een discussieonderwerp weet te vinden dat, zou het de agenda van de Tweede Kamer halen, nog voor leuke momenten kan zorgen.

Inmiddels is hem ook gewaar geworden dat de beperking van het burgerlijk huwelijk tot veel verdriet leidt bij groepen geliefden (zij noemen zich *polyamori*) die hun verbintenissen niet officieel kunnen maken. Die hebben als eersten alvast getekend. Camacho heeft nu vierduizend handtekeningen verzameld, in twee weken. Dus die veertigduizend, denkt hij, komen er wel.

Wat precies het kunstzinnige is aan dit project, kan hij uitleggen: "Ik ben begonnen als schilder, maar schilderijen zijn slechts een projectie van de realiteit. Ik wil werken met de realiteit. Het verzamelen van handtekeningen, het filmen van de discussieavond (die is 16 mei in De Inkijk, Ruysdaelkade 2 – red.) en die stapels handtekeningen straks in den Haag zie ik als één groot schilderij."

**www.groepshuwelijken.nl**

## De wet is streng

Trouwen in Nederland kun je maar doen met één persoon. Per keer dan. Tegelijkertijd trouwen met meerdere partners maakt je tot bigamist en bigamie is strafbaar (maximaal zes jaar cel).
Dus het wettig huwelijk valt vooralsnog af als een groep geliefden zich met elkaar wil verbinden.
Ook het geregistreerd partnerschap (ontworpen voor homo's toen die nog niet mochten trouwen) is voor groepsverbindingen niet bruikbaar. Het staat juridisch gelijk aan het huwelijk en is dus ook beperkt tot één partner.
Notaris Gerrit Mens, van het Amsterdamse notariskantoor Bakker Voorwinde Mens: "Alleen het samenlevingscontract mag vooralsnog wel worden afgesloten met meerdere personen. Daarin kun je regelen wat je wilt, met net zoveel deelnemers als je wilt.
In een samenlevingscontract worden afspraken en regelingen tussen partners formeel vastgelegd. Mens: "Als mensen gaan samenwonen, samen een huis kopen, misschien gezamenlijke bankrekeningen hebben, of samen kinderen groot brengen, dan moet je de zaken regelen. Maar meer dan onderlinge afspraken zijn het niet.
Mens: "Een samenlevingscontract heeft geen enkele status voor derde partijen, dus ook niet voor overheidsinstanties. Een pensioenfonds zal niet meerdere partners accepteren, de sociale dienst kan moeilijk voor zeven partners gaan zorgen. De wet gaat uit van één partner."

**Kunstenaar komt met petitie voor juridische status groepshuwelijk**

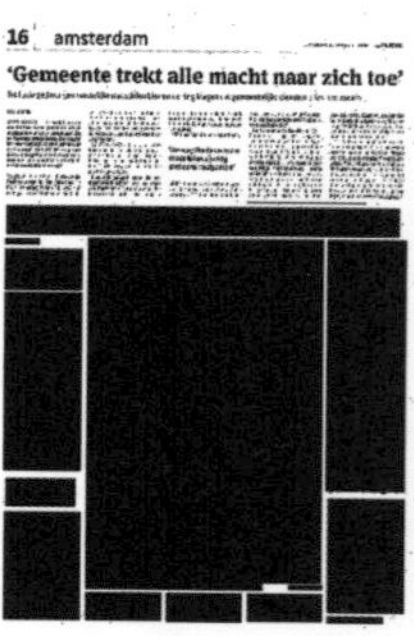
16 amsterdam
'Gemeente trekt alle macht naar zich toe'

- - - - - - - - - - - - - - - - - - - - - -

**MARRIAGE FOR TWO, THAT'S LIMITED**
a text by Loes de Fauwe

*Amsterdam: Why shouldn't you be able to get married to several partners? To two of them or—if you want to go wild—to four or five? That's the question posed by Colombian artist Francisco Camacho (1979).*

Asking the above question and subsequently gathering autographs in favor of opening up civil marriages to groups is not a stunt. A debate about matrimony is a tribute to the seventeenth-century Dutch philosopher and freethinker Baruch Spinoza, Camacho says.
Actually it is about art, claims the artist in residence of the Rijksacademie who has his studio in the Sarphatistraat. That we shouldn't think he's just chasing girls, he assures us—he grins: "No, I'm gay, no boyfriend"—because that is the impression one might get when seeing the "Yes, we want" leaflets that accompany his campaign. "A free citizen must be able to decide how many people he or she wants to spend his or her life with."
That is also the petition for which Camacho and his team, even today on the Elandsgracht, are gathering autographs. If it were up to him, a movement would be emerging which would make sure that 40,000 autographs will be presented in The Hague by September, obliging the Lower House to put the matter on its agenda.
And how did Spinoza get to Camacho? The foundation Kunst en Openbare Ruimte (Art and Public Space) and the Amsterdam Spinozacircle are organizing the art manifestation "My Name is Spinoza," in Amsterdam. It is impossible to think of an art form that is not participating.
Camacho thinks the philosopher should not simply remain present in the form of a statue on Waterloo Square, but rather that his ideas are what count. Liberalizing Dutch marriage laws would be a nice example, he feels. It was a train of thought that, via polygamous immigrants and Muslims, led him to group marriage: "In ancient cultures those women had no rights; they definitely should have the same rights as men. But why should matrimony be limited to two partners? It's a debate worthy of Spinoza."
It reads better than it sounds from Camacho, who is not fluent in English, but it's nice how a Colombian guest in The Netherlands manages to find a subject for a debate that, should it reach the Lower House, could produce some amusing moments.
Meanwhile it became clear to him that the limits of civil marriage lead to great sorrow among groups of lovers (they call themselves *polyamori*) who cannot make their union official. They were the first to sign. In two weeks, Camacho gathered 4,000 autographs, so getting to 40,000 shouldn't be a problem, he thinks.
What is so artistic about the project is something he can explain: "I started as a painter, but paintings are just a still projection of reality. I want to work with reality. Gathering the autographs, filming the public debate (on May 16th in De Inkijk, Ruysdaelkade), and the pile of autographs we will produce in The Hague are like one big painting."
*(www. groepshuwelijken.nl)*

- - - - - - - - - - - - - - - - - - - - - -

**THE LAW IS STRICT**

In The Netherlands you can only get married to one person. At a time, that is. Marrying several partners at the same time turns you into a bigamist and is liable to punishment (with a maximum of six years in jail).
Thus, a legal marriage is not an option for a group of loved ones who want to make their bond official. The legalized partnership (designed for homosexuals before they were allowed to get married) is equally useless. Legally it is equal to matrimony and therefore limited to a single partner.
Notary Gerrit Mens of the Amsterdam notary office Bakker Voorwinde Mens: "Only a cohabitation contract can be arranged for several people at the same time. You can put in it whatever you want and for any number of cohabitants, but this contract doesn't have any legal power."
A cohabitation contract formally lays down the agreements and rules between partners. Mens: "When people move in together, buy a house together, maybe open up a joint bank account or raise children together, you need to arrange your affairs." But it's nothing more than a mutual agreement.
"A cohabitation contract does not have any legal status for third parties, including public authorities. A pension fund will not accept several partners and a social service can hardly take care of seven partners. The law assumes only one partner."

- - - - - - - - - - - - - - - - - - - - - -

## Abdul Aziz's Holiday Cricket Club membership invitation

Dear friend who read this text,

You are invited to become a member of the Abdul Aziz's Holiday XI cricket club. To enjoy the many benefits of a club membership, please simply email miks111@yahoo.com with a "YES".

Board of organisers:
Simon Rees
Darius Mikšys

Members list:
(...)

The club inauguration was held on Friday 9 November at 6pm at the Contemporary Art Centre, Vokieciu g. 2, Vilnius. You are welcome to contact the organizers and club members with enquiries.

The Abdul Aziz's Holiday Cricket Club (Kriketo klubas "Abdulo Aziz Atostogos", Lith. lang.) is the first ever Lithuanian cricket club. It was named after the Abdul Aziz Invitation XL, cricket club based in London and "Holiday In" residency programme, initiated by Contemporary Art Centre (Vilnius, www.cac.lt), Gasworks (London, www.gasworks.org.uk) and Triangle France (Marseille, www.lafriche.org/triangle). Even though the art institutions have played major roles in the creation of the club, Abdul Aziz's Holiday is not an art project. It is just a cricket club, which served as the first in Lithuania. http://en.wikipedia.org/wiki/Lithuania_national_cricket_team

Over the years, Abdul Aziz's XI CC became a worldwide international cricket club, most famous among people who never played cricket. Although some of us are practicing the game, most important in our activities are the club aspect—being members of the cricket club you feel "cool" in some way.

Pic.: Pamela Echeverria, one of the first members of the club says: "Ven al Club!!" ("Come to the club!!")

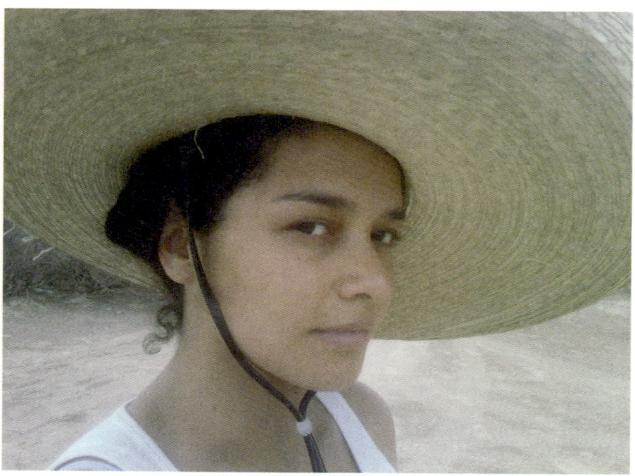

# Darius Mikšys

Darius Mikšys at Wollongong

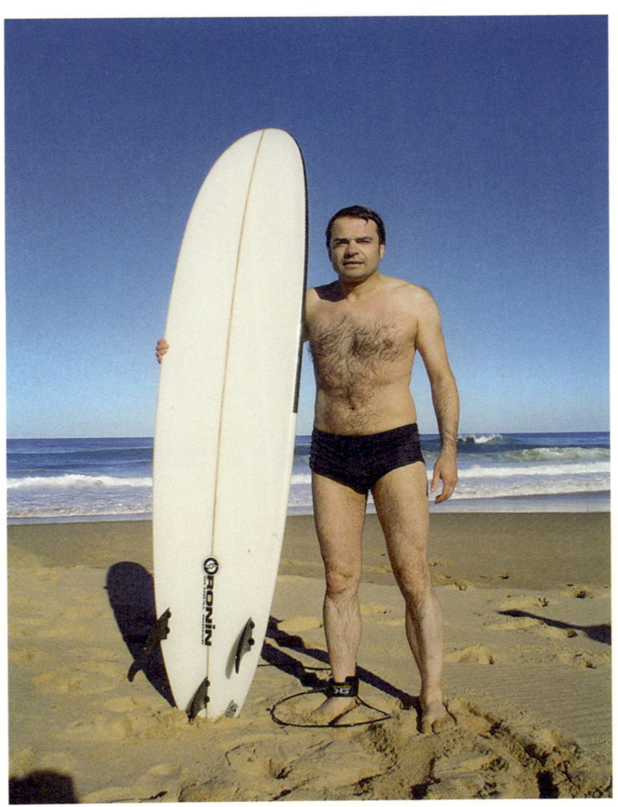

Before Darius Mikšys went to the Gasworks artistic residence in London, no one in Lithuania was playing cricket, and nor were expats from India seeing expats from the UK in a relaxed atmosphere often. The *Abdul Aziz Holiday Cricket Club* that Darius Mikšys founded upon his return is still active as a totally non-sequitur social event that gained its own life. It has the highest number of members not knowing anything about cricket than any other cricket club in the world. Hopefully Darius one day will become a president of a cricket federation of Lithuania.

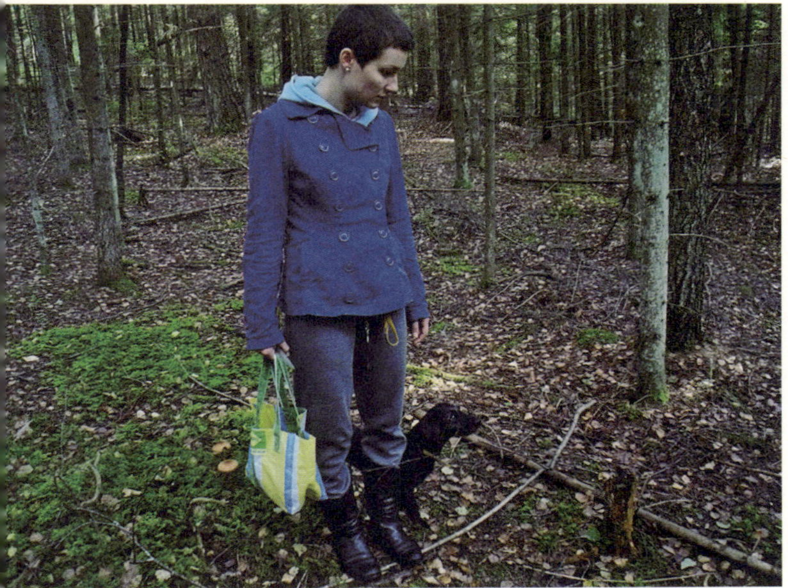

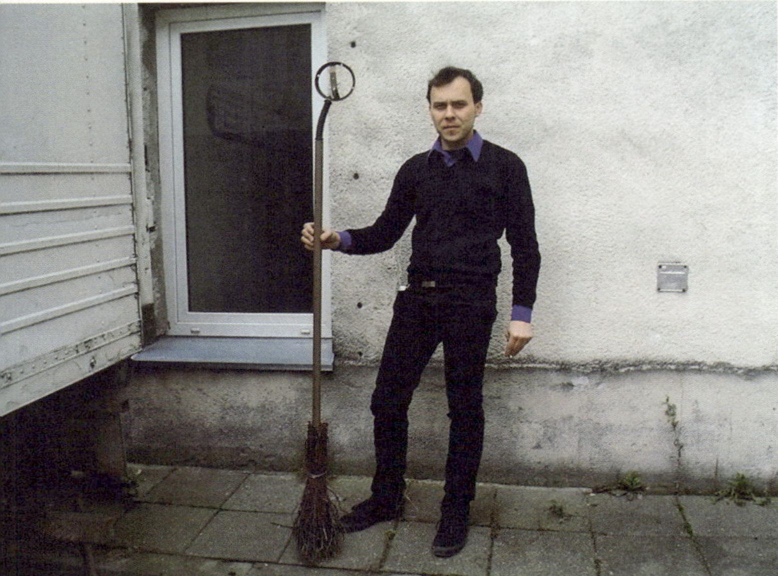

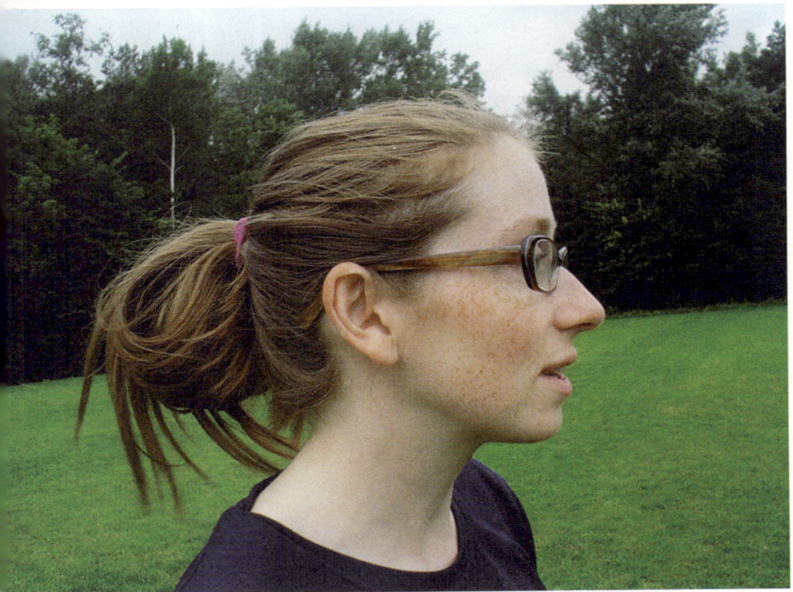

Julija Fomina, member of the cricket club, picking up mushrooms

Joe Micelli, member of the cricket club

Catherine Hemelryk, member of the cricket club, at the grounds

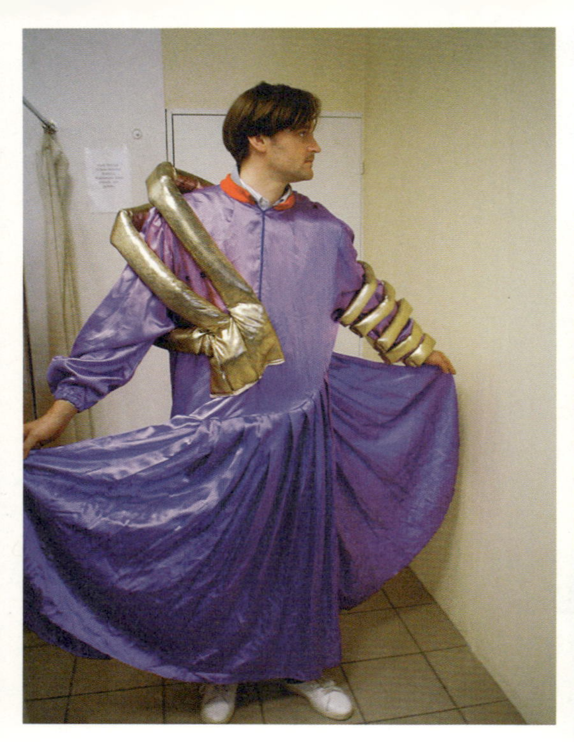

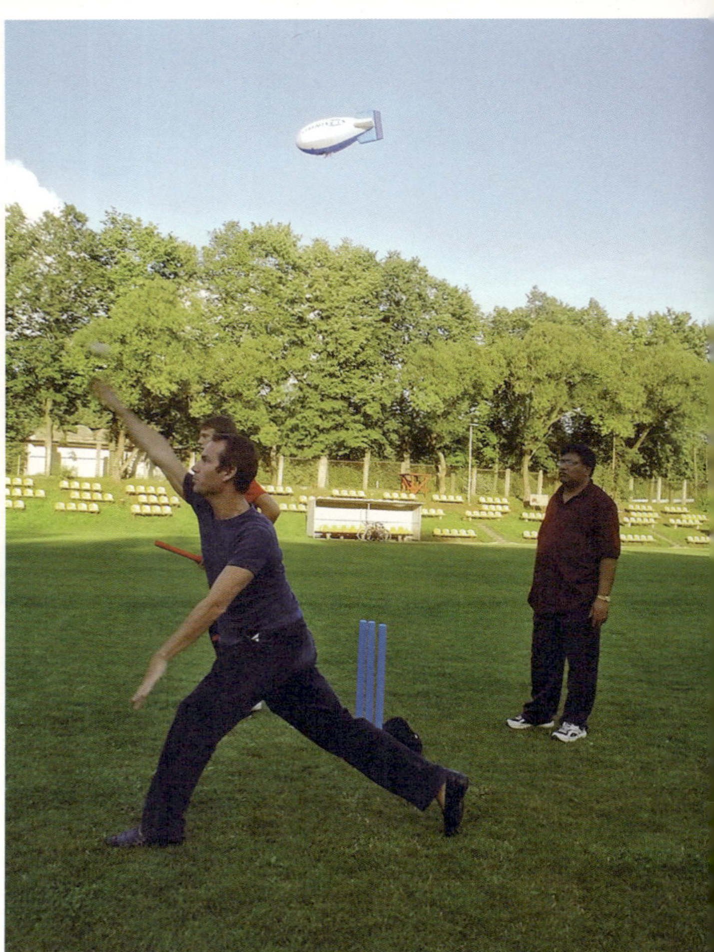

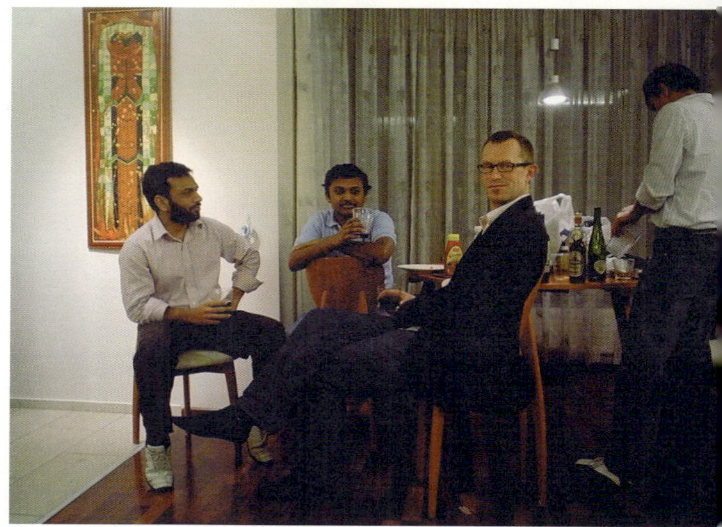

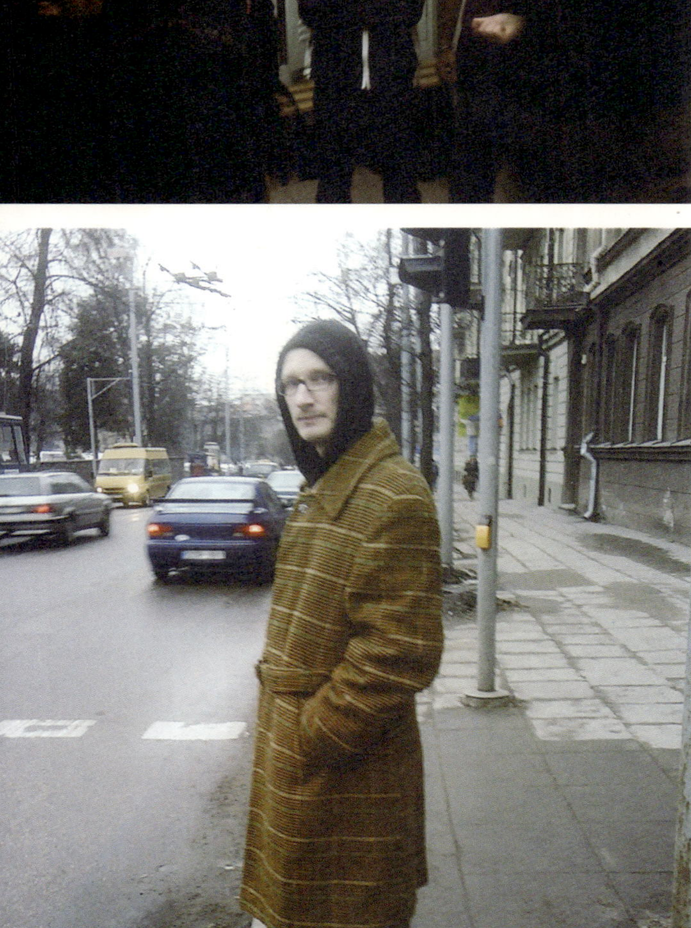

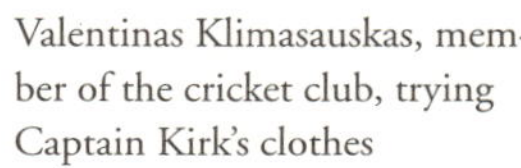

Valentinas Klimasauskas, member of the cricket club, trying Captain Kirk's clothes

During a game at Gelezinis Vilkas rugby ground: Tomas Maneke (left), Nair Padmanabhan (right)

Party at Nair's, from left: Asif, Saravana, Simon Rees, Siva Kumar

The members of Abdul Aziz's Holiday CC XI, Kauno Universitetai, and Vilnius Cricket Club, from left: Nair Padmanabhan, Saurabh, Anamjeet Singh (with a turban), Prateek Bobal, Satbir Singh, and Alistair Day-Sirrat, at the Vytauto Didziojo gymnasium sports hall changing room discussing the coming games

Rytis Saladzius, Pylimo St., Vilnius

## Manicurated

A nail salon was installed in the Bronx Museum's Permanent Collection Gallery. Ten works of art of the museum's holdings were selected, and visitors were invited to receive free manicures by professional manicurists. Miniature photographic reproductions of the selected works of art were applied to each participant's fingernails. The artworks were literally placed in the hands of the Bronx community.

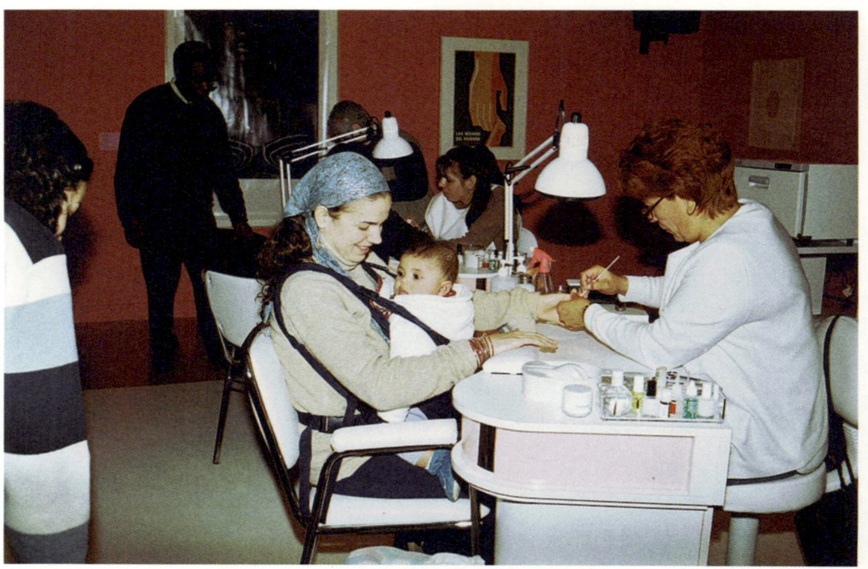

# Judi Werthein

*Manicurated*, New York, 2002

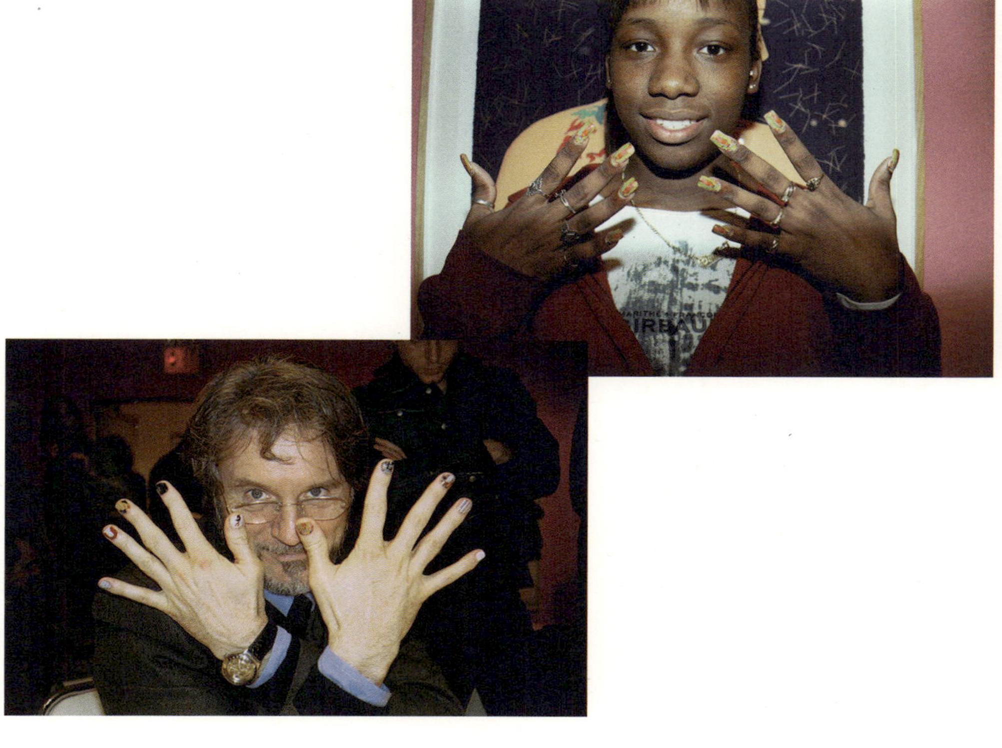

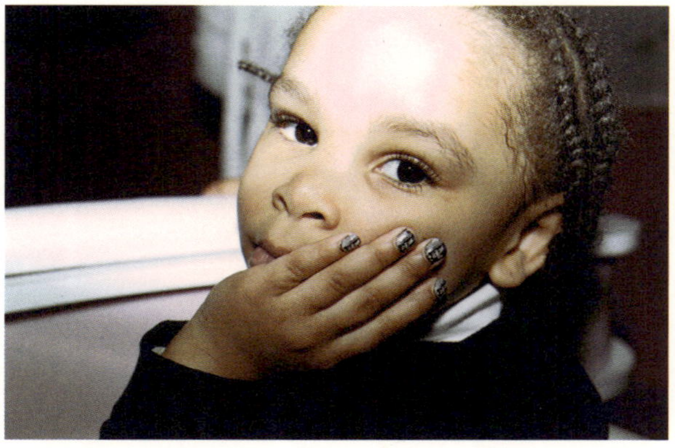

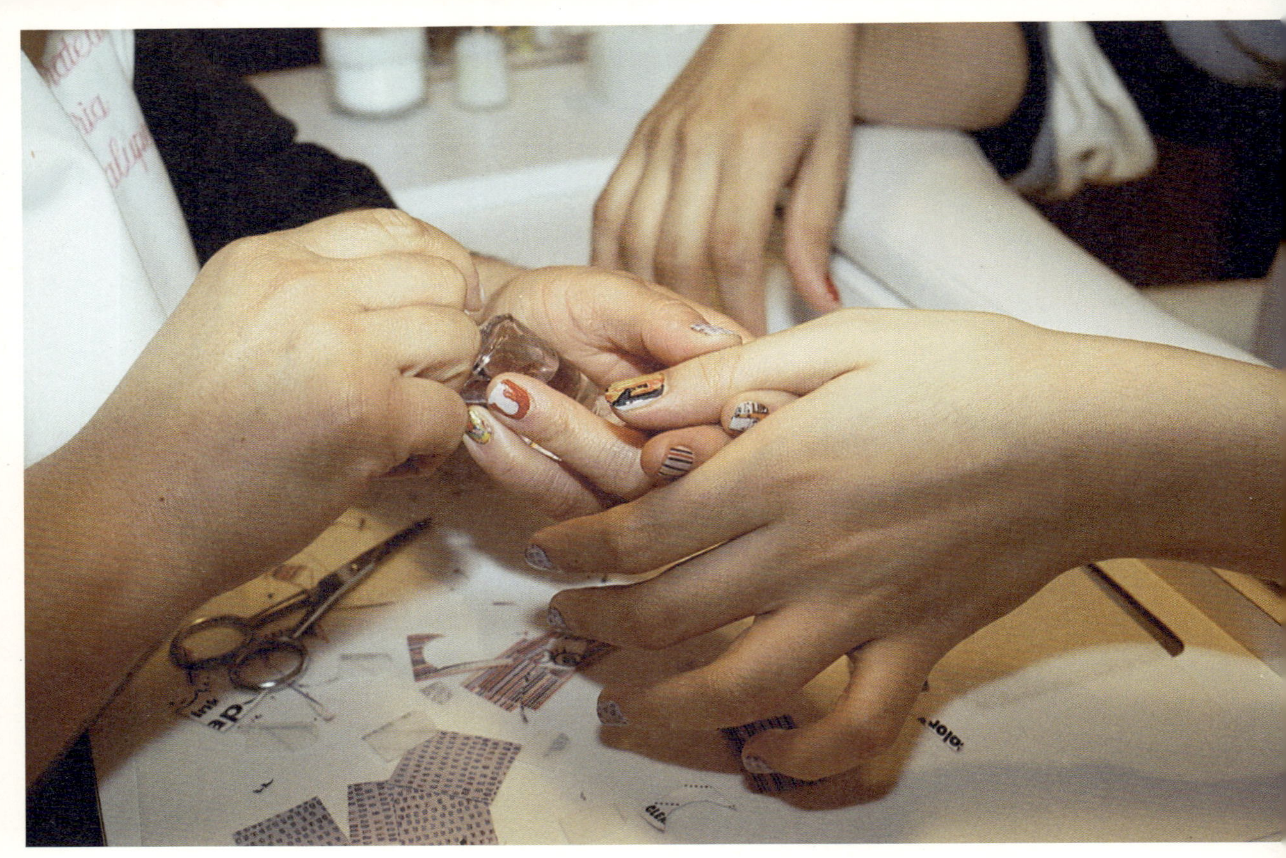

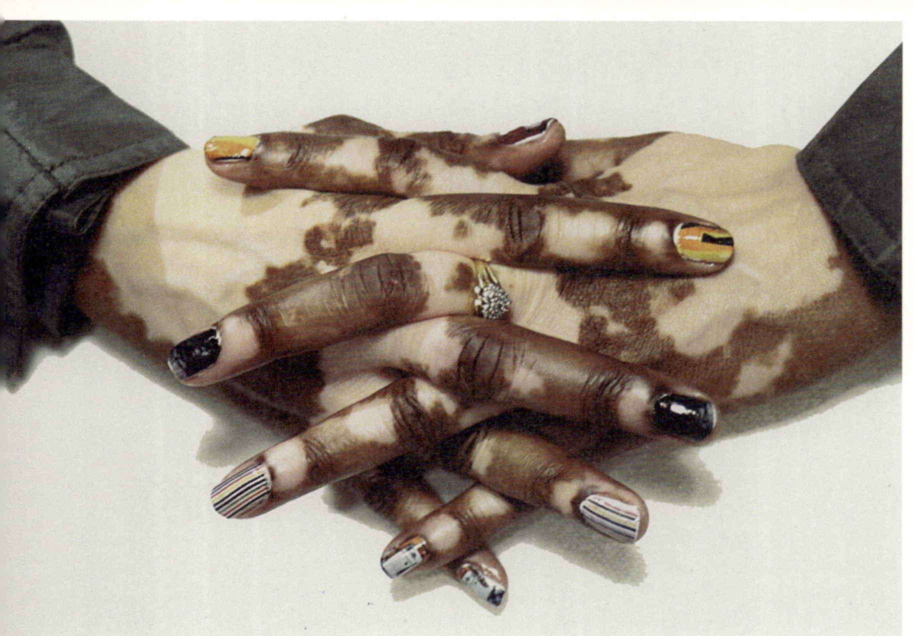

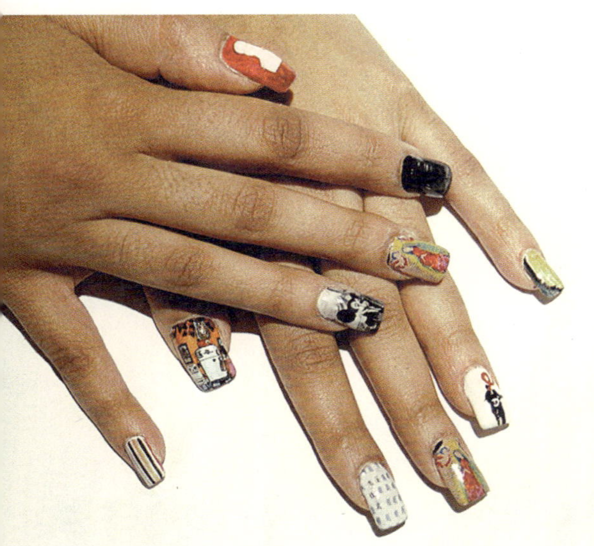

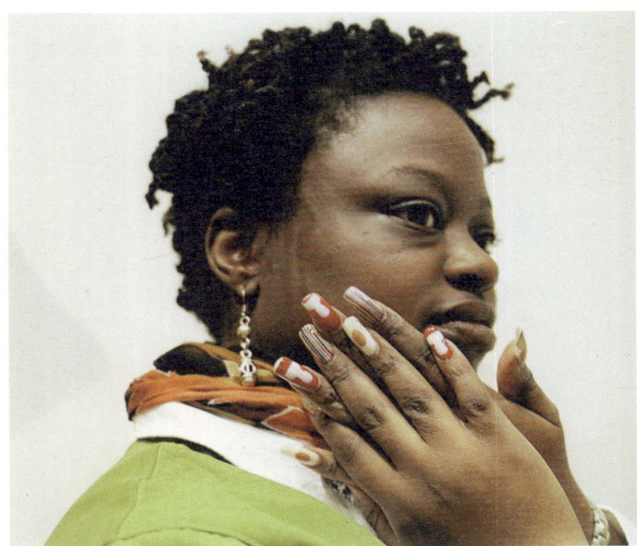

***Manicurated***, New York, 2002; participating artists: Byron Kim, Ester Hernandez, Zang Hongtu, Coreen Simpson, Tim Rollins & K.O.S., Tzeng Kwon Chi, Liliana Porter, Lynne Yamamoto, Jose Melendez Contreras, Larry Yañes

**Gabi Ngcobo** is an independent curator, writer, and artist from Durban, South Africa. She has worked as Assistant Curator at the South African Gallery, and curator and researcher for Cape Africa Platform. Other exhibitions include *Olvida quien soy*, co-curated with Elvira Dyangani Ose, Khwezi Gule, and Tracy Murinik for CAAM, Canary Islands, Las Palmas (2006), and *Titled/Untitled*, a curatorial collaboration with the Cape Town collective Gugulective. *Scratching the Surface Vol. 1* was curated under the collaborative platform manje-manje projects. In 2010 she co-curated *Rope-a-dope*, with Sohrab Mohebbi at Cabinet Project Space, New York (2010) and *Second Coming*, at the Center for Curatorial Studies, Bard College, 2010. She is currently completing a masters program at the Center for Curatorial Studies, Bard College, New York.

**Elvira Dyangani Ose,** born in 1974 in Spain/Equatorial Guinea, is an independent curator currently pursuing a PhD in History of Art and Visual Studies at Cornell University, New York, and holds a Master Diploma in Theory and History of Architecture, and a BA in History of Art. She is founding member of the *Laboratory for Oral Resources of Equatorial Guinea* and of the research group *Afroeuropeans* at the University of León, Spain. Her academic and curatorial research focus on Contemporary African Art and Culture. She has developed different interdisciplinary projects, focusing on the recovery of collective memory, intervention in public space, and urban ethnography. She has worked as a curator at the CAAC in Sevilla, and at the CAAM in Las Palmas de Gran Canaria, where she curated the exhibitions *Olvida quién soy* and *Tres Escenarios*. She was general curator of *Arte inVisible*, AECID, ARCO_Madrid in its 2009 and 2010 editions.

**Wanda Raimundi-Ortíz** was born in The Bronx, New York in 1973, where she currently lives. She studied at the Mason Gross School of Art at Rutgers University (MFA, 2008), and at the Skowhegan School of Painting and Sculpture (2002). She has produced a body of work that defies simple categorization in formal approach and narrative content. As an interdisciplinary artist, Raimundi-Ortíz has created works that address and explore the complexities of feminism, personal narrative, and Puerto Rican and Nuyorican culture. Awards include *The Bronx River Alliance Cultural Preservation Award* (2009) and the *El Diario/La Prensa Mujeres Destacada Honoree* (2008). Selected exhibitions include *Aqui y Ahora: Transcultura*, Centro Cultural de Espana El Salvador; *The S Files 05* and *No Lo Llames Performance*, El Museo del Barrio; *Artist in the Marketplace 25*, Bronx Museum of the Arts; and *The L Factor*, Exit Art, New York.

> www.wepawoman.blogspot.com

**Nástio Mosquito** was born in Huambo, Angola in 1981 and works between Luanda, Barcelona, and Lisbon. Mosquito's visual practice incorporates, music, film/video, and the spoken word. A self-proclaimed "communicator," Mosquito employs different media to critic and re-construct meaning located in art, politics, and history. His background in television and radio broadcasting allows Mosquito to utilize technology to his advantage by mimicking news reports, documentary film, and, to a certain degree, surveying mechanisms. Exhibitions and performances include *Urban Scenographies*, Johannesburg, South Africa (2009) and *Check List—Luanda Pop*, an exhibition from the Sindika Donkolo African Collection of Contemporary Art, Venice Biennale. His *DZzzz* live concert was first seen at Casa Africa in Las Palmas and in ARCO_Madrid, before he toured Johannesburg and Cape Town as part of the Speak Your Mind Festival.

> www.dzzzz.info

**Mlu Zondi** was born in Durban, South Africa, where he currently lives and works. He studied Performance Studies at the Durban University of Technology and creates performance indiscriminately for stage, gallery, and public spaces. Reluctant to get caught up in the embedded politics of these charged sites, Zondi nonetheless engages with its respective audiences and public, and calibrates concepts and works for each particular context. Awards include the *MTN New Contemporaries Award* (2006), and the *Standard Bank Young Artist Award*, Dance category (2009/2010). Selected exhibitions and performances include *Despotica*, a performance art video installation at Galerie KUB, Germany and at KZNSA Gallery, Durban (2009). *Experimenta* was commissioned and first performed at Bains Connective, Brussels and featured in group exhibitions including *Scratching the Surface Vol. 1* at AVA Gallery, Cape Town.

**Frente 3 de Fevereiro** is a multidisciplinary collective of cultural research and artistic intervention, the initiatives of which observe and critique the status of racism in Brazilian society. Its actions aim to eradicate prejudices inhered from slavery up until the present time. By creating new forms of protest against and alternative readings to racial issues as the media and the state narrate them, Frente 3 de Fevereiro attempts to generate social awareness of the outrageous living conditions of Afro-Brazilian communities, denouncing the "racial democracy" imposed by the authorities and the country's social bias. The *açoes* (actions) of Frente 3 de Fevereiro includes *Futebol/Desenho sobre fundo verde* (2006) and *Cartografia do Racismo para o Jovem Urbano* (2006). In 2007, it launched a book and film together entitled *Zumbi Somos Nós—Cartografia do Racismo para o Jovem Urbano.* Frente 3 de Fevereiro are Achiles Luciano, André Montenegro, Cássio Martins, Cibele Lucena, Daniel Lima, Daniel Oliva, Eugênio Lima, Felipe Texeira, Felipe Brait, Fernando Alabê, Fernando Coster, Fernando Sato, João Nascimento, Julio Dojcsar, Maia Gongora, Majoí Gongora, Marina Novaes, Maurinete Lima, Pedro Guimarães, and Roberta Estrela D'Alva.

> www.frente3defevereiro.com.br

**Fadaiat: Observatorio Tecnológico del Estrecho** (Technological Observatory of the Strait) is a multidisciplinary platform that aims to observe, by means of the creation of a permanent Media-Lab, the Strait of Gibraltar as a mirror-territory of the social, political, technological, and cultural transformations taking place in the world today. Exploring this European/Spanish border as a habitable territory, and as a radical transformative cartography, Fadaiat proposes to emphasize the state of emergency of certain social practices coming to pass in that area, persisting in the enrichment of the hybridization that those practices provoke. Fadaiat is Pilar Monsell Prado, Pablo de Soto Suárez, Joan Escofet Planas, José Pérez de Lama, Marta Paz Naveiro, Mónica Lama Jiménez, Helena García Rodríguez, and Sergio Moreno Páez.

**Gugulective** is an artistic collective found in 2006 in Gugulethu, South Africa. It is constituted by young artists coming from different areas of the country and sharing a range of diverse media and fine art. Gugulective arose from the need to bridge a creative and intellectual gap in places where cultural life has been situated apart from the official artistic mainstream, and to emphasize the roles of artistic and cultural events in transforming societies from the bottom up. Gugulective revisited *Shebeen's* historical meaning, turning it into a place of a political and sociocultural significance in which interaction with an audience is a primary objective. Gugulective has been displayed internationally, at events such as *Performing South Africa* (Berlin, 2008), *Subvision.Art.Festival* (Hamburg, 2009), and *Arte in-Visible* (ARCO_Madrid, 2009). Gugulective is Zipho Dayile, Unathi Sigenu, Themba Tsotsi, Khanyisile Mbongwa, Kemang Wa Lehulere, Dathini Mzayiya, and Athi Mongezeleli Joja.

> www.gugulective.net

# Everyone Is Welcome: Terms and Conditions May Apply

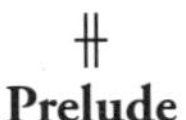

## Prelude

*For many of us, history is a rat race and "truth" is whoever gets there first. Every time we stop to catch some breath, someone else is speeding through, kicking dust and blurring the way to that illusive finish line. Many more of us do not have the "appropriate" attire to run the race, while others come titivated!*

ǂ

## Random selections in history

*Sometimes in April —*

In 1994, millions of people voted for the first time in South Africa's first democratic elections. I was one of them. I even worked as an enumerator and counted thousands of votes under the watchful eyes of international observers. I worked three-night shifts at a tabulation center somewhere in Chatsworth, a township near Durban. The experience was surreal, to say the least. My politics at the time were shoddy and I was really only in it for the money, so I didn't take notes and have no archival material from the experience. I bought a pair of expensive Nike sneakers, a movie ticket, popcorn, and Coca Cola with my earnings—that's it! Thinking about it in retrospect, I had no idea what awaited me. I only knew one thing: history had taken a sharp turn and it was taking me along with it. Long after those days, when I was learning that freedom was never going to come for free and that it's concept within that context was at my expense anyway, I discovered that I shared the memory of that exact time with those who survived the Rwandan genocide that left at least one million people dead. Now, I think twice before I commemorate. Indeed, where does one begin? This question has been asked by Ashraf Jamal, who has referred to South Africa as a "soap opera"—"a country that chooses to serialize itself into oblivion." How then to commemorate? Jamal asks this, and contends that "one doesn't commemorate, for South Africa, irrespective of the history it has constructed for itself, remains a society that lives with the terrible unease of never having begun. It may suppress this unease; indeed, it would seem that South Africa's finest talent is its ability to draw a rabbit out of a hat and call it history." As products of that history, many of us have had to step back, to be rabbits that choose to get back inside the magician's hat in order to find alternative ways to reemerge and to historicize that emergence from different perspectives.

*Sometimes in June —*

Growing up European sometimes makes one forget the color of one's skin and its significance. Believe it or not, that difference passes unnoticed to oneself, until somebody else decides it is time for one to pay attention. More than twenty years have passed by since the first *patera* or *cayuco* (ships used by immigrants to travel to Spain) arrived at the Canary Islands coast. "Good weather encouraged them to sail," somebody said. Ironically, the Canary Islands are called "islands of the everlasting spring." In those journeys from the West African coast to Europe, more than 90,000 immigrant people were arrested, at least 10,000 were reported dead, and hundreds were overlooked because of statistical reckoning and the selective memory of history. I have lived in the Canary Islands since I was seven years old. Never before was I was questioned as many times as in the past few years. Each time, I am asked to prove my political identity—Spanish, as I am obligated to deny any identity that inexorably puts me on the side of the forgotten. As sharp as history can be, placing me, a European black woman of African descent in opposition to them reveals history's deepest lack.

*Sometimes in September —*

Seven years and some months after I had cast my first and only vote (I shortsightedly spit on the following national elections in 1999), while in an artist residency program in Cape Town, the twin towers fell. It happened two days after the end of the World Conference against Racism, Racial Discrimination, Xenophobia and Related Intolerance, held in Durban. The news traveled so fast. My friends and I were watching as the second plane hit the second tower. In a bar on Kloof Street, while catching the first minutes of happy hour, we watched, mouths agape, and knew that history has just made another sharp turn and that it was taking us *all* with it. We did not leave the bar when the happy hour taps closed. In the morning, everything, including the Durban conference and its outcomes, was a blur, but the towers continued to tumble. That historical turn not only further intensified all that the Durban-held conference was against, but it also altered, among many other things, what we wear, how we behave, what we carry in our bags when crossing borders, and, most of all, the limits of our vulnerability at checkpoints. As a result, some people became, and even more are becoming, more random than others in "random" airport security checks.

*Sometimes in November —*

A year after the first "illegal" immigrant reached Fuerteventura Island's beaches, the acclaimed fall of the Berlin Wall was a reality. Europe staged a new political era, and freedom of movement acquired a completely different meaning. Nevertheless, free circulation proclaimed by the Schengen Agreement affected only the inhabitants of the countries signing the agreement. History collected a new apartheid experience. Europe constitutes an inexpugnable *metaborder*. The schema of a dual world, theirs and ours, was staged. "The figure of the unity of opposites (which is itself in many ways subtended by the schema or metaphor of the border) has never abolished this conception. On the contrary, it has confirmed that what can be demarcated, defined, and determined maintains a constitutive relation with what can be thought." So, choose your side of the border, and try to remain still. Damn, don't move!

ǂ

## Two: what have you done for me lately? (a duet)

*Gabi Ngcobo —*

The crisis of contemporary art is its fatal incarceration by discourse, which in turn alienates art from life. The crisis of life is lack of happiness. Experiencing art does not guarantee happiness but has potential to make the lives of people at least bearable. Let's face it: art and discourse are facing a pseudo–causality dilemma.

*Elvira Dyangani Ose —*

What if artistic discourses were able to establish alternative narratives through which to read the world? What if works of art were able to establish codes that help us consider ourselves and our prerogatives in a different manner? Who owns the capacity of telling? If given a chance, what types of histories would those people tell?

*Gabi Ngcobo —*

The challenge of history is that it never ends. It is a challenge because for a long time the kind of education that I received somehow affirmed that historical events were securely lodged in history and were never to be repeated. But the nature of history is that it does repeat itself. This is a known fact, a fact that makes Nelson Mandela's statement "Never, never and never again shall it be that this beautiful land will again experience the oppression of one by another and suffer the indignity of being the skunk of the world" unsettling. It is unsettling because it is excessively assuring. We cannot tell the future, but art has the capacity to reflect on historical experiences—to establish codes that can help us decipher the contemporary moment and narrate it to the world. "Articulating our contemporary experience," writes Jan Verwoert, "we cannot therefore be anything other than uncontemporary." What makes us uncontemporary, according to Verwoert, is our "insistence to not readily pass through the gates to enter the contemporary, without reservations." To put it mildly, I find Verwoet's observations refreshing. His reasons for this shared intuition to not readily enter into the contemporary is knowing that not entering—staying on the gates and taking a good look—might be a wiser decision. This reluctance to enter is also shared by the artists we have chosen for this project. If indeed they enter into the contemporary, they do so through other means: creating alter egos and pseudonyms in order to speak from and about that place, and through collaboration. The eleventh line in artist Nástio Mosquito's *Manifesto*, a video work, advises us to "collaborate, not because you have to share the bill, but because you'll grow taller with it." It is from this height, through these devises that we can have a glimpse of the contemporary and narrate it to the world.

*Elvira Dyangani Ose —*

That proves the unavoidable need of the art to be present, its crucial quality of being present. Those artistic practices are part of a long tradition of art and the artist's role in social changes. To those creators, everyday life is at the center of every discourse, and the narration of each society is of a crucial importance in the artist's critical practice. Works of art become part of a strong visual apparatus and a complex mechanism that came out from the experience of a collective social and political enthusiasm. Imagination is the necessary faculty for knowledge and change. Imagination is a social process. Art is a *fait social.*

*Gabi Ngcobo —*

At which point in history did art start relying so much on discourse for its survival? What can discourse do that art is not already doing for itself? What does it mean, for us so-called "postcolonial" beings, to bear witness to the critical discourse of postcolonialism being given a send-off? It has been over a year since this proposal was made public to an international audience as a curatorial departure point for the Third Guangzhou Triennial in China. What are we to expect next? So far I have not witnessed or heard of any major catastrophe of existence to those who have been deemed postcolonial by political history. This may mean several things, but one that topples all is that the colonial was never "post" in the first place. In fact, the only devastation I can detest is within the discourse itself. Life goes on, wars are fought, women are raped, anti-gay laws in places like Uganda are alarming, people are dying of AIDS, and the Pope's anti-condom claims are not only scandalous but deadly, to say the least. It is the artist's imagination that we can rely on, but not if the viewer is denied of much of the framework and left epistemologically bereft. The discursive aesthetics practices are, as Jacques Rancière sees them, "forms of visibility that disclose artistic practices, the place they occupy, what they 'do' or 'make' from the standpoint of what is common to the community."

*Elvira Dyangani Ose —*

Conceptually, colonialism was never "post." Colonialism was never over. It has been transformed into an accepted and broad coloniality. The coloniality of power, the coloniality of knowledge, as Walter D. Mignolo recalls. A coloniality which goes beyond temporal and geographical frames. I feel somehow that as postcolonial subjects—or, better said, as perpetually "colonialized" subjects, we are lost in the trap of discourse. However, art relies on a discourse that is more a "way of doing," a formula that distances ourselves from its spectacular dimension, a formula that is first of all experience. We need a discourse to call into question history, but history could be made using codes that are not necessarily written. Art interrogates history and regularly calls into question the visibility (or invisibility) of history's contributors and players. Contemporary artistic productions—mostly post-colonial initiatives—notably set out to excavate and uncover what Michel-Rolph Trouillot calls "silenced stories." For Trouillot, human beings participate in history both as actors and narrators. He refers to the ambivalence inherent in the definition of the word "history" to support his assertion that "History means both the facts of the matter and a narrative of those facts, both 'what happened' and 'that which is said to have happened.' The first meaning places the emphasis on a sociohistorical process, the second on our knowledge of that process or on a story about that process." Art proposes another reality to interfere with the sociohistorical process: the subjective reality of the art exhibition, the poetics of time and space of an artwork. It is in this realm of the subjective—as delimited by curators, by artists, by the political agendas of institutions, etc.—which is incapable of altering both discourses of the real, where the artist finds his or her place as an agent in the production of history. While critics may be quick to point out the constraints that such a discipline provides to dilettantes, some contemporary or postcolonial artists confirm Trouillot's assertions, when he recalls that alongside professional historians, there were other participants in the production of history that, even though they might not have dared to destabilize history's power, still added complexity to history-making. As I argue elsewhere, whenever the experience of the postcolonial subject is narrated, history and its silences go into crisis.[1]

1 Some of the thoughts reflected here were presented in a recent article, where Elvira Dyangani Ose reflects on Michel-Rolph Trouillot's book *Silencing the Past: Power and the Production of History* (Boston: Beacon Press, 1995). See more in: Elvira Dyangani Ose, *"On Travesía," Atlántica Magazine of Art and Thought,* No. 47. (2008), 24–35.

ǂ

**Three: teacher don't teach me nonsense**

*Gabi Ngcobo —*

History's silences intensify in places where historicizing beings meet and are shaped: the school or the academy. The dilemma of Western education as I have experienced it both in South Africa and in the Unites States is that it creates meaning from a Western perspective and of cannot grasp what that meaning may be for people on the other side—even when the subject is dealing with that other side. One of the things I found alarming, for an example, is that if people in the US have read or know any South African artist, that artist or writer is more often than not a white person. There is something comforting in learning that there were some white people who were involved in the struggle against apartheid, that whiteness was not totally doomed after all. But this is comforting at the expense of balancing with learning of the struggles from black perspectives, with learning from the people who suffered most under the brutality of that regime. If we were looking at becoming part of the "explosions of the posts," would it then not make more sense to propose a "post-white" moment?

*Elvira Dyangani Ose —*

A "post-white" moment or, better said, a "post-Western" moment is proposed from the experience of art, at the same time that it is articulated within the academy. Academy introduces new recipes to avoid getting lost in its own definition. Some of them challenge traditional conceptions, such us the exclusive modern universalism of the West, nowadays unpacked by theories on alternative modernities. Other dispute usual theoretical frameworks take Édouard Glissant's *Poetics of Relation* as a powerful example. However, "house specialty" seems to be the introduction of a persistent interdisciplinarity in art history departments.

For both of us coming from the other side, the side of "action"—(I have never been an artist, but my curatorial approach has always been linked to works engaging with intervention in public spaces, in real time and in life)—getting in the orthodoxy of the academy is a long process of struggling against our own skepticism, while performing a modus operandi that in changing the academy itself and our relation with it allows us to keep who we are and what we want safe.

ǂ

**Bonus track**

*The trouble with the rat race is that even if you win, you're still a rat.* (Written by Jane Wagner for Lily Tomlin's comedy act, 1977. The quote is commonly attributed to Tomlin and appeared in *People Magazine* in the December 26, 1977 issue.)

*Ask Chuleta* is a project consisting of a series of three videos featuring Wanda Raimundi-Ortiz as a self-made pseudo-character named Chuleta. Chuleta provides 101 (basic) lessons on contemporary art practices and jargon associated with it as an attempt to mediate meaning for the Latina and black youth from The Bronx, New York. This, for "Chuleta," is her way of "bringing gaps" between the art world and, as she puts it, "people like us"—opening a dialogue between the "white box" community and her non-gallery-going community. Performed within the seemingly non-mediated domestic setting of Ortiz's Bronx apartment, the videos are low-tech and straightforward. Chuleta's intervention launches with a series of attempts to define terms associated with contemporary art, terms whose meanings we take for granted until we are confronted with works such as Ortiz's.

A few years ago in Dakar, Senegalese curator Ngone Fall conducted a similar "experiment with language" in the form of a radio show. Fall undertook a series of discussions about art history using Wolof, one of the widely spoken languages in West Africa, as opposed to in the residual colonial French. This is not an easy task; in fact, it is almost impossible, as we realize through Chuleta, who is Nuyorican, a term ascribed to second- and third-generation Puerto Ricans born and residing in or around New York State, especially in New York City and its metropolis. Chuleta's accent reveals that Spanish—Nuyorican Spanish, to be precise—is her first language. Her performance is as much about language as it is about art as a place where we experience the limitations of language at work.

# Wanda Raimundi-Ortíz

*Ask Chuleta*, 2007–2008

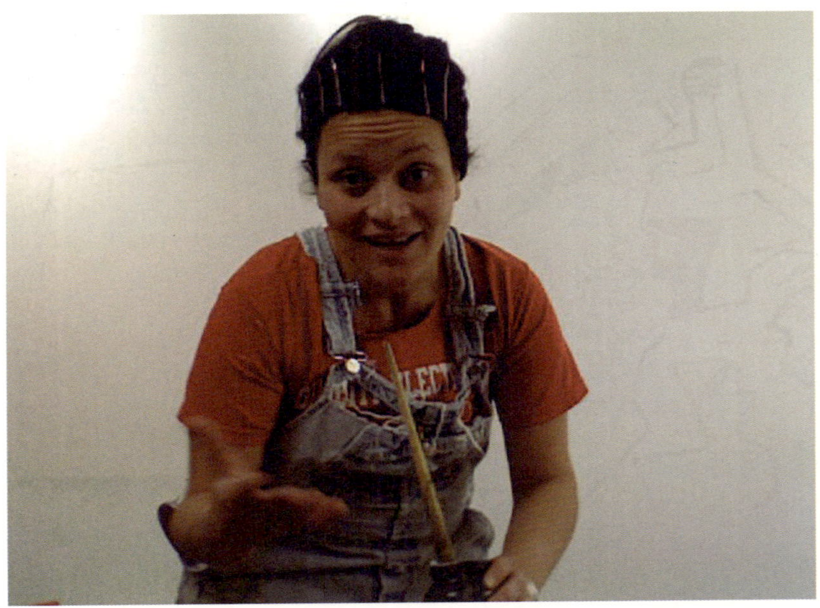

In this project, Chuleta discusses three topics. Topic 1 is "Contemporary Art," Topic 2 is "Pollock & Kahlo," and Topic 3 is "Color Field Painting." All three videos attempt to best educate Latino youth about the possibility of art and interpretation existing in things we do within our daily existence—things that do not need heavy philosophical background to understand in order to apply. In all three videos, Chuleta reiterates her mission: "To bridge the gap between the art world and everyday people." Although she refashions herself as a funny figure—an everyday type of woman who is fun and humorous—Chuleta's "lessons" are created for a more serious principle. They are gestures of generosity: a way to "give back" information to which others may not have access. The tension that is expressed by Chuleta's hand gestures as well as the struggle made obvious by facial expressions reveal the limiting and impenetrable nature of the language of art.

Explaining the concept of the "white box," Chuleta admits that "it sounds stupid." She takes risks and applies humor in order to reveal the superficial nature of the art world, a world of which she is part. Unpacking the concept of "posts" becomes a comical affair. "It's not like the *New York Post,* the newspaper, neither is it like posting stuff on your MySpace page," she warns. It is, rather, she explains, a "post" that marks something that occurs "after," something that is more like the last one "but different… like retro clothes or leftover food revisited the next day." The word "flipped" comes up often to highlight how it is all the same thing but turned around again and again—what Zine Magubane calls the "the explosion of 'posts'." Here Ortiz makes an argument about the contradictory nature of these explosions—for example post-identity, post-race, or post-black—as propositions that emerge when those described as "post" are making attempts toward creating their own forms of subjecthood. Chuleta's desperation takes her as far as letting out that hip-hop artist Jay-Z and R&B singer Beyoncé were spotted at Art Basel Miami Beach checking out the post-post-everything art inside the "white boxes," whose concepts she has been struggling to articulate. By referencing figures in popular youth culture, Chuleta seems to have driven her point home: "Go and see for yourself."

In "Pollock and Kahlo," dressed in denim overalls and carrying a hairbrush in her back pocket, Chuleta gives a spontaneous demonstration of how to make a Jackson Pollock painting. She tries without success to locate Pollock's "mess" within the American Abstract Expressionism movement and resorts, in desperation, to recommending that her viewers order the movie about Pollock's life on Netflix, an online DVD rental service. All of these attempts, whether we read them as failures of articulation or sites where meaning is transformed, have a twofold operation. On the one hand, they aim to empower those at the margins of discourses, and on the other hand also lay bare the superfluous distance art discourses have created between art practice and society.

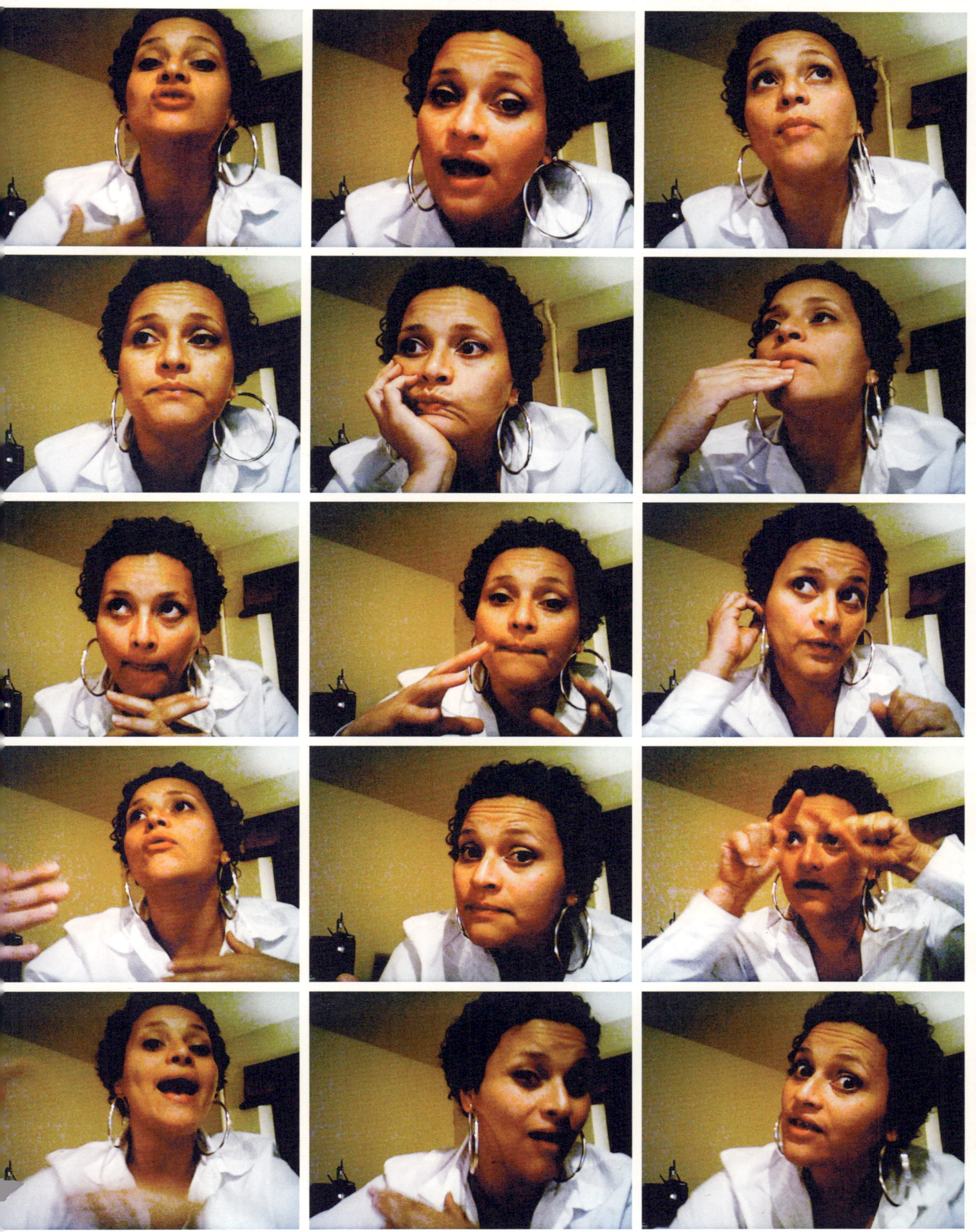

*Chuleta*, 2007–2008

"Hello, I'm here to tell you that Nástio Mosquito is dead." Thus begins Mosquito's video *The End of Nástio Mosquito*. Mosquito appears announcing his "own" death and introduces his alter ego Nástia, an alternative subject position within which his subjectivity can be reconsidered. He performs in front of a background projecting Web pages occasionally scrolling down to reveal written content, some projected on his body, and images of himself. Mosquito announces his death repeatedly throughout his performances; the more he dies, it seems, is the more he lives. Perhaps this frequency of the announcement suggests an afterlife, or Mosquito's refusal to stay dead. Perhaps Mosquito is making attempts at being "post-human" as a way of mimicking the "postcolonial" conditions that in turn have ushered in new forms of subjugation. His "post" is like a ghost that comes back to haunt the very place it is said to have transcended. This becomes apparent when he reemerges to admit: "unfortunately I'm inside this body, and that's a relationship *you* cannot run away from…" The performance of his own "murder" places him in a precarious zone of being and non-being, unfixed yet fixed, a zone that highlights his practice as operating within an intermediate position. Within this position he plays both victim and perpetrator by applying metaphors, narratives, and other interpretive linguistic modes, using them to help us make sense of the world around us. His practice as a whole is critiquing prevalent views of the African continent, dangerously historicized through a single lens as possessing the most terrible manifestations of human nature.

# Nástio Mosquito

***Manifesto***, 2008–2009, video stills; courtesy of DZzzz Enterprises and We Are Here Films

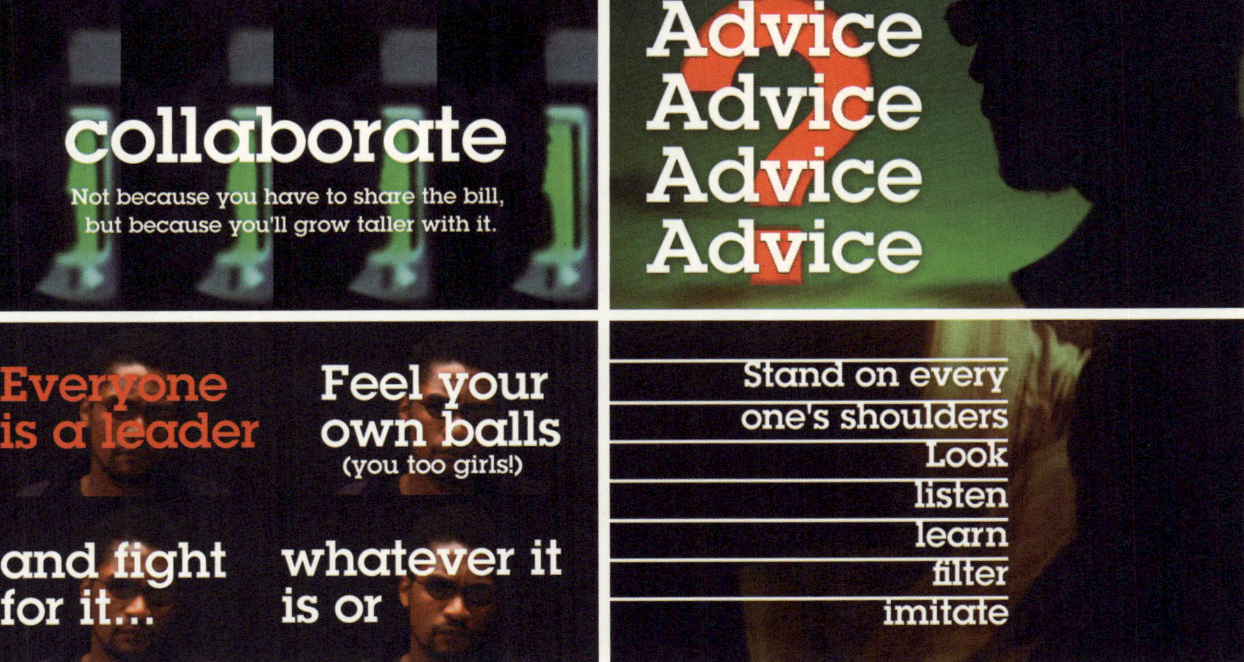

Mosquito's practice is an attempt to rearrange history by critiquing its narrative. He spares no one, not even himself, for he is aware that artistic creativity is not a luxury, nor can it be used as a discourse of development and poverty reduction. He thus resists the lure of spatial identification, the aspects of which are also integral to his practice. By justifying his actions by repeatedly reminding us that he is "the son of the Cold War," Mosquito places himself within the history of his country. Born in Angola when the Angolan Civil War had been raging for at least six years and was to continue for another two decades, Mosquito is aware that this history can both help him articulate his frustrations and hinder his creativity. "I know people in Africa have suffered with terrible wars but it's time to go to work. I'm sorry, *go to work*!" scolds Nástia, his alter ego.

In another live performance work, Mosquito, after again announcing his "death," makes a proposition to "Fuck Africa!" The performance is delivered in a fake accent and is accompanied by a live three-piece band. Here Nástia describes a scene in a marketplace where he effortlessly purchases Europe and America but snubs Africa when it is suggested that he also buy it. "What? Africa? You must be joking!" he retorts. From this point on he goes on a rant about the state of the continent, drawing from every imaginable stereotype and established but narrow-minded view of Africa. He then comes to a conclusion that seems to sum up the problem as lying in that many refuse to know, to investigate, and to get to the heart of the matter, which are gestures that say "Fuck Africa."

These acts and their delivery (he curses all the way through), help position Mosquito within a critical discourse of cultural criticism. Like Caliban, the protagonist in Shakespeare's *The Tempest*, Mosquito's use of the English and Portuguese languages, the colonizer's languages, is crude. Caliban's retort to Prospero, "You taught me your language and my profit on't is I know how to curse," has become over the years Mosquito's slogan for resisting the lures of postcolonial conditions that blur neocolonial curves. In *Dreams and Illusions* (2009), an intervention in the Cape Town public transportation, Mosquito attempted to put history into perspective by devising "radio shows" and installations in the form of history lessons. He started from scratch, following Franz Fanon's argument that the only way the colonized could become liberated and truly recognize themselves was first of all to fully acknowledge that what had initially been their culture and identity had been totally and irreversibly destroyed by the colonizers. His pre-recorded "lessons" thus were lessons about Africa's great civilizations and recent triumphs, many of which get obscured in the process of writing global histories.

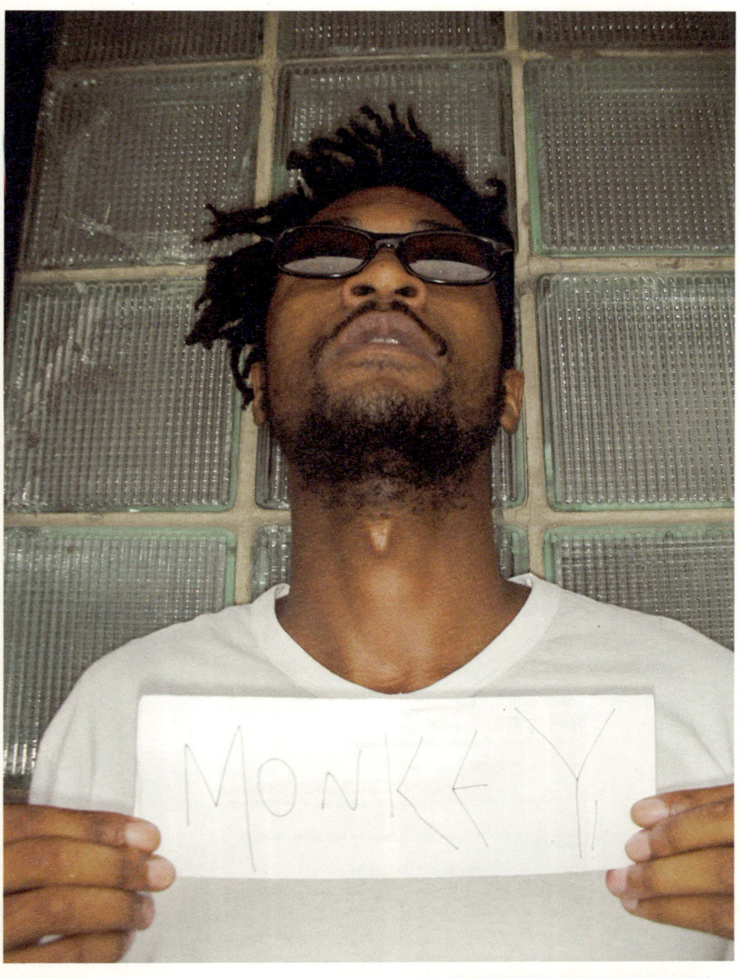


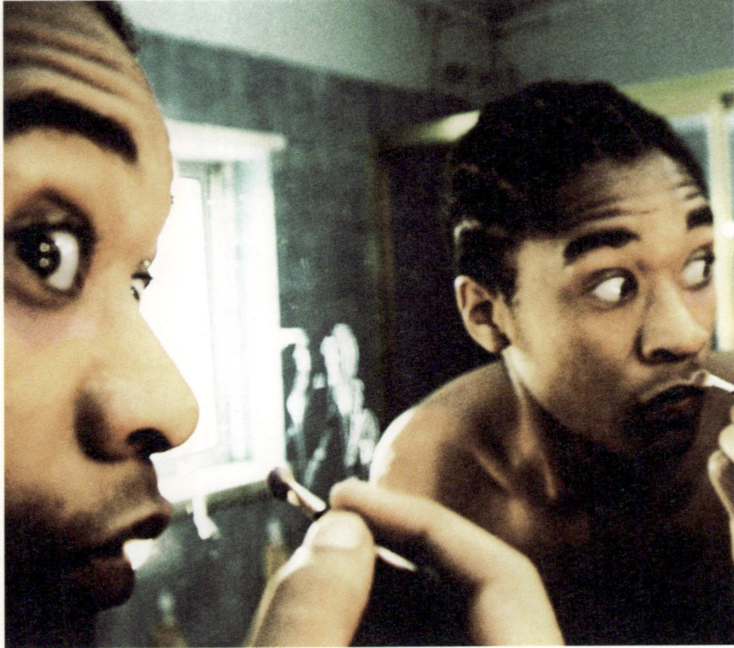

***Self Portrait (Monkey)***, 2008; courtesy of DZzzz Enterprises and We Are Here Films

***Untitled*** (photo by Tiago Figueiredo)

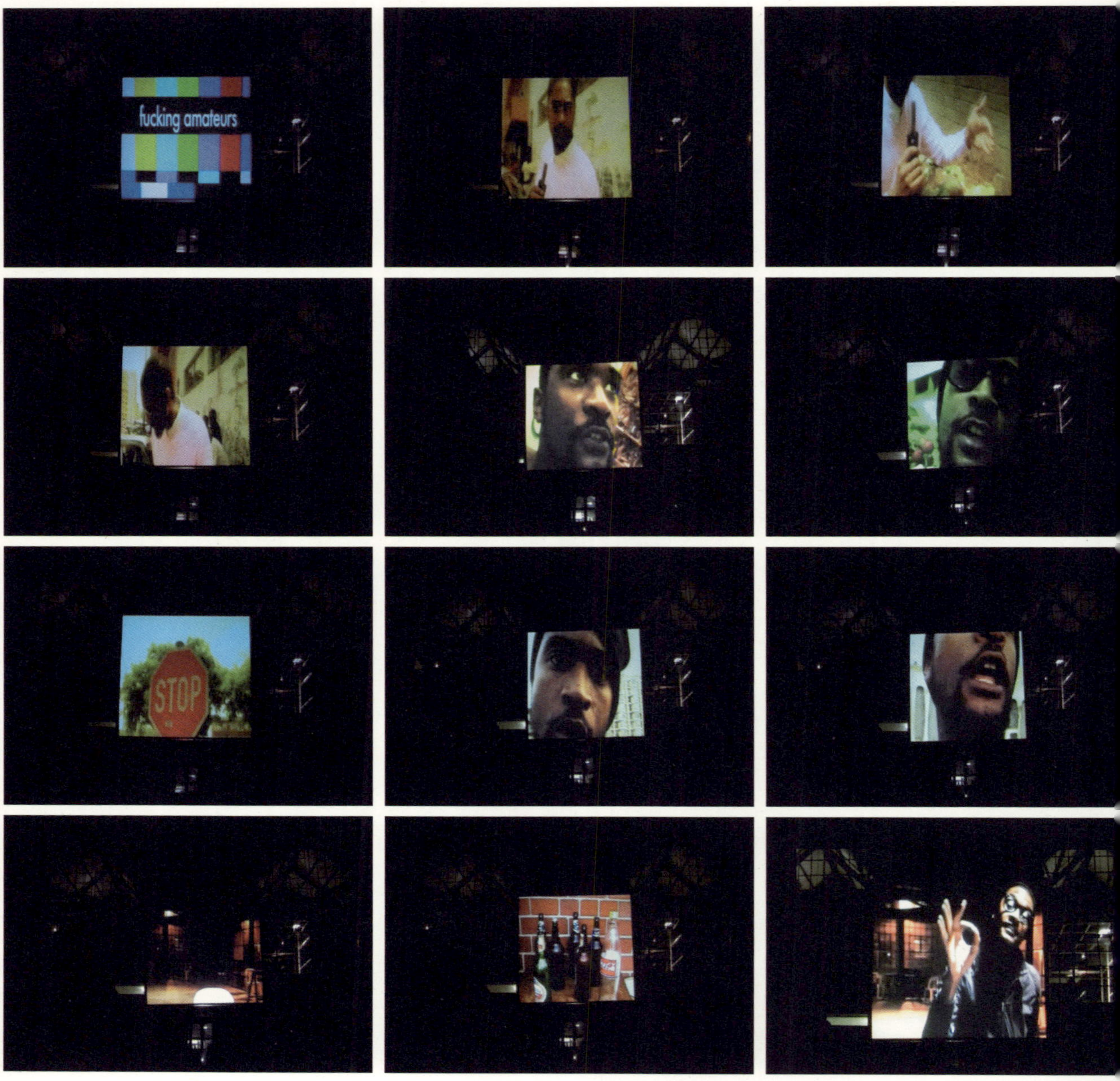

***Public screening of Urban Paradise,*** 2009, Drill Hall, Johannesburg (photo by Alastair Mclachlan)

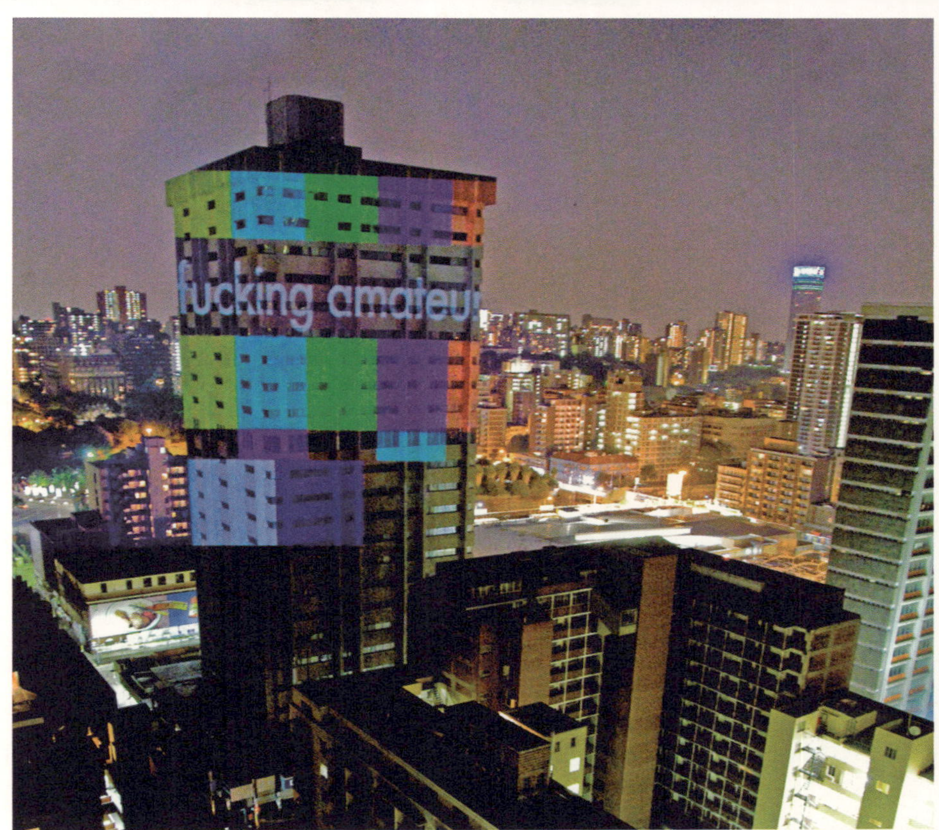


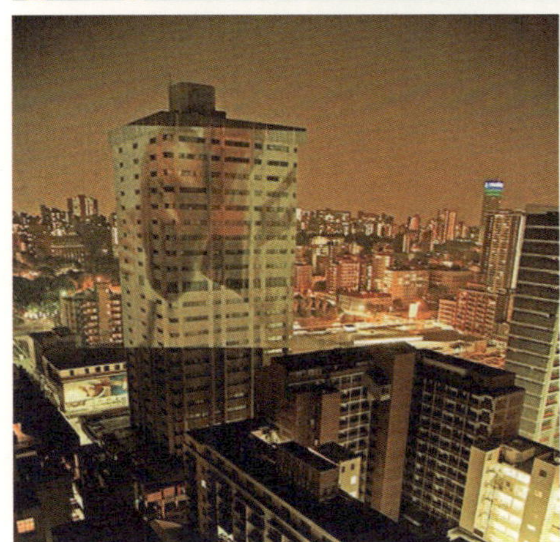

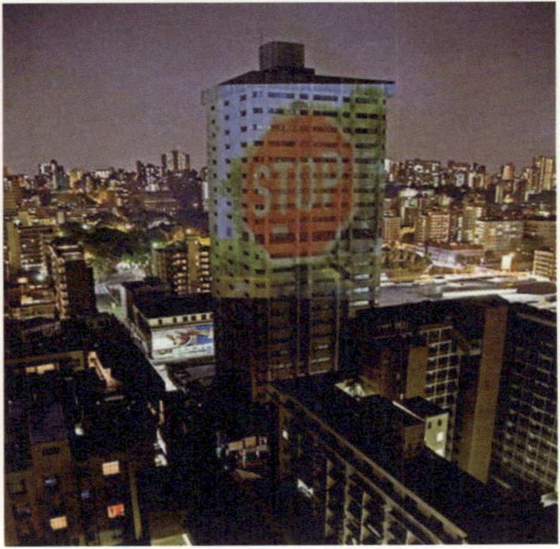


***Public screening of Urban Paradise,*** 2009, Drill Hall, Johannesburg

South African artist Mlu Zondi can be considered a product of a different set of "posts." As Rasheed Araeen observed, "There are historical conditions which apply to all the so-called postcolonial countries, including South Africa, but what makes South Africa different are its racial and ethnic components and the cultural diversities they represent." Thus for Zondi identity is key, both in its former construction under oppression and in how it is negotiated within a transforming society.

A performance artist with a background in theater education, Zondi is conscious about not limiting his work within one platform, and performs in theater stages, art galleries, and public and alternative spaces. His award-winning performance *Silhouette* has been seen in eight places in four countries over the past four years. The work is in collaboration with actor and writer Ntando Cele and features a video person who follows the characters around recording live transmissions of selected parts of the performance. In this performance Zondi and Cele negotiate gender roles that are a testimony of the fraught relationships between black men and black women, specifically in post-apartheid South Africa.

# Mlu Zondi

***Identikit***, 2004, Durban, South Africa (photos by Nathi Gumede)

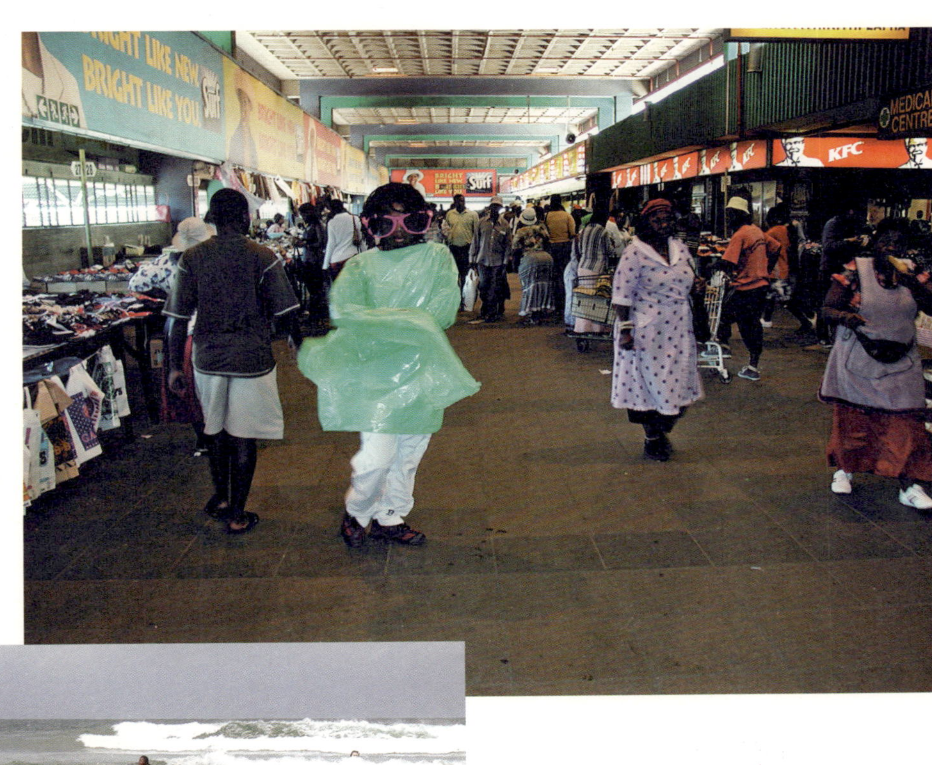


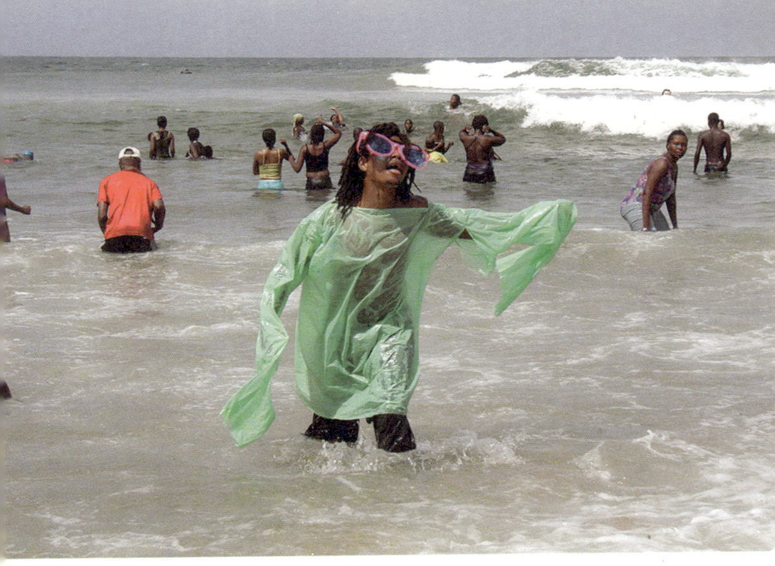

Silhouette – Part II

The constitution of a liberated South Africa introduced clauses that sought to correct many aspects of society, including by stressing women's freedom as authors of their own lives, as decision-makers, and as providers who may even earn more than men. From here on multiple crises surrounding black masculinities can be traced, this is what South African scholar of masculinities Kopano Ratele identified as "the male fear of democracy." These masculinity crises are unique compared to other crises that may exist in different parts of the world (not excluding South African male–identified people of other races), in that they are historico-racial in nature and emerge from subterranean movements underlying questions around cultural groupings, practices, habits, and identity. "I'm in the black and there's no getting out," muses Cele as confirmation of this. The title of the work, *Silhouette*, already suggests that what the work is addressing is indeed a black issue arising against a lighter background of the "miracle" that is South African democracy. Zondi's performance is mostly full of silent actions, as the only sounds that come out of him are whistles or a "hey" here and there to get a woman's attention. His movements are abstract but indicative actions that compel the woman to comply over and over again until, in the end, when she cannot take any more, she strikes back.

The man, Zondi, is terrified. It is, as Kopano Ratele observed, "a terrifying thought to be equal to others." He explains further that "It is a terror because it implies a revolution and revolution in turn implies death—the death of the old and the birth of the new. We can't imagine equality in the same way that we can't imagine our own death, that is to say social death." Cele's self-authored utterances during the performance attest to this terror, leading to contradictions and confusion about how exactly to claim her freedoms:

*I fizz at the thought of motherhood imagining my womb carrying another life then I look at those younger than me rushing to fresh produce. I, I, I, am the same being that brings life into the world yet I watch as my sons drown themselves in alcohol, down boy down!!! I play dead as my neighbour beats his wife to death. Amandla, amandla (power, power) I cheer on as we march to burn that witch to death. I nurture the homeless in winter, I pleasure my husband as if our honeymoon has just yet begun. I sing my brother to sleep and pray the lord my soul to keep for I'm fragile and can't save the world.*

*Silhouette* was devised as a project created under Zondi's performance company, Sololique Projects, established in 2002. He is the principal member, but incorporates other collaborators, such as Cele. It won the MTN New Contemporary Award and was devised around the time of South African president, then Deputy, Jacob Zuma's infamous rape trial. While Zuma was acquitted of criminal charges, his statements during the trial left a damaging social imagery around issues of women's rights to their bodies, around tradition, and around the AIDS pandemic. Sololique Projects has established an extensive body of works characterized by their play on contemporary political conditions, stereotypes, and tensions of "otherness" and difference.

*Silhouette*, 2005–2007, a Sololique Projects initiative

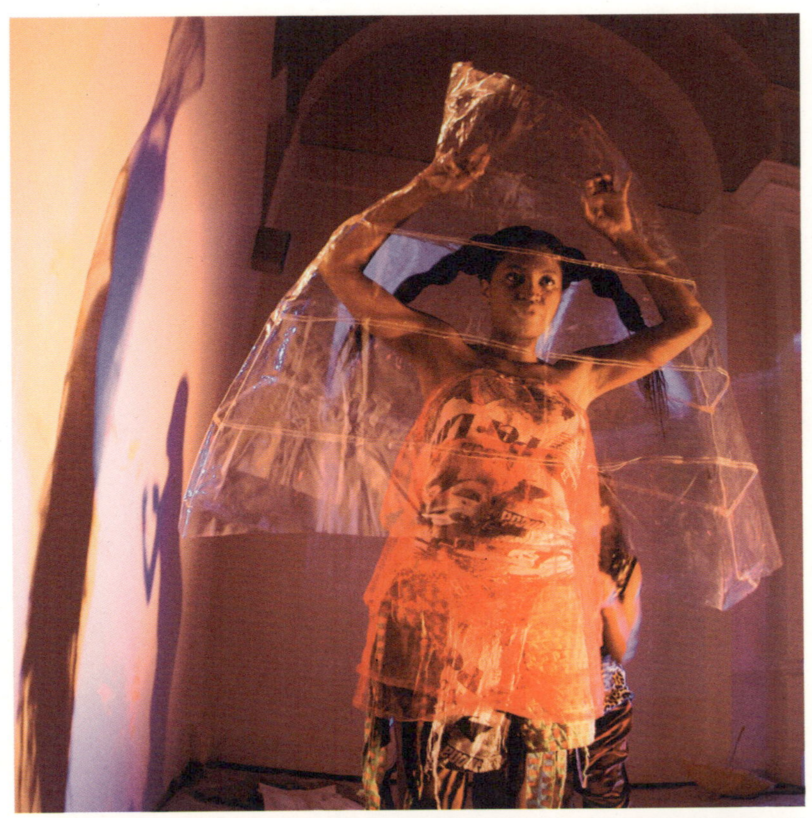

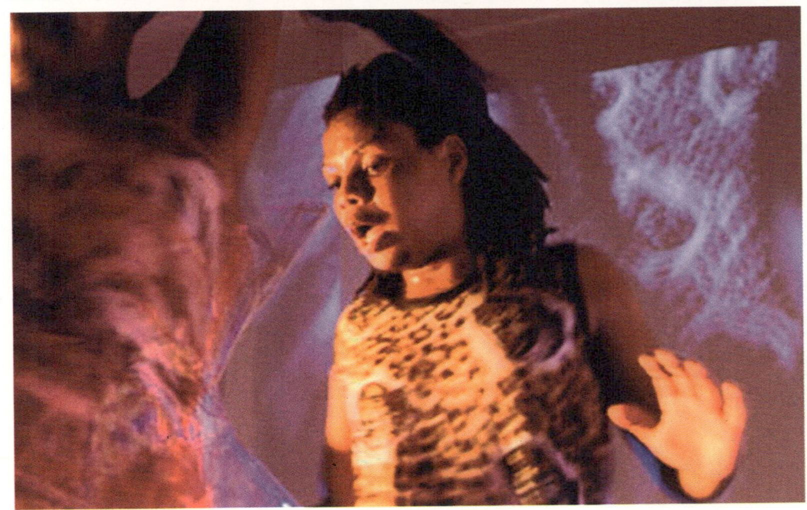

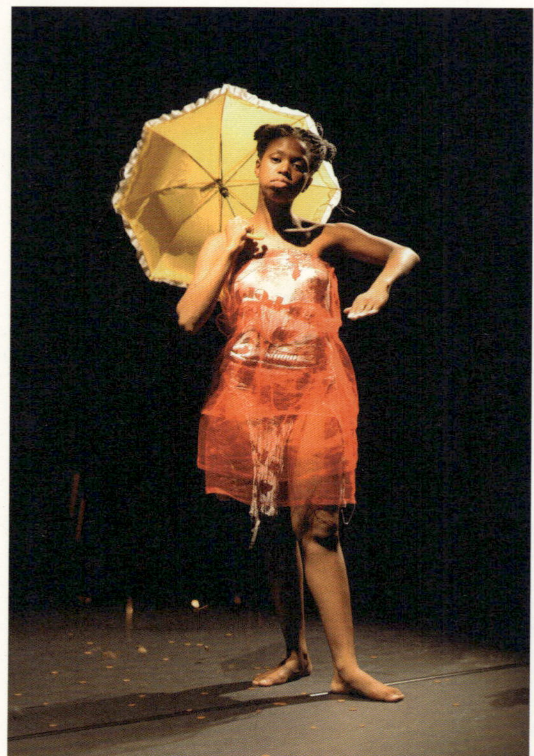

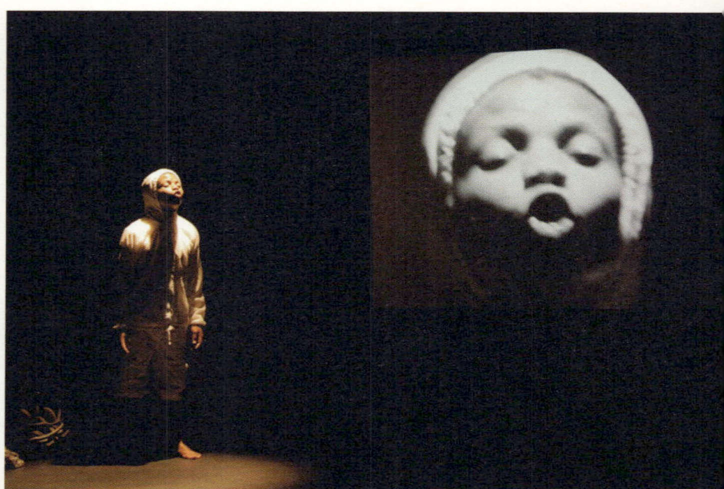

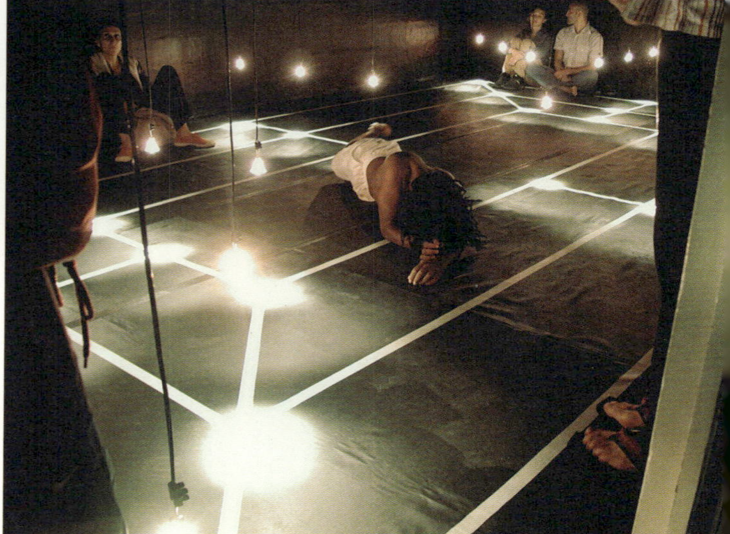

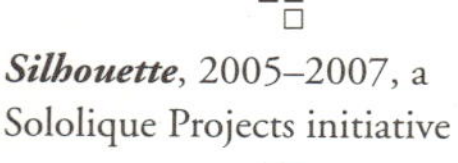

***Silhouette***, 2005–2007, a Sololique Projects initiative

***Identikit***, 2004, KZNSA Gallery Durban

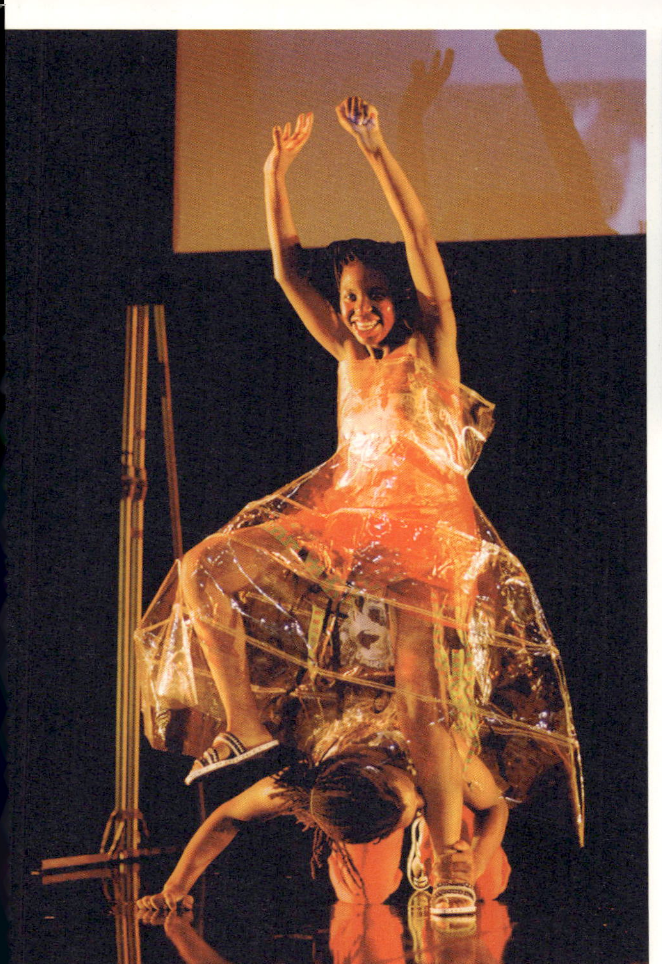

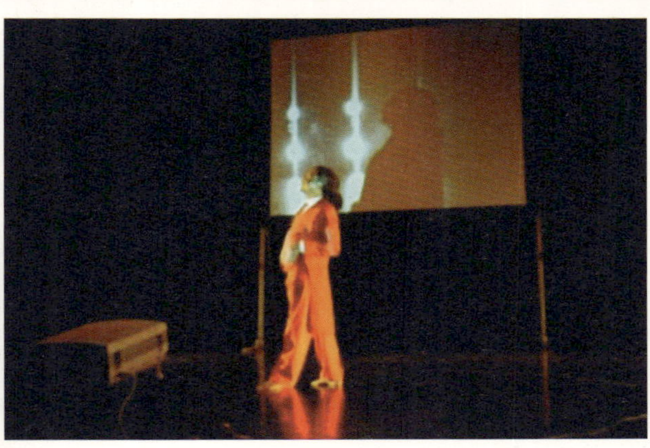

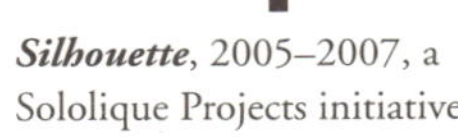

***Silhouette***, 2005–2007, a Sololique Projects initiative

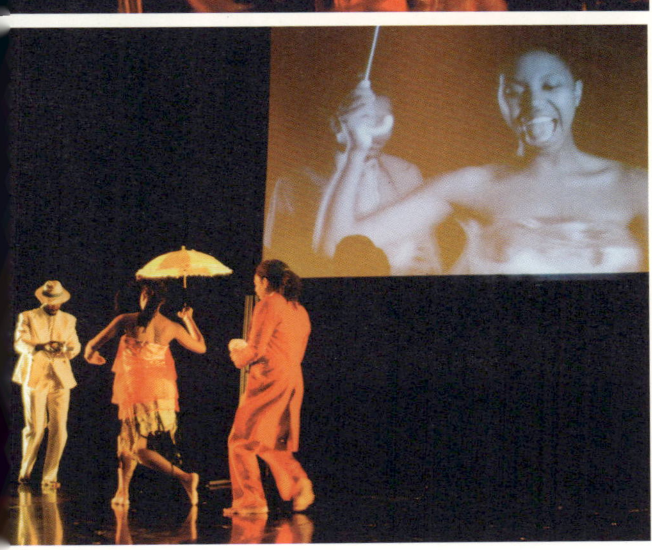

A dozen people are waving a banner at a crowded public square, the Praça João Mendes de Sao Paulo. Together, adults and youth, women and men, blacks, whites, native Indians, and foreigners emit cheering cries for justice and social unity. They are carefully guarded by the police of the city, who after a while force them to disperse. Before they fold the banner, it can be seen to read: *Zumbi Somos Nós* (We are all Zumbi).

*Zumbi Somos Nós* is a poetic manifesto of direct action against racism that the Frente 3 de Fevereiro created in 2006. This documentary film, produced by Gullane Films and retransmitted by the national channel TV Cultura as well as by more than a dozen television platforms around the country, combines multidisciplinary *açoes* (actions), artistic interventions in public space, and social criticism. All of these, along with vibrating musical compositions generated by some of the fifteen members of this multidisciplinary group, question the racial discrimination suffered by young black Brazilians at the hands of the authorities.

"Are we a racial melting pot? Are we a racial democracy? How could racial democracy emerge in a country that does not feature political democracy tradition?" Thus begins one of the songs that, along with interventions in urban space, are the most effective actions of this group.

# Frente 3 de Fevereiro

***Quem policia a polícia?*** ("Who polices the police?"), 2004, São Paulo, Poster

***Zona de Açao*** ("Action Area"), 2004, Police remove the posters "Gentrificado," by the collective Bijari, from Sao Paulo streets

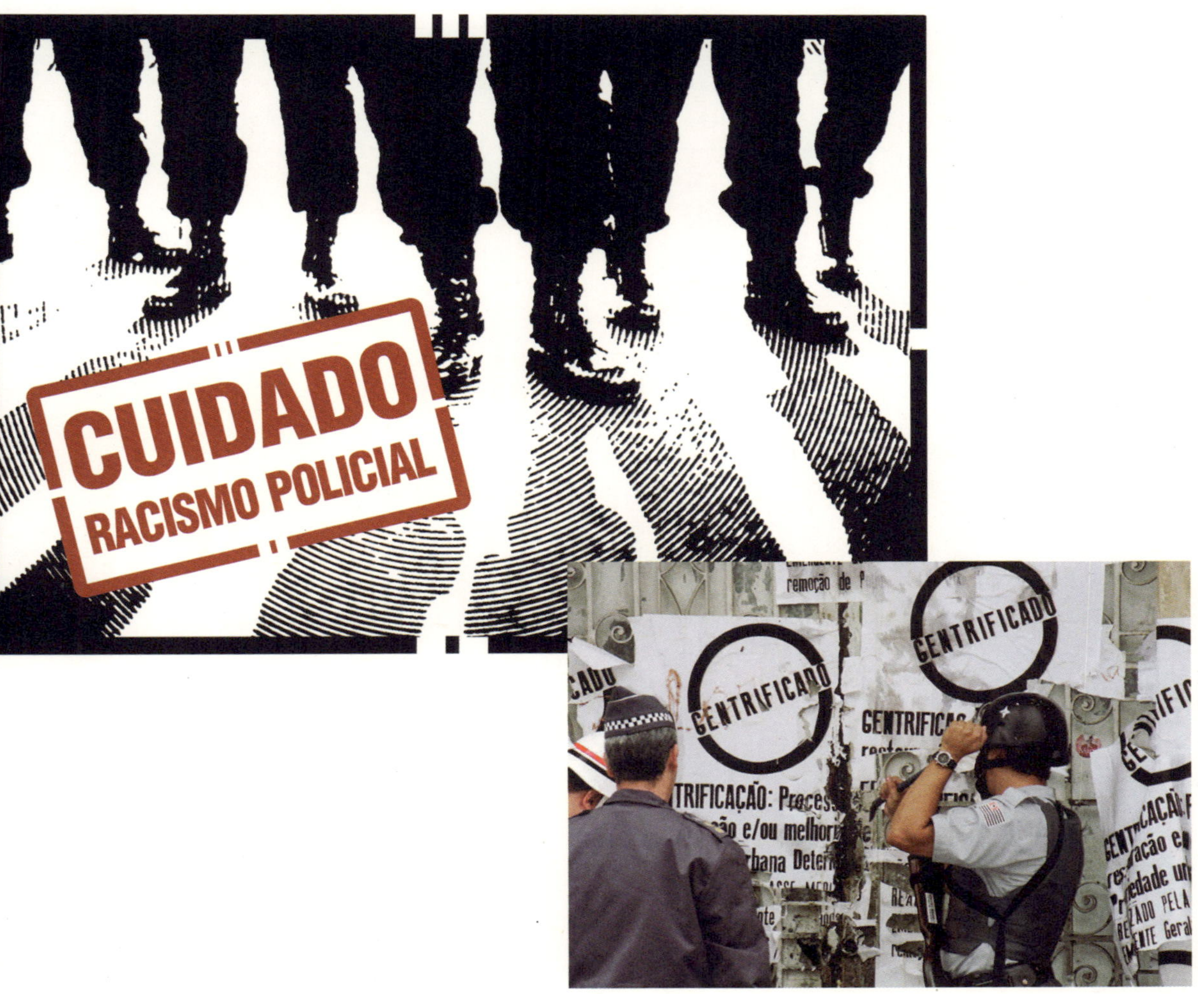

## Zumbi Somos Nós – Part II

Brazil is a country of the slave tradition, a tradition that has marked its culture, determined the relations between different communities (blacks, whites, native indians, etc.), and established a hegemonic power that racially demonizes and profiles black youth indiscriminately. This is a culture of racism established in Brazil in the days of the "Middle Passage," a culture that has hardly been erased by the imposition of laws and decrees. It is a tradition, denounced by Frente 3 de Fevereiro, that inscribes slavery in Brazilian day-to-day living.

The racial democracy has not served to accommodate the different communities living in Brazil. When we speak of democracy, a where are the blacks? Where is history? Where are the blacks in history? Somehow, as is criticized in the manifesto of Frente 3 de Fevereiro, society is repeating patterns of social repression that led to the creation of law enforcement. The Brazilian police force, since its inception, has existed to monitor the Quilombo. The Quilombo, organized since the sixteenth century by a system similar to an actual democracy, were the first settings where freed slaves lived together with their descendants and other ethnic minorities. They were spaces of resistance, bearers of the "afro" culture, whose presence is now also bound to a struggle for social awareness and respect for the contribution of black communities to Brazilian history and culture.

*Zumbi Somos Nós* is a clarion call to civil society about historical evidence of the people who sacrificed themselves for the vindication of their fundamental rights, or of those who were sacrificed in a clear denial of those rights. *Zumbi Somos Nós* ("We Are All Zumbi") is reminiscent of the name of one of the most important leaders of a Quilombo in the history of Brazil: Zumbi dos Palmares. So, the collective Frente 3 de Fevereiro was also created as a tribute to another innocent martyr, Flávio Ferreira Sant'Ana, who was killed by police who shot him outside his house because his physical description matched that of a criminal: Flavio was black. Frente 3 de Fevereiro was named after the date of his death.

The artistic actions of Frente 3 de Fevereiro are serving the citizenry beyond the origins of its various communities, and constitute a criticism of the social fragmentation proposed by the media and the state. Frente 3 de Fevereiro promotes new strategies for cultural relationships, interactions in urban space, and struggle and resistance for Afro-Brazilian culture.

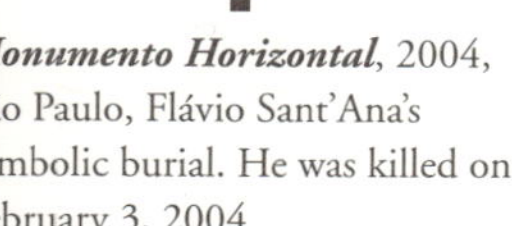

*Ionumento Horizontal*, 2004,
ão Paulo, Flávio Sant'Ana's
mbolic burial. He was killed on
ebruary 3, 2004.

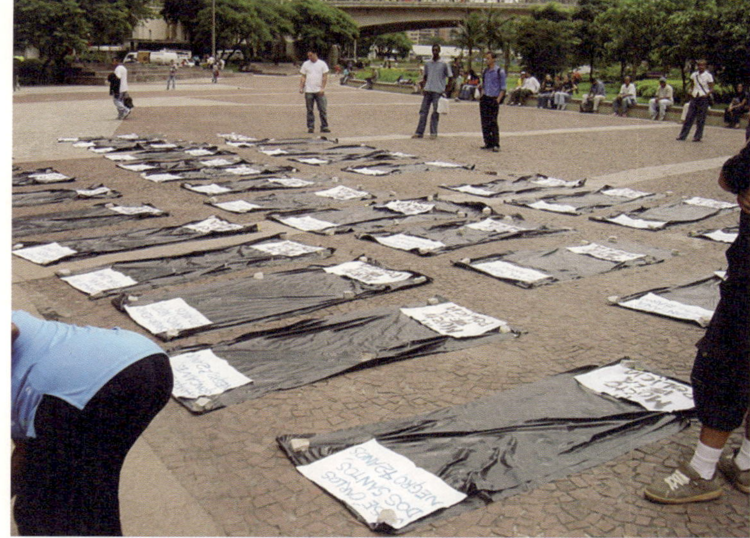

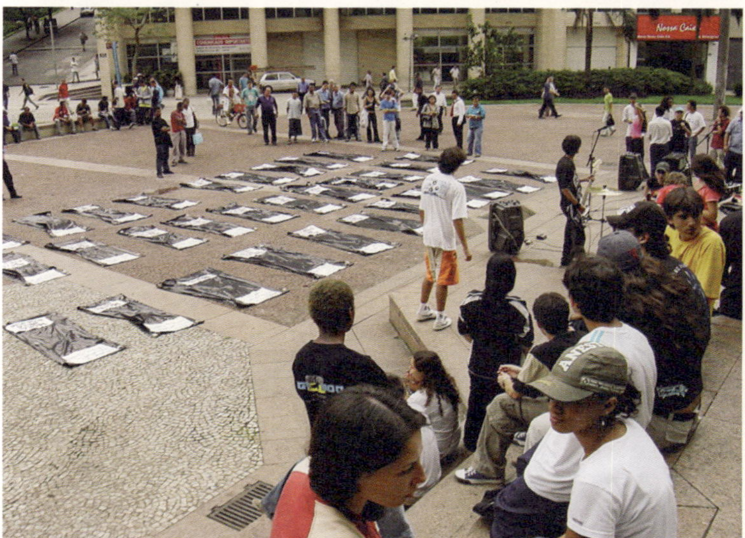

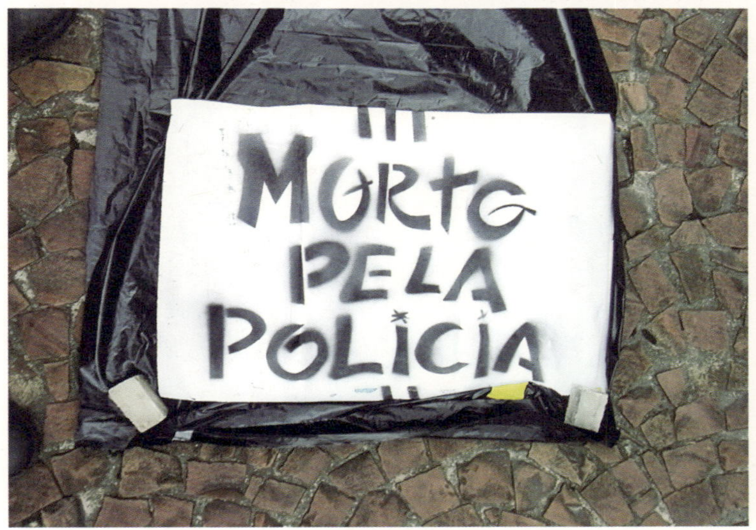

***Brasil Negro Salve*** ("Save black Brazil"), Final da Libertadores da América, São Paulo, Estádio Morumbi São Paulo x Atlético-PR, 14 de Julho de 2005

***Onde estão os Negros?*** ("Where are the blacks?") Campeonato Brasileiro, Campinas, Estádio Moisés Lucarelli Corinthians X Ponte Preta, 14 de Agosto de 2005

***Zumbi Somos Nós*** ("We are Zumbi"), Campeonato Brasileiro São Paulo, Estádio Pacaembú Corinthians X Internacional, 20 de novembro de 2005, Dia da Consciência Negra (photo by Peetssa)

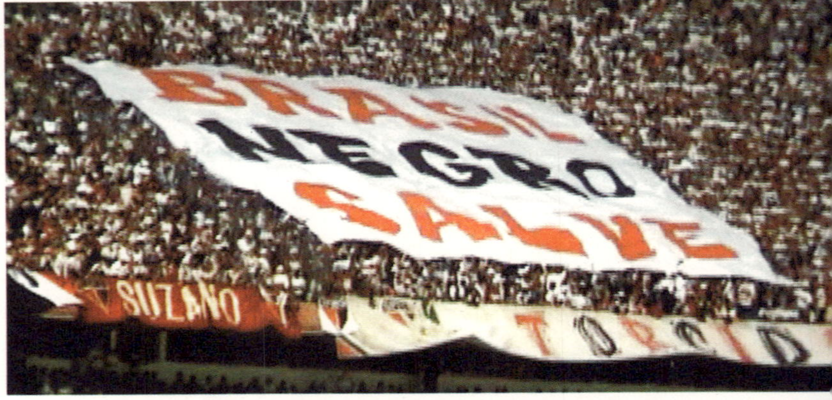


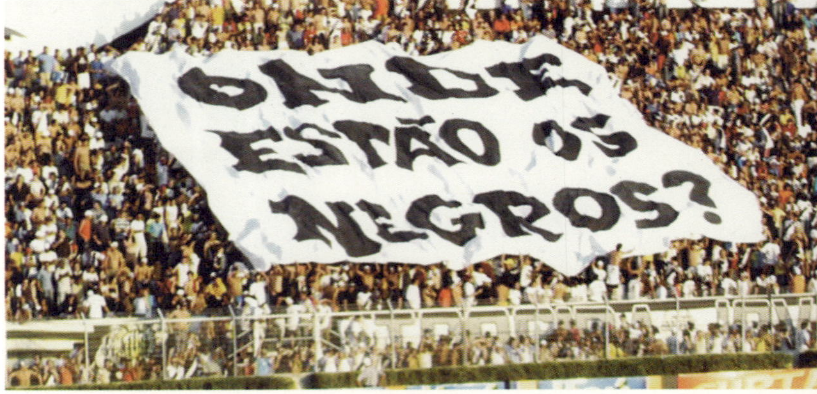


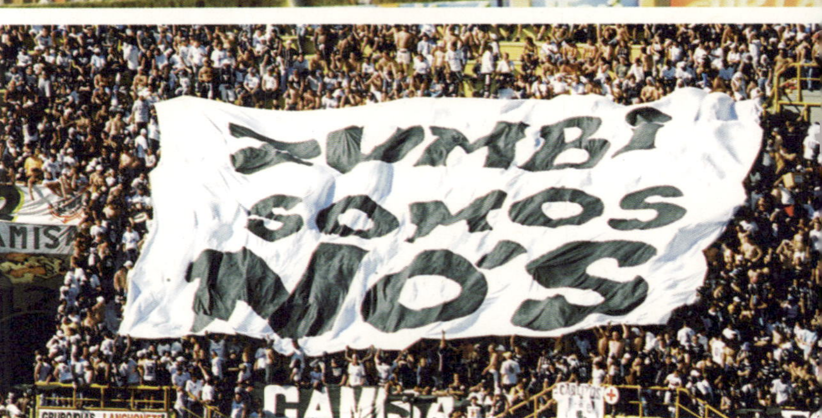

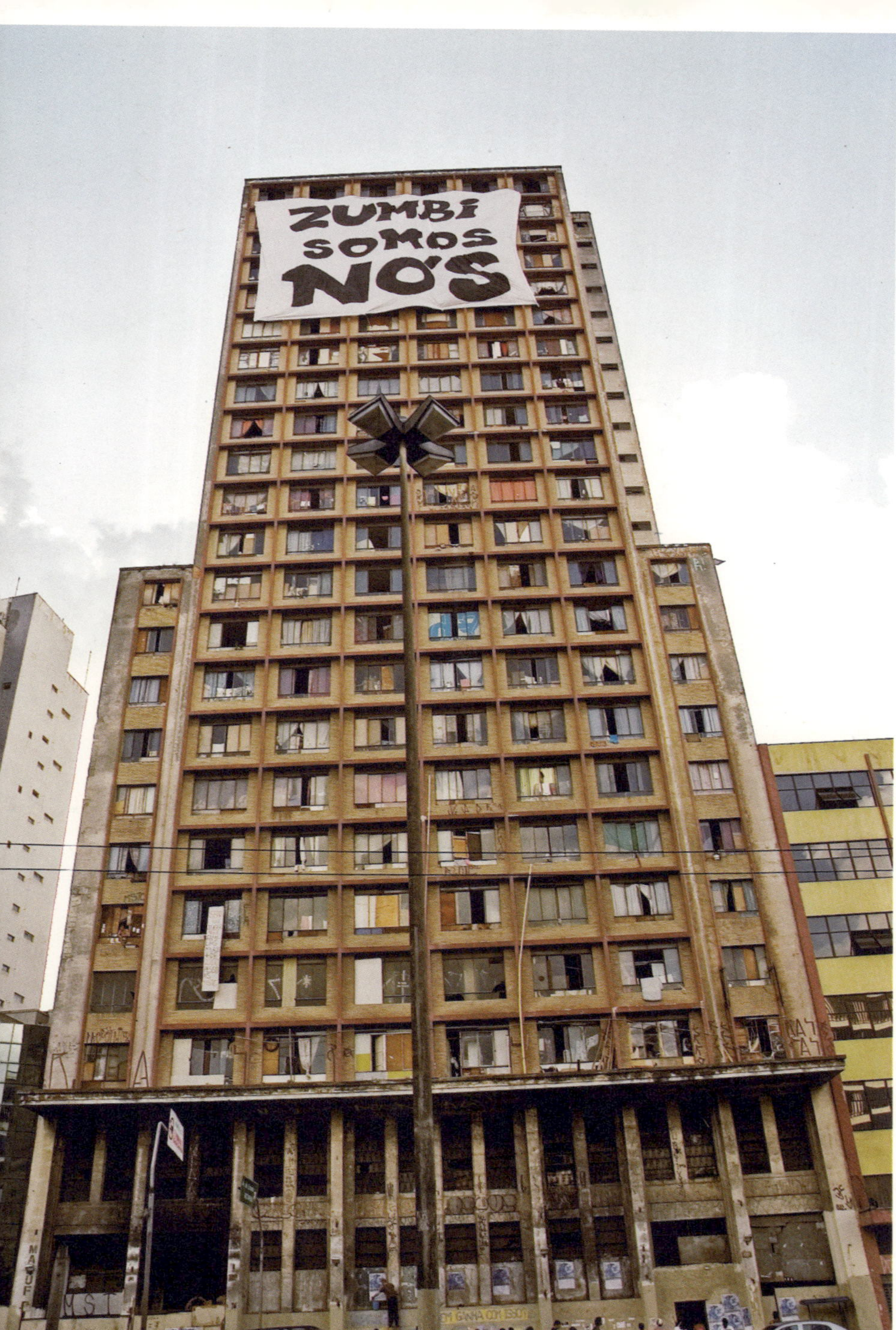


***Zumbi Somos Nós***, 2006, São Paulo, Prestes Maia Building, São Paulo's downtown homeless movement, Latin America's biggest vertical occupation (photo by Julia Valiengo)

On the night of September 28th, 2005, almost seven hundred immigrants furnished with more than one hundred ladders jumped the double fence that split Morocco from the Spanish city of Ceuta. Some of the witnesses said everything happened so fast that the only thing they were able to see were blurry figures searching for a new horizon.

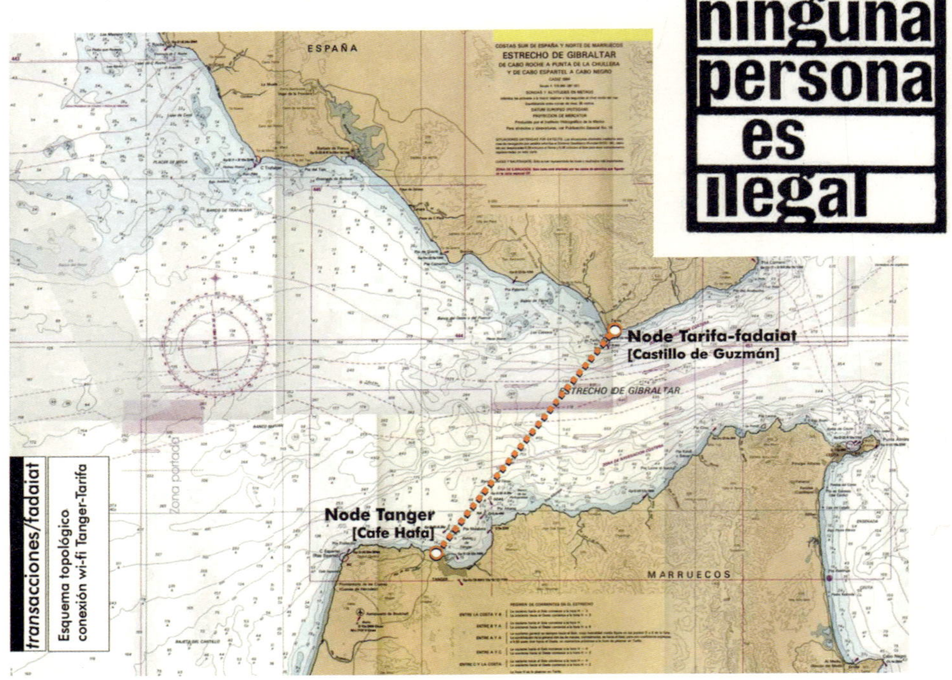

# Fadaiat: Observatorio Tecnológico del Estrecho

■□

***Transacciones, Tanger–Tafira***
(“Transactions, Tanger–Tafira”), 2006

□■

***Caravana Europea por la Libertad de Movimiento***
(“European Caravan for the Freedom of Movement”), 2006

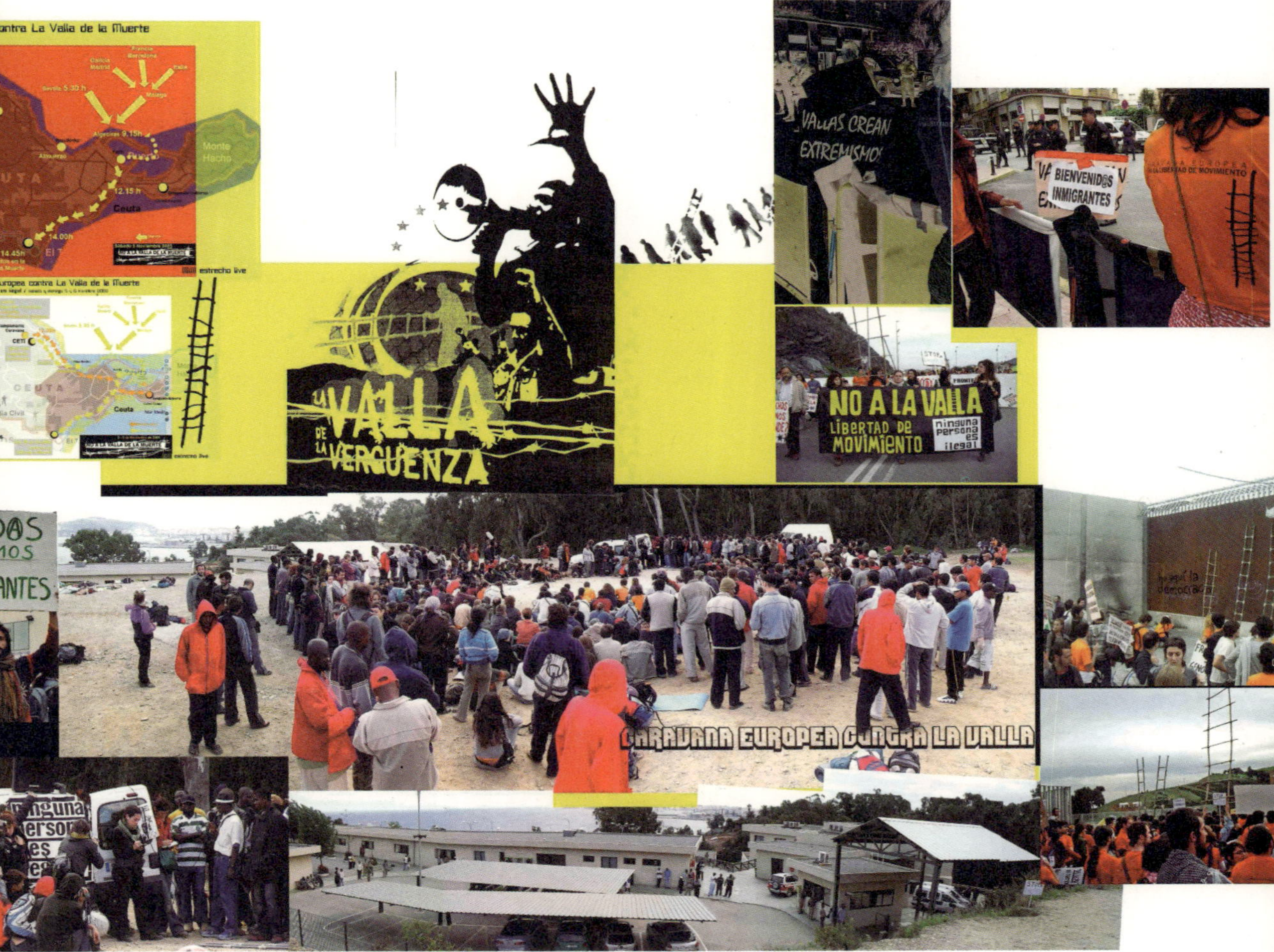

The "other" has always been a dominant figure in the Spanish visual cultural construct. Previously, the "other" was seen as a wild and distant person belonging to faraway territories, who rarely wandered the streets of Spanish cities. In the last three decades, the presence of that "other" is more intense. Images such as the one in the vignette above tell us about the fear that a so-called "phenomenon" provokes within society. It shows the ambivalence and the anxiety provoked by the idea of living irrevocably face to face with the "other."

That "living-together" acquires intensity in the territories close to the border, or at the border itself. Places such Ceuta, Melilla, Tanger, and Gibraltar are some of those scenarios. These settings are precisely where *Fadaiat: Freedom of Movement—Freedom of Knowledge* takes place. Fadaiat is an event-laboratory promoted by the *Observatorio Tecnológico del Estrecho* (Technological Observatory of the Straits), which took place in several cities in the southern part of the Spanish mainland, as well as in northern Morocco and on the Internet. It is a project that aims to provoke knowledge to avoid misunderstandings and biases among those communities. What makes this project powerful and intriguing is the fact that, in order to do so, Fadaiat does not pretend to aestheticize its discourse on migration. Furthermore, it displays the border—the territories of the Straits—as a stage where mimicry of transformations and changes in societies occur. This follows Etienne Balibar's thought that in revisiting the concept of the borders of Europe, one should consider Europe as a borderland territory in itself. The Observatorio considers the cross-cultural passing of the border as a habitable place, reflecting on the kind of social practices that emerge from cultural interactions taking place in that place.

As a formula against social immobility and in favor of civil self-awareness, the Observatorio produces, by means of its Media-Lab and its multidisciplinary workshops, experiences through which official political strategies and discriminatory states of exception are called into question. Moreover, the project aims to give visibility to critical conditions of immigrants in search of the acceptance of their full citizenship, and to the initiatives promoted by Spanish, Moroccan, and other international social activist groups, inside and outside of those territories.

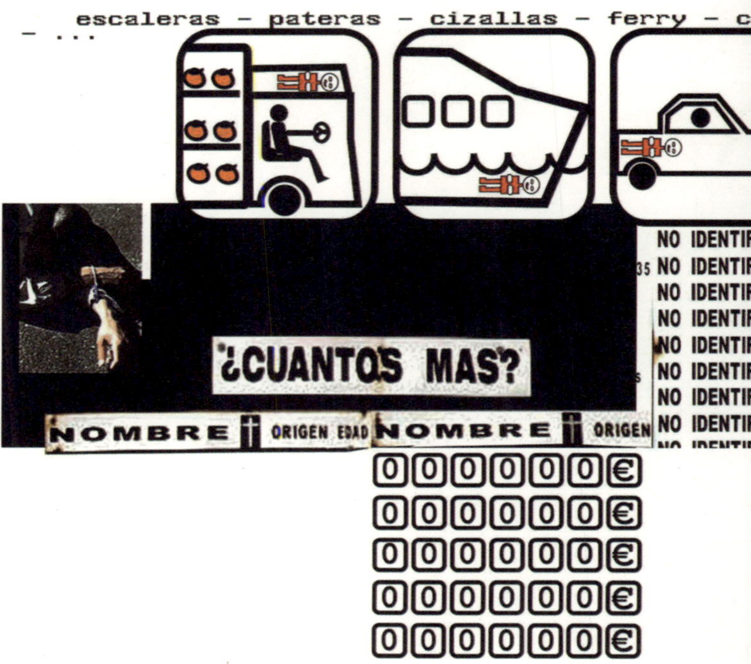

Fadaiat conceives its Media-Lab as a multicultural space, both local and global, the activities of which explore how creativity defines and address critical issues such as the media-sphere, ecology, globalization, immigration, land, and education, along with the effective use technologies of information and communication and the emergence of new forms of production and representation. Envisaged as a linking tool for Spanish and Moroccan (European and African) societies, Fadaiat uses various disciplines, such architecture, art, music, and new media, to articulate a social activist manifesto that proclaims, among other things, the capability of knowledge to liberate society from its immobility, and the reappropriation of liminal territories of the border—both conceptual and physical—by the citizenry.

After its 2004 experience, Fadaiat celebrated three more events: *Fadaiat Set-Up*, a modular ephemeral architecture installed in Tarifa, which provides another opportunity for workshops, conferences, and roundtables; and, two meetings in Barcelona and Malaga (*Casa de Iniciativas*) between the Observatorio members, activists, and collectives from civic society.

The book *Fadaiat: Freedom of Movement—Freedom of Knowledge*, published in 2006, gathers together the conclusions coming out of the several lectures, meetings, performances, manifestos, and workshops that constituted the whole project, with the contributions of Sandro Mezzadra, Roy Pullens, Helena Maleno, Florian Schneider, Brian Holmes, and members of Indymedia linked to the Observatorio Fadaiat. The contributors together discussed and presented alternatives to three interconnected areas of work: the territory Madiaq (new geographies); the border-factory, migration, and labor; and the "becoming cyborg" (new technologies and systems of communications).

As a cultural event, *Fadaiat: Freedom of Movement—Freedom of Knowledge* was both an in-situ laboratory and a virtual platform (still available on the Internet).

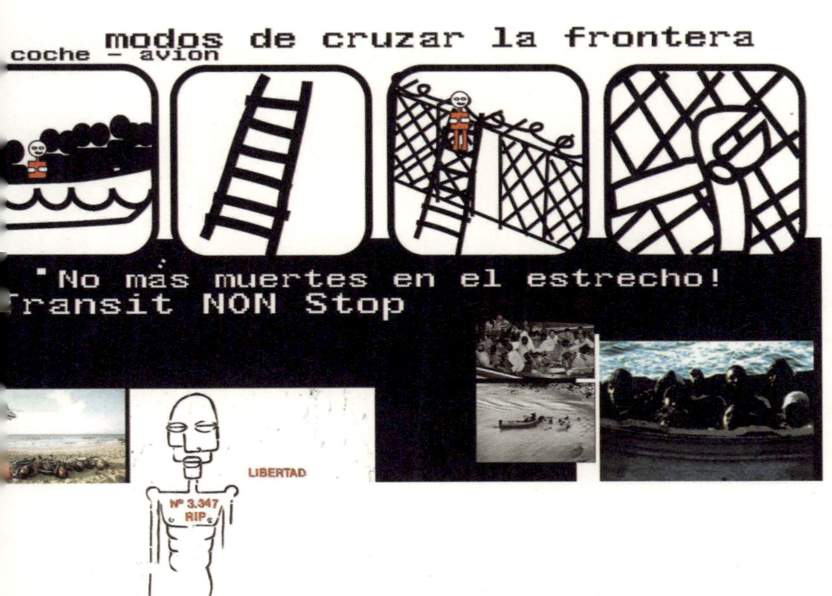


***Modos de Cruzar la Frontera*** ("Ways of Crossing the Border"), 2006

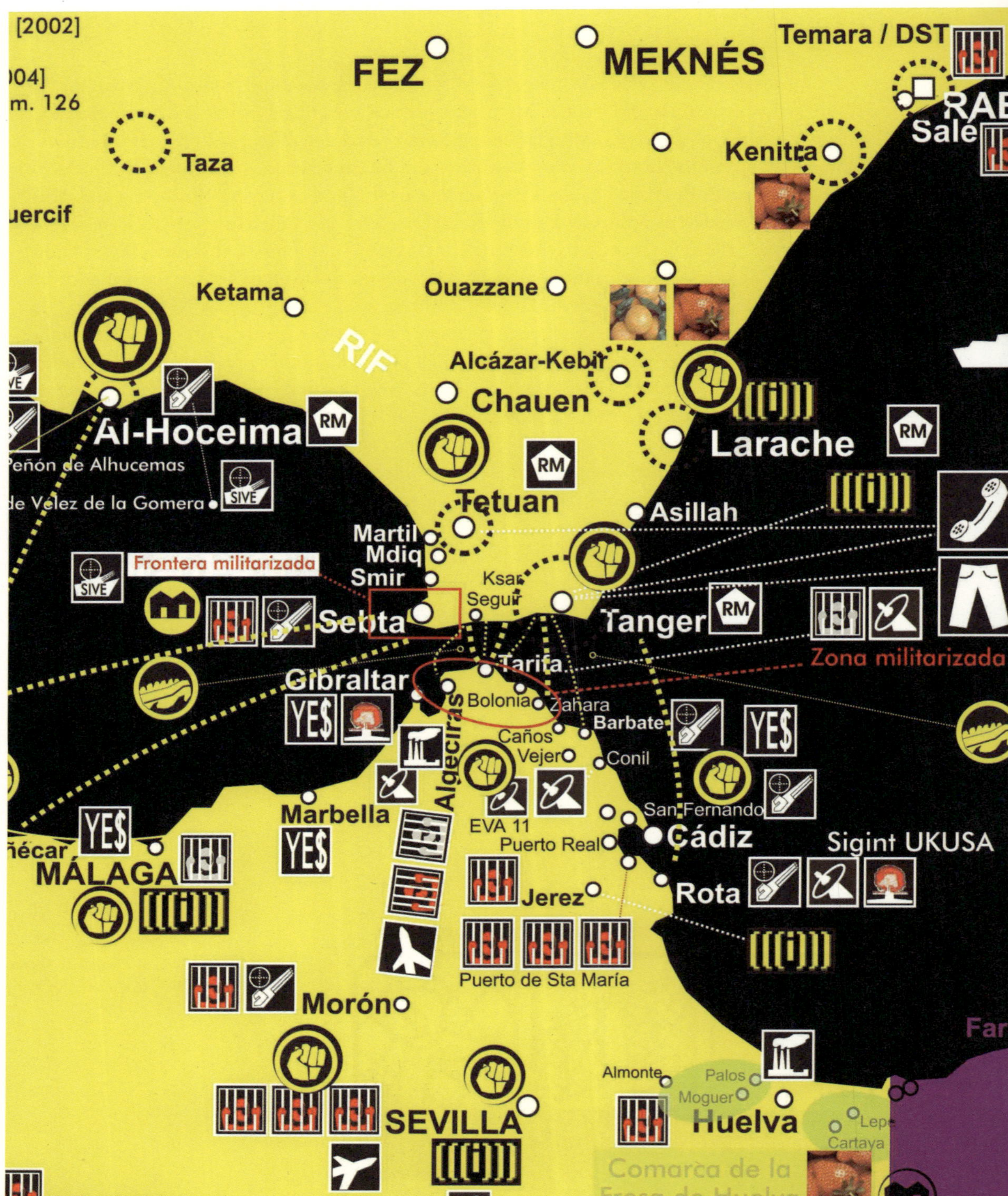

[2002]
04]
m. 126
FEZ
MEKNÉS
Temara / DST
RAB
Sale
Taza
Kenitra
uercif
Ketama
Ouazzane
RIF
Alcázar-Kebir
Chauen
Al-Hoceima
RM
Larache
Peñón de Alhucemas
de Velez de la Gomera
SIVE
Tetuan
Asillah
Martil
Mdiq
Smir
Frontera militarizada
Ksar Seguir
Sebta
Tanger
Zona militarizada
Tarifa
Gibraltar
Bolonia
Zahara
Barbate
YE$
Caños
Vejer
Conil
Algeciras
Marbella
EVA 11
San Fernando
Puerto Real
Cádiz
Sigint UKUSA
MÁLAGA
Jerez
Rota
Puerto de Sta María
Morón
Far
Almonte
Palos
Moguer
SEVILLA
Huelva
Lepe
Cartaya
Comarca de la Fresa de Huelva
Córdoba

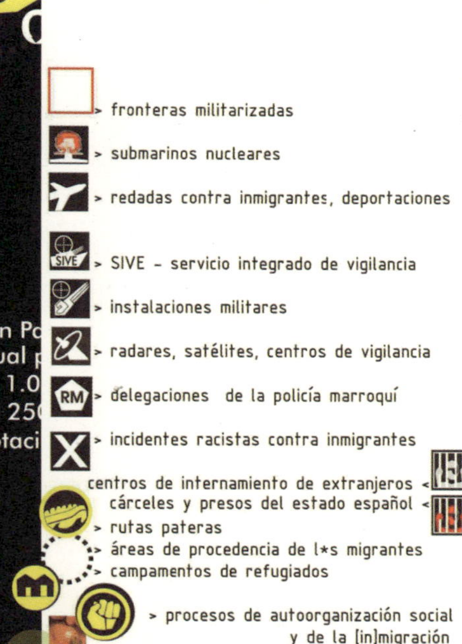


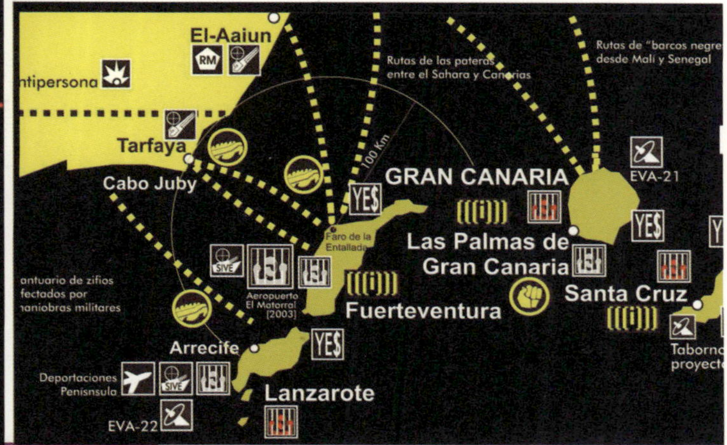


¿por qué cartografiamos?
¿qué? ¿quiénes?
imaginario, territorio (otro), rizoma, mundo...
real e imaginado
visualización, difusión, debate...
organización, hacer mapa (hacer rizoma?)
como modelo de organización, producción...
mapa vs calco

■

***Cartografía del Estrecho***
("Cartography of the Straits"), 2006

*legend translation for the graphic*

- Military frontiers
- Nuclear submarines
- Search on immigrants, deportation
- SIVE – Integrated Security Service
- Military bases
- Radar, satellites, surveillance areas
- Delegations of the Moroccan police
- Racist incidents against the immigrants
- Internment centers for foreigners
- Jails for Spanish people
- Navigation routes by boats of immigrants
- Refugee camps
- Trials on self-organization and immigration
- Shipping areas
- Mafias, connections on financial plots

Why do we make maps?
What? Whom?

- Imaginary, other area, rhizome, world...
- Real and imaginary
- Visualization, diffusion, debate...
- Organization, mapmaking (rhizome–making?)
- As an organization, production model
- A map versus a copy (an imitation)

*page 98–99*

■

***Migraciones Como Movimiento Social*** (Migrations as Social Movement), 2006

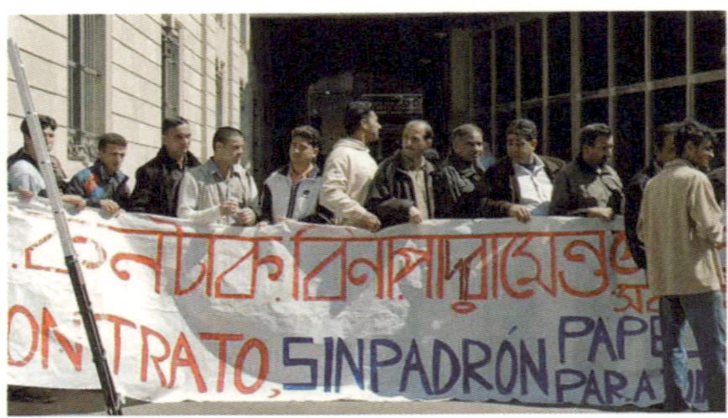
SINPADRÓN

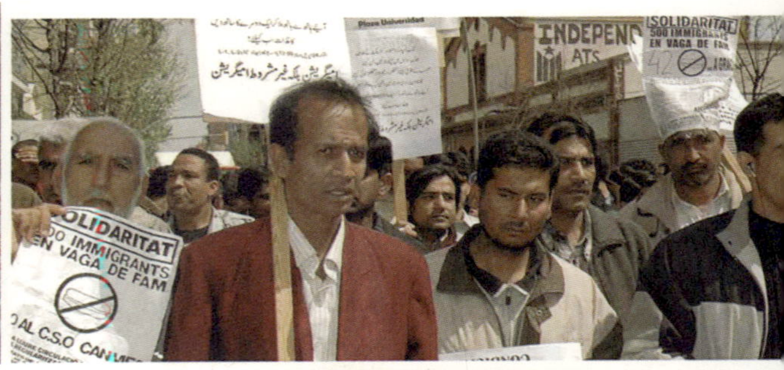
SOLIDARITAT
IMMIGRANTS
EN VAGA DE FAM

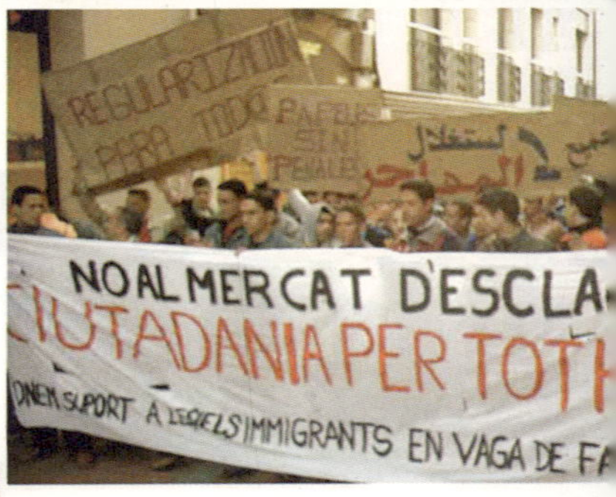
NO AL MERCAT D'ESCLA-
DONEM SUPORT A LES/ELS IMMIGRANTS EN VAGA DE FA

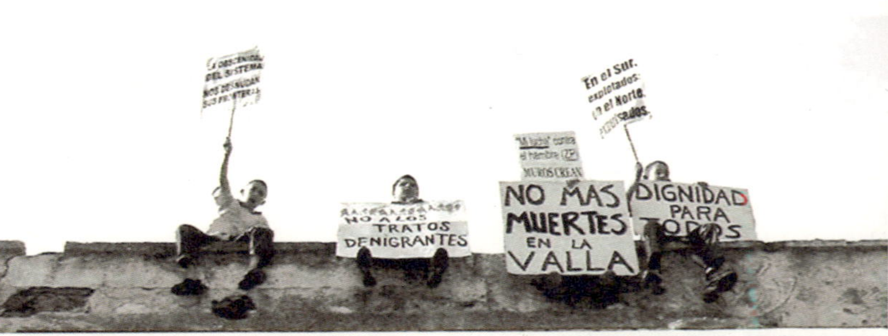
NO A LOS TRATOS DENIGRANTES
NO MAS MUERTES EN LA VALLA
DIGNIDAD PARA TODOS

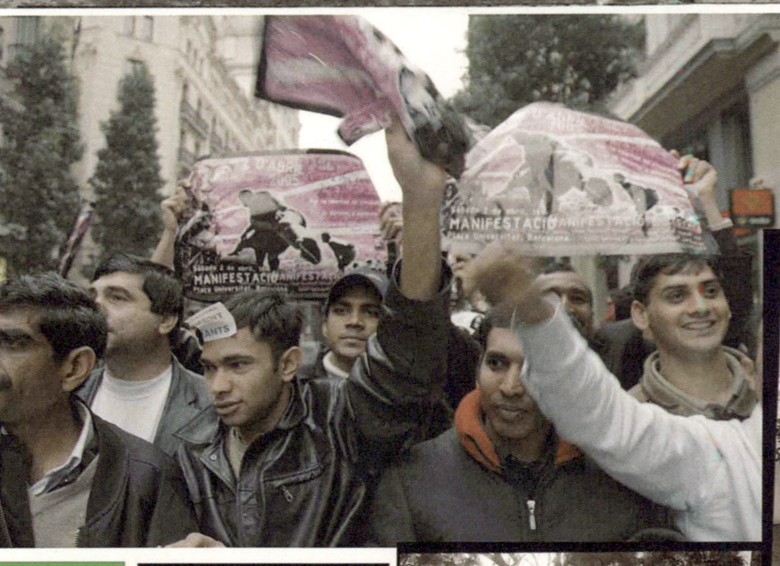
MANIFESTACIÓ

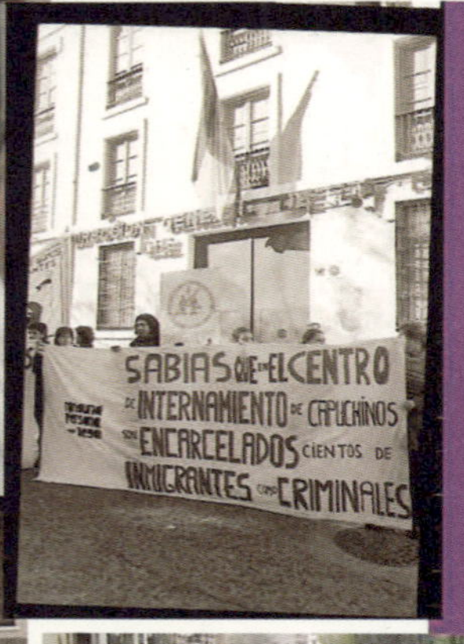
SABIAS QUE EN EL CENTRO DE INTERNAMIENTO DE CAPUCHINOS SON ENCARCELADOS CIENTOS DE INMIGRANTES COMO CRIMINALES

ninguna
persona
es
ilegal

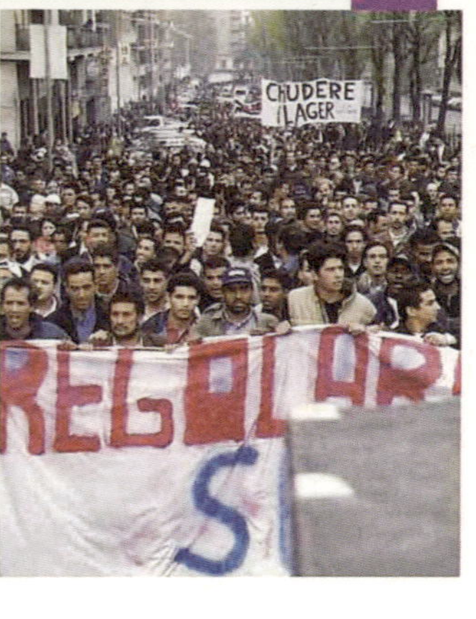
CHIUDERE I LAGER

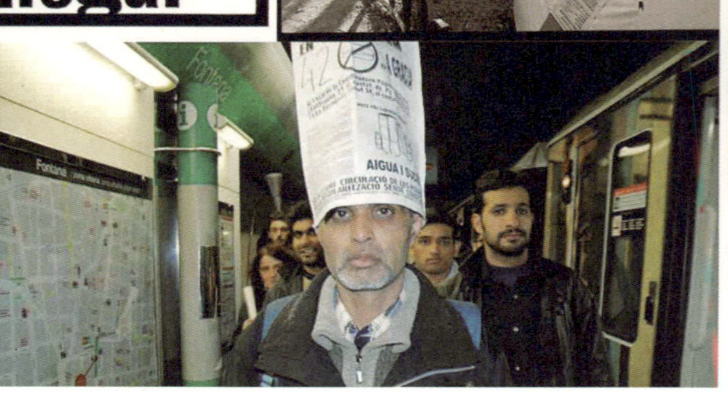
AIGUA I SUCRE
Fontana

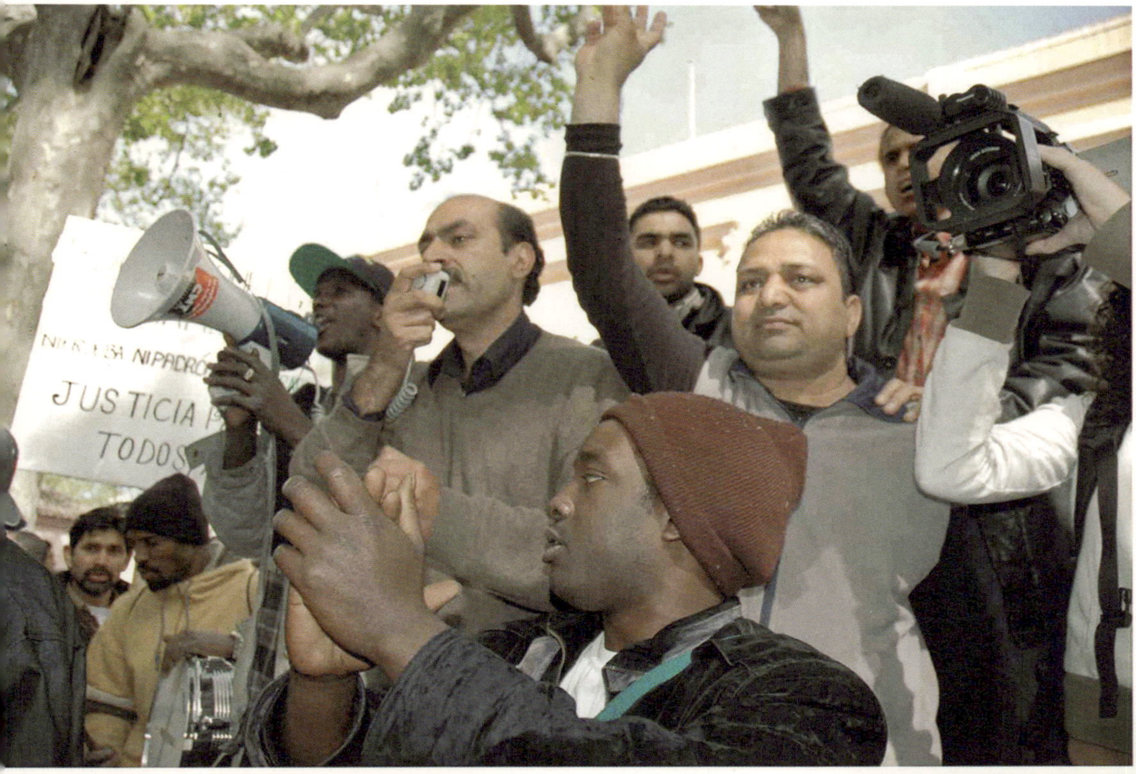

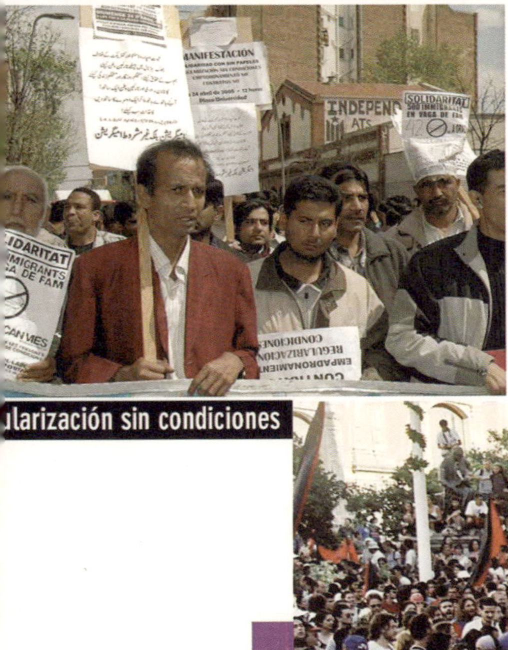

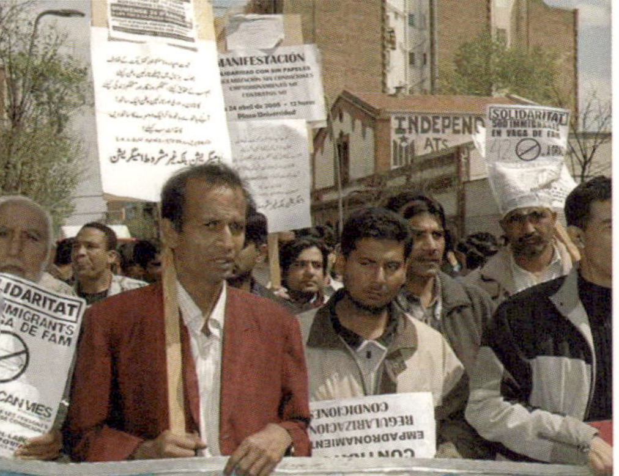


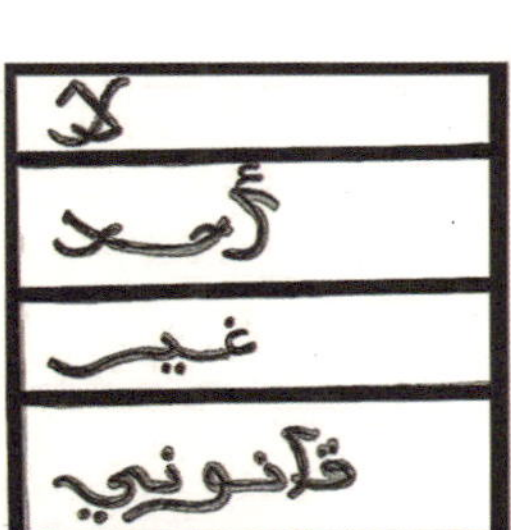


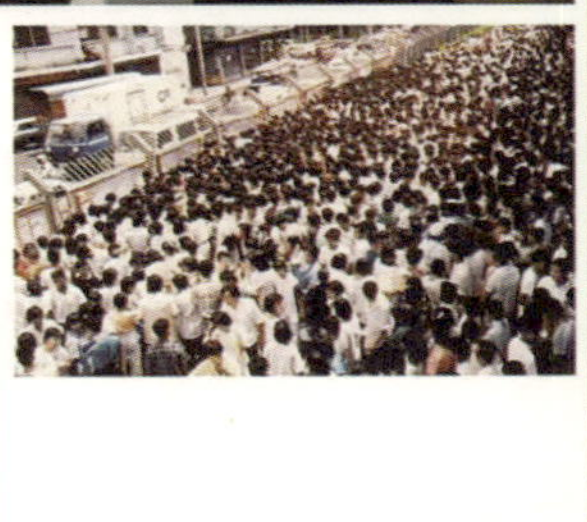

ularización sin condiciones

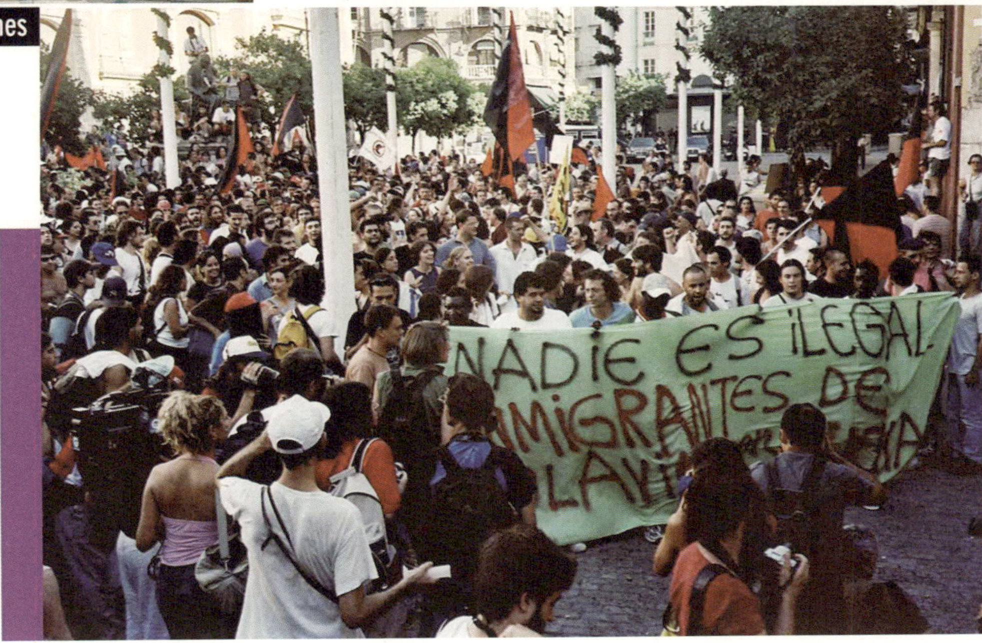

*Titled/Untitled* was a project curated by Gugulective with the curatorial assistance of Gabi Ngcobo at Kwa Mlamli and Blank Projects, Cape Town in 2007. The project, consisting in two different exhibiting venues, challenges issues of visual representation and sociocultural stereotyping. As one of Gugulectiv's initial projects, and despite its temporal framework, *Titled/Untitled* assembles the essence of this artistic collective's initiatives.

On the one hand, the *Untitled* aspect of the project calls into question perceptions and prejudices that places such as the *shebeens* have in institutional grounds. Known during apartheid as illegal clubs and located in black townships, the *shebeens* were bars where self-made alcohol was served and resistance to the old regime gathered together. Kwa Mlamli, the *shebeen* that Gugulective has transformed into a cultural and artistic center in an urban area of Gugulethu, was one of the project's main venues. The general misrepresentation of the *shebeens* diminishes the contribution of black communities to the official culture-making. With the reconceptualization proposed in *Untitled* of Kwa Mlamli, the space previously lacking aesthetic and recreational values acquires political and cultural significance. In effecting this, Gugulective assigns visibility to earlier situations in which *shebeens* have demonstrated their intellectual and political roles. As witnessed by the following initiatives, Kwa Mlamli Shebeen is the location of a trans-disciplinary program which includes presentations and interactions of agents of the most varied endeavors: music, spoken word, poetry, literature, and of course visual arts. *Untitled* also challenges the stereotype by which this collective has been classified as a "Black" artist collective. By means of the work presented in the exhibition displayed in the Blank Project gallery space, Gugulective brings attention to its rejection of that individual or collective imposed identity.

# Gugulective

***Gugulective Installation***, 2007, Upstairs/Downstairs

***Unathi Sigenu***, 2007, shackled, mixed media installation

***Themba Tsotsi,*** 2007, (foreground), untitled mixed media installation

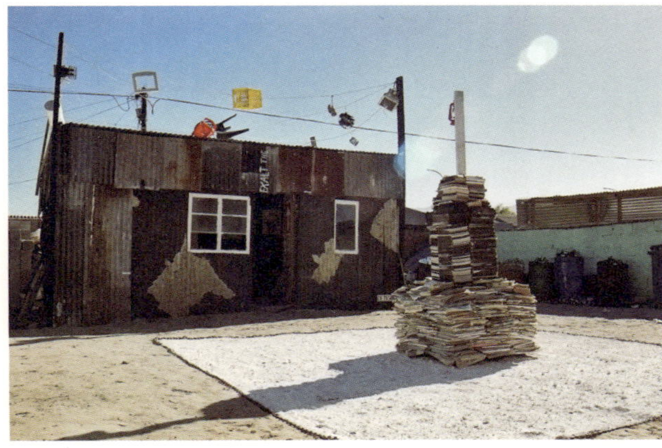

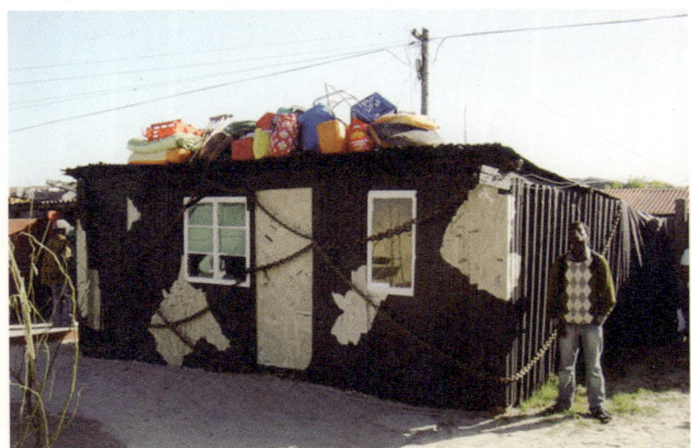

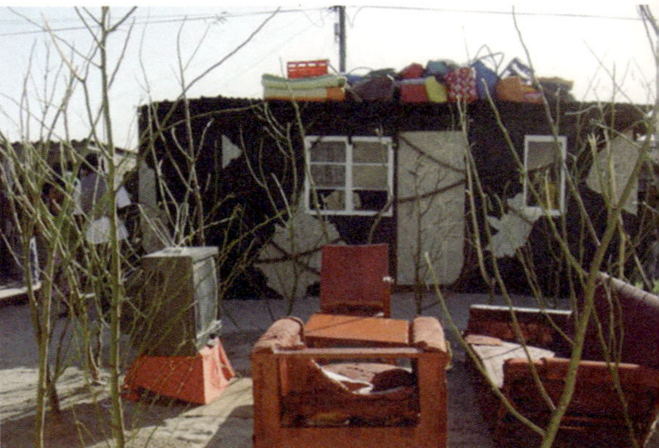

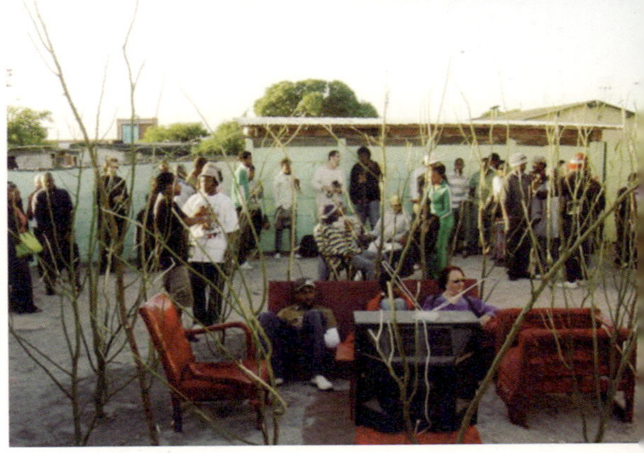

*Titled,* on the other hand, was a one-day event taking place in Kwa Mlamli Shebeen, where artists, curators, general audience, and other cultural practitioners gathered together to discuss issues on the accessibility of culture and institutional spaces. The main proposition was to establish Kwa Mlamli Shebeen a space for people to engage in social, political, cultural, and spatial issues in post-apartheid South Africa. *Titled* also included a peculiar installation in the *shebeen*'s bathroom, a study that reflects on how the bathroom environment is a major determinant in a person's emotional and mental state. "There, individual identity is cherished and strengthened in periods of solitude and conditions…" as Kemang Wa Lehulere recalls. That particular installation criticizes the general conception of an uneducated black townships resident.

*Titled/Untitled* was a cornerstone for the incipient trajectory of a collective, the strategies and projects of which aim to defy the South African art scene's prerogatives and general sociocultural bias.

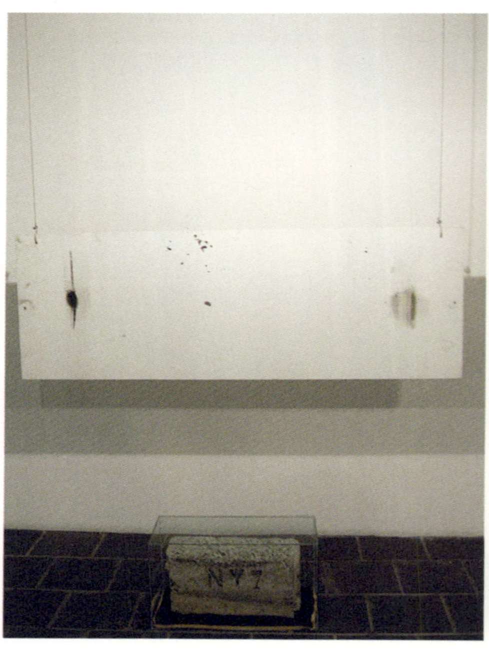

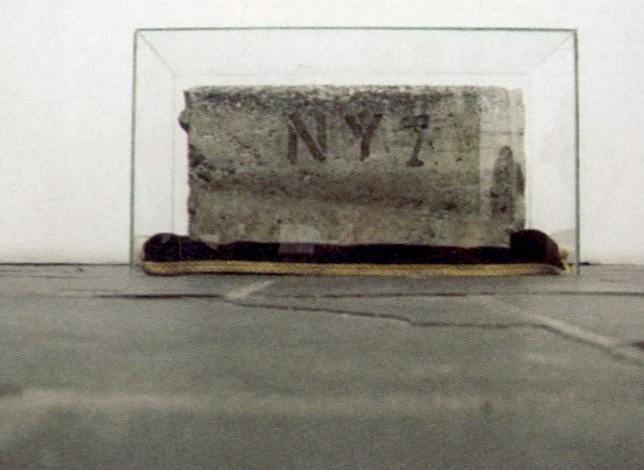

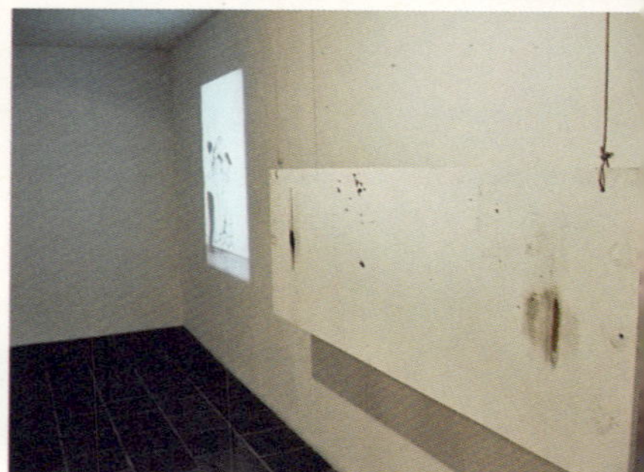

***Gugulective's* "NY7," *Scratching the Surface Vol. 1*,** AVA Gallery, 2008

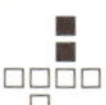

***Gugulective's* "NY7," *Scratching the Surface Vol. 1*,** AVA Gallery, 2008, being installed

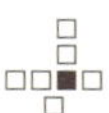

***Gugulective's* "NY7," *Scratching the Surface Vol. 1*,** AVA Gallery, 2008, performance

***Gugulective's* "Akuchanywa,"** 2007

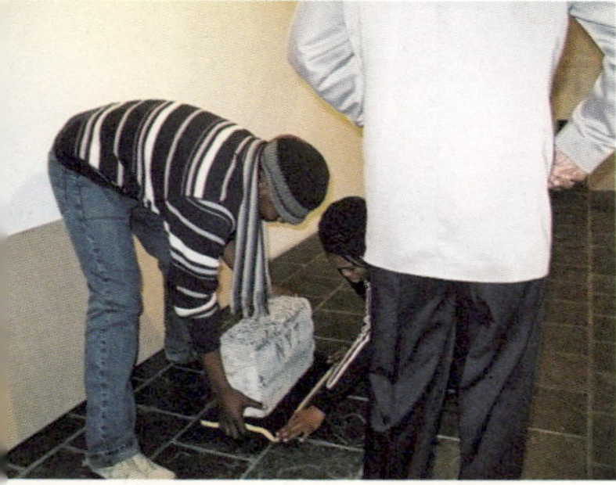

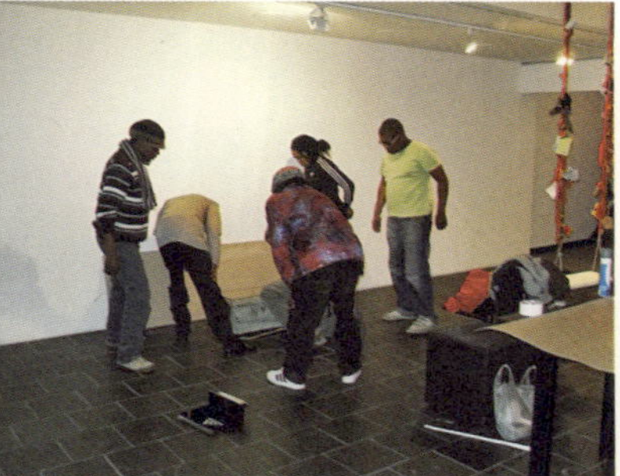

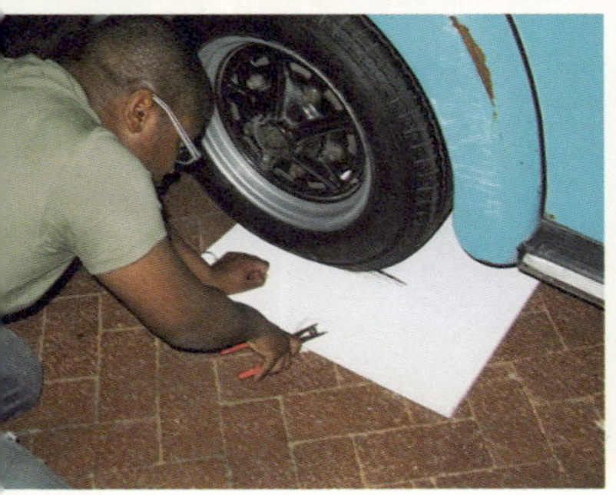

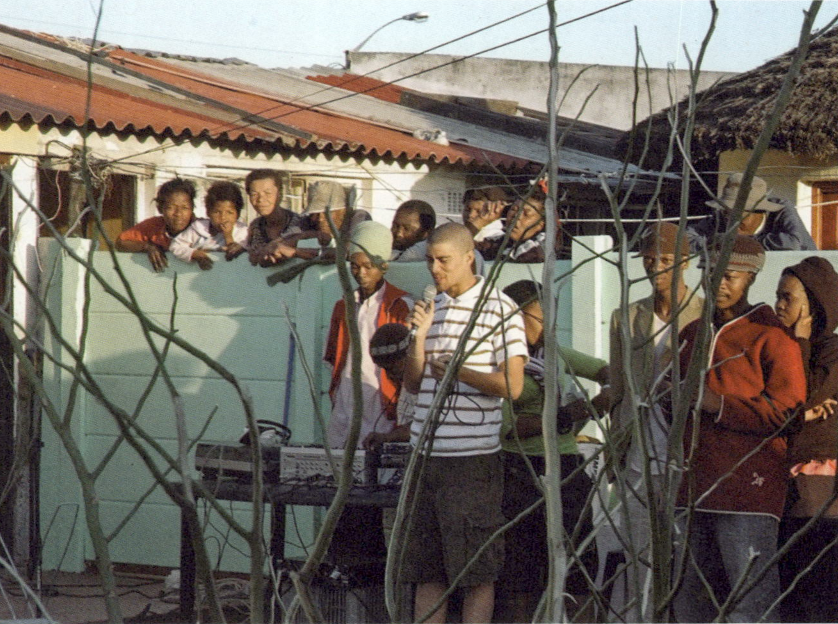

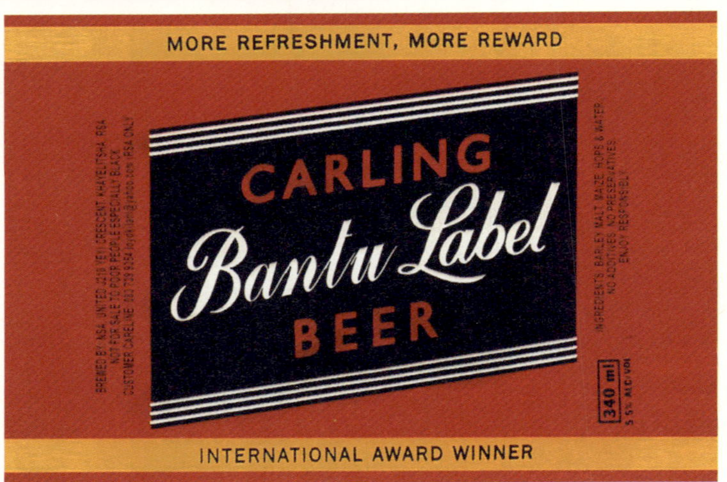


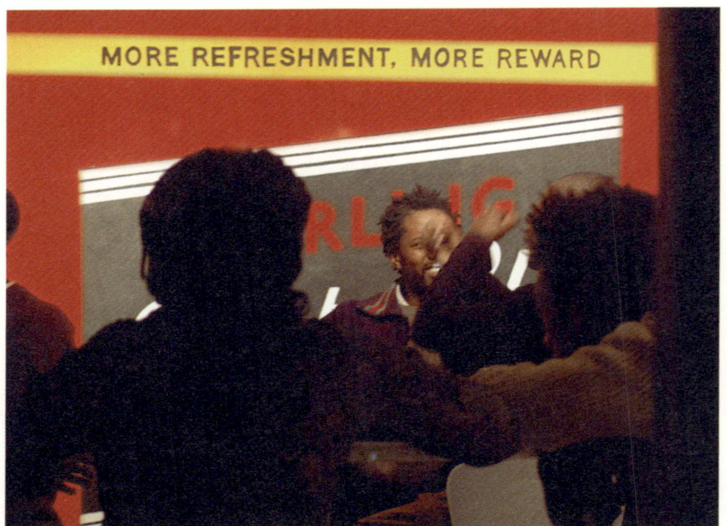


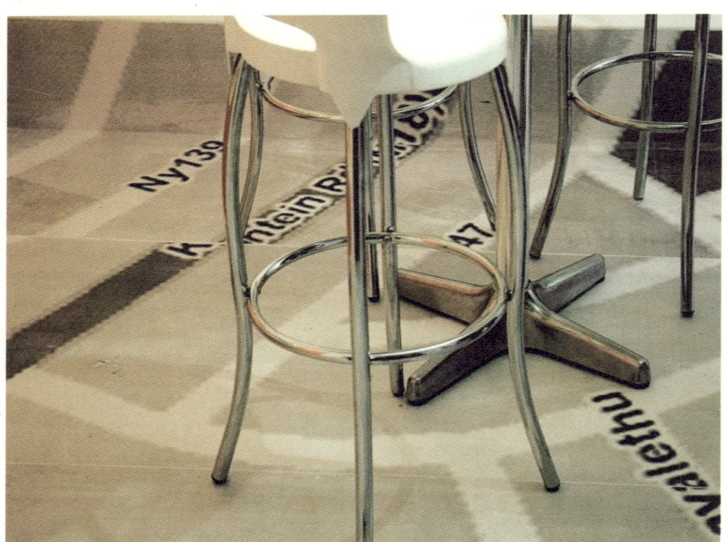

***Gugulective's Wall Painting after Lonwabo Kilani's* Untit *(beer bottles)***, 2008, Blank Projects

***Opening of Untitled***, 2008, Blank Projects

***Untitled***, Blank Projects, 2008 installation detail

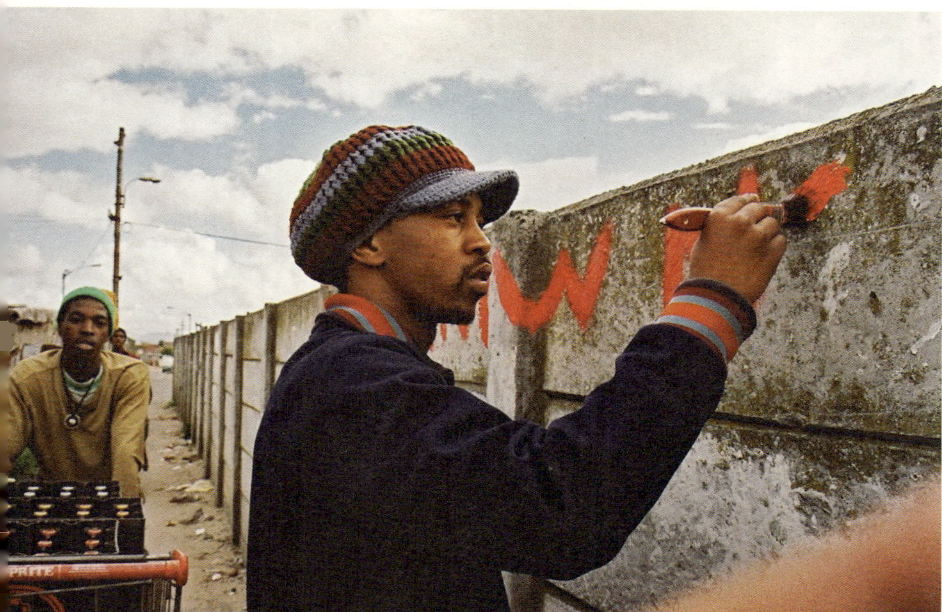

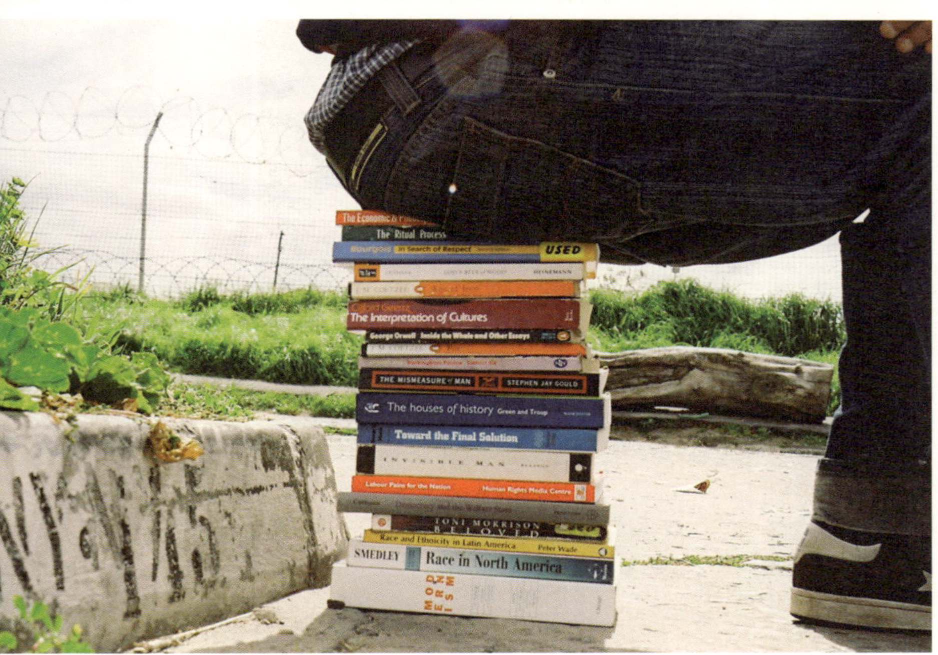

***Gugulective Public Intervention***, artist Themba Tsotsi, Gugulethu, South Africa

***Gugulective Public Intervention***, Gugulethu, South Africa

**Emiliano Gandolfi** is an architect and independent curator, co founder of *Cohabitation Strategies,* and member of iStrike. ultd.Gandolfi was co-curator of the 11th International Architecture Exhibition—Biennale di Venezia, and before this role, he was curator at the Netherlands Architecture Institute in Rotterdam, working on projects such as *Happening* and *Newer Orleans.* As part of the 2007 International Architecture Biennale Rotterdam, he curated *A Better World,* an exhibition and series of public events on architecture and activism. He was co-curator of the public program of the 2009 Tirana Biennial and co-founder of REbiennale, a cooperative platform created by a net of associations to share methods, processes and competences linked to self-construction. Over the past years he has been involved in a wide range of projects, exhibitions, and conferences that dealt with methodologies and interventions for urban transformation, on both theoretical and practical levels. He has lectured and organized conferences in many institutions worldwide; he is currently guest teacher at the National University of the Arts in Taiwan and advisor for the Curry Stone Design Prize. As a writer and critic he has contributed to several books and magazines such as *Volume* (Amsterdam), *Artforum* (New York) and *L'espresso* (Rome). He was the editor of *Spectacular City* (Rotterdam: NAi Publishers, 2006).
> www.cohstra.org

**Goddy Leye** is a visual artist and founder of artist-runinitiative *ArtBakery,* in Douala, Cameroon. Along with his individual work as an artist, Leye has initiated a series of community involvement projects with the aim of engaging contemporary art to foster dialogue and interaction between artists and local communities. *ArtBakery* is an artist residency program that includes public training sessions, public events, and exhibitions. Moreover it is also an extensive community project that is capable of taking art away from a self-referential stance and turning it into a common language with which to define the different aspirations of the Bonendale district. Leye's work has been exhibited internationally: it was featured in the Centre Pompidou and in the Havana, Sao Paulo, and Dakar biennales.
> http://goddyleye.lecktronix.net

**Teddy Cruz** is a Guatemalan-born architect, whose work dwells at the border between San Diego, California and Tijuana, Mexico. His research has focused on the trans-border urban dynamics between these two cities: where urbanities of immigration and surveillance, density and sprawl, wealth and poverty collide and overlap daily. Cruz has been recognized internationally for his research and work on housing and its relationship to alternative land use policies, modes of sociability, and economic processes. His work has been exhibited internationally, including at Archilab in Orleans; the architectural biennales of Rotterdam, Lisbon, and Venice; and at the San Francisco Art Institute and the San Diego Museum of Contemporary Art. He is currently an associate professor in Public Culture and Urbanism in the Visual Arts Department at UCSD in San Diego.
> www.politicalequator.org

**Jeanne van Heeswijk** works on socially committed art projects with a specific interest in the social, political, and economical relations that shape the public domain. In her projects she acts as an intermediary between situations, as well as places, and the people who inhabit these places. To achieve this aim, she often works closely with artists, designers, architects, software developers, governments, and citizens, and has herself coined the term "urban curating" for her interventions. Van Heeswijk's work has been exhibited in venues such as Witte de With in Rotterdam, PS1 Center for Contemporary Art in New York, and in the Taipei, Busan, and Venice biennales.
> www.jeanneworks.net

**Santiago Cirugeda (Recetas Urbanas).** With his *Recetas Urbanas* ("Urban Recipes") group, Santiago Cirugeda is engaged in carrying out subversive actions that point the finger at areas of dissatisfaction in urban contexts. Each project, in terms of housing or community space, is designed on the basis of the needs of its users and is built by the users themselves. His collectively produced projects allow people to demand an active role, and they range from systematic occupation of unused public spaces, to setting up prostheses on existing buildings, and to the construction of illegal housing and social spaces in containers. Most of these interventions, formally considered "art projects," benefit from a peculiar legal status and as such are safeguarded by the same laws that are used in swindling.
> www.recetasurbanas.net

**Bert Theis – Isola Art Center.** Bert Theis refers to his work as "audience-specific," an art capable of being sensitive not exclusively to the site (as for the "site specific" art works), but also to the social component: the people who live and work in that particular place. In 2001—together with artists, curators, architects, philosophers and neighborhood associations—Theis initiated the *Isola Art Center* and *out (Office for Urban Transformation)* in the Isola district, an area of Milan which is undergoing dramatic transformation. Daily discussions with the community, and the involvement of artists in public programs, has led to a process of greater awareness, thus legitimizing the role of the citizens. Theis has taken part in international art events such as Sculpture Projects in Münster, Manifesta, and, among others, the Venice, Istanbul, and Gwangju biennales.
> www.isolartcenter.org

# A Struggle on Two Fronts—Art as Collective Process

*What we demand is the unity of politics and art, the unity of content and form, the unity of revolutionary political content and the highest possible perfection of artistic form. Works of art which lack artistic quality have no force, however progressive they may be politically. We thus oppose both works of art with a mistaken political viewpoint and works of art with the tendency towards a "posters and slogan style," which is correct in its political viewpoint but lacking in artistic power. On issues of literature and art we must carry out a struggle on two fronts.*[1]

In Jean-Luc Godard's film *La Chinoise* (1967), Veronique decides to make use of her parents' vacation to set up a revolutionary cell in her home. She spends her days with her fiancé, Guillaume, and a group of militant friends searching for a clear political and aesthetic response to the immobility of contemporary society. Her large Paris attic home is turned into a political workshop. The walls are plastered with slogans; the sitting room is made into a conference hall; the corridor is assigned to "public enemies" like Novalis, Kant, and Descartes; and these opponents of the movement are vilified through their use as targets for suction-cup darts. Above the table, dominating the elegant dining room with its Louis XVI furniture, stand the emblematic words *Il faut confronter les idées vagues avec des images claires*,[2] while a list of "friendly" writers is written in chalk on a black wall, and the names are gradually rubbed out when they are no longer considered to be truly sympathetic.

The film is a succession of reflections on the formulation of a political position capable of bringing about radical change in society. In one scene, while reading an excerpt from Mao Zedong's speech at the Yenan Forum on Literature and Art in May 1942, Guillaume (Jean-Pierre Léaud) makes a terse comment: "...On issues of literature and art we must carry on a struggle on two fronts." On two fronts. How can one struggle on two fronts?

With different implications and in view of the way things are now—with undoubtedly less revolutionary intentions—the question posed in *La Chinoise* appears to have found an echo today. Artists and, to some extent, radical groups in the world of architecture are increasingly taking an interest in analyzing the relationship between an openly political position and an approach based on aesthetics and form. The works of artists like Thomas Hirschhorn, Marjetica Potrč, and Christoph Schäfer, to name but a few, and the works of those in the field of architecture, like Stalker, Collectif EXYZT, and Hackitectura, adopt a new approach to the contemporary and, in their different ways, seek to give form to their political commitment. A form that, to quote Hirschhorn, "touches truth."[3]

This vision of art has deep roots: it started taking shape in the mid-nineteenth century, when art (with Charles Baudelaire, Gustave Flaubert, and Gustave Courbet) came together, according to Michel Foucault, as a "place of emersion for what is at the bottom, for what is underneath, for everything that has no rights in a given culture, or at least no chance of expressing itself."[4] Here Foucault is talking in an evocative manner about "art as a place of the invasion of the elementary, as a stripping off of existence."[5]

**1** Jean-Luc Godard, in *La Chinoise*, a quotation from a speech given by Mao Zedong at the Forum on Art and Literature in Yenan in 1942
**2** "Vague ideas must be confronted with clear images"
**3** Thomas Hirschhorn, from *TateShots*, http://www.tate.org.uk/tateshots/episode.jsp?item=9115, (site visited on 12 August 2009)
**4** Michel Foucault, lesson held at the Collège de France on 29 February 1984, from *Il coraggio della verità*, Lettera internazionale, second quarter 2009, 2–5
**5** Ibid.

6 Ibid.
7 Cf. Nicolas Bourriaud, *Relational Aethetics* (Djion: Les Presses du Réel, 2002); *Participation*, ed. Claire Bishop, (Cambridge: MIT Press, 2006); and, on experimental communities: Carlos Basualdo and Reinaldo Laddaga, "Rules of Engagement: Art and Experimental Communities", Artforum (March 2004), 166–170

The unmasking that can be accomplished by art led Foucault—in one of his last lectures at the Collège de France, less than four months prior to his death—to talk of two themes that are decisive for outlining a reflection on the role of the artist with regard to the society in which he or she works: the *desire for truth* and the *aesthetics of existence*.

Reflecting on cynicism and on its transmission in Christian Europe, Foucault dwells on the means that have preserved and conveyed the ideas of Diogenes all the way through to the present day. These, he says, were religious movements up to the time of the Counter-Reformation, followed by revolutionary political upheavals. Lastly, Foucault examines a third means for spreading cynicism or for the idea of a lifestyle as a *scandal of truth* in European culture, which is that of art.

In art, Foucault is mainly interested in showing the convention of seeing the life of the artist, in its most essential form, as incontrovertible evidence of what art is in actual fact. This interest in the lives of artists is based on two considerations: art is capable of conferring upon existence the form of *true life*, and life itself is in turn a guarantee that all the works created within it, and as a result of it, fully belong to the domain of art.[6]

By reducing existence *to its primary elements*, art is opposed to conventionality in its *barbarous truth*. And I believe that, in this conflict, we can find one of the most interesting aspects of the work of those artists who now occupy political positions. It is a dramatic opening up of the field of art, often quite independently from the role of the institution (the museum or gallery), and the search for an area of autonomy in which to deal with reality. Art itself needs to establish a relationship with the real world—one that goes beyond mere embellishment and self-referential research within the context of art: it needs to become a stripping away, an unmasking, a scraping and excavation.

Here, we could further focus our attention on the work of artists who not only use art to tackle the present-day situation, but who also see art as an instrument to bring about a process of collective involvement on which they can then work. The work of these artists constitutes an extension of what Foucault mentioned in terms of the manifestation of the *scandal of truth* in the life of the artist. Artists who work in *relational* terms, who embark upon a *participatory process*, or who encourage the emergence of an *experimental community*—to mention but some of the definitions coined in recent years to define this phenomenon[7]—together bring about a *desire for truth* and this leads to research into the emerging conditions of our society. This becomes an aesthetic investigation that leads reality, or rather the community, to transform itself from being the object of artistic action into being an actively involved subject.

One recurrent aspect of these works is that they view the community as a dynamic element against which to measure themselves and by which they can constantly be influenced. Unlike public forms of art, the object or performance is not inserted into a particular context, but is rather a work on the actual dynamic nature of society, and it is sometimes prolonged indefinitely. The artist starts up the process and uses art as an instrument to legitimize the role of people in society, to respond to pressing needs, and to establish a form of reciprocity, an exchange of knowledge, a collectivization and cohabitation of the process. The aim is never to solve problems but rather to encourage new forms of interpretation and action in the local context.

**8** *Market of Tomorrow, Freehouse,* Jeanne van Heeswijk and Dennis Kaspori, Rotterdam, 2008–2009

**Jeanne van Heeswijk**'s projects fully reflect this approach. Her aim as an artist is to act as an intermediary between situations, as well as places, and the people who inhabit these places. She is not interested in producing events confined to a particular place, but rather in projects that can bring about an experimental condition within a specific group of people. As a result, her artistic work does not focus on accomplishing a predefined plan but rather on creating cultural models that address the problems involved in particular issues, such as the coexistence of different cultures for the establishment of areas of freedom within the urban fabric.

In her *Freehouse Markt van Morgen*[8] project, van Heeswijk selected as her field of action an open-air market in Afrikaanderplein, one of the areas of greatest immigration in Rotterdam. Her interest was in a series of problems that had made the market a place where conflict and unsolved issues tended to emerge. These issues, which also came out during consultation with the market users, defined the confines of van Heeswijk's work. Identifying this field of action meant entering personally into local dynamics, finding those who would be able to provide knowledge and make contributions, and starting up a series of actions that would be able to modify the state of affairs and, in turn, be modified by them. The market thus became the arena for a series of initiatives, proposals for new uses, and products that would be able to lead to possible developments in the area, starting out with collaboration between local salespeople, young designers, artists, entrepreneurs, and residents in the neighborhood, in order to create an innovative cultural program. Van Heeswijk's projects define a field of action that consists of a series of questions, and this leads to a process of change brought about by selecting *experts on location* (local people with knowledge, even though often latent, of the place) and with the contribution of specialists from different disciplines, such as artists, philosophers, sociologists, designers, and so on. Once sparked off, these processes lead to a series of consequences that are not necessarily controllable, and that to some extent acquire a life of their own.

Like van Heeswijk's, the projects of the Guatemalan architect **Teddy Cruz** start out by asserting the supremacy of collaborative processes over those of an individual nature. Bringing together groups of people with different types of knowledge and with different cultures brings about a highly stimulating level of complexity from an artistic and spatial point of view. Cruz's work in the border area between San Diego and Tijuana, where some of the richest districts in the world exist alongside areas of real destitution, is a workshop where new social, economic, and cultural models can be developed. The migratory flow of the Latin American diaspora enriches the suburban American landscape with informal economies and customs, while on the other side of the border, the urban waste of

9 Arjun Appadurai, *Modernity at Large* (Minneapolis: University of Minnesota Press, 1996), 31
10 See the interview with Bert Theis in this volume

San Diego (car tires, construction materials, and entire prefabricated houses) is used to build a vast, improvised housing area. In these exchanges, Cruz sees the emergence of new hybrid models in which the sterile life of suburban America can draw on the Latino social heritage, and he designs prefabricated frames that can be used as load-bearing structures to support temporary homes in Tijuana. A new paradigm may thus emerge from a rethinking of the architect's role: by mediating between entrepreneurs, authorities, and citizens, the architect is able to transform the intelligence and needs of these neighborhoods into economic policies and models that are capable of triggering off a process of empowerment. In the neighborhood of San Ysidro in San Diego, Cruz is experimenting with a new housing model in which, together with the inhabitants, he brings together ecological issues, new social possibilities, and the emergence of a new, endogenous entrepreneurship. Formal aspects become simply the underlying structure for a series of cooperation processes and for making it possible to try out new forms of aggregation.

Defining methodological and housing alternatives goes hand-in-hand with the possibility of creating new models to which to be aspired. This is what the Indian anthropologist Arjan Appadurai refers to as "the imagination as a social practice."[9] **Bert Theis**'s work in the Isola Art Center project comes from an attempt to imagine a world where a commonly shared understanding can be built up in the Isola district, an area of Milan which is undergoing dramatic transformation. By establishing the limits, potential, and objectives of the community, Theis has facilitated a discussion and a process of ideas about the future of the district, in both spatial and social terms. Daily discussions with the community, cooperation with neighborhood associations, and the involvement of artists and intellectuals has led to a process of greater awareness, emancipation, and self-determination, thus legitimizing the role of the citizens, but also encouraging different groups to interact.

The idea of using a space for contemporary art as a place for dialogue and interaction has led many residents to redefine the role of art and, at the same time, it has allowed a number of artists to start listening more carefully, and this has led to projects for the community outside of exhibition spaces. Since 2007, when the Isola Art Center was demolished[10], the project has continued with a series of art projects, events, and actions in the district, considerably broadening out the sphere of intervention. Projects like *Rosta*, in which artists such as Dan Perjovschi, Andreas Siekmann, and Christoph Schäfer made works on the shutters in the district, or *museo aero solar*, by Tomas Saraceno, could not have come about without the active cooperation of many local residents and a constant reappraisal of the role of art as a means of bringing about new collective ideas.

Sharing these intentions, even though in a profoundly different context, **Goddy Leye** has started up a series of projects of community involvement with the aim of making the aesthetic process a fundamental factor in development. In a city like Douala, the financial capital of Cameroon, in which there are no art schools or museums, art can become a new code for initiating dialogue with the community. This has been the case ever since the first projects in which Leye and a collective of artists showed their works in public spaces, stimulating debate about their content, and then in more complex projects such as *Bessengue City* and *ArtBakery*, in which he has become the coordinator of a complex network of operations and works by other artists, organizations, and local citizens.

In the *ArtBakery* project, Leye creates an experimental dimension in the Bonendale district of Douala. He has set up a community of artists which, along with local residents, has embarked on a process of emancipation from clichés of backwardness and marginalization in order to achieve a commonly agreed-upon definition of new expectations for the neighborhood. *ArtBakery* includes training sessions, public events, and exhibitions, but more than anything it is capable of taking art away from a self-referential stance and turning it into a common language with which to define the different aspirations of the district.

Interaction between art and local communities can also lead to clear conflict with the institutions, as is the case in **Santiago Cirugeda**'s work. With his *Recetas Urbanas* ("Urban Recipes") group, Cirugeda is mainly engaged in carrying out subversive actions that point the finger at areas of dissatisfaction in urban contexts. These particularly concern issues such as the gradual reduction of public spaces and the segregation of less affluent citizens into city suburbs. His collectively produced projects allow people to demand an active role, and they range from occupying unused public spaces to setting up prostheses on existing buildings and to the construction of illegal housing and social spaces.

*Un-Buildable House*, a self-construction project in the Poblenou district of Barcelona, provocatively shows how unused public space can be rapidly taken over for temporary housing. Cirugeda circulates detailed instructions on how to reproduce these housing units, and in some cases he also guarantees legal assistance. The project, which makes the front pages of all the local newspapers, meets its objective of inspiring debate about the problem of housing. Recently, the projects carried out by Recetas Urbanas have focused on the construction of facilities for community centers, collectives, and groups of activists. These premises, which are generally made of prefabricated containers, are demonstrations of the pressing need to establish new places of aggregation outside of the institutional context, creating opportunities for debate and for socializing.

Art as a collective process makes a complete break with the consolidated system of museum presentation, and creates conflict with the commercial dimension, establishing a practical alternative approach. The adoption of a particular field in which to launch a collective process, and in which to reformulate the relationship between artist and spectator by creating a dynamic and reciprocal dimension, gradually leads to new perspectives for development, and constitutes an alternative system of viewing the practice of art. As a collective process, art becomes committed, and defined by parallel networks that often arise out of the desire to create alternative operations with a view to defining contemporary society. Perhaps it is a synthesis of the two fronts of struggle raised by Mao Zedong: "the unity of politics and art, the unity of content and form."

*Emiliano Gandolfi —*

Even though you had an international career, your artistic development has been strongly connected to the specific conditions of your hometown, Douala [the economic and cultural capital of Cameroon]. In addition to this, your work is pervaded by different forms of engagement, in terms of your interest in working in a "collective process"—involving in your projects people from outside the art context—and your lifelong involvement in several artist collective groups. Could you tell us more about how this interest in collaborative work actually began?

*Goddy Leye —*

I must say that it started out of necessity. In Cameroon we don't have that many art galleries, so in order to bring our message through, we as a group of artists decided to start engaging the audience in a different way. We started working as a collective in 1993, with a group called *Prime Art,* focusing primarily on how to define new ways of experimentation in art. In those years I had the luck to study at the École Supérieure d'Art de Grenoble, so I brought back to Cameroon some groundbreaking experiences and new notions on art. In those years, in addition to painting, we started working more and more with performance, installations, and video. But the most important aspect was that we had the chance to come together regularly to discuss our works and perspectives, and this became vital for our personal growth. Another important aspect that we had to resolve was not having a real venue at which to exhibit, or an audience. So we decided to make our own art system by inviting the residents of the neighborhood where we had our studio to come over and to engage in a dialogue. These experiences were developed further after 1998 when we founded a collective called The Dreamers. My studio became a public space where people would come regularly and question our work.

*Emiliano Gandolfi —*

How did the attendance of the people from the neighborhood actually influence your work as an artist?

*Goddy Leye —*

It was a fundamental contribution. In an art gallery, at least in a place like Douala where there isn't really art criticism, there is not a sincere attempt to understand the message behind the work. But the people from the neighborhood shared with us observations on the content. To enlarge this dimension even more, we started making exhibitions in public spaces, like in a roundabout in the city center. In these events, many people became our supporters and many more were entering into contact for the first time with art and the relevance of its message. Also importantly, showing our works in public spaces was a way to train ourselves via the questions that were coming from the public. It was a way to have people engaged in a dialogue, which is something that in most cases doesn't happen in a gallery setting. On the other hand, we were learning through this process how to communicate more effectively—borrowing "informal" communication tools—and at the same time using this experience back in the gallery setting. By confronting the audience, we got used to receiving new ideas, but we also understood the importance of relating our projects to specific contexts and of considering making our own audience part of the work.

*Emiliano Gandolfi —*

It's interesting to take into consideration the shifting notion of art in a city where there are no art museums, or art academies, and where even freedom of speech is not a given. Art becomes a way to raise awareness on important issues. To what extent was this first attempt to open up the field to confrontation developed through an art practice in which people actually became part of the process, as in your *Bessengue City* project?

# Goddy Leye

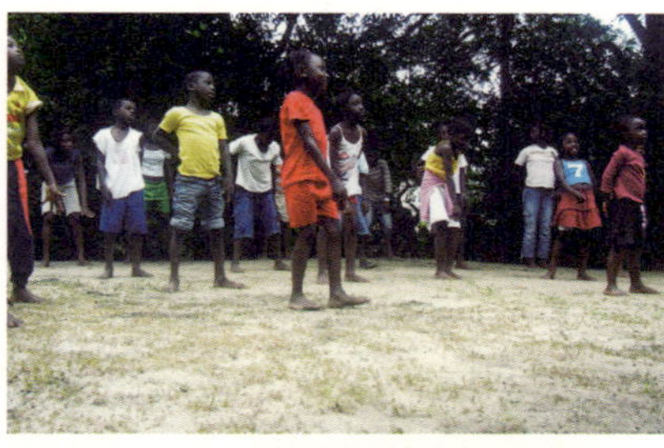

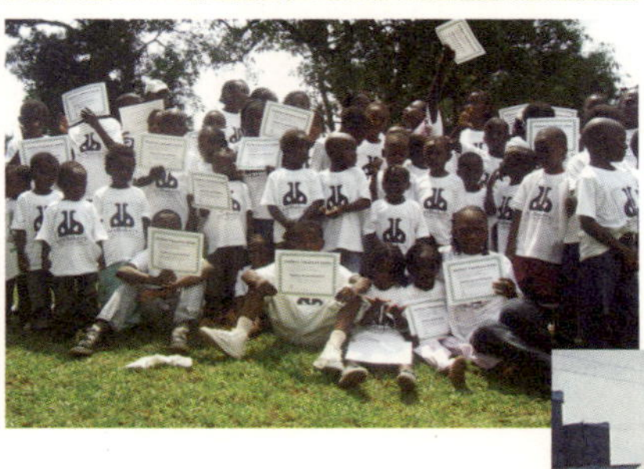

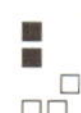

***ArtBakery***, founded in 2003 in Bonendale, Douala (Cameroun), has grounded its action on three main programs: a residency program for visual artists, training in art and visual culture, and support to young artists, critics, and curators. Most importantly, these programs are developed with a constant interaction with the local community of Bonendale and with the specific focus of developing art projects in public space. In these two images: a performance with children from Bonendale and students proudly showing their diploma at the end of a workshop at *ArtBakery*.

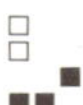

***Bessengue City***, 2002, a project by Goddy Leye with the contribution of James Beckett, Hartanto, and Jesus Palomino. With the support and validation of the existing Development Committee, the team worked with the people in the area to realize their pieces. Beckett worked on *Radio Bessengue City*, a radio with a range of one kilometer that was installed inside Palomino's shelter. Using this platform, groups of youngsters designed the program and the jingle, conducted interviews, and transmitted various recordings for over a year. These projects have been an important contribution for the activation of an empowerment process in the Bessengue district.

*Goddy Leye —*

*Bessengue City* came almost four years after the first experiences with The Dreamers, and it represented the beginning of a different type of engagement with the neighborhood. We soon realized that the participation of the public was not just providing a different understanding of our works, but that in fact the role of the public was vital to the existence of the works of art themselves. In those years I was in the Rijksakademie in Amsterdam, but I had the intention of going back to Cameroon immediately after the term of the residency program. I was already planning to start the *ArtBakery* project as a mayor engagement. But before starting this long-term project, I decided to test some of the ideas I was developing in a project that would involve the inhabitants of a neighborhood. I also wanted to work on a collaborative effort, including artists that I knew could bring to Douala a substantial contribution.

*Emiliano Gandolfi —*

So it's been a project intended as a tool for public involvement in a neighborhood of Douala. And how did it unfold?

*Goddy Leye —*

Bessengue is one of the poorest neighborhoods in Douala, completely self-built by its 10,000 inhabitants in an area that is dramatically flooded during the rainy season. In this neighborhood, a local non-government organization called doual'art was already working with art projects as means of development, and in 2001 I was involved in working on a project. It was an important occasion to reflect on what it meant to do art in an environment where people are suffering from problems related to poverty. Ultimately our conclusion was that it was certainly more relevant to act in neighborhoods such as this than in any other posh art venue. We decided to work on a medium-term project with the ambition of possibly achieving a long-term effect. To do this I called some of the artists that I met in Amsterdam and that could bring a contribution to the project. I challenged, for instance, Jesus Palomino—a Spanish artist well known for building shelters in museums—to rethink his practice in a new perspective and to build a shelter among thousands of other shelters. Most interestingly, he turned into a work of art something that in this environment is completely common, and by doing so he encouraged the local inhabitants to have a different perception of their own surroundings. Inspired by his broadcasting project in the Rijksakademie, I also asked James Beckett, an Amsterdam-based South African artist, to start a radio in the neighborhood. Lastly, I invited a third artist called Hartanto, who worked on establishing connections between people in Bessengue and inhabitants from his hometown in Indonesia.

*Emiliano Gandolfi —*

And what was the reaction of the local inhabitants to all of these art projects?

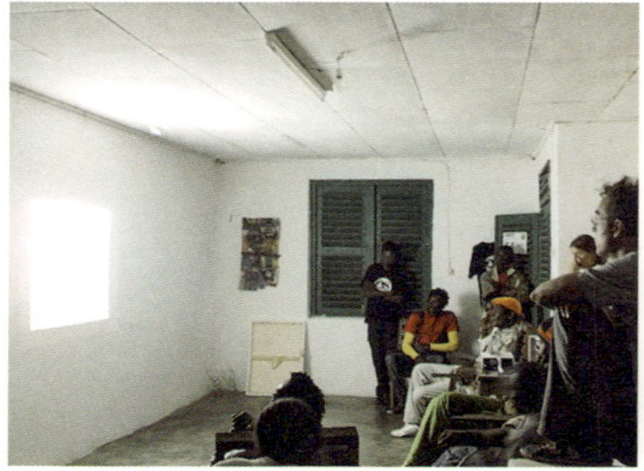

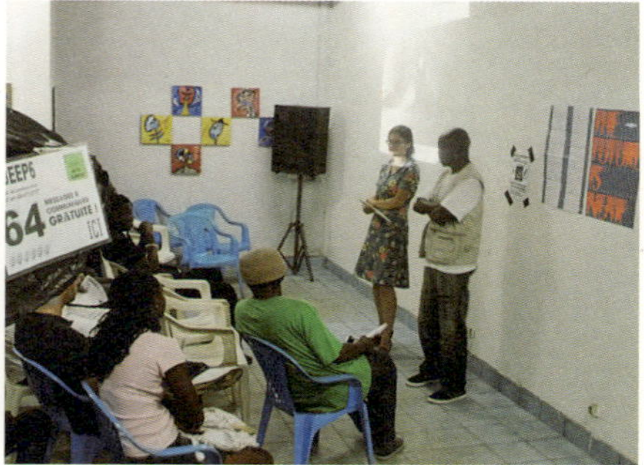

*Goddy Leye —*

The involvement of the people of Bessengue was in fact our main goal, and to be effective both the role of doaul'art and the relationship that we developed with the local council, the Development Committee, were fundamental. They would meet regularly to explain to the inhabitants what we were planning to do, so when the project finally started everyone was already informed and excited about helping us. The shelter by Palomino finally hosted the radio station by James Beckett. The radio station was engaged in involving the youth in broadcasting music and also in issues about their neighborhood. We couldn't talk directly about politics, but we could influence how the people perceived their neighborhood, developing—from a condition of illegality and marginality—a sense of belonging.

*Emiliano Gandolfi —*

Was it legal to broadcast?

*Goddy Leye —*

In fact broadcasting was illegal, and as a precaution we even limited the range of the radio to four kilometers, but that was enough to cover the entire district. We even received a visit by the regional delegate that had been alerted by a rumor that there was a pirate radio. But the fact that it was not a radio, but simply an "artistic project," defined a legal loophole within which we could operate freely. We started broadcasting every day from four to seven o'clock, and it was actually even a daily challenge to stop the transmission because the youngsters running the program were having too much fun! They had a huge number of programs every day, including rap shows, interviews, music, comedies, etc. After the first month, the project was meant to leave the equipment to a group of local youngsters that went on organizing programs and events for two more months. They took over wonderfully, looked for funding by themselves, and continued broadcasting regularly.

*Emiliano Gandolfi —*

In a way *Bessengue City* was a seminal project in terms of involvement of the local community and for the definition of art as a form of development. Do you think we could say that new skills were developed among the inhabitants of Bessengue?

*Goddy Leye —*

I must say that it is always difficult to define the causalities of these kind of projects. Even though some consequences are clearly referable to this experience. For instance, at least four of the youth that were involved in the radio project are now working in communication businesses, in radio and advertising companies. The radio brought different possibilities to their lives and stimulated new interests. Another

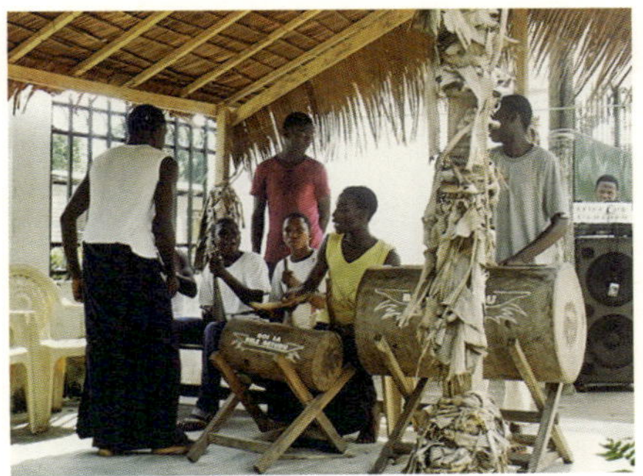

■■□
***ArtBakery,*** artists present their work at K-Factory, a space run by Cercle Kapsiki, a local collective of visual artists

□□■
***ArtBakery,*** community workshop on music organized by the Dutch artist Steven Jouwersma

clear consequence was that a water pump—as a communal space for women—was built in the neighborhood by doual'art and the architect that made the design drew direct inspiration from Palomino's shelter. Since all of these art projects were developed in Bessengue, the local inhabitants started seeing with different eyes their own neighborhood. Now the river bank is kept cleaner, and people are more receptive: they pay attention to the beauty of the space in which they live. For example, there is a young barber that decorated his shop in a terrific way; he makes sure to regularly change decorations because he believes that he is living in an environment where art is present. And he is proud of it.

*Emiliano Gandolfi —*

*Bessengue City* has been a testing ground for another important project held in Douala. With *ArtBakery* your interest in working with a collective and in involving local communities in making and understanding art was consolidated by the foundation of an art residency program.

*Goddy Leye —*

In order to work on *ArtBakery*, in 2003 I decided to move back to Cameroon and start a project that could function as a residency program for artists, and that could also become a place at which to give support to and train young artists and curators. These programs were imagined with the integral ambition of interacting with the local community as a fundamental aspect of the art process. The first stage was to define what an artist-in-residence program could be in a place like Douala, and this brought us instead to the initiation of a "portfolio program." We are helping young artists to develop the tools to enter the art world, and on the other hand we are inviting experienced international artists to share their own views, exchange ideas, and stimulate discussions. Parallel to this program, we are also organizing master classes.

*Emiliano Gandolfi —*

Bonendale is a neighborhood on the outskirts of the city, in a way perceivable as a separate village. In fact, the activities that *ArtBakery* produces are embedded in the place, but in a way it is also an invasive presence. How does the relationship with the community work?

*Goddy Leye —*

The work with the community is a fundamental aspect of *ArtBakery*. For us it is very important that the

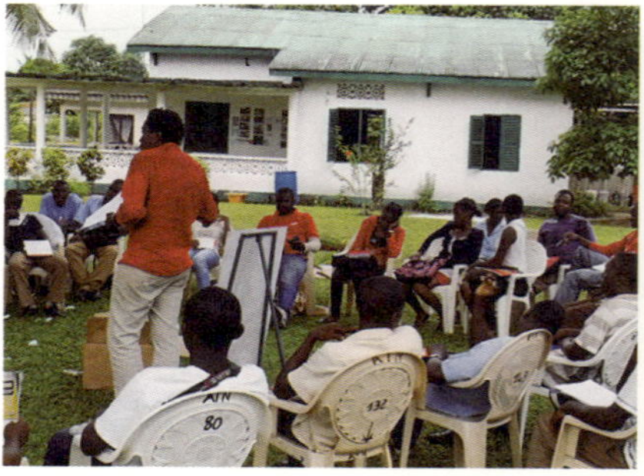

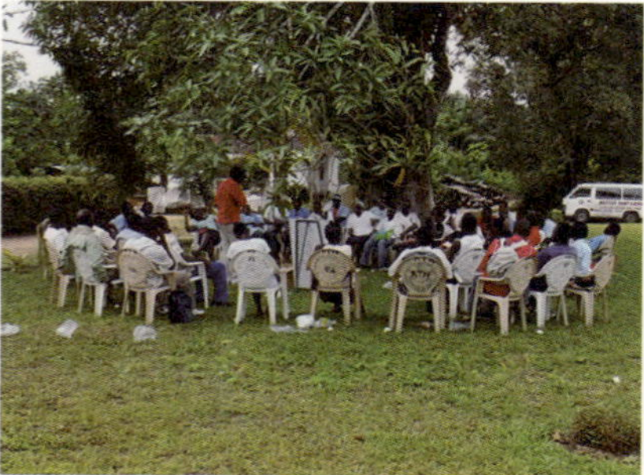

art that we produce has some kind of relationship with the local inhabitants; in fact, we consider them our first audience. That is why many of our programs are aimed at introducing an aesthetic vocabulary to the community. In order to do this we also organize a series of projects that we call "outreach." For instance, we have being doing a program called *Ateliers Vacances* for four years now, in which we gather thirty to fifty young people from the village from the ages of six to sixteen years (though sometimes it is difficult to keep the smaller ones from coming anyway). These kids have the opportunity to work with up to six artists who teach them how to draw, paint, and work with clay, and who also introduce them to poetry, theater, and dance. And in the past two editions, we also introduced them to environmental issues, in order to preserve ancient knowledge about the medical use of plants and to raise ecological awareness. In addition to these projects with kids, we have outreach projects with youngsters in which we teach them how to use cameras and video equipment, and how to do editing, whereas other courses develop writing skills and so on. It is crucial for the way they perceive themselves and their own habitat—through these skills they start being more critical of what they see, while also eventually using them to build a profession. We are also starting projects with local farmers and artisans, we have a library, and we have many more projects in collaboration with the local community. For *ArtBakery*, it is of primary importance to open the eyes of the community to the effects and possibilities of art, even though not everything we do is related to art, or is actually an art piece itself. We do public screenings—for example, we regularly show foreign films and documentaries—to expose the cliché that Europe is like paradise. This is not necessarily art, but it contributes to shaping a critical understanding. We even have a television broadcast called Bonendale TV.

*Emiliano Gandolfi —*

You frequently refer to the notion that "development is an aesthetic project." What role do you think art can have in shaping an alternative in Bonendale?

*Goddy Leye —*

With art you deal with images and visions, and changing an image of a place has a huge impact on people. Part of the trauma of most underdeveloped countries comes from the negative image their people have of themselves. So it is very important for artists to change this image, and if you succeed, confidence will follow, along with the demand for a better standard of life. One of the biggest problems is switching from one image that is purely negative, to a new one, which can be a spark of energy.

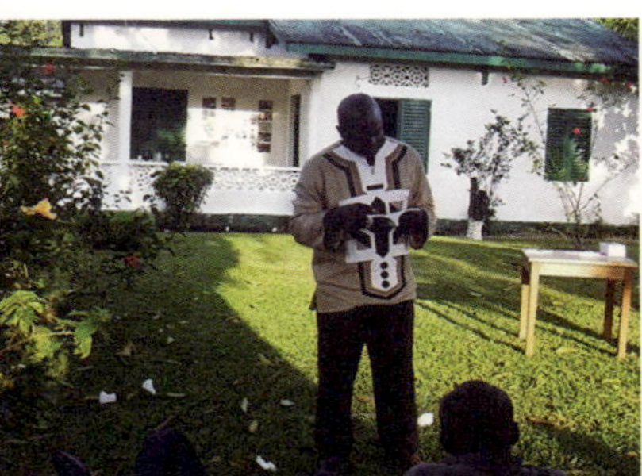

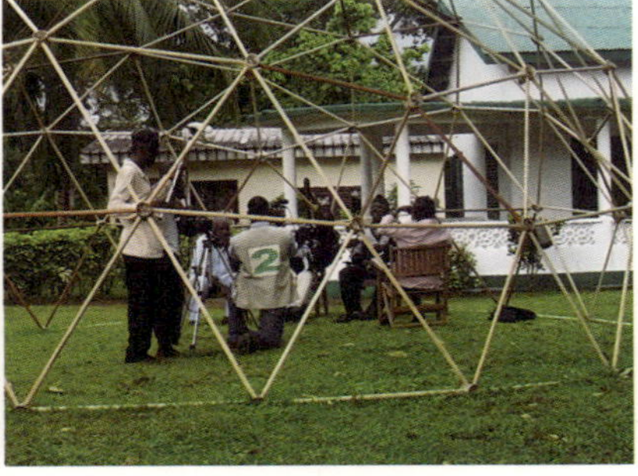

■■□□
***ArtBakery,*** poetry workshop with Lionel Manga

□□■■
***Ring,*** a project by the collective Autodafe (Dominique Malaquais, Goddy Leye and Art Bakery, Cercle Kapsiki, and Aretha Louise Mbango). A cross-disciplinary performance between scenography, choreography and songs from the village of Bonendale

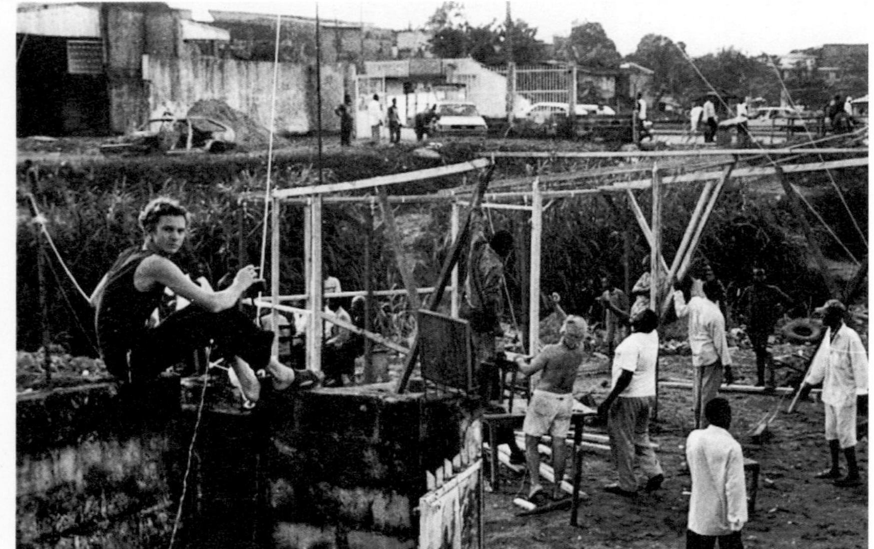

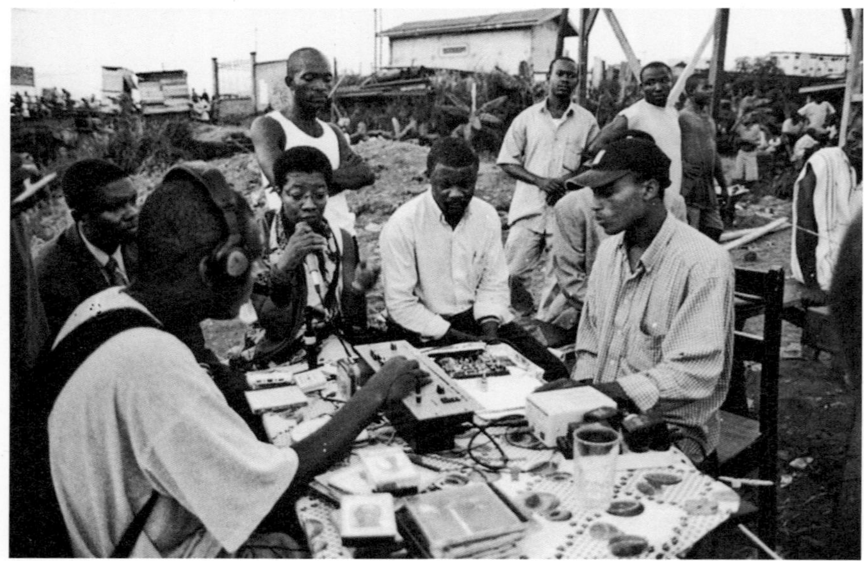

■
□
***Bessengue City***, 2002, James Beckett during the construction of Jesus Palomino's shelter

□
■
***Bessengue City***, 2002, a moment of the transmission of *Radio Bessengue City*, a project by James Beckett

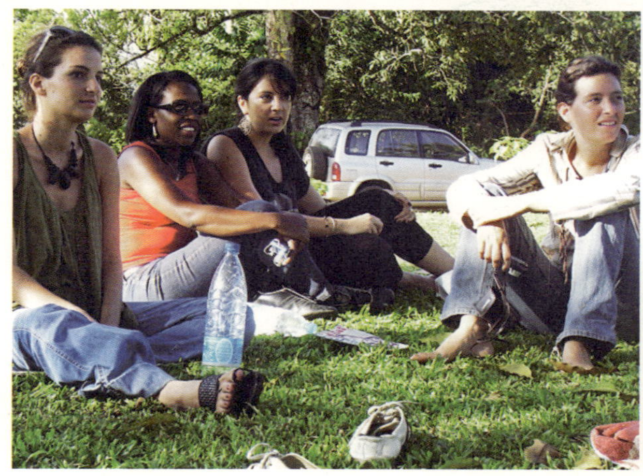

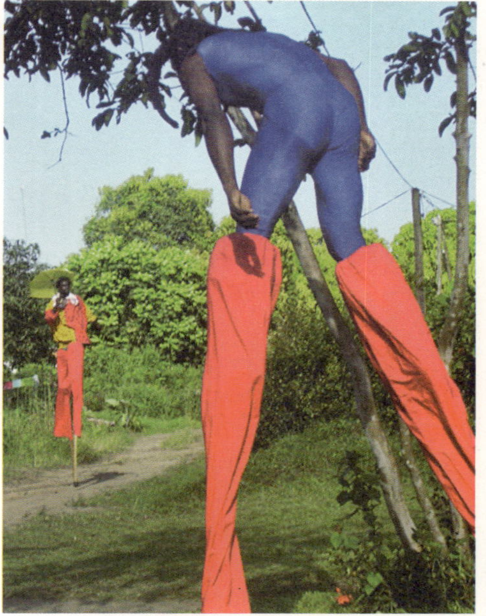

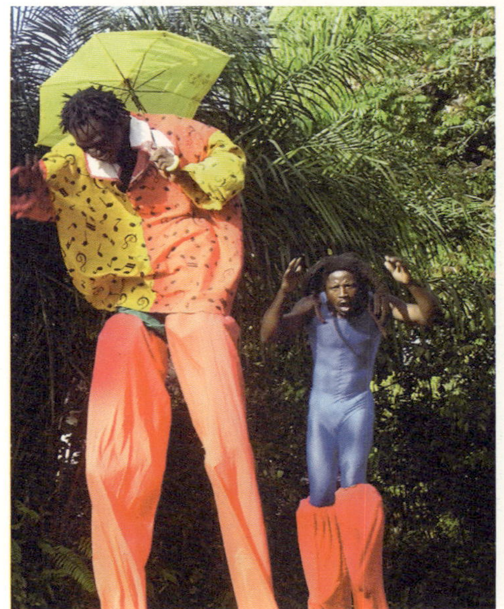

***ArtBakery***, a performance by *Koz'arts*, a Bonendale-based collective of performing artists, during their open studios in 2009

*Emiliano Gandolfi —*

Over the last number of years your research has been focusing on the definition of new operational devises. The border region between Tijuana and San Diego becomes for you a laboratory in which to imagine counter-spatial procedures, political and economic structures that can produce new modes of sociability and participation. What are the ties between your work and the specific localities where you are operating?

*Teddy Cruz —*

My practice first began, simply, as a desire to critically observe the specificity of the politics inscribed in the territory of the San Diego-Tijuana border, oscillating between some of the wealthiest real estate in the US and some of the poorest settlements in Latin America, barely twenty minutes away. These two different types of suburbia are emblematic of the incremental division of the contemporary city, and of the territory between enclaves of mega-wealth and the rings of poverty that surround them. Critical observation of this locality reveals issues that cannot continue to be ignored. The triangulation between the politics of immigration and labor and the redefinition of the American neighborhood by immigrants will point the way to a different idea of density and social justice which is at the center of our research and work: imagining a city where the neighborhood is the primary site of production toward new economic models and social and cultural relations.

*Emiliano Gandolfi —*

In your work, the flows of traffic across this border region, whether of people, goods, or services, could be seen as new opportunities for constructing alternative modes of encounter, dialogue, and debate. What would you consider to be the main lessons behind these phenomena?

*Teddy Cruz —*

I have been documenting these illegal flows, in one direction, by the informal land use and economies produced by migrant workers flowing from Tijuana into San Diego, and by "infrastructural waste" moving in the opposite direction to construct an insurgent, cross-border urbanism of emergency. This suggests a double urbanism of retrofit: in the South-North direction, the Latin American diaspora retrofits San Diego's first ring of suburbanization with informal uses and economies. In the North-South direction, by recycling the urban debris of the "other" city, Tijuana is constructing a secondhand housing urbanism made of waste, the foundation of which is not based on objects but on a process of threading topography, human and economic resources, social networks, and programs: the political economy of waste and housing. Behind the façade of poverty that characterizes the marginal communities on both sides of the border, there is a more complex idea of housing. Across these neighborhoods, housing is not conceived as generic units of dwelling thrown in the territory, but as a relational system grounded in social organization. A new paradigm can emerge here about sustainability, and which threads environmental, economic, and social issues, where housing can become the main armature to construct public culture and infrastructure.

*Emiliano Gandolfi —*

I find extremely fascinating how your work is a constant redefinition of the very nature of notions like community and citizenship. It's about sharing resources and suggesting how the recycling of the fragments and situations of these two cities can allow new ways of inhabitation. But it is also redefining the role and the tools of the architect.

# Teddy Cruz

***The Political Equator*** emerges as one extends the Tijuana-San Diego border across a world atlas between the 28th° and 32nd° parallels north. It produces a necklace of global conflict linking some of the most intensive border checkpoints in the world.

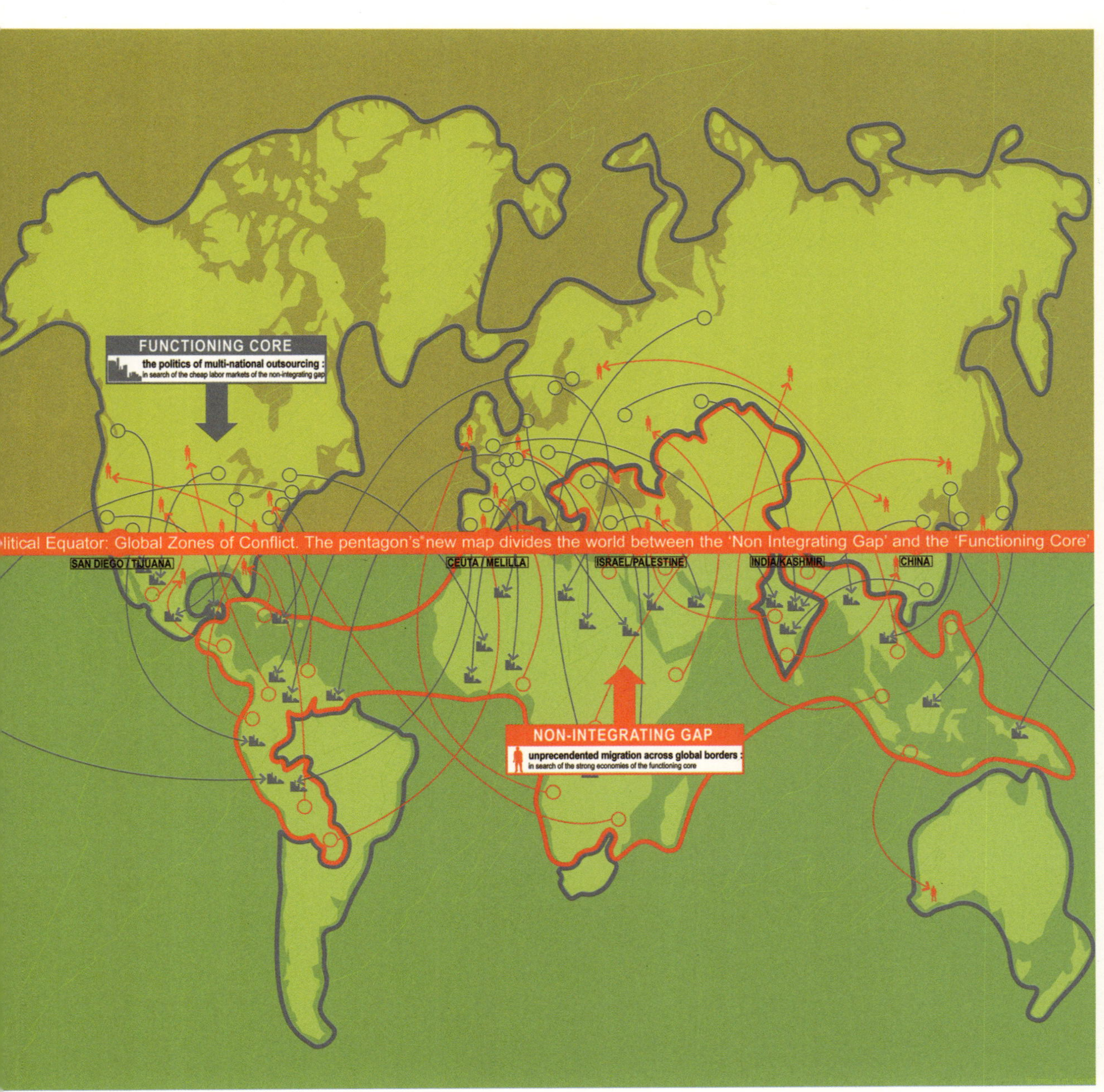

*Teddy Cruz —*

Recently, I have been recollecting a passage I read in the *New York Times* a couple of years ago. It somehow has become the most inspirational statement I have read in questioning my role as an architect within these zones of conflict. This quote came from the least expected place: the first report to the US Congress by General David H. Petraeus, the US commanding general, in those days, of the war in Iraq. In this report, Petraeus suggested to Congress that after the experience in Iraq, the contemporary US soldier should transform, no longer existing as a high-tech robot-like figure armed with the latest gadgets that can dominate the warfield from a distance. The contemporary soldier should instead engage the critical proximity of neighborhoods, transforming into an anthropologist, a social worker, versed in many languages! Now… even though this can sound scary, I thought, if the contemporary soldier is transforming, why can't architects transform? We need to appropriate the procedures of the "other," not becoming necessarily anthropologists or social workers, but borrowing their procedures so as to operate differently in constructing critical observational research and alternative spatial strategies.

*Emiliano Gandolfi —*

It is like changing the perspective, from a birds-eye view—or, carrying on your analogy, from a jet fighter—to a sidewalk viewpoint. What change would this different approach lead to?

*Teddy Cruz —*

We need to challenge our reductive and limited ways of working, by which we continue seeing the world as a tabula rasa on which to install the autonomy of architecture. We need to reorient our gaze toward the drama embedded in the reality of the everyday and in so doing engage the shifting sociopolitical and economic domains that have been ungraspable by design. Or, as artist Tania Brugera said to me recently: "It is time to restore Duchamp's urinal back to the bathroom!" We are in need of a more functional relationship between research, artistic intervention, and the production of the city. At a time when the institutions of urban planning need to be redefined, one particular topic that needs to be considered is the value of social capital (people's participation) in urban development, enhancing the role of communities in producing housing. These housing configurations would enable the development and emergence of local economies and new forms of sociability, allowing neighborhoods to generate new markets "from the bottom up," within the community, as well as to promote new models of financing to allow unconventional mixed uses. We have the urge to rethink existing conditions of ownership, redefining affordability by amplifying the value of social participation.

*Emiliano Gandolfi —*

What I am mostly interested in with respect to these procedures is how different ideas of empowerment, participation, and representation emerge. It's about sparking a collective creative process in which the citizens are empowered and the architect draws relations and opens possibilities.

*Teddy Cruz —*

The architect becomes the initiator of a new process. These processes give voice to communities that unfortunately often lack representation and the capacity to understand their own procedures. Through mediation between the stakeholders, we can problematize the debate, amplifying and explicating the ethical knowledge specific to a community. Ultimately, it is about translating the intelligence embedded in these neighborhood dynamics into new politics and economies, and initiating a fundamental empowerment process.

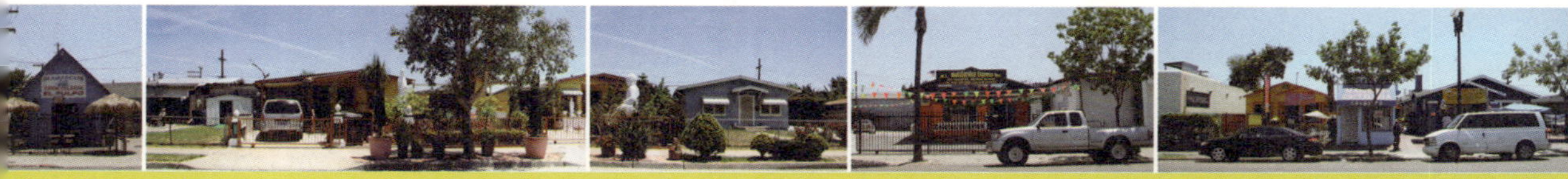

ctics of encroachment: as the Latin American Diaspora travels Northbound, it inevitably alters and transforms the fabric of San Diego's older bdivisions, generating non-conforming mixed uses and high densities that retrofit Levittown with difference.

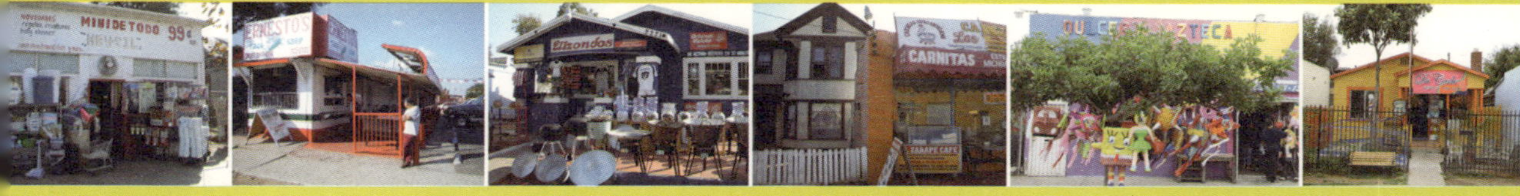

ɔn-Conforming Buddha: a tiny post-war bungalow in a San Diego mid-city nieghborhood has been transformed from a single-family residence into a ıddhist temple.

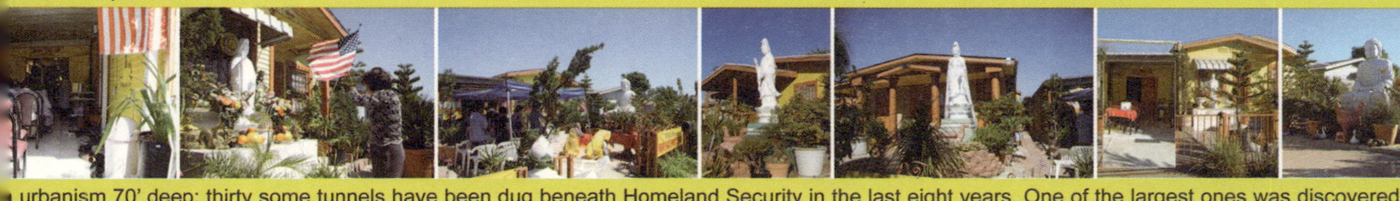

urbanism 70' deep: thirty some tunnels have been dug beneath Homeland Security in the last eight years. One of the largest ones was discovered st year. It had retaining walls, water and air extraction systems and electricity. It connected a house in Tijuana and a factory in San Diego.

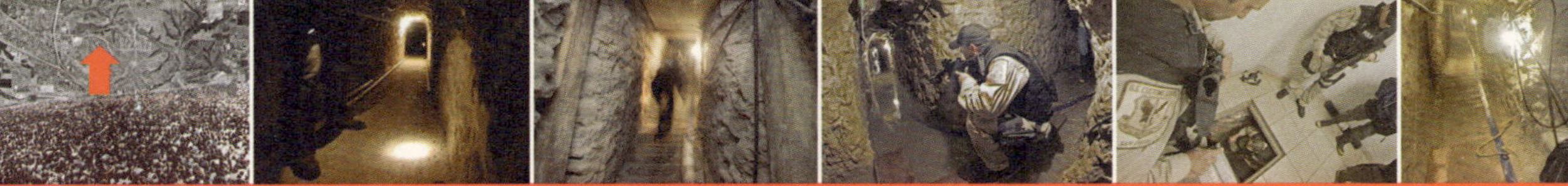

**outh to North:** Neighborhoods made of non-conformity. Tijuana's informal land use patterns encroach into San Diego's sprawl.

**orth to South:** Neighborhoods made of waste. San Diego's Housing waste is recycled into Tijuana's slums.

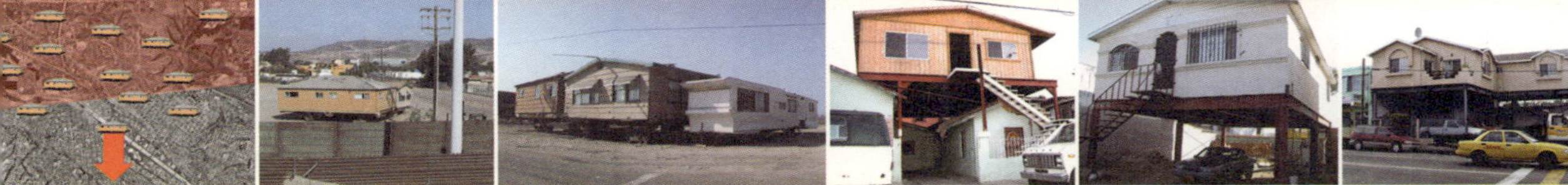

grant housing: Mexican builders recuperate post-war bungalows that are slated for demolition in San Diego, and bring them across the border. Once imported o Tijuana they are assembled above one story steel frames. These floating houses define a space of opportunity beneath them, that will be filled with other uses.

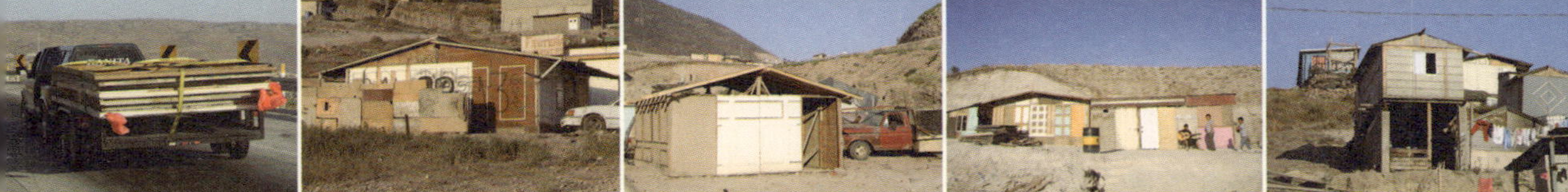

ɔusing urbanism made of waste: one city recycles the leftover of the other into a second hand urbanism. Used garage doors and wooden crates make ıll systems.

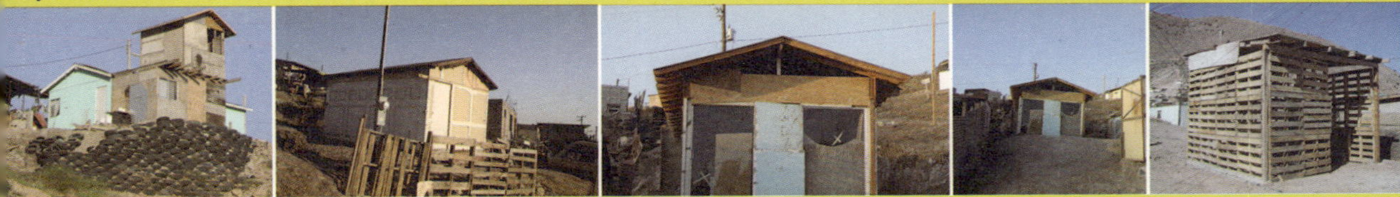

ecycled rubber tires are cut and dismantled into folded loops, creating a system that threads a stable retaining wall.

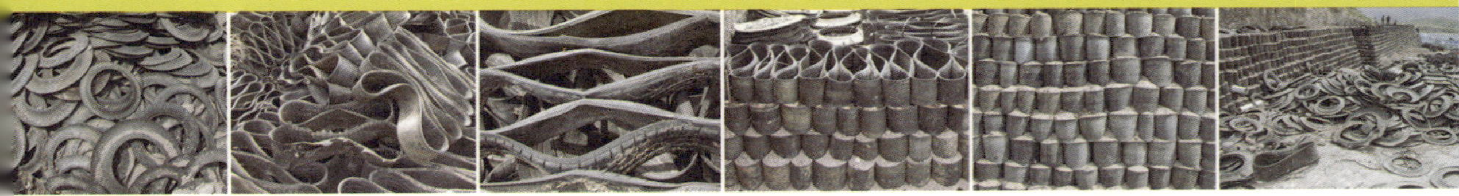

■

ns-border informal urban ıamics, as illegal zoning seeps ɹth to retrofit the large with the all, urban debris flows south construct a housing urbanism ıde of waste.

Emiliano Gandolfi
**Teddy Cruz**

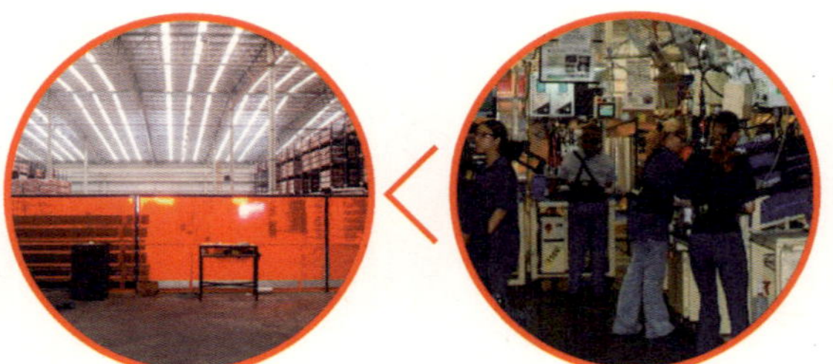

Tijuana a city of Factories
The politics of cheap labor/housing crisis
Maquiladoras extract labor from surrounding slums and do not contribute with housing infrastructure

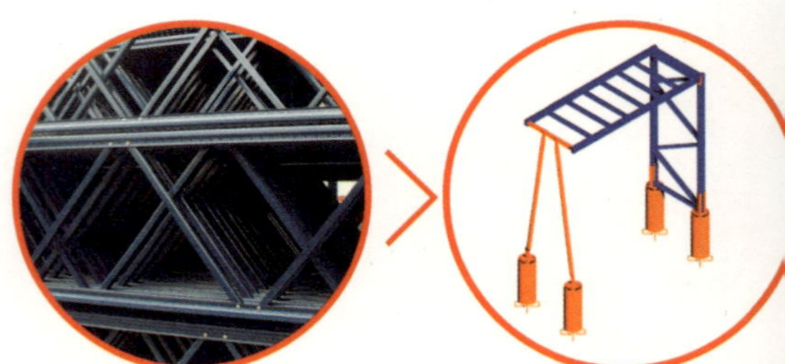

NAFTA North American Fair Trade Agreement
Labor = Housing
Encroaching into the 'Maquiladora' assembly line to produce support systems for dwelling

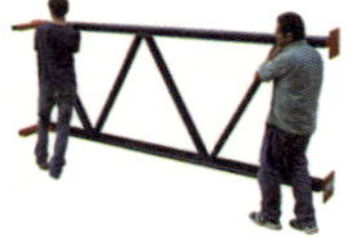

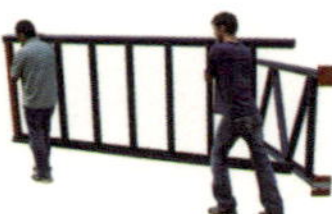

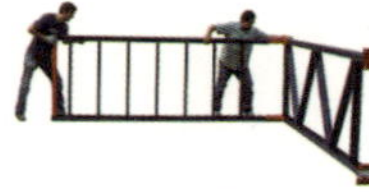

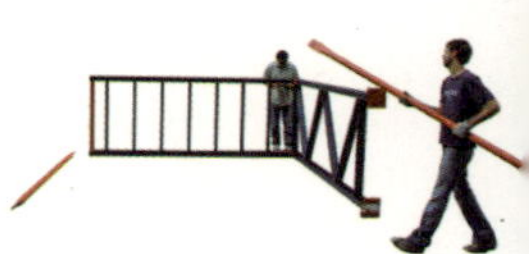

Teddy Cruz's research on the informal settlements in Tijuana has pointed to the factory as a site of intervention, designing new triangulations between systems of production, labor dynamics, community activism, emergency housing, and micro-infrastructural systems.

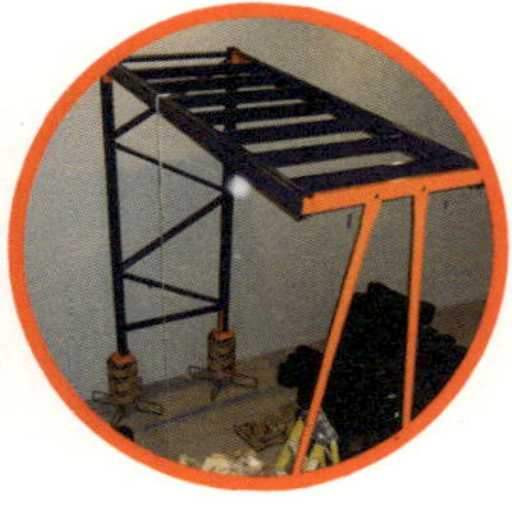

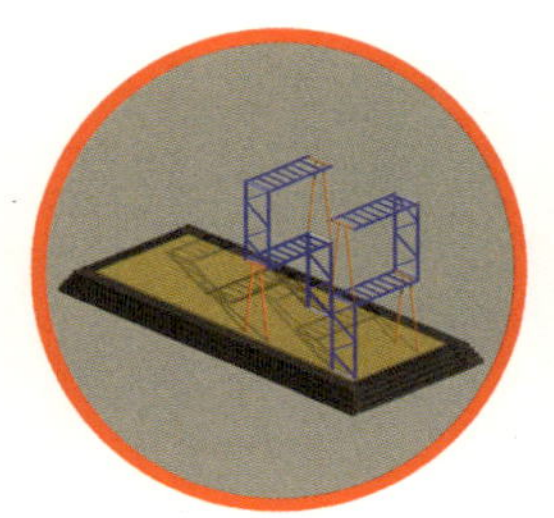

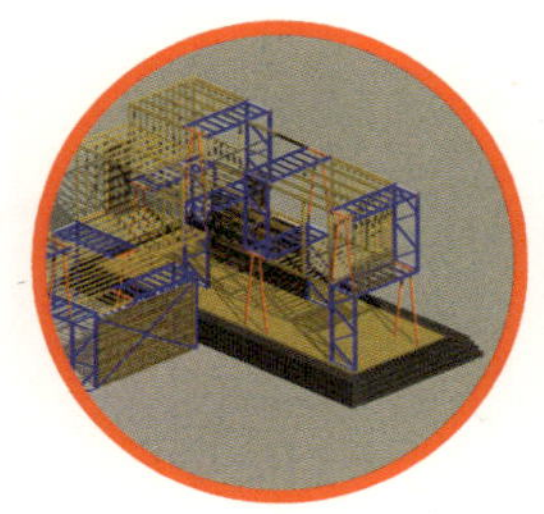

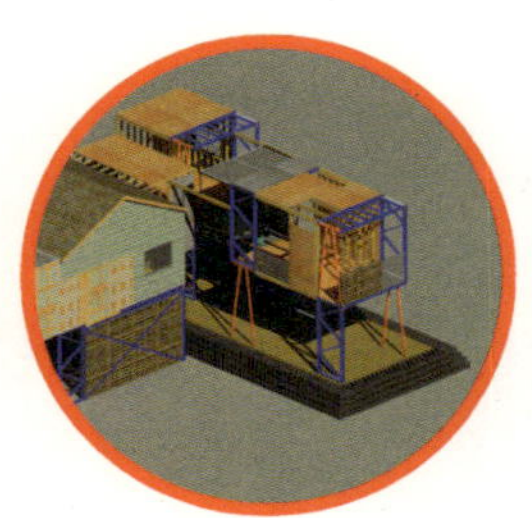

A factory–produced frame serves as a device with which to stitch the recycled systems imported to Tijuana from San Diego. Produced by factories, partly subsidized by the government, managed by factory laborers and distributed by activists, this frame is inserted into the political economy of waste that defines the sustainability of Tijuana's slums.

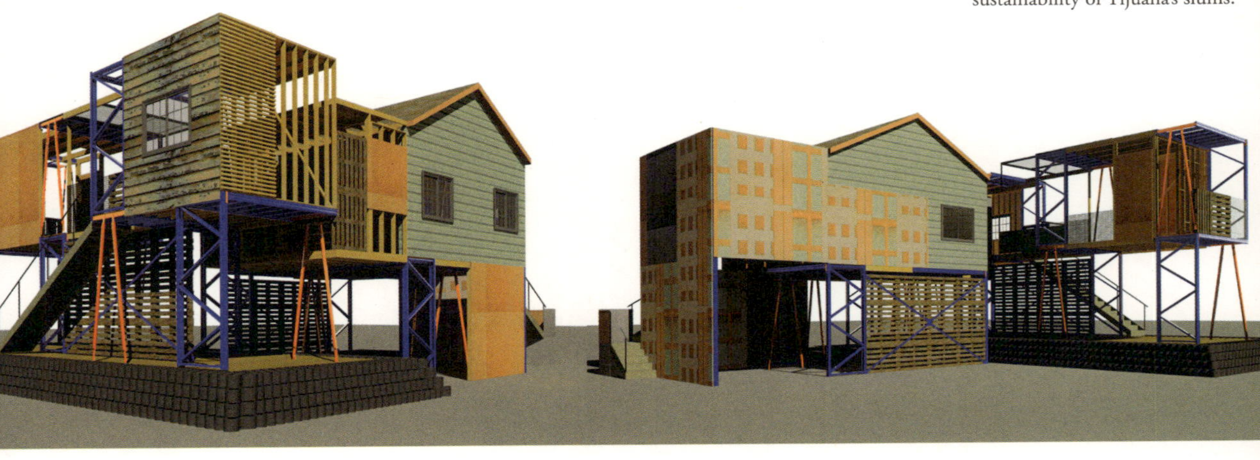

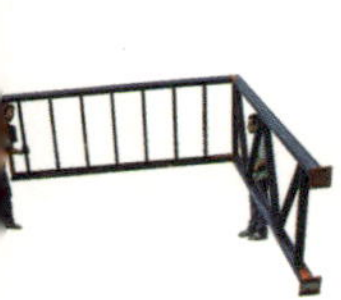

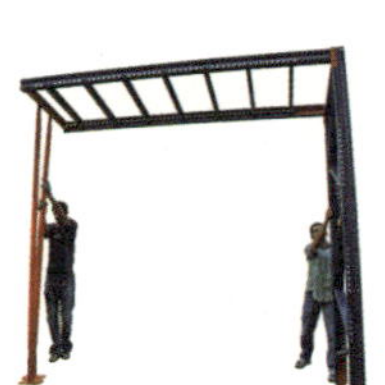

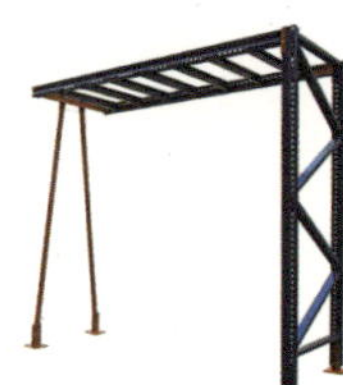

Emiliano Gandolfi
**Teddy Cruz**

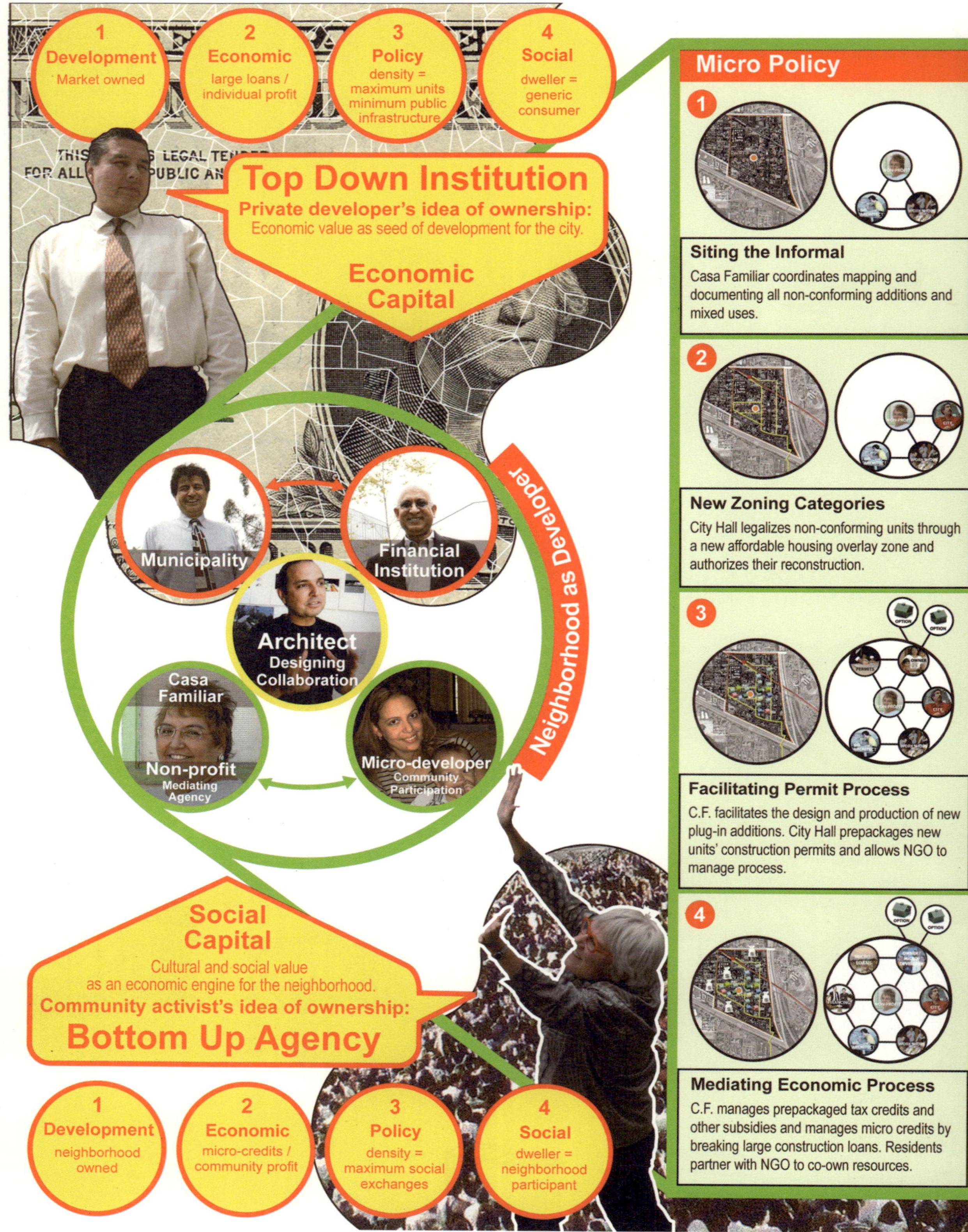

1
Development
Market owned
2
Economic
large loans / individual profit
3
Policy
density = maximum units minimum public infrastructure
4
Social
dweller = generic consumer
Top Down Institution
Private developer's idea of ownership:
Economic value as seed of development for the city.
Economic Capital
Municipality
Financial Institution
Architect
Designing Collaboration
Casa Familiar
Non-profit
Mediating Agency
Micro-developer
Community Participation
Neighborhood as Developer
Social Capital
Cultural and social value as an economic engine for the neighborhood.
Community activist's idea of ownership:
Bottom Up Agency
1
Development
neighborhood owned
2
Economic
micro-credits / community profit
3
Policy
density = maximum social exchanges
4
Social
dweller = neighborhood participant
Micro Policy
1
Siting the Informal
Casa Familiar coordinates mapping and documenting all non-conforming additions and mixed uses.
2
New Zoning Categories
City Hall legalizes non-conforming units through a new affordable housing overlay zone and authorizes their reconstruction.
3
Facilitating Permit Process
C.F. facilitates the design and production of new plug-in additions. City Hall prepackages new units' construction permits and allows NGO to manage process.
4
Mediating Economic Process
C.F. manages prepackaged tax credits and other subsidies and manages micro credits by breaking large construction loans. Residents partner with NGO to co-own resources.

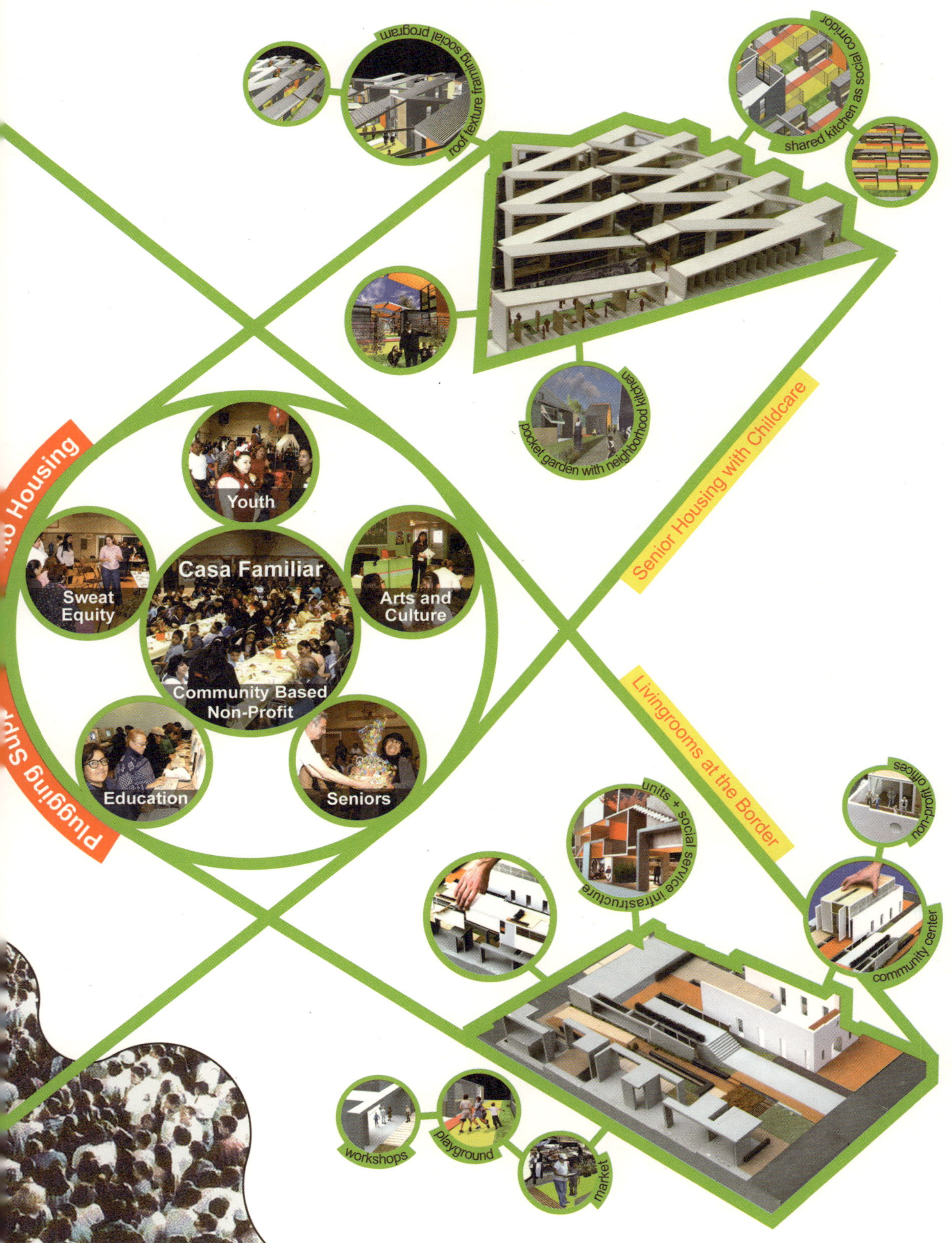


The neighborhood as a site of production of new cultural and economic configurations: informal economies and densities can be translated into new categories of property, land use and citizenship.

Micro infrastructures of social service are injected with social, economic, and pedagogical programming across time, serving as armature for housing.

Designing critical interfaces between top–down and bottom–up institutions and agencies: besides designing buildings, architects can design political and economic process.

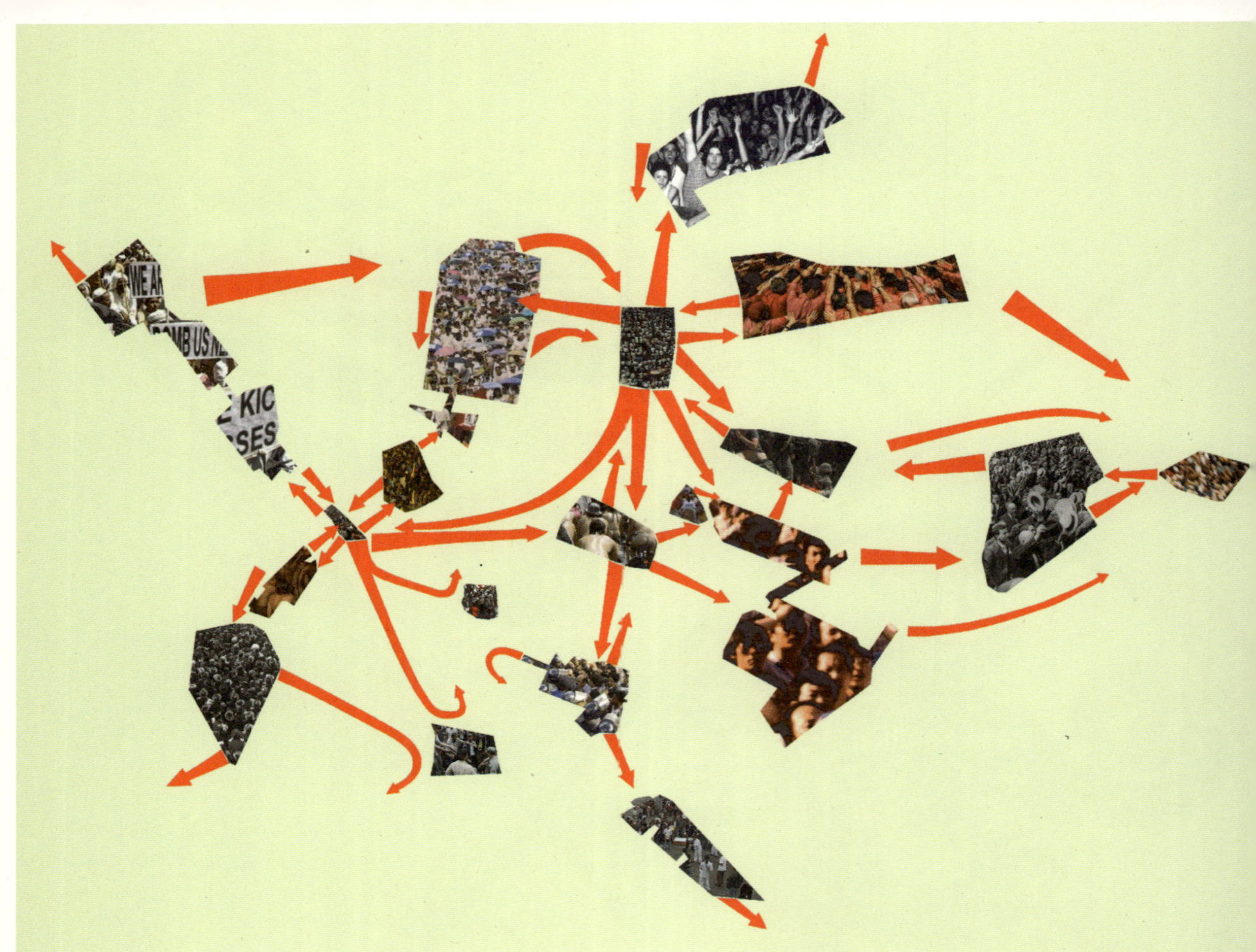

■□
***Guy Debord(er)***, searching for an urbanism beyond the property line

□■
***Practice Diagram***, conflict as an operational tool with which to redefine practice, exposing jurisdictional and economic power

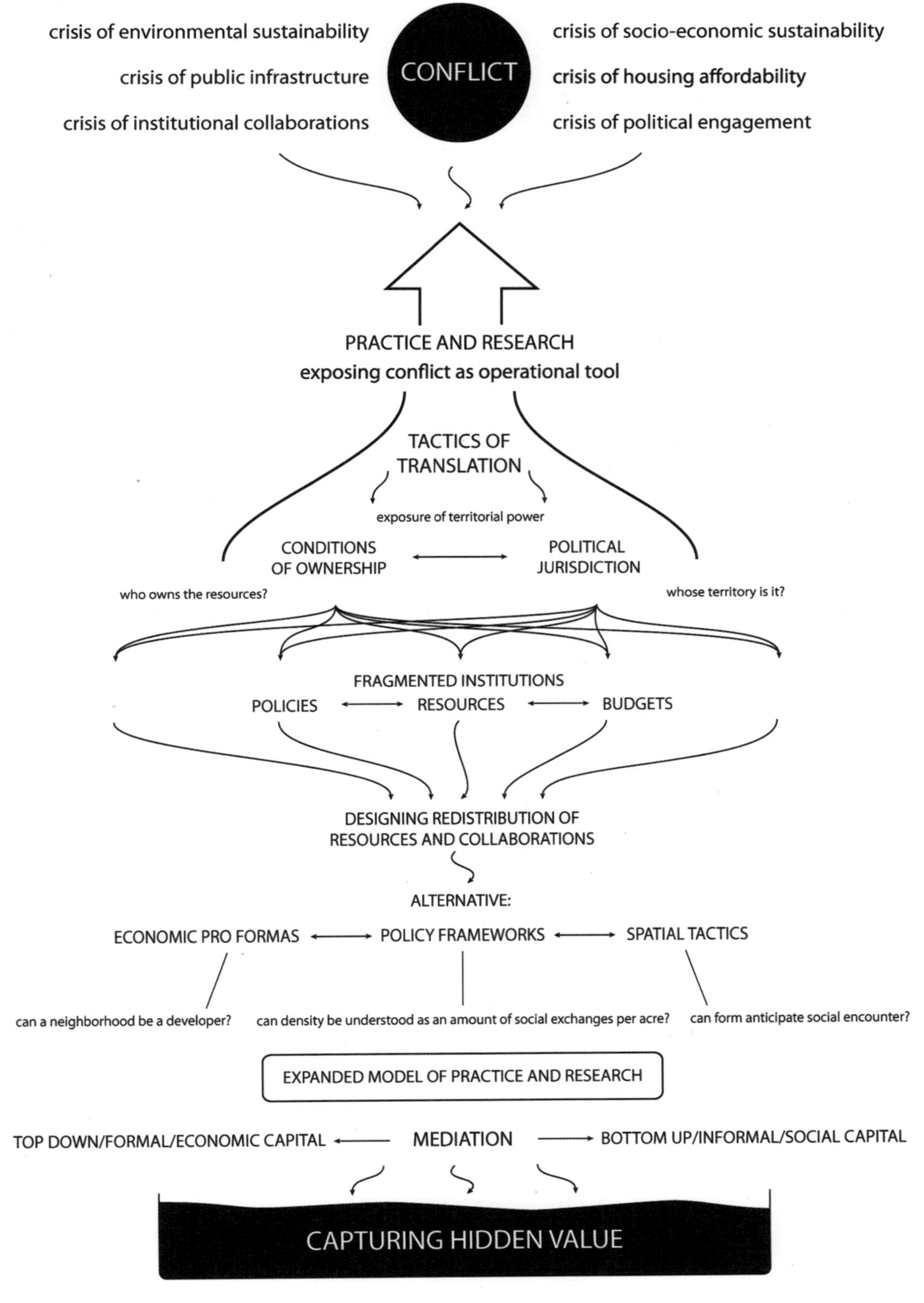


Emiliano Gandolfi
**Teddy Cruz**

# IT RUNS in the neighbourhood

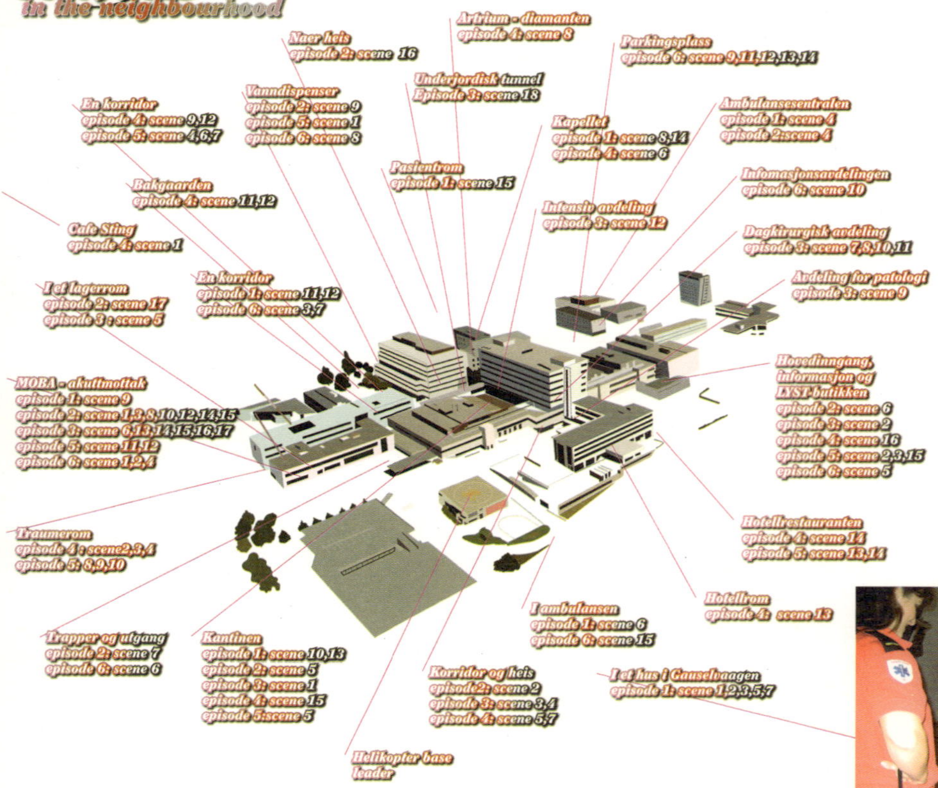

THE CITY OF SUS

Artrium - diamanten
episode 4: scene 8

Naer heis
episode 2: scene 16

Parkingsplass
episode 6: scene 9,11,12,13,14

Underjordisk tunnel
Episode 3: scene 18

En korridor
episode 4: scene 9,12
episode 5: scene 4,6,7

Vanndispenser
episode 2: scene 9
episode 5: scene 1
episode 6: scene 8

Ambulansesentralen
episode 1: scene 4
episode 2:scene 4

Kapellet
episode 1: scene 8,14
episode 4: scene 6

Pasientrom
episode 1: scene 15

Infomasjonsavdelingen
episode 6: scene 10

Bakgaarden
episode 4: scene 11,12

Intensiv avdeling
episode 3: scene 12

Cafe Sting
episode 4: scene 1

Dagkirurgisk avdeling
episode 3: scene 7,8,10,11

En korridor
episode 1: scene 11,12
episode 6: scene 3,7

I et lagerrom
episode 2: scene 17
episode 3 : scene 5

Avdeling for patologi
episode 3: scene 9

Hovedinngang,
informasjon og
LYST-butikken
episode 2: scene 6
episode 3: scene 2
episode 4: scene 16
episode 5: scene 2,3,15
episode 6: scene 5

MOBA - akuttmottak
episode 1: scene 9
episode 2: scene 1,3,8,10,12,14,15
episode 3: scene 6,13,14,15,16,17
episode 5: scene 11,12
episode 6: scene 1,2,4

Hotellrestauranten
episode 4: scene 14
episode 5: scene 13,14

Traumerom
episode 4 : scene2,3,4
episode 5: 8,9,10

Hotellrom
episode 4: scene 13

I ambulansen
episode 1: scene 6
episode 6: scene 15

Trapper og utgang
episode 2: scene 7
episode 6: scene 6

Kantinen
episode 1: scene 10,13
episode 2: scene 5
episode 3: scene 1
episode 4: scene 15
episode 5:scene 5

Korridor og heis
episode2: scene 2
episode 3: scene 3,4
episode 4: scene 5,7

I et hus i Gauselvaagen
episode 1: scene 1,2,3,5,7

Helikopter base
leader

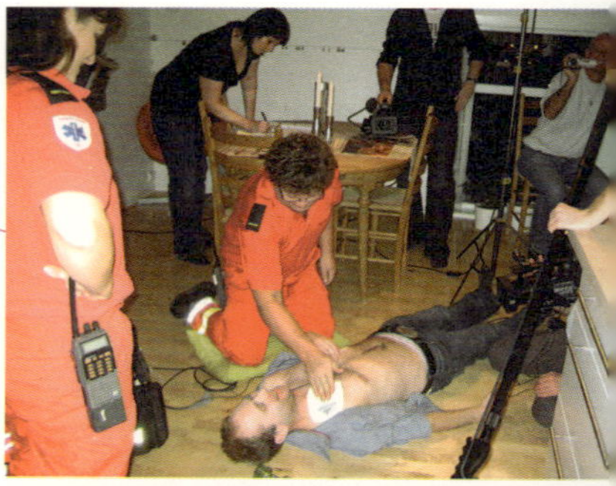

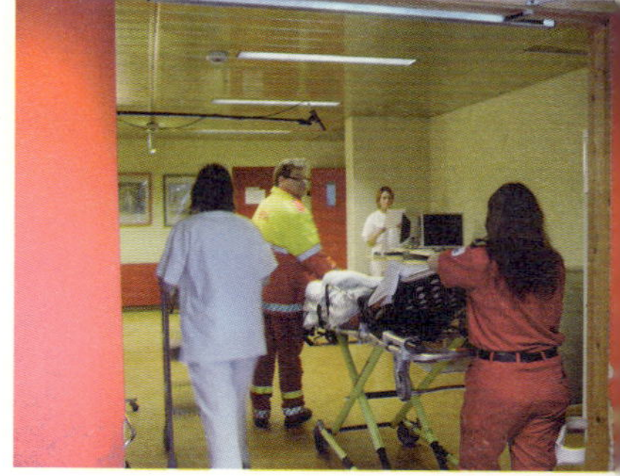

# Jeanne van Heeswijk

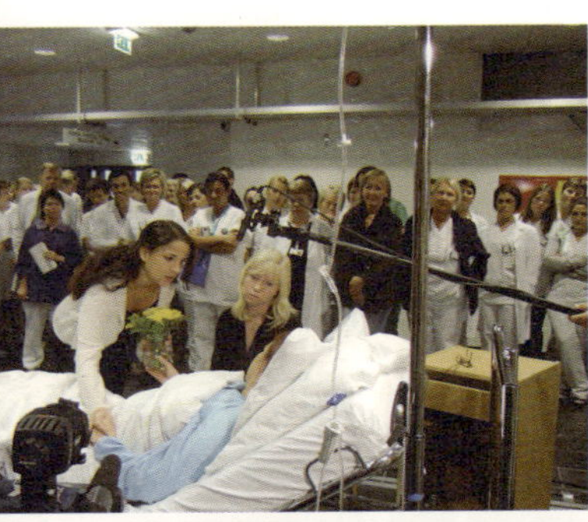

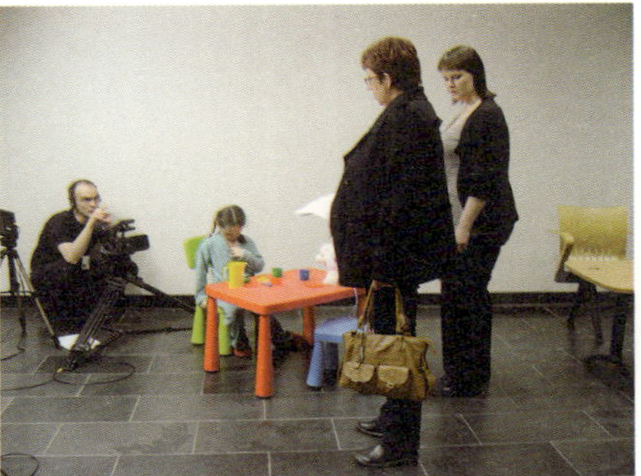

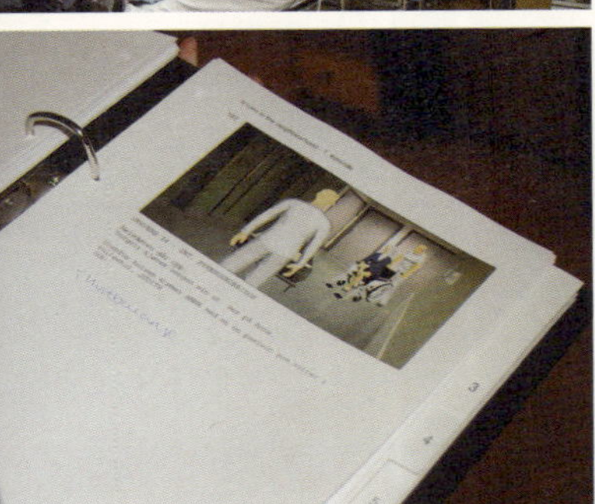

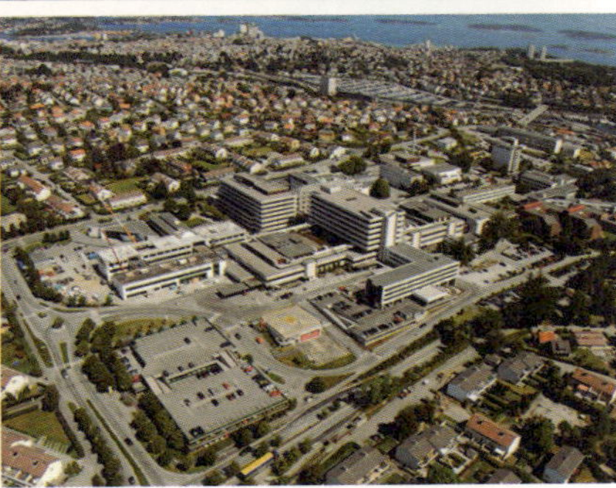

***It Runs in the Neighborhood***, 2008, Jeanne van Heeswijk and the employees of the Stavanger University Hospital (SUS), Stavanger, Norway, filming with employees of the SUS

In cooperation with the Stavanger University Hospital, Jeanne van Heeswijk developed the first hospital TV soap opera in Norway. With over 5,500 employees and almost 50,000 patients a year, the hospital can be seen as a community in itself, with its own communication structure and media. *It Runs in the Neighborhood* is a six-episode hospital soap based on real-life situations. The purpose was to give the public insight into the life inside the hospital and the medical and ethical dilemmas that the hospital employees encounter. The six episodes were shown on the Internet, on public screens, and on television. At the same time, the SUS communicated directly with the public via a new interactive Web site regarding the issues raised by the series. The crew consists of the artist Jeanne van Heeswijk and numerous volunteers from the SUS, who collected stories, wrote the manuscript, worked with cameras, lighting, sound, and other technical elements, and helped with makeup, the script, directing, and all of the other tasks involved in a fully fledged TV production.

*Emiliano Gandolfi —*

Projects like *Face Your World* and *Freehouse* reveal a radical attitude in your interest toward local dynamics. Apparently the final aim is always in terms of stirring a collective process, rather than on the definition of a specific result. How do you define your scope and what is your intent for these projects?

*Jeanne van Heeswijk —*

I am interested in immersing myself in a specific situation and stimulating a set of interactions between the people involved. In order to start to work on a certain location, I create what I call a "field of interactions." I pose a set of questions that circumscribe particular problematics or tensions, and when this field is defined, I step inside! For my work, this is a fundamental procedure. I am not curating the project, nor do I write a conception and produce a project. Instead, I *become part* of the field. This is where my work lies and is also the biggest challenge: how to be completely inserted within a collectivity.

*Emiliano Gandolfi —*

And how do you define the field of interest and why is it so important to establish this relation?

*Jeanne van Heeswijk —*

To define the questions that circumscribe the field is already a process that has to come from a specific circumstance and from the people involved. I am interested in identifying a group of people that I call "experts on location," and also in swindling the dreadful discussion on participatory practice. I am not working specifically with "inhabitants" in neighborhood communities. Last year, for instance, I worked on a project in a hospital in Norway that resulted in a TV soap opera—so it depends very much on the circumstances. These "experts" are people with knowledge of a place: usually they live there. Or they are people that have a peculiar purpose, such as working there, or that carry a certain knowledge that is needed for that specific place.

*Emiliano Gandolfi —*

So the experts are an entry point in order to understand the latent potentials of a specific condition and to activate a response. But which are the aspects that attract your interest? Is there something that emerges from a specific situation that strikes you?

*Jeanne van Heeswijk —*

Looking at certain areas, questions arise immediately about how these places can become public again. There are questions about publicness, social interaction, and politics that are constantly in my reasoning. What will publicness mean in these areas, and how can these areas be platforms again for meeting, discussion, and conflict? In that sense I would say that the approach of my projects is always similar, but they are completely different in execution, which is partially because they are not "executed." They are an ongoing collective research on these notions.

*Emiliano Gandolfi —*

The questions that you record or pose define the field, and then you empower local inhabitants that carry a specific knowledge to start a process. Do you have a specific aim in mind from the beginning of the process?

*Jeanne van Heeswijk —*

I am interested in processes of change. Through interactions, confrontation, and, eventually, conflict, ultimately a movement starts happening. And if a movement starts happening, change starts happening. For instance, in the case of the work in the market in Rotterdam, we identified a number of market sellers, people who might not live in the area, but who nevertheless through their roles have specific knowledge of

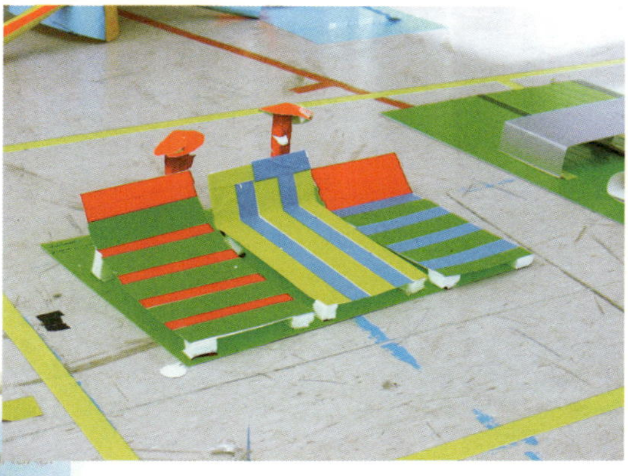

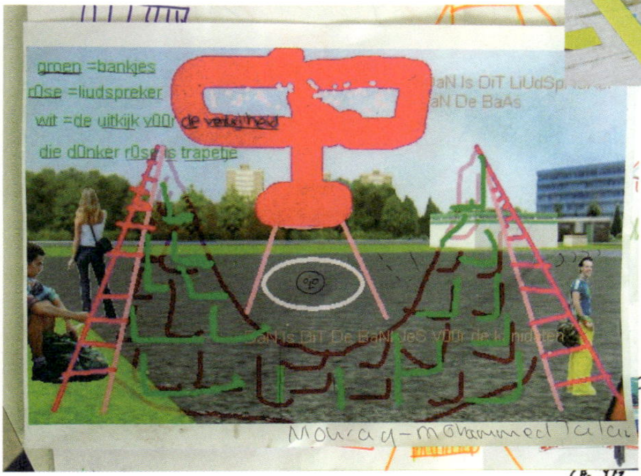

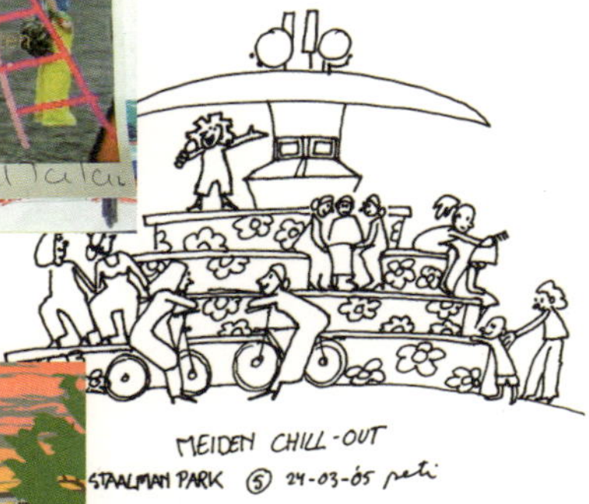

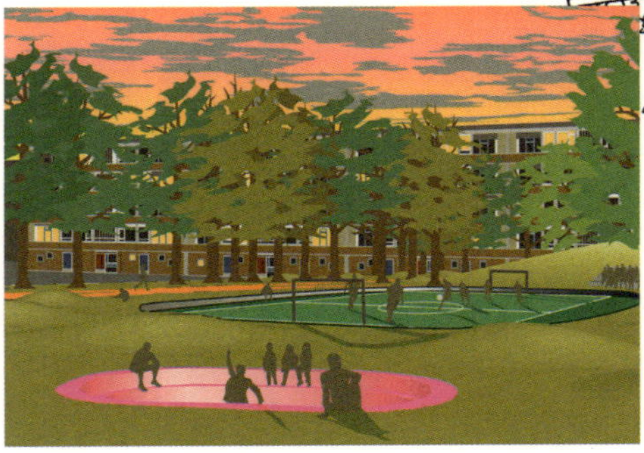

***Face Your World, StedelijkLab Slotervaart***, 2005 (UrbanLab Slotervaart), Jeanne van Heeswijk, Dennis Kaspori, and Maaike Engelen, Amsterdam

The *Face Your World* (2002) project, conceived in Columbus, Ohio offers children a collective learning environment in which they can learn how to investigate, as well as adapt, their living environment. The Interactor, a 3–D multiuser computer environment, allows children to "engineer" their surroundings. On the initiative of Stichting Kunst en Openbare Ruimte (SKOR) (the Dutch foundation for art and public space) and the Amsterdam Fund for the Arts (AFK). Jeanne Van Heeswijk, architect Dennis Kaspori, and philosopher Maaike Engelen developed a practical educational model for participation in urban renewal aimed at secondary school students (specifically middle-level, or lower secondary vocational education, students), devising a completely new version of the Interactor in collaboration with the interactive communication and media productions IJsfontein.

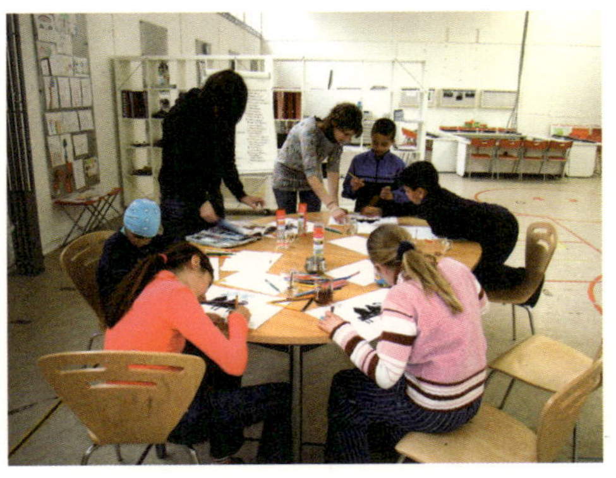

the place. My interest lies in how they can—through forms of interaction and conflict with other "experts on location"—become agents of change. And this can happen only if you are part of that process yourself. So for my practice this really means engaging, becoming part of that action/reaction, part of that conflict, to move toward the interaction process that is needed to get things moving. When I insert myself in these processes of "experts on location," I insert myself as an amateur. At the moment I am extremely interested in this notion of the amateur in a field of experts. I am not directing, and being an amateur means being completely open as much as you can, being submissive to anything you can learn, and being reactive to anything a person wants to bestow upon you and wants to teach, even with things that you think are unnecessary to learn.

*Emiliano Gandolfi —*

In this way you are making things emerge from the local context and asking people to take positions in a process.

*Jeanne van Heeswijk —*

In this process it is important to let go of any grip and to wait for the spatial conditions to emerge. You have to let go within your subjectivity, and that is something that as an artist I try to practice all the time. When we all attempt to lose our subjectivity, it is, at least partly, the precondition for generating something between us that is actually an agent of change.

*Emiliano Gandolfi —*

In other words, we could say that your work is an effort to make people lose their subjective position. And how do you develop this process when you are commissioned to work within an art institution?

*Jeanne van Heeswijk —*

I must say that I don't see very much of a distinction between working inside or outside the museum framework. Sometimes a project is commissioned and I am interested in the question framed by the commissioner. I rarely stick to that question—I think of it as one of the questions that might be part of the framework, and then I extend, rework, rethink, or counterbalance the question. When you start to speak with the people that are involved, more and more questions emerge, and at last you have the frame of questions into which we can step and start a process. Eventually I find other partners to match up with whatever the commissioner is lacking. I even think that sometimes it is good to bring reflections on certain projects back to the institutional context. It's always hard, but I definitely try to avoid displaying documentation as an art piece.

*Emiliano Gandolfi —*

Every project that you are doing is in fact related to a certain framework that generates a set of questions, which fosters a field. But not everything that is generated by this process is actually art.

*Jeanne van Heeswijk —*

No, not everything is an art piece, in the sense of a commodity that you could put on display or sell. But I do believe that the whole process in itself is art. So if you talk about art and how art can effect social change, that is more than a chain of commodities, of art pieces. To me, art is the production of social change. And that occasionally can also result in art pieces, books, discussions, a festival, and many other things. Differently from politics, art has a specific framework derived from aesthetics, from the imaginary, and in that it elevates ideas into imagination and its relation to ethics. That is a whole field that comes with it, and it is a whole different one from the one of politics, or of city planning, if you will. All works derive from a continuous interest in the world and from seeing art as a very important part of that world. In that sense, I always say that I am a believer. I do believe that art is an important catalyst for social change.

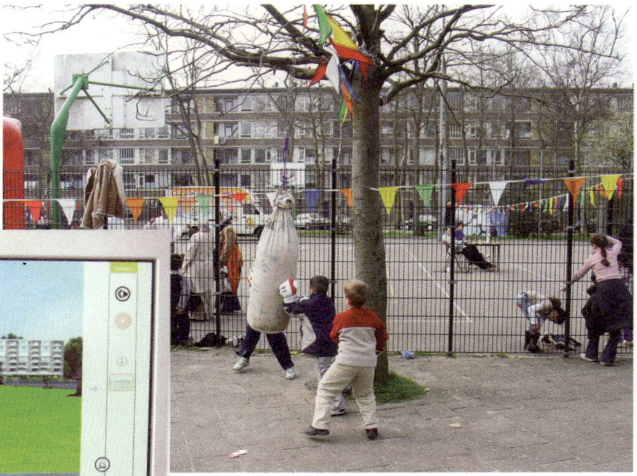

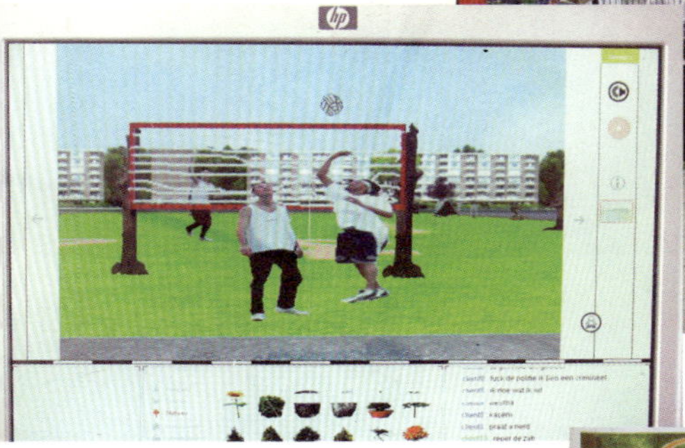

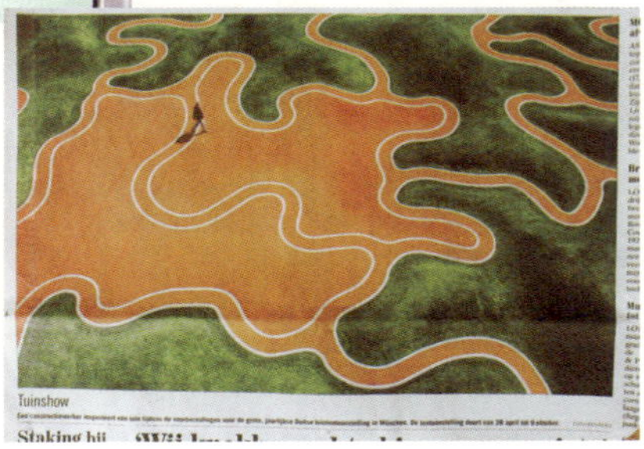

***Face Your World, StedelijkLab Slotervaart*** started in early 2005 in the Staalmanplein neighborhood, an area undergoing drastic urban renewal, including the planned creation of a park of about 13,500 square meters to serve as the district's new public heart. Van Heeswijk worked hard to ensure that this commission went to *Face Your World*, in order to create an urban-planning process based around intensive participation by local residents. *Face Your World* set up camp in an old gymnasium, on the site of the future park, and transformed it into an "urban lab": a place to discuss and work on the design of the park with students, local residents, and other interested parties. Each day, pupils from different vocational schools in the neighborhood, along with residents, explored their surroundings with invited experts. Collectively they worked on the design of their future park, addressing not only what facilities should be available, but also how it should look, and their personal roles within it. StedelijkLab Slotervaart provided a learning environment as part of a public process of planning for the neighborhood's future. Six months later the participants presented their design to the local authorities and other local residents. After some minimal modifications, the borough council officially approved the communal design for the "Staalman Park" on March 1, 2006.

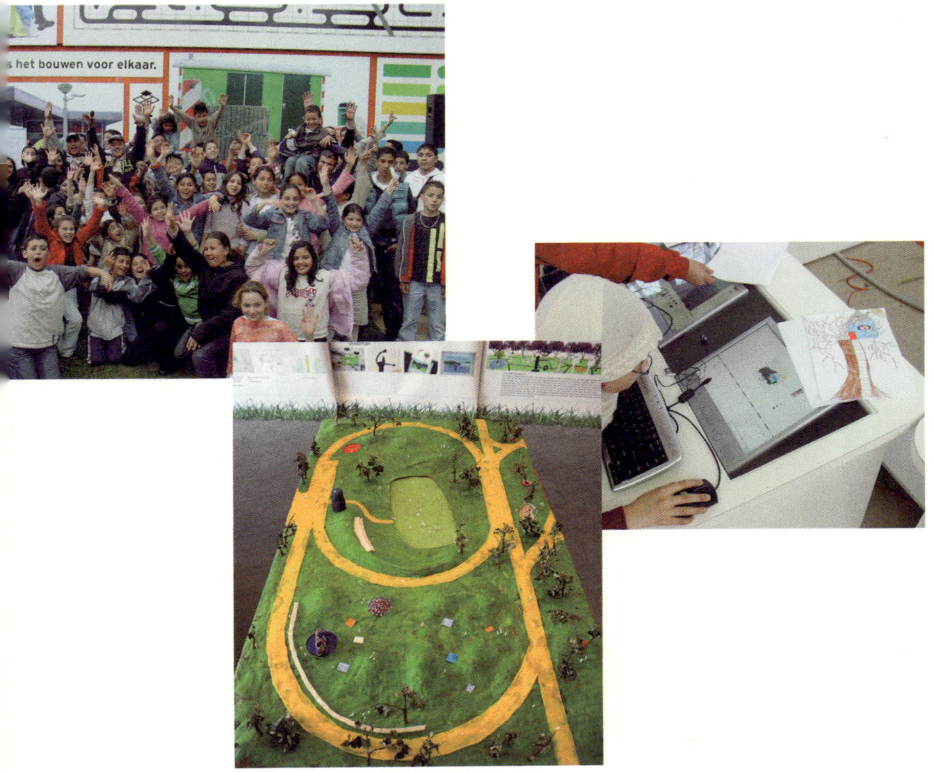

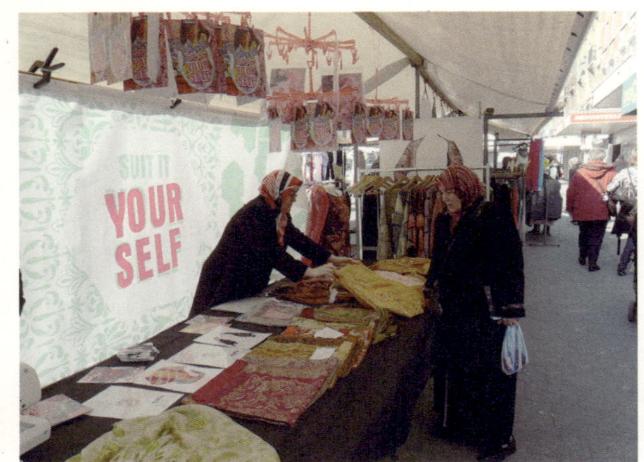
SUIT IT
YOUR
SELF

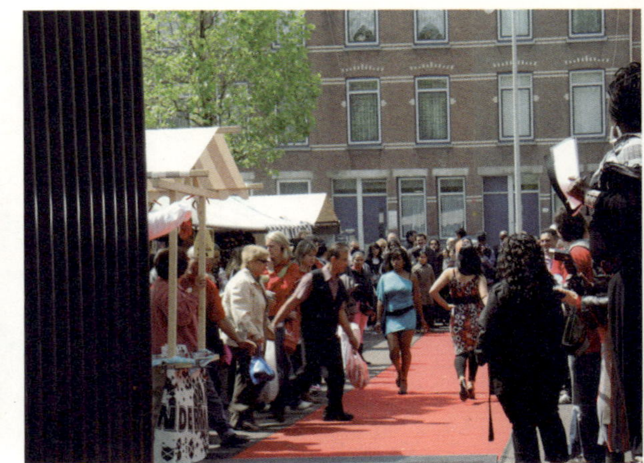

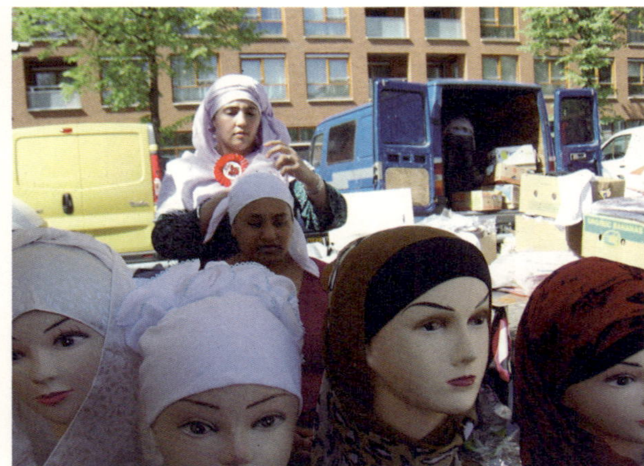

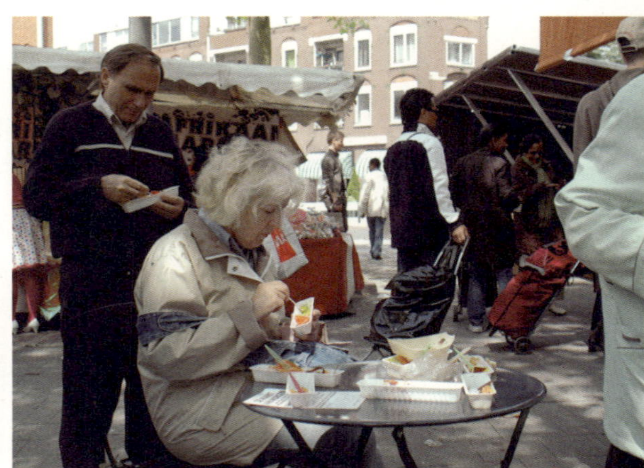

***Market of Tomorrow Freehouse***, 2008–2009, Jeanne van Heeswijk and Dennis Kaspori, Afrikaanderplein, Rotterdam

Afrikaandermarkt as model for the future—the Afrikaanderwijk in the south of Rotterdam is currently going through a process of transformation. By focusing on its small and multicultural character the neighborhood could distinguish itself from the newly developed suburbs that will surround it. One of the strongest and most recognizable points of the area is the Afrikaandermarkt. With over 300 stalls, it is one of the biggest markets in The Netherlands. Twice a week, it has for years brought the most exotic products to the city. But it is also a run-down market in need of attention.

*Freehouse*, a project that is based on cultural production as a means for economical growth, developed a plan for an innovative programmatic design of the market. Along with market salesmen, local entrepreneurs, people from the neighborhood, designers, and artists, they developed new products and services, in order that the market again becomes a site of cultural production and a meeting place for the neighborhood. For a whole year, all kinds of interventions took place in the market to test these new products, actions, and arrangements. On June 7, 2009 the plan was presented in a full-scale in which the *Market of Tomorrow* is reenacted as a living model.

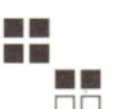

New products and services presented on the *Market of Tomorrow*

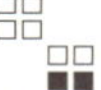

Exhibition Knowledge center at the *Market of Tomorrow*

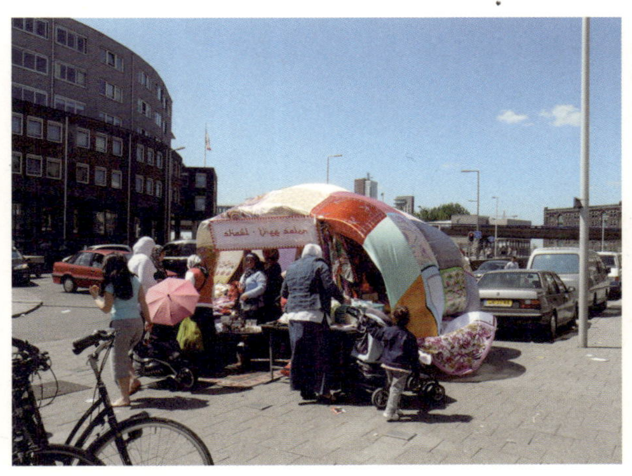

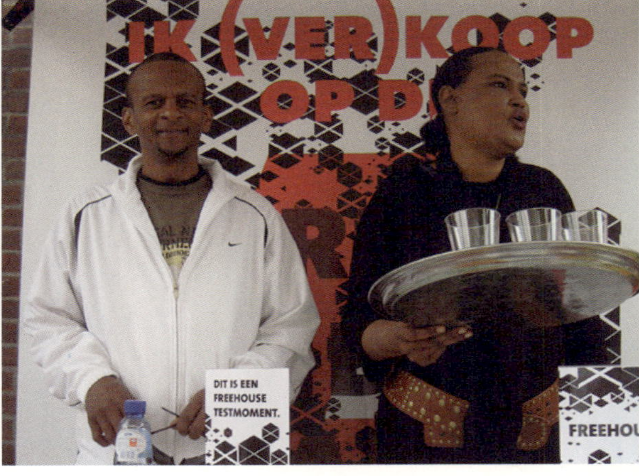


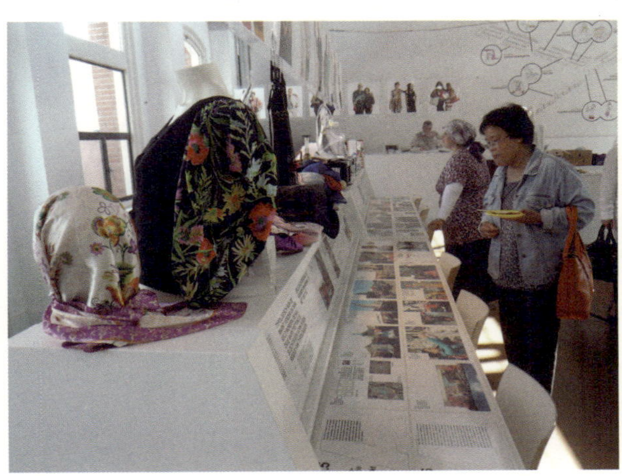

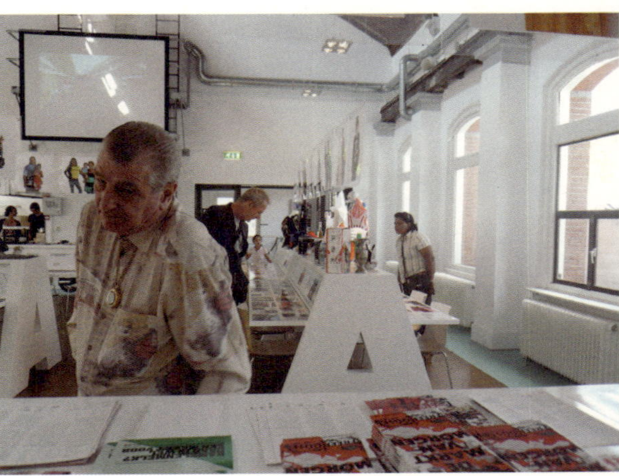

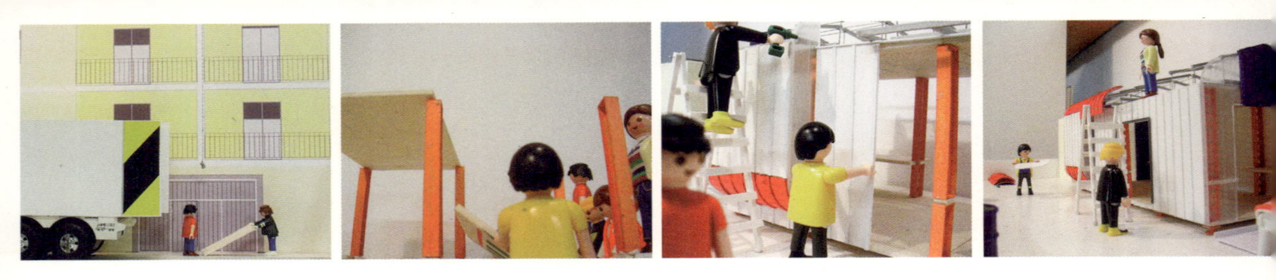

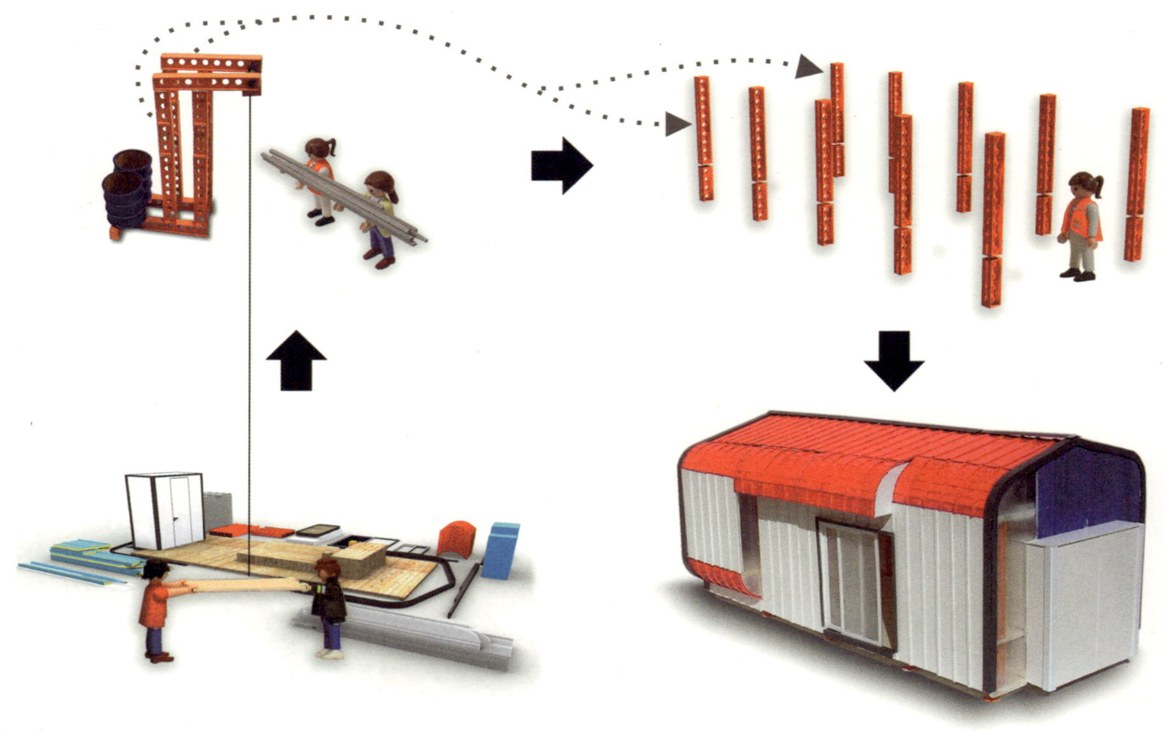

# Santiago Cirugeda (Recetas Urbanas)

***Roof Housing*** is an architectural solution to the issue of affordable housing. Santiago Cirugeda proposed using the flat roof terraces of existing buildings to build small houses using very light materials. This solution, while enabling residents to avoid paying land costs, raises questions around public and community space. And it becomes legal as long as all residents in the surrounding buildings agree on the new construction, and it is reversible at any time.

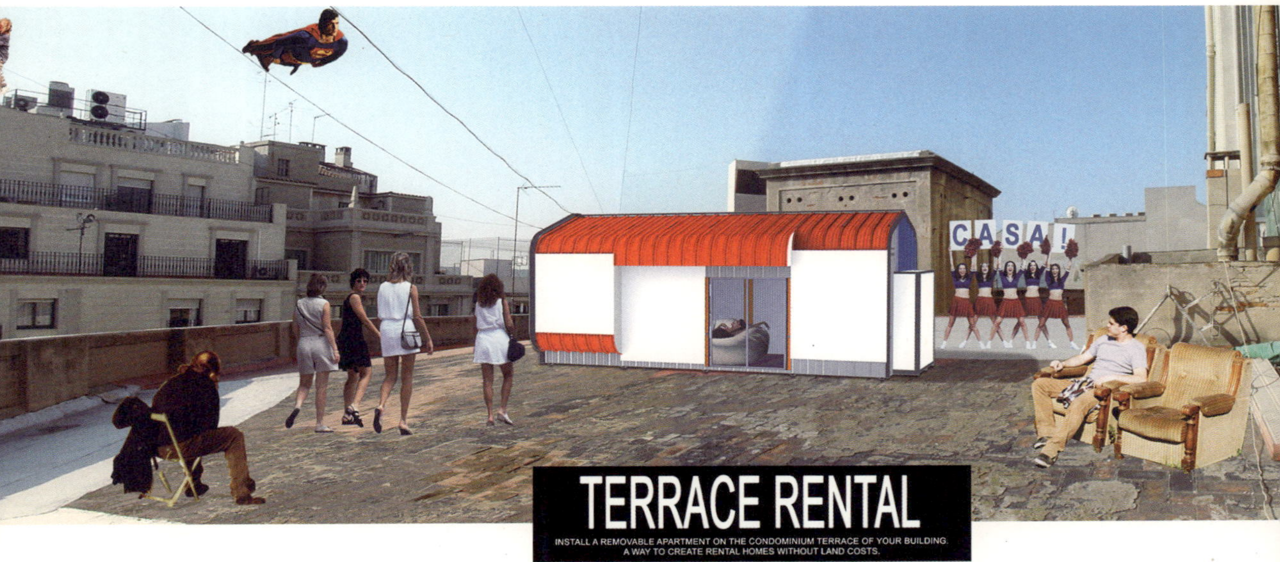

*Emiliano Gandolfi* —

There are two sides to *Recetas Urbanas* ("Urban Recipes"). On the one hand, the work is appreciated in international museums and biennales, and on the other, it gives voice and visibility to social movements at the local, neighborhood level by constructing unauthorized installations in public places. There's an evident contrast between these two worlds. How do you relate to these two very different platforms?

*Santiago Cirugeda* —

I never turn down an invitation! And every time I act accordingly! Operations with activists play a fundamental role, which is that of showing the institutions and public opinion that the city needs to be viewed in an all-inclusive manner. We must all open out our own sphere of interest and consider as an integral part of our social fabric those minorities who have so far been neglected. Work with museums has a dual purpose. On the one hand, it follows the same principle, which is that of giving media visibility to these issues. On the other, it allows us to redirect the contributions that the institutions make to collective projects in order to encourage different ways of using the city. The support of the institutions also allows us to provide legal protection for some projects in the field. Referring to a temporary operation as a "work of art" gives us a legal means of legitimizing an unlawful intervention.

*Emiliano Gandolfi* —

Your urban actions are often constructions that encourage a different way of using the city—a "parallel" way, one might say. They introduce original aggregative functions into the public arena: temporary homes, constructions often bordering on illegality and indeed at times openly illegal. Do you consider these operations important for bringing about a new use of public spaces, or do you see them more as urban actions that attract media attention to issues such as the lack of community spaces or cases of urban segregation?

*Santiago Cirugeda* —

I don't see a distinction between these two positions. One is a medium-term strategic decision, while the other is a tactic that has an immediate effect. Every action is viewed as an attempt to meet a need and, at the same time, to give media visibility to the particular issue. I started working on illegal projects to respond to precise demands from part of the population, but every action is also a search for new accomplices with whom to put on even more sweeping, ambitious operations. Our work is part of a broader network of associations that share the same sort of vision and who have the same sort of approach. Our ambition is both to increase our visibility and to enter into greater contact with other networks further afield, as well as to expand our sphere of influence toward institutions and organizations in the world of politics. This network of ours has expanded enormously over the past three years. The die-hards in collectives working with architecture have been joined by collectives of squatters, hackers, artists, performers, social organizations, and lots of others. By opening up like this, the network has become more complex and varied, and this makes us more effective, but it also requires more work to coordinate everything and to create the right interaction so that we can launch common communication strategies to reach the public institutions. Our aim is to draw up intervention protocols based on a number of local experiences, and to channel these experiences in a clear and reproducible manner also at an international level.

*Emiliano Gandolfi* —

Many of your projects have been created by the end users, such as in the case of the *Un-Buildable House* or the project for the two illegal halls you built over the Faculty of Fine Arts in Malaga.

*Santiago Cirugeda —*

The first self-construction project we worked on was the one for the *Aula Abierta* in Granada. This was the first time we'd experimented with a collective process of this type, and indeed it led to the creation of an association. This experience taught me the importance of drafting a cultural program around the construction of a collective space. The methods we use in our work have gradually changed over time. Experience has shown me that, when you start building a structure or a space for the community and you adopt a collective, self-construction approach, the projects you make end up producing lasting results and consensus. It must be said that collective work is very tough going, especially when you're working on an urban scale, and thus in situations that are rather delicate from a legal point of view. In these cases in particular, it's essential to put up a united front in order to ensure both the conservation of the spaces and their upkeep. Another important aspect to be considered is that of using the construction process to encourage a sense of appropriation in people, as well as a sense of dignity, even when the places are right out on the fringes.

*Emiliano Gandolfi —*

Over the past two years, you've started up a series of works using prefabricated items such as industrial containers. What made you decide to do this?

*Santiago Cirugeda —*

In many of the projects we've worked on in our network of activists and militants, we don't consider ourselves as designers, but rather as consultants for urban interventions—we're builders. In this sort of operation we're interested more in the process that arises from the construction of a shared space than in the actual aesthetic outcome. Many of these projects with containers are the result of precise needs and of the necessity to be quick and efficient in the shortest time possible, spending as little as we can. The rest normally comes from decisions made on the spur of the moment. Over the past few weeks we've have been putting together the stories of these projects and of the more than twenty group exhibitions that have been part of the urban actions. The result is a book to be entitled *The Clash*, available for free online. We're also working on a self-construction project in a gypsy village. The project is the result of a group initiative and it respects the tastes and needs of those who will inhabit it. We're certainly not going to be winning the prestigious Mies van der Rohe Award with these operations, but I still think they are both necessary and urgent.

*Emiliano Gandolfi —*

In terms of the social repercussions of your work, your interest in a collective process when creating your operations overshadows their physical and material aspects. Rather than becoming a result, the installation is simply a means to inspire a collective social movement.

*Santiago Cirugeda —*

The creation of a movement is certainly our objective. But we need to work by degrees. A situation has been coming about over the past few years in which political power is subject to economic power, and it controls most communication media, but fortunately it doesn't have a complete monopoly. The work of the political organization in our network will continue to generate counter-information and procedures that can bring about a critical mass with regard to these issues. The initiatives undertaken by the social movements to tackle issues such as human rights, the environment, and indigenous rights have had significant effects. Over the past fifty years, thinkers such as Henri Lefebvre and Jane Jacobs have been describing ways to expand people's rights to the city, but these lessons have mostly been ignored by politicians. Our work aims to focus on these issues through physical operations, sit-ins, debates, media actions, and public events that can have a real influence on local policies.

Emiliano Gandolfi
**Santiago Cirugeda**
**(Recetas Urbanas)**

# UN-BUILDABLE HOUS

Architect - who collaborates with an international construction festival - to prese a new type of housing that can be grouped and assembled collectively

CONFLICTO POR UNA PROPUESTA ARQUITECTÓNICA EN SANT MARTÍ

## BCN prohíbe habitar el prototip de piso de 30 m2 del Poblenou

- El ayuntamiento alega que el solar es para equipamientos, no para viviendas
- El contenedor de Cirugeda será retirado tras el festival de arquitectura Eme3

JORDI SUBIRANA
BARCELONA

El minipiso de 30 metros cuadrados en forma de contenedor ideado por el arquitecto Santiago Cirugeda no se podrá usar como vivienda en Barcelona, al menos por ahora. El consistorio ha denegado el permiso para que la construcción, ubicada en el número 11-17 de la calle de Àlaba, pueda ser habitada. El motivo es que el prototipo de minipiso está en un solar cuyo uso «está destinado para equipamientos y no para viviendas», indicó un portavoz municipal.

El minipiso de Cirugeda se encuentra en ese solar del barrio del Poblenou desde el pasado julio, ya

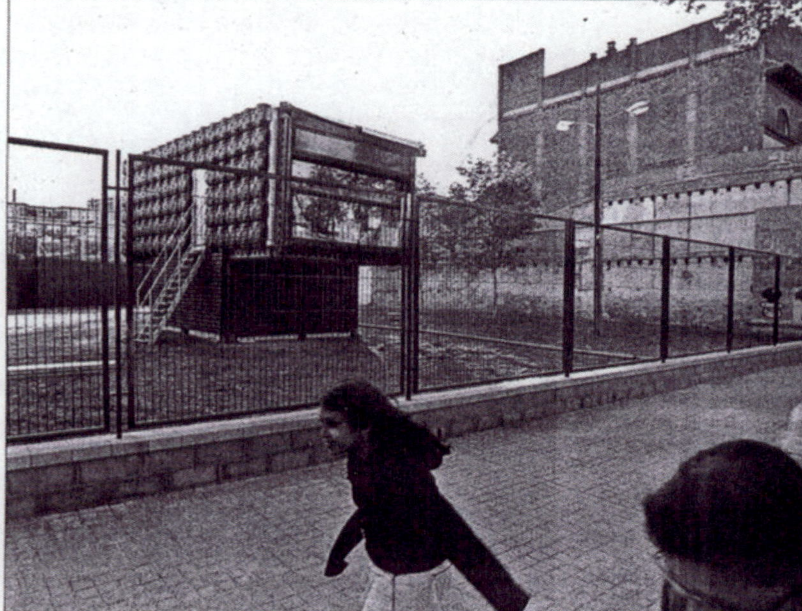

►► El minipiso del arquitecto Santiago Cirugeda, ayer, en el Poblenou.

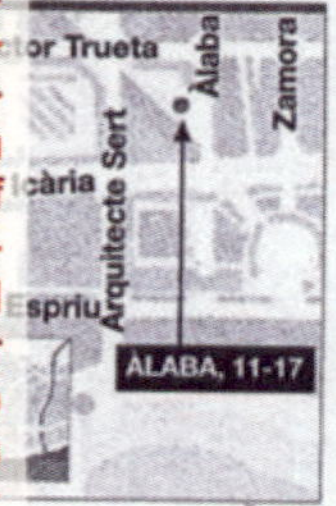


a ceder el solar co- aunque sea provisio- local quiere evitar ilino se niegue des- r el habitáculo. etrás de la negativa municipal se esconden también quejas de algunos residentes de la zona contrarios al habitáculo. Sin embar- reu, presidente de la ecinos del Poblenou, e constancia de ninguna protesta por parte de vecinos y negó que desde su asociación se ha-

ya presentado protesta alguna tra el prototipo. Andreu opinó minipisos como el de Cirugeda son una solución al problema « vivienda».

PLATAFORMA CREATIVA // Javier nas, director del festival Eme3, firmó la negativa municipal y guró que ahora sólo utilizará contenedor para enseñarlo y c una plataforma creativa abie Según Planas, la construcción d rugeda se desmontará muy pos mente a finales de octubre, tras bar la muestra arquitectónica.

El minipiso de Cirugeda, u quitecto con alma social, se pres con mucha polémica en la pas edición del salón Construmat abril del 2005. Construido –en nas una semana– con materiale ciclados, tiene lavabo, cocina, do torio y espacio para un come Está destinado a personas con e sos recursos y busca ser una sa económica para acceder a un vienda. Hay quien considera qu es un lugar digno para vivir.

An architect collaborated with an international construction festival to create an economical prototype of minimal housing units. They can be grouped in clusters to create collective residential nuclei, easy to assemble and install. After a press campaign raised to alarm over a housing ministry without an urgently needed plan for new housing, a hijacked media campaign proved that the units can function independently on a plot of Barcelona public land under private management. It called for an alternative supply of housing for sectors of the population with limited financial resources or who are willing to rent property without the hope of ever owning it. They can be given with the option of actively participating in the physical assembly of the prototype, so lowering expenditures as well as personalizing and dignifying the houses themselves. Materials include: collapsible steel structure, wooden double T joints, sandwich panel (water-repellent board – polyester – OSB), auxiliary steel structures, aluminium frames, sandwich panel (steel – polyurethane – steel), plasticized PVC steel sheet; PVC cases; cellular polycarbonate, glass and sandwich plate (aluminium – polyethylene – aluminium); as well as coordination by friends, family members or helpers to allow prototype to be assembled rapidly with the necessary machinery and auxiliary materials.

Subject: citizen//Collaborators: Pepe, friends, and a group of illegal construction workers//Materials: leftovers from US 5, brick, mortar, bathroom fittings, heather, fiber cement, Cuba libres//Description: housing unit for 2 people//Approximate surface area: 22 m² of housing and a balcony of 13.5 m²

**Palacio de Exposiciones de Barcelona, Feria Construmat, 11-17 April 2005 Festival eme3, Calle Àlaba 11-17, Barcelona, June 2005-March 2006**

*Un-Buildable House,* stackable housing module for the temporary occupation of plots of land

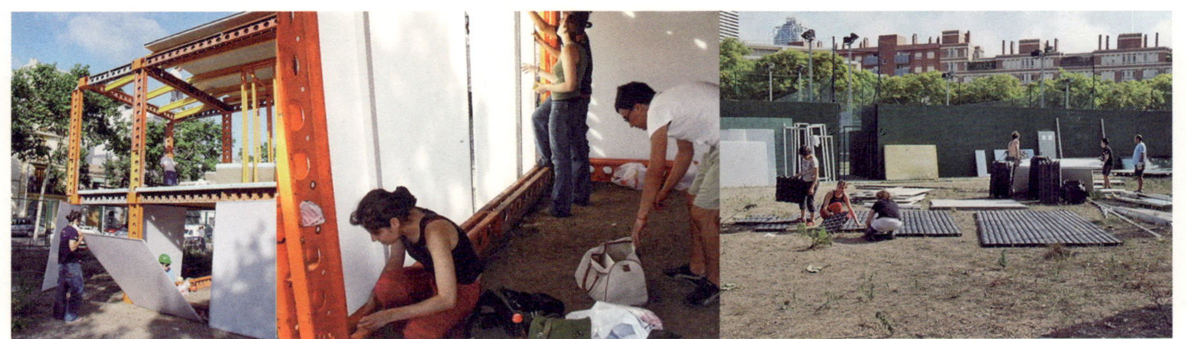

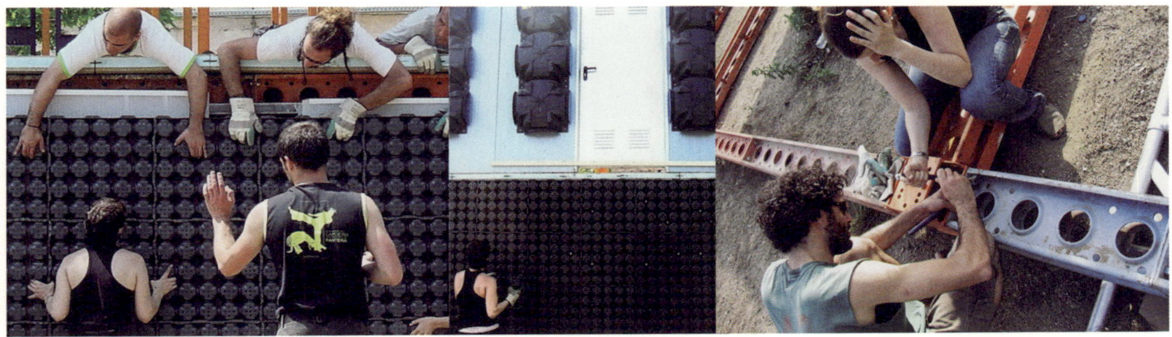

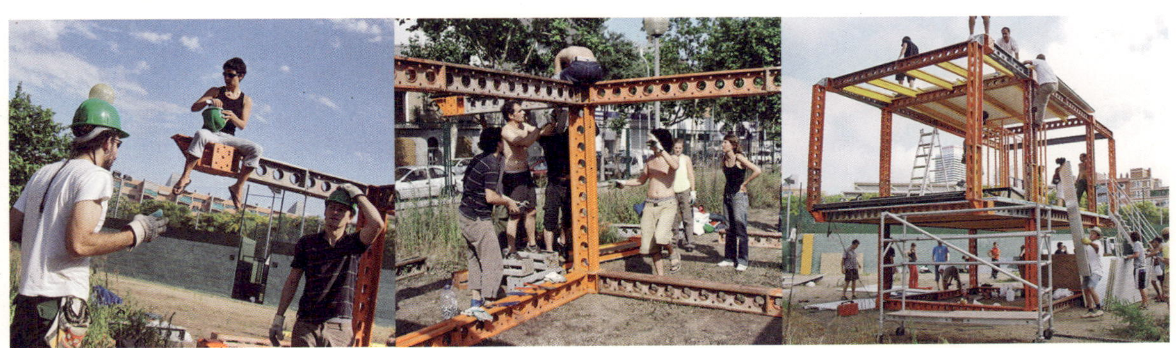

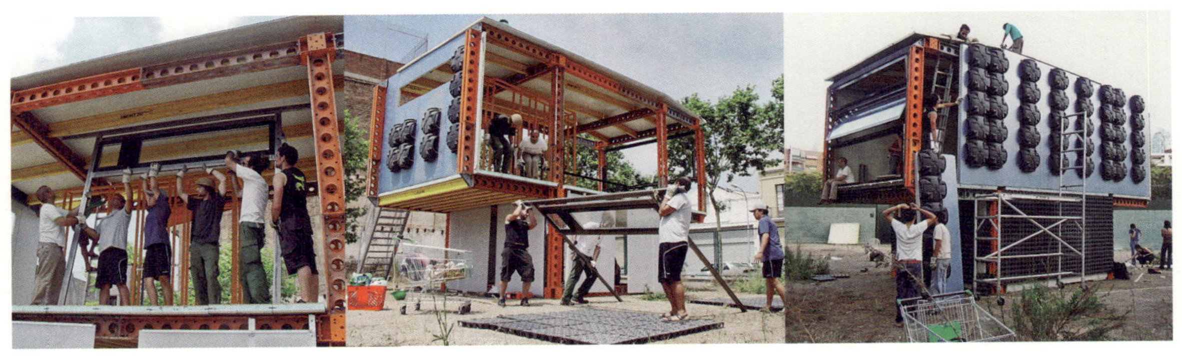

Emiliano Gandolfi
**Santiago Cirugeda (Recetas Urbanas)**

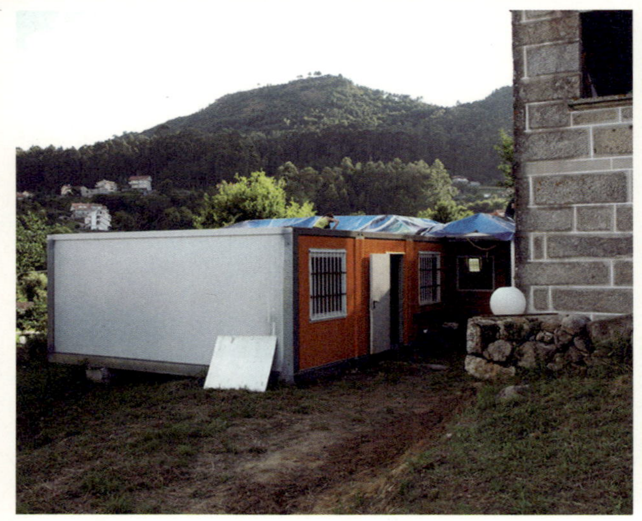

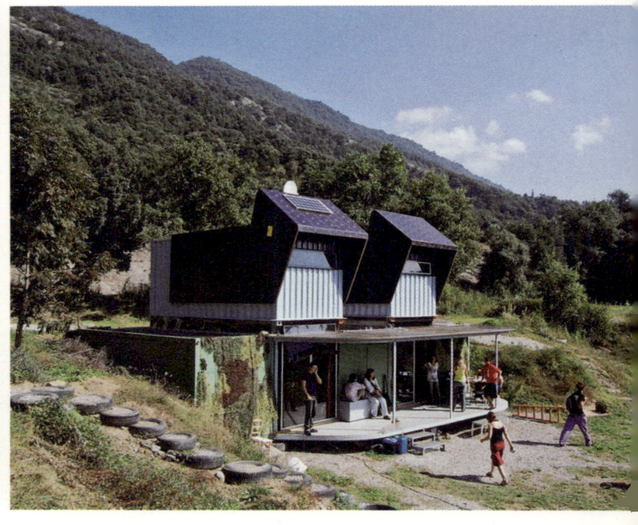

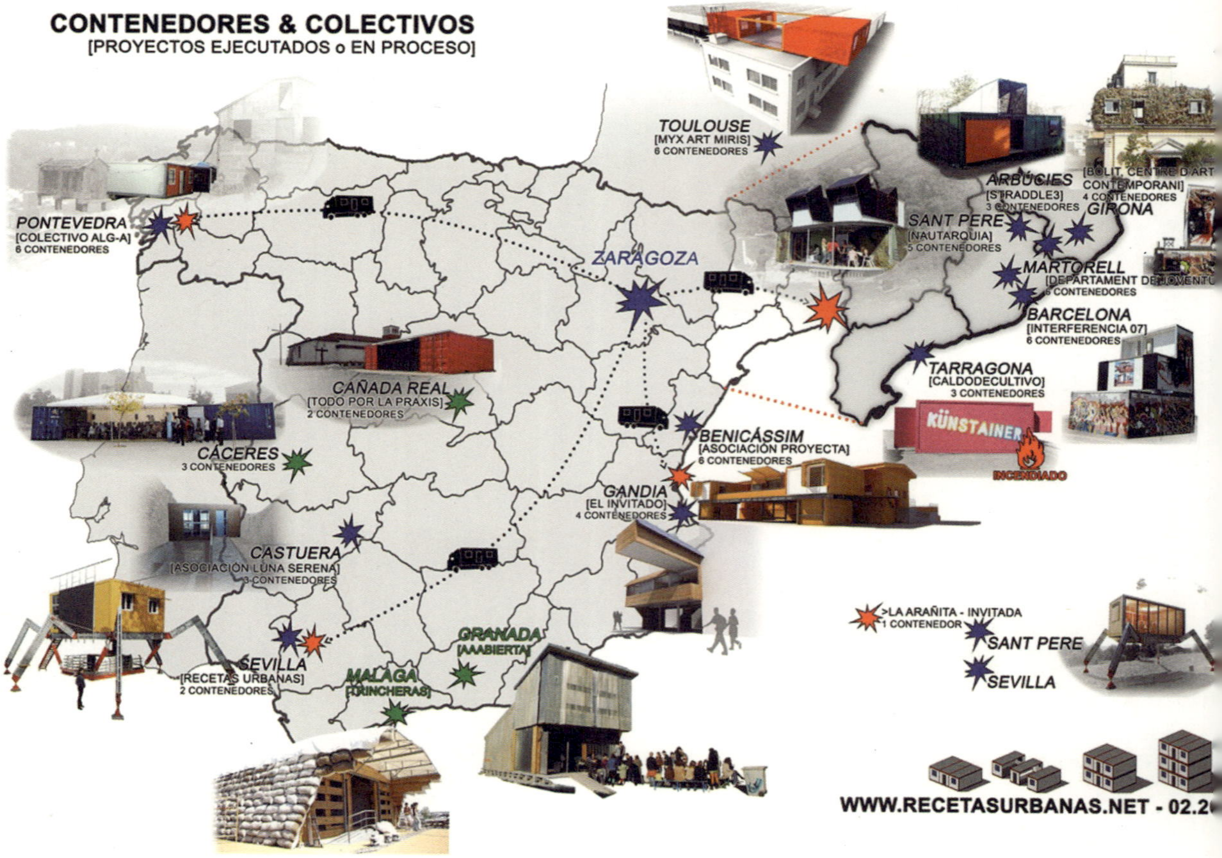

## CONTENEDORES & COLECTIVOS
[PROYECTOS EJECUTADOS o EN PROCESO]

TOULOUSE
[MYX ART MIRIS]
6 CONTENEDORES

PONTEVEDRA
[COLECTIVO ALG-A]
6 CONTENEDORES

ZARAGOZA

ARBÚCIES
[STRADDLE3]
3 CONTENEDORES

[BOLIT, CENTRE D'ART CONTEMPORANI]
4 CONTENEDORES
GIRONA

SANT PERE
[NAUTARQUIA]
5 CONTENEDORES

MARTORELL
[DEPARTAMENT DE JOVENTU
6 CONTENEDORES

BARCELONA
[INTERFERENCIA 07]
6 CONTENEDORES

TARRAGONA
[CALDODECULTIVO]
3 CONTENEDORES

KÜNSTAINER
INCENDIADO

CAÑADA REAL
[TODO POR LA PRAXIS]
2 CONTENEDORES

CÁCERES
3 CONTENEDORES

BENICÁSSIM
[ASOCIACIÓN PROYECTA]
6 CONTENEDORES

GANDIA
[EL INVITADO]
4 CONTENEDORES

CASTUERA
[ASOCIACIÓN LUNA SERENA]
3 CONTENEDORES

SEVILLA
[RECETAS URBANAS]
2 CONTENEDORES

GRANADA
[AAABIERTA]

MALAGA
[TRINCHERAS]

>LA ARAÑITA - INVITADA
1 CONTENEDOR
SANT PERE
SEVILLA

WWW.RECETASURBANAS.NET - 02.2

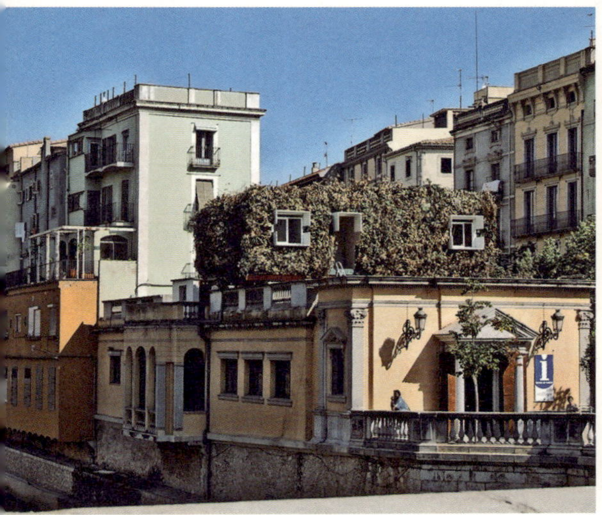

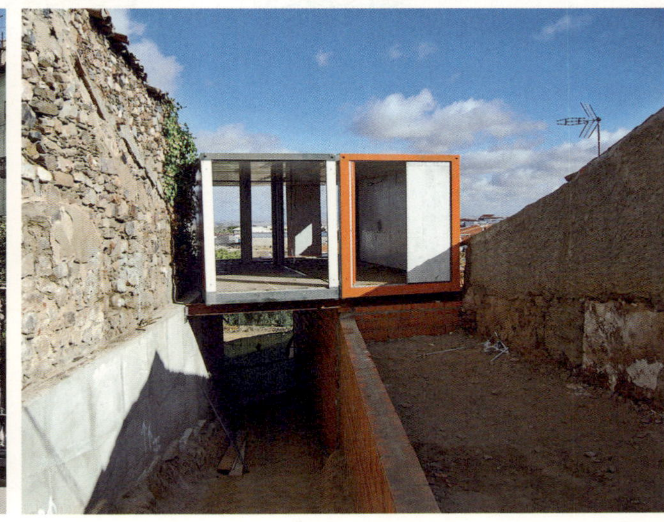

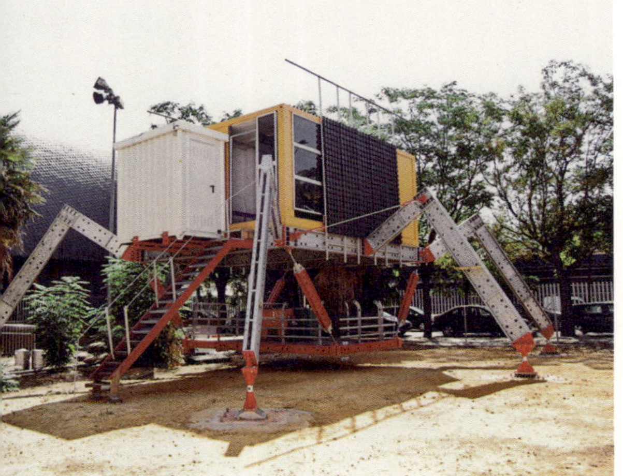

***Camiones, Contenedores, Colectivos*** ("Trucks, containers, collectives") stems from an exceptional opportunity in the heritage of street furniture recovery: a series of housing- containers handed over by the Municipal Society for Urban Rehabilitation of the City Hall of Saragossa, for different collectives, associations, and citizen groups to use. The initiative's success and viral expansion shows the importance of self-management processes as supplements or proposals for social and political work, using self-construction as a weapon for collective involvement. The range of situations experienced so far is wide and heterogeneous. To begin with, the groups involved in the experiment stem from very diverse fields. Some of them are linked to alternative education, such as *La Fundició* co-operative and the youth collective *SpaiDer3**, while others are creative networks such as *Alg-a* or cultural associations such as *Caldodecultivo*. There are activist groups, such as *Todo por la Praxis* collective or *Alien Nación*, and unconventional architectural studies such as *Straddle3*. The wide range of case studies for projects carried out illustrates different ways of operating, constructing, and managing spaces in very diverse situations, thus involving different types of occupation and agreements, funding and management, and relationships with the local context.

***Coelctivo Alga***, Pontevedra, 2008–2010

***Nautarquia + Straddle3***, San Pere del Torelló, 2009

***Recetas Urbanas + El Bólit***, Girona, 2008—2009

***Luna Serena + Recetas Urbanas***, Castuera, 2010

***Recetas Urbanas***, Sevilla, 2009–2010

■
***Untitled/Untitled***, 2001–2007, "permanent" urban installation, Isola district, Milan; the work was destroyed by the real-estate company Hines

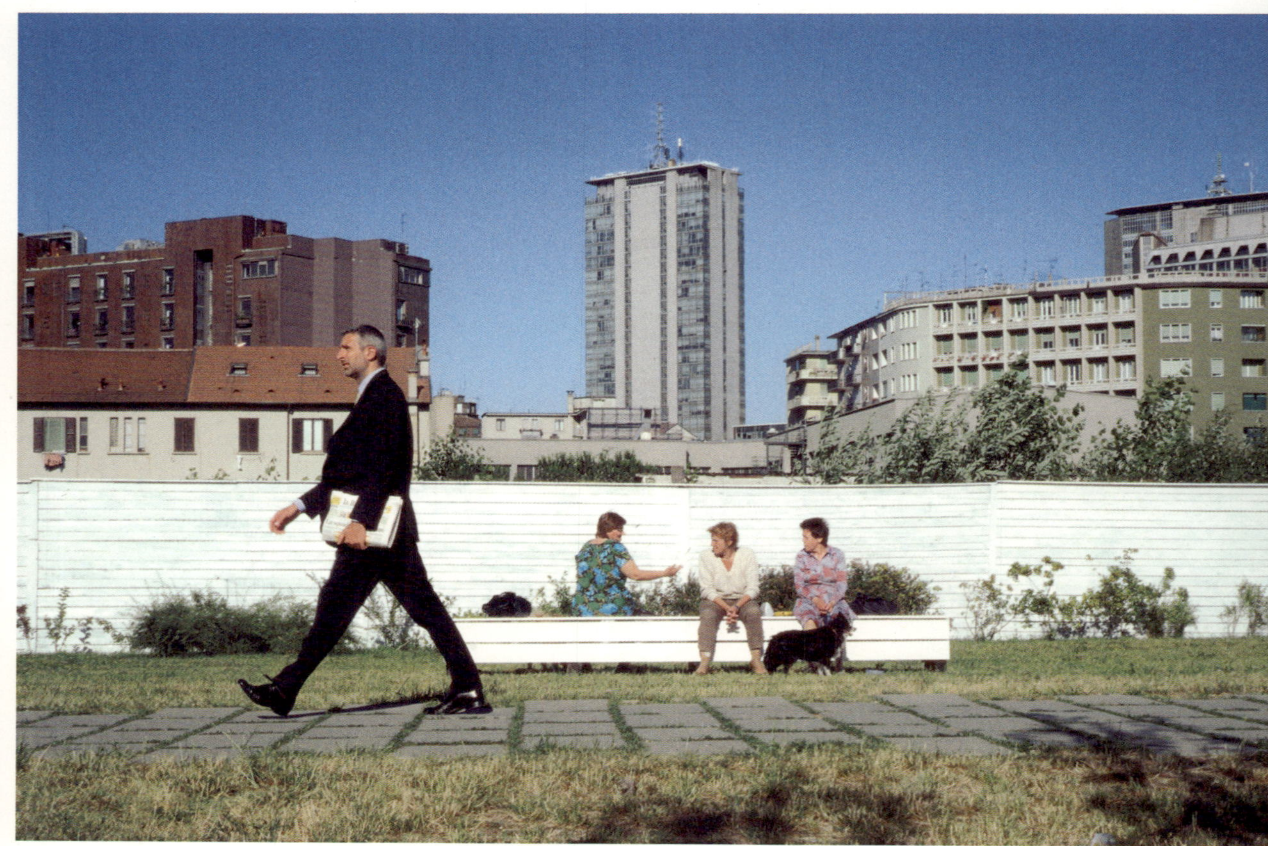

# Bert Theis

Craftsmen expelled from Isola Art Center's building and standing in front of a work by Urban Blooz Project, as part of the exhibition *Situazionisola*, co-curated by Bert Theis, 2007

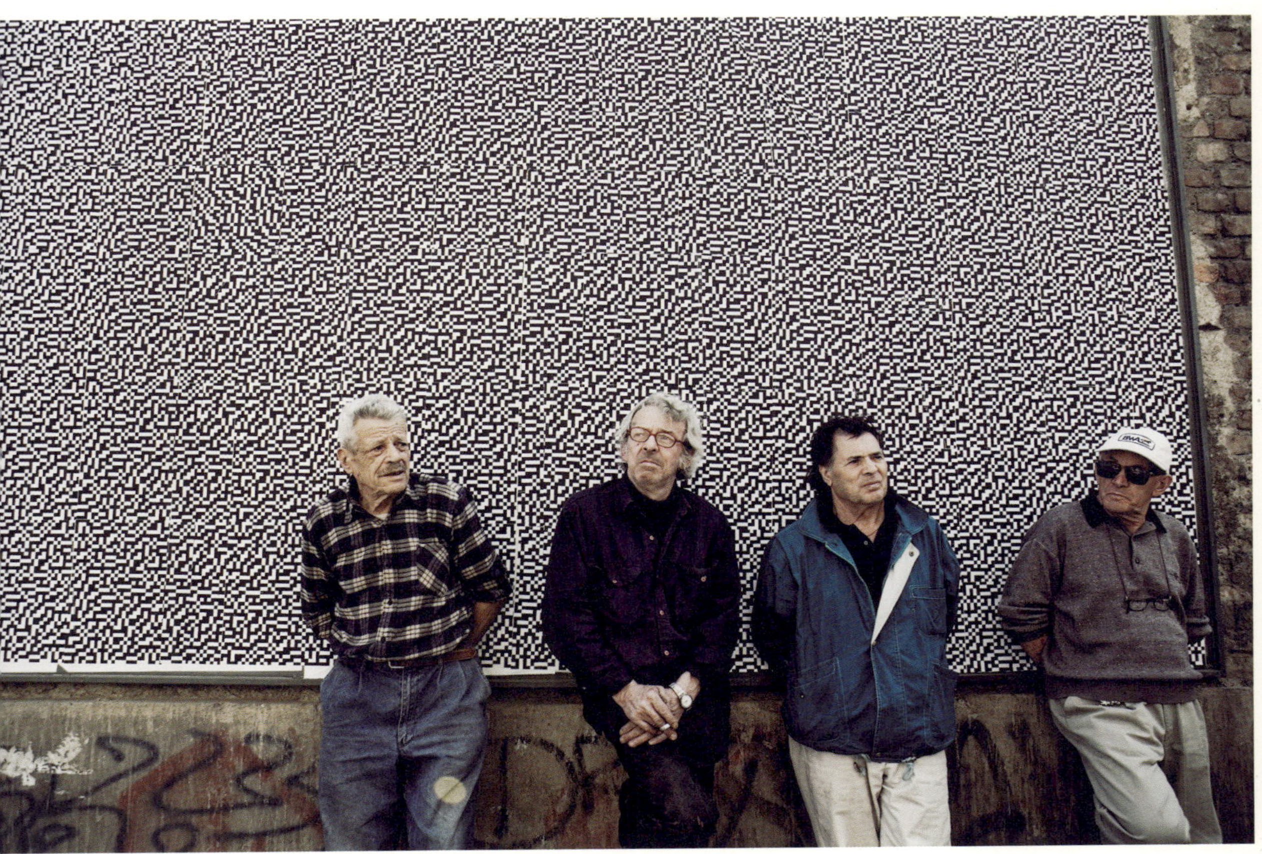

*Emiliano Gandolfi —*

Bert, in your work you've always challenged the use of the public domain—from your works in the 1990s, such as the *Philosophical Platform* and the *Skulptur Projekte* in Münster, Germany to works that are more complex in relational terms, such as the *Isola Art Center* in Milan and *Territoria* in Prato.

*Bert Theis —*

I'm part of a generation of artists who, in the 1990s, wanted to go beyond the distinction between representation and the production of real things. I've always been interested in creating structures in which the borderlines between art, design, and architecture disappear. This means I've never been interested in creating sculptures for people to admire. In the 1970s, site-specific art was already taking an interest in the particularities of places. But this approach, especially when applied to an urban context, often neglected one decisive aspect, which was that of the social component: the people who live and work in that particular place. I prefer referring to my approach as "audience-specific," and my work is sensitive to both the spatial and the social domains. And in this case, when there's the active participation of the inhabitants, one can aspire to works that are "fight-specific"!

*Emiliano Gandolfi —*

As regards the *Isola Art Center*, how does an audience-specific work turn into a "fight-specific" neighborhood movement? In other words, was it the project that brought about a change, or was it the change itself that influenced the project?

*Bert Theis —*

When I started working on the Isola in 2001, you could already sense the tension and protest in the neighborhood against the plans for urban redevelopment. In this precarious situation, I thought it would be interesting to create a long-term contemporary art project that would be able to establish a dialectical process with the inhabitants of the neighborhood and promote the creation of alternatives. I had no preconceived ideas about what approach to adopt—it all needed to be invented. In 2001, I created the first collective operation with the groups working at the Isola. This was a one-hundred-meter-long palisade in white wood—a sort of symbolic barrier that would give tangible form to where the road dividing the neighborhood in two would pass. But the symbolic barrier wouldn't have lasted a minute against the power of an earthmover. So it was quite clear that this symbolic barrier also had to be accompanied by a social, political, and cultural barrier. And that was something that could not be done by a single person. To start off with, there were just a few of us—Stefano Boccalini, Gruppo A12, Marjetica Potrč, and Thomas Hirschhorn as foreign artists, and Marco Scotini, Roberto Pinto, and Emanuela De Cecco as curators—but many others joined us later.

*Emiliano Gandolfi —*

In your work, the idea of "audience-specific" had already been clear for a number of years, both in the platforms and in the project for the fake Luxembourg Pavilion at the Venice Biennale in 1995. The greatest change in the project for the Isola district was probably the idea of involving other artists. How did this collective approach come about?

■□
***Philosophical Platform***, 1997, Skulptur Projekte, Münster

□■
***Potemkin Lock***, 1995, Luxembourg fake Pavilion, Venice Biennale

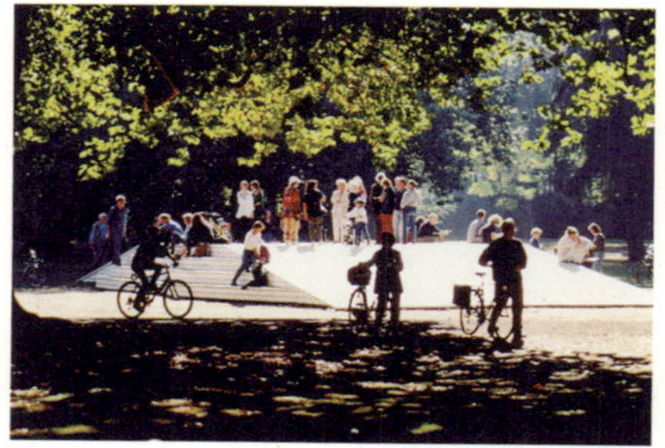

*Bert Theis —*

In actual fact, it was a gradual process. We occupied the second floor of a former industrial building known as the *stecca degli artigiani* ("building of the artisans") and, with the agreement of some neighborhood associations, we started creating a center for contemporary art and for the neighborhood.

*Emiliano Gandolfi —*

*Isola Art Center* was the result of a very ambitious idea: an art project that works in an integral manner with the neighborhood and neighborhood associations. How did the relationship between the artists and the people living in the neighborhood work out?

*Bert Theis —*

There was a huge gap between the artists and the local people to begin with. They were worlds apart and didn't know each other. But, through our work and through the habit of putting on an art event whenever there was some public occasion in the neighborhood, these two worlds started coming together, and in 2004 this led to the setup of the center for art and for the neighborhood. Now, after eight years of work, we've been able to set up a network of people—called *Forum Isola*—which has turned art into an instrument of struggle for the neighborhood. This is an extraordinary success if one thinks that art is normally used as an instrument of gentrification rather than as something that brings people together. We regularly have meetings which are attended not only by artists and curators, but also by inhabitants, shopkeepers, representatives of associations, and so on.

*Emiliano Gandolfi —*

How has the participation of the neighborhood influenced the work of the artists you've involved? And do you believe that the works that have been made would have been different in a traditional museum?

*Bert Theis —*

To give you an example, one of the works that involved the neighborhood to an extraordinary degree was Tomas Saraceno's *museo aero solar*. We involved the entire neighborhood in the creation of this hot-air balloon of used plastic bags—the children helped us collect the material and put it together in a huge collective work. Tomas maintains that he could never have carried out this project with a traditional museum. The work of these artists is of course fundamental, but the neighborhood too makes a significant contribution to those artists who are interested in opening up to greater involvement.

*Emiliano Gandolfi —*

In 2007 the *Isola Art Center* was evicted and the building later demolished. The municipality and builders decided to go ahead with development despite the protest movement and the suggestions for alternatives that would have preserved the *stecca* and the park. How did you work to put together an alternative?

*Bert Theis —*

The position adopted by the neighborhood is moderate but firm. The people have never objected to new

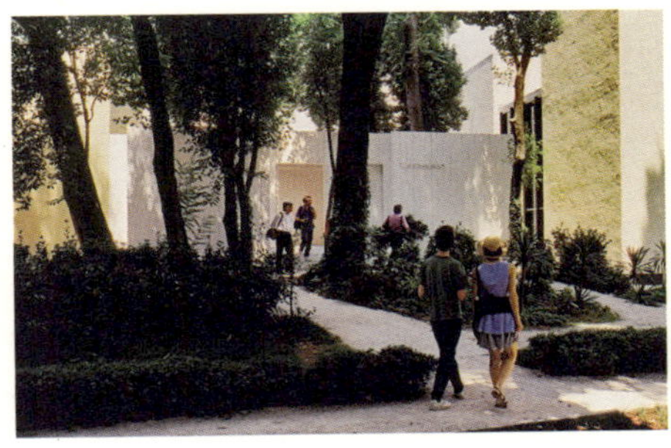

buildings. We submitted to the municipality an alternative plan which would have maintained the same disposition of masses, with the aim of preserving the gardens and the *stecca* as a public space for the neighborhood. And we also set up an *Office for Urban Transformations (out)*—a place where we could meet with various associations. A place for discussion and interaction. The aim of *out* is to give visibility to an alternative that can gain widespread approval and, in order to achieve this, we have worked on a series of projects with the associations, architects, and artists. The latest one was *Il Parco Possibile* ("The Possible Park").

*Emiliano Gandolfi* —

After your building was demolished, what instruments have you used to continue with your work?

*Bert Theis* —

Ever since the *stecca* and the fencing around the gardens were removed, the extraordinary effectiveness of our work has become quite evident. We're still attempting to get the municipality and Hines (the American constructors involved in the building works, along with Salvatore Ligresti, the entrepreneur) to make some compromises. We've made a series of appeals to the Tribunale Amministrativo Regionale (TAR), the regional administrative court—some of which we've won—and we've submitted alternative plans and put on public debates and a series of events. Now we're fighting for new spaces and for the services that are lacking in the neighborhood, such as sports and social areas.

*Emiliano Gandolfi* —

And what about the art projects in the neighborhood? For example the project in which you are involving artists to produce works on the shutters of the shops?

*Bert Theis* —

Since we no longer have our gardens, we've organized a series of events in the streets and squares of the neighborhood. The shutters project is going at full steam. Now we're being hosted by a large number of shops, associations, restaurants, and bookstores. The project is called *Rosta*—a name borrowed from a project in the 1920s, when artists such as Vladimir Mayakovsky made posters that were shown in the windows of the Soviet telegraph company. We also involved artists like Dan Perjovschi, Andreas Siekmann, and Christoph Schäfer, and it was an overnight success. Many people in the neighborhood were hospitable to the artists, offering them spaces and even helping them make their works. There is no lack of space where art can be created, but none of the neighborhood's problems have been solved. We're hoping that the cases still going through the courts will enable us to start negotiating with the municipality for a self-managed public space where we can continue to work.

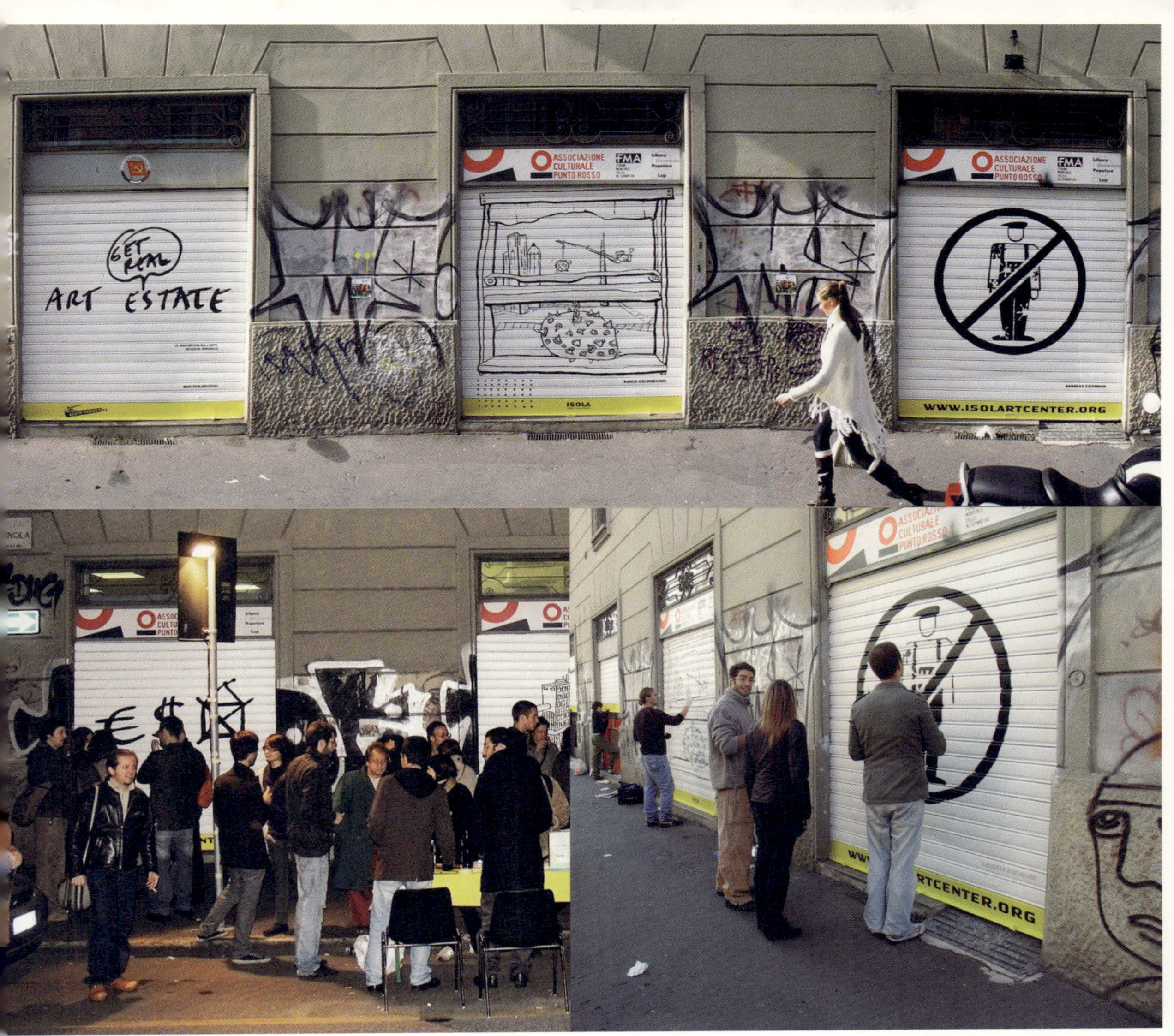


*Isola Rosta Project*, 2008–2010, permanent exhibition on the shutters of the Isola district, curated by Bert Theis

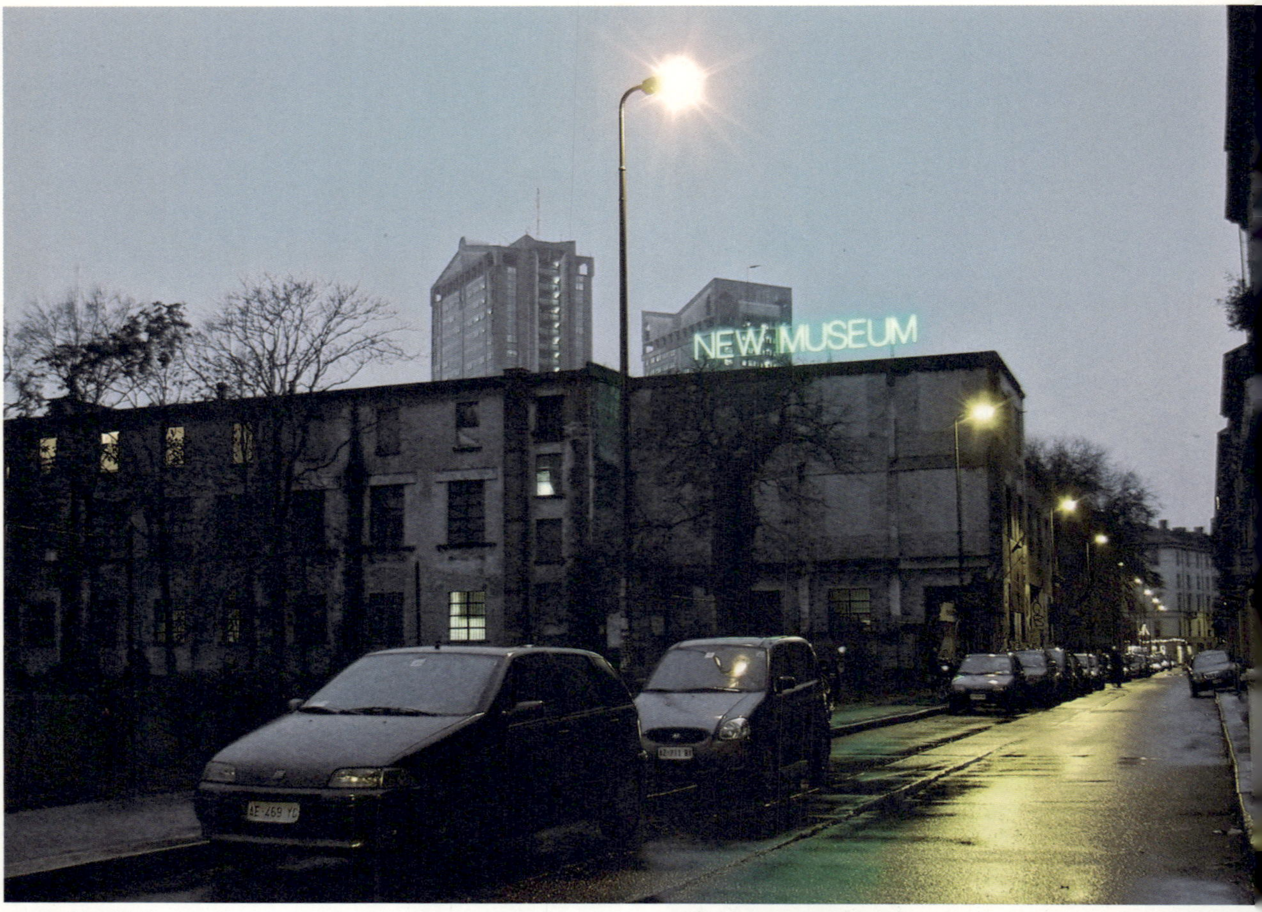

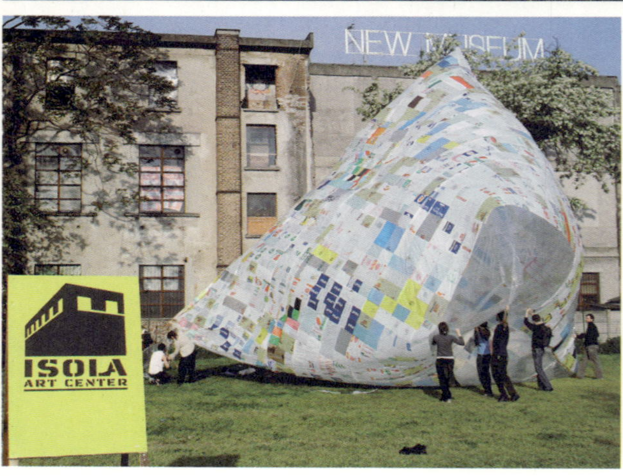


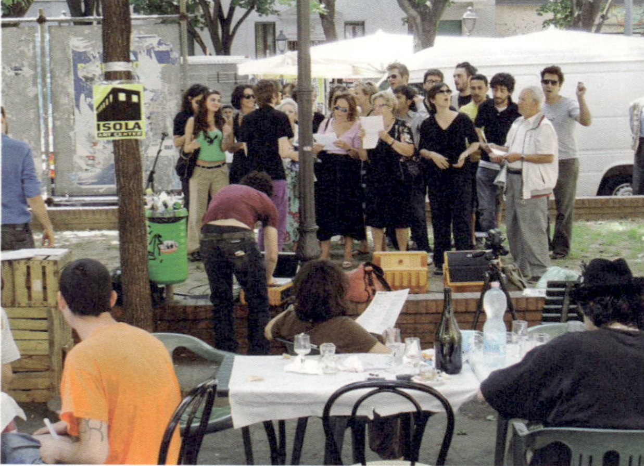


***Kings, New Museum***, 2006, neon installation on the Isola Art Center, curated by Alessandra Poggianti

***Tomas Saraceno, museo aero solar***, 2007, Isola Art Center, as part of the exhibition *Situazionisola*, co-curated by Bert Theis

***The Milan Complaints Choir,*** 2009, from a project by Tellervo Kalleinen and Oliver Kocht-Kalleinen, Isola Art Center, part of the exhibition *Public Turbulence*, presented by Matteo Lucchetti

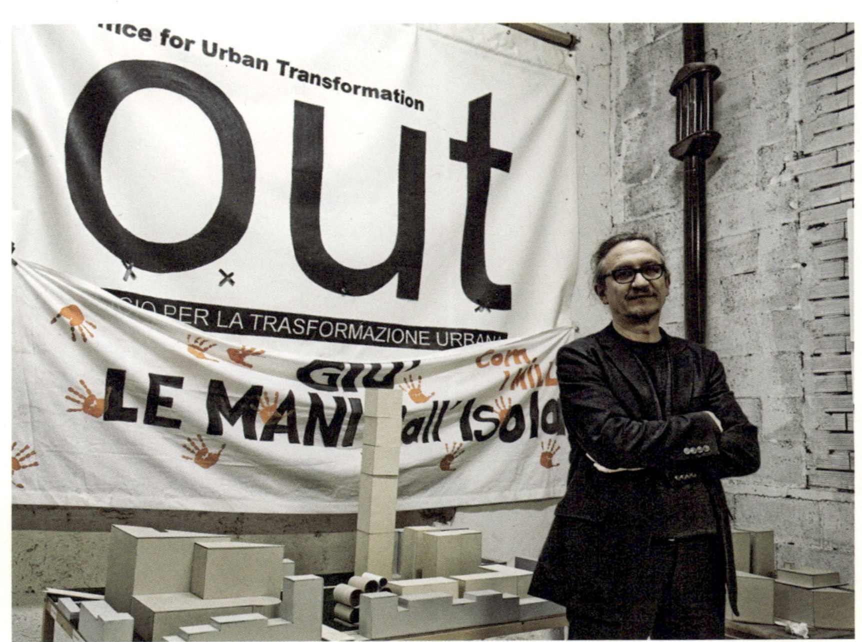


***Office for Urban Transformation (out)***, 2007, the artist Bert Theis in front of a working model for the Isola district

**Hu Fang** was born 1970 in Zhengjiang, China. He graduated from the Chinese Literature Department of Wuhan University in 1992, and now lives and works in Guangzhou and Beijing. He is a fiction writer and one of the conceivers of Vitamin Creative Space as well as of *the shop* in Beijing. As a novelist and essayist, Hu Fang's recent publications include the novel *Garden of Mirrored Flowers* and an anthology of fictional essays *Pavilion to the Heart's Insight I*. He is a frequent contributor to art magazines such as *Yishu, Abitare China,* and *Art Asia Pacific*. His curatorial practices are widely reflected on his variety of exhibitions at Vitamin Creative Space and his projects engaged in different situations within international contexts. He was coordinating editor of documenta 12 magazines, a "player" of Lyon Biennial 2007, one of the correspondents of Venice Biennale 2009, as well as the co-curator of Yokohama Triennale 2008.

> www.hufangwrites.com www.vitamin-creativespace.com

**Zheng Guogu** was born 1970 in Yangjiang, China. Lives in works in Yangjiang. Zheng Guogu is a conceptual artist of globalization, staging the world as opportunity in the endless universe of the acceptable. His functioning comparable to the work of a stage director surprises the spectator of his artistic works with a reality permeated by the ficticious. In cooperation with the other artists and friends he often experiments with different media and materials to resolve the frontier between art and everyday life in another dimension.The respective projects he has participated in recently include: *Breaking Forecase: 8 Key Figures of China's New Generation Artists,* Ullens Center for Contemporary Art (UCCA),Beijing, China, 2009; *Biennales de Lyon* 2009; *Sprout from White Nights,* Bonniers Konsthall Stockholm, Sweden, 2008; *Third Guangzhou Triennial,* 2008; *Brave New Worlds,* Walker Art Center, USA, 2007; *Documenta 12,* Kassel, Germany, 2007.

**Xu Tan** was born in Wuhan, Hubei Province in 1957 and currently lives in Guangzhou. Since the early 1990s he has been part of "Big Tail Elephant Group," an experimental art team in Guangzhou. Xu Tan has insisted on his lifestyle as "outcast," maintaining sensitivity to the changes in social life and culture, and questioning the boundary of contemporary art. Over the years this has led his working style to appear more like that of a social theorist than a purely visual artist. His work has been shown around the world, including at the 53rd Biennale di Venezia, the 50th Biennale di Venezia, the Berlin Biennial, and the Gongdong Triennial.

> www.xutan-keywords.com

**Ming Wong** (1971) is an artist exploring the performative veneers of language and identity, through his own "world cinema." He lives and works in Berlin & Singapore. Ming Wong was awarded Special Mention (Expanding Worlds) for his solo show at the 53rdVenice Biennale. Following his success, Ming Wong has rapidly drawn invitations from the international art world. They include *Modern Mondays at MOMA NY* 2010/11 Season (a prelude to exhibiting in *Projects at MOMA NY*). He will also show at Sydney Biennale 2010, Singapore Biennale 2011, and Oberhausen Film Festival 2010. In the last six months, his works have screened in Centre Pompidou Paris, Museum of Contemporary Art Taipei, Tokyo Metropolitan Museum of Photography, Tropenmuseum Amsterdam.

> www.mingwong.org

**Sou Fujimoto Architects** is an architecture studio based in Tokyo, Japan. The studio has a solid history in residential projects which demonstrate a Japanese flair. They have also produced a number of conceptual structures that push the limits of housing and space conventions.

> www.sou-fujimoto.com

**Cao Fei** (1978) is a Chinese artist based in Beijing. She is known for her multimedia installations and videos, and is acknowledged as one of the key artists of a new generation emerging from Mainland China. She mixes social commentary, popular aesthetics, references to Surrealism, and documentary conventions in her films and installations. Her works reflect on the rapid and chaotic changes that are occurring in Chinese society today. Her recent work includes a Second Life project entitled *China Tracy* that has been exhibited in Deutsche Guggenheim, 2010; Shiseido Gallery, Tokyo, Japan, 2009; Serpentine Gallery, London, 2008; a 52nd Venice Biennale, Chinese Pavilion; *RMB City— A Second Life City Planning* has been exhibited in 2007 Istanbul Biennale; Whose Utopia, TATE Liverpool, 2007; and Nu Project, Lyon Biennale, 2007. Cao Fei also participated in the 15th Biennale of Sydney, 2006; the Moscow Biennale, 2005; Shanghai Biennale 2004; and the 50th Venice Biennale, 2003. She also exhibited video works in the Guggenheim Museum, New York; the International Center of Photography, New York; MoMa New York; P.S.1 New York; Palais de Tokyo Paris; Musee d'Art Moderne de la ville de Paris; Mori Art Museum Tokyo. Cao Fei is the finalist of Hugo Boss Prize 2010, and won the 2006 Best Young Artist Award by CCAA (Chinese Contemporary Art Award).

> www.caofei.com

# New Species of Spaces

*The five colors blind the eye.*
*The five tones deafen the ear.*
*The five flavors dull the taste.*
*Racing and hunting madden the mind.*
*Precious things lead one astray.*

*Therefore the sage is guided by what he feels and not by what he sees.*
*He lets go of that and chooses this.*

—

Lao Tsu, *Tao Te Ching,* Chapter 12
Lao Tsu, *Tao Te Ching,* trans. Gia-fu Feng
and Jane English, (New York: Vintage Books, 1989), 14

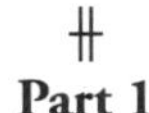

**Part 1**

*He took his eyes off the blinking computer screen to look at the gray skyline outside the glass-curtain wall. Thick clouds were slowly turning bright in the soft setting sun. Densely constructed tall buildings stretched off into the distant horizon and, as if they were cells capable of self-reproduction, defined the boundaries of our lives amid quick duplications and constant hybridizations. He pressed the keyboard and a theme park stumbled into view, assembled, spun around, and scattered in the middle of colors. A city was constantly being destroyed and rebuilt, adding one history on top of another, until it finally became too blurred to be distinct.*

—

Hu Fang, *Garden of Mirrored Flowers* (Hu Fang, *Garden of Mirrored Flowers*, Guangzhou: Vitamin Creative Space, 2009), 115)

I begin by imagining how the protagonist, who is an architect, has discovered the labyrinth of life that has revealed itself to him gradually during his building a theme park called *Garden of Mirrored Flowers.*

Going further than Jorge Luis Borges's *Garden of Forking Paths*, the labyrinth of life in this novel entitled *Garden of Mirrored Flowers* can be directly reality itself. Perhaps this novel is a "documentary" of reality, in that it simply collects traces in reality. Those traces (television advertisements, stock market information, cell phone text messages, shopping lists, etc.) are always revealing rather dramatic events to us; from political shows to economic crises, the ability of reality to produce stories seems to be overpowered today.

Therefore, this novel will become the "script" of this reality, just like the great tradition in Russian literature that the Russian writer Victor Pelevin pointed out in the preface to the Chinese edition of his novel *Generation "П"*: "In Russia, what writers write are not novels, but scripts."

Therefore, "I" am not the author of this novel. It is possible that reality is using my hand to write its own novel—this reality is increasingly becoming "surreal" and "beyond-reality," and is increasingly becoming saturated to the extent that it is void of values. If the reality in which we exist is increasingly becoming the secretions of people's crazy brains, can we still see reality?

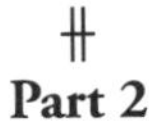

**Part 2**

*As the central architecture of the complex, the cinema is the largest luminous architectural body. Lights and the lights of movies are projected to the sky above the complex, and intermingle with the lights of the city. Naturally, they also shine upon people, upon their faces and bodies from above. It is like the setting for the finale of the TV series*

At the Threshold of an Era*: before our eyes is the prosperous metropolis, under our feet is success and fame, a prominent position that cannot be exceeded...*

—

*Contemporary MOMA* (a Beijing-based real estate ad magazine), No. 8, 2009

The Linked Hybrid building, also known as *Contemporary MOMA,* is a residential building complex designed by American architect Steven Holl for Beijing. This huge residential container is more like an epochal allegory of the imaged space of reality. It proclaims: 1. REALITY WILL BECOME A SET IN A FILM. 2. RESIDENTS WILL BE THE STARS OF THE FILM. 3. THE ARCHITECT WILL BECOME THE FILM'S DIRECTOR.

Therefore, the architect and the real estate developers encourage people to take part in the process of creating this script of contemporary life of "watching" and "being watched." If watching is a conscious activity, today this conscious activity seems to create its own reality: mirror images. Through his artistic work, Dan Graham sensitively reveals the important psychological impacts of the semi-reflective glass of shopping malls and office buildings, particularly at moments when one's own reflected image fuses with that of the goods displayed behind the glass. This fusion produces an entirely new self-image. While Graham of course shows that this new self-image is of someone who wants to purchase the goods behind the window, he also touches upon the most fundamental cultural condition of urban life, namely that urban living space has become a continuous system of self-reflection in which "I" can never perceive the existence of other people beyond my own mirrored image, just as the city itself cannot perceive any other parts of the world, but only its own reflection.

Man indulges in revelry with his own mirror images, a city indulges in living in its own mirror images—this is the beginning of the exhausted experience of the self. Is it still possible for us to be truly related to reality?

ǂ

**Part 3**

*Spaces have multiplied, been broken up and have diversified... To live is to pass from one space to another, while doing your very best not to bump yourself.*

—

Georges Perec (Georges Perec, *Species of Spaces and Other Pieces*, ed. and trans. John Sturrock, London: Penguin, 1997)

You walk through a jungle or a mountain range. At the end of the road are two forking paths: the left pertains to the "first life" and the right to the "second life."

Had there not been **Cao Fei**/China Tracy's *I/Mirror*, I would not have encountered the life called "Second Life" that soon. There seem to be new views of life and death, of history, and of the world there, but quickly we find that "Second

Life" is no new world; it's like the "first life": a life. *I/Mirror* shows the beautiful scenery of the end of the wasteland, but it is a metaphor not about the future, but about the politics of daily life here and now. To put it another way, the aesthetics of the future is actually not mysterious. It lies in the increasingly blurred and mixed-up frontier between reality and imagination; it will disappear into the same horizon as life. More and more, artists are engaged in the flow of life—no longer the single meaning of solidified reality in the past, but a moving, unresolved process.

To show **Cao Fei**, **Ming Wong**, **Sou Fujimoto**, **Xu Tan**, and **Zheng Guogu** on paper, to explore conversations among them, is to cast a new light on the complexity of relationships between art and reality. Art is no longer an artist's manipulations in a laboratory, but his instinctive, active participation in a "possible life." I think that today our question about art should turn from "what is it?" to "what can it become?" We may say that, from the start, the purpose of these creations is not to become "works of art." As a force toward integrating different situations, an art creation must and will inevitably constantly raise questions about social life and encourage our conscious activities.

Zheng Guogu in *The Age of Empire*, **Xu Tan** in *Keywords School*, **Cao Fei** in *RMB City*, and **Ming Wong** in *Life of Imitation* somehow all regard life as a process of experience, and develop a singular perception of the world from it. By the same token, for **Sou Fujimoto**, the exhaustion of living spaces does not mean the end of architecture. Perhaps it is the beginning of architecture returning to "mother earth" and the dwellings of man to a "cave." It is in this sense that his architectures have proposed the possibility of a new living space. Each of these art creations embodying vastly different concepts becomes a unique space of its own. Yet they all call forth a truly diversified new species of space.

These individuals regard life itself as a process of experimentation and develop their own unique ways of perceiving the world. As opposed to an unconscious involvement, these figures always have the ability to "intend" movement in a certain direction, which is to say that they are always likely to construct a dynamic relationship between and around, to generate an integration of multiple relationships through their art practices, making the work itself a kind of Post-fact: both the result of a transformation and a proposal, which will in turn touch, and deeply influence, the relevant groups, and reality itself. Based on such a premise—that is, if we regard the practice of art as a reconstruction of a relationship to life (such a relationship is no longer a definite social determination, but a fundamental and philosophical understanding)—it must be bound to the direction of its spaces and groups, and become a proposal for constructing the possibility of life.

These different forms of creativity with different orientations respectively become different spaces, but they also suggest the existence of a truly diverse *New Species of Space*—one that will inspire a new space for life.

Zheng Guogu is regarded as something of a legend in contemporary Chinese art. Not only has he created unique art objects, but he has also created a sustainable ecology initiative environment for contemporary art development. In 2004, he bought about two hectares of land in the suburb of the city of Yangjiang in southwest Guangdong province and started his *Empire Time*, a project initiated with a conceptual garden–esque space idea, and he is devoting his life to developing it during the process.

Reflecting the computer game *Age of Empires, Empire Time* in reality integrates more complicated spatial modalities and social relations. It is not a fixed, viewable work enclosed within an interior space, but rather a project that extends into an even truer living space, which comprises the entire process of dwelling in a spatial location, from conceptual ideal to practical implementation to day-to-day living.

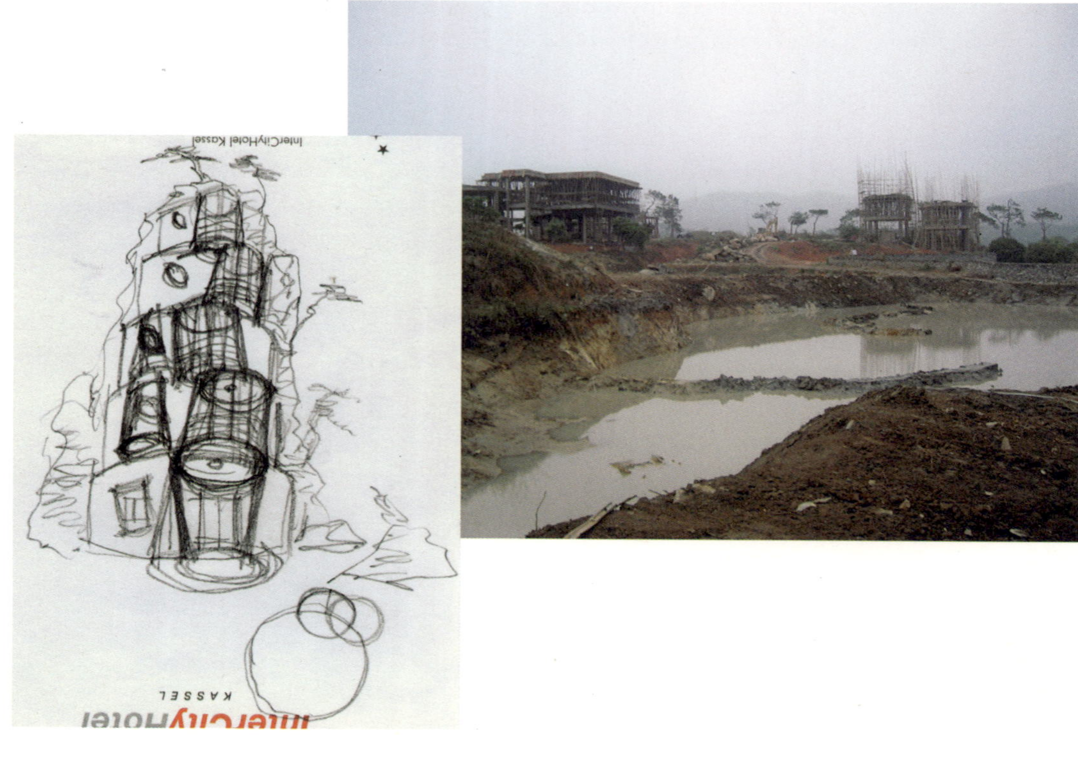

# Zheng Guogu

***Plan of the Empire***, Drawing, 2006–2007

***The Age of Empire***, ongoing Land Project, 2004–present

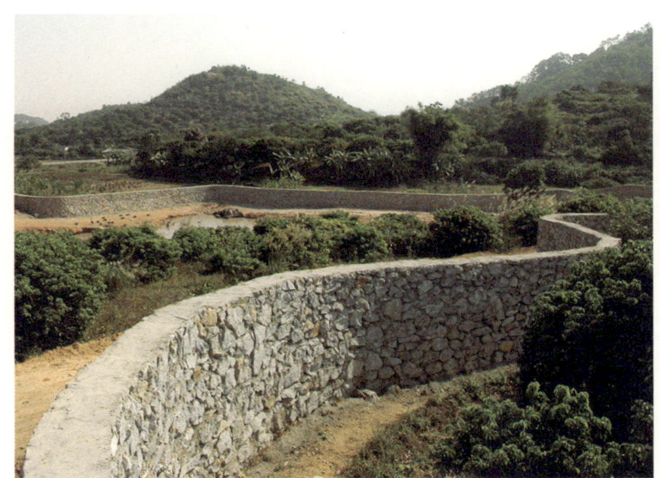

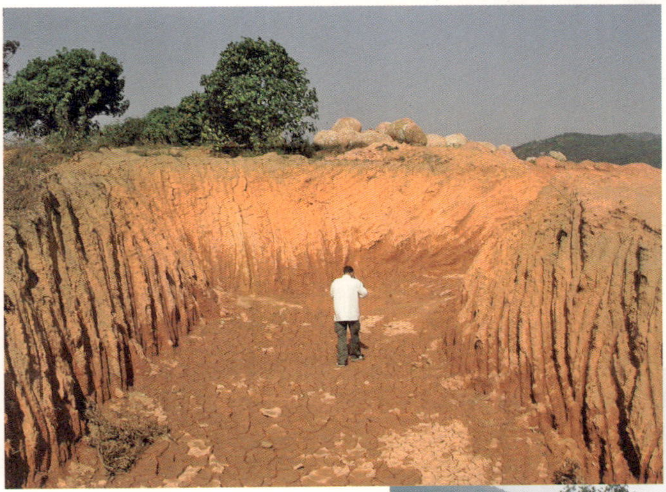

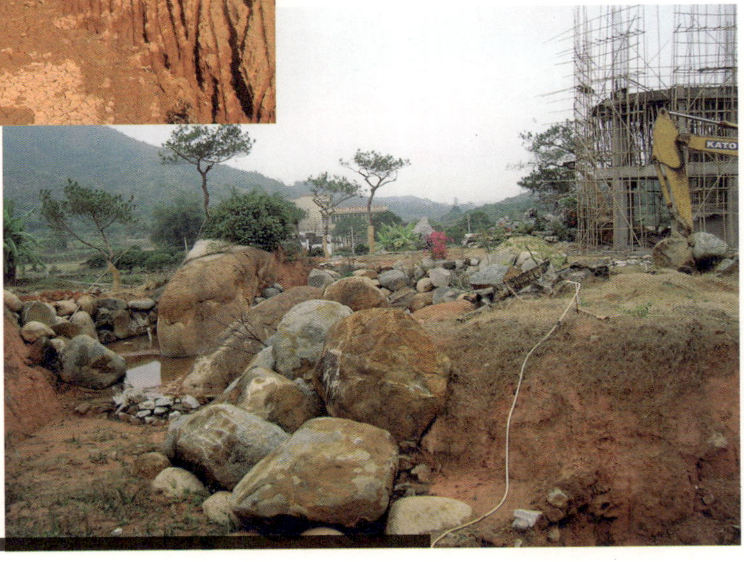

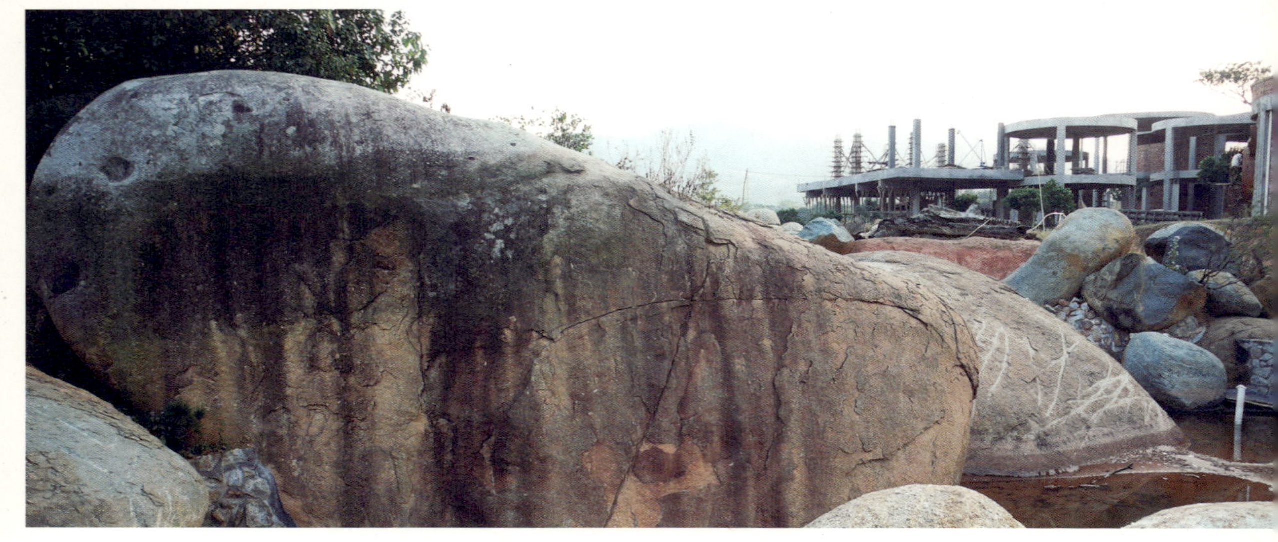

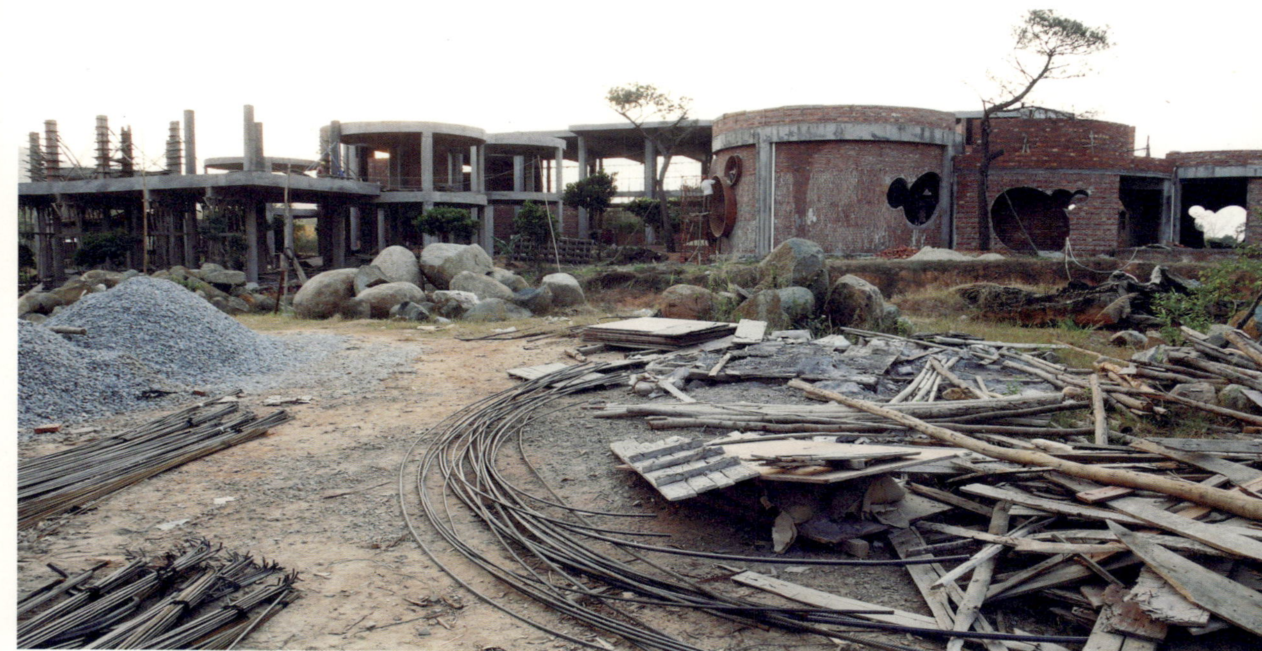

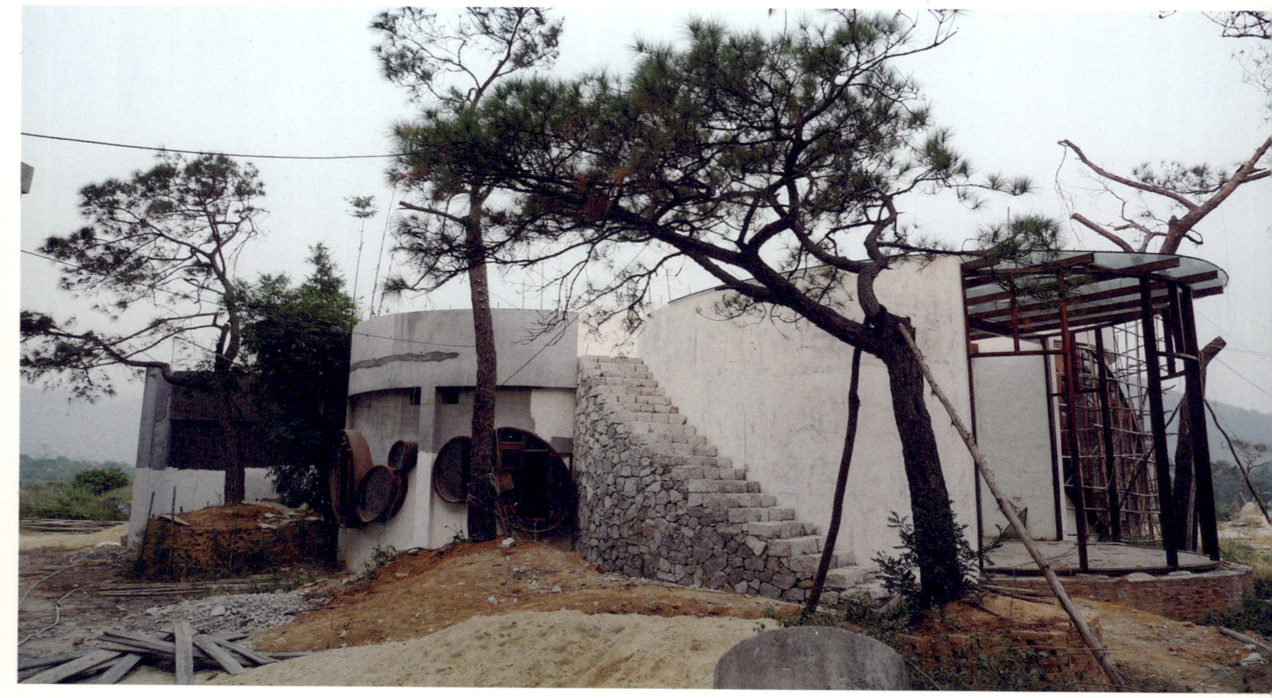

***The Age of Empire***, ongoing
Land Project, 2004–present

Annex: A Dialogue Between Hu Fang and Zheng Guogu

*Hu Fang —*

What's the relationship between the present land ownership situation in China and your *Empire*? Without owning land, you would never be able to create the *Empire...*

*Zheng Guogu —*

I bought land from a peasant, which as you know is illegal in China. So the *Empire* is illegal at the moment. I will somehow have to make it legal! This is the object of my project—that by making use of public relations, it can become a legal entity.

*Hu Fang —*

Public relations with who, the government?

*Zheng Guogu —*

*Empire* is a time that will ultimately disappear. Through stamps and signatures, it is being transformed into law, and it will undoubtedly exist through the communications I have had with various public departments in government, such as the Bureau of Land Resources and the Department of Urban Planning and Design.

*Hu Fang —*

Doesn't all land have to go through this process to a degree before it is able to be established?

*Zheng Guogu —*

Absolutely. Unless you have good connections it's impossible to get a license to develop land.

*Hu Fang —*

No public relations, no empire.

*Zheng Guogu —*

Unless you are going to plant vegetables on a barren mountainside or a trackless plain. Once you make architecture, problems arise. For example, my painting *Landscape of the Age of Empire* is an ideal, but in reality, in the real construction of *Empire*, everything depends on good public relations.

*Hu Fang —*

We might see the birth of a new kind of landscape with *Landscape of the Age of Empire*—we could call it "the individual landscape"—that until now there has been very little space for in China's policy. It's very interesting that after breaking all the rules and regulations, you are still going to legalize your *Empire*.

*Zheng Guogu —*

I want to become a peasant, or become a new intellectual going "up to the mountain, down to the village." [Mao's policy, begun in 1968, of ordering some seventeen million privileged students from the cities into the remote countryside to learn from workers and farmers.]

*Hu Fang —*

I remember actually that *Age of Empires* is the name of a computer game; you were interested in it a lot.

*Zheng Guogu —*

There is no barbecue in the computer game, yet you can find it in my real *Empire*.

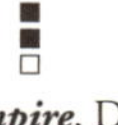

***Plan of the Empire***, Drawing, 2006, 2007

***Zheng Guogu in his empire***; all images courtesy Vitamin Creative Space

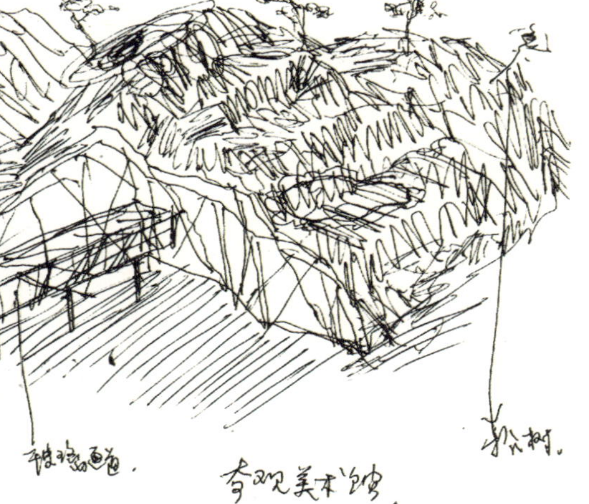

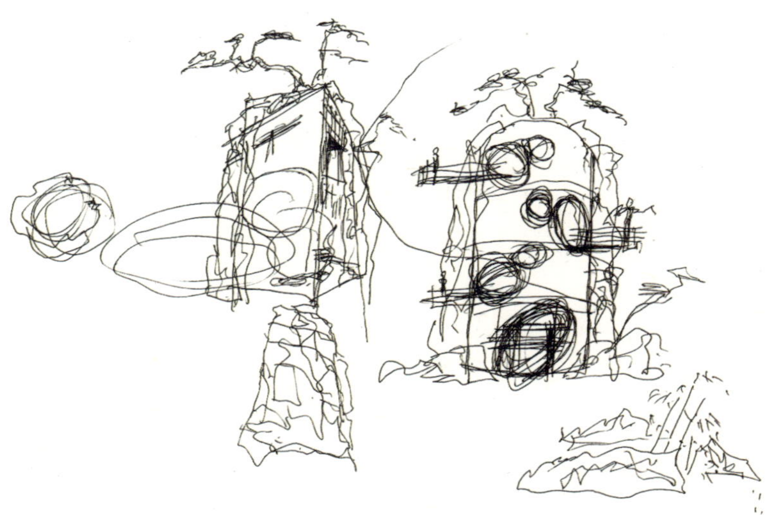

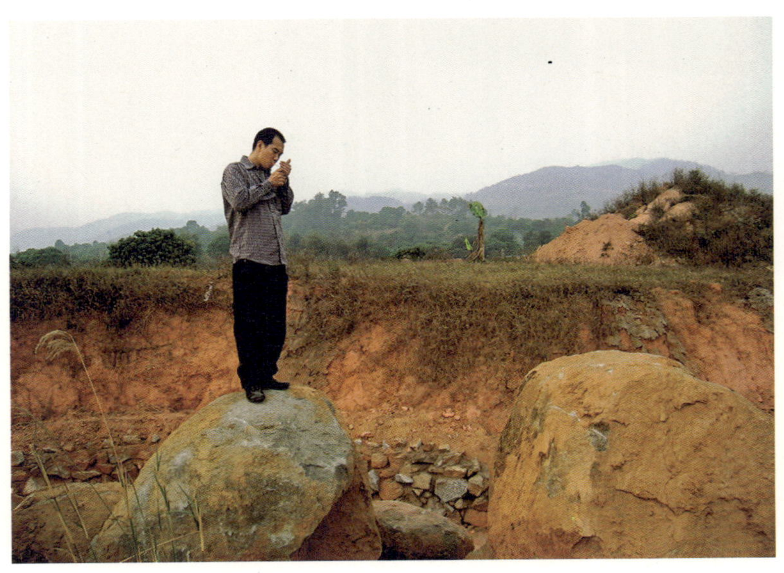

*Xu Tan: Flaneur of Keywords* — Until today, Xu Tan has kept his lifestyle as a Chinese flaneur. He is sensitive to social transformations, and has never stopped questioning the boundary of art. Born at the end of 1950s (1957), Xu Tan experienced the Cultural Revolution, the economic reforms of the 1980s, and the commercial flurry of the 1990s. Before Chinese society moved to a new global age, "transformation" had become not only a way of Chinese society but also a way of life for Xu Tan, as he constantly asks the question: What does "contemporary art" mean? And where is the relationship between "contemporary art practices" and the "Chinese living system"? Xu Tan constantly contrives his own answers. Western Conceptualism was once an important source of inspiration for Xu Tan (and for an entire generation of the first group of Chinese avant-garde artists), allowing this generation not only to free its hands, but also to free itself from certain definitions of art which were supposed to contain the truth of art. This does not imply any sort of answer to China's "reality," but rather Xu Tan's own works grow out of Chinese "reality" in an organic process that present art-historical knowledge fails to answer.

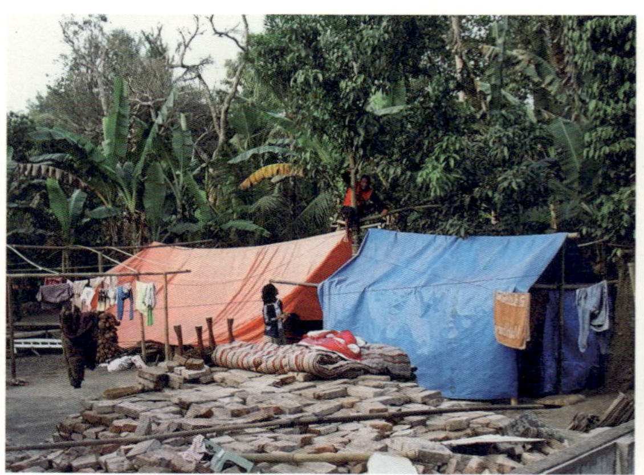

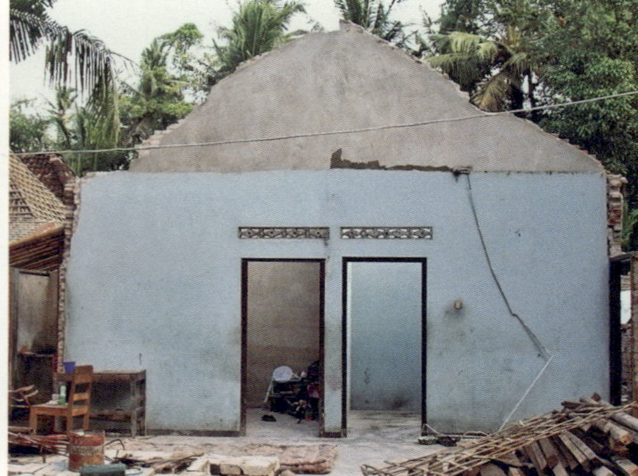

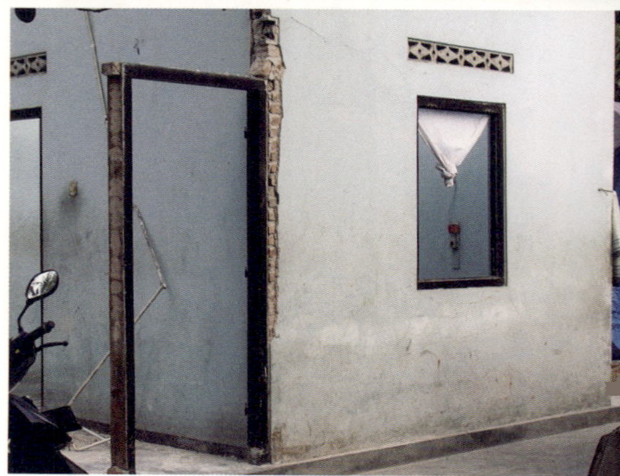

# Xu Tan

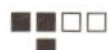

***Research for* "Searching for Keywords: Life, Survival,"** Photo, Indonesia, 2007

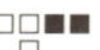

***Searching for Keywords: Life, Survival***, Installation, 2008

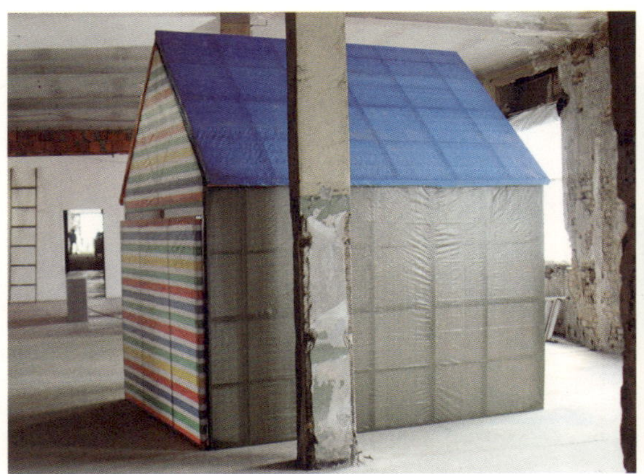

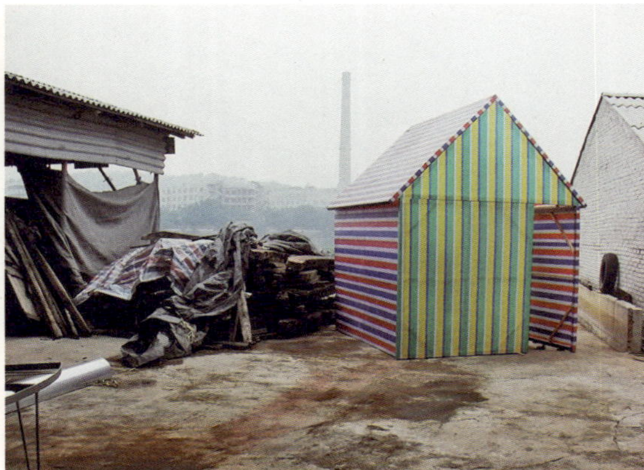

In the early 1990s, Xu Tan joined the “Big Tail Elephant Group” in Guangzhou with Lin Yinlin, Chen Shaoxiong, and Liang Juhui. The aim of this group was to develop critical strategies for negotiating the rapidly changing economic and cultural life in southern China, where the first wave of urban development had been stimulated by a special economic policy. They started to turn bars, outside restaurants, and underground parks into exhibition venues, and the activities they brought into Chinese art scenes made them become some of the radical artistis of the 1990s. Xu Tan acted more as a thinker rather than as a visual artist. Some of his works were difficult to define “as art or not” at that time, but they become more significant today.

Since 2000, Xu Tan has been interested in rediscovering the Chinese life value in the new historic context through multimedia, which always reflects the invisible conflicts of daily life within the Chinese context in a new global age. He started to become interested in the relationship between vocabulary systems and the system of living in 2005: “Suppose you could find the simplest and most essential vocabulary structure to help a person accomplish his or her basic ex-

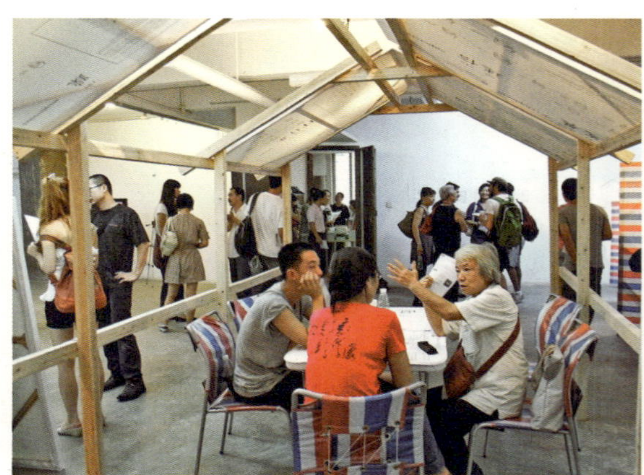

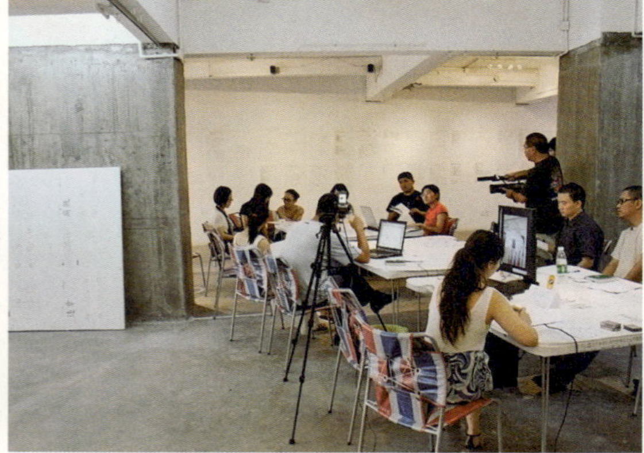

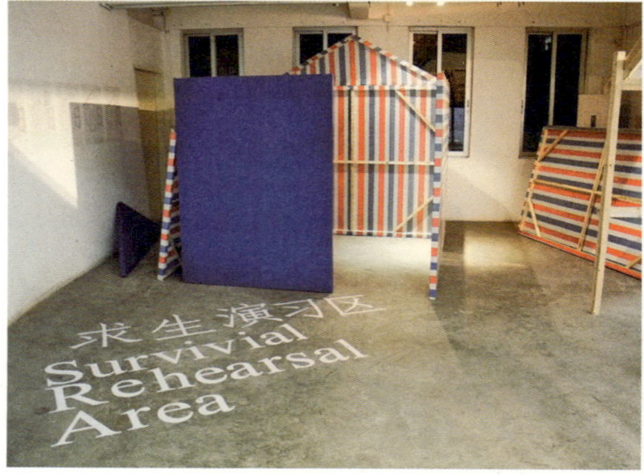


*Keywords School—Guangzhou*, Vitamin Creative Space, Guangzhou, 2009

istence in society. The point is that this kind of vocabulary system is actually of vital importance, and we have to think about at what point and from which side the vocabulary system intersects with the system of existence." Based on this interest, he authored his *Searching for Keywords* research based on his observation of Chinese society: he develops an unique method of "Searching for Keywords" as a communication tool to generate group discussion and different kinds of dialogues. This has ultimately shaped the first version of the Keywords School—a school as a new model of public space. There have been 125 Chinese keywords collected by the artist within the last two years of his research, and these keywords have been used as the basic interactive study material for communication in classes, as they reflect collective social consciousness and the multi-social landscape within the Chinese context. It's a school without predetermined goal; the artist, the "students," and all of the participants shape the form of the school together, through discussion and dialogues. "We" are creating art. Nevertheless, Keywords School is not the end of the project, but rather a temporary outcome of the process which will lead to new paths in a journey.

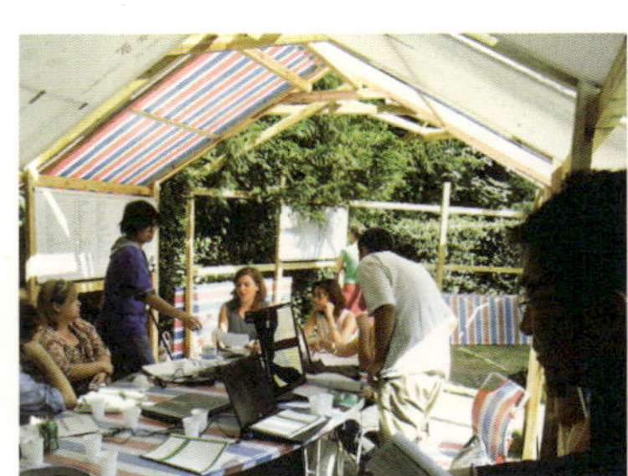

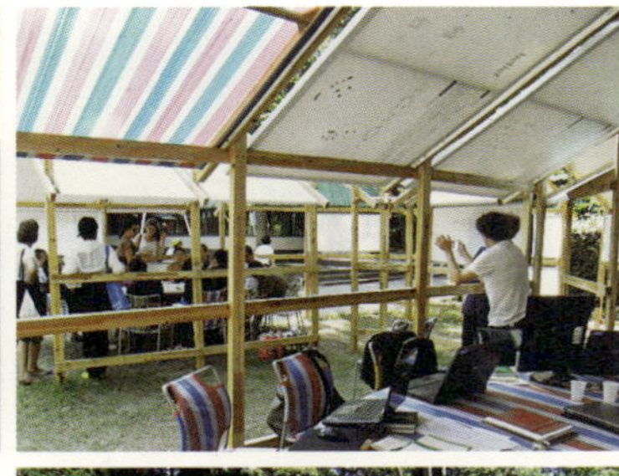

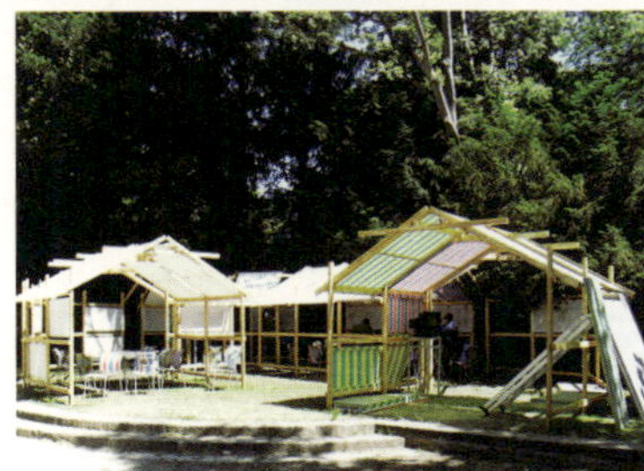

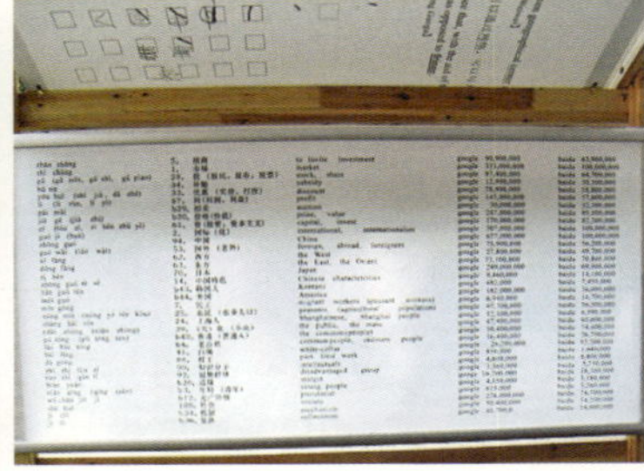

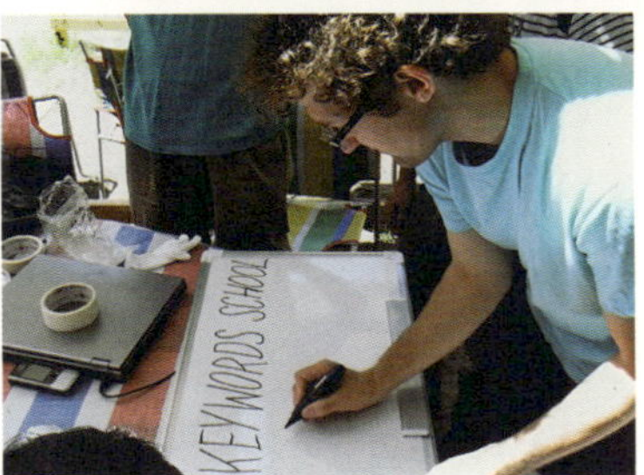


***Keywords School—Venice***, Giardini, the 53rd Venice Biennale, Venice, 2009; all images: Courtesy Vitamin Creative Space

*Hu Fang —*

How many people have you interviewed altogether during the *Searhing for Keywords* process in the last two years?

*Xu Tan —*

At the moment, some of the words and texts are merely a portion of the project. I reckon there must have been about twenty or so people interviewed in Zhang Jiang (Shanghai), and about twenty or so artists all over the country. Aside from those, there had been more interviews done in Guangzhou and Shenzhen.

*Hu Fang —*

The main method of research for *Keywords* was through the medium of interviews and dialogues. Are interviews, for you, a methodology that is more vivid and effective?

*Xu Tan —*

I do attempt other methods, for instance through Google or Baidu, to do my research. However, the videotaping of an interview produces a visual medium which is very important to me. A voice recording without images would be a totally different thing altogether. For me, this image, the expression of a person and his environment, are absolutely integral factors in the linguistic realm. Moreover, all of the interviews were direct, impromptu ones, and the immediacy of them is also very essential.

*Hu Fang —*

Yet the final video work that was exhibited had some post-production work which you had done, notably the slowing down of the speed of the dialogues.

*Xu Tan —*

I altered both the speed and pitch of the recordings, but that did not change their sense of immediacy and directness. This is because I want to accentuate people's self-consciousness and their surroundings. Also, I had specially chosen specific angles for the shots, such that I can film the person in such a way that is in accordance to the final presentation.

*Hu Fang —*

*Dictionary of Keywords* is basically developed through these interviews and dialogues. When you were editing the work, did you carry out a process of analyzing the words?

*Xu Tan —*

Yes, the process of developing *Dictionary of Keywords* includes looking for various keywords and then categorizing them, which in itself is a sort of analysis. However the kind of records I create is not based on a kind of scientific research or investigative sampling of society. The manner with which we encounter our material samples is not the same as the social sciences' investigations. Perhaps this indicates some sort of simulation at play—after all, simulation is related to the notion of play and gaming.

On another note, I think it could be meaningful too if we analyze this from the perspective of linguistics. However this could well be a very demanding job. For instance, in Chinese, many important phrases have a strong "a" intonation in them, such as "prosper" ("fa da"), or "to beat" ("da"); some words that possess a deeper, unspoken meaning have a more modest sound to their vowels. Conjectures like these would be regarded as unprofessional by professional linguists, but it renders itself interesting when viewed from the perspective of video art.

*Hu Fang —*

In fact, do the keywords that emerge from this work reveal your personal interest in the link between social consciousness and individual mindfulness? A lot of words have concrete conversational meanings in a linguistic environment. However, they can transcend these concrete meanings from their common realm of understanding and take on a symbolic significance.

*Xu Tan —*

From another perspective, this whole project is similar to a kind of linguistic game. But through this sort of game, it can develop a kind of symbolic correspondence with reality. We always say that art is mythology. Well then, language is like a kind of structure too. I feel that we cannot view keywords as a real reaction of contemporary society. We call them "keywords"—"keywords" are "key." What this says is: you can derive some things from these sorts of linguistic games, and these things are provided for according to the rules of the game. You could, for instance, say that a lot of Chinese artists talk about "relations"—work relations, public relations. The word "relations" is used very frequently, and perhaps it cannot really explain any problems. Maybe this community of people use it more often, or maybe the folks who were interviewed today uttered this phrase more often today; this is something we can't be sure of. However, by treating them as keywords, an intriguing situation arises. You can sense some sort of symbolism within. That is to say, we Chinese people have a great interest in relations between people, one which is evident and fascinating. I'd mentioned before that our society is really one that is collective and communal, yet there are some artists like Wang Jianwei, who in his interviews repeats the phrase "collective" numerous times. That is why in fact, through this method—which is akin to spotting the ball that falls off-court—you can begin to sense such conceptual matter. You may vaguely wonder how these artists have entered the world of art or how this road toward entering the art world is structured.

Hence, I didn't really want to embark upon a discourse about society through the idea keywords. Rather, I feel that there is a relatively large proportion of possible linguistic games here. I recall something I saw while on a train: some young people looking very serious as they played a game of "killer," and the people around them all found this hard to believe. I feel that through keywords, we can construct a kind of game akin to this.

*Hu Fang —*

I think the topic of keywords comes a lot from your perspective in your personal practice, to look for a kind of immediate understanding of the situation as well as a way of participating in it at once. Words are therefore regarded as a sort of crucial material for your work. They link up the flow of consciousness with changes in the society as a whole.

*Xu Tan —*

Yes, I feel that this "linking up" which you speak of is an urgent and essential concept. Hans Ulrich Obrist once asked me: What is the difference between what you do and Western conceptual art? I think that this is a very important question because it compels us to consider our understanding of conceptual art. For me, I reckon that conceptual art of the 1970s placed more importance on the play within the concept itself, whereas for us today, our game with conceptual notions deals more with linguistic games. Our direction for works is built from there on, and hence we create a closer relationship with our own construction of concepts and that which determines their contents.

Therefore, whether conceptual art is still in its framework is no longer important. What we are doing is something that deals with consciousness in our reality and environment today. I feel that to force this into a set model would be detrimental. I also feel that this activity into consciousness is not merely happening among Chinese artists; many young artists in the West influenced by globalization and intercultural exchange are also creating similar works.

The reason why I still want to use the phrase "game" here is that we were just talking about how it is a notion that is used in linguistics and conceptualization of social realities. Art is indeed a great game, but it differs from the usual fun games of daily life. The two "games" certainly have disparate meanings in this case.

*Hu Fang* —

The state of constant change in Chinese society today makes it appear like it possesses infinite potential. It is precisely this potential which results in its being in a seemingly unresolved state. So this strong sense of fluidity can affect the way in which art enters society, as well as foster a more vibrant and optimistic environment.

*Xu Tan* —

I don't believe that whatever it is we are optimistic about will definitely become a social reality. When we are feeling positive, all it indicates is that we believe we may have a chance, and to say that we have a chance is, like you mentioned, an indication that the future is not bright. Moreover, on the one hand, this future—which isn't necessarily brilliant—accentuates to the whole world how unresolved it is; on the other hand, it precisely proves that this society still possesses some sort of energy. I feel that in its entirety, this situation is very meaningful. I think that this aspect is evident in the works of artists such as Cao Fei.

*Hu Fang* —

Should this sort of change also provide a sort of suggestion to activities related to the new perspective on knowledge and meaning—that is, to reject strict definitions and either/or propositions?

*Xu Tan* —

I feel that in terms of the developments and vicissitudes of human culture, when it is at its brightest, it also means that it will be on the decline soon. I reckon that there are two parallels in the epistemological activities of humankind. For instance, just as we need two legs to walk, there are logical ways of acting and their illogical, crazy diametrical opposites. These two are constantly mutually reacting. What is interesting is: in China, the formulation of a logical construct and that of a counter-logical one lies in the consciousness of the same person, who is building up a very fascinating mode of thinking for the future.

This is what I told an artist yesterday, and he said that the concept of keywords is one that comes from the West, and isn't suitable for use or consideration in China. What I meant to say earlier is precisely this: the concept of keywords is indeed invented by the West, but this term doesn't hold much importance in the environment of Western linguistics; rather, it is extremely appropriate in China, and is a term used often in Chinese. In China, keywords are used widely—you can see keywords in the newspapers and magazines everyday—and this is simply because in China, keywords are themselves unclear entities. They are not the sort of products derived from logic and analysis in the manner that the West is used to. If we say that the West specializes in the invention, use, promotion and development of tools, then we can also claim that we are already used to not having a crutch to aid us in our progress.

Hence, because keywords are such fuzzy conceptual tools in our context, I feel that this methodology for thought coincides well with the kind of inner consciousness that we are accustomed to.

*Hu Fang —*

As I was reading these keywords, I could sense their connection to some sort of collective consciousness. But this relationship is within this project, which seems rather ambiguous. I can feel that these keywords are not actually entities meant for analysis, but rather are meant to be media to be encountered and experienced by everyone.

*Xu Tan —*

Right, the meanings of these keywords are really manifested within the ebb and flow of collective consciousness. For instance, I sense that Chinese people are more concerned about societal living than ways of creation. I also feel that this in itself is a kind of collective consciousness and knowledge. I think this covers quite an extensive arena and a lot of things are not really the way I imagine or believe them to be. At the same time, the sort of investigations that we do cannot accurately depict the movement of this collective consciousness. However, you can vaguely sense the movement itself, and it is precisely why this experience seems so much more alluring and intriguing.

*Hu Fang —*

The whole research process of keywords is a comprehensive effort, and includes a live workshop, a dictionary, and a Web site. It has become a multimedia process-led project. If the dictionary and Web site provide audiences with means of "self-learning" or "self-discovery," then what is the focus of the live workshop in terms of interaction with audiences?

*Xu Tan —*

I don't think the project is solely a sort of discourse or exchange on a linguistic level. It touches on myriad experiences that entwine the Chinese language with corresponding information emerging from Chinese society. This so-called artistic experience involves elements of knowledge, but can certainly also be attributed to the current interest in China in being "hot" or "hip." If people had absolutely no interest whatsoever with Chinese society today, then the workshop would never had happened. Furthermore, the live workshop also presented propositions for culture and collective knowledge in the future. If everyone is not keen on the various modes of thinking and whether these can create true culture of value, then the workshop would also be hard to execute. This particular point is something that I am interested in discussing further with the audience. At the same time, through these participants, I can learn about the disparate keywords that they offer from various societies with different backgrounds and culture. Therefore, the workshop itself has become a means of extended research for me.

*Hu Fang —*

Through this process, the research into keywords has become a means for self-learning and individual growth, while finally you aim to capture some essence that is constantly altering.

*Xu Tan —*

Why not create another meaningful game in the linguistic environment of our society today? In this game, the way you play, the things you discover will always be fascinating. The future will not be the same as today's reality. Perhaps it will have more meaning than what we have today—this is absolutely possible. That is exactly why this project presents a sense of vigor as well.

The proposal is for a new video installation featuring the Singaporean artist Ming Wong's one-man reinterpretation of the Italian film *Teorema*, made in 1968 by Pier Paolo Pasolini, a distinguished Italian writer, poet, and filmmaker. This new work will combine Ming Wong's exploration of performativity, language, and identity with the dissection of one of the most "visionary" films from Italy.

Teorema

The story of how a handsome stranger with a mysterious divine force enters the lives of a typical upper-middle-class Italian family, and transforms their lives. Then, one day, the "guest" leaves, as suddenly and mysteriously as the way he came, and each member of the household loses the identity he or she had before. The daughter goes from a dancing free spirit to a rigid catatonic state, the son abandons his studies to become an artist, the mother rediscovers her sexuality in her life with young men off the streets, the father leaves all material things behind and walks alone in a volcanic landscape, and the maid goes back to her village and performs miracles.

This video installation is a contemporary take on the film *Teorema* made fifty years ago. Ming Wong will play all the characters (the "guest," father, mother, teenage son and daughter, and maid) in five separate videos representing the trajectories of each member of the household, so that all five journeys will be observed concurrently. The linear narrative is thus spread out to show the effects that the "guest" has on the Italian hosts.

This will be a development from what the artist started with his reinterpretations of the films of P. Ramlee in *Four Malay Stories* (selected for the Jakarta Biennale 2009), and with his recent video installations in Berlin, inspired by the German filmmaker Rainer Fassbinder.

The artist Ming Wong will portray all the characters and deliver his lines, this time in Italian. With very little knowledge of the Italian language, his struggle with the pronunciation and the repetition of the words and phrases will form a key aspect of the work. The audience will observe a male Chinese Singaporean attempting to portray different Italian characters *revealing themselves at the point when they have lost their sense of identity*. It is not a "spoof" or "send-up," as the attempts by the artist, though humorous to watch at times, are sincere, serious, and laborious.

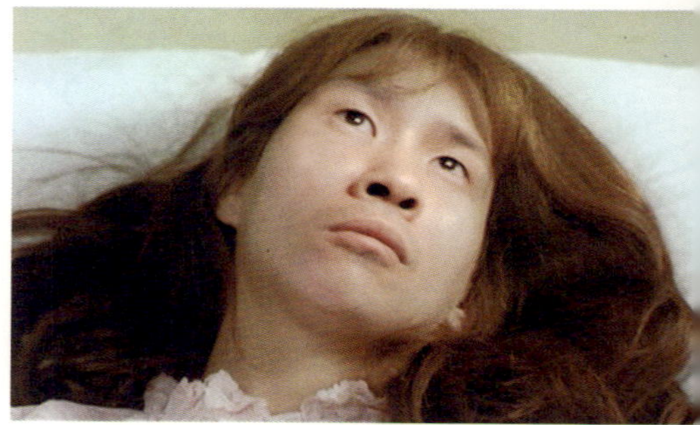

# Ming Wong

***Devo Partire. Domani. / I must go. Tomorrow.*** / 明天， 我要走。Cast of characters

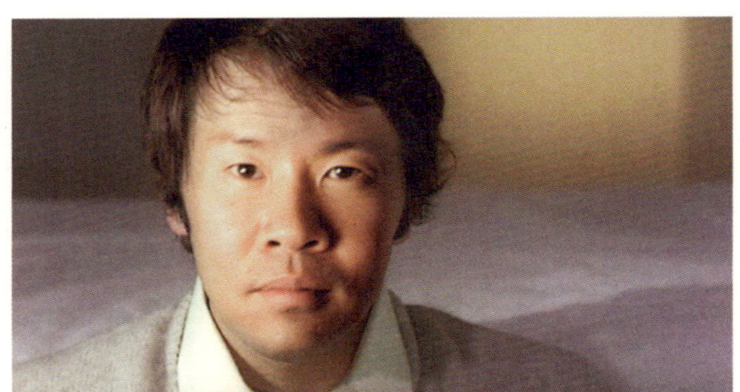

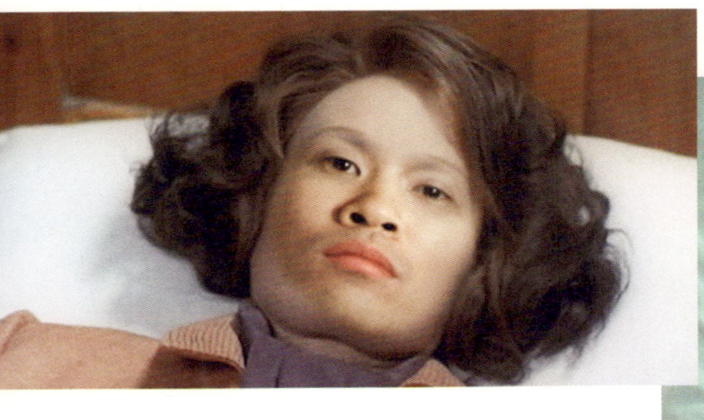

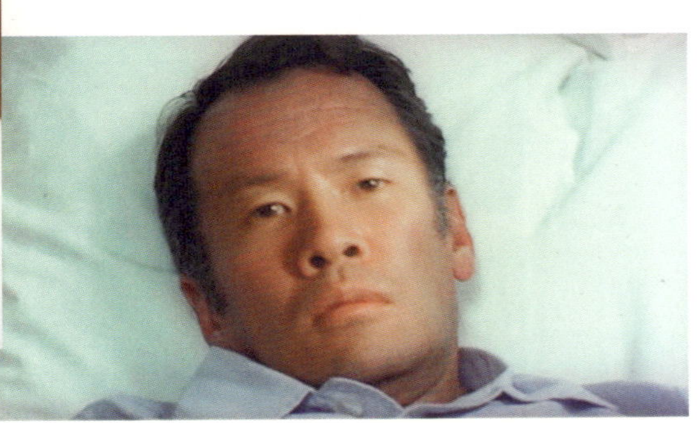

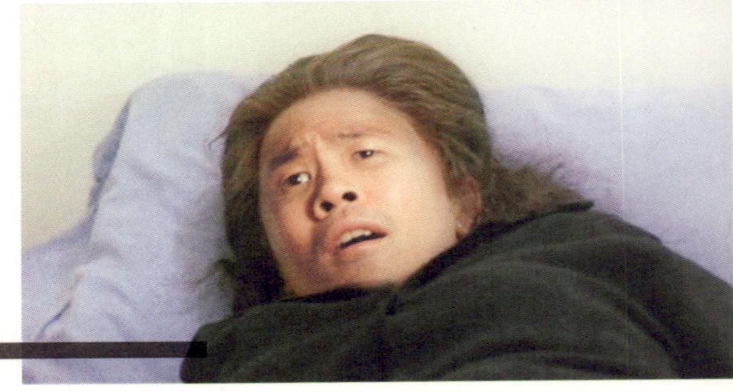

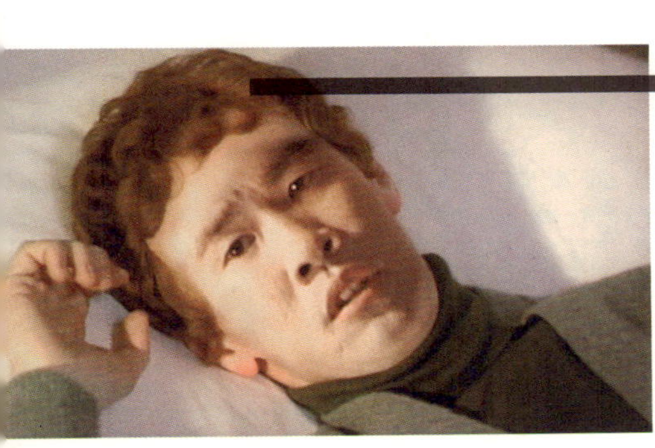

The tagline of the film on its release is: “There are only 923 words spoken in *Teorema*—but it says everything!” Most of the dialogue relates to the confessions by each character to the “guest” on how his or her life has been transformed thanks to the “guest.” The lines are non–naturalistic, and have a timeless, poetic resonance to them, which when being delivered imperfectly by the artist, refocuses the audience on the words themselves and on their possible meanings. The film that Pasolini created is itself open-ended and ambiguous; Ming Wong’s “transformation” of the film, as the “guest” himself (from Singapore), will add another layer of meaning to the work.

Each video will trace the character’s trajectory: seduction, revelation, transformation.

> Example of the son’s revelation:
>
> “I don’t recognize myself anymore. Because what made me like the others is destroyed.
>
> “I was just like anybody, with so many faults perhaps, mine and those of the world. “You made me different, took me out of the natural order of things.
>
> “While you were near me, I did not realize it. I understand it now that you’re leaving me. And the awareness of losing you, has become the awareness of my diversity.
>
> “What will become of me from now on? What will the future be like living with a me, that hasn’t anything to do with me?
>
> “I have to get to the bottom of this… diversity which you have shown me, which is my true, frightened nature, and even if I don’t want it, won’t this put me against everything and everyone?”

The artist’s past work has mostly been shot indoors in studios. For this project, he would like to extend his practice by shooting *on location* in Italy. This is in response to his time spent in Italy preparing for the Venice Biennale, his contact with the country, and his introduction to its people, language, culture, and politics. He believes that the landscape and setting play important roles in the Italian identity; he would like to film himself as different archetypal characters against the “real” setting in Italy—as a stranger in the locations of Italy—in order to heighten the distance between the real and the supposed, and to reveal gaps in the authenticity of “Italian-ness.”

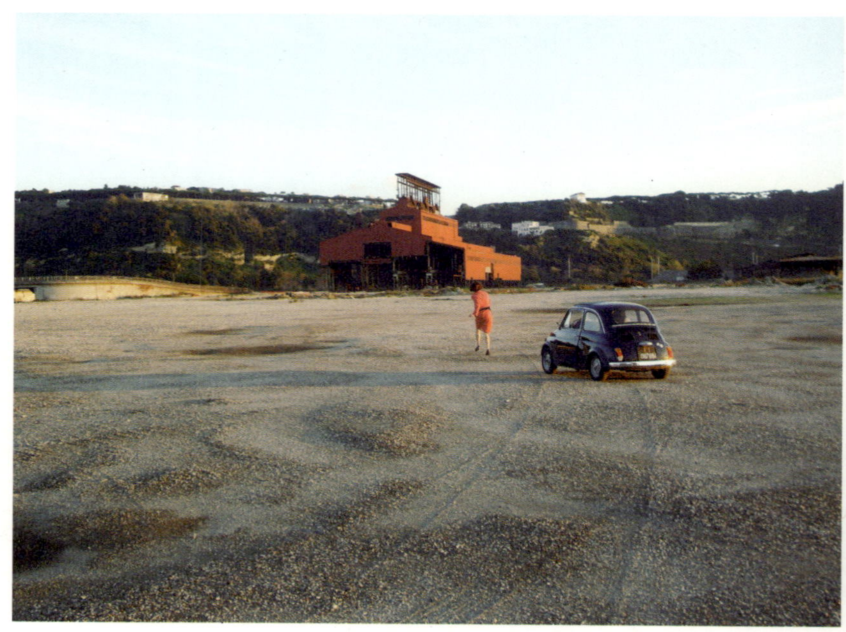

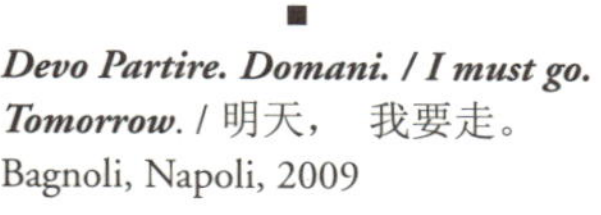

■

***Devo Partire. Domani. / I must go. Tomorrow.*** / 明天， 我要走。
Bagnoli, Napoli, 2009

Ming Wong’s latest film installation *(Devo Partire. Domani.)* is co-commissioned by the Napoli Teatro Festival Italia, premiering in June 2010; all images courtesy the artist

Proposal PART 2

*Filmic Structures*

The film scenes are deconstructed into five linear narratives, one for each member of the household: father, mother, son, daughter, and maid.

Each narrative comprises three parts:

1—**Temptation**: When the stranger appears in their lives and seduces them.

2—**Confession**: When the stranger announces his departure, they each communicate their internal conflicts

3—**Revelation**: When the stranger has departed and each character embarks on his or her own journey into the unknown.

*Technical/Physical Structures*

Each narrative is played concurrently on separate plasma screens, located next to each other. Hence the viewer is able to follow the characters' narratives together—that is, five temptations and five confessions happen concurrently on five screens.

However, when the narratives arrive at Part 3: Revelation, as each character embarks on his or her own journey into the unknown, the five plasma screens begin to move in separate directions. This will force the audience to choose which character to follow. The breakup of the household signals the breakup of the audience, as individuals within it move in different directions. The maid ascends to a height, viewable only at a distance, and this should be timed to coincide with the image of the maid floating above the farmhouse. At the end of the cycle, the videos go black, and the screens return to the original starting point, and the cycle starts again. (Please refer to the sketches on page 180 and 181 to have an idea of distances and directions.)

*Some notes*

The Revelation allows the characters to make choices about their lives, and to embark on their individual journeys into the unknown, in order to escape the crises in their identities. The members of the audience also then must make decisions about which narrative they want to follow, to find out which narrative means the most to them, and to disperse the passive viewing crowd.

As the artist plays all the characters, and as the artist is the stranger, he is, in effect, seducing himself, confessing to himself, and embarking on his own journeys into the unknown. Here, the artist is the "divine" figure, the stranger with the mysterious ability to make one forsake all that one knew about his or her own identity.

Part I (Temptation) & II (Confession)
Ming Wong—Sketch for *Devo Partire. Domani. / I must go. Tomorrow. /* 明天， 我要走。

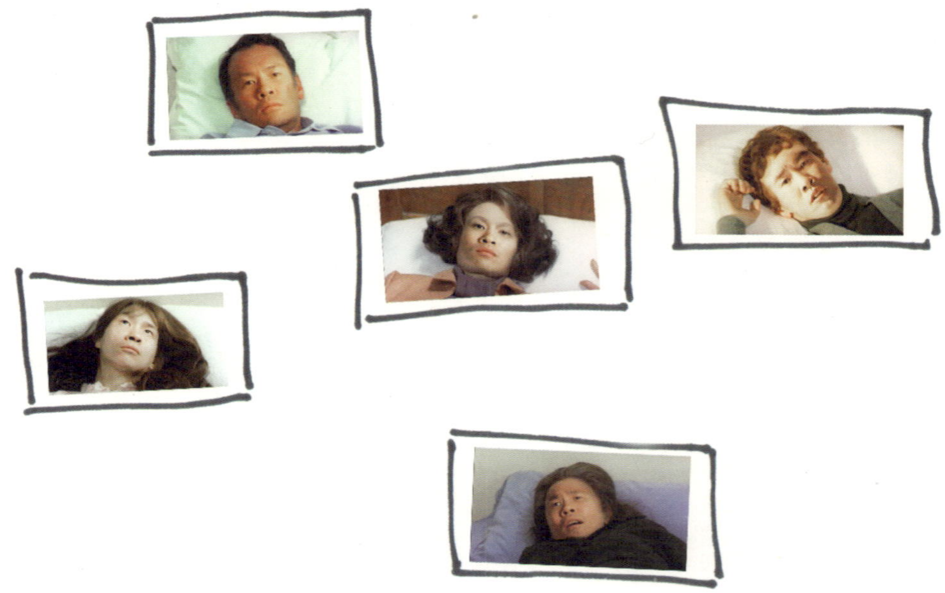

Part III (Revelation)

Ming Wong—Sketch for *Devo Partire. Domani. / I must go. Tomorrow. /*
明天，　我要走。

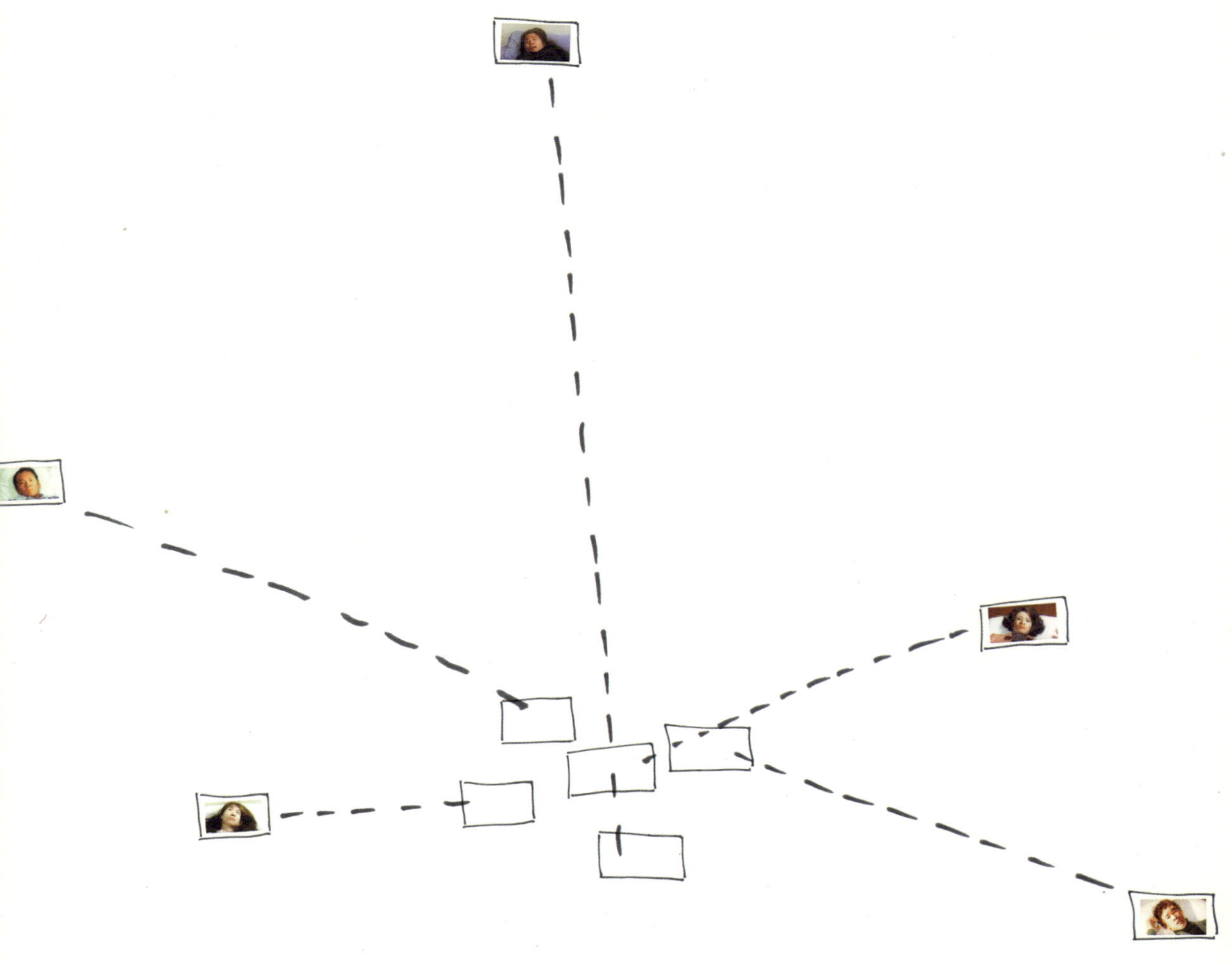

The building is composed of slabs layered at 350-millimeter intervals. These slabs can be used as chairs, desks, floors, roofs, shelves, stairs, lightings, openings, gardens, and structure. The 350 millimeters are based on the size of human activities. For example, 350 millimeters is the height of chairs, and 700 millimeters (350 multiplied by two) is the height of desks, and 175 millimeters (350 divided by two) is the height of the steps of stairs. This succession of such different levels creates a variety of places. As they seek out functions for these places by instinct, the inhabitants manage to dwell in this topography called a "house."

We made this plan not to create a functional machine but to create a more fundamental "place for living." "Place" might be said as "prompt" or "key," in other words. This is a primitive place like a cloud, a nest, or a cave. We believe that this project can be a trial of a new prototype of residences.

This house can be said to be inconvenient. However, in this project, inconvenience does not have any negative meanings, such as "impractical," "uncomfortable," or "not well equipped." We think that inconvenience can prompt multiple human activities. It is similar to the relationship between nature and men. Inconvenience serves as a possibility, then.

Now, is it possible "to design" such inconvenience, indefiniteness, and unexpected surprise? For this purpose, we tried a method of "relationship between parts." By using this method, we design architecture from local orders, not from the whole one but from a relationship between parts. Then we can make ambiguity, imperfectness, and order live together in one building. The most complicated and ambiguous thing is the simplest, which amounts to new simplicity. Here, 350 millimeters (the intervals of slabs) serves as the local order. 350 millimeters is the new module of architecture. It is about one-tenth of the conventional story height. The new relationship between architecture and the human body is born there.

Principal Use: **Residence** / Structural Composition: **Steel** / Design Period: **2001** / Design Team: **Sou Fujimoto Architects** / Consultant: **Jun Sato, Structural Engineer**

# Sou Fujimoto Architects

*Primitive Future House*, 2001

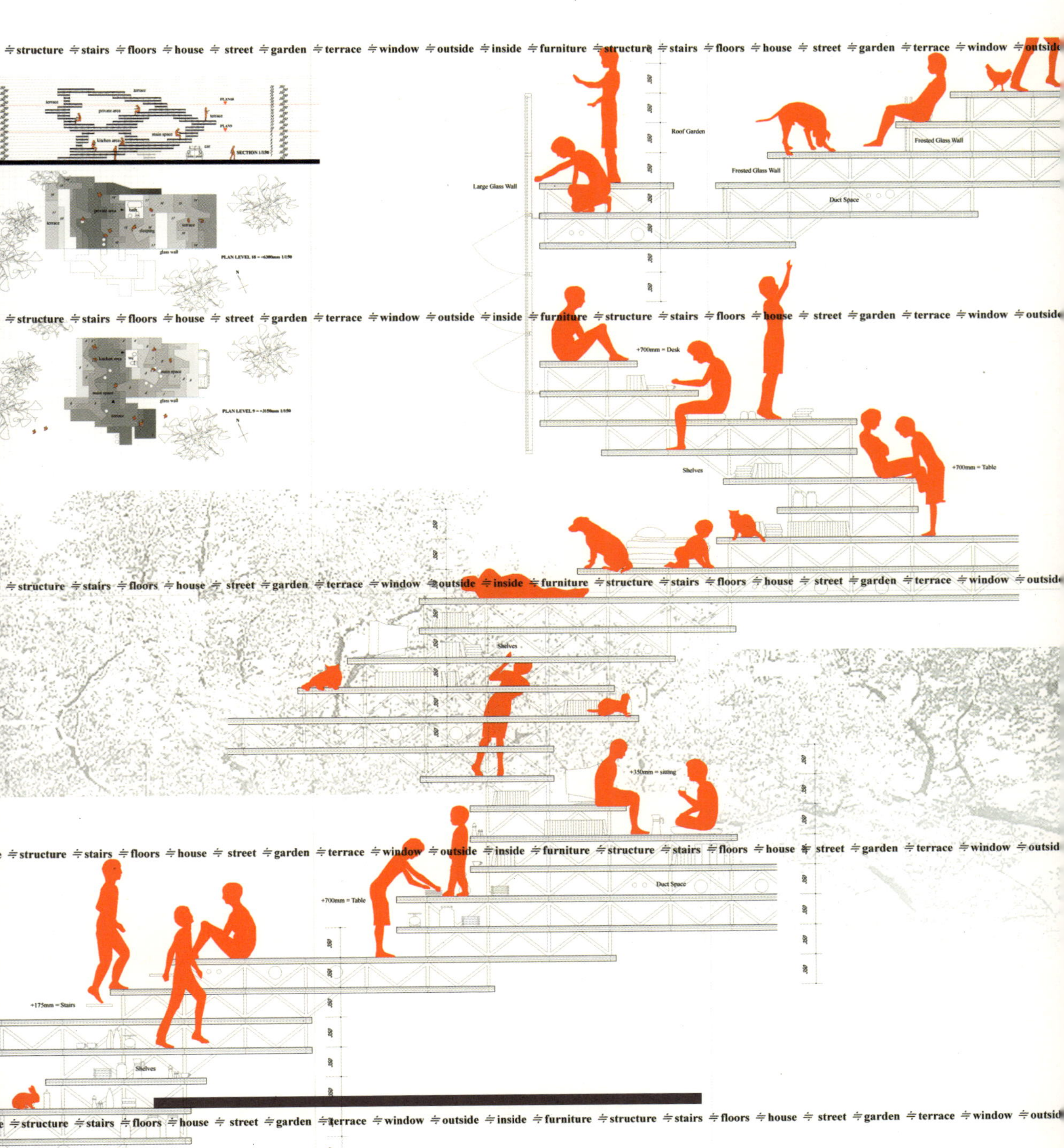


Hu Fang
**Sou Fujimoto Architects**
Primitive Future House

# Futuro primitivo
# Primitive future
## Sou Fujimoto

**1. ¿NIDO O CUEVA?**

El nido y la cueva son estadios primitivos de la arquitectura, pero, en cierto sentido, representan realidades opuestas.

Para la persona (o animal) que lo habita, el nido puede describirse como "lugar funcional" acondicionado de forma acogedora. En cambio, la cueva es ajena a sus habitantes. Es un lugar que acontece de manera natural, sin tener en cuenta si es acogedor o no para que una persona lo habite. No obstante, tampoco es un lugar poco apropiado para vivir. La cueva presenta huecos y requiebros, así como expansiones y contracciones inesperadas del espacio. Al entrar en una cueva, la gente redescubre cómo habitar estos accidentes geográficos: en esos huecos parece que se puede dormir, esa altura parece apropiada para comer, esos rincones parecen un poco más privados, aquí podría poner este libro. Así, las personas empiezan a habitar gradualmente estas características geográficas. En otras palabras, una cueva no es funcional, sino heurística. En lugar de un funcionalismo coercitivo, consiste en un lugar estimulante que permite una gran variedad de actividades. Cada día sus habitantes descubrirán nuevos usos para un mismo lugar.

Por tanto, nido y cueva parecen conceptos similares pero en realidad son opuestos. Un lugar funcional, hecho para la gente, y un lugar que existe antes que la gente y que es distinto, ajeno a ella. Y precisamente porque es distinto, existen oportunidades de descubrimientos imprevistos. Por eso, al decir cueva no estamos diciendo que el aspecto externo deba ser el de una cueva, sino que esa cualidad de cueva puede imaginarse como una forma pura que podríamos denominar la caverna transparente.

Más que en nidos, creo que la arquitectura del futuro debería consistir en espacios parecidos a cuevas. Sería más enriquecedor. El problema es que la caverna en sí es una topografía natural que produce efectos de otredad inesperados en las personas. ¿Es posible una "cueva artificial" en "una arquitectura creada por el hombre"? La gran incógnita es si se puede realizar de forma intencionada algo que exista sin propósito, o algo que vaya más allá del propósito.

Es precisamente la idea de una caverna artificial y transparente lo que anuncia las posibilidades de la arquitectura del futuro.

**1. NEST OR CAVE?**

The nest and the cave are both primal states of architectu but in a sense these two are opposites.

For the person (or animal) living in it, a nest can be described as a hospitably arranged "functional place." By co trast, a cave is there regardless of people. It is a place tha occurs naturally irrespective of whether it is hospitable o inhospitable for a person to inhabit. Yet neither is it uns able as a place in which to live. In a cave there are variou contours and hollows, as well as unexpected expansions and contractions. When people set foot in a cave, they re cover how to inhabit these geographical features. These h lows seem like they can be slept in, that height seems go for eating, those nooks are slightly more private spaces, I could put this book here; in this way, they gradually beg to inhabit these geographical features. In other words, a cave is not functional but it is heuristic. Rather than a co cive functionalism, it is a stimulating place in which var ous activities are enabled. Each day, people will discover new usages for a place.

Thus, the nest and the cave seem similar but are actually opposite concepts. A functional place made for people, a a place existing prior to people that is for people an "oth place. And because it is other, it is suffused with chances for unanticipated discoveries. Therefore, having called it cave, its outer appearance does not have be like a cave, bu rather the quality of a cave itself might be imagined as a pure form that we could call a transparent cave.

Rather than nests, I think that in future architecture should comprise cave-like places. I think that would be ri er. The problem is that a cave itself is a naturally occurri topography that provides people with rich discoveries of otherness. Is an "artificial cave" possible in "architecture made by people"? The big question is whether something that is without purpose, or something that exceeds purpose, can be made intentionally.

It is precisely an artificial, transparent cave that indicate the possibilities for future architecture.

■

***Sou Fujimoto**, 2G International Architecture Review,* no. 50 (Barcelona: Gustavo Gili, 2009), 130–131

Casa del futuro primitivo, proyecto, 2001.
Primitive Future House, project, 2001.

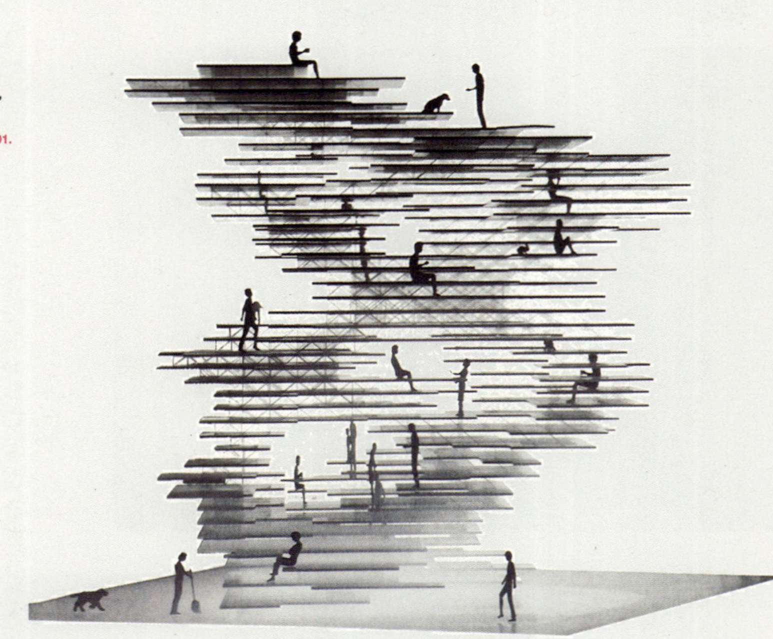

Casa Dom-Inó, estructura estándar, Le Corbusier, 1914-1915.
Dom-Inó House, standard structure, Le Corbusier, 1914-1915.



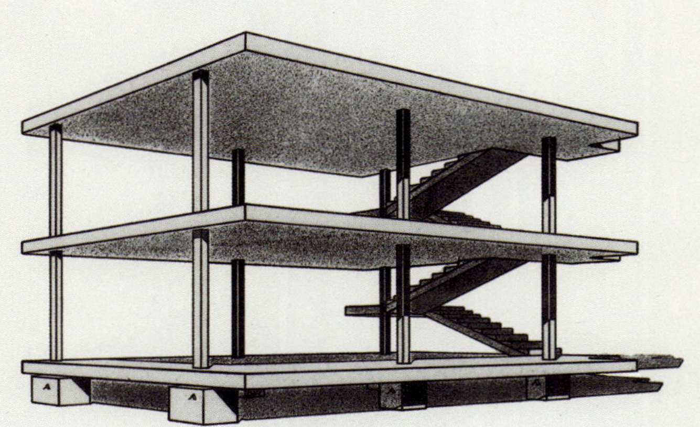

131

***Final Wooden House***, 2008
Kumamura village, Japan
(photos by Iwan Baan)

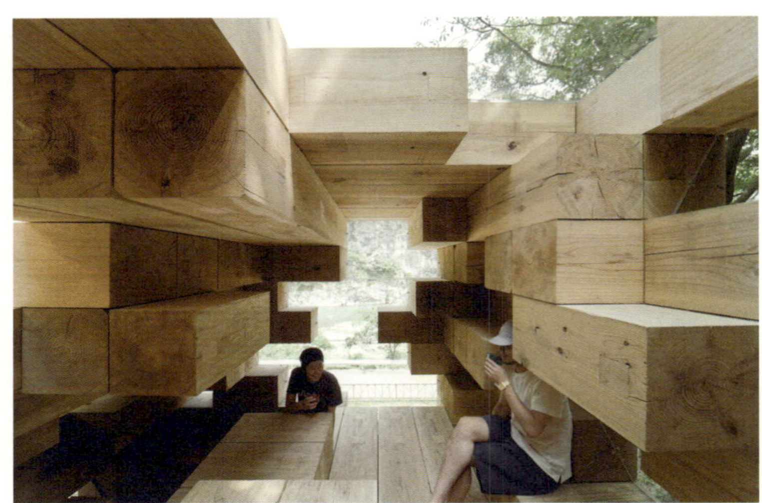

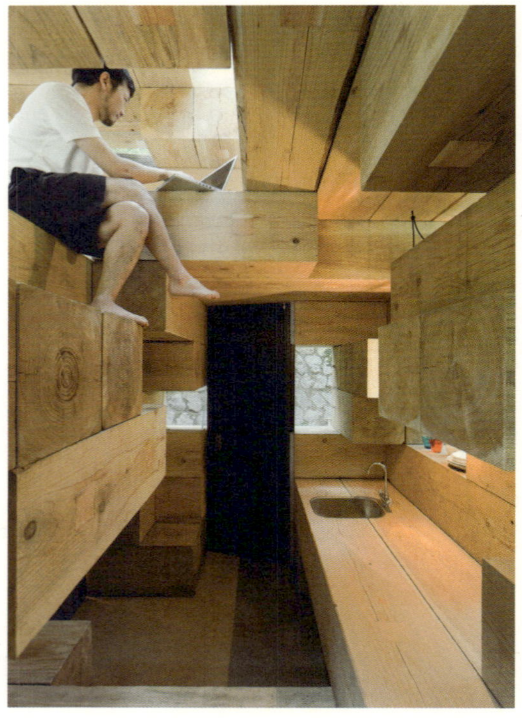

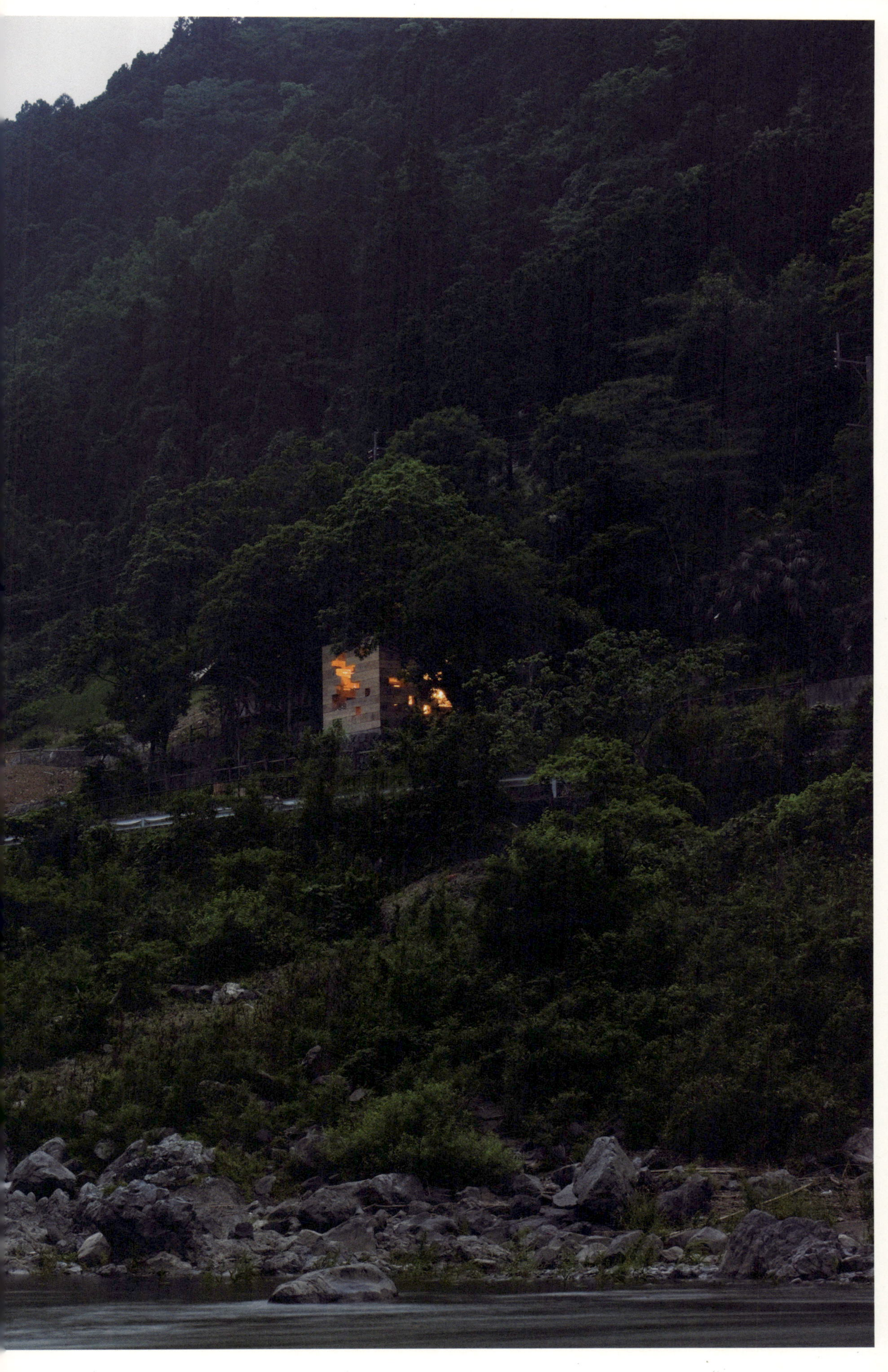

*RMB City* is a virtual art community in the online world of Second Life, initiated by the Chinese artist Cao Fei (Second Life: China Tracy) as a public platform for creativity. Officially launched in late 2008, it will continue to grow and change over its two-year run, with the participation and support of leading international art institutions and networks. The city is a laboratory for experiments in art, design, architecture, literature, cinema, politics, economy, society, and beyond.

Life is brought to *RMB City* in a few different ways. As a public space, it constitutes a contemporary, virtual version of the museum or theater, but at the same time it is itself the work that hangs on the wall or that flickers across the screen. Currently, *RMB City* is undergoing a new phase of rebirth and regeneration in which it is constantly nourished by projects that offer groundbreaking perspectives on avant-garde urban planning, and that utilize the newest forms of communication media.

Recently, cooperation with a heterogeneous group of artists, sound professionals, architects, poets, and other generally creative minds laid the foundation for the brand new video *Live in RMB City*. Officially presented at The Shiseido Gallery on the occasion of Cao Fei's solo exhibition in October 2009, *Live in RMB City* is a touching cinematic tale about the mysteries of (virtual and real) life. While wondering through the city and its new buildings, China Tracy unveils the secrets of existence to her newly born baby avatar, China Sun, in a magical journey on the border between dream and reality.

Constantly watched over by the attentive guidance of its mayor and rebalanced by oriental feng shui experts, *RMB City* has also recently trodden on the theatrical stage. Performed for the first time last November at Artissima, *RMB City Opera* is an experimental live performance work that combines real-life acting with film taken in Second Life. Its style draws from Chinese social and cultural history (specifically, Chinese Cultural Revolution propaganda operas), while its subject matter permeates the thoroughly new identity crises of our current digital era.

Within these projects, the artist questions the meaning of public space in contemporary time and pushes further the idea of public art projects for future societies.

# Cao Fei

***The Birth of RMB City,*** Video stills, 2009, 10'31"

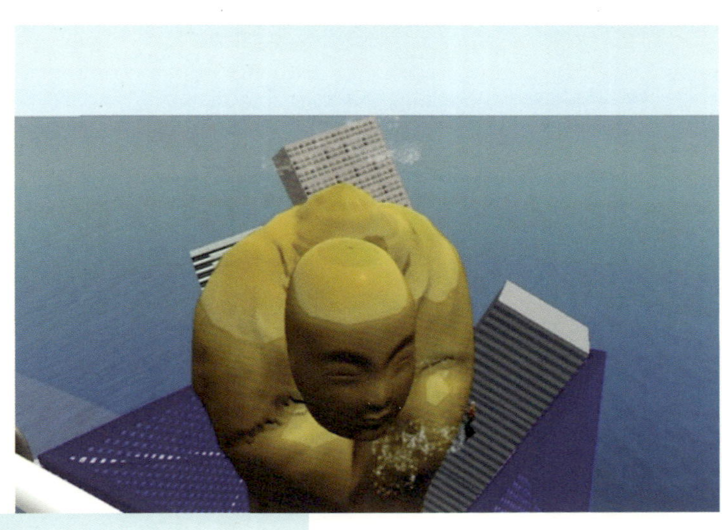

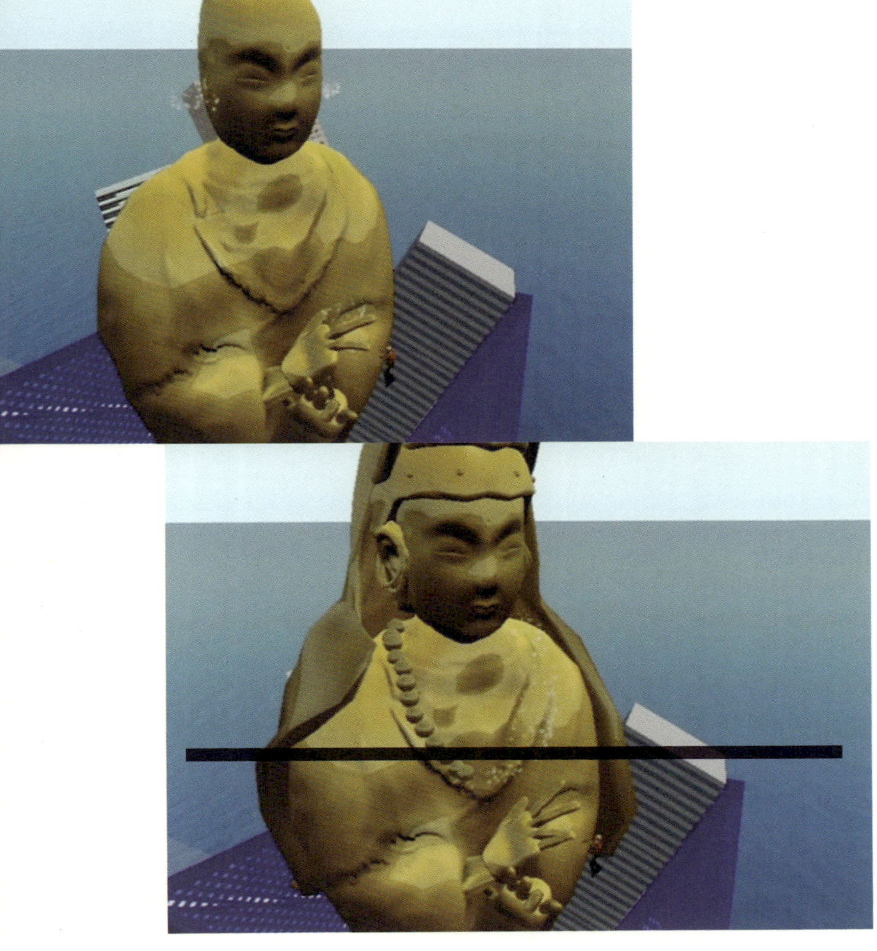

People's Limbo in RMB City

**by Cao Fei (Second Life: China Tracy)**

"People's Limbo" is a new series of interactive, experiential activities that take place in Cao Fei's *RMB City*, a fantastical community in the vast virtual world of Second Life. A reaction to the global economic crisis, the project is an exploration of the feelings of despair, denial, and loss of control that accompany financial catastrophe, as well as the simultaneous potential for progress toward rebirth, self-reliance, and freedom. In the words of Lao Tsu, "If you empty the self and relax your desires, you will know more clearly where you are heading."

Some of these games are competitive and reflect the influence of past economic realities, like one in which the visitor is thrown into the middle of a dense bubble of chaotic, bouncing balls, only to find it increasingly difficult to maneuver his or her way out, mirroring the quick loss of control that occurs as an economic bubble builds (and quickly collapses). Others, like a sustainable community garden, are meditative, and represent idealized visions of the future.
Videos of the ten new People's Limbo activities, brought to life by avatars representing such characters as Karl Marx, Mao Zedong, and a Lehman Brothers banker, serve as the real-life manifestations of the People's Limbo experience.

Master Q's Guide to Virtual Feng Shui in RMB City

**by Cao Fei (Second Life: China Tracy) and Huang He (Second Life: QueenShoe Voom)**

In this special project coinciding with the opening of *RMB City*, young Guangzhou-based artist Huang He (as Master Q) explored ways to manipulate the qi (invisible energy flow) of *RMB City* and the digital realm, while *RMB City*'s creator Cao Fei (Second Life: China Tracy) created a video interpreting this intervention.

Master Q extends feng shui, a system based on three-dimensional spatial reality, into *RMB City*, where space is compressed into folds on a flat screen, and its only genealogy is the cohesion among pixels. In this way, Huang He's virtual feng shui project looks more like a rupture than a piece of continuity. Traditional feng shui pays high respect to harmony, a presupposed optimum in which displeasure is avoided and pleasure is obtained, just as in Freud's pleasure theory. But the harmonic ideal also indicates that too much pleasure will become tension that is turned into pain, and that people should not chase pleasures limitlessly. In the virtual world (where typical physical harm is not a concern), we say we don't mind taking risks to pursue *jouissance* (unlimited pleasure and freedom). How then do we maximize the comfort or safety of the "people" in a virtual space? Or should this even be the goal at all? Through Huang He's project, we may even journey back to the origin and ask: what is well-being? What is comfortable? What is a space?

Interview Marathon in RMB City

**Cao Fei (Second Life: China Tracy)**

On March 20, 2009, to mark *RMB City*'s reinstallation in Serpentine Gallery, London, China Tracy (Real Life: Cao Fei), JuliaPeytonJones Popstar (Real Life: Julia Peyton Jones ) and HansUlrichObrist Magic (Real Life: Hans Ulrich Obrist ) had an interesting dialogue which took the form of a marathon in *RMB City*. The marathon started at the "Bird's Nest" (People's Park), after which China Tracy decided to bring the group to *RMB City*'s People's Entertainment Television (the CCTV tower replica hanging in the air), with the event finally wrapping up at one of Huang He's virtual feng shui devices—the Gourd of Wood—where three tree-shaped green beams appear when they are activated by three people. China Tracy, JuliaPeytonJones Popstar, and HansUlrichObrist Magic all enjoyed the "wood element qi," which brings kindness and peace.

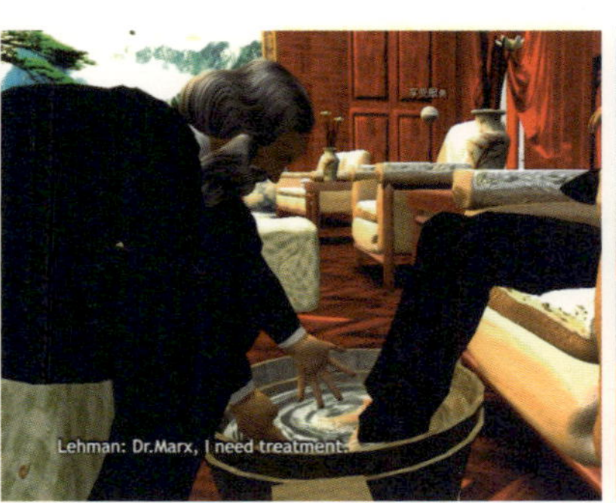


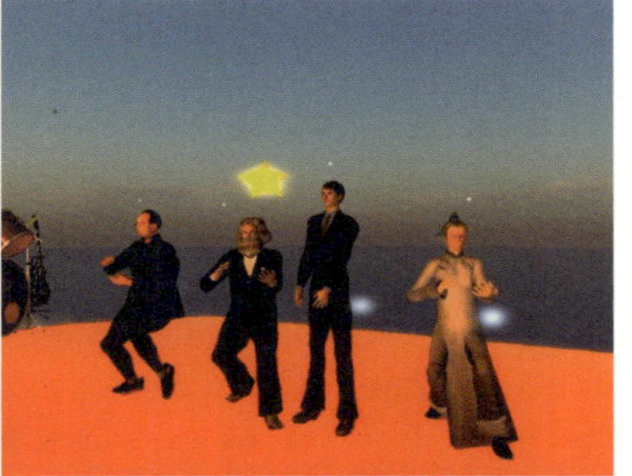

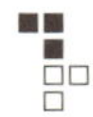

***People's Limbo in RMB City,*** Video stills, 2009, 18'58"

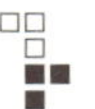

***Live in RMB City***, Video stills, 2009, 25'

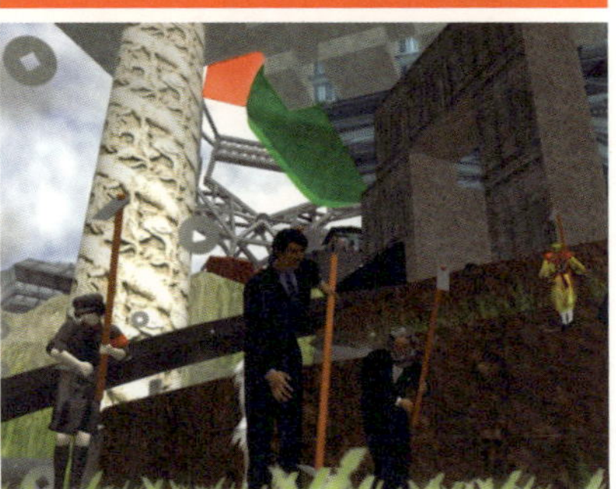

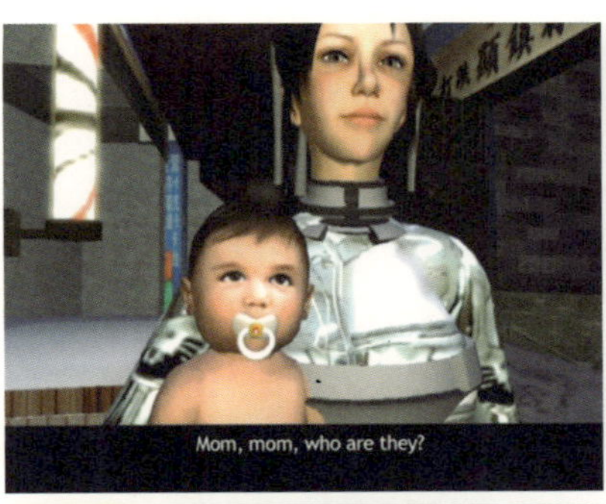


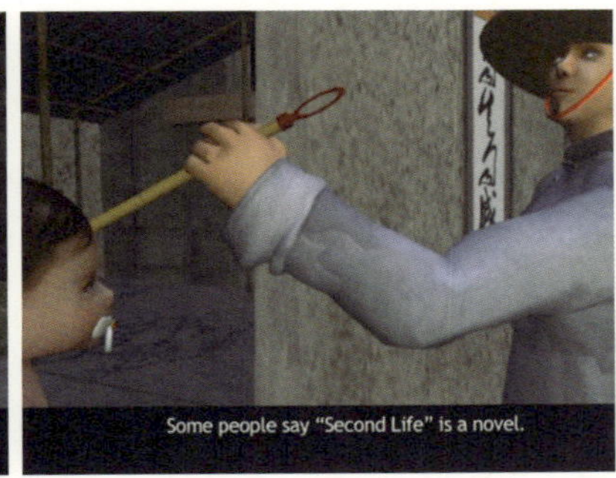


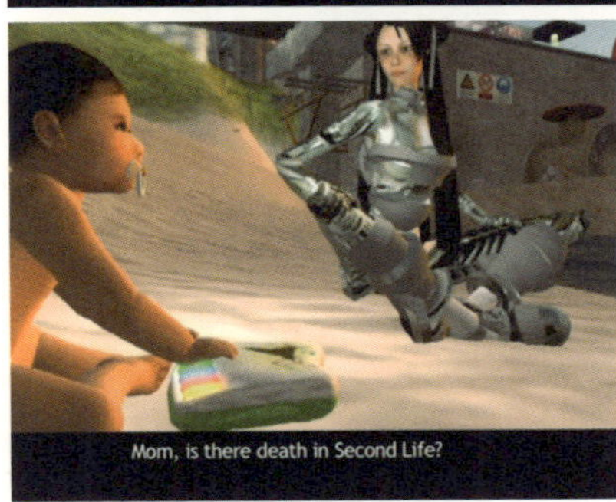

To fully utilize the possibilities of an interview in Second Life, and to touch on the issues of virtual representation vs. reality that the *RMB City* project seeks to explore, the goal of the project was to conduct an "Interview Marathon"—or rather a "relay race." The avatars HansUlrichObrist Magic and JuliaPeytonJones Popstar would be chatting with the avatar China Tracy, but who would know who was really behind the keyboard? For this event, China Tracy temporarily became the "People's Avatar," a psychic medium channeling multiple voices and visions. In the space of one hour, several real-life participants "played" China Tracy, passing the digital mask of her avatar on just as an Olympic Torch is passed from one runner's hand to the next. The resulting dialogue may form a sort of exquisite corpse, with China Tracy as the literal (virtual?) body, challenging conceptions of identity, performance, and narrative. The event was documented as an episode of RMB-TV, a new conceptual platform to examine *RMB City* as a theatrical stage. In a world where nothing is real, isn't everyone an imposter?

## Live in RMB City

**Cao Fei (Second Life: China Tracy)**

Imagine that you could be reincarnated into a new life, that you could go back to birth and take your first steps in a new world... A fantastic, exciting and unpredictable journey, the video *Live in RMB City* follows the first breaths, fears, and curiosities of newly born China Sun, the baby of China Tracy, in Second Life. The camera follows baby China Sun's wanderings and explorations in a revived *RMB City*, inspired by brand new additions created by a team of artist, writer, architect, and philosopher collaborators, and infused with a fresh stream of life.

Commissioned by Tokyo's Shiseido Gallery for a 2009 Cao Fei solo exhibition, *Live in RMB City* is a dreamy children's tale on the mysteries of (real and virtual) life. Accompanied and instructed by the attentive guidance of an extravagant cyber-mother, *RMB City*'s newest-born baby wonders through old and new buildings, weaving the net of an articulated journey between past, present, and future.

The secrets of virtual existence are slowly unveiled in *RMB City*, a world where mothers never grow old and buildings can become ice-creams, and yet the deeper meanings of life remain unanswered because, as China Sun starts to learn, there is only one way of explaining it, and that is through poetry and imagination: "If my little boat sinks, it has gone to another sea."

## Mayor Project

Every city has a mayor, and there is no exception for *RMB City*, a city that exists in the crevice between reality and virtuality, and that exchanges different values of the two different worlds. Every three months, *RMB City* inducts a new mayor, and each brings a different set of skills, ambitions, and styles to the table. We regard our mayors as leaders for *RMB City*, but not as manipulators. What we expect from our mayor is a change that he or she initiates: maybe something better, maybe something worse, but nothing stagnant. During each mayor's three-month term of office, we hope it is ultimately possible to witness the transformation in the city from a perspective of virtual virtuality.

Our mayors to date have been media executive and art collector Uli Sigg (Second Life: UliSigg Cisse), financial consultant Alan Lau (Second Life: AlanLau Nirvana), art institution director Jerome Sans (Second Life: SuperConcierge Cristole), and senior researcher in the Auto-ID Lab University of St. Gallen / ETH Zürich Erica Dubach (Second Life: E3A Digital).

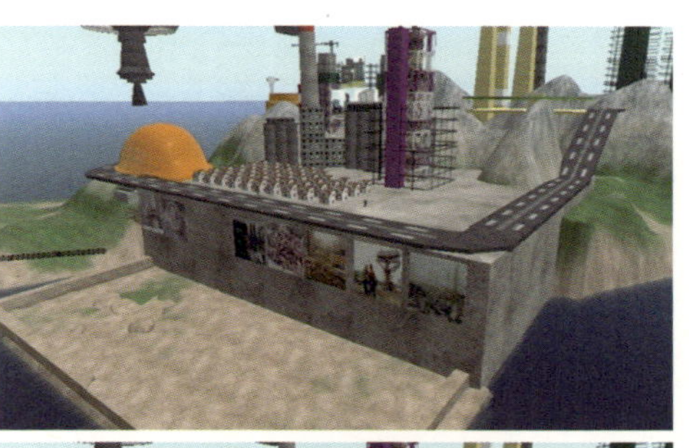

***RMB City: A Second Life City Planning***, Video stills, 2007, 6', all images courtesy RMB City and Vitamin Creative Space

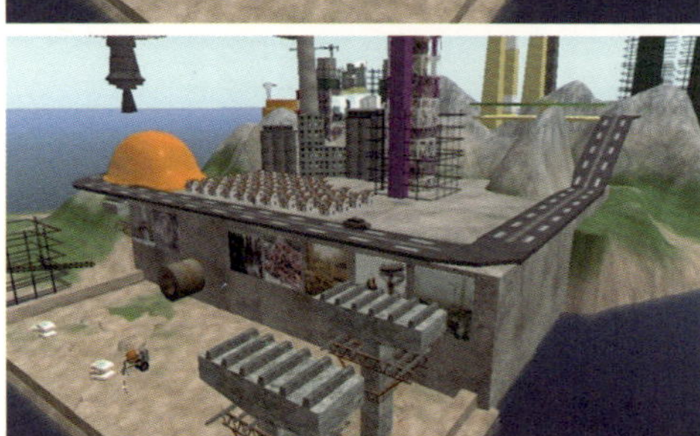

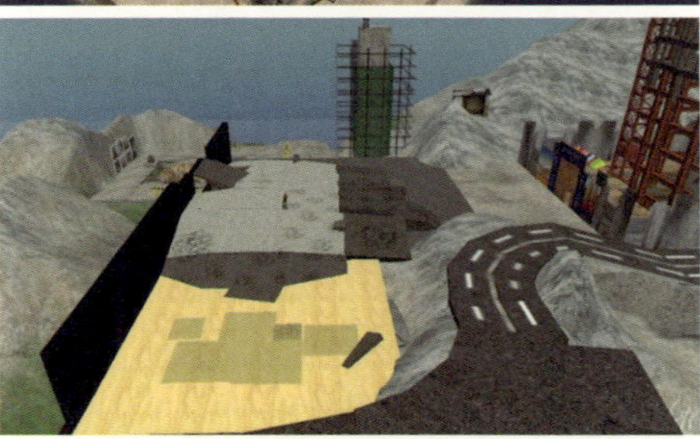

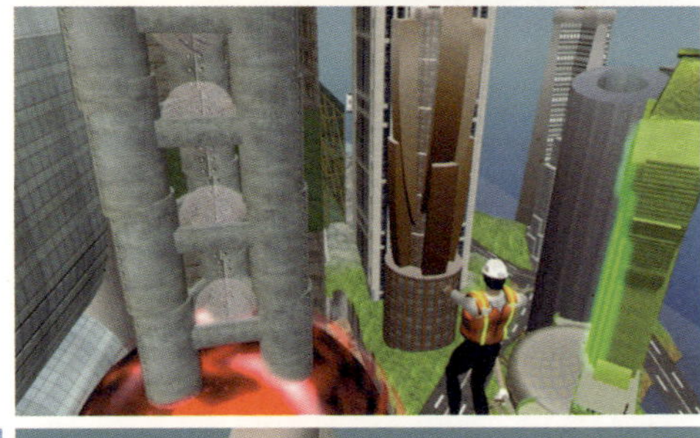

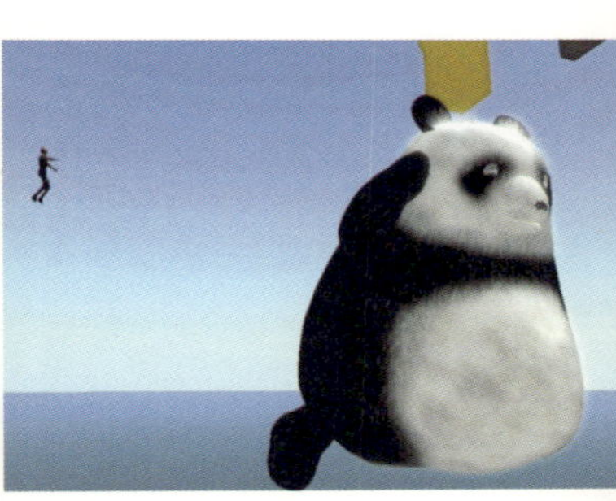

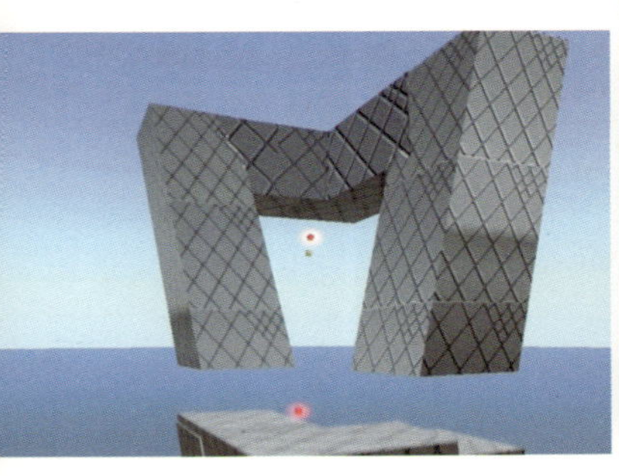

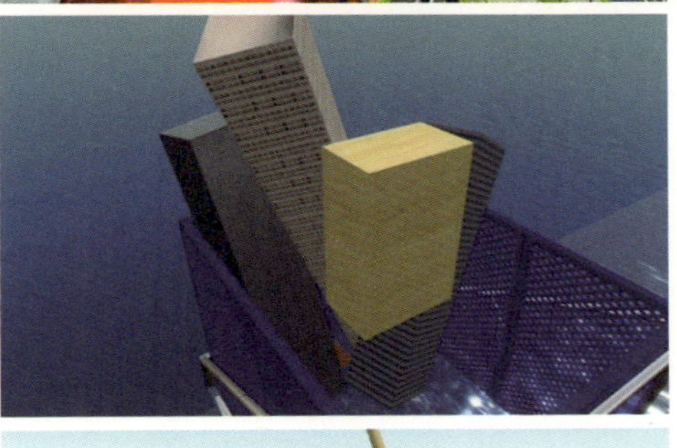

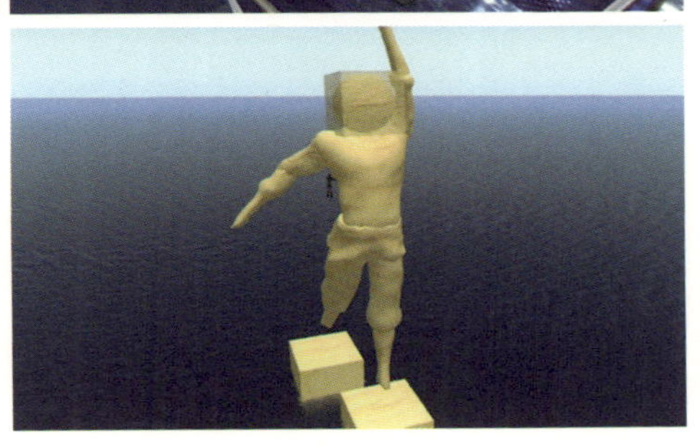

- - - - - - - - - - - - - - - - - - - - - - - - -

**RMB CITY MARATHON**

Time: March 20th, 2009
Location: RMB City in Second Life

Hans Ulrich Obrist and Julia Peyton-Jones had a one-hour interview with China Tracy, a character performed by six different individuals in real life, to experiment with a multi-identity conversation in the unique virtual context of Second-Life.

….
[3:03] You: Hello HansUlrichObrist Magic!
[3:04] You: Hello Hans Ulrich, why don't you take a stroll with us?
[3:04] You: walking walking walking is healthy!
[3:04] You: nonstop walking, we never stop walking
[3:04] You: wrong way wrong way!
[3:04] You: that's not the direction of the future!
[3:05] You: are you lost?
[3:05] You: Hans Ulrich, walk with us! not backwards!
[3:06] You: Yes!
[3:07] You: Can we start?
[3:08] You: Now we are in sync
[3:08] You: How do you feel?
[3:08] JuliaPeytonJones Popstar: Hello, we're going to be two minutes, just getting ready here.
[3:09] You: OK great
[3:09] You: Now we're having our warm-up jogging
[3:09] You: Before the real race begins.
[3:10] You: How do we name our gang?
[3:10] You: We look like we're on our way to a hit-job.
[3:10] Selavy Oh: lol
[3:13] comet Morigi: She's wearing a Heaven-4D the brand.
[3:13] Hansulrichobrist Magic: Hurricane
[3:13] JuliaPeytonJones Popstar: So great to be with you all here in RMB City.
[3:13] Hansulrichobrist Magic: parallel realities
[3:13] You: same reality
[3:13] Hansulrichobrist Magic: David Deutsch Fabric of Reality an urgent book urgent
[3:14] You: but now we are in the book
[3:14] Hansulrichobrist Magic: same reality? can you tell me more
[3:14] Hansulrichobrist Magic: China Tracy same reality?
[3:14] You: yeah we are in the same reality
[3:14] Hansulrichobrist Magic: a rendezvous of questions marks
[3:14] JuliaPeytonJones Popstar: Let's start the interview, shall we?
[3:14] You: yes we came from different realities
[3:15] You: but we are here
[3:15] You: the race to the future
[3:15] JuliaPeytonJones Popstar: Tell us, what has happened in RMB City since we last spoke?
[3:16] You: what you have seen here is part of the outcome after the opening of RMB City
[3:16] Hansulrichobrist Magic: yes we are so curious we want to know everything
[3:16] Hansulrichobrist Magic: as Dieter Roth said EVERYTHING the magazine of everything
[3:16] You: there have been different kind of cultural activities which are shaping the new life in rmb city
[3:16] Hansulrichobrist Magic: which cultural activities
[3:16] Hansulrichobrist Magic: exhibitions
[3:16] You: then probably we should go everywhere in the city-
[3:16] You: so we are starting here
[3:17] You: but we will take you on a great journey
[3:17] Hansulrichobrist Magic: yes lets start the journey it has only just begun only just begun
…
[3:18] Hansulrichobrist Magic: EveRRevolution
[3:18] JuliaPeytonJones Popstar: Revolution is everything!
[3:19] You: infiltration is better
[3:19] JuliaPeytonJones Popstar: It's part of the everyday here and always
[3:19] Hansulrichobrist Magic: Beuys said La Rivolutzione siamo noi We are the Revolution does China Tracy agree
[3:19] JuliaPeytonJones Popstar: Subversion the best
[3:19] Hansulrichobrist Magic: or Resistance
[3:19] You: daily life becomes the way that revolution exists
[3:19] Hansulrichobrist Magic: Lyotard did les Immateriaux after that he wanted to do a show on Resistance it remained unrealised
[3:19] Hansulrichobrist Magic: RESISTANCE IN SECOND LIFE
[3:19] JuliaPeytonJones Popstar: Revolve daily life
[3:20] Hansulrichobrist Magic: can Second Life be Resistance
[3:20] You: for a revolutionary means of

transport, do you want to try to fly?
[3:20] Hansulrichobrist Magic: China Tracy Resistance?
[3:20] JuliaPeytonJones Popstar: yes lets fly
[3:20] Hansulrichobrist Magic: Yes lets fly
[3:20] Hansulrichobrist Magic: totally fly
[3:20] Hansulrichobrist Magic: fly totally
[3:20] Hansulrichobrist Magic: Urgent fly
[3:20] Hansulrichobrist Magic: fly urgently
[3:20] You: click fly on the bottom of your screen - follow
[3:20] JuliaPeytonJones Popstar: fly now
[3:20] Hansulrichobrist Magic: We are into Second Life lists
[3:20] Hansulrichobrist Magic: we chat and fly
[3:20] You: timelessness is the way of resistance?
[3:20] You: you will see the CCTV still well preserved in our city--
[3:21] You: but actually in real life, it was consumed by fire
[3:21] You: let's fly to the tower and back-
[3:23] You: Lost in RMB City?
[3:23] You: Were you lost in RMB City?
[3:24] JuliaPeytonJones Popstar: No, we were walking in the air, and now over the sea
[3:24] You: actually i would like to take you to City Hall
[3:24] Hansulrichobrist Magic: China Tracy did my last 8 messages reach you we are deeply worried
[3:24] JuliaPeytonJones Popstar: fantastic!
[3:24] Hansulrichobrist Magic: the silence cannot be transcribed
[3:25] Hansulrichobrist Magic: Silence in second life WOW
[3:25] Hansulrichobrist Magic: silence and flying
[3:25] You: and to experience the new value of our first Mayor UliSigg Cisse
[3:25] You: I am happy if you dont get lost in Rmb sity
[3:25] You: city
[3:25] Hansulrichobrist Magic: China Tracy are we a community
[3:26] Hansulrichobrist Magic: production of community
[3:26] Hansulrichobrist Magic: community production reality production
[3:26] Hansulrichobrist Magic: China Tracy did your identity change
[3:26] You: Don't do things that I would not do
[3:26] Hansulrichobrist Magic: What does freedom mean
[3:26] You: this is the first value of our mayor
[3:26] Hansulrichobrist Magic: the freedom of China Tracy
[3:26] Hansulrichobrist Magic: liberte
[3:26] Hansulrichobrist Magic: la liberte
[3:26] Hansulrichobrist Magic: the freedom
[3:27] You: !!!!!!!!!!!!!!
[3:27] You: our freedom includes the option not to have any opinion on what is freedom means in a virtual space
[3:27] Hansulrichobrist Magic: This is a break we are taking a picture now we are back in a nano second
[3:27] China Rehula is Online
[3:27] Hansulrichobrist Magic: what is a nanosecond on second life
[3:27] Hansulrichobrist Magic: nanosecond life
[3:27] Hansulrichobrist Magic: ever nanosecond ever life
[3:27] You: because that would represent a reduction of freedom
[3:28] Hansulrichobrist Magic: china Tracy can you tell us about all the RMB city citizens
[3:28] Hansulrichobrist Magic: where are you what do you see
[3:28] You: i think that's a very useful unit on Second Life, because we chose a next age, and that's what we're trying to approach in second life, so I like the idea of a nanosecond, and let's communicate this way
[3:28] Hansulrichobrist Magic: China Tracy where are you what do you see
[3:28] Hansulrichobrist Magic: what else is useful? Is second life a UTILITY
[3:29] You: does a visitor make a citizen?
[3:29] You: does RMB indicate a chinese identity of the city? so the question is a very chinese one -
[3:29] Hansulrichobrist Magic: China Tracy this is an homage to ALighiero Boetti
[3:29] You: then the chinese answer would be no
[3:29] Hansulrichobrist Magic: the Velocity of Boetti in Second Life
[3:29] Hansulrichobrist Magic: lets type faster and faster
[3:29] Seductive Dreamscape: a citizen is someone who contributes in a useful way to SL
[3:30] Hansulrichobrist Magic: the peoples Avatar I am dying to know more about the peoples avatar please tell me more am dying to know The Peoples Avatar
[3:30] You: Not yet, but that would be the ideal future if it became a utility, utility meaning a necessity in our daily

life - that would be a true Mayor's vision
[3:30] Hansulrichobrist Magic: channeling other voices
[3:30] You: I'm grateful for this strong Mayor's vision provided to us
[3:30] Hansulrichobrist Magic: how does that reflect how your identity has and may have changed during this project
[3:31] Hansulrichobrist Magic: What about multiple identities
[3:31] Hansulrichobrist Magic: the Mayor is also a Collector
[3:31] FlyKnifeModelsDream Oh is Offline
[3:31] You: i think we are exactly reflecting the fact - probably my stupidity is different from other people's stupidity - in that way we represent the people, different stupidity
[3:32] Hansulrichobrist Magic: Seductive Dreamscape you talk about useful contributions Cedric Price said its important to make useful mistakes what can be useful mistakes on SL
[3:32] Hansulrichobrist Magic: useful mistakes
[3:32] You: china tracy can be hu fang or mianmian
[3:32] Hansulrichobrist Magic: can China Tracy bring us to Third Life what is Fourth Life
[3:32] Hansulrichobrist Magic: lets push it further
[3:32] Hansulrichobrist Magic: second life is not enough
[3:32] Hansulrichobrist Magic: Super string theory has 11 dimension
[3:32] You: useful mistakes? It would be to do something so that people like it for the wrong reason -
[3:33] You: And that they could share with a collector, who likes things for the wrong reason
[3:33] Hansulrichobrist Magic: where is Popstar Popstar is in World RMB City ONE
[3:33] Hansulrichobrist Magic: Totally wrong reason great
[3:33] Hansulrichobrist Magic: China Tracy what is next when will you take us to Third Life
[3:34] Hansulrichobrist Magic: China Tracy can you tell us about your unrealised projects
[3:34] Hansulrichobrist Magic: projects which are too big to be realised
[3:34] Hansulrichobrist Magic: to small to be realised
[3:34] Hansulrichobrist Magic: censored project
[3:34] Hansulrichobrist Magic: is there censorship in secon dlife
[3:34] Hansulrichobrist Magic: is there self censorship
[3:34] You: may be would be the project in fourth life
[3:34] Hansulrichobrist Magic: Doris Lessing said we have self censorship the books we never wrote
[3:34] comet Morigi: test/ comet
[3:34] Hansulrichobrist Magic: is Panda there
[3:35] Hansulrichobrist Magic: Panda the novelist
[3:35] Hansulrichobrist Magic: totally Panda
[3:35] Hansulrichobrist Magic: urgent Panda alert
[3:35] Hansulrichobrist Magic: Comet Hurricane
[3:35] Hansulrichobrist Magic: Comet Typhoon
[3:35] Hansulrichobrist Magic: Test Test
[3:35] Hansulrichobrist Magic: Silence there is so much silence in second life
[3:35] You: i want to explore humanbeing's desires in every aspect, it
[3:35] You: but you see, sl is not enough
[3:35] Hansulrichobrist Magic: Multidimensional DESIRE
[3:35] Hansulrichobrist Magic: how Many dimensions does desire have
[3:36] You: it depends on where our desires are
[3:36] You: but can we talk about spriti
[3:37] Hansulrichobrist Magic: yes spirits
[3:38] Hansulrichobrist Magic: China Tracy Spirits
[3:38] You: well it depends what country that you are at
[3:38] Hansulrichobrist Magic: a spirit always hides another spirit
[3:38] You: like for Japan, desire is about getting married
[3:38] Hansulrichobrist Magic: desires are context specific
[3:38] You: in Hk, is more like it's about financial stuff
[3:38] Hansulrichobrist Magic: and in Bejing?
[3:38] Hansulrichobrist Magic: and in RMB City?
[3:39] JuliaPeytonJones Popstar: I'm back !
[3:39] You: desire in Beijing... and in rmb city...
[3:39] You: i think a lot of people want to see CCTV tower rebuilt
[3:40] Hansulrichobrist Magic: CCTV leads us to RMB TV can you tell us about this theatrical city new theatrical city ever
[3:40] You: Desire is about acting out and making it your own utopia-- in RMB City
[3:40] JuliaPeytonJones Popstar: TV is a

new theatrical stage here in RMB City?
[3:40] You: i think RMB City is a great setting for experimental performance and you can really go beyond the boundaries of the real world and act out the craziest dramas you can think of
[3:41] Hansulrichobrist Magic: Re Desire NIETZSCHE wrote art is the desire to be different the desire to be elsewhere
[3:41] Hansulrichobrist Magic: China Tracy what is your definition of art do you agree with Nietzsche ever
[3:41] JuliaPeytonJones Popstar: An obscure object...
[3:41] Hansulrichobrist Magic: Craziest drama sounds hurricane and valerio
[3:41] You: being different is nice, but sometimes it's about moving together in a pack and having a common core-
[3:41] Hansulrichobrist Magic: what has been the craziest drama so far in RMB CITY
[3:42] You: behind every interesting movement, there has always been a common theme that drives it
[3:42] Hansulrichobrist Magic: are there new words in Second Life NEOLOGISMS RMB NEOLOGISMS we need to invent new words
[3:42] You: i think it has yet to be acted out---
[3:42] Hansulrichobrist Magic: the necessity to invent new words
[3:42] JuliaPeytonJones Popstar: Crazy desires reflected in the world of TV in the world of RMB... how many channels? chat show hosts? documentaries?
[3:42] JuliaPeytonJones Popstar: adverts?
[3:43] Hansulrichobrist Magic: adverts for?
[3:43] You: i think - it may not be a new word, but it's a word hasn't been used here yet- RMB City needs a stimulus package,
[3:43] You: just like all the governments are getting right now
[3:43] JuliaPeytonJones Popstar: and the financial sector?
[3:43] Hansulrichobrist Magic: Lets introduce VALERIO to Second Life
[3:43] Hansulrichobrist Magic: Valerio was an urban rumor
[3:43] Hansulrichobrist Magic: it all started in a night club in RImini in the 90s
[3:43] Hansulrichobrist Magic: many kids screamed Valerio that night in the streets
[3:44] Hansulrichobrist Magic: it became a phenomenon all over Italy VALERIOOOO
[3:44] Hansulrichobrist Magic: Hundreds of thousands of people screaming VALERIOOO
[3:44] You: is Valerio a post-pop in Second Life?
[3:44] Hansulrichobrist Magic: it was a new word very positive energy as Paolo Fabbri explained later
[3:44] Hansulrichobrist Magic: Yes a neologism for ENERGY VALERIOOOOOOOOOOOOOOOOOOOOOOOOOOOO
[3:45] You: energy... hm.... energy is what the real world needs the most at this point
[3:45] JuliaPeytonJones Popstar: and how are experiments recorded?
[3:45] You: maybe Second Life is a way to achieve it-
[3:46] JuliaPeytonJones Popstar: a reimagination of energy
[3:46] You: memory is something that everyone has, that directs all our future actions
[3:46] Hansulrichobrist Magic: Is RMB City new OPtimism
[3:46] You: it's part of you that stays with you forever
[3:46] Hansulrichobrist Magic: Memory is a protest against forgetting
[3:46] JuliaPeytonJones Popstar: but warps in retrospect sometimes
[3:46] JuliaPeytonJones Popstar: so important to protest!
[3:46] You: important to protest...
[3:46] Hansulrichobrist Magic: More information does not mean more memory
[3:47] Hansulrichobrist Magic: on the contrary information can lead to amnesia
[3:47] Hansulrichobrist Magic: how to transform information into knowledge
[3:47] You: life
[3:48] JuliaPeytonJones Popstar: information and knowledge woven together as a background around us here
[3:48] Hansulrichobrist Magic: Live? Life? Both?
[3:48] You: so for me, when i find information, or i find knowledge, i understand this is wisdom, or not wisdom
[3:49] You: my body and my brain will tell me if it has wisdom, or has no wisdom-
[3:49] You: because wisdom is different from knowledge, and from information
[3:49] JuliaPeytonJones Popstar: bodies are key to knowledge and wisdom, a way of knowing that can't be forgotten easily
[3:50] Hansulrichobrist Magic: is there a beginning and an end

*(Excerpts from original documentation of the online chat)*

- - - - - - - - - - - - - - - - - - - - - - - - - - -

**Anna Colin** is a curator living in London and working at Gasworks since 2007. There, she has programmed solo projects and exhibitions by artists including Martin Beck, The Otolith Group, Olivia Plender, and Ana Laura Lopez de la Torre, and has curated group exhibitions and seminars such as *Disclosures* (2008, co-curated with Mia Jankowicz) and *Everything has a name, or the potential to be named* (2009, co-curated with Catalina Lozano). Parallel to Gasworks, she has developed two more installments of the project *Disclosures*, one in collaboration with Nottingham Contemporary (2008) and another in partnership with The Whitechapel Gallery and The Women's Library (2009). As a critic, she was London's correspondent for *Art Press* (Paris, 2002–2007) and co-editor of the magazine *Untitled* (London, 2007–2008), and has written for art magazines and publications internationally.

**Neil Cummings** was born in Wales, lives in London, and when not working as an artist is a part-time professor at Chelsea College of Art and Design, London. He is a member of Critical Practice, a trustee of Nottingham Contemporary, and is on the editorial board of *Documents*.
> www.criticalpracticechelsea.org www.neilcummings.com

**Marysia Lewandowska** is a Polish–born, London-based artist. Since 2003, she is a professor at Konstfack in Stockholm, and part of a team responsible for a Art in the Public Realm, a new MA program. Most recently, Marysia Lewandowska took up a six-month residency at CCS Bard to complete her long-term project *Womens' Audio Archive*:
> www.chanceprojects.com www.marysia-lewandowska.com

Neil Cummings and Marysia Lewandowska collaborated from 1995 to 2008.

**Goldin+Senneby** (since 2004) is a framework for collaboration set up by artists Simon Goldin and Jakob Senneby, exploring juridical, financial, and spatial constructs through notions of the performative and the virtual. Their collaboration started with *The Port* (2004–2006), a series of insertions into the online world Second Life. Acting in an emerging public sphere constructed through digital code, *The Port* critically reflects on community-based production within "social software." In their more recent body of work, known as *Headless* (2007), they look at strategies of withdrawal and secrecy, and approach the sphere of offshore finance and its production of virtual space through legal code.
> www.goldinsenneby.com

**CAMP** seeks to create platforms beyond the binaries of commodity markets versus "free culture," and of individual versus institutional will, in order to think and to build what is possible, what is equitable, and what is interesting, for the future. CAMP is not an "artists collective" but a space of production, where energies and ideas may gather, even temporarily. CAMP was set up in November 2007 in Mumbai as a small "startup" in collaboration with Khoj Delhi.

CAMP's founding members are: Shaina Anand, filmmaker, artist, and founder of www.chitrakarkhana.net; Ashok Sukumaran, who trained as an architect and artist, and who now does speculative technical and conceptual projects (http://0ut.in); and Sanjay Bhangar, who trained in independent media and urban studies, and who now works as an independent Web developer and technology writer.
> www.camputer.org

**Ana Laura López de la Torre** is an artist and writer based in London since 1995. Using the overlooked and the underrated as a starting point, her work creates visible and unexpected connections between things, people, and places. Her practice is process-based, often acting as a catalyst and involving disparate constituencies with common interests but conflicting agendas. López de la Torre's work explores the meaning of the local as a critical and politicized context for artistic production. She works collaboratively with other artists, community organizations, and people from all walks of life.
> www.rememberolivemorris.wordpress.com

**Maria Thereza Alves**, a Brazilian artist and cofounder of the Green Party of Brazil, lives in Europe. Alves researches social and cultural phenomena through site-specific works which address local histories and the environment, and which at different times have engaged botanists, civic officials, and the involvement of communities. Alves's works are attempts to create a public forum at an individual level for active investigations and participation. She has worked in the Pantanal swamps of Brazil, the mountain village of Matsunoyama in Japan, the industrialized mega-port of Guangzhou in China, the indigenous village of Amatlan in central Mexico, the agricultural village of Fadiouth in Senegal, and throughout Europe. Alves has recently exhibited at the Lyon Biennale (2009), at the Guangzhou Triennale, and at Manifesta 7 in Trento (2008). Maria Thereza Alves is represented by Galerie Michel Rein, Paris.

# Unveiling the Past, Disclosing the Present, and Envisioning the Future: On Strategies of Openness

*"It started in an effort to theorize a paradigm of the artist, which is well under way in practice. Under this paradigm the artist serves as conduit between specialized knowledge fields and other members of the public sphere by assuming a role I have called the Public Amateur.*

*In such a practice the artist becomes a person who consents to learn in public. It is a proposition of active social participation in which any non-specialist is empowered to take the initiative to question something within a given discipline, acquire knowledge in a non-institutionally sanctioned way, and assume the authority to interpret that knowledge, especially in regard to decisions that affect our lives. The motive is not to replace the specialist, but to augment specialization with other models that have legitimate claims to producing and interpreting knowledge.*

*The idea is to pursue knowledge with very transparent stakes in a space where the interest of the parties involved can be exposed to scrutiny."* [1]

Since first reading the text by Chicago-based artist and writer Claire Pentecost, these introductory sentences have stayed with me for their belief that artists have a constructive role to play in society, and because of their ability to connect modes of action that have been key to the practice of artists who, in turn, have given my own work its meaning. With this text, the formulaic question "Is it art?" seems to be brushed aside once and for all and replaced by a more tolerant, fresher space from which to operate culturally. And yet, many artists for whom this space is important do not rest on their laurels for all that: they make a particular point in aligning their work ethos and methods with those of the disciplines with which they choose to interact. They often do so transparently—sharing with others their learning process with their highs and lows—and make it an integral part of the work.

Besides being transparent and "perceptible to the eye," "visible" is, among other definitions, what is "on hand," what is "available."[2] Availability depends upon access, which itself depends on a plethora of factors, whether physical, intellectual, financial, legal, political, religious, ethical, cultural, bureaucratic, or arbitrary. The atmosphere of "discouragement from knowing," to use more of Pentecost's words, has given artists and activists alike a particular incentive to investigate the terrain of knowledge and information access. The hard task of identifying what falls into the public domain when records don't even exist, the act of turning common knowledge material into formats that will resist the passing of time, and the act of exposing and archiving the present and the trivial for our own sake as well as for future generations have in recent years been a favored form of action for cultural practices embedded in the sociopolitical present.

ǂ

My particular professional and creative engagement with the topic of visibility possibly started in 2002 when I co-presented a fortnightly radio program on

1 Claire Pentecost, "Oh! The Public Amateur is Not Afraid to Let On That She Just Figured it Out," 2007, published on http://publicamateur.wordpress.com/about/ (last accessed 26 July 2009).

2 See: http://www.thefreedictionary.com

visual arts on the London-based independent radio station Resonance FM. Programming visual arts on the radio, and without any budget, limited us to a few possible formats: the chat show (interviewing or setting up discussions with artists, reporting on exhibitions); playing live or pre-recorded works oriented toward sound art, spoken word, music, and other speech-based forms; and commissioning artists to do radio-specific works for no fee.

Three years of radio programming and one break down the line, I launched a three-month-long radio project of a more consistent curatorial nature with a grant from Arts Council England. It was titled "Radio Gallery," in reference to Gerry Schum's *Fernsehgalerie* (Television Gallery), which had famously attempted to make artists' works accessible to all via TV broadcast and also to start a sustainable market for video art.[3] With similarly optimistic plans, "Radio Gallery" commissioned twelve artists and curators engaged with immaterial and/or non-exhibition specific practices to treat one hour of radio as exhibition space. The project was a pilot and, despite the positive feedback, was not repeated.[4]

What makes talking about this project particularly relevant is a small yet significant episode, which denotes the different understandings of the concept of visibility depending on the side on which one stands. In fact, as a condition to obtain the Arts Council England grant, I had had to agree to come up with some sort of visualization of the project, as it was deemed too impalpable and not visible enough by the funders. Instead of the expected exhibition, which would have defeated the object, I proposed a launch, a panel discussion, and a closing event with live music and performance. In contradiction with the funders' well known quantitative measurement of success, three events which attracted as many people as a six-week-long exhibition in a small-scale public space satisfied the funders more than the tens of thousands people who actually heard the programs when they went on air or who have downloaded the podcasts since 2006.

This experience, as well as a few years of engagement with the marginal field of sound art, stimulated my liking for practices and ideas which struggle to be accepted by common definitions—for practices which set themselves apart, whether to retain their autonomy or out of enthusiasm for learning about anything that is not directly related to their own professional territory.

ǂ

The next step was *Disclosures*, a project initiated at Gasworks (London) in Spring 2008 together with Mia Jankowicz (then residencies curator at Gasworks and now working independently).[5] *Disclosures* set out to scrutinize the notion of openness across fields of cultural production at large—to look at how open-source methodologies translate to practices located outside of the Internet.

The project was launched with a two-day seminar which brought together practitioners from the fields of visual and media art, philosophy, urban sociology, and

3 Broadcast on German television in two parts: *Land Art* for Sender Freies Berlin in 1968–1969 and *Identifications* for SWF Baden-Baden in 1970.

4 See: http://www.radiogallery.org

5 Following the first edition of *Disclosures*, the project has since become ongoing in addition to becoming detached from one particular institution. While still investigating cultural practices committed to knowledge sharing, the disclosure of hidden and forgotten social histories, both old and recent, is a subject that has gradually become a recurrent motive of this long-term project. See: http://disclosuresproject.wordpress.com/

social history studies. Linked by a commitment to enriching the public domain and increasing flexibility as far as the flow of information and knowledge is concerned, the participants also aspire to reconciliation of intention and methodology—in other words, to using means of production, presentation, and dissemination which reflect the work's artistic and/or ideological ends. Commissions were made to collectives and individual artists, including by **CAMP**, Open Music Archive, Critical Practice, Petra Bauer, and Marysia Lewandowska in response to the following four phases which composed the seminar:

1

The points of connection as well as the divides between critical media practice and socially responsive work in the visual art field, both aspiring to acting in response to—or potentially securing a place outside of—the market economy and the main sociocultural circuits.

2

Intellectual property laws and the current licensing system; the public availability of information and knowledge; the factors that have forced public resources out of civic reach; and the implications ensuing from the release of cultural material and alternative genealogies to those written by Western history.

3

The socioeconomic, political, and cultural conditions for the technological underpinning of openness—Free/Libre Open Source Software (FLOSS)—to exist and become widespread across various global contexts; the limitations of FLOSS as a tool and model.

4

Experiments with the blurring of authorship and with cross-referencing in the field of literature; horizontal collaborations through which the relationship between the fan, the author, and the author's creations are reconfigured.

Due to the project's engagement with the concept of openness, we had hoped to implement an open curatorial platform, similar to two relatively successful models of collective, consensus-based curating we had come across, one set up by the research cluster Critical Practice in London for "Open Congress" at Tate Britain in 2005, and the other by Iaspis and Konstfack in Stockholm for the performative seminar titled "Who Makes and Owns Your Work?" in 2007.[6] Following their example, we created a "wiki" on which we scrupulously posted the project's latest bibliography, synopsis, agendas of meetings with practitioners, and a wish list of participants, and started to solicit critical input and content from the people we were approaching.

For us, as curators working in a competitive and often highly custodial art world, making our hesitations, weaknesses, and desires public was a liberating experiment. But there was a drawback: the wiki was hardly used by anyone other than us. If this misuse of open-source tools and the naive belief that if you go "open," participation will follow naturally taught us a few lessons, it didn't annihilate our willingness to share curatorial processes and research. In fact, one of the project's

6 See: http://opencongress.omweb.org/modules/wakka/HomePage and http://www.whomakesandownsyourwork.org/

7 See: http://pipeline.gasworks.org.uk

8 Claire Pentecost, "Oh! The Public Amateur is Not Afraid to Let On That She Just Figured it Out," 2007, published on http://publicamateur.wordpress.com/about/ (last accessed 26 July 2009).

commissions led to the creation of Pipeline, a second online presence for Gasworks. Edited internally, Pipeline (re)publishes research material generated by and around Gasworks's projects, making accessible resources beyond commonly available biographical or searchable texts. As an evolving archive, its principle is to share knowledge with anyone interested in engaging with similar topics, in order to advance it rather than replicate it.[7]

## The five projects

**Neil Cummings and Marysia Lewandowska**, **CAMP**, **Ana Laura López de la Torre**, and **Goldin+Senneby**, whose work is presented in this publication alongside that of **Maria Thereza Alves**, all took part in the first edition of *Disclosures*, and some of them in subsequent ones. If their ways of operating are hardly comparable—for instance, at a decision-making level, some will opt for a ground-up consensus, while others will adopt a more editorial approach—all are dedicated to establishing a direct dialogue between their sociopolitical and historical surroundings and the production of cultural material. They may work in response to a need, issue, or a shortfall; to uncover hidden histories; to resist the normative and reshuffle the expected; or to help construct the future by feeding the social imaginary.

According to varying principles, these projects are entirely built around participation, and often exist through their capacity to rally other enthusiasts, with the view to creating collective knowledge and/or memories. They are "public amateurs" opposing selfhood and engaged in a learning process which "in public [...] has a chance to be collective, thereby deeper and finally more subversive."[8]

**Anna Colin**

Unveiling the Past, Disclosing the Present, and Envisioning the Future: On Strategies of Openness

For its jubilee year in 2008, Moderna Museet in Stockholm commissioned a new work from Neil Cummings and Marysia Lewandowska. "Instead of reinterpreting Moderna Museet's illustrious past—a task of mourning—we have vividly imagined the museum's future, the future of all public museums. Eighteen months research, and interviews with all the key employees of the museum, from Director to maintenance staff, has resulted in *Museum Futures: Distributed*."[1]

"*Museum Futures: Distributed* is a machinima record of the centenary interview with Moderna Museet's executive Ayan Lindquist in June 2058. It explores a possible genealogy for contemporary art practice and its institutions, by imagining the role of artists, museums, galleries, markets, manufactories and academies."[2]

*Museum Futures: Distributed* takes the form of a film and a transcript, presented in this publication. Interviewed in 2058 by Ms. Chan from the Asian Multitude network, Ayan Lindquist, the museum's executive, revisits the past hundred years of Moderna Museet's history and her own more recent trajectory in cultural governance. During that period, the art market and the art institution have divorced once and for all. Commercial galleries have become "a competing meshwork of global auction franchises," while "public/private museum hybrids" and other nodal cultural entities, in addition to their engagement with so-called "art-artefacts," "exhibitionary practice," and "embedded coproduction," have been dedicating their time to activities as varied as cooperating "on a draft amendment to Article 39 of the United Nations Declaration of Human Rights" or distributing "regenerative medical technologies."[3]

1 Quoting from: http://www.chanceprojects.com/node/406 (last accessed on 18 July 2009)
2 Quoting from: http://www.neilcummings.com/content/museum-futures-script-0 (last accessed on 18 July 2009)
3 Quoting from: *Museum Futures: Distributed*, transcribed by Neil Cummings.

# Neil Cummings and Marysia Lewandowska

***Ms. Chan***, 2008–2009, still from Museum Futures, distributed by Moderna Museet Stockholm, Sweden, HD video 32'

***Ayan Lindquist***, 2008–2009, still from Museum Futures, distributed by Moderna Museet Stockholm, Sweden, HD video 32'

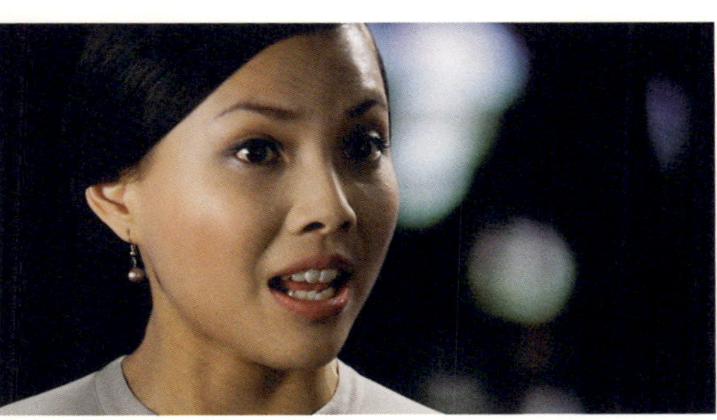

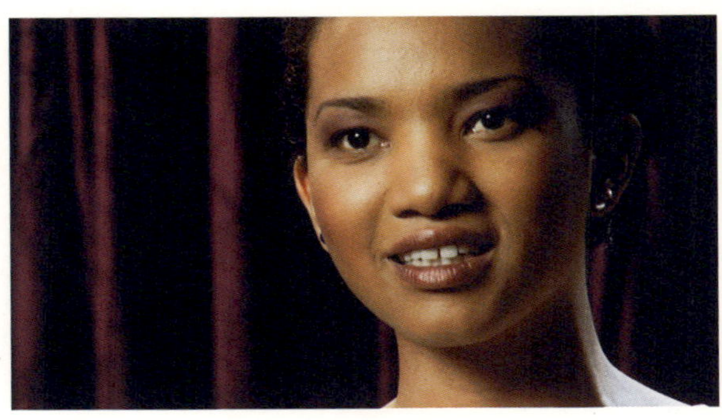

- - - - - - - - - - - - - - - - - - - - - - - -

**MUSEUM FUTURES: DISTRIBUTED**

Neil Cummings and Marysia Lewandowska.
Centenary Interview 2058 transcribed by
Neil Cummings

Interior: The common room, Moderna Museet v3.0. A beautiful lounge, comfortable seating, local lighting, graduated windows with breathtaking views of the sea.
*The Executive of Moderna v3.0: Ayan Lindquist, is waiting to be interviewed in real-time from Guangzhou, in the Asian Multitude network.*
*She is browsing screens as a face fades-up on the wall window.*

MS CHAN
Nihao, hej, hello!
Hello is that Ayan Lindquist?

AYAN LINDQUIST
Nihao, hello.
Yes Ms Chan, this is Ayan.
We are in sync.

MS CHAN
Thank you so much for finding time…………
You must be very busy with the centenary launch

AYAN LINDQUIST
It's a pleasure.
We really admire your work on mid $20^{th}$ C image ecologies.
Especially your research on archival practice

MS CHAN
Well I'm flattered.
For many Asian non-market institutions, your pioneering work with long-term equity contracts has been inspirational too!

AYAN LINDQUIST
Oh, there was a whole team of us involved…………… So, lets begin.

MS CHAN
Ok. Just to refresh, for the centenary I'd like to archive your live-thread recall of Moderna.

AYAN LINDQUIST
Yep, that's fine,
I've enabled about 20 mins.

MS CHAN
Ok, live.

Maybe we could start with some personal history.
What were you doing before you became executive at Moderna Museet 3.0?

AYAN LINDQUIST
Well, I joined Moderna 2.0 in 2049, almost ten years ago.

First as adviser to the development working group.
Then as part of the governance team.
I participated in the forking of Moderna 3.0 in 2'51.
And was elected fixed-term executive in 2'52, …….uhmm,……until today.

I've got another four years in the post.

MS CHAN
And before that?

AYAN LINDQUIST
Immediately before joining Moderna I collaborated in the exhibition programme at the MACBA cluster in Mumbai for six years.

Although, more in resource provision.
That's where we worked on a version of the equity bond issue you mentioned.

MS CHAN
And before that?

AYAN LINDQUIST
In programming again at Tate in Doha for four years, particularly developing exhibitionary platforms.

And even before that,

I participated in research on cultural governance, for the Nordic Congress of the European Multitude for six years.

I suspect exhibition agency and governance are my real strengths.

MS CHAN
Maybe we should dive into the deep-end.

Could you briefly say something of why Moderna 3.0 devolved, and why was it necessary?

AYAN LINDQUIST
As you can imagine there was a lot of

consultation beforehand.
It's not something we did without due diligence.

For almost forty years Moderna v2.0 has explored and developed the exhibitionary form.
We pioneered the production of many collaborative exhibitions, resources and assemblages.

We helped build robust public - what you prefer to term non-market cultural networks.
And scaled those networks to produce our *i-commons*, part of the vast, glocal, Public Domain.

We have continually nurtured and developed emergent art practice.

Moderna can proudly, and quite rightly say that we participated in shaping the early 21st century movement of art. From an exhibitionary practice based around art-artefacts, spectacle and consumption - to that of embedded co-production.

MS CHAN
Do you mean that…………..

AYAN LINDQUIST
Of course there are many complex factors involved…………

But we were agent in the shift from a heritage cultural mind-set of 'broadcast', to that of emergent, peer-to-peer meshworks.

Following the logic of practice, we became an immanent institution.

MS CHAN
Could you say a …………..

AYAN LINDQUIST
Uhmm……..
Although having said all of that……….
We've not really answered your question, have we?

Given that Moderna 2.0 continues its exhibitionary research, some of us believe that exhibition as a technology, and immanence as an institutional logic needed to be subject to radical revision.

So this is what we intend to explore with Moderna 3.0, we want to execute some of the research.
To enact. To be more agent than immanent.

MS CHAN
Ok. I wondered if you could you say a………

AYAN LINDQUIST
Sorry to over-write, but in a way the forking follows something of the tradition of Moderna Museet.

Moderna 2.0 mutated through 1.0 because the tension between trying to collect, conserve, and exhibit the history of 20th Century art, ***and*** at the same time trying to be a responsible 21st Century art institution proved too difficult to reconcile.

Moderna 1.0 continues its mandate.
Its buildings and collection has global heritage status.
In turn, this early hybridization enabled Moderna 2.0 to be more mobile and experimental.
In its organizational form, in its devolved administration, and its exhibition-making practice….

MS CHAN
Could you just expand on the 'more complex factors' you mentioned earlier….

AYAN LINDQUIST
That's a big question……….

Let me re-run a general thread from composite…………[…]…uhmm

*Ayan taps the terminal/tablet*

Well, a good place to start might be the bifurcation of the market for 'contemporary art' from emergent art practices themselves.

Although the public domain has a long genealogy.
Waaaay……. back into ancient European land rights, 'commons' projects and commonwealth's.

It was the advent of digitalisation, and particularly very early composite language projects in the 1980's which - and this appears astonishing to us now, were proprietary - that kick-started what were called 'open', 'free' or non-market resource initiatives.

Of course, these languages, assemblages and the resources they were building needed legal protection. Licenses to keep them out of property and competitive marketization.

The General Public License, the legendary GPL legal code was written in 1989.

MS CHAN
It's not so old!

AYAN LINDQUIST
So then, text and images - either still or moving; artefacts, systems and processes; music and sound - either as source or assembled; all embedded plant, animal and bodily knowledge; public research, and all possible ecologies of these resources began to be aggregated by the viral licenses into our Public Domain.

*Enumerate on fingers?*

Landmarks include the releasing of the sequenced human genome in 2001.
The foundation of the 'multitude' social enterprise coalition in 2'09.
Intellectual Property reform in the teen's.
The UN-Multitude initiated micro-taxation of global financial transactions in 2'13 - which redirected so many financial resources to Public Domain cultural initiatives.
well I could go on, and on, and on.

But anyway, most participants will be over-familiar with this thread.

MS CHAN
Remind me, when did Moderna affiliate?

AYAN LINDQUIST
In-Archive records suggest Öppna dagar or Härifrån till allmänningen, with Mejan…….
I'm sorry.

We did some collaborative 'open' knowledge projects with *Mejan* in Stockholm in late 2'09.

And when Moderna 2.0 launched in 2'12 we declared all new knowledge *General Public License* version 6, compliant.

MS CHAN
Wasn't that initiated by Chus Martinez, one of your predecessors?
She seems to have shaped early Moderna 2.0, which in turn, became an inspiration globally.

AYAN LINDQUIST
It's nice you say so.

Since 2'12 we collaborated with the fledgling Nordic Congress, in what was to become the European Multitude, to form the backbone of the Public Domain cultural meshwork.

It eventually convened in late 2'22.

So we were at source.

MS CHAN
Ok. Uh ha, thanks.

AYAN LINDQUIST
Now, simultaneous with the exponential growth of the Public Domain, was the market for what we still call 'contemporary art'.

Many historians locate one of the sources for this 'contemporary art' market, as the auction in New York in 1973 of the art-artefact collection of Robert and Ethel Scull.

An extraordinary collection of paintings by pop-male-artists like Andy Warhol, Claes Oldenburg, Ed Ruscha, and……er……I recall……..Jasper Johns.

MS CHAN
Ok. From composite I'm streaming the John Schott analogue film of the sale, from New York MoMa's Public Domain archive.

AYAN LINDQUIST
It's a great film, and many of the art-artefacts have subsequently devolved to Moderna.

MS CHAN
I have the catalogue.
It's present,……….I'm browsing.

AYAN LINDQUIST
That auction set record prices for many artists.
It also connected art-artefacts with financial speculation in a way previously unimagined.

By 1981 one of the 'big two' auction houses, Sotheby's, was active in 23 countries and had a 'contemporary art' market throughput of 4.9 billion old US dollars.

Soon, global Trade Fairs mushroomed. Commercial galleries flourished and a sliver of 'branded' artists lived like mid 20th Century media oligarchs.

By 2'06 complex financial trading technologies were using art-artefacts as an asset class. And most public Modern Art Museums were priced out of the 'contemporary art' market.

In retrospect, we wasted an enormous amount of time and effort convening financial resources to purchase, and publicly 'own' vastly overpriced goods.

And we wasted time wooing wealthy speculators, for sporadic gifts and donations too!

MS CHAN
That connects!
It was the same locally.

The conflictual ethical demands in early Modern Art Museums were systemic.
And obviously unsustainable.

Reversing the resource flow, and using Transaction Tax to nourish Public Domain cultural meshworks seems, ......................well, inevitable.

AYAN LINDQUIST
Ahhh, sometimes, rethreading is such a wonderful luxury!

Anyway, auction houses began to buy commercial galleries.
And this dissolved the tradition of the primary - managed, and secondary - free art market.

As a consequence, by 2'12 the 'contemporary art' market was a 'true' competitive market, with prices for assets falling as well as rising.

Various 'contemporary art' bond, derivate and futures markets were quickly convened.

And typically, art-asset portfolios were managed through specialist brokerages linked to banking subsidiaries.

MS CHAN
Ok. I also see some local downturns linked to financial debt bubbles bursting. Spectacularly in 2'09, again in 2'24 and again in 2'28.

Market corrections?

AYAN LINDQUIST
Probably. Market corrections and their repercussions.

Overall the market expanded, matured in 2'27 and has remained sufficiently resourced ever since...................... More or less.

By 2014 formerly commercial galleries, the primary market, had became a competing meshwork of global auction franchises.

By 2'25 they needed to open branded academies to ensure new assets were produced.

MS CHAN
I can see the Frieze Art Academy in Beijing. Was that was one of the earliest?

AYAN LINDQUIST
The market for 'contemporary art' became, to all intents and purposes, a competitive commodity market, just like any other.

Of course, useful for generating profit and loss through speculation.
And useful for generating Public Domain financial resources, but completely divorced from emergent art practice.

MS CHAN
Ok. This might be a bit of a dumb query.

But does Moderna feel that in the self-replication of the 'contemporary art' market, that
something valuable has been lost from public Museums?

AYAN LINDQUIST
To be perfectly honest, no.
No, we only experience benefits.

You see, through the UN Multitude distribution of Transaction Tax, we're much better resourced.

Which in turn, has enabled us to develop our local cluster and node network.

Generally, competitive markets thrive on artificial difference and managed risk.

They are just too limited a technology to nurture, or challenge, or distribute a truly creative art practice.

And just take all these private art-asset collections, built by speculator-collectors, and supported through private foundations.

Apart from the hyper-resourced, they all ultimately fail.

Then they're either broken-up and recirculated through the 'contemporary art' market.
Or, more usually, devolve to the multitude and enter public Museum collections.

Here at Moderna, we have benefited enormously from a spate of default donations. Consequently, we've a comprehensive collection of 'contemporary' art-artefacts through reversion.

MS CHAN
Ok. Then this was the basis for the amazing Moderna *Contemporary Art* exhibition in Shanghai in 2'24.

It was reconstructed as a study module while I was at the Open University in 2'50.

I can still recall it. What a collection! What an amazing exhibition!

Ok, so maybe here we could locate an ethic approaching something like a critical mass.

As Moderna Museet's collection. exhibitions and activities expanded - and of course other Museums too - the ethic of public generosity is distributed, nurtured and also encouraged.

Everyone benefits.

I can see that when the Ericsson group pledged its collection for instance, it triggered a whole avalanche of other important private gifts and donations.

Like the Azko - la Caixa collection, or the Generali Foundation gift.

Or, like when the Guggenheim franchises collapsed as the debt-bubble burst in 2'18, and the Deutsche Bank executive reverted their collection.

AYAN LINDQUIST
*[laughter]*

We think that's a slightly different case, and certainly of a different magnitude!!
Although it's a common trajectory for many public/private museum hybrids.

MS CHAN
Ok, it's certainly true of museums locally.

The former Ullens Center for Contemporary Art in Beijing,..........and MOCA in Shanghai for instance.

AYAN LINDQUIST
That connects, the increased resources, and the gifts, donations and reversions enabled us to seed our local cluster devolution.

From 2'15 we invested in partnerships with the Institutet Människa I Nätverk in Stockholm; with agencies in Tallin and also Helsinki.

With the early reversion of the *Second Life* hive, and with *Pushkinskaya* in St Petersburg.

We created, what was rather fondly termed, the Baltic cluster.

MS CHAN
Ok, from composite I see there had been an earlier experiment with a devolved Moderna. During the enforced closure in 2'02 - 2'03, exhibitions were co-hosted with local institutions.

There was even a Konstmobilen!

AYAN LINDQUIST
Ja, and it was always considered something of a success.

Distributing and re-imagining the collection through the cluster - incidentally we cut our carbon debt to almost 12 - radically scaled our activities.

So, while developing locally, we also began to produce a wider Moderna Museet network.

The first Moderna node opened in Doha in the United Arab Emirates.
We participated in the local ecologies restructuring of resources; from carbon

to knowledge. That was in 2'18.
In 2'20, Mumbai emerged with the *Ex Habare* three-year research project.
In cooperation with several self-organised Research Institutions - I recall *Nowhere* from Moscow, the *Critical Practice* consortium in London, and *Sarai* from Delhi.

And as you already mentioned Shanghai launched in 2'24 with the landmark *Contemporary Art* exhibition, then the Guangzhou node went live in 2'29 with *La Part Maudite: Bataille and the Accursed Share*.

A really timely exhibition!

It explored the distribution of trust and 'well-being' in a general economy. The ethics of waste and expenditure; and the love, and terror, implicit in uninhibited generosity.

Isn't that node's location near your present Guangdong Museum hub?
On Ersha Island, by the Haiyin Bridge?

MS CHAN
We're almost neighbours!
As for the *La Part Maudite:* much of that source work is still live, and still very present.

AYAN LINDQUIST
We saw you did some restoration to the image server codecs recently, thank you for that.

MS CHAN
Ok. A pleasure.

AYAN LINDQUIST
Our most recent node emerged in San Paulo in the Americas in 2'33.
Through the agency of the Alan Turing Centenary project *Almost Real: Composite Consciousness*.

MS CHAN
Ok, if I may, I'd just like to loop back with you, to the 20's and 30's. It's when many academic historians think we entered a new exhibitionary 'golden age' with Moderna.
You co-produced a suite of landmark projects, many of which are still present.

AYAN LINDQUIST
We're not too comfortable with the idea of a 'golden age'. Maybe our work became embedded again.

Anyway, if there was a 'golden age' we'd like to think it started earlier, maybe in 2'18.

We set about exploring a key term from early machine logic - 'feedback'.
And we made a re-address to the source, the legendary *Cybernetic Serendipity* exhibition at the Institute of Contemporary Art in London; on the exhibition's 50th anniversary.

MS CHAN
From composite - I see Tate has many Public Domain archive resources - it's recorded as the first exhibitionary exchange between visual art and digital assemblies.

AYAN LINDQUIST
For us at Moderna, that exhibition set in motion two decades of recurrent projects exploring *Art, Technology and Knowledge*.

Its most recent manifestation, linked to the Turing research, has resulted in Moderna 3.0's cooperation on a draft amendment to Article 39 of the United Nations Declaration of Human Rights.

We are seeking to extend certain rights to organic/synthetic, intelligent composites.

MS CHAN
You're co-producing sovereign composites!

AYAN LINDQUIST
Yes, yes that's what I was hinting at earlier; about Moderna being more agent, and executing as well as exhibiting.

MS CHAN
Now I understand, sovereign composites!

I can see Moderna's centenary proposal for a *Museum of* ***Their*** *Wishes*.

It's absolutely amazing!

I know it's a very common thread, but definitely still worth rerunning.

The one about the foundation of the Moderna Museet's collection with the *Museum of Our Wishes* exhibition in 1962.

And how this was revisited in 2006 with the *Museum of our Wishes II* - to address the lack of women artists within the collection.

AYAN LINDQUIST
We see our legacy as a resource, not a burden.
It's something we have been working with for a while, recursive programmes.
It's at root.

Actually, *Wish II* was finally fulfilled in 2'22, when some Dora Maar photographs reverted.

But, with the emergence of self-conscious composite intelligence, addressing 'their' wishes seemed appropriate, even necessary.

And it's true, if the draft amendment is ratified, it will be an amazing achievement.

MS CHAN
Ok. Even if you don't like the term, maybe a new 'golden age' is beginning?

AYAN LINDQUIST
For that, we'll all just have to wait and see.

But earlier, you were right to suggest that in 2'20, with *Ex Habare The Practice of Exhibition*, we consolidated the idea of emergent art.And, distributed new institutional practices.

MS CHAN
In the Asian network it's common knowledge that *Ex Habare* reaffirmed the role of the Museum in civil society.

AYAN LINDQUIST
Well to start, we un-compressed the Latinate root of exhibition, *ex habare*, to reveal the intention of 'holding-out' or 'showing' evidence in a legal court.

It's obvious, that implicit in exhibition is the desire to show, display and share with others. By grafting this ancient drive, to desires for creative co-production, we enabled exhibitions to remain core to Moderna's aspirations.

It's also true that to source, participate, co-produce and share, to generate non-rivalous resources, are vital to the constitution of a Public Domain. And indeed, a civil society.

There's a neat homology.

*Ex Habare* distributed these values, and it's also true, they replicated at an astonishing speed.

MS CHAN
It's so good to be reminded!
Even I tend to take the power of exhibition as a technology for granted.

Do you think that this is because artists and others moved into collaborative relationships with Moderna?

AYAN LINDQUIST
Var ska vi börja?

Artists and others realised………..that the 19th Century ideological construction of the artist, had reached its absolute limit.

As configured, art as a 'creative' process had ceased to innovate, inspire or have any critical purchase.

Quite simply it was irrelevant!

MS CHAN
Everywhere, except in the 'Contemporary Art' market!

AYAN LINDQUIST
*[Laughter]*

That heritage 'broadcast' communication model of culture that we mentioned earlier, privileges creative exchanges between artist and media in the studio / manufactory.

Exchanges which were distributed through competitive trade and collecting institutions.

At best, 'broadcast' extended a small measure of creative agency to the encounter between audiences - often referred to as passive 'viewers'- and artworks.

MS CHAN
Ok, I have material from composite.

So even when this model was disrupted; like in 1968, the *Modellen; A Model for a Qualitative Society* exhibition at Moderna for example. It looks like we fell back into, umm.................

Perhaps the wider creative ecology was just not receptive enough.

AYAN LINDQUIST

You might be right Ms Chan

It was really when artists began to imagine art as a practice, and explore creativity as a social process.........

MS CHAN

Sometime around the late 1990's perhaps?

AYAN LINDQUIST

.........Yes, yes, then we could detect something of a change.

Artists began to engage creatively with institutions, and vice versa.

With all aspects of institutional practice; of course through co-producing exhibitions, but also through archival projects - which you've done so much to research Ms Chan - through organisational engagement, administration, and so on.........

MS CHAN

Ok, I'm browsing material from composite on *Institutional Critique*.

Michael Asher and Hans Haacke, they seem to be mostly artists from the America's in the 1970's -1980's

AYAN LINDQUIST

Not sure if those are the appropriate resources?

Artists associated with *Institutional Critique*, I recall Michael Asher and Hans Haacke, but also Julie Ault and Group Material, or Andrea Fraser.

They had a much more antagonistic and oppositional relationship with exhibitionary institutions.

They resented being represented ***by*** an exhibitionary institution.

Especially those linked to a 19th Century ideology.

MS CHAN

Ok, now I'm browsing material on Sputniks,...... EIPCP, Bruno Latour, Maria Lind, Arteleku, Van Abbe Museum's Plug-Ins, Superlex, Franc Lacarde, Raqs and Sarai, Moderna's projects, Bart de Baer........

AYAN LINDQUIST

Yes, this constellation feels more relevant,

As artists rethought their practices, they recognised themselves as a nexus of complex social process.

And that creativity was inherent in every conceivable transaction producing that nexus.

At whatever the intensity, and regardless of the scale of the assembly.

The huge challenge for all of us, was to attend to the lines of force, the transactions, and not be dazzled by the subjects, objects or institutions they produced.

We recall that it was under these conditions that artists' practices merged with Moderna. Merged into relations of mutual co-production.

And so in exchange, Moderna began to think of itself as a creative institution.

Subject to constant critical and creative exploration.

MS CHAN

Ok, so these were the forces generating Moderna 2.0 in 2'12.

AYAN LINDQUIST

You're right,

We simply stopped thinking of ourselves as a 19th Century museum - which had to constantly expand, commission signature buildings, evolve huge administrative hierarchies - exhibition, education, support, management and so on.

And more on instituting - in the ancient sense of the word - of founding and supporting.

On instituting creative practice.

So, we started to play, risk, cooperate, research and rapidly prototype.

Not only exhibitions and research projects, but ourselves.

Some values were lost - which is always painful, and yet others were produced.

And those most relevant maintained, nurtured and cherished.

We learnt to invest, long-term, without regard for an *interested* return.

And that's how we devolved locally, and networked globally.

We've had some failures; either exhibitions couldn't convene the necessary resources, or we made mistakes.

But as an immanent institution, most experiences were productive.

Ahm.........Not sure if that jump-cut thread answered your query............,

MS CHAN
Sort of.....

AYAN LINDQUIST
The short answer could be that artists have transformed Moderna, and we in turn transformed them.

MS CHAN
Ok, but that last sound-bit is rather banal. Although, the thread's not uninteresting.

AYAN LINDQUIST
Ironically, our playful devolution of Moderna 2.0 reanimated the historical collection displayed in version 1.0.

We freed art-artefacts from their function, of 'recounting' the history of 20th Century Art; however alternative, discontinuous, or full of omissions we imagine that thread to be.

And once free, they engaged with realtime discursive transactions.

They became live again, contested nodes in competing transactions of unsettled bodies of knowledge.

MS CHAN
Um........., I'm not sure I'm following this......
As time is running out, and there's so much to cover.

I just wonder if you could mention......
Could you recall, even briefly, some beacon exhibitions.
Like *Transactional Aesthetics*, or the *Ecology of Fear*.

AYAN LINDQUIST
*Rädslans ekologi*, or the The *Ecology of Fear* was timely, given the viral pandemic throughout DNA storage - so many systems were compromised; and the various 'wars' that were being waged, against difference, and public attention......for material resources, energy,.........

And I guess the same with *Transactional Aesthetics*. It was the right moment to be participating in the production of local social enterprise and well-being initiatives......

MS CHAN
Could you just mention the legendary Alternative Research in Architecture, Resources, Art and Technology exhibited at Moderna in 1976.
Which you revisited on its 50th anniversary, in 2'26.

From composite I can see archive materials.
They're present.

AYAN LINDQUIST
There's not much to add.

Obviously the first version of ARARAT explored appropriate local technologies for buildings and urban systems - using sustainable resources.

In 1976, this was the beginning of our understanding of a global ecology, and of the finite nature of mineral resources; especially carbon.

Given our population reached 8bn in 2'26 it was vital to revisit the exhibition.
To somehow, take stock..............

The first shock was that so little of the initial exhibition was recoverable - we invested in reconstruction and archival research - it's all Public Domain composite now.

And the second, was the realisation that so little of the source exhibition had had any real effect.

We suspect a serious flaw in the exhibitionary form.

MS CHAN
The lack of resources from those early exhibitions is always disheartening.
It's hard to imagine a time before,

even rudimentary Public Domain mesh-works, embedded devices,..........and semantic interfaces.

AYAN LINDQUIST

Well, one of the great outcomes of the Moderna Golden Jubilee celebrations in 2'08, is that they revisited and reflected on the preceding fifty years.

We recently found shadow-traces for a Moderna History book.
And for reasons that are not entirely clear, it remained unpublished during the Jubilee celebrations - so, we intend to issue a centenary heritage publication,

we'll be sure to send you a copy.

MS CHAN

I see we have overrun, I'm so sorry.

I just wonder before we disconnect, what is Moderna re-sourcing in the near future?

AYAN LINDQUIST

Well, for us, there are some beautiful assemblies emerging.

Real-time consensus is moving from a local to regional scale.
Triangle in the African Multitude is distributing amazing regenerative medical technologies.

Renewable energy has moved through the 74% threshold.
Um ….. live, almost retro, music performance is popular again

Nano-technology has come of age, and 1:1 molecular replication will soon be enabled, linked to scanning technology hardwired to the manufactories in the Asian network.

Outside of heritage, singularity will be overwritten by difference.

Now that's exciting!

MS CHAN

Exciting indeed!

Thank you so much Ayan. Its been a privilege, really.
Enjoy the centenary celebrations, we'll all be there with you in spirit.
Zai Jian, goodbye

AYAN LINDQUIST

Thank you Ms Chan.

Goodbye, zai jian, hejdå

Goodbye, zai jian, hejdå



*The text can be downloaded from here http://www.neilcummings.com/*

\- - - - - - - - - - - - - - - - - - - - - - - - -

Known as a space of "sovereign bifurcation" or juridical construction; a space of low taxation, anonymity, and deregulation; and as "a safe haven for the proceeds of political corruption, illegal arms dealing, illegal diamond trafficking, and the global drug trade"[1], the complex world of the offshore has been an inexhaustible source of inspiration for Goldin+Senneby's ongoing project *Headless*. As curator Lisa Rosendahl wrote, "Goldin+Senneby are interested in how the juridical construction of offshore financial centres can be seen as performative acts of fictionalizing place and staging realms of invisibility."[2]

*Headless* started in 2007 as an investigation into the offshore company Headless Ltd, incorporated in the Bahamas in 2002, and its possible connections to Georges Bataille's secret society Acéphale (meaning "headless"), founded in Paris in the late 1930s. The artists' enquiries and findings are continuously traced in a docu-fictional murder-mystery novel titled *Looking for Headless*. The novel is ascribed to the fictional author K.D., who used to work in offshore management before turning to writing. *Looking for Headless* will be K.D.'s debut novel, exploring the dark sides of global finance.

*Headless* is an ongoing performance and meta-fiction which has generated a number of public and physical manifestations—from talks and interviews to novels, films, and exhibitions—produced and presented in line with the strategies of the offshore economy: invisible, withdrawn, and delegated. The artists have been consistently absent from the public aspects of the project, while the aforementioned outcomes have been delegated to, or have involved the contribution of, writers, curators, designers, actors, lawyers, detectives, economic geographers, pirates, and journalists.

1 Ronen Palan, *The Offshore World* (Ithaca: Cornell University Press, 2003), 48

2 Lisa Rosendahl's introduction about *Headless* at: http://www.goldinsenneby.com/gs/?p=72 (last accessed on 18 July 2009)

# Goldin +Senneby

***Headless***, 2007–present, Logotype

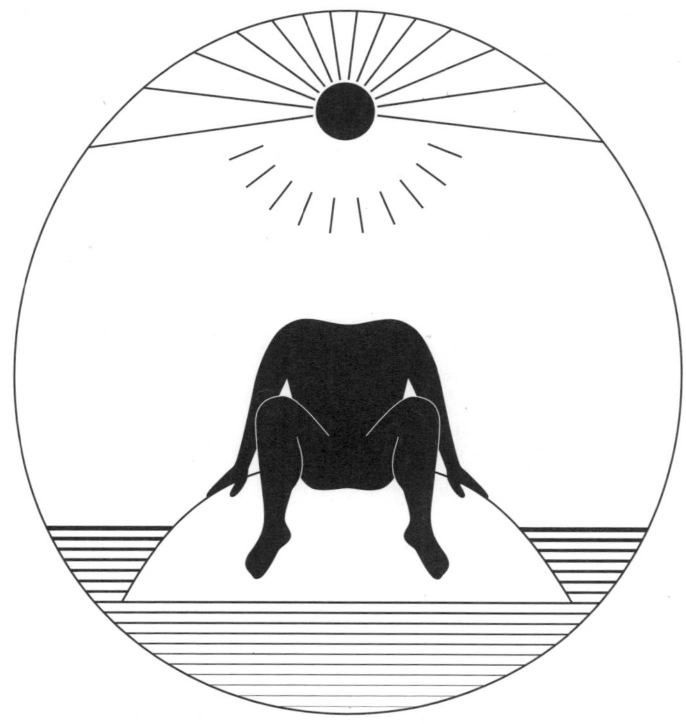

- - - - - - - - - - - - - - - - - - - - - - - - -

**LOOKING FOR HEADLESS**

A lecture given by Goldin+Senneby, produced for *visible*

Looking For Headless: Artistic and Legal Strategies of Withdrawal in the Context of the Production of Fiction

*(Simon and Jakob take their seats. Simon has a large surgical patch bandage covering one eye and the area above and below it.*

*They spend a few moments whispering to each other. Jakob seems to be concerned about Simon, but Simon nods, indicating that he is fine and wants to do the talk despite his injury. Once this is agreed they settle in their chairs.*

*Jakob has some sheets of printed paper in front of him, which he now arranges. Simon has two half-liter bottles of mineral water and a packet of 1mg Paracetamol with him, and nothing else.)*

**SIMON:** As you can see, I had a violent disagreement with a door handle today, and my eyesight is a little bit impaired.

**JAKOB:** (*Amused*) He's also just had about a hundred pain killers.

**SIMON:** Yeah, well I was in pain.

**JAKOB:** So, instead of both of us reading jointly from this paper, as we had intended to do, we've decided to initiate an open discussion between ourselves, and see where that takes us.

(*Pause*)

But first of all, I'll just say something about us. And I <u>can</u> still read, so I think I'll just read this. (*Reads somewhat flatly from printed paper*) Our names are Simon Goldin and Jakob Senneby. We are artists, and our artistic practice, goldin+senneby, explores juridical, financial, and spatial constructs through a variety of performative and virtual forms.

For the last three years, we have been working on a project called *Headless*. In it, we've been investigating an offshore company called Headless Ltd, which is registered in the Bahamas.

**SIMON:** (*Interrupts*) Could I just say, this company, Headless Ltd., really exists.

**JAKOB:** Yes, it is really registered in the Bahamas.

**SIMON:** We have copies of the registration documents, and we know the company that registered it, the names of people who signed those documents. We know about a lot of the people involved.

**JAKOB:** Ehm, yeah. (*Slightly disconcerted, pauses to look at his papers and collect his thoughts*) Right.

**SIMON:** Right!

(*They both laugh*)

**JAKOB:** What interests us is the fictitious character of offshore businesses, and the legal issues raised by such companies. But also, we are interested in the act of investigating them and what this says about the space they occupy. (*Pauses, noticing that Simon is fidgeting*) Do you want to say a bit about the fictional element in our work?

**SIMON:** Me? Yes. I'd like to say that we are all characters in the investigation, and all characters in the novel. (*He looks out across the audience*) When we give a talk at a conference in Maastricht, or smash up an eye, you know, whatever, it's all part of the project. We base things on fact. And that means you become part of what you are investigating.

**JAKOB:** But we also need to make clear that the outcome of this investigation is unusual. We are writing a murder-mystery novel about the investigation. And that, clearly, is fiction.

**SIMON:** It's both. Fact and fiction.

**JAKOB:** But, I mean, just to be <u>perfectly</u> clear, the project leads to a novel. What we are producing is fiction. No one actually dies, for example.

**SIMON:** We don't know that! Really, we don't. That's the thing about offshore. You can't know anything absolutely for sure about many things.

**JAKOB:** OK. (*Begins reading from his pa-

*per again*) Such an approach has proved fertile for the exploration of the questions of authorship, identity and its uses and abuses, and, perhaps most importantly, the idea of withdrawal, especially in the context of a fiction about the "offshore" industry. (*Stops to think*) I think I'm just going to read this next bit as well, because it serves as an introduction. (*To Simon*) Is that all right?

(*Simon is busy taking another Paracetamol. He nods as he glugs down water from one of his bottles.*)

**JAKOB:** The offshore sector has an important role in the global economy. It makes possible the anonymous reallocation of capital. Offshore companies are nurtured and protected largely by the finance industry, in offshore financial centers, or "tax havens." Such companies are officially registered, yet the owners' identities and the nature of their businesses remain secret.
Companies can be set up in this way because local political history has established offshore financial centers as legal exceptions, in which legal secrecy is guaranteed. Creative interpretations of concepts such as nationhood, legal responsibility and affiliation, and citizenship mean that capital can evade domestic political regulation entirely, whilst the companies themselves operate as legitimate businesses. The whole system is a fiction upheld by the many players who act it out.

(*Pause*)

Simon, do you want to say something about the particular company we've been looking at?

(*Simon seems a little surprised; perhaps he hasn't been listening.*)

**SIMON:** Right... Yes, the company is called Headless Ltd. Registered on the Bahamas. The word "headless" is also the English translation of the Greek word *acephale*, meaning "headless" or "beheaded." *Acephale* was a surrealist publication and secret society established by the philosopher Georges Bataille in the late 1930s.
We know almost nothing about Bataille's secret society because, y'know, it was secret. We <u>do</u> know that they wanted to create a new world order in which there was no central authority, no God. They actually planned to decapitate one of their own members as a symbolic act of making society headless. Apparently they were all willing to be the victim, but no one wanted to be the executioner. The current business activities of Headless Ltd are just as secretive and unknown. (*As an afterthought*) And dangerous.

(*Pauses*)

**JAKOB:** I think it's fair to say that this project has been more difficult for us personally and artistically than we thought it would be. Would you agree?

**SIMON:** I dunno about difficult. I've enjoyed it. Some bits have been painful (*Indicates injured eye*) and others have been frustrating. I dunno, difficult? Sure, there are difficult things, I guess. Quite difficult... (*Laughs quietly to himself as he drinks more water*)

**JAKOB:** (*Tries to keep going*) Ehm... Perhaps it's the fact that... that investigating something like an offshore company is almost impossible. I mean, just as a proposition it's undoable.

**SIMON:** Because that's the point about 'em!

**JAKOB:** Exactly. These companies are set up so the US tax authorities or whoever can't find out about them. What chance have we got?

**SIMON:** But it's also about the risks, right? This is not a risk-free area. And the risk makes the search more exciting.

**JAKOB:** (*A little defensively*) There are some potential risks... Everything has risks.

**SIMON:** But not everybody goes out chasing them. That's the thing about this project. Part of it is that you are looking at institutions that <u>really</u> don't want you to look.

**JAKOB:** Well...

**SIMON:** And we don't know why that is. We just don't know why. What we <u>do</u> know is that a lot of people tried to stop us, one way and another.

**JAKOB:** Okay, yes, looking into the unknown is a risk, but what for us was more important was the question how such companies manage to be so secretive.

**SIMON:** (*Ignoring Jakob*) The risk is actually worse for some of the collaborators we work with. Some of them are already ex-collaborators! We've had people doing investigative stuff in the Caribbean, in Hong Kong, Gibraltar, you know, and you just don't know for certain what's gonna happen when they knock on a door or they get invited in somewhere. Especially when you think about the ethical conflicts involved.

(*Jakob looks at him, confused*)

**SIMON:** I mean, looking for something hidden brings with it certain questions of ethical responsibility. (*Pause*) For example, we employed a firm of private investigators. I can say this, right?

**JAKOB:** I don't know. (*Amused*) This wasn't actually in the paper. But, I guess you just said it, so...

**SIMON:** I mean, it wasn't illegal. And this is a part of how offshore works. It's just, when you start to get into private surveillance and that kind of thing, you've sort of opened yourself up in some way.

(*Pause. They look at each other, slightly quizzical.*)

**SIMON:** So anyway, we got some detectives to shadow an employee of the company we are looking at. An individual who we think is involved in Headless in a significant way. We got video footage and everything, full investigator's report.

**JAKOB:** Then we had it turned into a chapter of the novel.

**SIMON:** (*As if ignoring Jakob*) You've got to try and get inside this closed, inaccessible world using detectives and covert stuff. It's the only way. We've also tapped email accounts, even a company intranet at one point. I mean, we didn't do anything, there was no real motive sometimes. But you have to try things, to look at ways of getting behind the secrets. It opens you up, is all I'm saying.

(*Pause*)

**JAKOB:** Because there are no legitimate entry points to offshore. This is what is so brilliant about how offshore is set up. It's a legal exception, it exists kind of around normal law. So investigating it is quite an interesting proposition in itself.

**SIMON:** Another thing we know is that we are being watched. By taking an interest in offshore, we ourselves have attracted interest. For me, this is where it gets absorbing. I mean, apart from all the warning letters from Sovereign's lawyers...

**JAKOB:** Sovereign Trust, just to clarify. Sovereign is the offshore management company that administers Headless Ltd.

**SIMON:** And we know for a fact that Sovereign have sent someone to snoop on us, most recently during an exhibition.

**JAKOB:** Let me say, nothing came of that. It's a free country. They sent someone, apparently.

**SIMON:** We've had a few cease and desist warnings from them.

**JAKOB:** But in this case nothing happened.

**SIMON:** It was there, though. I mean, the surveillance was there. It's interesting that they needed to do that. And it wasn't the only time there've been people looking into our work.

(*Pause*)

**SIMON:** Oh, and another thing. It was also interesting who sent that observer. Howard Bilton sent him. Howard Bilton sent him personally. Bilton is the chairman of the Sovereign Group, a leading offshore management company.

**JAKOB:** (*Holding up a hand to subtly stop Simon speaking*) Ehm, could I just ask... (*humorously but nervous*) do we have any libel lawyers in the audience, because I think we might be needing one soon!

**SIMON:** (*Laughs*) It was Bilton, chairman of the Sovereign Group, *allegedly*. Is that better?

**JAKOB:** (*Speaking as if to Simon, but also to the audience*) The point is that you don't actually know who's in the audience. Ever. (*More to the audience*) We're not actually very accustomed to talking about this project in public.

(*Simon drinks more water. The topic seems to be closed.*)

**JAKOB:** Anyway, perhaps we should talk a bit about the outcome of the work itself, which is a commercial murder-mystery novel. Because, on one level, we have been trying to look into offshore generally. On a more specific level, we're trying to explore the implications of its fictional nature.

**SIMON:** Incidentally, we haven't even come close to uncovering the truth about the company we're investigating. We had someone go over to the Bahamas and look for it physically. And since then, wherever else the search has gone, the walls seem to have gotten higher and thicker. Perhaps we need to blow them up!

**JAKOB:** It certainly feels like there's some pretty strong pressure not to let anyone spy on this very clever and complicated world. But, as we said, it's more the...

**SIMON:** (*Interrupts*) I mean, offshore companies are usually about tax avoidance. But all this to avoid tax? We still feel that there's some other reason for Headless to exist. And I'm not the only one. (*Turns to Jakob*) Can we mention KD?

**JAKOB:** (*Not quite believing what he's heard*) Err, I...

**SIMON:** I'll take that as a no!

**JAKOB:** Just to say that there are other people looking at Headless Ltd. A novelist called KD, as it happens, is also looking into the same company. It's an interesting subject. (*With strong emphasis*) But, there's also a point at which our project *Looking for Headless* as a work of artistic exploration has to stop. Which, in a sense, is why we are talking about it now. Our own work is about withdrawal, and I think we've shown the lengths that Headless and its owners have been willing to go to to maintain that withdrawn status.

**SIMON:** That's true.

(*Jakob returns to papers and then speaks, still looking down*)

**JAKOB:** Okay. We are artists, and the originators of this project. We are also interested in the nature of art as a commodity.

(*Looks up, as if speaking without notes now*)

Outsourcing is one focus of this interest. Throughout the history of Western art, the artistic process has often been one of collaboration. Most artists do not work in a creative and practical vacuum. They require assistance of one kind or another, however peripheral. In fact, one of our collaborators, the novelist who's ghostwriting the novel...

**SIMON:** Was. He kinda got scared.

**JAKOB:** Well, he's... The roles have changed a bit recently. But I think for us here at the moment the idea of outsourcing creative work clearly raises interesting issues about authorship. In the *Headless* project we outsourced as much of the work as possible. Even this paper, which we are not giving exactly, was written by a ghostwriter for us. This naturally leads to the question of how far from the actual process of creating art the originating artist can be while still having the title of artist.

There are also ethical and perhaps legal questions of whether an outsourced worker merits attribution as an artist, and, you know, whether a work of art requires that all its artists—rather than just the originating artists—should be identified. In other words, what do we mean by the category "artist" when we consume art?

**SIMON:** Ehm, if you were investigating a secret company and some thug working for that company beat you up, you know, if you were trying to get past the security desk, for example. I dunno, some act of violence. Would he deserve a credit? Because he is an actor in your fiction.

**JAKOB:** That's actually quite an interesting point, because the outsourcing we have used spans a wide range of levels of artistic commitment. But also a range of levels of consciousness. There are people, the company's lawyers for example...

**SIMON:** Howard Bilton, or, you know, the odd police officer here and there...

**JAKOB:** (*Tries to ignore Simon*) Anyone who has been drawn into the work we are doing is effectively part of it. We're not legal experts, but it seems to me that at least in some cases these actors might have a legitimate claim to artistic input. If, for example, a huge amount of money was concerned, let's say they made a movie from our project and it generated millions of dollars. Who should get the money? Everyone here is potentially part of the narrative. Some more than others, perhaps. There might be people here who at some point, past or future...

**SIMON:** Or present, if you like. (*Grins*)

**JAKOB:** ...people who actually have a material influence on the plot, hence on the work as it stands. Not just the crafting of it, but the ideas. And that would be a pretty decent description of what an artist does.

**SIMON:** The most interesting would be those who are not aware of it. And that's almost all the people involved in making offshore work. For example, offshore is protected by a legal system, but that legal system knows nothing about what it maintains and protects. These people are part of our fiction.

**JAKOB:** The whole process of protecting the offshore world is about perpetuating myths—fictions, if you like—to conceal what is within. These companies are not registered in <u>places</u>, not really. When you say you have a business in Lichtenstein, you don't go there, the business doesn't have any material connection to that territory. They are not part of the normal legal structures of these countries at all. They exist in a specially created legal hole or exception, one which grants them special privileges of secrecy. But what they require is a whole performance—managers, lawyers, governments, officials—a continuous performance of people whose job is essentially to maintain the pretence.

(*Pause, as if both trying to think what to say next*)

**JAKOB:** Perhaps it seems that we have taken a critical position relative to offshore. In fact, we have tried very carefully to take no position. We are interested in how offshore functions in terms of its own fictive self, not in terms of the ethics involved.
I'd just like to read from the paper we were going to give. Err... (*finds place*) This is about the approach we have taken to authorship and the way our fiction has evolved in response to the fiction of offshore. Err... Yes: we intuitively feel drawn to the multi-headed author. This is evident in the various strands of the *Headless* projects, which have included all of the following, from various outsourced "workers": documentaries, academic lectures, an expert colloquium, gallery installations, a short book, translations, a travel blog, staged interviews, literary readings, a fine etching entered in an international art prize.

**SIMON:** That's in addition to all the unknowing actors, who are generally actors in this fiction only because they are actors in offshore's fiction.

**JAKOB:** But the central strand of all this is a novel, one that we want to be mainstream enough to publish with a mainstream publisher. For such an aim, all these narrative standpoints, the multi-headed nature of the narrative poses a problem. Because we as artists have to stand in some visible relation to the novel. Are we artists? Are we actors in the performance? Or are we just directors, handing out roles in this drama to other people? Of course, we play all these parts, directing the action by arranging the events that are then played out. But we can never retain control of the sequence of events, or the reactions that arise.

**SIMON:** Like having a door handle slam violently into your eye.

**JAKOB:** Shit happens, don't they say!

**SIMON:** Yeah, like even the hotel door becomes an actor in our fiction!

**JAKOB:** You know, just to go off the topic for a minute. I just thought, we are inspired here by a secret society founded by Georges Bataille, whose most famous work is *The Story of the Eye*.

Right? And, just to explain this a bit, we sent our ghostwriter John Barlow to the Bahamas last year to research *Headless*, and while he was there he got an eye infection, which meant he couldn't go to a concert and then he lost his camera and that led somewhere else... Now you have this accident with your eye.

**SIMON:** Cool, so now the story has taken over and is imposing its own themes! (*Adopts a mock-dramatic tone*) The eye as symbol of knowing, seeing as knowing... We definitely never planned this. (*Points at is injured eye*).

*(Confused, Jakob returns to the script and reads.)*

**JAKOB:** There are various points at which our work intersects with legal issues on a more practical level. The very notion of publishing a "docu-fictional" work is problematic. To the extent that the work is documentary in nature, a publisher will require authors to confirm the truth of facts presented; the James Frey and other cases have recently underlined the importance of contractually established truthfulness in works of nonfiction. Yet as a work of fiction, exactly the reverse is true: the fictional nature of the work, its characters, and the institutions therein will have to be declared.
Our control in this project, though, is severely limited. The investigation takes the shape of an ongoing performance where subject, method, and artistic narrative cannot be separated, and are not under the control of the originating artists.
Our "withdrawal" from the normal position of the artist is an attempt at mimicking the withdrawal of our subject—offshore companies—from the visible economy. It is somewhere between appropriation and parody of the methods, language, and strategies of offshore. The novel *Looking for Headless* will be published next year. Thank you.

*(They turn and talk. Simon appears animated, as does Jakob. But Simon is very amused about what he has just seen, and Jakob isn't.)*

- - - - - - - - - - - - - - - - - - - -

*Context —*

A large number of ships leave from the Sharjah Creek to Somalia. Presently, Somalia is a gathering of semi-state entities, where formal tariffs and customs are not applicable (and thus the entities are similar to "free trade zones"). With war up ahead and crisis at its tail (and with pirates in between), the movement of goods and sailors may trace old trade routes, but also map out something new: a contemporary landscape of new and used objects, labor, charcoal (the only bulk item on the return journey), Asian and African diasporas, and giant wooden ships being built in Salaya, Gujarat.

The zone of exception that defines Somalia and its waters, and the impact such status has on global trade, form the subject of *Wharfage*. The project consisted of two parallel pieces: *Wharfage*, a book containing two years of port records related to Somali trade;[1] and *Radio Meena*, four evenings of radio transmissions from the port.

*Wharfage —*

"The idea of the book was to dig out state records to produce an official litany, a register of 'facts,' that serve as testament of this commerce and movement. This was our way into the politics of representation and the act of 'making visible.' The idea of the book was born out of an early conversation we had at CAMP, where during our initial research we were often confronted with pirate litanies.[2] This seemed to be the dominant trope of engagement with sea trade and Somalia, something the book quite obviously counters by bringing attention to other sets of operations and trade."[3]

1 A PDF of the book can be downloaded from: http://www.camputer.org/event.php?this=wharfage

2 See for instance: http://en.wikipedia.org/wiki/List_of_ships_attacked_by_Somali_pirates

3 Words by CAMP member Ashok Sukumaran

# CAMP

**Notes**

The following annotations are based on research and interviews carried out with Sharjah Creek's workers, unless otherwise stated.

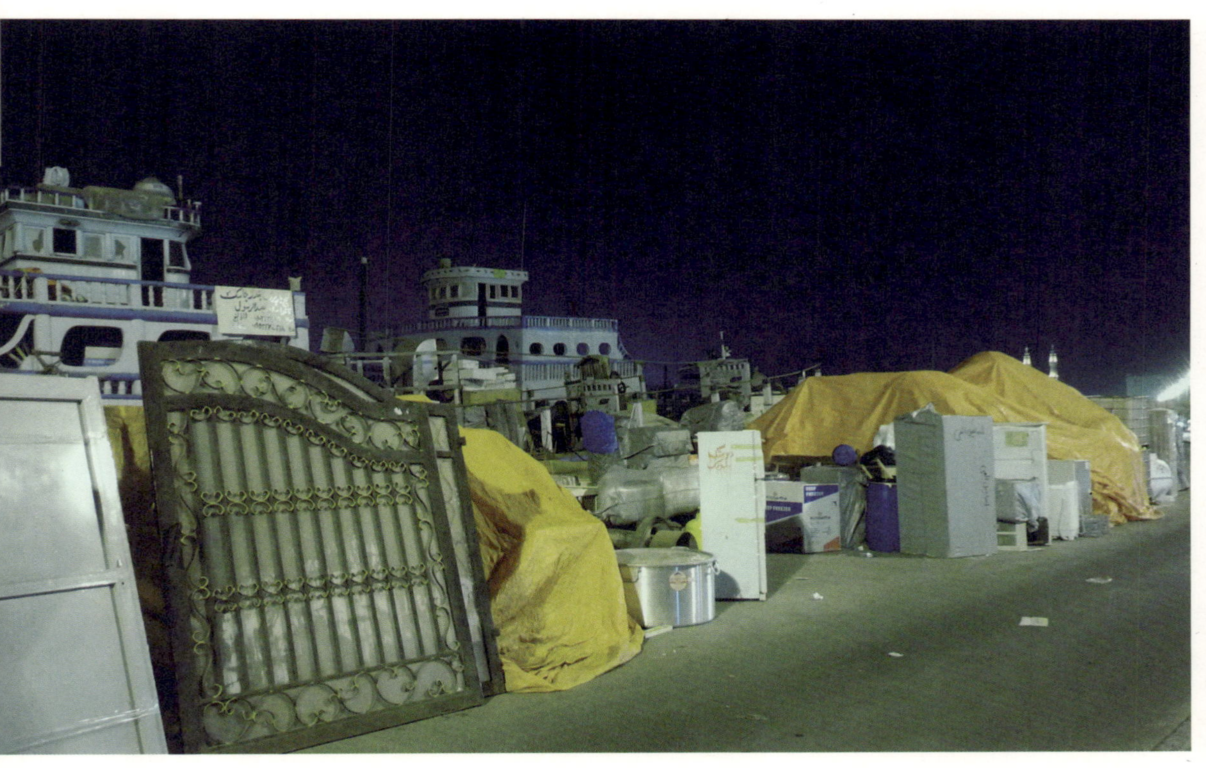

***Goods in the port of Sharjah***, 2008

"We take a whole supermarket with us. Sometimes even used medical dispensaries on the boat with us. *Vahan pe kuch bhi nahin hai*, there is nothing there."

"Focusing on things that are exchanged, rather than simply on the forms or functions of exchange, makes it possible to argue that what creates the link between exchange and value is politics [...] This argument [...] justifies the conceit that commodities like persons, have social lives."—Arjun Appadurai, *The Social Life of Things: Commodities in Cultural Perspective*, (Cambridge, UK: Cambridge University Press, 1986), 13.

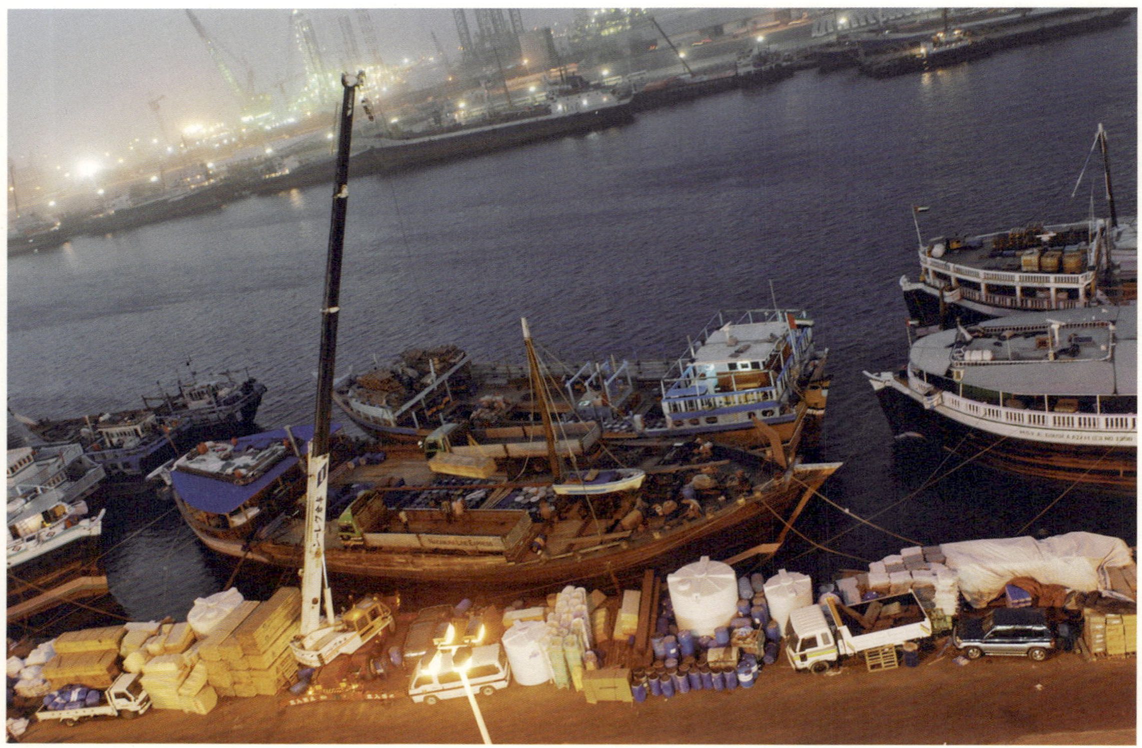

■
***Sharjah Creek*, 2008**

In the wake of a global financial crisis, business in the string of shops across the Sharjah Creek has slowed down. Around sunset, migrant workers from South Asia hang around a couple of empty plots, clustered under streetlights. Many of them have started buying tickets to return home, unable to cope with the pressure of paying back their guest-worker loans at a time when their salaries are also being withheld. Of late, many have even approached sailors on the old Sharjah port to ask if they could sail back to India on the boats with them, offering themselves as ship hands in exchange for passage. On the port, trucks line up, offload wares, and leave. The loading of dhows goes on well into the night: a strange scuttle of human bodies carrying sacks around a maze of stacked boxes, up a slim ramp, and onto the deck. Seemingly unaffected by the economic turn, dhows traverse pirated waters, as trade with war-torn Somalia goes on. Sailors from Salaya say that had it not been for the demand from Somalia, their dhows would not have much to carry, or many places to go. For Salaya, Somalia is then, in a sense, somehow symptomatic of possibilities. Though sometimes troubled by pirates, there seems to be a consensus among sailors, agents, and traders that when compared to container traffic and navy vessels, these relatively "small" dhows are rarely ever a desirable target, bound as they are for Somalia, carrying essential supplies and commodities. And that, after all, this is business, and that it will go on.

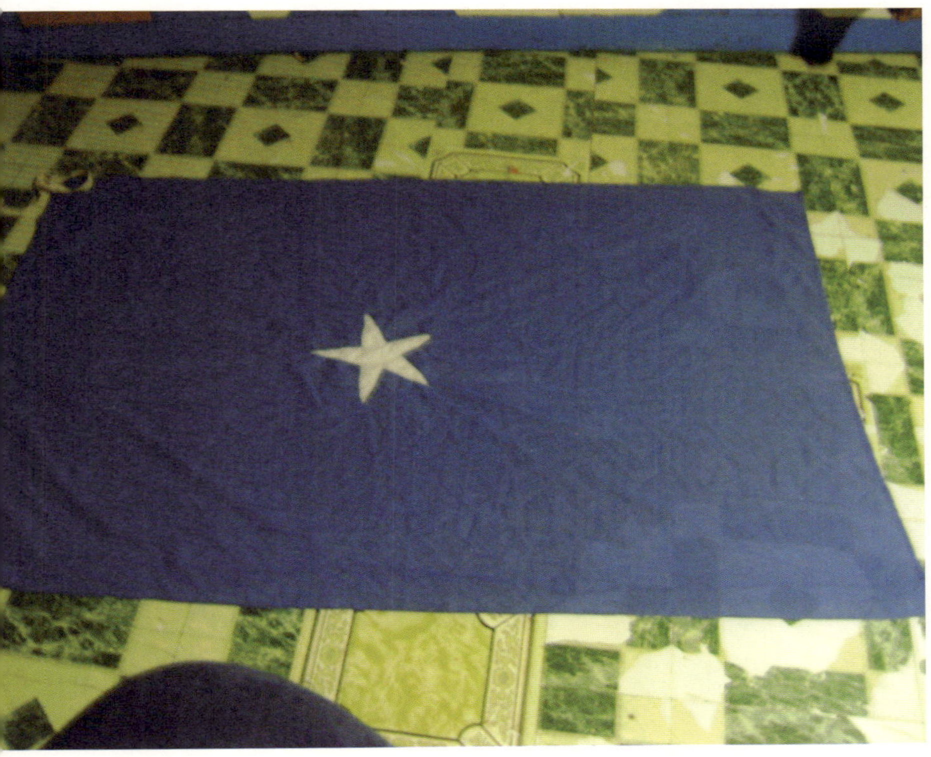

■

***Somaliland Flag***, 2008

Somalia, a collection of quasi-governmental and semi-state entities, has an economy based largely on the export of livestock from the region, a private telecommunication system with the cheapest cell phone rates on the continent, and a post-war diaspora interconnected and spread all across the world.

"When we sail out of Sharjah we put back the Indian flag as we are in international waters. When we enter the waters of the nation whose port we are to dock at, we have to mount their flag. It's the law. If it's Mogadishu or Kismayo we use the blue flag, it's really simple with a white star. We made one on our own."

What about Somaliland?

"Ah, for Berbera, it's just like the Indian flag with a black star. But upside down, with *La ilaha il allah* written on it."

*Radio Meena —*

"Members of CAMP, even prior to its formation, have done extensive work with micro-media and broadcast. (See most earlier works here: http://www.chitrakarkhana.net.) As with the book, our interest was to produce particular communication and information with and about other sets of agents, and other constellations of people. The radio station was to drop down on a boat, its broadcast slowly growing from fifty meters to beyond, carried forth by word of mouth, congregations, and "musafirs" (Arabic, Persian, Hindi, and Urdu word for "travelers") who came into contact with it. What we enjoy most about micro-radio is its ability to close distance on its various nodes of creation and reception. Thus, the spectrum is not so much a frequency one can tune into from a distance, but rather it has the ability to activate the listeners as contributors."

"Our status of artists working within the biennial framework conferred on us unique access to the port records, and the authorization to bring in a transmitter, set up an antenna, and broadcast Radio Meena. The idea of having radio receivers and books on the roof or the art cafe was our way of giving the biennial crowd a 'safe' distance from the station, or rather an initial point of reception. For them it was about reading the book first, sensing that there was something more immediate and visceral happening elsewhere—in languages they may not understand—and if they cared to venture forth, they could follow the sounds up to the clusters on the port."[4]

4 Ibid.

A project on the creek in Sharjah, United Arab Emirates, developed for the 9th edition of the Sharjah Biennial, 2008

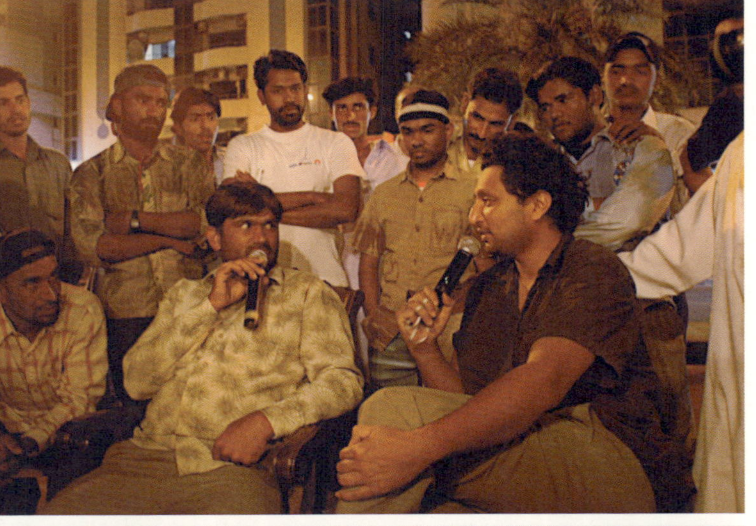

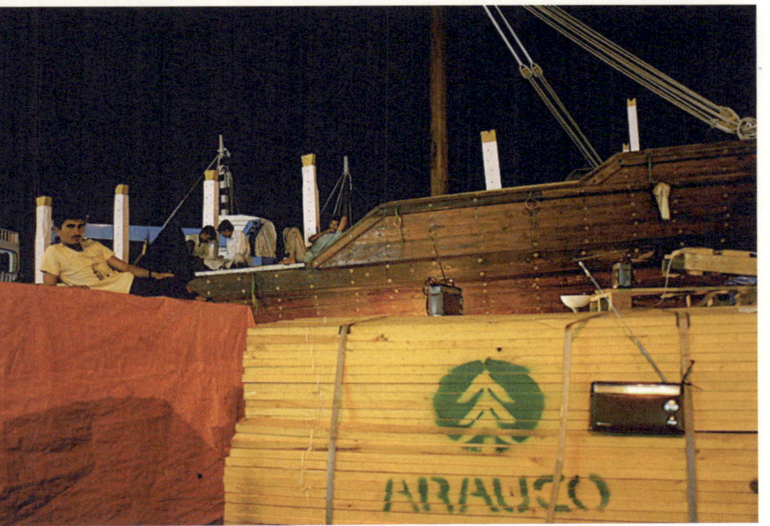


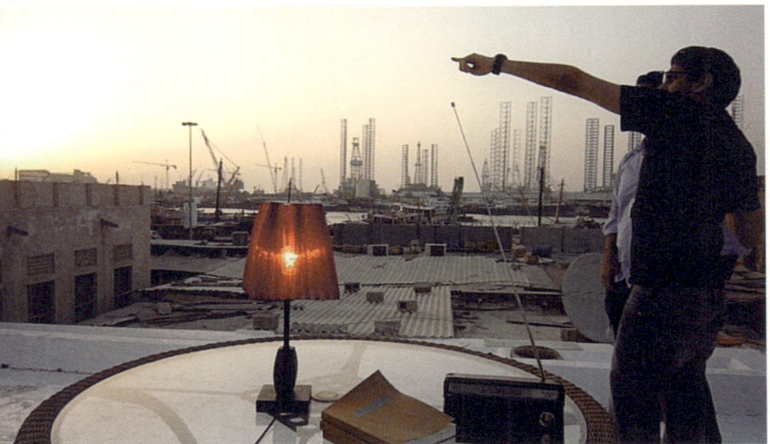

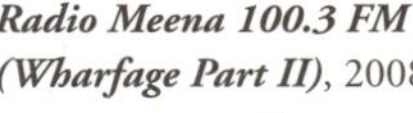

***Radio Meena 100.3 FM (Wharfage Part II)***, 2008

***Safe distance***, 2008, a listening and reading post on top of the art cafe in the museum quarter

← Date of arrival: November 20, 2008

Vessel name: M.S.V. Nigah e Makdumi
Manifest no. missing
Flag: India
Coming from: Somalia
Duty (AED): 000
Landing fees (AED): 1435

| Goods | Quantity |
|---|---|
| Charcoal | 28679 bags |

→ Date of departure: November 20, 2008

Vessel name: M.S.V. Prem Sagar
Manifest no. 10317/10348
Flag: India
Going to: Bossaso, Puntland
Docked at Sharjah Creek for: 17 days

| Goods | Quantity | Weight (tonnes) | Value (AED) |
|---|---|---|---|
| Food supplies and home appliances | 300 packages | | |
| Candy | 400 cartons | | |
| Chairs | 10 bundles | | |
| Chicken stock | 200 cartons | | |
| Clothes | 1500 packages | | |
| Cooking oil | 2500 cartons | | |
| Furniture | 20 bundles | | |
| Hair oil | 100 cartons | 160 | 400000 |
| Lighters | 100 cartons | | |
| Macaroni | 2700 cartons | | |
| Metal | 30 bundles | | |
| Milk | 500 cartons | | |
| Pens | 30 cartons | | |
| Shoes | 1000 cartons | | |
| Soap | 200 cartons | | |
| Textiles | 500 bundles | | |
| Wood | 5 bundles | | |
| Food flavourings | 930 cartons | 17.67 | 11613 |
| Medical supplies | 6 packages | 2.392 | 6042 |
| Milk | 1634 cartons | 20.328 | 40846 |
| Plastic bags | 108 cartons | 3.204 | 5950 |
| Shampoo | 1712 cartons | 29.53 | 16975 |
| Shoes | 130 cartons | 2.587 | 60494 |
| Tent fabric | 300 bundles | 11.386 | 12339 |
| Textiles | 180 bundles | 11.5 | 17187 |
| 16 vehicles: | | | |
| Toyota Hilux Surf | 2 units | 3.84 | 15600 |
| Nissan Caravan | 1 unit | 1.73 | 4790 |
| Nissan truck | 2 units | 5 | 18000 |
| Suzuki Escudo | 1 unit | 1.3 | 10570 |
| Toyota Hilux | 3 units | 4.99 | 28950 |
| Toyota Land Cruiser | 1 unit | 1 | 11000 |
| Toyota Mark II | 6 units | 7.534 | 40276 |
| | Total weight of goods: | 285.931 | |
| | Total value of goods: | | 700632 |
| | Customs paid: | | 860 |
| | Docking charges: | | 220 |

(The weight 160 and value 400000 are bracketed together for all goods from Food supplies and home appliances to Wood.)

← Date of arrival: November 22, 2008

Vessel name: Taufeej
Manifest no. missing
Flag: Sri Lanka
Coming from: Somalia
Duty (AED): 000
Landing fees (AED): 1015

| Goods | Quantity |
|---|---|
| Charcoal | 20320 bags |

← Date of arrival: January 28, 2008

Vessel name: M.S.V. Al Bashir
Manifest no. 1744
Flag: India
Coming from: Kismayo, Somalia
Duty (AED): 000
Landing fees (AED): 605

| Goods | Quantity |
|---|---|
| Charcoal | 12048 bags |

→ Date of departure: February 06, 2008

Vessel name: M.S.V. Madeef
Manifest no. 1017
Flag: India
Going to: Bossaso, Puntland
Docked at Sharjah Creek for: 32 days

| Goods | Quantity | Weight (tonnes) | Value (AED) |
|---|---|---|---|
| Engine oil | 1000 cartons | | |
| Television sets | 50 units | | |
| Cardamom | 50 cartons | | |
| Clothes | 10 bundles | | |
| Fish nets | 35 bundles | | |
| Garlic | 100 cartons | | |
| Medical equipment | 200 cartons | | |
| Rice | 1200 bags | 85 | 100000 |
| Rope | 100 bundles | | |
| Shoes | 30 cartons | | |
| Tomatoes | 1000 cartons | | |
| Tyres | 200 units | | |
| Washing machines | 20 units | | |
| Water | 1200 cartons | | |
| Wood | 40 bundles | | |
| Beauty products | 2100 cartons | 14.507 | 127318 |
| Kettles | 567 cartons | 11.235 | 63747 |
| Kettles | 531 cartons | 10.035 | 15560 |
| Kitchen items | 409 cartons | 6.963 | 44611 |
| Linoleum | 629 rolls | 22.833 | 12367 |
| Macaroni | 5300 bags | 53.759 | 23590 |
| Macaroni | 5100 cartons | 52 | 22700 |
| Macaroni | 5300 packages | 53.742 | 198535 |
| Macaroni | 5300 packages | 53.742 | 198535 |
| Matches | 2375 cartons | 19 | 16740 |
| Mats | 365 bundles | 10.77 | 56862 |
| Metal rods | 17 bundles | 45.45 | 143507 |
| Metal sheets | 18 packages | 54.99 | 195340 |
| Notepads, papers, metal doors, mattresses and glass shelves | 268 units | 8.5 | 12486 |
| Plywood | 24 bundles | 35.328 | 139586 |
| Textiles | 180 packages | 12.5 | 12686 |
| Tyres and tubes | 550 units | 17.617 | 17939 |
| | Total weight of goods: | 567.971 | |
| | Total value of goods: | | 1402109 |
| | Customs paid: | | 1140 |
| | Docking charges: | | 760 |

← Date of arrival: February 10, 2008

Vessel name: M.S.V. Shah e Kalandar
Manifest no. 3431
Flag: India
Coming from: Berbera, Somaliland
Duty (AED): 000
Landing fees (AED): 1302

| Goods | Quantity |
|---|---|
| Stone | 651 tons |

← Date of arrival: February 10, 2008

Vessel name: Al Adnan
Manifest no. missing
Flag: Comoros
Coming from: Somalia
Duty (AED): 000
Landing fees (AED): 800

| Goods | Quantity |
|---|---|
| Stone | 651 tons |

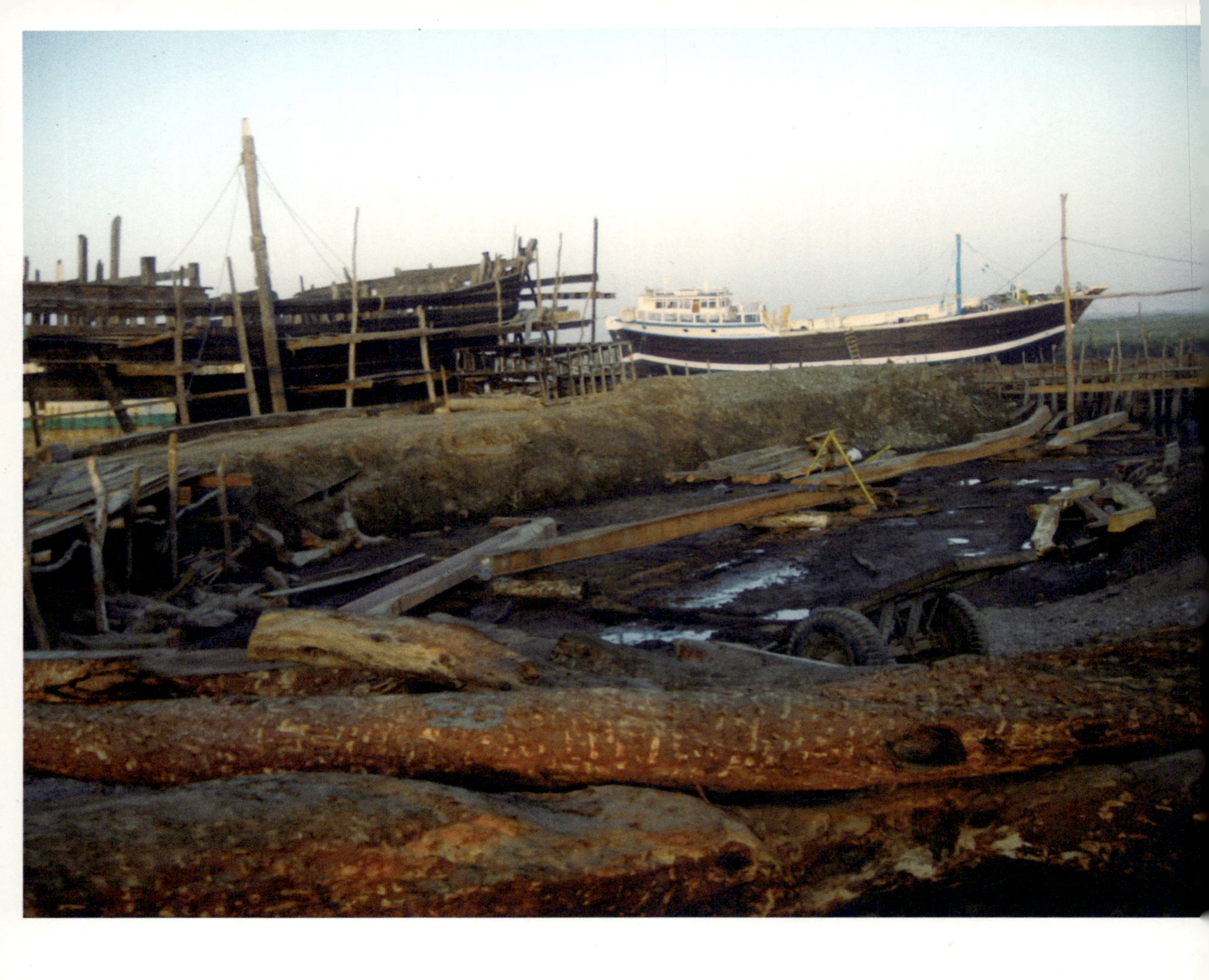

***Salaya***, 2008

"The boat business in Gujarat is more of a family business. It is passed on from father to son or to nephews. In Salaya, children usually make their first trip on a boat at twelve to fourteen years old, accompanying either their father or uncle. After the first trip, most of them drop out of school and start working on the boat itself. For them, the boat is their home. Even when they are in Salaya, they end up spending more time on the boat than at their home. Staying on the boat is also a way to avoid family tensions and frustrations."

Salaya's population of 20,000 is predominantly Muslim. Literacy, as in the rest of Gujarat, is low; almost all of the village's young men work on boats as ship hands and crew, as carpenters and gaiders (contractors), or as fishermen. Often, a new dhow (a type of boat) fitted with a tiny motor sails from Salaya, only to be refurbished with a far more powerful one in the United Arab Emirates. And the ships spend a great deal of time on the Sharjah Creek, as this has become their most frequented docking bay. During their nine-month period at sea, families communicate with the crewmen via VHF radio on bands that are assigned to ships. Down time occurs during the monsoons, when ships and crew return to Salaya to rest and repair. For sailors, this is a time to marry.

"In those two months back home, a lot of us get married and begin families. All the eligible bachelors are back home then and their marriages are arranged by their families. Like this boy here—we have to get him married when we return. But often when we leave, it's as good as giving *talaaq* (divorce) to our wives."

Initiated and led by London-based artist Ana Laura López de la Torre, *Do You Remember Olive Morris?* is a project that takes as a starting point the historical figure of community activist Olive Morris (1952–1979). Olive Morris was a key figure in 1970s South London. She set up the Brixton Black Women's Group and was a founding member of the Organization of Women of African and Asian Descent (OWAAD). She was also part of the British Black Panther Movement and was central to the squatters' campaign of that decade. She died tragically young at the age of twenty-seven.

The project started in 2006, when Ana Laura López de la Torre came across a photograph of Olive Morris standing at a Black Panther Movement demonstration in Coldharbour Lane, Brixton and holding a placard reading: "Black sufferer fight police pig brutality." From then on continued long, often frustrated, but mostly enlightened research around this character who had not found her place in history books, and who, despite having had a council building in the London borough of Lambeth named after her, has been largely forgotten.

The artist started piecing together a fragmented and under-documented history through primary research; through meeting and talking to people who had lived, worked, demonstrated or travelled with her; and through secondary research, browsing the slim sections dedicated to Britain's black history in archives and libraries around London.

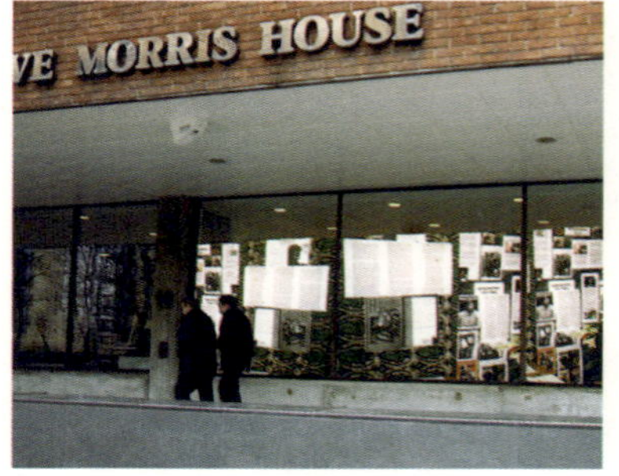


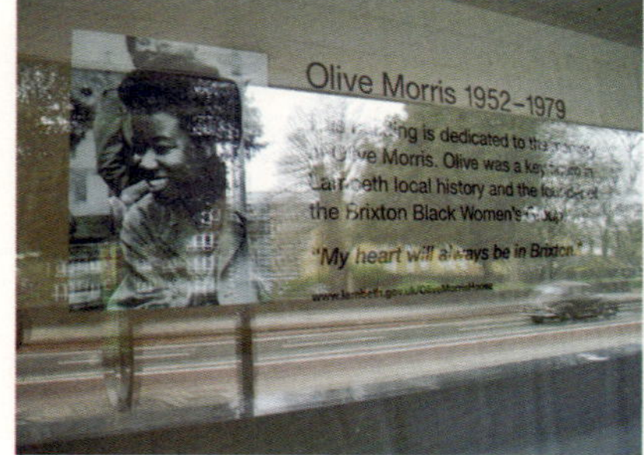

# Ana Laura López de la Torre

■□□□
New window display at 18 Brixton Hill after the re-instatement of the plaque
□■□□
Proposal for a new façade at Olive Morris House
□□■□
Olive Morris at a Black Panthers' demonstration on Coldharbour Lane, (photo by Neil Kenlock)
□□□■
Olive Morris

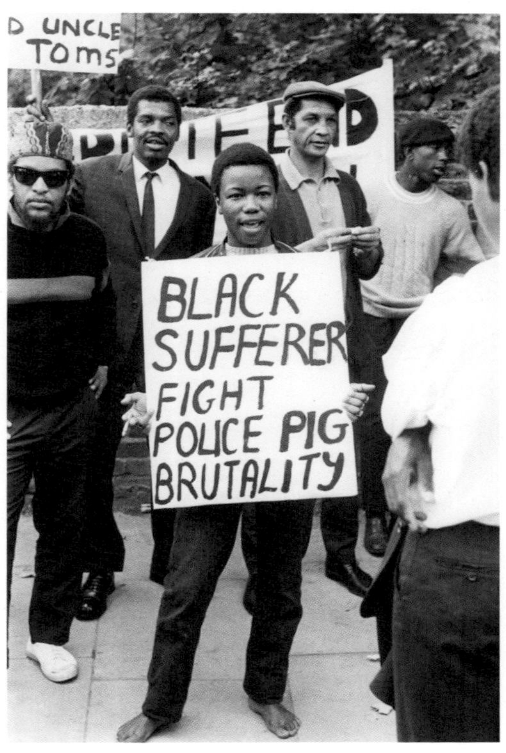


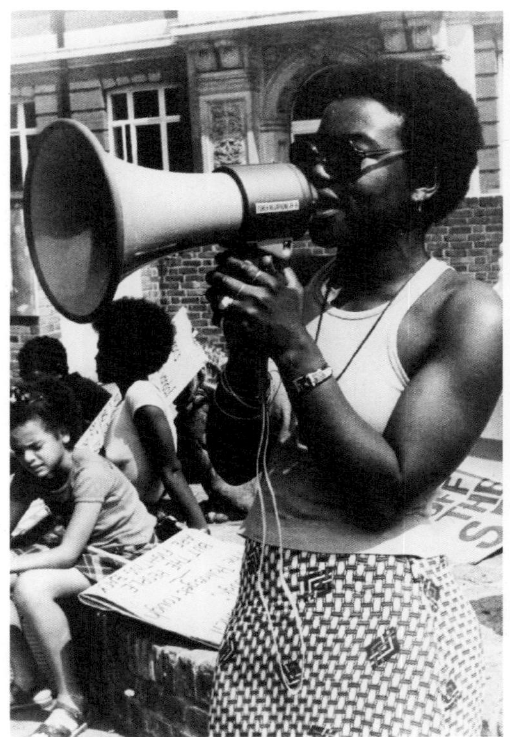

In October 2008, the Remembering Olive Collective (ROC), a women-run volunteer group, was created. ROC is so far composed of some twenty members, including artists, activists, sociologists, archivists, curators, cultural theorists, and community workers of varied generations. The group meets once a month and is involved in extensive archival and oral history research around Olive Morris, and by extension around black activism in 1970s South London. The archive, the basis of which is formed by a collection of documents related to Olive Morris currently owned by Liz Obi, a friend and colleague of the late activist, is currently being catalogued and complemented by ROC, and was made available at Lambeth Archives for permanent public use in October 2009, along with the oral history archive. The other outcomes of the project include the project's blog, first launched in 2007; regular presentations of the project as well as fundraising events at cultural and political events, festivals, and fairs; a radio series which will be broadcast in autumn 2009; an exhibition and series of events presented in November 2009 and January 2010 at Gasworks; and a publication released in early 2010.

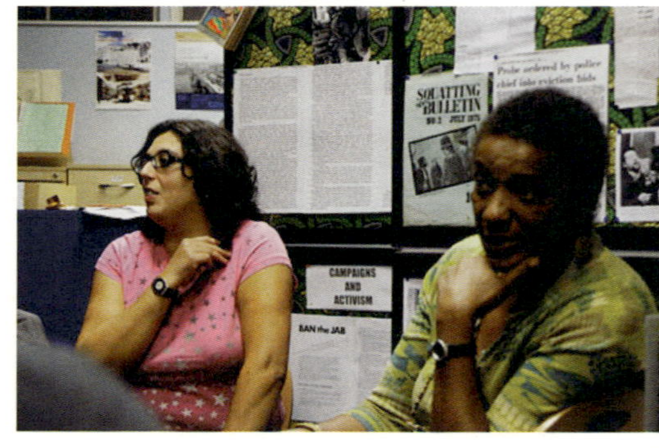


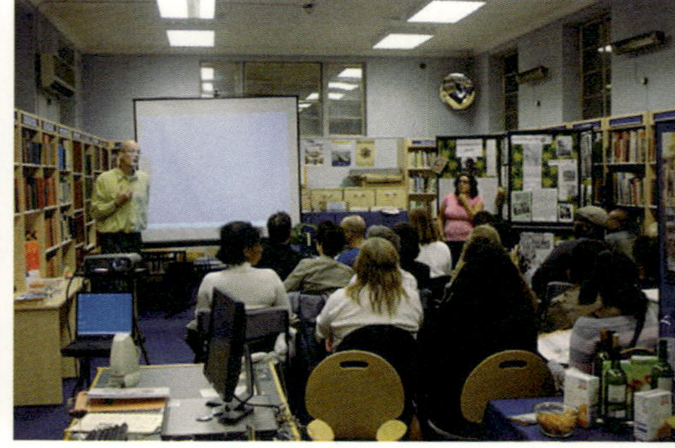

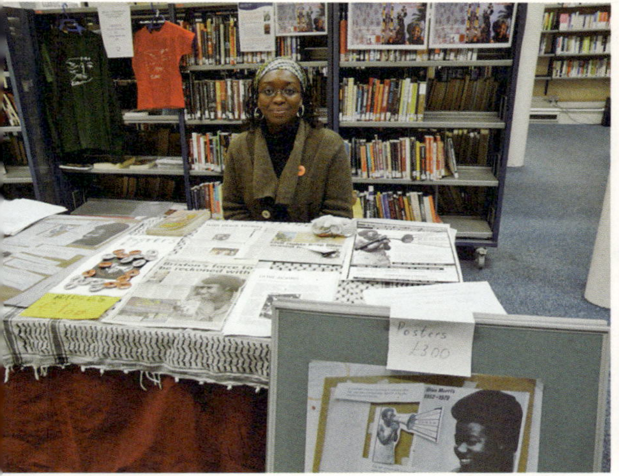


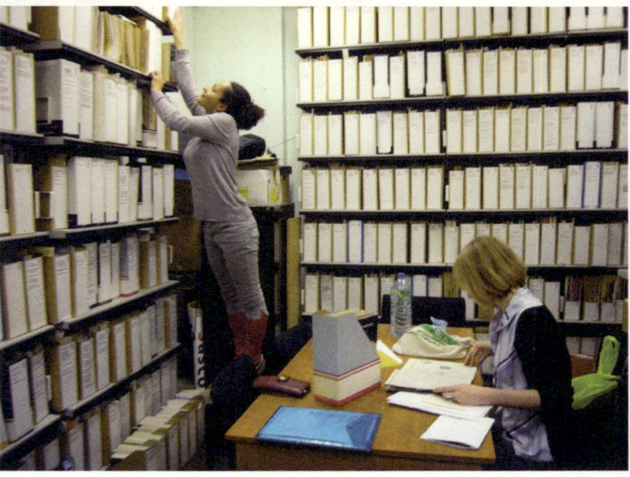

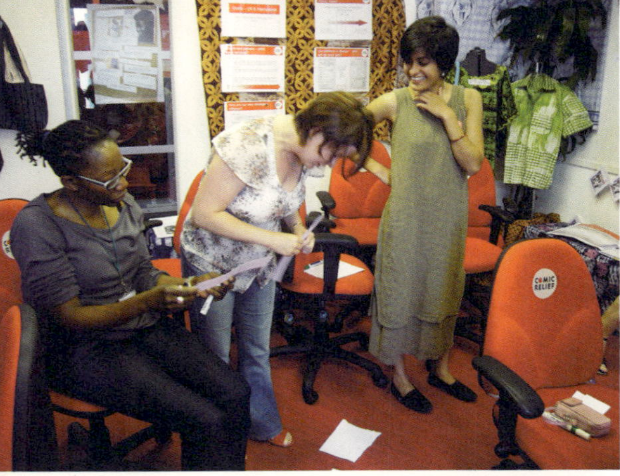


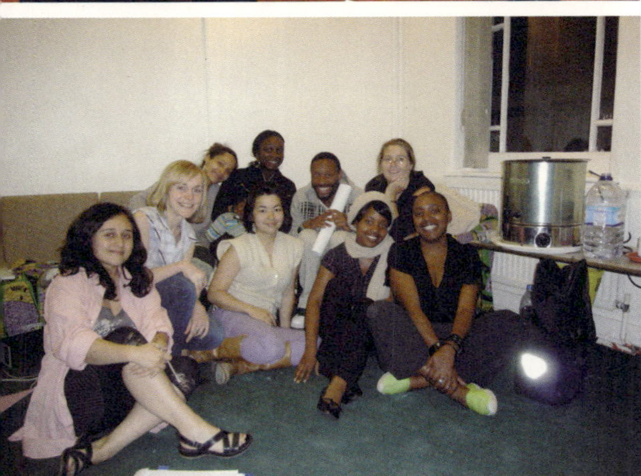

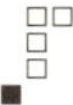

Weblog launch at Minet Library, 2007

ROC member Emma Allotey running a stall at Brixton Library, Launch of International Women Week in Lambeth, 2009

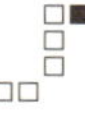

ROC members Sheila Ruiz and Altair Roelants doing research at the Feminist Library, 2009

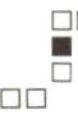

ROC member Rakhee Kewada with Comic Relief staff, during a workshop on Olive Morris as part of Comic Relief Staff Learning Week, 2009

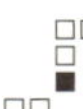

ROC members with Ferron Morris (Olive Morris' nephew) visiting ROC's monthly meeting at Lambeth Women's Project, 2009, Brixton Hill after the re-instatement of the plaque

Derrick Anderson - Chief Executive
London Borough of Lambeth
Lambeth Town Hall
Brixton Hill, London SW2 1RW

13 February 2009
Dear Derrick Anderson

I write on behalf of the Remembering Olive Collective (ROC) in respect of the rebranding of Olive Morris House, 18 Brixton Hill as the Customer Service Centre, 18 Brixton Hill. Please see enclosed photocopies of Lambeth Council stationary, as evidence of this.

ROC was formed in October 2008 by a group of women, led by Ana Laura de la Torre—a Brixton resident and artist—out of a concern to keep the memory of Olive Morris alive in our community.

In September 2007, as part of Black History Month, Ana Laura launched the "Do you remember Olive Morris?" blog, in partnership with Lambeth Archives. Please visit www.rememberolivemorris.wordpress.com for full details of Olive Morris and the work of the Remembering Olive Collective.

From December 2007 through to May 2008, Ana Laura and other people involved in the project had several meetings with council officers responsible for the new Customer Service Centre in Olive Morris House, and form the Corporate Communications Team. The focus of these meetings was to ensure that Olive Morris's memory was continued and honoured in the newly refurbished building. In addition to suggestions for the rededication of the building by reinstating the dedication plaque and photograph, a proposal was made to incorporate a visual display in the public area of the building, highlighting Olive's unique contribution to Brixton's black community during the 1970's. Please see enclosed minutes of those meetings.

Despite the support and endorsement from Catherine Miller-Bassi (Head of Arts), the Black Cultural Archives and Gasworks (local cultural organisations of recognised status), the discussion was discontinued when the Communication Team informed us that they did not have any funds to support our proposal and that they were also concerned about a potential clash with their corporate style guidelines. This last communication was in response of a formal proposal we had been asked to submit, including visualisations and a budget. Please see enclosed our submission.

At the time of those meetings we were reassured that there were plans to reinstate the Olive Morris plaque and photograph in the lobby of the staff entrance. We were disappointed to hear that the large number of Lambeth residents who visit the building daily were not going to benefit from learning that the building is named after an inspiring leader of the Black community.

To this date, we haven't got any indication about Lambeth Council plans to rededicate the building. We are therefore requesting you to investigate on our behalf. We would like a timetable from you for the rededication of the building together with an explanation as to why Olive Morris's name appears to have been dropped from the address of the building. See also enclosed a letter from Yana Morris (Olive's sister), and a recent article from the South London Press, in which important community leaders (Linton Kwesi Johnson and Clarence Thompson), also express their worries about this matter.

We hope you will appreciate our concern that Lambeth Council appears to be involved in removing Olive's name from our local history at a time when we should be honouring her activism and selfless contribution to the community, as an inspiring role model for our young people.

We would hope to be involved in the plans to rededicate the building and are actively fundraising towards the commissioning of an information display honouring Olive's memory. We would be happy if we could meet with you to discuss our concerns and the future plans for Olive Morris House.

We would be grateful if you could respond to us before the 4th of March 2009, which is the date of ROC's next meeting, so we have an opportunity to discuss your response with the members of our group.

Yours Sincerely,
Liz Obi
Chair Remembering Olive Collective

---

Derrick Anderson - Chief Executive
London Borough of Lambeth
Lambeth Town Hall
Brixton Hill, London SW2 1RW

Dear Mr Anderson

My name is Yana Morris sister to Olive Morris after whom Olive Morris House is named. I am writing on behalf of my brothers and sister, the rest of Olive's family and her friends.

We understand that Olive Morris House recently underwent refurbishment and that the Olive Morris picture and original dedication plaque is supposed to be reinstated in the staff entrance to the building. It has also come to our attention that the public area of the building has been re-branded as Brixton Customer Service Centre, with large size signage at street level. We have also received reports that correspondence issued from the building not always carries Olive Morris House name on it, instead referring exclusively to the new Customer Service name, followed by the street address.

I am writing to enquire about Lambeth Council's intention with regard to reinstating the plaque, photograph and maintaining the public presence of the building as Olive Morris House. We strongly believe that it will be of great importance to our community to preserve the memory of Olive Morris and her achievements in a manner and location that is informative and accessible to the general public and not just Lambeth Council employees.
We are concerned that like so many other monuments commemorating the achievements and contributions of African Caribbean people in Britain this dedication to Olive might be about to be dismantled and forgotten. We have already seen the sadly demise of Mary Seacole House and Paul Robeson House. When defending the importance of preserving the memory of Olive Morris, we would like to point out that not only was she a remarkable African Caribbean woman—but unlike Robeson and Seacole—she was also a member of the local community, who dedicated her short life to working with and for the people of Lambeth.

We believe that publicly reinstating her name and achievements will not just be a tribute to her remarkable life, but also an inspiring role model for our local youth. It would be a great disservice to Lambeth's history as well as a travesty in today's climate of inner city youth crime and dysfunction, should the visibility of her name and history be compromised, or reserved exclusively for Lambeth Council staff.
I would like to appeal against any plans to phase out or obscure the current name attached to the Lambeth Directorate building. We would welcome any discussion about this issue and would point

you in the direction of www.rememberolivemorris.wordpress.com for information and history about Olive's life and why this building was named after her.

I look forward to an early response to my letter and hope this matter will be settled amicably.

---

DERRIK ANDERSON REPLY
(SAME LETTER TO ROC AND MORRIS FAMILY):

Dear Liz / Dear Yana

Thank you for your letter of 13 February 2009 regarding how we are remembering the contribution of Olive Morris to our local history.

I appreciate the issues that you have raised and I have asked colleagues to update me on what we are doing to preserve her memory. I agree that it is important that the building does not lose its connection with Olive and her contribution to our local history.

The building will continue to be called Olive Morris House. The customer centre simply sits within the Olive Morris building. I have been reassured that the plaque is now re-instated alongside her picture. There will also be a window display and words explaining the significance of her contribution. This will also include a website address for further information, including the Remember Olive Morris site. Within the customer centre we will have a number of slides on our plasma screens again promoting the website and the significance of Olive Morris.

In terms of preserving the memory of Olive Morris more widely, Lambeth Council has also positively promoted her in many other ways in recent months. There have been two feature articles in our fortnightly resident newspaper, Lambeth Life. The most recent article on International Women's Day features Olive Morris as a local female icon.

Again can I reassure you that there is no intention to ignore the memory and contribution of Olive Morris and I am sorry for the delay in getting the plaque re-instated and responding to your other requests.

Yours sincerely

Derrick Anderson

- - - - - - - - - - - - - - - - - - - - - -

**FINDING OLIVE**
**THE STARTING POINT**
text by Ana Laura López de la Torre

I came to live in London in 1996 and settled in Brixton (1), where I still live. I come from Uruguay and I found myself naturally at home in Brixton, joining a neighborhood that has been shaped by the continuous influx of immigrants from all corners of the world. Like many Lambeth residents, I have had my fair share of waiting time at Olive Morris House. (2) I never thought much about the building's name. In fact, at the back of my mind there was an unformed idea that the building was named after a man: Oliver Morris, perhaps an English gentleman of political or philanthropic leanings.

In August 2006, I was at Peckham Library doing some research about the history of black activism in the UK. I was looking for images of people holding placards, when I came across a picture that stopped me in my tracks. It was a small black and white photograph, printed toward the back of *The Windrush Legacy: Memories of Britain's Post-War Caribbean Immigrants*, a book published by the Black Cultural Archives in 1998. In the picture there was a young woman with short-cropped hair, and her mouth open in a defiant gesture. She had the physical build of a teenager, and looked almost like a boy. She was holding a placard that read: BLACK SUFFERER FIGHT PIG POLICE BRUTALITY. She held a cigarette between her fingers and was barefoot.

The caption said that the picture had been taken at a Black Panther Movement demonstration in Coldharbour Lane, but there were no further references to Olive Morris in the book, apart from a dedication to her on the last page for her contribution to the black struggle—from which I learned she had passed away.

I was startled. Could this be the same person whom the Lambeth Housing Services building was named after? I was puzzled and excited about the idea that a council building had been given the name of a woman who—if one were to judge from the image—had been involved in radical activism within the borough.

But who was this woman? I asked my friend Hurvin Anderson, who was working with me on the research, if he knew her. He told me that the name was familiar and he thought she was an activist who had died very young. He asked a friend who had been active with the Brixton Black Panthers Movement, and he confirmed that Olive had been a Black Panther herself and was known for her fearlessness in confronting police abuse.

A council building named after a female Black Panther. It seemed to defy belief in this age of non-confrontational politics. I wanted to know more. I searched and scoured the Internet for more information, but nothing came up. I found a brief comment in a forum for squatters that mentioned Olive Morris and Liz Turnbull as the first successful squatters of private property in Lambeth. A council building named after a female Black Panther and squatter. A building dedicated to Housing Services.

I visited Olive Morris House and saw the dedication plaque under a framed picture of Olive smiling. The plaque mentioned her as the founder of the Brixton Black Women's Group, and from her date of birth and death (1952–1979) I understood that I was in the presence of a remarkable historical figure, who in the span of her short life had managed to make an impressive contribution on many fronts.

The research that brought Olive Morris to my attention was for a participatory arts project that went on to win an Archives Landmark Award from the London Metropolitan Archives. One of the prizes was the opportunity to use an actress or actor to perform a character of the period researched. I asked for an actress to perform Olive Morris to a live audience. I envisioned the actress in a Brixton street, barefoot and telling the audience the amazing story of her life, possibly in October to coincide with Black History Month. I was asked to provide the actress with a biographic script. My request for a street performance was denied on the account that October is a cold month, and I was asked to arrange for a suitable venue. I ap-

proached Brixton Library and the organizers of Black History Month, and they were keen to host the performance during Black History Month 2007.
With all practicalities seemingly resolved, I set out to compile a biography of Olive Morris to give to the actress. Up until then I had presumed there would be plenty of public sources of information about Olive Morris: records in archives, libraries, perhaps even a book or two written about her. The Black Cultural Archives had their archives in storage waiting for a new home. Lambeth Archives and Brixton Library did not have anything on file, although they knew of Olive Morris and her importance. The Women's Library had some papers related to her, but they were not catalogued and as such inaccessible. Nothing on the Internet, nothing on file.

I therefore set out to search for Olive Morris. The idea of a weblog came about as the first step toward the performance which, to this day, I still have not been able to put together. The blog was set up to keep a record of the search for Olive Morris. Hopefully, the blog would grow to be a reliable public repository dedicated to Olive Morris, enlarged and enriched with the stories and memories of all the people who had the privilege of knowing her.

Lambeth Archives supported the creation of this blog in several ways, and put me in touch with Liz Obi. Liz had once been a close friend of Olive, and in 2000 she had organized an exhibition at Brixton Library titled *Remembering Olive, Remembering the Times*. When I met Liz, the door I had been seeking for a long year suddenly opened wide.

Tim O'Dell of Brixton Library and Jon Newman of Lambeth Archives had been in touch with her to source some images for the Black History Month program. After a few emails and phone calls, I met Liz for coffee at Brixton Market. On that morning I learned more about Olive Morris than in a whole year of searching in archives and on the Internet. Liz and Olive had squatted together at 121 Railton Road, and in 1972 had hitchhiked their way to North Africa in search of a Black Panther in exile.

After questioning me and listening to my story and my reasons for wanting to do this project, Liz agreed to help me. I invited her to speak at the launch of the weblog, and she kindly offered also to bring some of her exhibition materials to arrange a display on the day.

Liz invited me to her house to see the materials she had. When she had organized the exhibition at Brixton Library, Liz had added to Olive's personal archive photocopies of items that she had found in libraries and other archives. Having lived through those years, Liz knew where to look for information. She had also contacted Mike McColgan, Olive's partner. Mike had in his possession several documents belonging to Olive, including school notebooks and college essays, correspondence with several community organizations, albums of personal pictures, and notes of condolence received after Olive's death. He gave all this material to Liz, to complement the materials she had already gathered for the exhibition.

For my visit, Liz had taken all the documents out of storage, and pinned up several items on the exhibition boards. She had also prepared a selection of books that were influential to her and Olive in the 1970s. Liz talked me through the items I was picking up at random, answering my questions and adding her personal comments and stories. I was like a kid in a toy shop, and Liz had more or less to throw me out of her house. I could have stayed there all day going through this amazing collection. I left with a handful of borrowed pictures and documents to scan, including Olive's passport. Having her passport in my house was especially moving for me; after a year looking for Olive, here she was.

Of the many things that Liz had to say about Olive, there were two that stood out for me. The first one was Liz's description of Olive, and how she always visualized her whenever she thought of her: silver bangles on her arms and forever riding her bike. The second one had to do with what Liz had learned from Olive: never to be afraid of anything.

On a tip from Liz Obi, I managed to track down Yana Morris, Olive's sister, who works as a head teacher in South London. I made contact with her and sent

her information about the project and the weblog. A few days later I received an email from Jennifer Lewis, another of Olive's sisters:
*Dear Ana Laura, my name is Jennifer and I am Olive's other sister, I was pleased to hear of your intentions from Yana. Funnily enough my daughter Tamara had a similar idea some time ago and did try to contact Liz but to no avail. Unfortunately I will not be able to attend the launch in the Minet Library however my daughter will attend and I would be happy to contribute in any way I can.*

- - - - - - - - - - - - - - - - - - - - -

**Blog launch at Minet Library, Brixton**

On Monday, October 1, 2007, on a very wet London evening, a group of people braved the weather to gather at Minet Library for the official launch of the weblog http://rememberolivemorris.wordpress.com.

I arrived early to set up equipment and was soon joined by Liz, who brought the exhibition about Olive Morris that she had presented in 2000. Liz also brought some candles, incense, and some of her plants. The exhibition boards were covered in African textiles. As an artist, I was pleased to see (and gently reminded of) how little it takes to give a personal touch to what we do, when we take temporary occupation of an institutional space.

The presentation was introduced by Jon Newman, who explained why Lambeth Archives had chosen to support the project. The use of weblog technology was an innovative tool that they were keen to engage with, but also the fact that it was an artist-led project brought "a different sensibility" to their job of collecting and preserving local history.

I started the presentation by welcoming the audience, and as an introduction and a form of setting the wider background against which this project was conceived, we showed a six-minute-long video, made the previous week in collaboration with Liz Obi. The video was made outside Olive Morris House, and in it we asked people in the street if they knew who Olive Morris was, inviting them to volunteer a guess. (3)

I went on to tell the story of how I came to be interested in Olive Morris, and then showed the blog and its contents to the audience, explaining the different sections in which I had tried to organize the information. I wanted to give a sense of the breadth of Olive Morris's work and interests, but to try to keep a non-linear, or non-chronological, order. I described the fragmented way in which I had compiled the information, and that I hoped the blog maintained that open structure, in which snapshots from Olive's life and her times could be connected through the personal journeys or interests of those reading and contributing to the blog.

Following the more formal part of the presentation, Liz Obi spoke to the audience about her personal relationship to Olive Morris, and about the journey on which she had embarked a few years ago when she decided to put together the *Remembering Olive, Remembering the Times* exhibition. Liz also spoke about Olive's legacy, and about what she had learned from her. She went on to tell the audience about her initial reticence when we first met: "What does this white woman want to do with Olive's story?"—but that understanding my motivations, she had agreed to collaborate and share her knowledge with me. Liz's initial words of support and her engagement with the project went on to become a real collaboration between us, and led to the founding of the Remembering Olive Collective in October 2008.

In contrast to Liz's own search for Olive's history, where she both had the personal knowledge (dates, places, names) and the trust of and access to those who had known and worked with Olive, the issue of me being an "outsider" is—I feel—quite central to the success or failure of the project.

We had the pleasure of counting Sandra Hurst amongst the audience. She had known Olive despite being several years younger. Sandra told us how she had moved into the 121 Railton Road squat after Liz and Olive moved out, and was involved with her partner in setting up and running Sabarr Bookshop. Sandra was a founding member of Black Roof, which was started as a community organization to protect the rights of squatters, and which went on to become a housing cooperative. There was quite an animated discussion about the lack of awareness of the story of black squats, and of the paradox of having a housing building named after Olive Morris. A lineage of black squats was traced from 121 Railton Road to the recently closed Rastafarian Centre at St Agnes Place.

There was also some debate as to whether the naming of buildings and streets is actually a positive thing and a desired recognition of the achievements of black people, or whether—as Jon Newman pointed out—it could simply be a political gesture that can be easily undone, as it is actually happening in South London nowadays (the renaming of Mary Secoale House was given as an example). The current situation of Olive Morris House's refurbishment was discussed, and this was one of the areas in which the audience felt some concrete outcome could come of this project.

Neil Kenlock, the author of the photograph that brought me to Olive, also present, kindly offered to go through his archive and make his photographs of Olive available free of charge for this blog. Neil reminded the audience that it would be a pity if Olive Morris went down in history just as a squatter, because above all, her fight was "a fight for equality, and this is how she should be remembered." Neil spoke about his photographs of Olive, and told us about Olive's courage and fearlessness. *"It took a lot of courage for her to stand there holding that placard. Those were tough times and many big and strong men didn't have the guts to do it, but Olive did. She even took her shoes off."*

Tamara Lewis was also in the audience. Tamara is Olive's niece, but was born after her death. She said, "Seeing and hearing all this, I keep thinking how happy Grandma would have been if she was here today." This prompted some comments about Doris Morris, and her own engagement with political activism, as the source of both the inspiration and the support that Olive found in her own family.

There was a sense, especially for those who knew little about Olive Morris, of the importance of recuperating her figure within our local community—not just as an inspiration for black people, but as an example for everyone. As Liz said, what was most important about Olive's legacy is that she showed us that we all can, as individuals, make a difference. That this power we had as individuals to stand up against injustice is a very real power, and that we should not hesitate to use it on our own and in collaboration with others.

With the good atmosphere amongst the audience—a gathering of people paying respects and honoring the memory of Olive Morris—it was easy for all of us to push away the chairs and carry on chatting over a drink, to the sound of some classic reggae tracks.

When it was time to go, a small group of us started on the search for a local pub. We stumbled by chance upon an "old style Brixton pub" of the kind that has now vanished from Brixton city center. Just as we walked into the pub, Liz shouted and ran after a man who was walking out to smoke a cigarette. He had been a friend of Olive, and had gone out with her when they were very young. Over a few cigarettes shared in the outdoor cold, Hurley pieced together with Liz some memories of Olive's early youth and later years. It seemed to us that it had been Olive's spirit guiding us to that pub, to another encounter.

Just after midnight, Liz Obi, Oniel Williams, and I walked together all the way to Brixton, still talking about Olive and her times, the fate of "the 1970s struggle," contemporary politics, the third world, and the reality of life in Brixton as experienced by our children. Just as we were coming into Coldharbour Lane, we saw a police van and several police officers in the process of searching two young black men. One of the police officers was feeling the youth's toes over his white sport socks, and another was holding in his silicone-gloved hand a forensic evidence bag with a small amount of weed in it. We walked past them and a third police officer volunteered—with a smile—some community-relations nicety to us, as we continued our journey without making any fuss.

There it was in a nutshell: the sign of the changing times. Much talk was made on this night about what Olive Morris would be doing nowadays, were she still

alive. For sure, she would have something to say.
Ana Laura López de la Torre. September 2007 (text revised in July 2009)

**Notes**

(1) Brixton is an area of South London, England, in the London borough of Lambeth. It is predominantly residential with a prominent street market and substantial retail sector. Brixton is a multiethnic community, with around 24 twenty-four percent of Brixton's its population being of African and/or Caribbean descent, which has givening rise to Brixton its status as the unofficial capital of the British African-Caribbean community in London. (Wikipedia, the free encyclopedia - http://en.wikipedia.org/wiki/Brixton. Accessed: 25 July 2009)

(2) Olive Morris House is one of several council buildings in the borough of Lambeth and serves as the Housing and Council Tax Benefit center for people who have to pay rent or who are receiving benefits or on low income.

(3) http://www.youtube.com/watch?v=rfwcaZ5TozU

- - - - - - - - - - - - - - - - - - - - - - -

Olive Morris with other Black Panthers in North London, c. 1972 (photo by and copyright: Neil Kenlock)

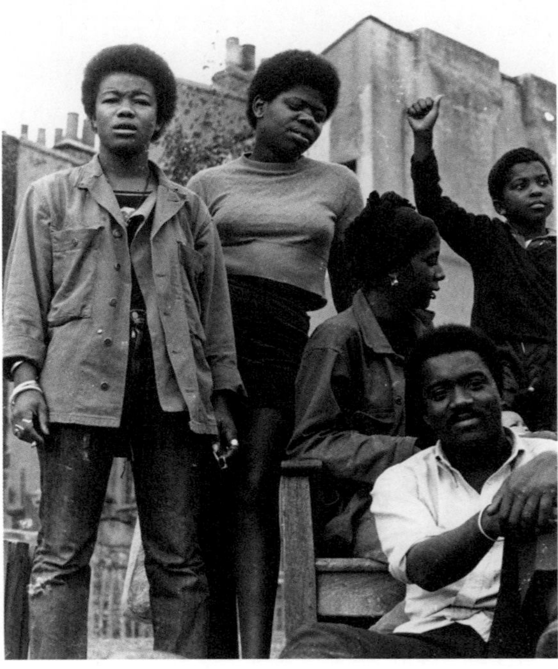

The project investigates the origin of the seeds found on the site of Huangui Lu in the Liwan district in Guangzhou's city center, where today one hundred wholesale markets exist. The artist's investigation resulted in an installation occupying two long walls in the Museum of Contemporary Art in Guangzhou, as well as the museum's inner courtyard, in which five cubic meters of earth excavated from the site of Huangui Lu was transferred.

Conceived as two walls of documentation, the indoor element of *Wake in Guangzhou* brought together material belonging to the realm of scientific evidence, as much as that of speculation: from research images, maps and records, to notes and drawings made by the artist in an effort to piece together an episode in the history of botany that had not been previously addressed. Recording the artist's intervention and tracing the contemporary migration of the seeds, a large photograph of the excavation site and a dozen images of the seeds movement in the site further featured in the display.

The documentation in the installation begins with Ibn Battuta, a Berber from Algeria, who was a world traveler in the twelfth century. Having visited Damascus, Cairo, Bethlehem, Iraq, Aden, Zanzibar, Oman, Anatolia, and Maldives, seeds could have arrived with him in Guangzhou, and more specifically in Huangui Lui, from any of these places. We also learn from Alves's research that Guangzhou, formerly named Canton, was for a long time the only port where foreigners were allowed to disembark into China. Similarly, the neighborhood from which Alves took the sample was the only part of the city where foreigners were allowed to work and live in Guangzhou.

Another trajectory in the research concerned itself with the birthday parties of the Emperor of China, which the emperor preferred to be big. Foreign guests would have to come via Guangzhou to make their way to the capital, and they came with gifts, sometimes living ones such as elephants or giraffes, which may have carried seeds from their home country on them. The seeds may have fallen off of them along the way, most probably upon disembarking. Also, rice was imported

# Maria Thereza Alves

*Excavation Site*, 2008, Huangui Lu

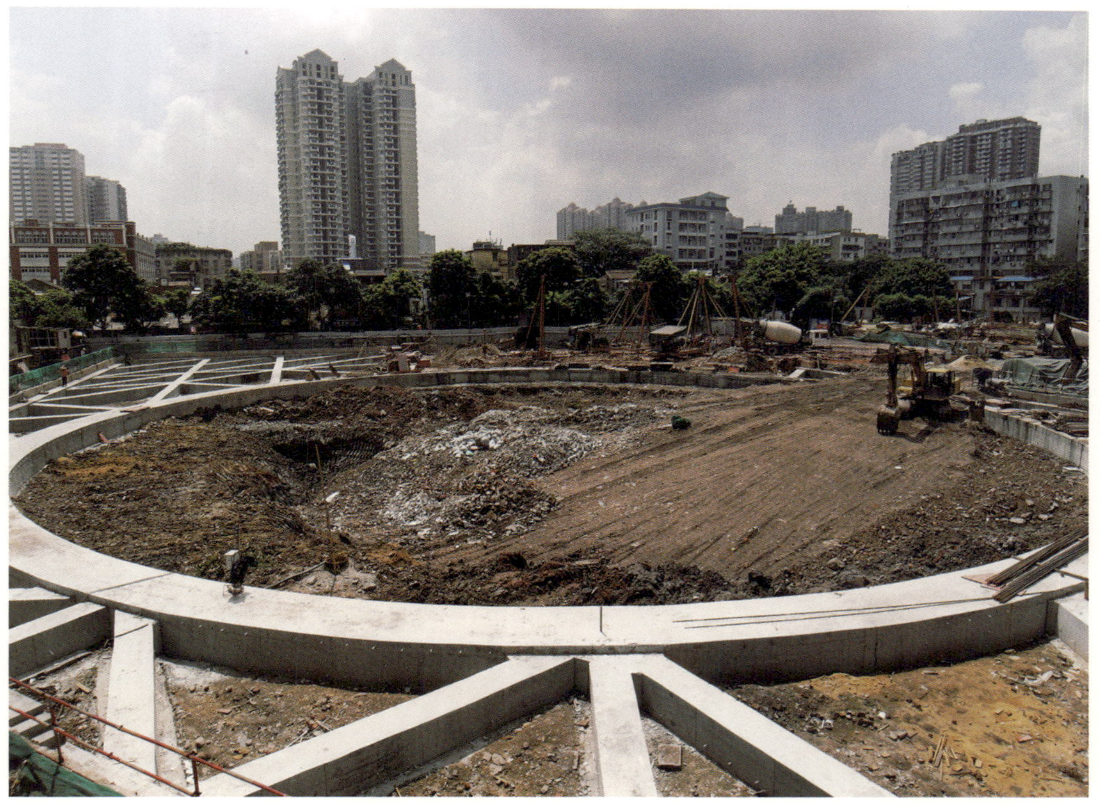

into China through the port of Guangzhou, and there are sixty different types of weeds that grow among the rice from Vietnam, any of which could have grown in Guangzhou. Further afield, Mr. Wu, a Chinese merchant with authorization to trade with foreigners, collected the work of the artist Tinqgua, who had a studio in the foreign quarters. Tinqgua was also collected by a business associate of Mr. Wu, Augustine Heard, who was from Massachusetts in the United States and who did business with Australia. These people provided more opportunities for the arrival of seeds.

*Wake in Guangzhou* unearths further narratives and possible itineraries explaining the landing of foreign seeds in Guangzhou, and by extension in rest of China. Through this historiographic work, as well as through other projects in which the artist has invested her time as researcher of a history without records, Alves relies on what she calls "borderless history." Borderless history is what sometimes fails to be recorded, catalogued, archived, and/or written about. As the artist puts it, "Borderless history must also consider our friends, their lovers, where we travel and who we meet there, how the wind blows, and where the fruits we eat come from, all contributing to the complexity of history and the current landscape."

Excerpts from a statement by Maria Thereza Alves
A project by Maria Thereza Alves commissioned for the 3rd Guangzhou Triennial, China, 2008

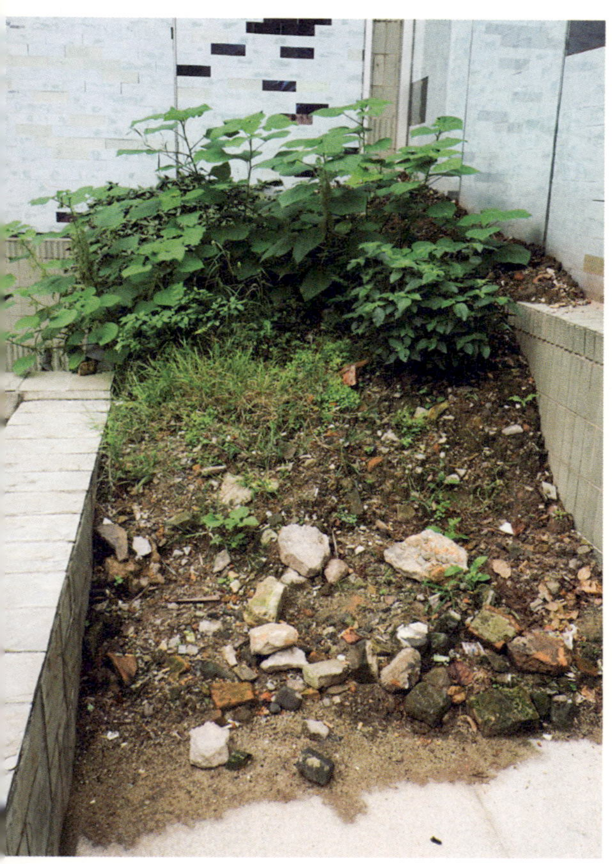

***Earth Sample,*** 2008, at the monumental garden of the Museum of Contemporary Art in Guangzhou

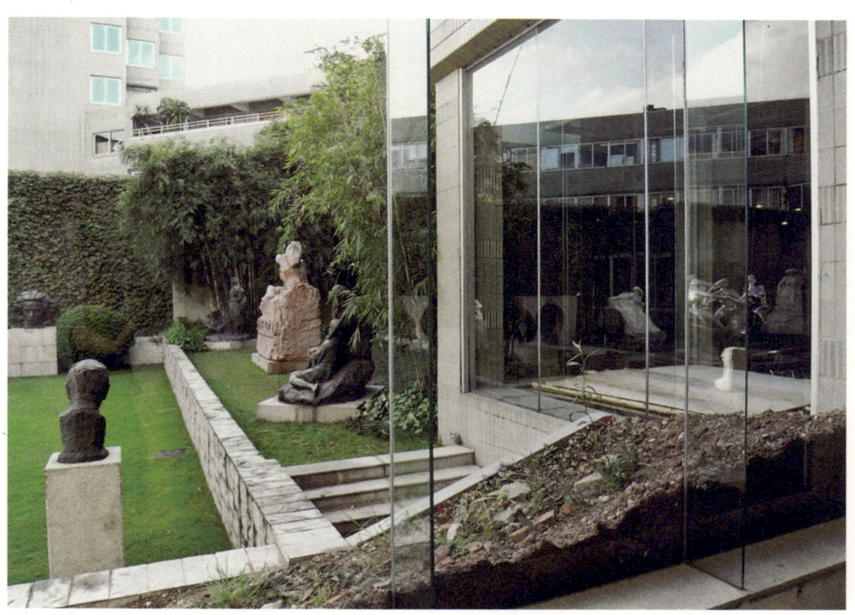

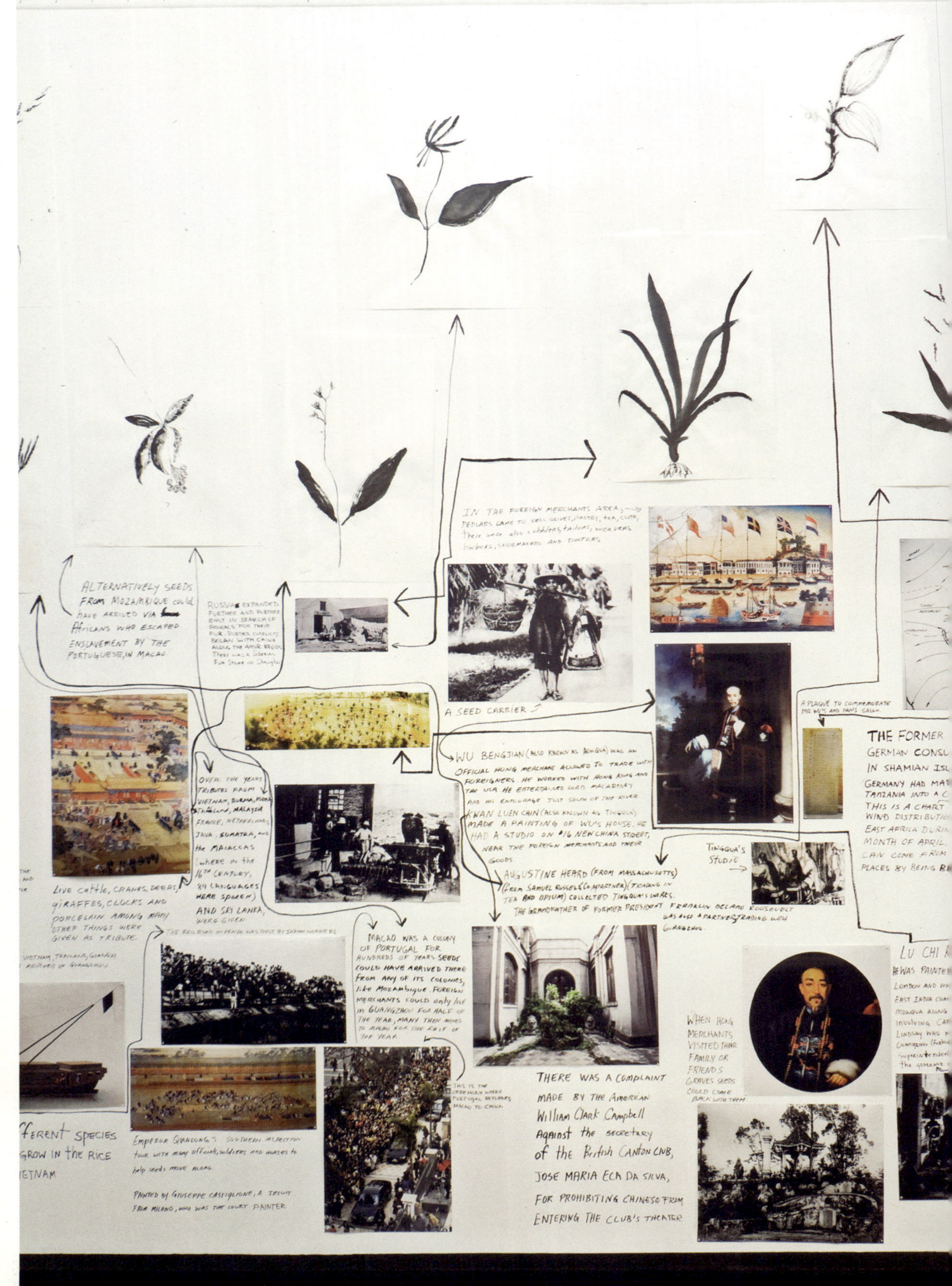
IN THE FOREIGN MERCHANTS AREA, PEDLARS CAME TO SELL OLIVES, PASTRY, TEA, CLOTH, there were also cobblers, tailors, weavers barbers, SHOEMAKERS AND DOCTORS
ALTERNATIVELY SEEDS FROM MOZAMBIQUE could HAVE ARRIVED VIA Africans WHO ESCAPED ENSLAVEMENT BY THE PORTUGUESE, IN MACAO
RUSSIA EXPANDED FURTHER AND FURTHER EAST IN SEARCH OF ANIMALS FOR THEIR FUR.
A SEED CARRIER
A PLAQUE TO COMMEMORATE
THE FORMER GERMAN CONSU IN SHAMIAN ISL
GERMANY HAD MA TANZANIA INTO A C THIS IS A CHART WIND DISTRIBUTIO EAST AFRICA DURIN MONTH OF APRIL CAN COME FROM PLACES BY BEING
OVER THE YEARS TRIBUTES FROM VIETNAM, BURMA, KOREA, THAILAND, MALAYSIA FRANCE, NETHERLANDS, JAVA, SUMATRA, AND the MALACCAS (where in the 16th CENTURY, 84 LANGUAGES WERE SPOKEN) AND SRI LANKA, WERE GIVEN.
WU BENGJIAN (ALSO KNOWN AS HOWQUA) WAS AN OFFICIAL HONG MERCHANT ALLOWED TO TRADE WITH FOREIGNERS. HE WORKED WITH HONG KONG AND THE USA. HE ENTERTAINED LORD MACARTNEY AND HIS ENTOURAGE JUST SOUTH OF THE RIVER
KWAN LUEN CHIN (ALSO KNOWN AS TINGQUA) MADE A PAINTING OF WU'S HOUSE. HE HAD A STUDIO ON #16 NEW CHINA STREET, NEAR THE FOREIGN MERCHANTS AND THEIR GOODS.
TINGQUA'S STUDIO
AUGUSTINE HEARD (FROM MASSACHUSETTS) (FROM SAMUEL RUSSELL & CO. PARTNER) (TRADING IN TEA AND OPIUM) COLLECTED TINGQUA'S WORKS.
THE GRANDFATHER OF FORMER PRESIDENT FRANKLIN DELANO ROOSEVELT WAS ALSO A PARTNER TRADING WITH GUANGZHOU.
Live cattle, CRANES, DEERS, giRAFFES, CLOCKS AND PORCELAIN AMONG MANY OTHER THINGS WERE GIVEN AS TRIBUTE.
MACAO WAS A COLONY OF PORTUGAL FOR HUNDREDS OF YEARS. SEEDS COULD HAVE ARRIVED THERE FROM ANY OF ITS COLONIES, like MOZAMBIQUE. FOREIGN MERCHANTS COULD ONLY live in GUANGZHOU FOR HALF OF THE YEAR, MANY THEN MOVED TO MACAO FOR THE REST OF THE YEAR.
LU CHI
WHEN HONG MERCHANTS VISITED THEIR FAMILY OR FRIENDS GRAVES SEEDS COULD COME BACK WITH THEM
THERE WAS A COMPLAINT MADE BY THE AMERICAN William Clark Campbell Against the secretary of the British CANTON CLUB, JOSE MARIA ECA DA SILVA, FOR PROHIBITING CHINESE FROM ENTERING THE CLUB'S THEATER
ferent species GROW IN THE RICE IETNAM
Emperor Qianlong's southern inspection tour with many officials, soldiers and horses to help seeds move along
Painted by Giuseppe Castiglione, a Jesuit from Milano, who was the court painter

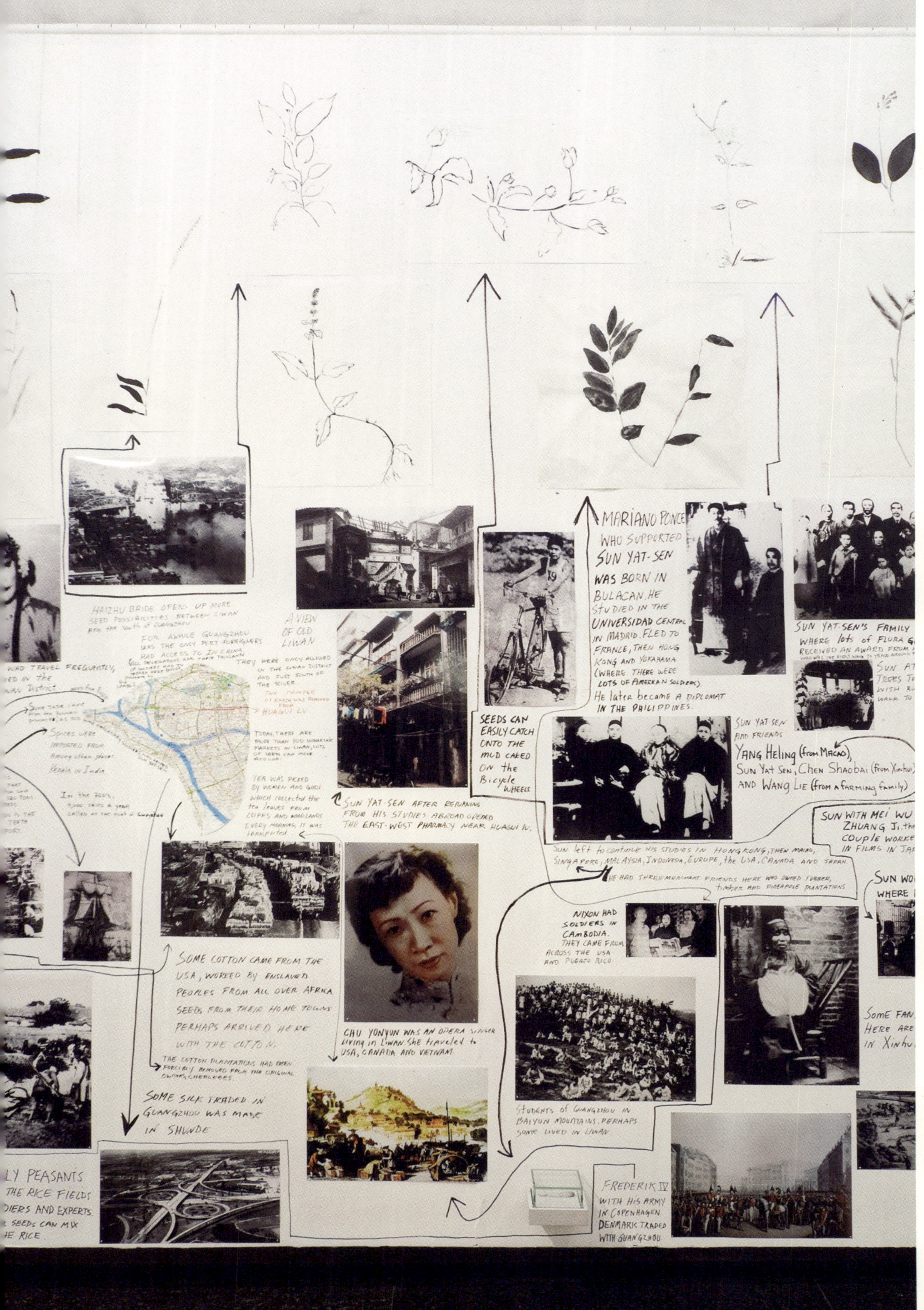
HAIZHU BRIDE OPENS UP MORE SEED POSSIBILITIES BETWEEN LIWAN AND the South of GUANGZHOU
A VIEW OF OLD LIWAN
FOR AWHILE GUANGZHOU WAS THE ONLY PORT FOREIGNERS HAD ACCESS TO IN CHINA
THEY WERE ONLY ALLOWED IN THE LIWAN DISTRICT AND JUST SOUTH OF THE RIVER
HUAGUI LU
TODAY, THERE ARE MORE THAN 100 WHOLESALE MARKETS IN LIWAN, LOTS OF SEEDS CAN MOVE AROUND.
TEA WAS PICKED BY WOMEN AND GIRLS WHICH collected the tea leaves FROM CLIFFS AND WOODLANDS EVERY MORNING. IT WAS transported.
Spices were imported from among other places Kerala in India
In the 700's, 4,000 ships a year called at the port of Guangzhou
MARIANO PONCE WHO SUPPORTED SUN YAT-SEN WAS BORN IN BULACAN. HE STUDIED IN THE UNIVERSIDAD CENTRAL IN MADRID. FLED TO FRANCE, THEN HONG KONG AND YOKAHAMA (WHERE THERE WERE LOTS OF AMERICAN SOLDIERS). He later became A DIPLOMAT IN THE PHILIPPINES.
SEEDS CAN EASILY CATCH ONTO THE MUD CAKED ON the Bicycle WHEELS
SUN YAT-SEN AND FRIENDS YANG Heling (from Macao), Sun Yat Sen, Chen Shaobai (from Xinhui) AND Wang Lie (from a farming family)
SUN YAT-SEN AFTER RETURNING FROM HIS STUDIES ABROAD OPENED THE EAST-WEST PHARMACY NEAR HUAGUI lu.
Sun left to continue his studies in HONG KONG, THEN MACAO, SINGAPORE, MALAYSIA, INDONESIA, EUROPE, the USA, CANADA AND JAPAN.
HE HAD THREE MERCHANT FRIENDS HERE WHO OWNED RUBBER, timber AND PINEAPPLE PLANTATIONS
NIXON HAD SOLDIERS IN CAMBODIA. THEY CAME FROM ACROSS THE USA AND PUERTO RICO.
SOME COTTON CAME FROM THE USA, WORKED BY ENSLAVED PEOPLES FROM ALL OVER AFRICA SEEDS FROM THEIR HOME TOWNS PERHAPS ARRIVED HERE WITH THE COTTON.
THE COTTON PLANTATIONS HAD BEEN FORCIBLY REMOVED FROM THE ORIGINAL OWNERS, CHEROKEES.
CHU YONYUN WAS AN OPERA SINGER LIVING IN LIWAN. SHE traveled to USA, CANADA AND VIETNAM.
SOME SILK TRADED IN GUANGZHOU WAS MADE IN SHUNDE
Students of Guangzhou in Baiyun Mountains. Perhaps some lived in Liwan.
FREDERIK VI WITH HIS ARMY IN COPENHAGEN DENMARK TRADED WITH GUANGZHOU

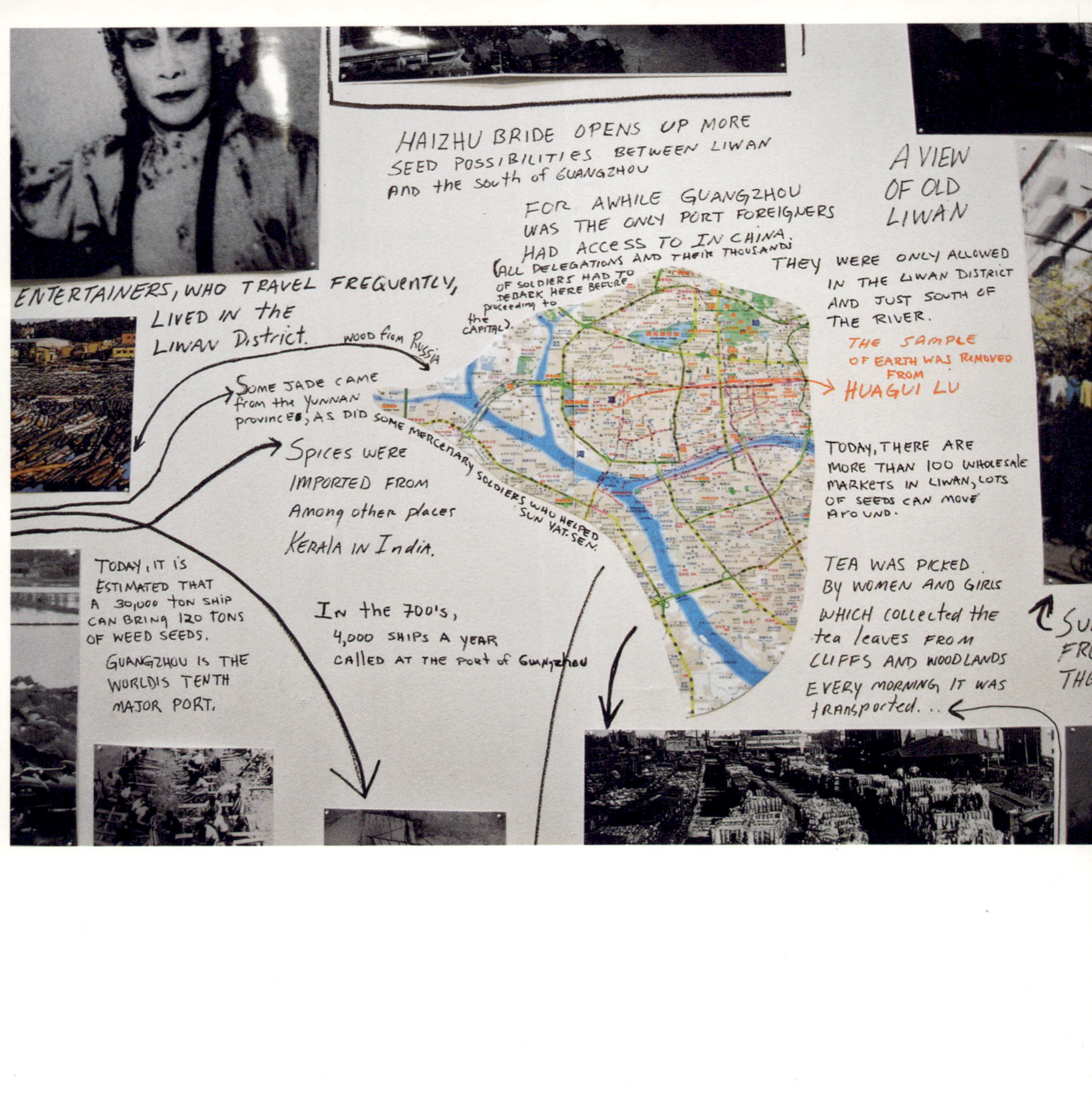
HAIZHU BRIDE OPENS UP MORE SEED POSSIBILITIES BETWEEN LIWAN AND THE SOUTH OF GUANGZHOU
A VIEW OF OLD LIWAN
FOR AWHILE GUANGZHOU WAS THE ONLY PORT FOREIGNERS HAD ACCESS TO IN CHINA.
(ALL DELEGATIONS AND THEIR THOUSANDS OF SOLDIERS HAD TO DEBARK HERE BEFORE proceeding to the CAPITAL).
THEY WERE ONLY ALLOWED IN THE LIWAN DISTRICT AND JUST SOUTH OF THE RIVER.
THE SAMPLE OF EARTH WAS REMOVED FROM HUAGUI LU
ENTERTAINERS, WHO TRAVEL FREQUENTLY, LIVED IN THE LIWAN DISTRICT.
WOOD FROM RUSSIA
SOME JADE CAME FROM THE YUNNAN PROVINCE, AS DID SOME MERCENARY SOLDIERS WHO HELPED SUN YAT-SEN.
SPICES WERE IMPORTED FROM AMONG OTHER PLACES KERALA IN INDIA.
TODAY, THERE ARE MORE THAN 100 WHOLESALE MARKETS IN LIWAN, LOTS OF SEEDS CAN MOVE AROUND.
TODAY, IT IS ESTIMATED THAT A 30,000 TON SHIP CAN BRING 120 TONS OF WEED SEEDS.
GUANGZHOU IS THE WORLD'S TENTH MAJOR PORT.
IN THE 700'S, 4,000 SHIPS A YEAR CALLED AT THE PORT OF GUANGZHOU
TEA WAS PICKED BY WOMEN AND GIRLS WHICH COLLECTED THE TEA LEAVES FROM CLIFFS AND WOODLANDS EVERY MORNING. IT WAS TRANSPORTED...

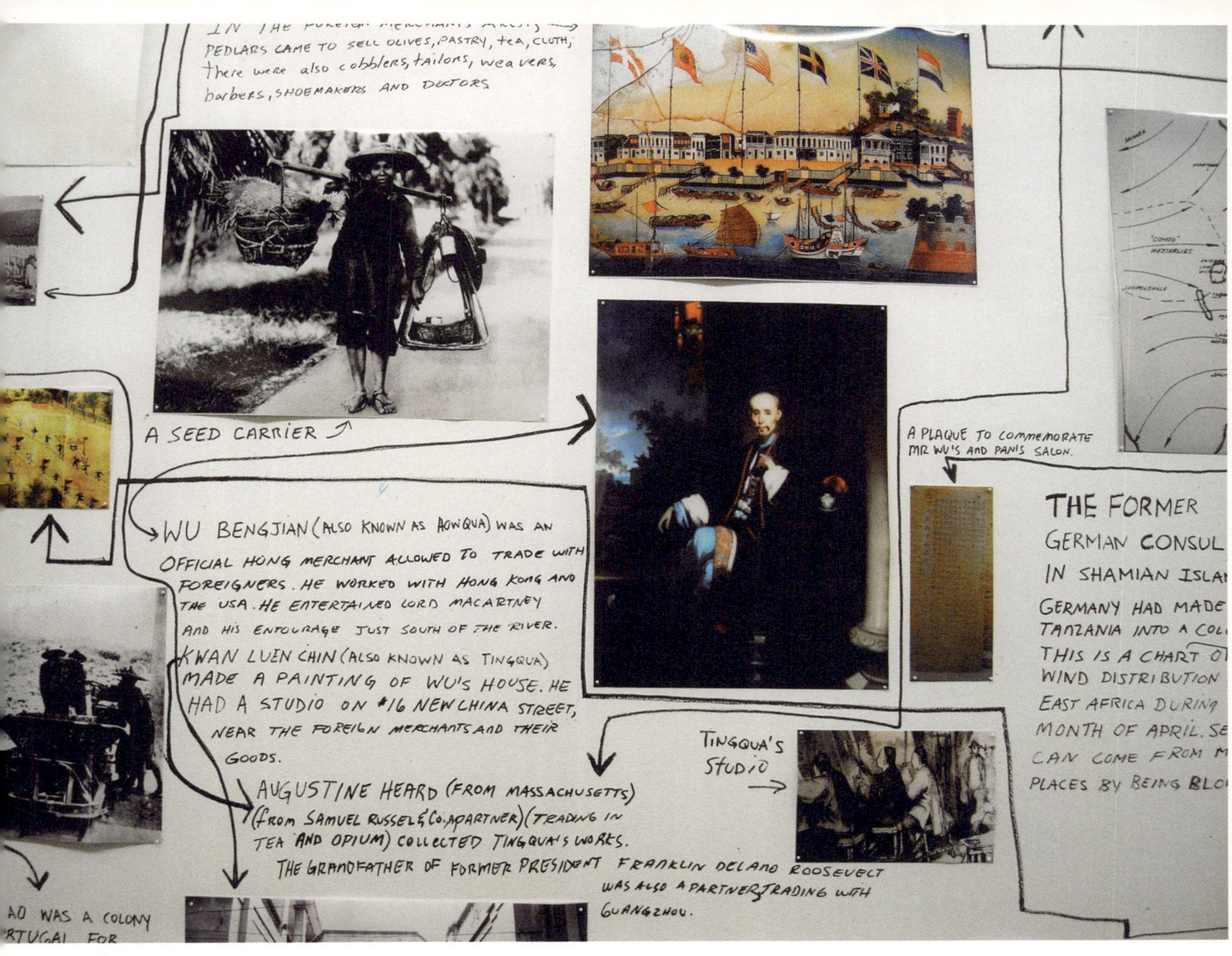


*page 252–255*

■

***Wall Detail***, 2008, Museum of Contemporary Art in Guangzhou; all images are by Maria Thereza Alves and Mr. Ho

**Cecilia Canziani** is a curator and writer. Co-director of the program at Nomas Foundation, Rome, she is founding member of the independent space 1:1projects, and member of the Ada network for nonprofit initiatives. She has held several courses on Art History, Art and Economy, and Museology at universities and art academies in Italy and abroad. She contributes to *Flash Art* and *Arte e Critica* magazines.

**Daniele Balicco**, PhD and essayist, contributes to the *Allegoria*, *L'Ospite Ingrato*, and *Alias* magazines and to the daily *Il Manifesto,* for which he has published *Non parlo a tutti: Franco Fortini intellettuale politico.* He devised the *Normali Marziani* project.

**Alterazioni Video** (Paololuca Barbieri Marchi, Alberto Caffarelli, Matteo Erenbourg, Andrea Masu, Giacomo Porfiri) was established in Milan in 2004. Alterazioni Video is a platform which combines art with social and alternative functions of new electronic media. Culture jammers, neo-situationists, and media activists, the members of Alterazioni Video infiltrate through the meshes of society, ready to hijack messages and information of official communication by stepping from one medium to another: from street art to Web space, from DJ live sets to physics laboratories, and from urban inquiries to the production of community image saboteurs, they focus their work on the use of representations rather than on the production acting as a collective figure trying to open and repossess spaces for communication techniques and a social imaginary otherwise controlled and disciplined.

> www.incompiutosiciliano.org

**Anna Scalfi** views and experiences art as the "frame" that profoundly changes the actual confines of permitted action. The entire organizational process of her projects constitutes an analytical approach to the mechanisms of negotiation between art and society. An independent artist, she creates site-specific projects capable of inducing forms of participation that go beyond the strictly artistic context. She is working in London on the *From Inside (I Like the System)* project, a PhD project at the Essex Business School. Her research is the outcome of her interdisciplinary education at the Brera Academy of Fine Arts, at the S. D'Amico Academy of Dramatic Arts, and at university faculty of sociology of Trento.

> www.indeposito.net

**Cesare Pietroiusti**'s work focuses on issues of interaction, community, social engagement, and the alteration of prescriptive economies in the art world. Since 1977, he has been showing his works in Italy and abroad, in institutional and alternative spaces, both public and private.

> www.evolutiondelart.net www.nonfunctionalthoughts.net

**Progetto Diogene** brings together individual artists who work together toward the creation of a space of reflection and listening. Members of the group are Donato Canosa, Ludovica Carbotta, Andrea Caretto, Manuele Cerutti, Sara Enrico, Davide Gennarino, Luca Luciano, Laura Pugno, Andrea Respino, Raffaella Spagna, Monica Taverniti, Cosimo Veneziano. Progetto Diogene fosters the reduction of that which is unecessary, autonomy of thought, alert observation of the world, cosmopolitism, and awareness.

> www.progettodiogene.eu

**Matei Bejenaru** employs a socially engaged practice to frame discussion on the effects of globalization in the organization of labor in post-communist countries. He is the initiator of Periferic Biennial in Iasi, Romania and is one of the founders of Vector Association, a contemporary art institution which supported the local emerging art scene to become both locally and internationally visible.

> www.bejenaru.context.ro

**Aspra.mente** (Eva Cenghiaro, Giulia Gabrielli, Gabriella Guida, Alessandra Saviotti) originated from the idea of "work in progress," intended as the conception of interdisciplinary projects that develop over time. The work that arises is often the product of in-depth preliminary research connected to the sociocultural context of the site at which the project is proposed, aiming at directly involving the public and searching for a type of collective assignation of responsibility which renders the artistic act as participatory as possible. Aspra.mente's artistic investigation is predominantly concerned with food consumption as connected to the earth and capable of generating agricultural projects.

> www.aspramente.blogspot.com

**Bik van der Pol** (Liesbeth Bik and Jos van der Pol) have worked collectively since 1995. Their working method is based on cooperation and research methods regarding how to activate situations in order to create a platform for various kinds of communicative material. They have exhibited widely, developing projects and commissions with various international institutions. Part of their practice includes publishing books and curating. They live and work in Rotterdam, Netherlands.

> www.bikvanderpol.net

**Publink** is an art collective initiated by Roberta Bruzzechese, Maddalena Vantaggi, and Maria Zanchi. Publink investigates through art the limit between public and private space, collectivity, and the individual. Publink offers strategies to formulate new readings of the public space, through projects studied for urban and suburban specific contexts.

> www.rifiutoconaffetto.it

**Manuela Ribadeneira** (born in Ecuador and currently living in London) views her artistic work as a social, political, and spatial investigation. Her practice is based around constructions of objects and sound, also utilizing strategies of participation and performance in work that comments on or intervenes in social and public spaces. As part of her practice, with Nelson García she founded *Artes no Decorativas*, a shareholding company that was legally established in 1998.

# An Antidote to the Crisis: Suggestions and Solutions From a Generation Born in the Desert

*Cecilia Canziani —*
"There is undisputedly a common social denominator behind the movement, but it is also true that, in psychological terms, this generation appears to be universally filled with sheer courage, a stunning desire to act and a no less surprising confidence in the power of change." This is an excerpt from Hannah Arendt's *On Violence*, and it might just as well refer to the artists I have chosen for *visible*. The research project took quite a long time to prepare and covered a vast area to begin with, until I realized that something interesting and new really was happening in Italy. I also saw that it was important to seize these strategies and analyze them as breaks with the recent directions in which art has been moving, and in the context of contemporary Italy.

A number of artistic experiences with significant social and political components are currently emerging in Italy. Their premises and outcomes are not that different from projects which, in other countries, and particularly in The Netherlands, the UK, and the US, have been a well defined and widely practiced and studied area of contemporary art ever since the 1960s. But the world in which Italian artists work is very different, and it has a different social, economic, and political vision. It is just that the difficulties that have so far faced the development of artistic processes along the lines of "new genre public art" are no longer an obstacle. And, what is more, over the past five years many independent spaces and many collectives have opened their doors, in a country in which art has traditionally been characterized by cumbersome individual personalities. And this is something very new and important. Going back to the words of Arendt, we certainly cannot talk of an organized movement and yet the courage, resolve, and foolhardiness of the younger generations in Italy cannot fail to astonish. This is a country that is witnessing the collapse of a political system, for which the left—the political parties and trade unions, which failed to understand the changes that society and the labor market were heading toward—is also responsible. And from this point of view it seems to me that, especially in Italy, these experiences should be seen not only, or at least not so much, in relation to what is happening in the visual arts but more in relation to how, in this moment of crisis of democracy, the public sphere is reorganizing with grassroots initiatives. This is as true of the left as it is of the right (as we see in the case of the vigilante groups). And possibly we need to look for the roots of these directions in Italian history.

*Daniele Balicco —*
What strikes me most about the artistic experiences that you have selected is the presence within all of them of an inheritance that is implicit, because it is not declared, but also, I would say, especially because it is not known. This may appear to be paradoxical, because in art, and basically in life too, we become adults when we see ourselves as parents. In other words, when we make choices rather than submit to tradition: no one is ever heir to someone if they do not consciously take from them, even in transgressing the code of their legacy.

And yet, even though in an enigmatic manner, an inheritance is present in this road map that you suggest. I don't mean in the immediate, of course. Each of these artists has a clear idea of their international models, with whom they actually enter into direct collaboration. By "inheritance" I mean something different: belonging to a broader history, one that is not just artistic but cultural in general terms. A mechanism that, just like the unconscious, and even against the wishes of those who act, obliges one to be part of a context that one may not like, want, or even know entirely. It's like a sort of magnetic device that attracts and directs every genuine feeling of expression and gives it an initial, elementary form. The ability to react against this force, and to transform it, really makes the aesthetic result a compromise.

We can only assess the actions of the aesthetic subject, its expressive power, and the quality of its gesture, if we manage to define, at least in general terms, the opposing force from which its desire for autonomy and freedom arises and takes shape. Compared with the map that you suggest, the legacy is there, but it's like a hieroglyph that needs to be deciphered. And this is no coincidence. Because hereditary tradition does not belong to the world of art, but to that of political experience. What I have in mind here is the galaxy of intellectual, social, and political experiences that, especially in international theory, are referred to as *operaismo* ("workerism"), which is the great and tragic history of the anti-system movements in Italy from 1967 to 1977. It might also be worth taking a quick look at what Italy was like in those years. The nature of the historic trauma that these experiences unwittingly work on will become clear. For countless reasons, in those years, Italy was of strategic geographical and political importance. Now it is simply a downgraded province of NATO on the border between Europe and Africa, but then it was one of the key theaters of the Cold War. And, what is more, it was a country that was undergoing rapid economic and social change, in an international political context that, in spite of itself, placed it in a strategic area of intersecting borders: first along the East-West divide between the United States and the Soviet Union, and second along the North-South divide between Europe and Africa/the Middle East. All of this was complicated by the presence of the largest communist party in the West and, to its left, social movements against the system that was the largest in terms of extent, potential, and duration.

Perhaps it is no accident that an area with such an overload of tensions, power relationships, and transformations generated the highest levels of experience in all sectors. This ranged from industry—as typified by Olivetti—to culture and entertainment—and here as an example anyone can make his or her own choice, from Michelangelo Antonioni to Giò Ponti, Franco Fortini and Pierpaolo Pasolini, Arturo Benedetto Michelangeli, Bruno Munari, or Giorgio Strehler. In such a rich and interesting Italy, protest became central. Disillusioned hopes of social improvement, which were somehow betrayed by the economic boom, entered into a short circuit with fierce trade union and student protests and a genuine desire to change and to live differently. But history, as we know, took a different course. This process of change was cut short by military violence by the state and by the United States. The tremendous and terrible 1970s, with their clashes of extremes and political violence, are now viewed by public opinion as one of the causes of the disastrous state in which Italy is now—but the *doxa*, as any third-year high-school student might suspect, does not normally coincide with the truth. Even the anti-authoritarianism of 1968 is blamed, as though financial speculation and military policies had no impact on the real life and history of the country. Because if one takes a closer look, with neither bitterness nor partiality, at what really happened in those years, one can immediately see that an end was put to the joyful, intelligent, and creative experience of a student and (from 1969) workers' movement of unprecedented size. It was put to an end by state-sponsored terrorism: the Piazza Fontana bomb attack on December 12th, 1969. It was the fear of a coup d'état that armed and transformed the social movements of those years. And this was a well founded fear, as one can see from documents, especially those of NATO, that have recently been declassified. I believe that anyone who wants to understand what has happened in Italy, from the 1980s through to the desolation of today, should see the ghastly present we are living in now as the end result of a ferocious reaction to the *real* potential of a radically autonomous and progressive country. But at the end of this long and convoluted reasoning, I shall try to return to my original point: Why do I see a quite clearly pervious and by no means consciously adopted legacy in what comes under the name "workerism"—or better, *operaismo*—and the artistic experiences that you have selected? Because I believe that social history works more or less like the history of an individual. The experiences, desires, dreams, and traumas of a community all settle into a sort of social subconscious, without entirely disappearing. There they continue to exist and transform, until they reappear, sometimes in an unrecognizable form, when external conditions change. In other words, some experiences, which are destroyed by force, disappear from the horizon, but they do not go away. They remain as a trauma that needs to be given new form. I realize that this is a specious form of reasoning, but I would like to see the artistic experience that you have chosen as *the unconscious aesthetic reformulation of a historical trauma*. That of Italy as an unfulfilled country, as Guido Crainz famously described it. The themes that your artists revolve around include the reversal of disadvantaged situations into creative potential, the ironic experimentation of forms of intelligent and sustainable life, and group work as cooperation and autonomy. As a result, once they are shifted onto the aesthetic level, they all restore the practical means with which the finest people in the generation before ours wished to view and experience the world. It's a specious interpretation, I realize that. And yet is it not possibly through its ability to free the dreams of liberty and emancipation that history has inhibited one of the most profound reasons for the existence of art?

*Cecilia Canziani —*

If it is true that art can represent a precise *mise en image* of society, the emergence of institutional criticism with undercurrents of social commitment may at least tell us something that breaks down the hard surface of the times we are living in. Whether or not it is specious, I do like your interpretation of these practices as a return of what has been removed: if we shift our eyes from the history of Italian politics to the art system, we can see that the problems are really not that dissimilar. Over the past thirty years, the visual arts in Italy have suffered from the effects of three main interlinking factors: the excessive power of the market, the absence

of institutions, and an educational system that is incapable of escaping from obsolete academic mechanisms. The inevitable consequence of this has been the provincialization of Italian art, which in any event has been turned into a dangerously self-sufficient cultural economy, one that is on the fringes and mainly focused on its domestic market. It is not possible to think of culture as separate from politics, and this hardly edifying image of art clearly reflects the general trends of our history from the 1970s onward. And yet, in an increasingly appalling political situation like that of Italy, areas of resistance do emerge—as we are discussing right now. And, even though the art system promises no radical changes, it is increasingly less hard to see the work of artists who promote alternative ways of producing and distributing culture by introducing virtuous processes that use existing resources and ensure positive effects for the broader community.
This seems to me to be both interesting and worthy of attention, because the last time that visual art in Italy asserted its political nature and was recognized and promoted within the system was in the case of Arte Povera. That was back in the 1960s when, as you were saying, Italy spoke with an authoritative voice in the international cultural debate. The generational element has its weight in this proposal, but we need to find some form of continuity with those lines of research that were able to resist the hegemony of a market based on an unequal relationship between private galleries and institutions. The work of Cesare Pietroiusti is one of those threads between what you ascribe to the legacy of the movements and the situation as it is today. In this project, he is involved in a conversation with **Anna Scalfi**, but he is also indirectly present in the approach adopted by **Aspra.mente** and **Publink**, of which he was a lecturer at the University Iuav of Venice, where he teaches. In an interview I read in a book called *What We Want is Free: Generosity and Exchange in Recent Art*, he said something rather interesting for this discussion: "I like to think that an art practice is the only work with the freedom to consider side effects as a positive part of the project." In a certain way his work is a side effect of a prescriptive market. Earlier on I used the term "New Genre Public Art," which Suzanne Lacy describes as "an integrative critical language through which values, ethics, and social responsibility can be discussed in terms of art." It may be a rather dated phrasing, but I still like it; it seems to me more precise than others, partly because of a word that only Lacy uses: ethics.

The ethical use of resources is something that has struck me in the work of many artists and collectives in Italy, because it places the work on a level that is very different from the welfare-oriented stereotype that the institutions and even the art system have in mind when they think of operations in the public sphere. I have therefore chosen projects that bring about participation and interaction, based on three parameters: projects that induce an alternative economy by introducing sustainable processes, projects that involve the virtuous use of existing resources for the benefit of the community, and projects that turn into resources that which cannot currently be defined as such.

*Daniele Balicco —*

Two years ago, Bollati Boringhieri published a little book by Luigi Zoja, an important Jungian psychoanalyst, entitled *Giustizia e bellezza*. The concept is very simple: justice and beauty are concepts that ancient and Christian thought have almost always viewed together, inextricably binding them together. There is a precise Greek term that expresses this combination, which actually also coincides with excellence—the highest level to which human experience can aspire. The term is *kalokagathìa*. Modern thought, on the other hand, gradually separates out the two terms, confining justice to the legal field and beauty to the aesthetic. Without entering into the merits of Zoja's reasoning, it seems quite clear that this process has today reached its peak, placing us in front of a double impasse. The modern legal system, with the deception of a contract, of procedural democracy, and of personal liberty (which is formally guaranteed but actually, as Marx explains, is basically only the freedom to sell one's own time), has provided extraordinarily powerful instruments for preventing the conscious understanding of the fundamental injustice of modern forms of power. And the most important of these is "liberal democracy." Quite frankly, the modern legal system makes justice unthinkable. This is one of the arguments put forward by Walter Benjamin. We are not free in a world that is incapable not only of enforcing, but also even of conceiving of justice. And this is why today's institutional politics is what it is: an empty shell, a bit more or a bit less than a wretched and arbitrary show of power. Something similar could be said about the transformation of "beauty" by our industrial culture: from an object that could give the individual independence and freedom to a sophisticated mechanism for the colonization of the unconscious. With hindsight it could be said that Theodor Adorno and Max Horkeimer were not entirely wrong about this. In our advanced state of modernity, mass aesthetics has been given the task of compensating for the alienation of individuals, by aestheticizing their desires, and by preshaping their cravings and their imaginative powers. The double impasse is thus quite clear: it is impossible to think of justice and thus of the common good, and it is extremely difficult to achieve an authentic relationship with aesthetics as a realm for the creation of free individuality. When faced with this double incapacitation, it seems to me that the experiences you have selected are ironically attempting to bring back to life an older concept of art and politics. They appear to be going back to an artistic practice that is incapable of separating out "beauty" and "justice." And indeed, in all these works there is an ironic educational intent. In this perception of the objective limits of the mandate, which is defined and expressed through irony, there is an attempt to educate and bring about a higher level of social coexistence through these aesthetic forms. There is a desperate, though almost silent, search for access to an atrophied common consciousness. This is actually a healthy view of the profession, of the role, and of the goals to which one can aspire. Once again, we cannot exclude the fact that an objectively disadvantageous situation can be reversed in these young artists (and in this case I am thinking in particular of the world of contemporary-art training, criticism, and production in Italy). For those who are creating today, it is possible to introduce a more levelheaded and adult vision of the real arenas of action and transformation.

*Cecilia Canziani —*
I like to think that artists can deal with social issues precisely because of their main function, which is that of working with images. *Home Front*, the first of three exhibitions organized by Martha Roesler at the headquarters of the Dia Foundation at 77 Wooster Street in New York, opened in February of 1989. This was just when the SoHo area was beginning to be affected by building speculation, which led to a staggering number of evictions, creating a dramatic rise in the number of the homeless, and it came with the connivance of the political parties. The project, which brought together artists, activists, and district committees, questioned the ability of art to intervene in society, stemming from the the idea that no social problem can avoid being represented, and that one step toward the resolution of a problem starts from a correct reflection on its representation. In a recent text, Chantal Mouffe wonders if art can still play a critical role in a society in which artists and cultural practitioners have become necessary elements in the capitalist production system. I however believe that it is precisely an awareness of being a part of this system that is the key factor of an art that is capable of really intervening in the public domain. This is why I am interested in projects that deconstruct economic processes from within: these projects are capable of creating short circuits in the system by interfering on the visual plane. One example of this is *Incompiuto Siciliano*, by **Alterazioni Video**. As chance would have it, one of the first stages of the project was a photographic campaign. At the same time, the other projects in question appear as sustainable and achievable models: the Parco dell'Incompiuto (literally, "the park of the unfinished") in Giarre, Siciliy, has institutional partners and the town hall recently created the Department for the Incompiuto Siciliano. *Vaccinium*, by **Aspra.mente**, works on the world of the popular imagination of the Trentino region but, in practical terms, it tackles the problem of single-crop farming and its effects on the environment. **Anna Scalfi**'s *indeposito* (literally, "on deposit") transforms the sum of two zeros into a cultural resource: unused spaces and works that artists and museums do not know where to place. *Rifiuto con Affetto* ("Recycle with Love") breaks the cycle of consumption by introducing an ecology of exchange. Lastly, **Progetto Diogene** grafts the economic and cultural potentials of residences in the cracks in the city, which are seen as resources. I also think that the fact that these works demand legitimization not only from the art system but also from users is important: **Publink** and Manuela Ribadeneira discuss this in their conversation, saying that they do not even think it is necessary for those who use *Rifiuto con Affetto* to know that they are actually taking part in an art project, and that verification comes about by using the services offered by the project itself. This aspect necessarily involves self-sustainability too. But in the dialogue of many voices that makes up this text, the words of the artists also revealed the limits to what art can and cannot do. This brings to mind the words that Hans Haake wrote in 1968, just after the assassination of Martin Luther King, against a backdrop of protests against the war in Vietnam, in which the art community had taken part most energetically. He said, "Nothing, but really absolutely nothing is changed by whatever type of painting or sculpture or happening you produce on the

level where it counts, the political level. Not a single napalm bomb will not be dropped by all the shows of Angry Arts. Art is utterly unsuited as a political tool too. No cop will be kept from shooting a black by all the light-environments in the world. As I've said, I've known that for a number of years and I was really never bothered by it. All of a sudden it bugs me. I am also asking myself, why the hell am I working in this field at all? Again an answer is never at hand that is credible, but it did not particularly disturb me. I still have no answer, but I am no longer comfortable." It is worth remembering that artists are not social workers, nor can they replace the institutions or provide the services that should be, but are not, provided to the population. This does not, however, mean that culture cannot constitute an area of resistance. When faced with an excess of realism, I think it is necessary to bring in the idea of *if it were*, and to imagine a different culture and different policies, with references to ethics as possible rather than as utopian. I believe I have done this by engaging in initiatives that advocate ethical polices for the production and distribution of independent contemporary culture. You yourself have done it with *Normali Marziani* ("Normal Martians").

*Daniele Balicco —*

Deleuze says somewhere that the toughest thing for a generation is not crossing the desert, but being born in the middle of it. It's not so much being obliged to go through dark, hostile periods of history so much as being born into them without direct experience of other forms of historical time, other forms of coexistence, other forms of culture, and other forms of life. This means growing up without desiring anything other than what is there, except for an undefined, aimless escape. To some extent this is our problem too. Perhaps the only desire that many of us have—and it may be more or less explicit or equivocal—is precisely that of escaping. And above all escaping from Italy, which really does seem to be precipitating into an incomprehensible and vicious nothingness. But this makes us subject to a power that is exercised against us. We do not stop it, and we do not express anything of ourselves. They kick us out. And out we go.

But actually it should be we who make them go away. We need to direct our own capabilities and our intelligence against those who are governing our country and wasting enormous potential and intelligence. In *Parva Aesthetica*, about one of his travels around Italy, Adorno is amazed by the elementary forms of everyday life in Italy—its gestures, colors, harmonies, food, and the encumbrance of a magnificent art whose presence grows wild in everyday life. Thinking about the millions of Italian emigrants scattered all over the world, he more or less says: inexorably and against all reason, the expulsion from the terrestrial paradise continues. And that's it. That's the point.

We're trying to transform the space around us, trying to find out about it, to control it, to love it, and to transform its centuries-old history into a cognitive and existential privilege. Let's try changing our point of view, just as the artists you've chosen have done. Every obstacle can be turned into an opportunity, and every disadvantage into an opportunity for change. It is up to us. Being adults in Italy might appear to be a disadvantage today; they portray us as eternal *enfants*, incapable of growing up. That's fine. Since we are adults and since the reality around us is getting worse by the minute, we are indeed "Martians." There's a great book, written a few years ago by Luciano Gallino, called *L'impresa irresponsabile*, in which the word "irresponsible" is used to describe the dominant characteristics of our ruling classes, who act irresponsibly toward the state, toward work, toward culture, toward the environment, and toward the future. We are part of this appalling normality. And, at the same time, we neither seek nor adore some mythical, exotic, or anthropological "elsewhere." It's the normality of the present world, built up with passion, responsibility, intelligence, and creativity, that we are trying to pursue and live in. This is why we live under the injunction of this permanent oxymoron: we are indeed "Normal Martians." It does of course take time to understand, to know, and to tackle any given problem. Rests must be taken. It is an idea of time and work that clearly clashes with the media world we live in, which has already gobbled up all cultural work, imposing the same sporadic superficiality everywhere. To some extent, the world of the media is chronophobic. On the contrary, I think we need to claim a self-assured chronophilia as our own distinctive feature. Every natural, chemical, artistic, or cognitive process has a time and a rhythm of its own—one that cannot be accelerated. With *Normali Marziani*, we are trying to focus on the best that our generation has created and experimented with: we have looked into the world of invasive journalism and singer-songwriters, political and digital video-art documentaries, cinema and theater direction, macrobiotic foods and new forms of farming. In other words, this project is conceived of as a sort of spaceship capable of intercepting all the best that is around us and sending warning signals to our present, so that things stop going on like this.

*Cecilia Canziani —*

At the heart of this strategy, which is decidedly anti-economic if we only look at it in terms of profits, there is a need to give time and to take it for oneself. After all—as Liesbeth Bik and Jos van der Pol explain later on—there's no saying that certain or even expected results will be achieved when there is enough time and when it is used properly. I am absolutely fascinated by the potential for failure that is an integral part of these projects. Possibly it's rather like the side effects that Cesare Pietroiusti was talking about. I am interested in it in that that we always start out from suppositions that need to be verified, and in non-institutional contexts this verification comes about in terms that go beyond the realm of art history and aesthetics.

Time is required for the formation of those communities that are not simply comprised of the end users of the work, but that contribute to its creation and look after it. And time was also useful for bringing about these conversations, which I thought might offer better ideas than a text written by a single author, by bringing in a range of different voices and visions which the projects we are talking about need, prompt, and produce.

Arendt's idea of a community—one that is created around a common action—appears to be what networks and groups of various kinds all have in common, at whatever latitude, and now appears to constitute the last fragile bulwark in defence of democracy. At the beginning of our conversation, you traced out a line between the movements of the 1960s and 1970s and the different experiences that are coming about today in the world of culture. But times have changed, and I wonder what the differences are, quite apart from the similarities. A few months ago, on the phone, Matei Bejenaru told me a lot about Romania and its shift from a totalitarian regime to a capitalist country. He insisted that all actions need to be placed precisely in their time, in a particular place, and in a given context if we are to understand their causes and their effects. What does this need for community mean today in Italy?

*Daniele Balicco —*

There is an ever-increasing need for a sense of community, I believe, because we can all perceive the continuous, explicit (or invisible) expropriation of what we share: space and time, first and foremost. These days, the commercialization of every aspect of our lives is not even seen anymore in terms of extortion and exploitation. And this is why, when compared with the social movements I mentioned earlier, we have made a great step backward in social terms. We're closer to the lives of the *carbonari*—secret, revolutionary workers in the nineteenth-century —than to the *operaismo* militants in the 1960s.

A whole world of values, achievements, and rights, which were considered by our fathers to be second nature, have simply vanished into thin air. We stand naked in front of an increasingly arbitrary and narcotizing power. At the same time, the Martian normality we are tending toward only exists as a fragmentary form of expectation: in actual fact, it still needs to be built from scratch. And that's the rub. We need to try not to be naive, and we need to learn as much as we can about the real hierarchies of power in our own country and around the world. We need to experiment with everything that we believe is right, fully knowing that, at least for the moment, we are moving within clearly prescribed spaces. In other words, there is no point deluding ourselves and yet, at the same time, we must also continue to search for the Archimedean point beyond which our intelligence, our passion, and our ability to build will be stronger than their violence.

*Incompiuto Siciliano* is a project in progress that aims to identify and classify the aesthetic and formal characteristics of unfinished public architecture in Italy. An initial survey resulted in the classification of around 500 unfinished architectural projects. The Italian region with the highest number of unfinished public works is Sicily.

The project aims to promote dynamic acceptance of the phenomenon in order to trigger virtuous response mechanisms. The initiative has received support from a number of local and national governmental agencies, thus transforming the initial mapping into a cultural and economic resource for Sicily.

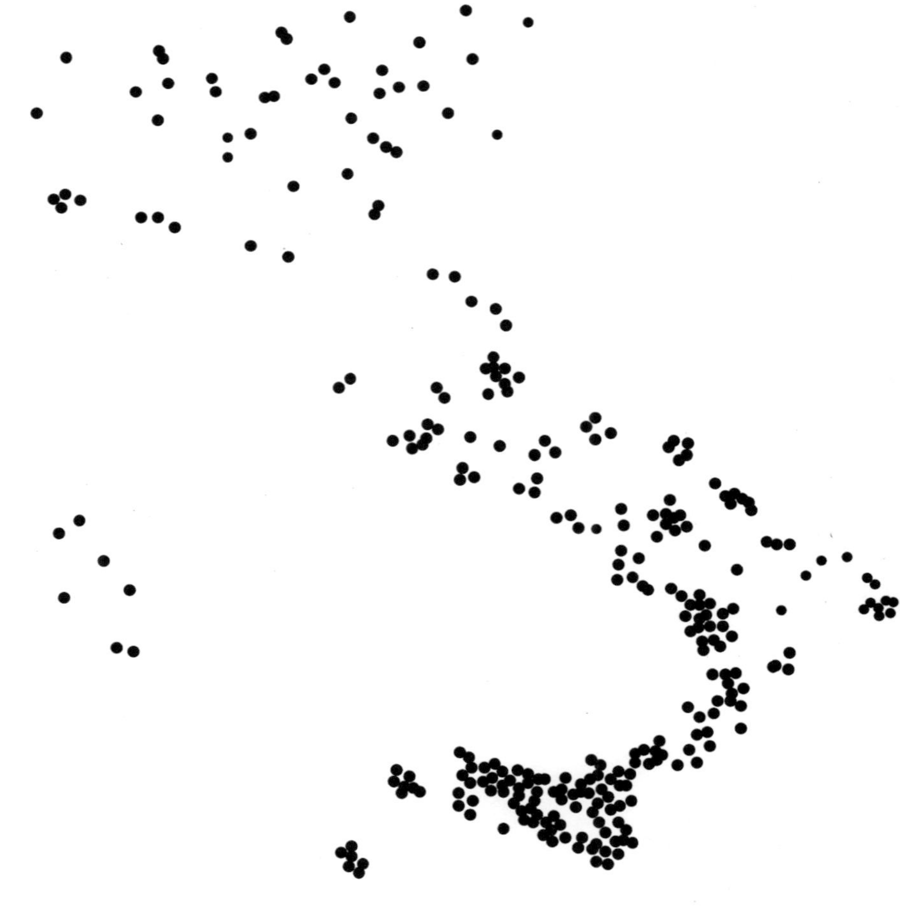

# Alterazioni Video

■□
*Map*, Density of the unfinished buildings in Italy

□■
*Ponte Incompiuto*, 2006, S. Maria di Lanciano, Italy

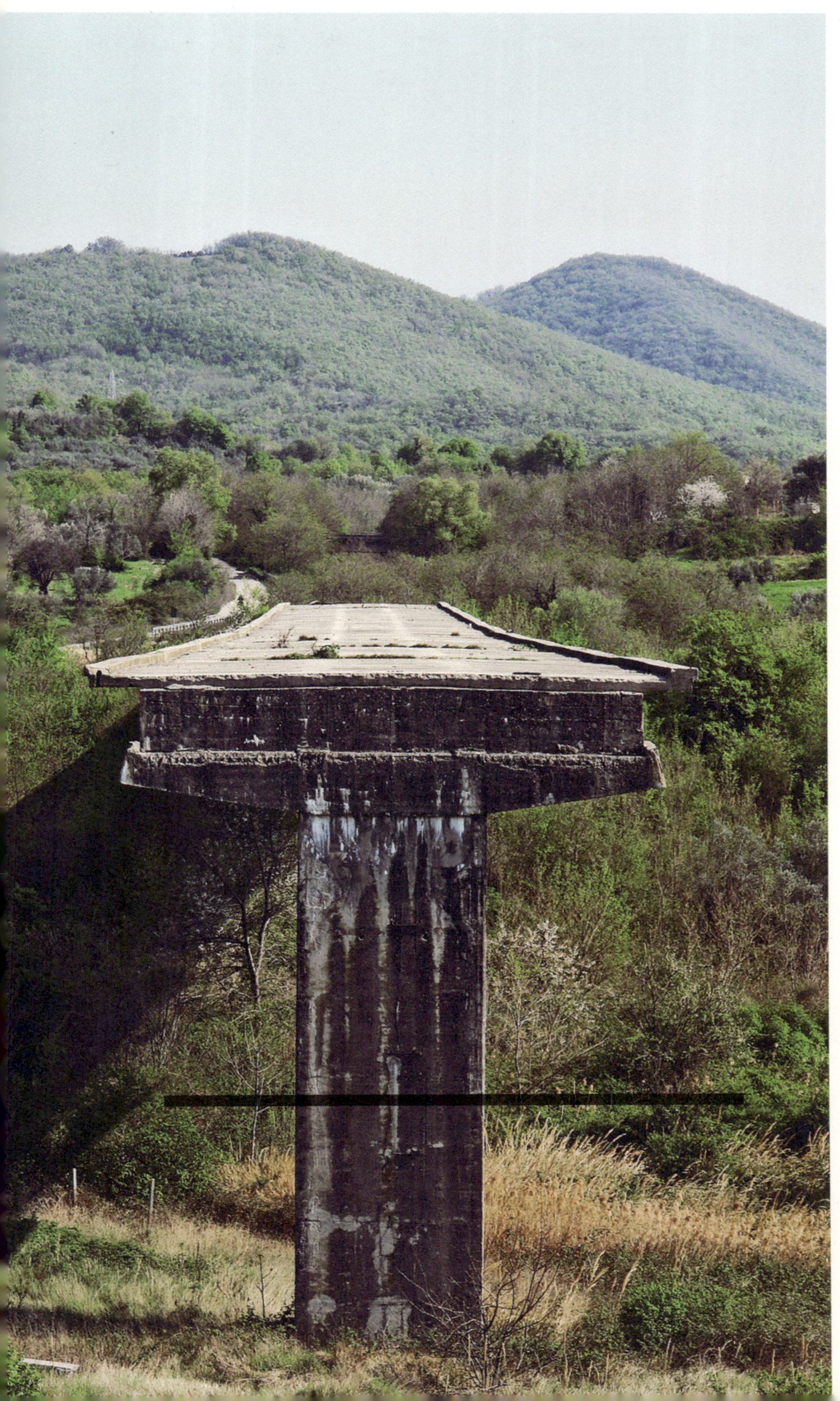

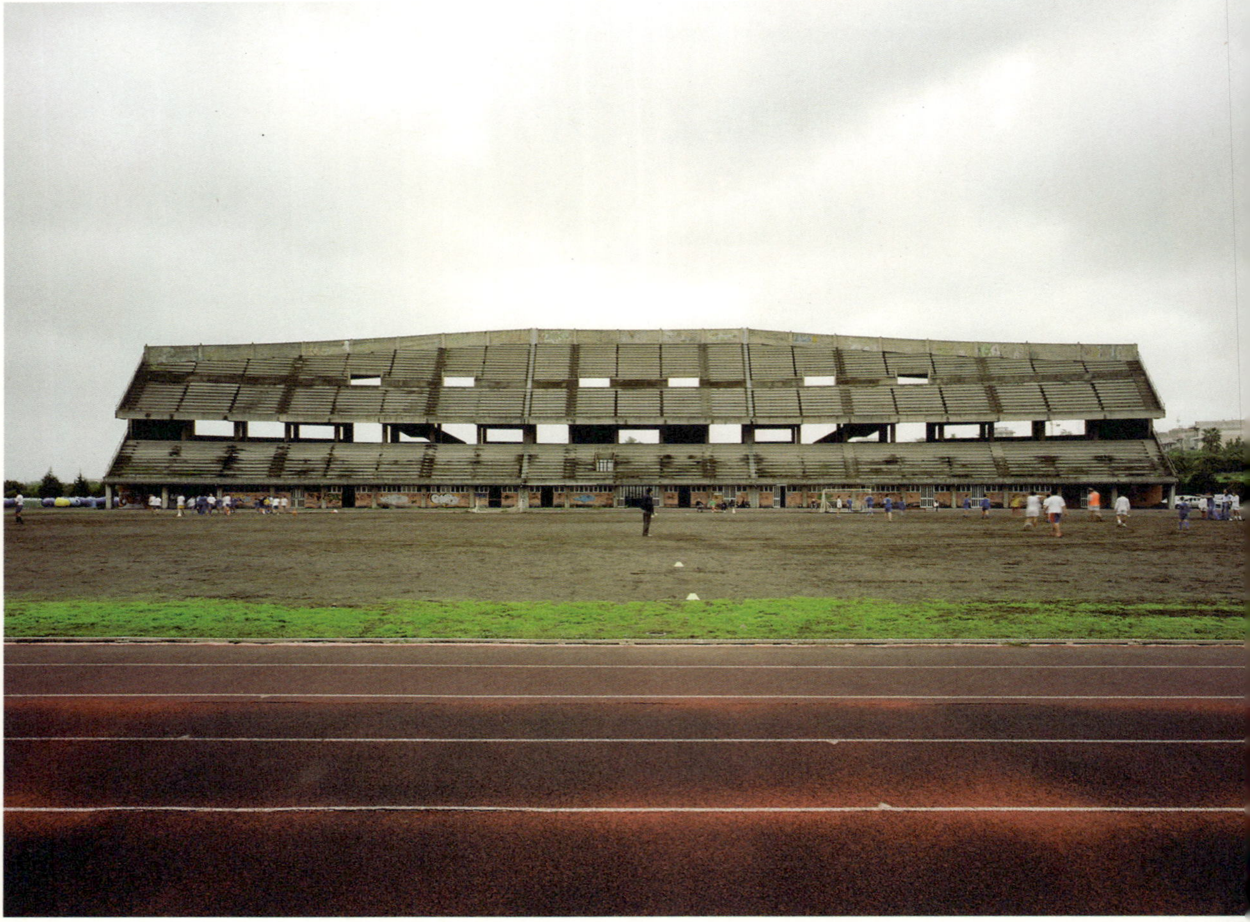

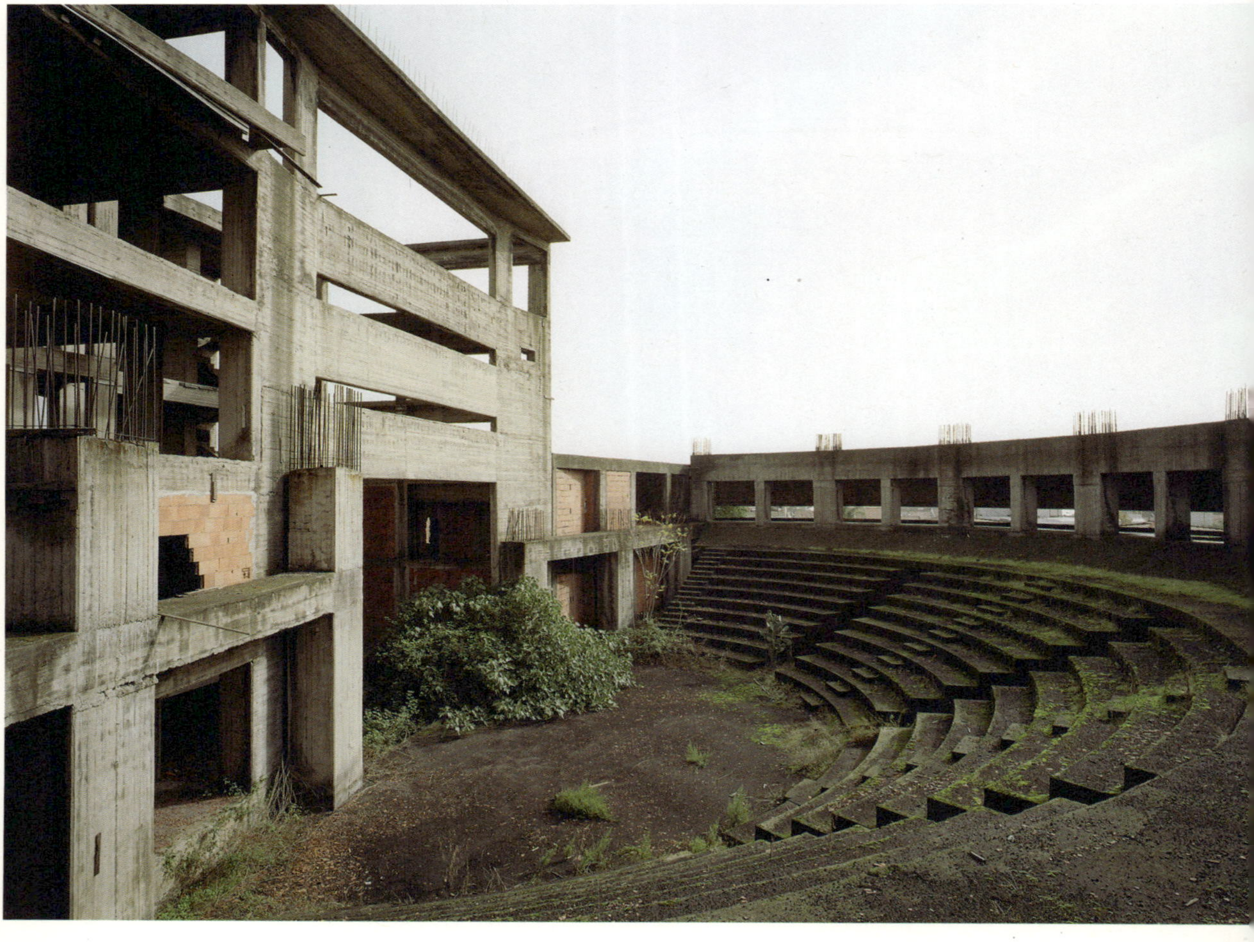

***Giarre—Stadio del Polo***, 2007, Giarre, Italy (photo by Gabriele Basilico)

***Giarre—Teatro Nuovo***, 2007, Giarre, Italy (photo by Gabriele Basilico)

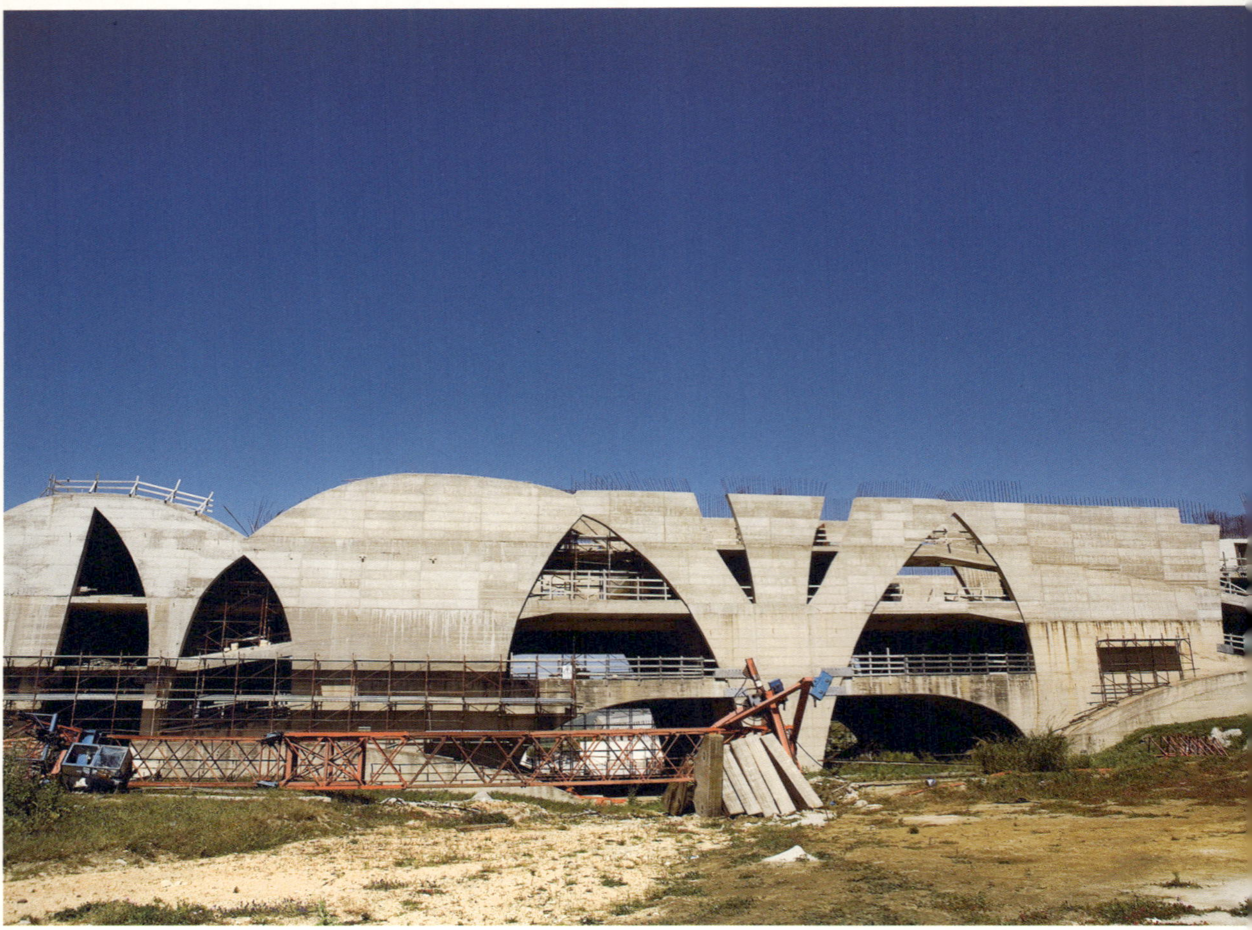

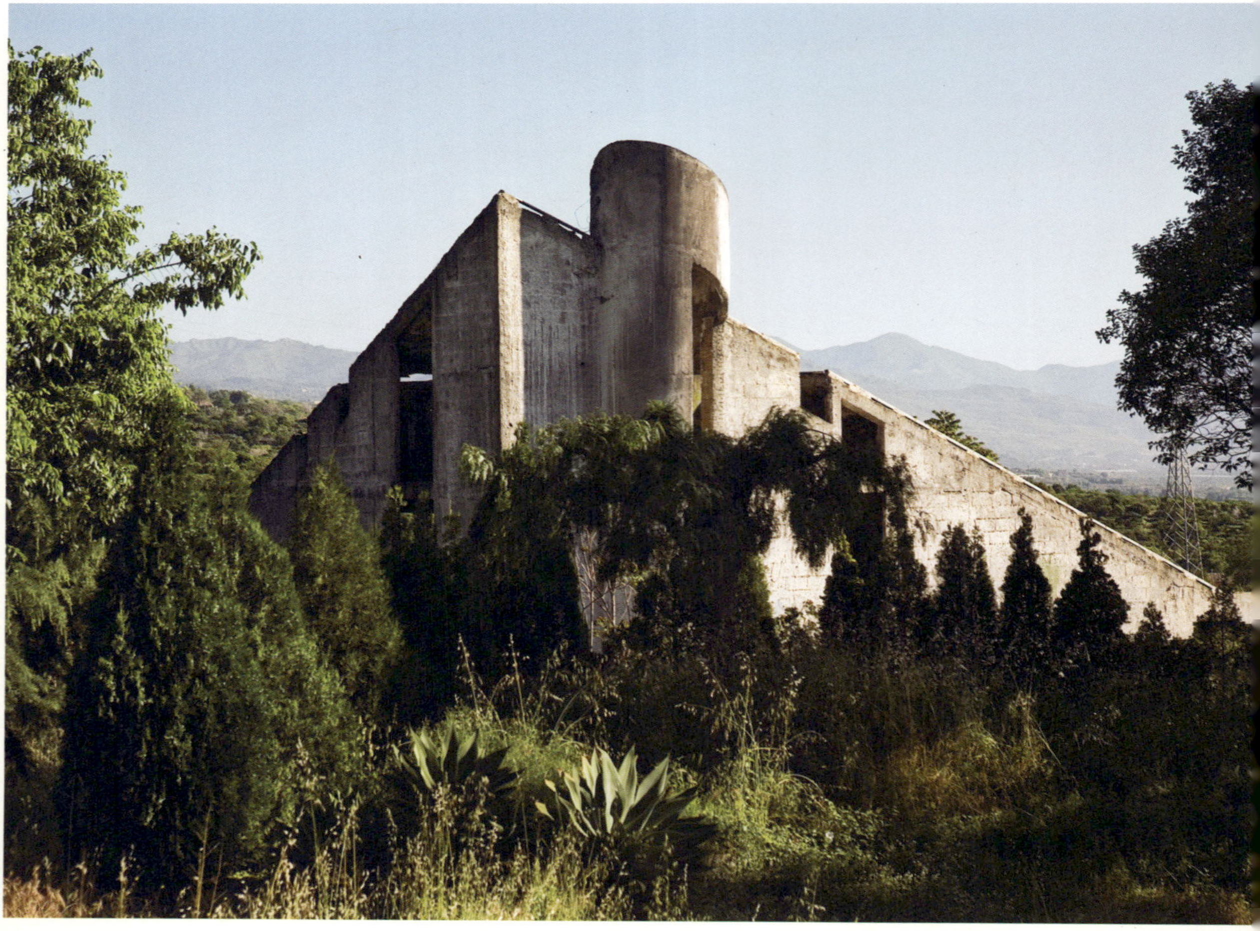

■
□

***Gibellina—Teatro***, 2007, Gibellina, Italy (photo by Luca Babini)

□
■

***Giarre—Bambinopoli, Parco Chico Mendes***, 2007, Giarre, Italy (photo by Luca Babini)

Annex: A text contribution by Cecilia Canziani

*Soliloquy*—As we were saying a few pages back, the risk of failure is an aspect that is often inherent in projects that focus on the public realm. Indeed, *Incompiuto Siciliano*—unfinished works in Sicily—which opens my selection of works, breaks away from the structure I had formed, which was based on the idea of having artists discuss with others about similar issues. The aim was to avoid an authorial text of my own, which seemed to conflict with those openly dialogical and collective processes we are talking about here. However, due to deadlines and busy schedules, this time the original plan did not work out: neither with Julieta Aranda, with whom we had an intense exchange of ideas in Rome about how the various communities can interpret *e-flux Video Rental* and *Pawnshop*, two projects worked on with Anton Vidokle, nor with 0100101110101101.ORG—who have in common with Alterazioni Video an ability to intervene on the level of reality, based on an interrogation of the world of the imagination.

As a result, this project for an almost spoken form of writing remains *unfinished*. And yet it does have a side effect, for some months after I started this research it offered an opportunity to re-examine some aspects of the creative vision that I have constructed. Mediation, for example, is one of these aspects. It is no coincidence that the sore point in this stumbling-block of an approach is that, as curators, critics or, more in general and more properly, as cultural practitioners, we cannot afford to shirk our role. This is because while the encounter between a work and the public in a place with a stable atmosphere like that of a museum cannot take place without intermediation, it becomes all the more necessary when the work comes into contact with different audiences in the infinitely more complex context of the public realm. As part of this research, *Incompiuto Siciliano* was a starting point for me, precisely because it multiplied the figures and places of intermediation by involving the institutions themselves and making them look after an anomaly that they did no more than register: in Italy there is a law that classifies the degree of incompleteness of public works, but once the taxonomic zeal that is so typical of our bureaucracy has died away, no solution is offered. In *Incompiuto*, together with Enrico Sgarbi and Claudia d'Aita, Alterazioni Video starts with a mapping process that illustrates the extent of the phenomenon in Italy, and then goes on to concentrate on the little municipality of Giarre. This town holds the record of having—in just three hundred hectares—twelve of the 160 unfinished public works in Sicily, a region with an extraordinary density of unfinished works. However, Alterazioni Video starts out by reporting a problem, but then reverses the view: what happens if we start considering this wounded landscape as a sculpture park?

Early on in the project, Alterazioni Video commissioned Gabriele Basilico to carry out a photographic campaign in Giarre that transformed this architecture (which is deconstructed since it is devoid of function) into a monument. This initial action was followed up by a documentary video in the form of an investigation which involved the inhabitants and administration of the town, all of whom are jointly responsible for the construction of sometimes useless public works, and yet hope lies in them to bring new life to the little municipality. As Martha Roesler shows, artists can act on society by working on its representations. As a document, a photographic image is an effective means of questioning reality: the unfinished work becomes an effective metaphor for understanding the society that produced it. It is a faithful, perfect *mise en image* of Italy over the past fifty years. And as such it is a monument: an invitation never to forget that in Italy, and especially in Sicily, concrete very often means mafia—and that it is neither something else nor somewhere else. We are all involved in it.

The third stage of the project is the creation of an archaeological park of unfinished works in Sicily—the *Parco Archeologico dell'Incompiuto Siciliano*, the creation of which was jointly put forward by Alterazioni Video and the municipality of Giarre. It is sponsored by MIBAC, Darc, and Regione Sicilia.

The *Parco dell'Incompiuto* is a complex work, in which the roles of author, public and intermediary are interchangeable. It reminds us of the concept of shared care and responsibility, transforming an undermined territory into an economic resource based on informed cultural tourism. Verification will take place not in the world of the imagination but in that of reality and of time: it will work *if* the park really is created, *if* it is funded on a regular basis and, more than anything, *if* it is accepted and used, and if its potential is understood first and foremost by the local community, which is its main target and, at the same time, its mediator.

*indeposito*[1] is a temporary space made available for the storage of works that would otherwise be dispersed. Artists who for different reasons do not know where to allocate their works, and would otherwise destroy it, can make use of *indeposito* services. There is no charge for the use of the storage space, the directors reserve the rights to decide whether or not to accept the works, and the transactions are regulated by a legal contract.

*indeposito* builds upon aspects of precariousness and invisibility that characterize the contemporary, using them as resources, which gives it the form of a temporary, flexible, disseminated space.
*indeposito* reactivates spaces that are not used, and the works in deposit are accessible and engage in a new dialogue with the public.

1 *indeposito* exists in its use, and it manifests itself as a subtraction of a void. Even in its written form it adapts itself to the given context. It does not have a specific font, color, proportion and is characterized only by an action of resizing. The logo *indeposito* is defined in relation to the text of the page where it appears, by using the same font and color, minus three points of size, and always appears in small caps.

# Anna Scalfi

***indeposito Trento***, 2009, directed by Denis Isaia; via Brennero 159, 38100 Trento, Italy

***indeposito Trento***, 2009, Gianfranco de Bertolini, Denis Isaia, and Claudio Bortolotti (Presidente Patrimonio del Trentino SpA)

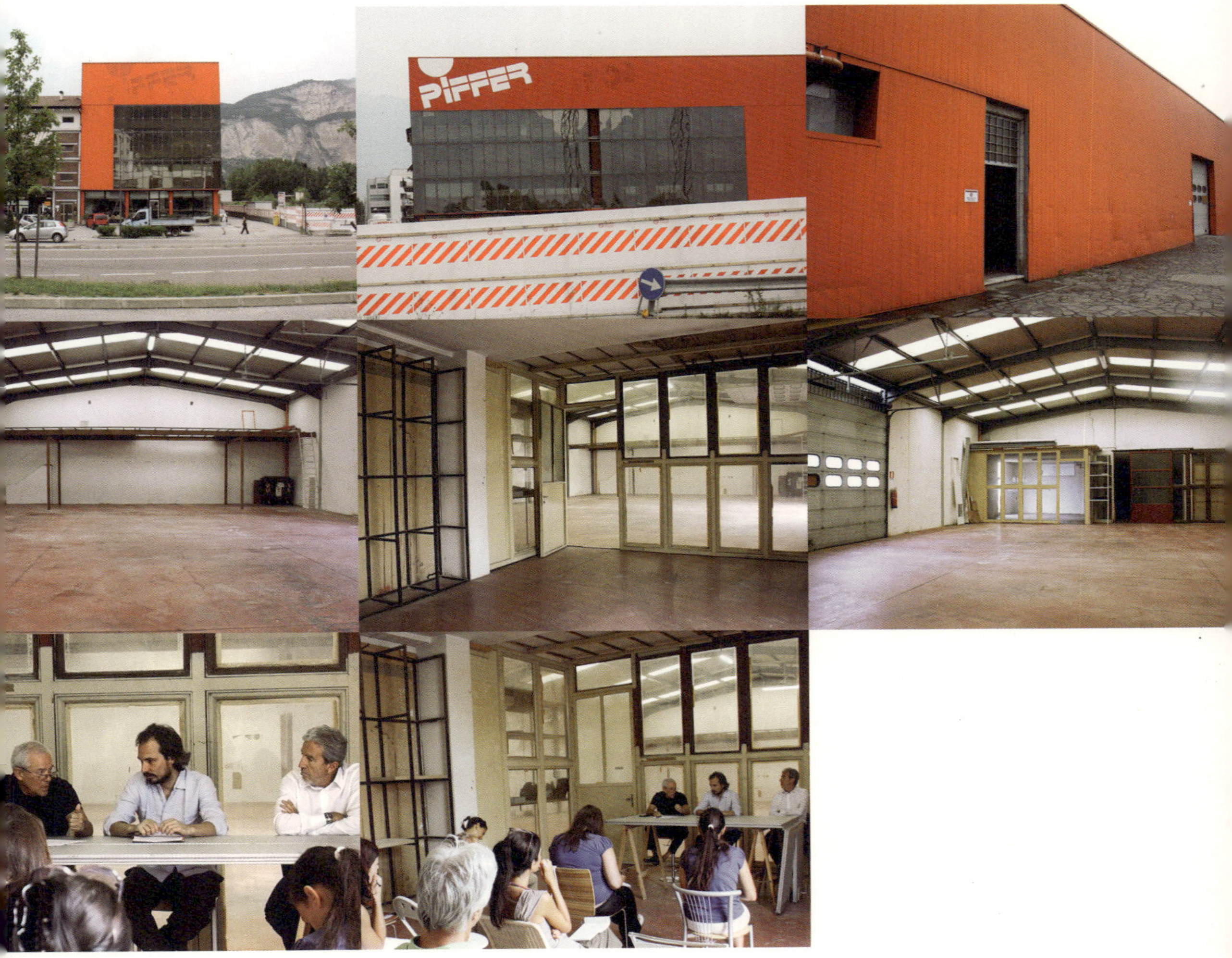

Annex: A Dialogue Between Anna Scalfi and Cesare Pietroiusti

*Cesare Pietroiusti —*

*indeposito*, which might translate as "instorage," is a project you have devised and which has its own art director, Denis Isaia, who also supervises the Trento headquarters. The *indeposito* site on the Internet is created and run by Cristian Pozzer, and Patrimonio del Trentino SpA has temporarily offered a currently unused space. The lawyer Gianfranco de Bertolini has provided legal assistance. It seems only right that I should start with a counterintuitive question, which needs to be interpreted in the broadest manner possible: in terms of your expectations, your fears, or possibly your superstitions, in what way do you think that *indeposito* might *not* work?

*Anna Scalfi —*

At the moment, I have no expectations, fears, or superstitions. What I am certain about is the 600 square meters, cleaned with sorghum brooms, buckets of water, and blisters on our hands; two trash bins filled with what is termed "non-recyclable waste" because of its unclear biological or synthetic origin; an inch of water in the bathroom, flooded on Friday afternoon, just two days before the press conference; and, last but not least, forty-eight euros worth of brooms, buckets, detergents, and bags that cannot be refunded. Perhaps it is already *not* working. By normal criteria, which allow one to make reassuring projections in terms of time, innovation, or religious beliefs, it is certainly *not* working right now. Statistics, percentages, numbers—the rhetoric of the system ensures standard conventions, and the model of non-functioning is standardized by market rules. This is why if *indeposito* does *not* work, its necessity will be ensured. This is why Denis and Chiara have broken their backs dancing in the dust. Luca, from the furniture shop next door, took fifteen chairs from his window and lent them for the conference, and a very kind plumber, requested by the company that gave us free use of the warehouse for *indeposito*, also came along. You could say we might consider the *non*-functioning of *indeposito* as pretty mediocre.

*Cesare Pietroiusti —*

*indeposito* is a priceless intuition. Even at the cost of quoting myself, I really do believe it could be referred to as a non-functional space. And you're right: this is exactly why it's necessary. It is indeed a potential space, because it clearly offers possibilities but gives no guarantees of productiveness or investment, of definition or role. More than anything, it is a space that is constantly waiting, and thus in a state of suspension with regard to any possible conclusion or result. *Indeposito* is always waiting: like any empty space, it is waiting for something to fill it—in this case, works of art that no one knows where to place. But, unlike all other spaces, once the works have actually arrived, the space is also waiting for them to leave. Paradoxically, *indeposito* really does "want" to be continually and repetitively emptied. This is what makes it different from museums, but also from our homes. This makes it just as necessary as any other place whose meaning needs to be sought, deposited, and introduced on each occasion—as necessary as any place we see in the current plethora of self-celebratory, fake, and clearly defined sites. This is true at least in terms of the spectacular impact that museums seek when they "communicate" what they are doing or what they are going to do.

*Anna Scalfi —*

Your reference to expectation makes me "long-circuit" ecstatically, and I will try to transcribe the concept by converting it into language. In terms of the definition of roles, what I am interested in is how *indeposito* offers an opportunity for the self-attribution of a role—in terms not of privileges but of responsibilities. It is no coincidence that the term "director" comes from institutional organizations. Those who are inspired to become the "director" of a local venue can find a place and manage their own collections, working on their own curatorial vision. When I say that the fact that *indeposito* does *not* work is a guarantee of its necessity, I mean "necessity" as an alternative to the system. It is necessary as a logical way of deviating from the expected results. A non-functioning of the system is a local functionality, given context in the form of special significance, and thus one that responds to a system of significance rather than of economics. A market of significance that is agreed upon, and one that can be proposed and accepted—an alternative significance at the heart of the decision-making process, which deals with its context and thus with the mechanisms of relational, rather than coercive, consensus. The idea of expectation and of disengaging the mechanism from changes over time leads to a break from any retroactive economic assessments and, in its logical ramifications, it anticipates the identification of the space in an attribution of significance itself. I have been able to create these projects thanks to this currency of significance—which can be agreed upon, and which runs through all their roles and functions—and thanks to its acceptance as a result of acknowledgement. Yes, you're right: "on deposit," "introduced on each occasion." The current value of meaning and of its common utility is confirmed by action and use. Like in a bank: *on-deposit, on-deposited.*

*Cesare Pietroiusti —*

As Adorno has repeatedly and mercilessly explained, the issue here is one of "de-mythicization," one of realizing that the means of thought, convictions, and even desires that appear to be "ours" are induced, at least in the first instance. What we believe to be true (or beautiful, or whatever) is almost always false. So the only thing we can do, patiently and without any great hope, is to attempt to reveal the (external, but firmly internalized) mechanisms that "make" us think, feel, or want something. We need only think of places that are built. In other words, of "buildings": What happens when a political power without any idea, culture, or vision, attempts to assert its presence? It will build a monument around an empty meaning, and the inconsistency of this monument will be compensated for as much by its name (maxxi, mega, macro) as by its architectural appearance. The more this senselessness emerges, the more it is disguised by monumentalism, high-tech solutions, and exorbitant costs.

First point: the more something costs, the less sense it makes. Definitions, like product labels, are invented to disguise this lack of meaning. "Museum of contemporary art" is no longer anything like a myth; it is a label. I think we can free ourselves of this label and—I say this as an artist—from any subservience to it. We need to blow the lid off the shams of those who attribute to themselves (and to whom we attribute) the power of legitimization, and we must first of all do this within ourselves. The "museum of contemporary art" (and any other place that is defined and delegated) actually delegitimizes.

Second point: the more an institution claims to give one legitimization, the more it takes from one. So I consider *indeposito* to be precious because it is non-functional, illegitimate, and not appointed. In other words, its uses and values are potential (because they are open to suggestions from anyone) and not guaranteed (because they need to be assessed each time).

*Anna Scalfi —*

This contradiction comes out in everyday life and the raw nerves of the system emerge from the details. They are sweet-filled decaying voids, they are universes. I start from there, imagining more, and introducing a minor disturbance into the mechanism. By negotiating everything in offices, in compliance with all the standard rules, procedures, and permits. And often by provoking legitimate exceptions, in that thin slice of discretionary power that remains in the hands of the official. With no experience, one can act outside the rules of the system. I accuse the concept of legitimization in the broadest way. I like it, it is

required, I consider it, and I adapt to the rule: I legitimize myself. And I do so in order to enter the system and interact. In education, in permits, in the human negotiation of collaboration. My first experience: the total lack of a budget is worth more than the limited presence of a sponsor. Sometimes I've made my works in spite of and only thanks to the guarantee of not having any cover for my budget. It is only this that has allowed people who are completely alien to the world of art to listen to ideas and to be persuaded by them, and to end up contributing materials and services. The less-than-partial presence of a sponsor would have made any assistance impossible, changing the prices and making the project as a whole quite unfeasible, and that is exactly what was happening. A system that believes it needs to safeguard and regulate economic profit legally and commercially makes anything else unpredictable and difficult to achieve. It is not contemplated. A whole array of solutions need to be created, with the assistance of experts.
My second experience: skepticism about contemporary art is the best form of vetting for the significance of the project. Normally, those I contact to solve some problem first feel the need to make it quite clear to me that they have nothing to do with contemporary art, which they consider incomprehensible, costly, and absurd. Then they go silent, because they have suddenly come up with a solution for my problem: they go back to what they were saying, now completely caught up in the project, seeing it from within. And I smile: it's done. In spite of all the terrible prejudice against contemporary art. And, depending on their own particular abilities, they all add their own forms, colors, and materials, while I smugly hold in check my supposed control over aesthetic decisions.
I like the "frame" of art because it allows otherwise impossible, unimaginable, and prohibited actions. I like sparking it off in unofficial places, bringing the context into it, free from any positive prejudice about art, free from the reassuring boundaries of artistic nature in this environmental anomaly, where attribution wavers between insult and surprise. I like the predicament and the break from eternal commonsense, the holding back from the automatic controls that distract you, so that you can understand what borderline you're walking on. I like leaving this margin empty so that you can negotiate with yourself about the meaning of what you see.

*Cesare Pietroiusti —*

I'll ask for hospitality at *indeposito* in the coming months. "The Museum of Italian Art in Exile" is a project of mine that aims to start up a research project throughout Italy, and later it intends to acquire a certain number of works by (Italian) artists who are not represented in any museums in Italy and who have no (or almost no) visibility in the art-media system. This traveling museum will be taken in by a number of institutions. Before it goes into exile, however, I'd like the collection to stay, at least for a while, at *indeposito*.

At least in Italy, nowhere could be more suitable.

*indeposito Malpensa*, directed by Alessandro Castiglioni and Francesca Marianna Consonni; Via Padova 9, Cardano al Campo, Varese

*indeposito Mumbai,* directed by Andrea Anastasio; super–processor compound, Lalbaug industrial estate, Mumbai 400012, India

*indeposito Goa,* directed by Arun Jothi; 33/1, Gaunsawaddo, Sodiem, Siolim, Goa 503417, India

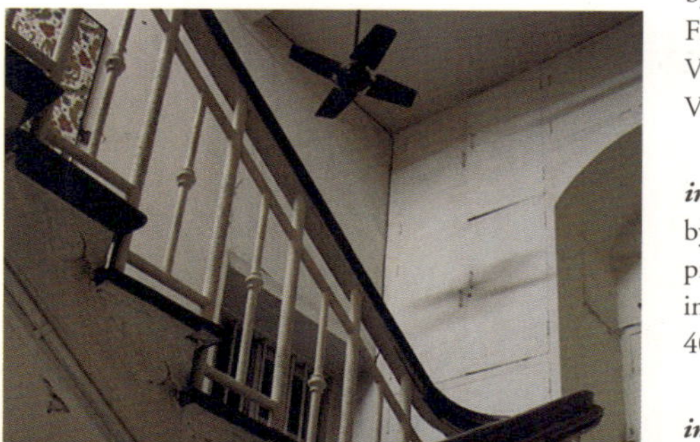

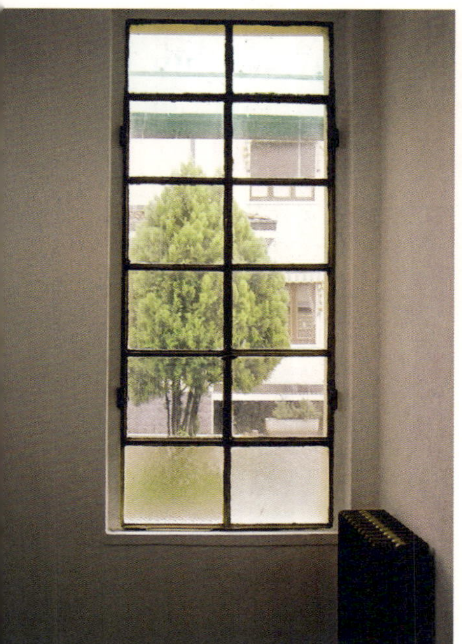

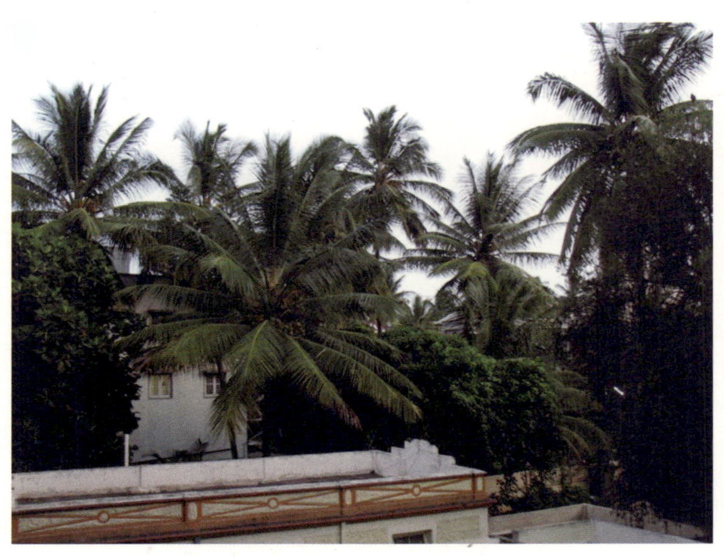

The *Diogene bivaccourbano* ("Diogene Urban Bivouac") is an international residency program that intends to promote artist exchange and mobility, cutting down the number of structures for this purpose to a few basic elements by using the network of existing public services that characterizes a particular urban space with the aim of reducing costs and allocating funds to realize an essential living structure, avoiding the construction and management of complex permanent systems.

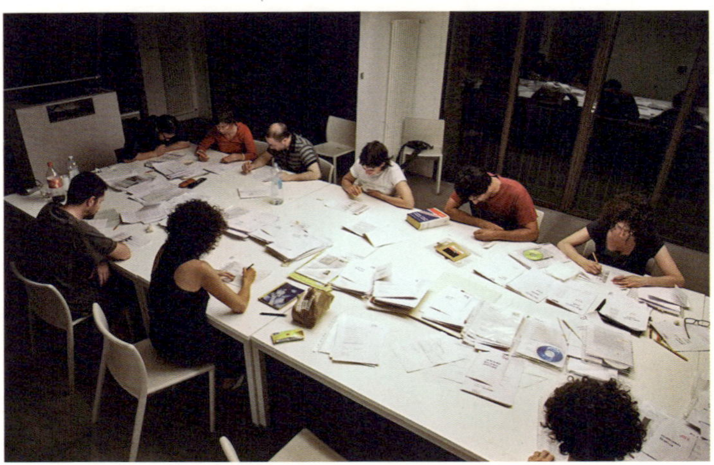

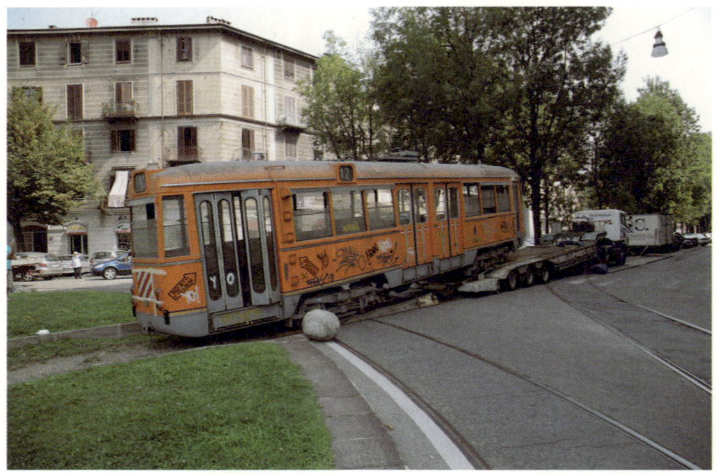

# Progetto Diogene

***bivaccourbano***, 2009, positioning of the tram in the roundabout

***bivaccourbano***, 2009, selections of the applications for the residency

***bivaccourbano***, 2009, Corso Regio Parco, corner of Corso Verona, Turin

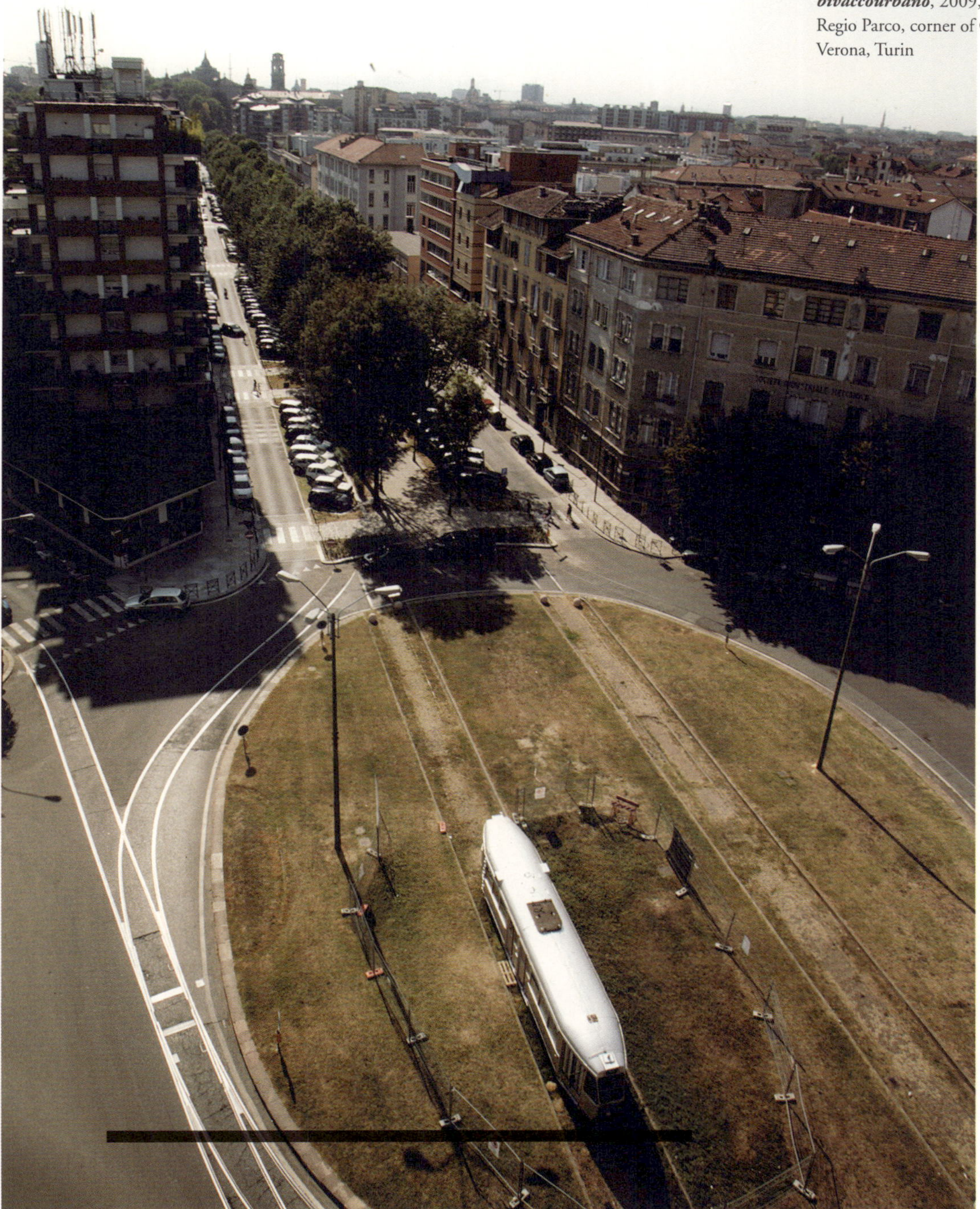

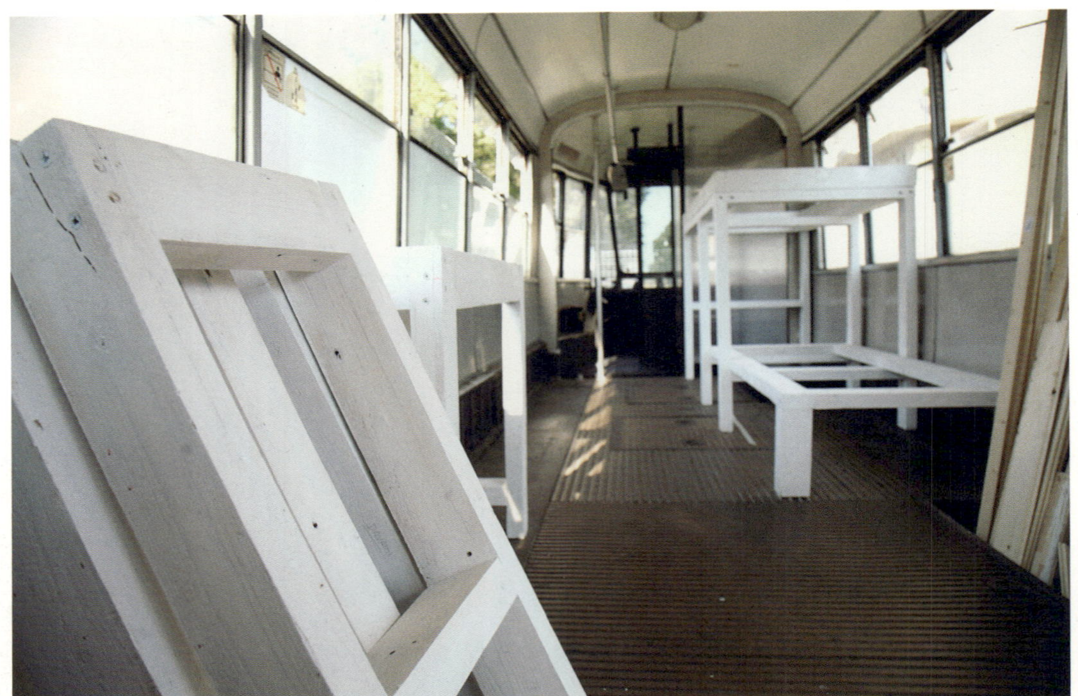

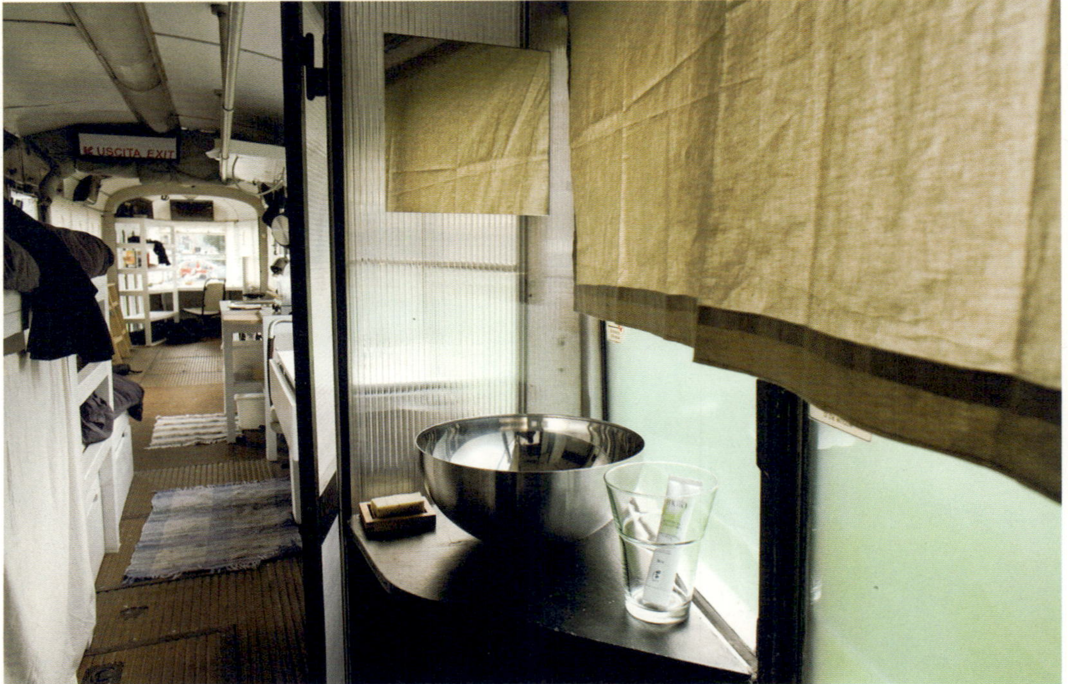


***bivaccourbano***, 2009, interior and exterior view of the bivouac

***bivaccourbano***, 2009, presentation of the "Bulding Transmissions Team," with Nico Dockx (Artist in Residence 2009) and Pol Matthè, at Blank, Turin

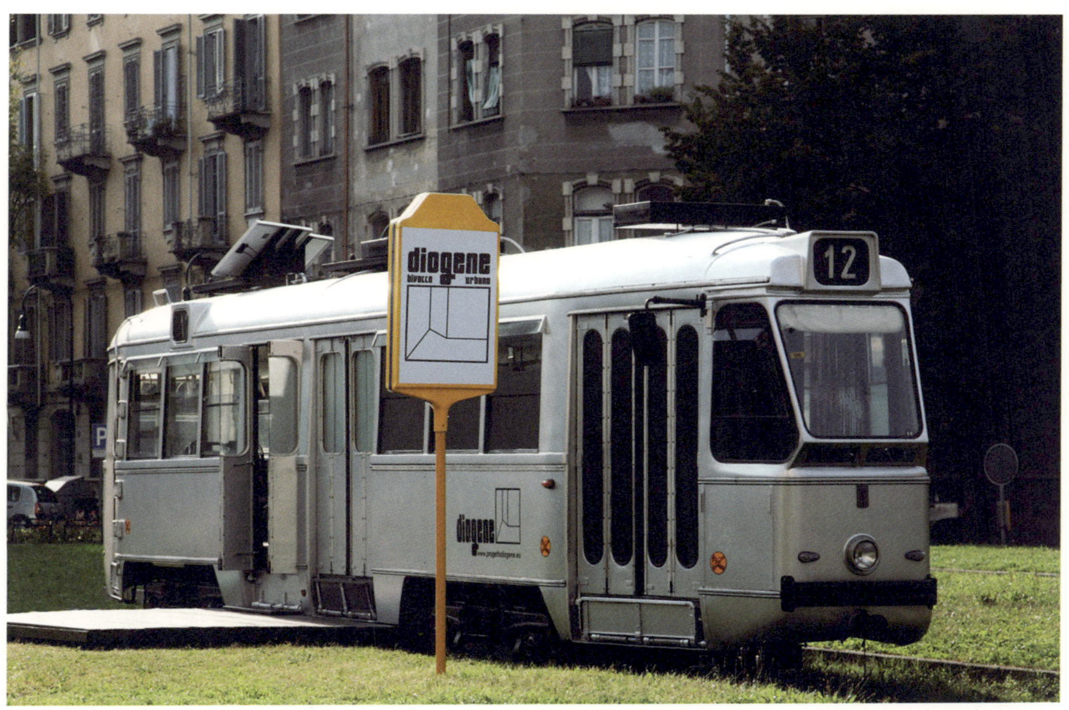


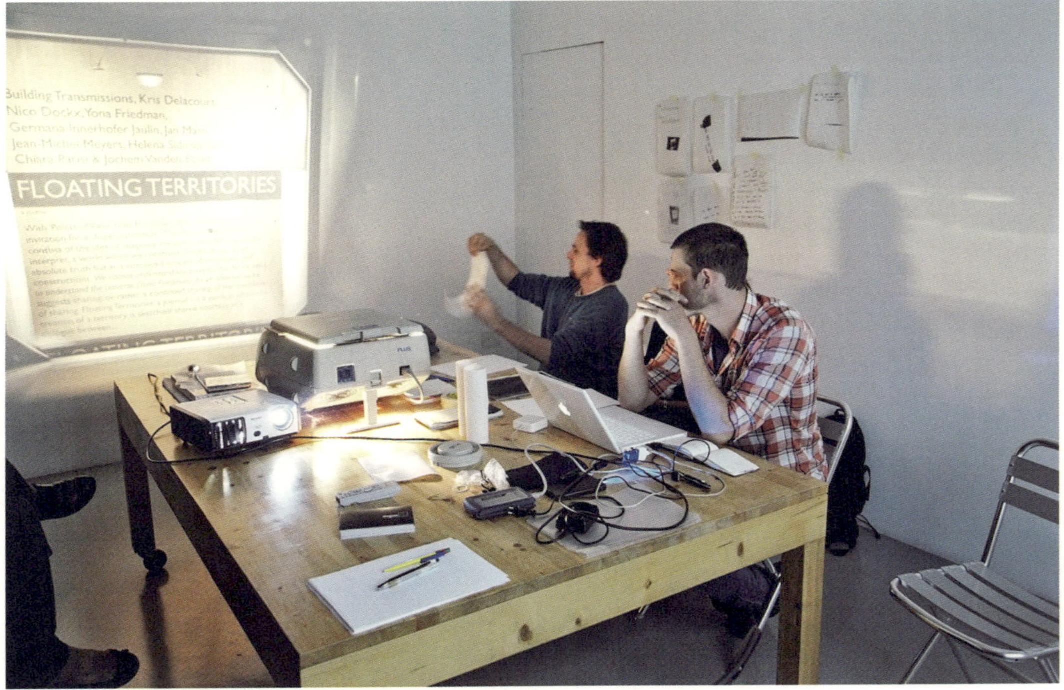


Cecilia Canziani
**Progetto Diogene**
Diogene bivaccourbano

Annex: A Dialogue Between Progetto Diogene and Matei Bejenaru

*Progetto Diogene —*

Researching the Peripheric Biennial, we think that we focus both on the economic processes in the art field and on the construction of self-organized projects. From our side, we are working to create a dialogue space that focuses attention on an artist's work and poetics, offering the possibility to an artist to work in a good situation with a budget and a space, without any complex structure. What do you think about the economic situation of artists nowadays?

*Matei Bejenaru —*

I live in Iasi, Romania, a university city of 400,000 inhabitants situated in northeastern Romania. There, at the end of the 1990s, with a group of visual artists and philosophers, I found Vector Association, which produced the Periferic Biennial, and Vector, an art-and-culture-in-context publication. During the past decade, we ran a four-year gallery program as well as different residency programs involving artists and theorists from southeastern Europe, Turkey, and Lebanon.

Art has different functions according to context and historical time. In our post-communist society, the main function of art is social and emancipatory. In other words, art relates to social and political issues in a time of deep transformation from a totalitarian regime to a neoliberal society. Also, different from the spirit of the 1990s, when artists' discourses were critical to the human condition under communism, after 2000 the critical discourse shifted to the "parameters" of the newborn society: consumerist, corrupted, full of contradictions, socially polarized.

In communist times, independent artists were producing art as a strategy for intellectual survival. In the 1990s, they (including me) came down to the street to promote social change and to invent institutions. Since 2000, most artists produce art to sell, and to get international visibility and recognition. The Periferic Biennial developed a local art scene and put the name of Iasi on the map. Its presence also applies pressure within Romania toward the development of a professional infrastructure for contemporary art, which is still very weak in Romania twenty years after the fall of communism. That is why, in comparison with the artistic strategy of the Progetto Diogene, our aim is to get financial and logistical support from the existing power structures for the development of an institution that is needed but that is not yet born. We do not have a museum or a center for contemporary art, and there are only two commercial galleries in the city, which primarily promote traditional forms of art. This is the main reason why a priority is to enhance the quality of art education in the university, as well to have a professional center for contemporary art with medium-term secured budgets to help stabilize the personal subsistence of artists.

I took a look at your Web site and I liked the way you presented the project. For me, your artistic approach (building a living economically independent structure in the post-industrial city

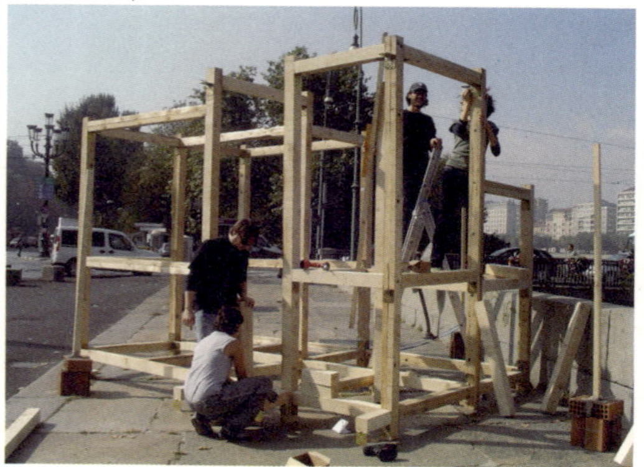

■■

***bivaccourbano***, 2008, Piazza Gran Madre, Turin

and offering it as a residency program for artists) is the dominant part of the project. I also like the idea of building it from found material from art institutions and events (Artissima or the Venice Biennial, for example). It gives a necessary criticality to the project.

*Progetto Diogene* —

Our art scene is quite different from the one you describe. We start from different needs, but in some ways we work in the same direction. We work into a structured art system composed of museums, foundations, commercial galleries, and not-for-profit spaces, all of which, except for the commercial galleries, are promoted by public or private institutions. From the beginning of our project, we felt that some things are changing, that the sensitivity to cultural producers from public or private institutions is growing. There is more interest in new projects with low economic budgets. We try to work in this moment of transformation with a practical proposal for the creation of a network of artists who work on different types of research. We work as a collective and try to do something different from institutional work, and that in Italy is still missing. We attempt to use our economic and intellectual resources for selected artists' work. The goal is to give value to the selected artist's work and approach through discussions and meetings. The 2009 edition of *Diogene bivaccourbano* will be located inside a small self-contained module—the Bivouac—an out-of-use tram carriage set on an abandoned section of track at the corner between Corso Regio Parco and Corso Verona in Turin. The tram could be seen as an empty shape of the city that will the starting structure from which the living and working place will grow up. This organism, at the end of the residency, will become a platform that welcomes and develops an international artistic network. We are not sure, however, that the criticality of the project, which you highlight, is our main goal; to build the bivouac from found materials is mainly a practical necessity but is also linked with our intention to cut the surplus.

*Matei Bejenaru* —

What are the criteria and the procedures for selecting the artists? Do you expect them to produce new work? For this, in my opinion, they need a longer period of time, or to come several times to Turin, starting with a research visit, and moving to realization and presentation of the project. Very personally, I think that it is more important that you create a space for artists to listen to other artists, than for the artist to produce a new piece. I can imagine that it is difficult to live in the bivouac for more than a few days and that this can affect creativity. By the way, how do the artists go to a toilet or go to have a shower?

*Progetto Diogene* —

The competition is open to all artists currently working in the specific sector of the visual arts, without restriction of approach or medium. Usually we require a portfolio, artistic curriculum, statement of the artist's work, and description of a project that the candidate intends to develop during his or her stay as the motiva-

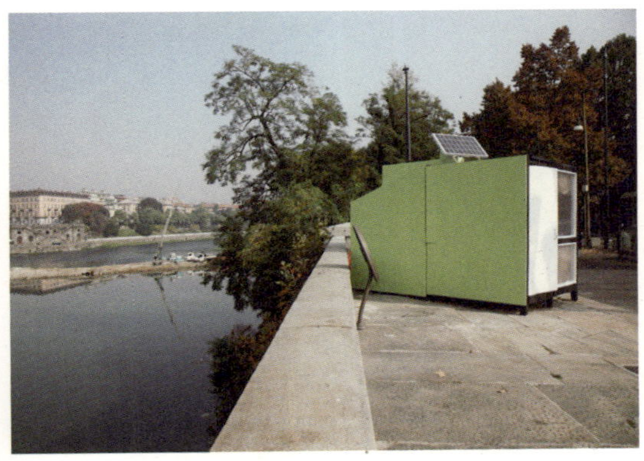

tion for applying. The main criteria are the originality of the artistic works and the coherence of the artist's statement with the proposed project; only in the final phase of selection do we consider the curriculum of the artist. During the residency, the selected artist takes advantage of the urban and natural resources (sun, water, public toilet, Internet points): the bivouac is self-contained and self-sustained, with a little kitchen, a chemical toilet, and a system for hot water and a shower. The dweller's life is conditioned by the weather, with energy derived from a solar panel that powers all the mechanisms in the residence.
The listening space that we aim at creating, and which, as you said, is crucial, is almost accidental, and resembles more the concept of nearness. Building a real place and developing a program of meetings and conferences constitute an official, working hypothesis of exchange, while the physical closeness with the artist brings a different quality of listening. Producing a new piece is not a fixed goal, but is like an occasion of sharing a work. This happens or does not happens depending on the subjectivity and wishes of the selected artist. And beginning this year, the time of residency is longer in order to allow the artist more time to familiarize him- or herself with the context.

*Matei Bejenaru —*

To whom are you addressing meetings and conferences? To the academic world? To artists and students? To the art crowd?

*Progetto Diogene —*

The conferences are addressed to other artists, students, and art professionals. Beginning this year, it will take the shape of a discussion between fewer people. The entire project and its processes are also addressed to the community—the building of the bivouac-tram at the period of residency awakes interest and curiosity in inhabitants of the city. The bivouac is inside the public space, making visible the artist's work space. The aim is to communicate to inhabitants that the artist works in a real place, essential for him and not so far from the world. We show in some ways the entire process of work of art.

*Matei Bejenaru —*

Can we go back to the idea of criticality in art? You said that you do not intend to be critical. I am not referring to critique in a *stricto sensu*. In the moment, you analyze your art context and decide to produce something that doesn't fit with the rules of the system, you have a critical attitude. It is also important to control the meaning and the ways of "reading" of your project. In my opinion, this can be done if the producer defines from the beginning the finality of the project. If a project like yours is proposing to be out of the economic circuit of art, I think that it has a criticality. This was the reason I asked you for more details about the conferences and

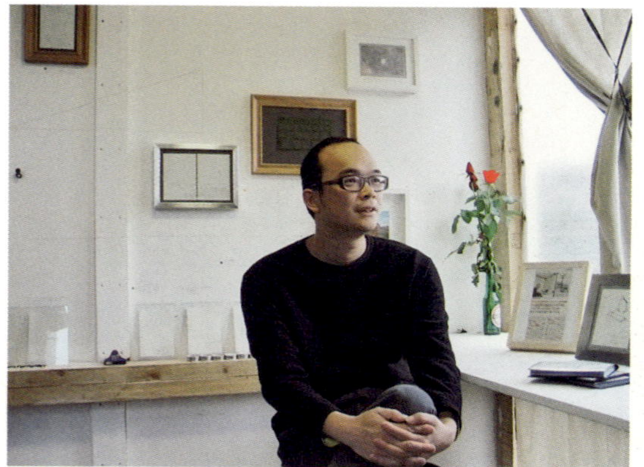

■■
***bivaccourbano***, 2008, open studio with Pak Sheung Chuen (Artist in Residence 2008), Piazza Gran Madre, Turin

presentations: there is a focus point where the project can be discussed and contextualized. With reference to the Urban Bivouac, I would like to better understand what is more important for you: the functionality of the bivouac; the design; or the communication, awareness, and new forms of sociability it can produce? What is the message you want to transmit? Would you accept the reproduction of the project inside a successful commercial gallery in Turin or Milan?

*Progetto Diogene —*

As you said, we do have a critical aptitude, and that was one of the starting points of our project. When we said that criticality was not our main goal, we were referring to the fact that we are not interested in becoming socially responsible designers; we just try to work with the strictly necessary, which is the main reason for using disposable waste to build the bivouac. In such a frame, we think that this attitude has in itself some elements of criticism. We do not want to be a replacement for something that already exists, like galleries or museums, but at the same time we don't criticize *a priori* the art system. We prefer to act in practice, activating processes based on alternative dynamics, to show that it is possible to act in different ways, furnishing new points of view. To be critical for us means working together through individualistic behavior, focusing the attention on the work of the artist and on the rule of the artist in the society.
For us is important to work together and, through our practical engagement, to give a new life to an interstitial space of the city, creating places of exchange. Above all that, our collective work is a proposal, a new way for producing culture and for sharing ideas, works, and projects with other artists. Concerning the possibility of presenting the project in a successful commercial gallery, we think it would be possible, depending on the kind of intervention. We could, for example, hold a lecture in a gallery to communicate our project to a larger number of people, or have a theoretical discussion with a small number of experts, but what we are doing, as a collective, is not for sure something that can be sold.

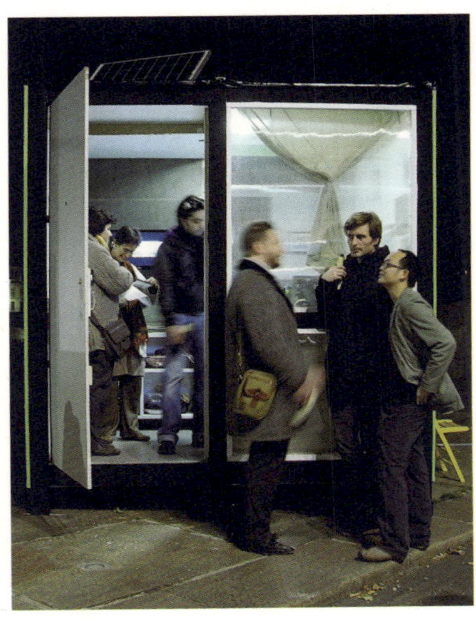

Presented in the frame of Manifesta 7, *Vaccinium* relates to the cultural identity of the region of Trentino, known for the production of apples, which determined the creation of a stereotyped image of the region and left no space for other products to emerge.

Aspra.mente operated a recovery of local tradition and concentrated its attention on the blueberry. The project aims to deal with the idea of agriculture and modern tools of production and commercialization in relation to artistic practice. *Vaccinium* intends to open a critical perspective on the idea of traditional and alternative medicine. The blueberry was proposed as a medicine, in the form of juice, and was accompanied by a leaflet of instruction.

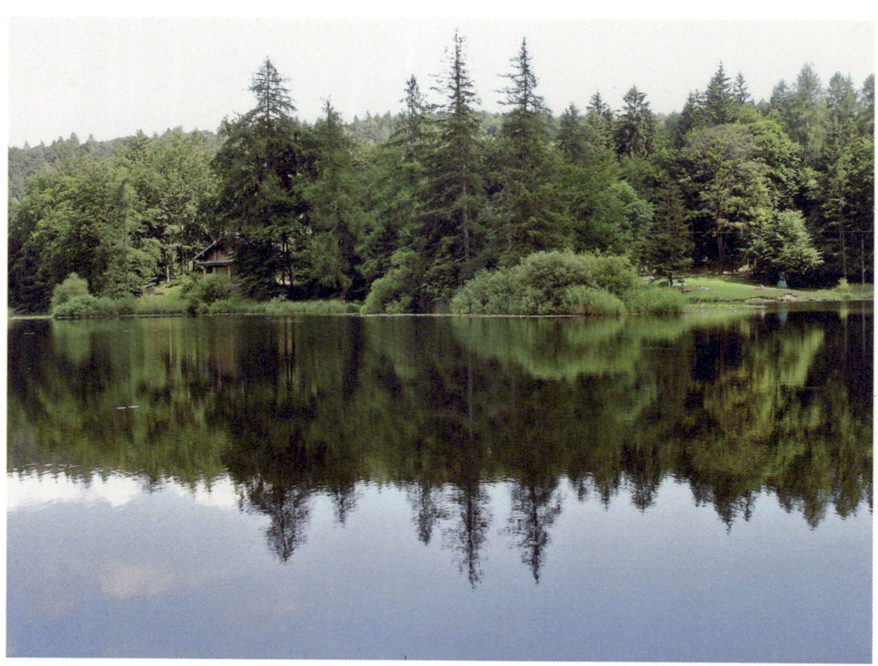

# Aspra.mente

Vaccinium, 2008, Manifesta 7, Rovereto (Italy)

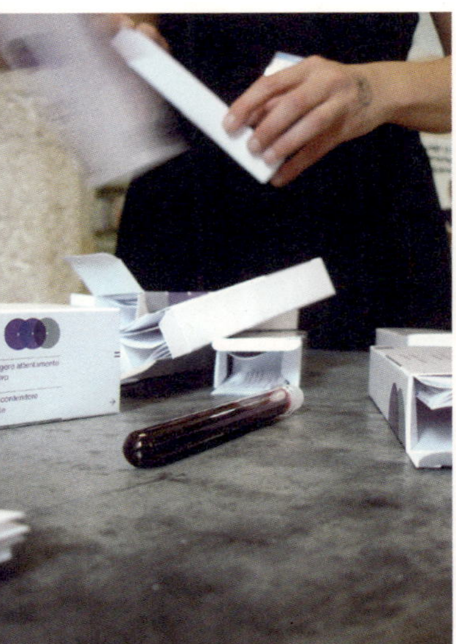

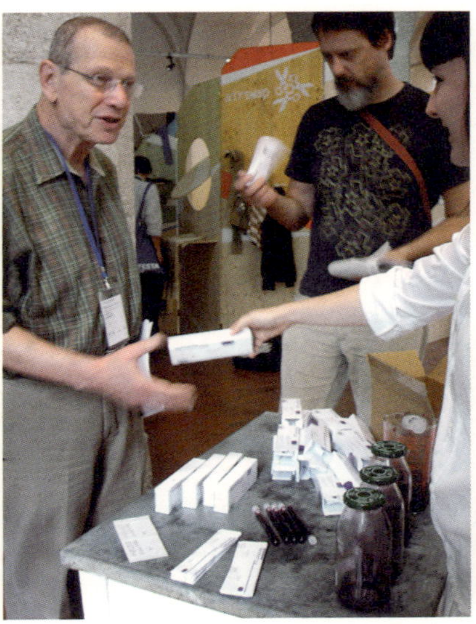

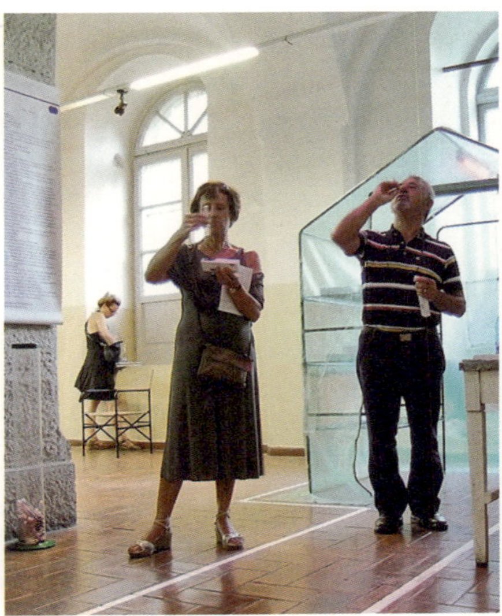

Annex: A Dialogue Between Aspra.mente and Bik Van der Pol

*Bik Van der Pol —*

We saw your work during *Manifesta* and tasted from the glass tubes with blueberry. How do you work together? How do you communicate, and do you keep each other engaged, on top of things? Does your blog operate as a tool in creating a collectivity? And what is the relation between your collective, your community, and the community you are trying to establish through your work, when focusing on the content?

*Aspra.mente —*

We employ guerrilla tactics and marketing strategies to enhance existing resources, transform the imaginary of local contexts, create communities, and potentiate sustainability. An important aspect of our practice is the fact that we don't live in the same place. We have different characteristics that stem from personal experiences as individuals living in our small cities. Maybe for this reason trust is a very important aspect of our work in developing a relationship with the public. We use e-mails and Skype to comunicate, and use the Internet as an ethical tool. That's why we chose to create a blog—it is open to comments and collaborations and it serves as an archive for our work.

Works such as *Flower Salad*—an act of guerrilla gardening—aim to generate a spontaneous community around a small edible garden. We developed a flower bed as a public space and the public is in turn invited to interact with it in order to acquire awarness of common resources. *Flowerbed* is also a way to reclaim space and perhaps this is a link with your practice (we are mostly thinking of *City Oasis*). In *Flower Salad*, the participation is active, but the aim is to generate a community.

*Vaccinium* has a similar approach, and an emphasis on the element of trust: we asked people to consume blueberry juice as a medicine and we demanded from the public that it believe in the treatment. I see an analogy with your work *Laughing Gas* (2007), presented in Graz, Austria, where you sprayed the gas as a sort of positive energy and people had to trust you and your action. Of course, you could not see a physical change, but maybe a humor change or a change in behavior. Once we find a theme, we spend time in researching and analyzing the topic from different points of view. Only then do we meet, have dinner together, and spend as much time as is needed to get to the point. To describe an example of the way we work, for *Vaccinium* we wanted to find a dialogue with the Manifattura Tabacchi, and with the space and history of the factory in relation to the local agriculture. We found that it was interesting how tourism and images of the region, Trentino Alto-Adige, were related to the idea of well-being. The research on history and science became more about medicine and the trust that people generally put in traditional as well as natural or alternative drugs.We are used to working with other people, so we create this community around the work itself. Designers, farmers, spectators, and people working in markets or other places are all invited to interact with us. Some of them work in making the performance or installation, some leave comments or make new proposals, and some interact with us through the fruits that we give as gifts. I saw that your work relates to public space. Let's say that our focus is more on common goods, even if it deals with the space, the environment, and the region.

*Bik Van der Pol —*

We think there is an overlap of common goods and public space. You are right that our work deals with public space, and with the developments regarding issues connected with public space, the public, and publicness, in the broadest sense of the word. Common good also touches upon

**■■**
***Flower Salad*, 2009**

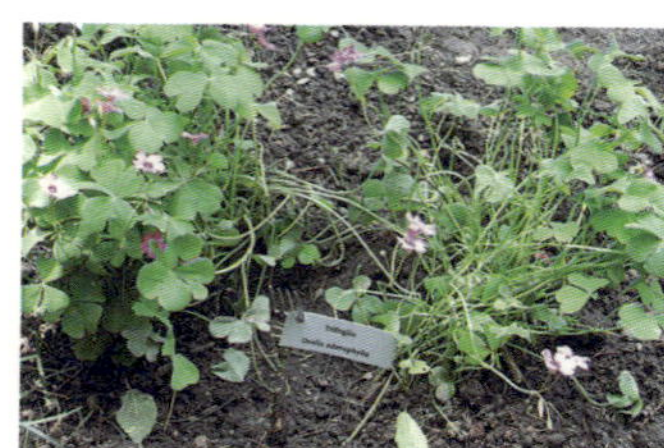

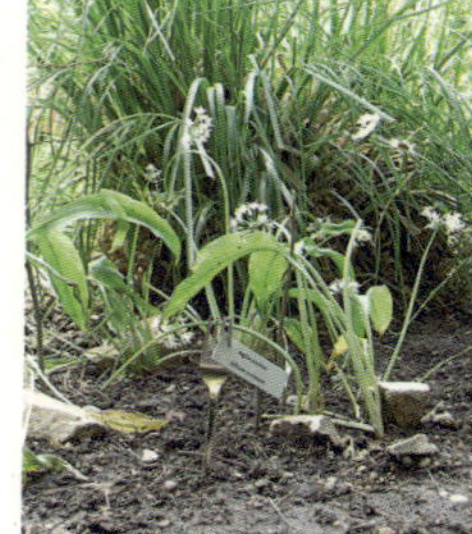

"the public," since "common" and "public" can be understood to be similar, we feel. We would like to share our thoughts on publicness with you, and we have reedited part of a previous text we wrote not so long ago. Around 1980, the art magazine *Artforum* circulated a questionnaire among artists asking them for their opinions and experiences regarding changes in their audiences. The public was an issue even then. Institutions asked themselves who their audiences were, where they went when not visiting museums, why they did not visit museums, and what that meant for the raison d'être of those institutions and artists.

The artist Vito Acconci said that if the gallery and art spaces could still be seen as spaces of activity, there were two options: one is to use the gallery as a "language," as an imparter of meaning, and the other is to use the gallery as a space in which art "occurs," where art has a place while the viewer looks on. He chose, as we still do, the second option, although we would like to note that art also occurs in areas other than galleries and art spaces. The gallery, therefore, mutates. In Acconci's words, it becomes "a community meeting place, a place where a community could be formed, where a community could be called to order, called to a particular purpose." Roughly translated, art occurs, or better still can occur, where a community can be formed by convening it for a specific purpose. In a certain sense, this is very close to what you do.

What does it mean if, as artists, we abandon the museum and the gallery, and unleash our observations, our "anthropology," into our everyday surroundings, into communal spaces shared by different communities, into the space that we call public? It is not a coincidence that we use the term "anthropology." Despite the fact that anthropology and art are different entities, we believe that they also have similarities. In modern anthropology, culture is understood to be central to human nature. In other words, our species has developed the capacity to view our world in symbols. We can learn and teach these symbols socially and we can transform the world (and ourselves) on the basis of such symbols. Sometimes situations can provide us with the means of imagining that what we see can be seen differently. And when we say "differently," we don't mean in the same sense as Marcel Duchamp's declaration that the Woolworth building, for a long time the highest in New York, was a "readymade." Transformation, which for Duchamp signified a transformation from building to objet d'art, can occur other than via the readymade. One could also see it as meaning that the strength of an object, in this case a building, is already implicitly present in the object itself. The way the publicness of public space as space seems to be that any space that is not occupied by the capital is still space that is geared toward the same goals as is the capital: quick and efficient transportation, of people and of goods. There is idealism, which is the ideal of the capital. This idealism creates the symbols. Access to any kind of public is in principle guaranteed but is in reality reserved for the target groups that are part of this machinery. The question is more and more how we want to deal with this type of public realm that makes up a growing part of our surroundings, of our collective consciousness. A type of space that maybe even creates a specific type of imagination. We believe art cannot just fill a gap. If we want another type of public realm, we should approach this realm as something crucial, and we should not allow it to be just a streamlined leftover area in between buildings and highways. If public interest interests us, we need to start to make these places an actively important part of the public domain, and look at things from a totally different angle, in order to equip ourselves with the tools of imagining that what we see can be seen differently. Many of our projects have circled around our questions, doubts, and criticisms regarding this issue. If the public space cannot be traced, as we just stated, except for in the only space that is vaguely called "public" (namely its streets and its squares), is it then productive to think of the "public sphere" as something symbolic, as something that generates a transformation, we wonder?

*Aspra.mente —*

Regarding the audience and the role of art spaces, we spent a long time, during *Manifesta*, speaking about the way to "fit" in the space at our disposal. We were used to working in public spaces, or in other words with spaces that have nothing to do with the art world and with people (still not "audiences") not properly educated in the art language. Our goal was to create, even though *Manifesta* was such a big exhibition, that same spontaneous interaction with the audience in order to speak about the world in which we live. That which is public is mainly connected with access to resources and, above all, to food. We work with food since it makes it possible to deal with economy, everyday life, and social behaviors and relations in a very easy and immediate way. Looking back to the future, we would like to underline how food lies at the basis of the society, from everydaylife and social interaction to economies and politics on a large scale. What if we become conscious that this "idealism of capital" controls food culture and what one eats? What if it makes one believe that one can be healthy just by buying medicines and that drugs can cure almost everything? We are what we eat and our identity is connected with taste. Why don't we go back to nature and take it to the streets?

I agree with you that every leftover space can be seen with new eyes. In our recent work, *Flower Salad*—which incidentally stemmed from research on wild edible plants growing in urban settings—we set up a garden made up of several wild edible flowers of the region. What you need is free and everywhere around us.

*Bik Van der Pol —*

Without becoming too generalizing, we think it is interesting that all the aspects mentioned during our conversation, back and forth, are so much connected. You mention food as your "tool" to work with, to investigate the relationship between those who produce, sell, and mediate food along what we'd like to call the "foodline" (first of all, the farmers/producers, but above all, the industry, the transporters/distributors, and the public, which is in this case the consumer). Despite the power that different players in this foodline have, we'd like to think that the consumer is, in the end, the boss: he/she decides what to eat. At least, that is what we'd like to think. If the consumer wants to have organic food on the plate, the food industry answers that need by producing organic food, and does even more: guided by principles of profit, this need is incorporated in the foodline just as easily as any other product that either seems to be needed, or that is decided to be needed by the consumer. So we'd say that the public is sensitive to "wanting to do good," but what is good has to come to them as easily as what is not good. So, yes, we agree with you that food is one of the products at the basis of our society, next to housing and energy, and it is probably no coincidence that all these industries are major players on the stock market as well.

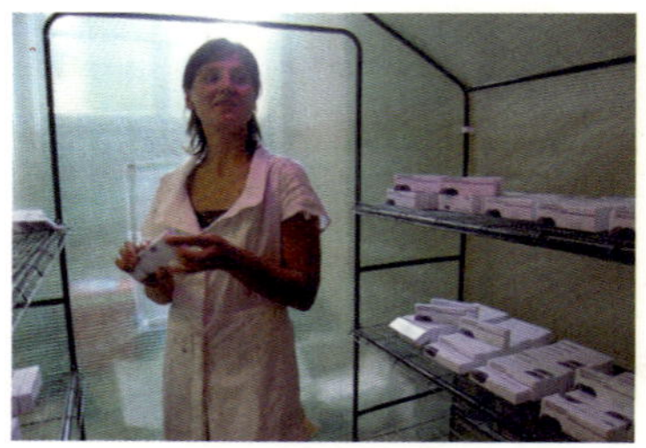

■■■

***Vaccinium***, 2008, Manifesta 7, Rovereto (Italy)

We think it is so fascinating to see the developments in these three fields, now that fossil-fuel-based energy is coming to an end (though it is not yet clear when), and new sources have to be invented and developed. The big energy companies, who thus far have earned their money with oil, have to find other ways. And they need to keep that idea central in order to survive and stay powerful, which means that all that is developed and invented will eventually not be developed without their commitment and involvement. If oil from seeds or palm trees have to replace fossil-based oil, they will be the producers of that oil as well, with the blessing of our governments. Economy depends on that. It seems there is no way out. Which is why we think "time and communication" are important notions, not just hollow empty issues. Where time and communication (speed) means money on a global scale, it generates a rethinking, a rediscovering, and at best a start of a re-consciousness on a small human scale, even if this does not bring change or a solution or make a difference.
Attempts such as making people more conscious of what they eat or grow or read or believe, through the arts, seems bound to fail, since it makes no difference in how the world around us develops. On the other hand, what defines if something is a success or a failure depends so much on how you measure it, and from what point of view. Why is something considered a failure? Why is something considered a success? Who measures success or failure? Why him/her/them and with what reason or interest? From where is this person or public opinion (formed and molded by whom?) speaking? Whose voice is the loudest, and why is it that we only hear that voice? (For example, politicians like Berlusconi). Chantal Mouffe speaks of public space as an agonistic space, as public space not as a space where everybody agrees, but where conflict is incorporated, even necessary to create public space, agreeing to disagree. If other voices are being excluded, ridiculed, reduced, and silenced, the public realm no longer exists. This might be very efficient for global economic reasons and for reasons of finance (for a select few), but dangerous for human reasons. This is why other voices continuously need to explore, investigate alternatives, and find ways of making these findings public. That takes time, and ways of communication have to be explored, sometimes even invented, to go around the mainstream of voices, the mainstream that is always there, also in the art world. We have to insist on taking the time required (we do not mean only in the context of this conversation), and we have to resist that thoughts, which eventually become products whether one wants them or not (think of conceptual art, for example) get picked up too soon, commodified too fast, and taken into the stream of global production immediately as soon as they appear. They can be taken into this stream—lets not be naïve—but they must be taken in according their own premises and conditions, otherwise they are made innocent, useless, and ineffective.

Wild cards, wild salads, yes.

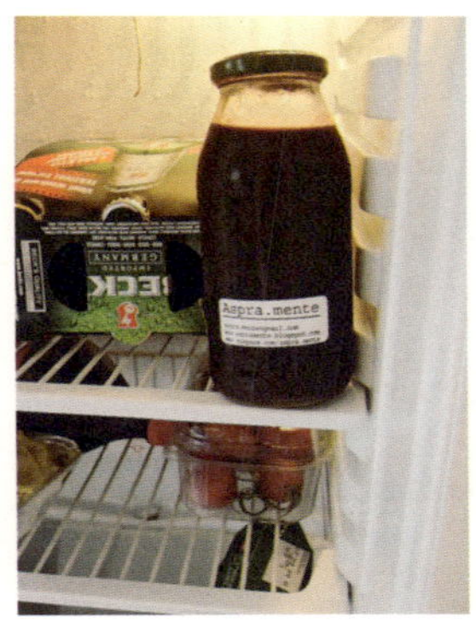


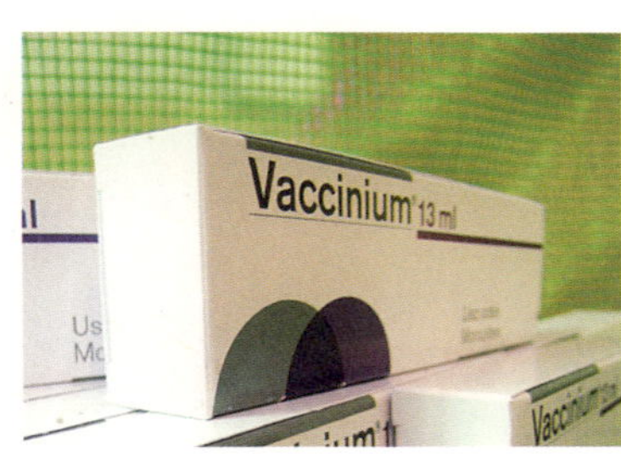

*Rifiuto con Affetto* (Recycle With Love)—RCA—is a trash bin that creates the occasion for an exchange transaction and that creates awareness of the increasing amount of rubbish that is produced and of the importance of disposing of waste in a critical and conscious way.

RCA is a work of public art that reinterprets a socially common gesture—discarding, refusing—in an intervention in the public sphere. Objects that are not used anymore can be placed in the bin for other people to take and use, thus giving them new life.

RCA can be found in Venezia, Mestre, Rivignano (UD), Matelica (MC), Rovereto, and Ravenna, all in Italy.

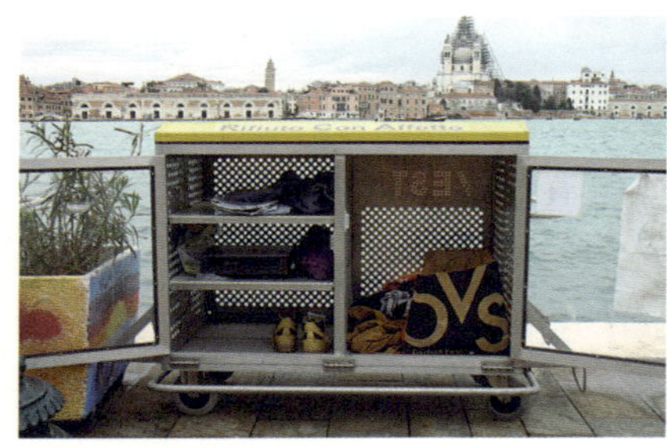

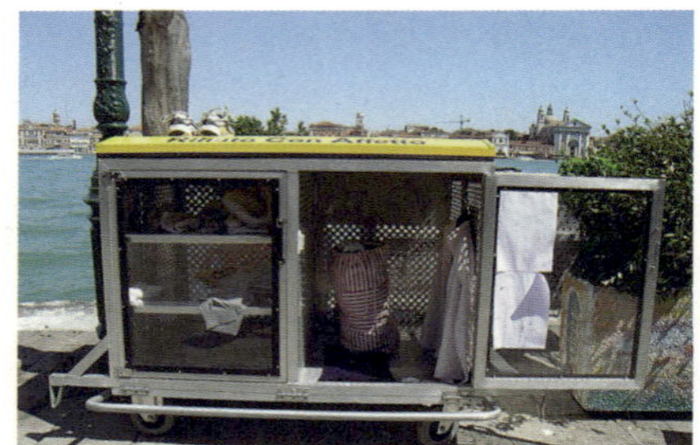

# Publink

*Rifiuto con Affetto*, 2009, Venice

*Rifiuto con Affetto*, 2009, placing the first bin at Palanca-Giudecca, Venice

*Rifiuto con Affetto*, 2009, inauguration of the second bin at Zitelle, Venice; the inhabitants of the neighborhood ask information on the use of the service

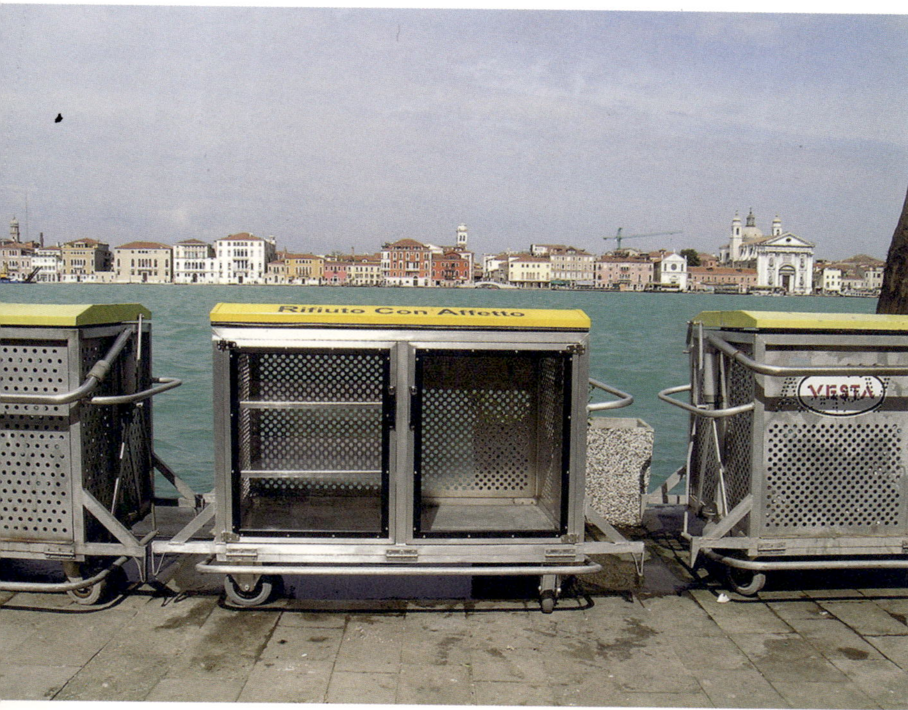


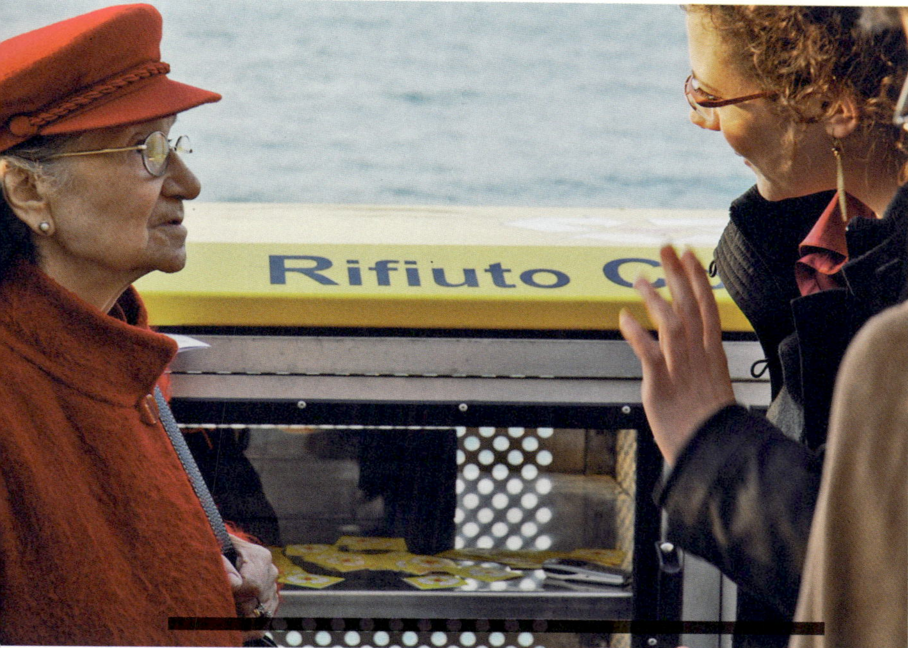

*Manuela Ribadeneira —*

"Society functions and always has without the artist. No artist has ever changed anything for better or for worse," said Georg Baselitz. What is interesting to me in this quote is the function of art in society and how this relates to work like yours or mine (some of it at least). In our works, there is the underlying idea that art can change society—there seems to be that desire or will—and I ask myself the question of whether that is a true premise to start with, whether changing society is the role of art. Your projects come from the idea of service and public service, more specifically, and both require a negotiation with the authorities, a process of convincing but also of insertion in the "real" social service, of legitimizing (in the eyes of the authorities and the public). I believe this is probably a very important aspect of your approach and it determines the way it circulates and the way it is funded.

*Publink —*

*Rifiuto con Affetto* (RCA) is a dustbin that works at the disposal of the citizens: instead of throwing away and ransacking; you can just leave an item and choose another one in exchange, and the entire community is responsible for it. The dustbin is an object that can be located everywhere, and therefore every space becomes potentially appropriate for it. We are not interested in situating art in public space, but in creating a new public space. Formerly seen as a place where rubbish is stored, the dustbin becomes a place of exchange. The interaction between the people is not physical, but rather is emotional. When you re-love an object, you give a second life to something that has already a story and you continue it. The "virtual community" that RCA creates is a net of stories that cross each other. In our projects, the public interacts with the work of art, becoming a responsible actor in a potential social transformation of the territory. We do not forget the formal and poetic side of creation, but we try to give a different meaning to the art fruition. We tested the RCA dubstin in Venezia, Rovereto, Mestre, and Codroipo. For us, artistic success comes second; if our projects don't work at the social level, they cannot have an artistic value.

*Manuela Ribadeneira —*

I see. The creation of community or interaction happens at the level of the objects, and in the emotion (*affetto*) that goes to the object. One of the things that I ask myself is that if this kind of work has the pretension of being really and truly and honestly a social service, a service to the community, then it has to be measured as such. And then, what is the cost in relation to the benefit to society? Is the efficiency of the project measured in the same way a social project (not artistic) is measured? Is art as such a service? Are we as artists being too lazy, or is it too easy not to be accountable for what we label as a service to society? Should these projects be measured in this way especially if they are funded by public money? Is this efficient? Or, if the idea is really and truly to provide a service, is it not more logical and perhaps more honest to work in

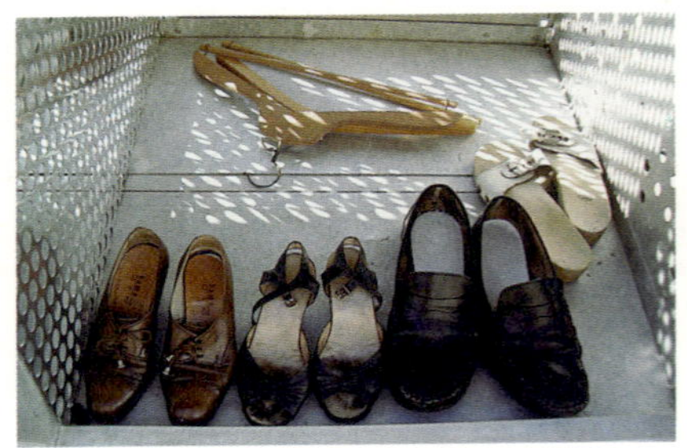

■□□
***Rifiuto con Affetto***, 2009, Venice

□■■
***Rifiuto con Affetto***, 2009, Rovereto

the public service sector or in grassroots politics? Or do you believe that the service lies more in raising the question, in raising the issue through art? But there is still the question of the usefulness of it all. Is art supposed to be useful and socially efficient?

*Publink* —

Art can't change the world, but it can generate or at least give representation to social alternative. We are not political or activists; we have a specific way to propose an art piece. We think that RCA can represent an alternative solution in our context—our country—but that doesn't mean it is the solution for everybody. It is of crucial importance for us to put a project to test, and that it works. For us, "to work" means that there is a process, use, and utility of the project. First, process: the work of art doesn't have a definitive form, but it lives as process, able to activate new relationships among the authors, in itself, and in the new space generated by this encounter. Second, use: the concrete use of the work begins a necessary instrument between user and work of art. And finally, utility: the user interacts with the work of art, becomes a responsible actor in a potential social transformation of the territory.

*Manuela Ribadeneira* —

I come from a third-world country, where one sees people looking in the rubbish for food and clothes and anything else, who live only by "recycling," by using, reselling, and giving a new existence to that which others throw away. The recycling, the re-loving (I like this word very much), and the redistributing processes of things are done by necessity by all those who have no alternatives. The poorer the country, the more recycling there is, and less is wasted and less thrown away. By making the dustbin so beautiful, don't you influence the public that will use it? Don't you think that the public can be preselected by the look of the bin, and that the design determines the objects that go in it? So perhaps my question is: Why the choice of that bin? The giving of new life to an object is something that is now very much in the air in crisis times. Out of curiosity: The things I see in the dustbin seem very slick and new—are they things people have thrown away?

*Publink* —

We throw away a lot of things that still can be used by others. What is useless for me, could be useful for you. In contemporary society the idea of "useful" has changed. An object becomes useless not because it is broken, but because it is not in fashion, or simply because we don't like it anymore. We want to give a second life to objects that can still be useful as an alternative to increasing the amount of waste. We like think of RCA as a new category of differentiating garbage: you have bins for paper, bins for glass, and with RCA you have a bin to put objects that you refuse with love. We are interested in the ecological impact of the project. RCA aims to reduce the quantity of waste heading to incineration or to the dump, to prolong the life cycle of an item for a more sustainable use of the resources, to put used items back on the market, and to avoid the exploitation of raw materials for the production of new ones.

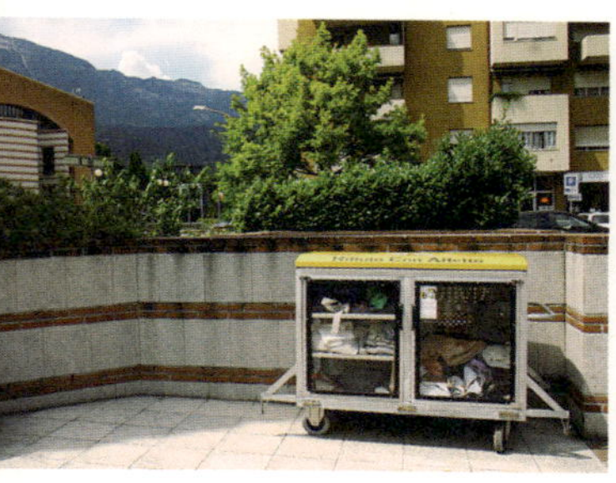

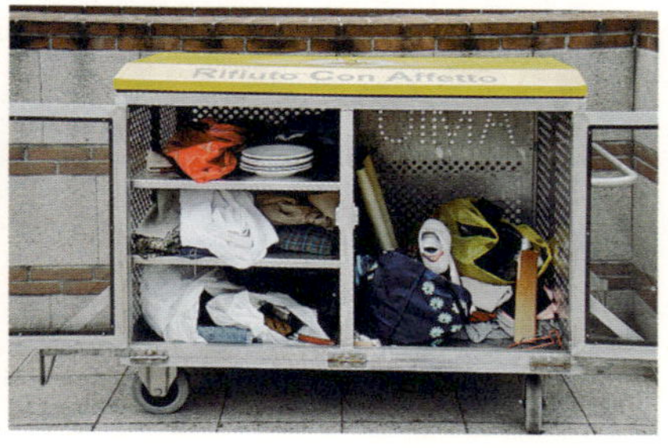

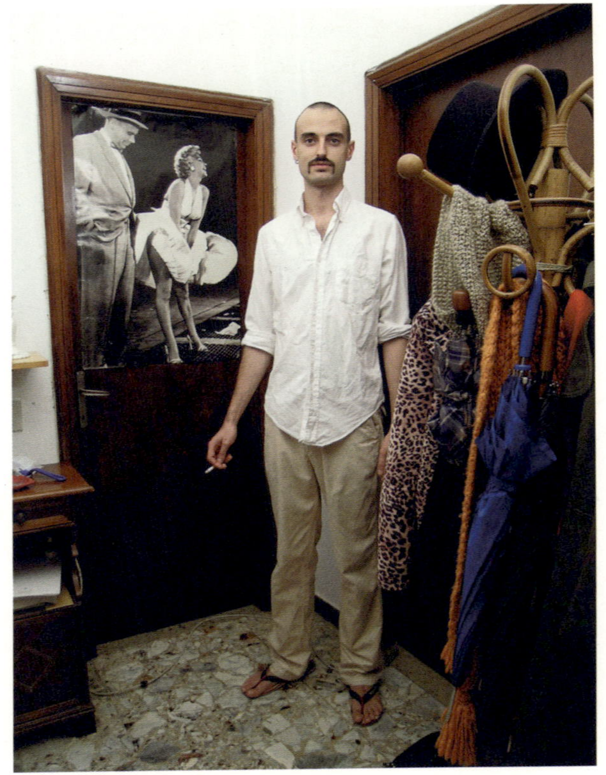

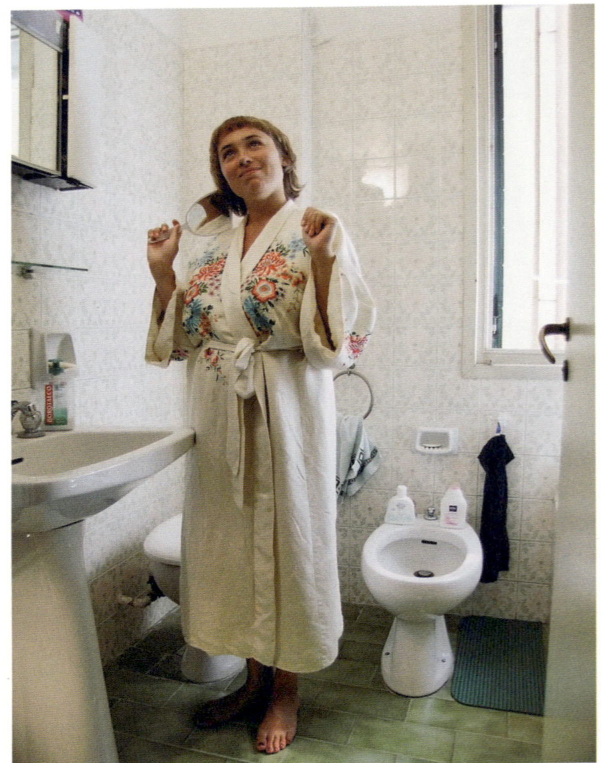

***Rifiuto con Affetto***, 2009, people are wearing the clothes acquired through *Rifiuto con Affetto*

We don't think that the design aspect of the bin—a designed object indeed, as one of us is a product designer—defines the public, but that its sleekness can foster respect for it and its use. From our experience of RCA, it seems that the project is used by all sorts of people without distinction of class.

*Manuela Ribadeneira —*

I find it important to understand the "economy" of this object. How is it financed?

*Publink —*

Like any public service, RCA is cofunded by public and private sponsors, and we communicate the project as a new public service through TV, radio, newspaper, and flyers. Is your work with *Artes No Decorativas* concerned with the creation of a community?

*Manuela Ribadeneira —*

Part of our practice is to organize events, residencies, talks shows, etc., and such activities come from the desire to accelerate things in order to create movement, and mostly to create conversation and thus community. Most of the works I did with my associate came from frustration with the art world and with the role of the artist. To our surprise *Artes No Decorativas* did have an effect on the way art was done and perceived in Ecuador. We changed the image of artist a bit by becoming super-professional (not a common practice at the time in Ecuador), by becoming super-efficient, and most importantly by using strategies that had not been used before. The irony is that we did change something there, but our intentions and our thinking had never been directed toward the possibility of change. We just did not think it was possible, although we wanted the art world to change. My way of thinking is changing with time. For a long time I thought that my work as an artist had a mission, that through my art and my artistic production I could change the rules of the game, that perhaps society would be better through the effects of what I do through art, that I could change what people think or how they think. Today I think that is not my role as an artist, and I think there are more efficient ways to change society. I think art changes society in spite of it, not because of it, and I think the thinking or intention of art should not be to change anything.

For me art is intentionless. I still think that one of the amazing byproducts of all art practices and objects is the creation of communities, and the RCA or pieces done in this similar vein are perhaps, in my eyes, monuments to this desire for community.

**Julieta González** was born in Caracas in 1968. González is currently Associate Curator of Latin American Art at the Tate Modern as well as an independent curator. She has worked as adjunct curator for *Farsites: Urban Crisis and Domestic Symptoms in Recent Contemporary Art*, Insite San Diego/Tijuana 2005; co-curator with Adriano Pedrosa, Jens Hoffmann, and Beatriz Santiago. for the 2da Trienal Poligráfica de San Juan, in Puerto Rico; guest curator at the 1st Prague Biennale, 2003, in Prague, Czech Republic; and the Lyon Biennale 2007 in Lyon, France. She was also curator of contemporary art at the Museo de Bellas Artes de Caracas in Caracas, Venezuela, and at the Museo Alejandro Otero in the same city. Julieta González lives and works between Caracas, Venezuela and San Juan, Puerto Rico.

**Jesús Bubu Negrón** was born in Barceloneta, Puerto Rico, in 1975. He has participated in group shows including Puerto Rico 2000, Puerto Rico 2002, and Puerto Rico 2004 in Puerto Rico; the 2006 Whitney Biennial in New York; the T1 *The Pantagruel Syndrome* show at the Castello di Rivoli in Turin, Italy; the 8th Sharjah Biennale in Sharjah, United Arab Emirates; and the 2da Trienal Poli/Gráfica de San Juan in San Juan, Puerto Rico, among others. He has had solo exhibitions at Galería Comercial in San Juan. Negrón lives and works in San Juan, Puerto Rico.

**Paul Ramírez Jonas** was born in California in 1965 and raised in Honduras, and returned to the United States in 1983. Ramírez Jonas has participated in group shows at the the 53rd Venice Biennale in Venice, Italy; the Xth Baltic Triennial in Vilnius, Lithuania; the Museu Serralves in Porto, Portugal; the Whitechapel Gallery in London, Englad; the 28th Bienal de São Paulo in São Paulo, Brazil; Media City Seoul 2000 in Seoul, South Korea; and Insite San Diego/Tijuana 2005, among others. He has had solo exhibitions at the Aldrich Contemporary Art Museum in Connecticut, the Jack Blanton Museum in Austin, Texas, and Ikon Gallery in Birmingham, UK. Paul Ramírez Jonas lives and works in New York.

> www.paulramirezjonas.com

**Javier Téllez** was born in 1969 in Valencia, Venezuela. Téllez has participated in numerous group exhibitions, including the 2007 Whitney Biennial, the 49th and 50th Venice Biennales, the 16th Biennale of Sydney, Manifesta 7, and Insite San Diego/Tijuana 2005, among others. He has had solo exhibitions at the Museo Rufino Tamayo in Mexico; the Bronx Museum in New York; the Museo de Bellas Artes de Caracas in Caracas, Venezuela; the Sala Mendoza in Caracas, Venezuela; Gasworks in London, UK; and the Calouste-Gulbenkian museum in Lisbon, Portugal. Téllez lives and works in New York.

**Anna Best** was born in London in 1965. Anna Best has organized numerous events in venues as diverse as gas stations, pubs, and museums under construction, among others. These have included the Ice Cream Van Convention, the Festival of Lying, Statoil Moonlight Love, and Texaco Ball. She has participated in group exhibitions at the ICA London; Apex Art, New York; and South London Gallery and Gasworks, London, among others. She has had solo projects at the Barbican Centre and the Tate Modern in London. Anna Best lives and works in Dorset, UK.

> www.annabest.info

**Tercerunquinto** formed by Julio Castro (b. 1976), Gabriel Cázares (b.1978), and Rolando Flores (b. 1975) in Monterrey, Mexico. Tercerunquinto has participated in a number of group shows at La Maison Rouge in Paris, Casa del Lago in Mexico City, Museo de Arte Carrillo Gil in Mexico City, the 2nd Prague Biennale in Prague, and the 4th Bienal de Mercosur in Porto Alegre, Brazil. They have had solo shows at the Museo de Arte Carrillo Gil in Mexico City and at Ikon Gallery in Birmingham, UK.

> www.tercerunquinto.org

# Visible: A Question of Agency

What is the real dimension of art's agency beyond its specific audience, and its institutions? How does the act of making things visible effect real change within a given society?

Raising the question of art's agency inevitably leads to a discussion of the idea of visibility, as one of the defining aspects of art is precisely that of making things visible. Likewise, curatorial practice, exhibition formats, and display apparatuses are also articulated around the premise of visibility. This constant negotiation of subjectivities in the public sphere leads one to wonder about the potential of art for social agency and the real effectiveness of our roles as cultural mediators.

The twentieth century and its particular socioeconomic changes problematized the role of art in society and affirmed its discursive condition; more than aesthetic objects and commodities, art works could trigger social change. As the social context of art's production, circulation, and reception has become a fundamental aspect of artistic practice, artists have increasingly sought to go beyond the space of the museum and the conventions of the exhibition in order to engage in interdisciplinary modes of address that aim to cause an impact upon society at large, including interventions in the social and urban fabric and forms of artistic collectivism among other diverse manifestations that abound in twentieth-century art history. And in this sense, art's call for agency outside its specific realm implies the cancellation, to a certain extent, of curatorial and institutional mediation.

However, as much as I have been interested in these forms of collective organization, institutional critique, and interventions outside the exhibition space, as a curator working in Venezuela during the late 1990s and early 2000s, I felt the need to contend with ideas related to agency and the visible in terms of our somewhat marginal position vis á vis the history of contemporary art and the fragility of our institutions, of which museums were but a small part. First and foremost, the thorny question of self-determination and autochthonous production of cultural discourse led me on a more abstract quest restricted to the confines of art history that has addressed, among other issues, a revision of the recent art history of our continent, a renegotiation of genealogies, and the historicizing of the until-now largely ignored narratives of conceptualism. My interest in this particular approach resides in the power of the archive to reveal obscured histories and to summon a reflection on a wider set of issues that transcend the merely art-historical: suppressed histories, the anti-monumental, and failed utopian undertakings have all been central to my practice as a curator.

More concretely, during the years that I worked in a fine arts museum in Caracas, a lot of my work involved making permanent collections more dynamic and visible by proposing that artists work with them, exploring minor histories embedded in the collections' formations that could provide insights on the construction of a cultural identity in Venezuela. I was very interested in the museum itself as a site for critical inquiry and as a site susceptible to deconstruction, es-

1 As is the specific case of Taller Popular de Serigrafía, a Buenos Aires group of artists who lent their formal expertise to the different constituencies in conflict with the government during the crisis in Argentina in 2002.

pecially in a country where the "elite status" of museums was being paraded as an excuse for their disintegration at the hands of government bureaucrats whose "mission" was to create museums of "popular culture." The idea of agency more than ever became important and fundamental, and the questions about the museums' audiences and reach of curatorial work became vital arguments for their survival. I did think museums there reached a wide audience and were not "elitist" by any account. However, an agenda for the production of a critical discourse by the museum was sorely absent. So in a certain way, my practice really centered itself on the institution, and how forms of institutional critique could actually provide ways to strengthen the ideological standing of our museums, and become a vehicle for preserving these spaces, which were ultimately lost to so-called "revolution." It is interesting to note, in passing, that during the critical period before the final disintegration of Venezuelan museums (a process that has been gradually taking place since 2002), artists whose work engaged in a reflection around the profound changes that were stirring our society and country did so introspectively and by focusing precisely on our institutions and their histories, on the visual codes implied in the construction of a national identity and of our much-touted modernity which seemed to vanish before our very eyes while the country swiftly and unstoppably marched backward toward darker and very premodern ages. The more incisive critiques of the involution of our country were not in the streets, or linked to any kind of protest[1], but instead took the most discreet forms and formats: they were subtle interventions in our disappearing institutional fabric, an aesthetics of failure that has yet to be come to terms with.

In this regard, I have found myself divided between a practice grounded on institutional dynamics and a fascination for interventions that inscribe themselves in contexts that go well beyond the space of art and its more conventional circuits of dissemination. My choice of artists for this book reflects this ambivalence, as many of the artists seem to move seamlessly across this divide. With the exception of **Tercerunquinto**, at one point or another in my career I have worked with these artists in different exhibition projects for which they have all produced thought-provoking and compelling works. I am specifically interested in the ways they eschew lofty aspirations of social change for the masses but instead focus more on micro-interventions, chance encounters, and poetic situations in a world that all too often neglects the beauty of randomness.

Each one of these artists addresses the visible from a very singular perspective, but most of the projects I have selected in conjunction with the artists have in common the fact that the public as well as other more specific audiences not only become subjects of the work but also take up an active role in the production of meaning. **Javier Téllez** works with marginal communities stigmatized by mental or other illnesses. The logic of his work points toward a consideration of madness not as an illness but rather as an "other" state of consciousness and of being in the world, shedding a different light on the spaces of madness, the confinement of patients, and the complexities of what society has defined as "mental illness." **Anna Best**'s "actions" engage the active participation of the community and the spectator in the sense that they become the real performers; her work is very specifically situated in the context of the public space and as such is a work that tends to be invisible in terms of conventional exhibition spaces but very visible, even though randomly, to the passersby that are able to experience and participate in it. **Jesús Bubu Negrón** works with outcasts and people at the very bottom of the social and economic ladders that our post-industrial society has imposed, making their plight and cause visible to a larger audience. **Paul Ramirez Jonas** engages his audience in actions that require trust and a renegotiation of the meanings of private and public, and he also addresses the notions of collective commemoration and the monument in a very particular way. The members of Mexican collective **Tercerunquinto** locate their practice at the intersection between architecture, urban intervention, and public sculpture, engaging the public in the production and modification of their immediate surroundings. The interviews I have conducted with these artists provide insights into their particular approaches to the idea of the visible both in their work as well as in the projects selected for this publication.

## Cigarette-butt Street-rug

*Cigarette-butt Street-rug* was produced as part of Jesús Bubu Negrón's participation in the 8th Sharjah Biennale in 2007. The artist was invited to participate in the biennale under the general theme of "Still Life, Art, Ecology and the Politics of Change." After a preliminary trip to Sharjah and the rest of the United Arab Emirates, the artist decided to work on a piece that reflected not only the underlying theme of the biennale, related to ecology, but also the tensions around the class distinctions in the rapidly modernizing cities of the UAE, specially regarding guest workers, which are a somewhat taboo issue in the UAE. In this sense, he decided to employ the different guest workers (Muslim and non-Muslim) who work in the lower end of the labor pyramid in Sharjah in the recollection of cigarette-butts and later production of an "oriental" rug with this urban waste.
As with many of his previous works, a labor-intensive object maps out a series of socioeconomic dynamics and tensions at play in a given context and inscribed in the formation of the work, literally in its fabric. Besides being socially conscious, the work also addresses the idea of the "other" and the persistence of stereotypes in terms of the representation of other cultures from a Western perspective.

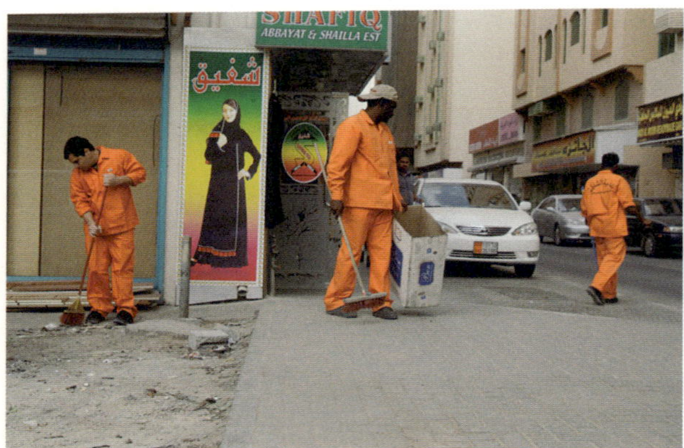


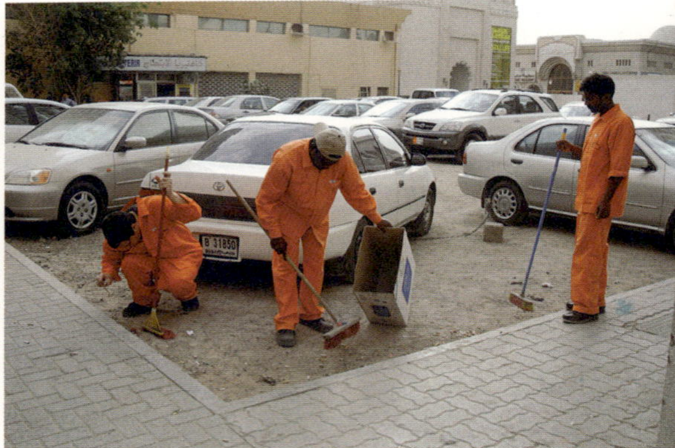

## Cruce Frontera

During an artist residency in the settlement of Frontera Corozal in the Chiapas region, Jesús Bubu Negrón collaborated with its inhabitants to construct a pedestrian crossing in one of the intersections of the town, which only has dirt roads. With this "urbanizing" action,

# Jesús Bubu Negrón

■■□□
***Cigarette-butt Street-rug***, 2007, 8th Sharjah Biennale, Installation
□□■■
***Cigarette-butt Street-rug***, 2007, 8th Sharjah Biennale, guest workers; courtesy of the artist and Pablo León de la Barra

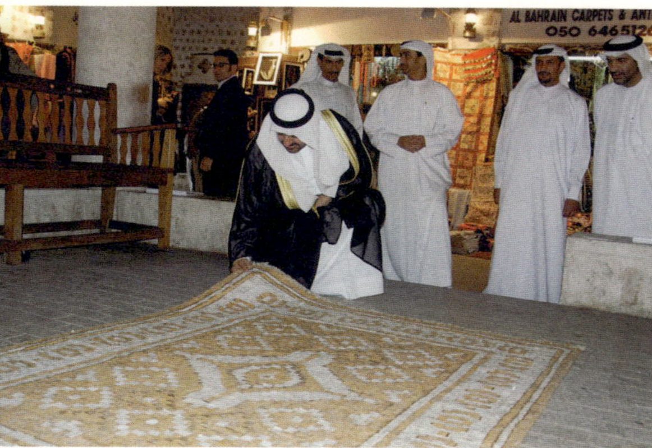


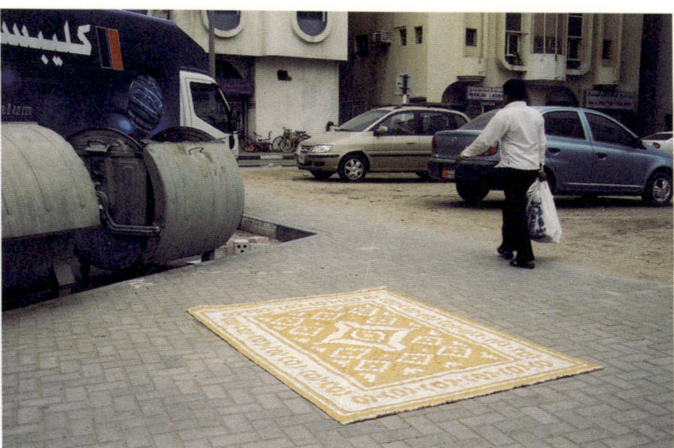

the artist attempted to consolidate the incipient city, creating a type of structure codified within the language of the modern city, where there are areas for vehicles and for pedestrians.

## Igualdad

Jesús Bubu Negrón addresses the sugar-based economy of Puerto Rico's past in order to give visibility to a community that is condemned to eventual disappearance in what was once one of the most important sugar mills in the area of Añasco. It thrived for more than fifty years, from the beginning of the twentieth century until the 1970s, when it was dismantled and when the community that had organized itself around it—which already spanned a few generations—progressively began to disintegrate. However, some of its old inhabitants still live there and a few of the mill's structures are left standing in ruins. Negrón organized this project with the collaboration of the inhabitants of Igualdad and neighboring towns, and proposed giving visibility to the mill in a very simple way: by lighting its chimney once again for seven days. This discreet action, visible from many kilometers away, triggered multiple reactions from neighboring communities who thought that the mill was up and running once again. The community organized a festival to commemorate the lighting of the chimney, an act that they proposed to continue every year.

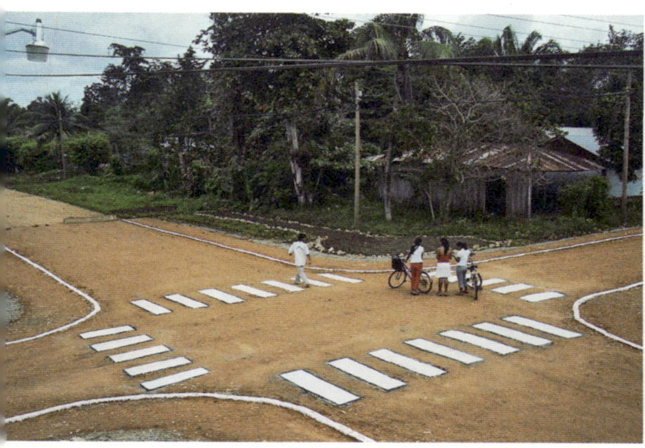

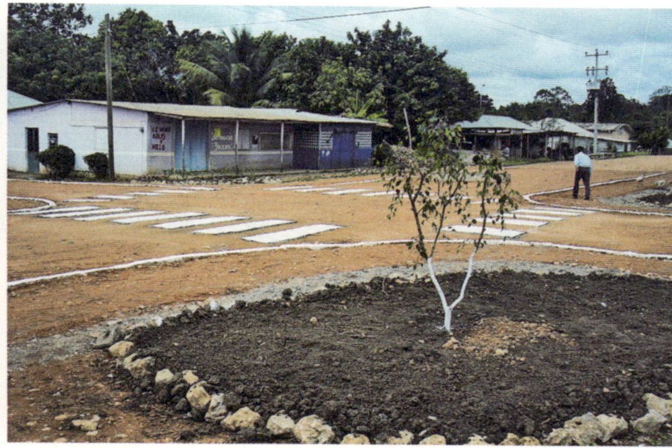

*Cruce Frontera*, 2006, Frontera Corozal, Chiapas

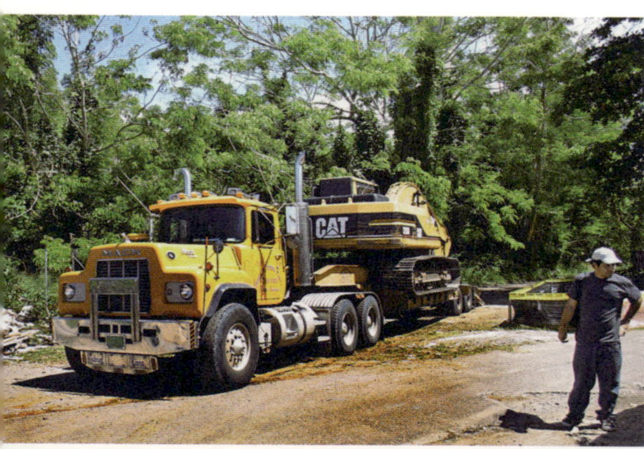


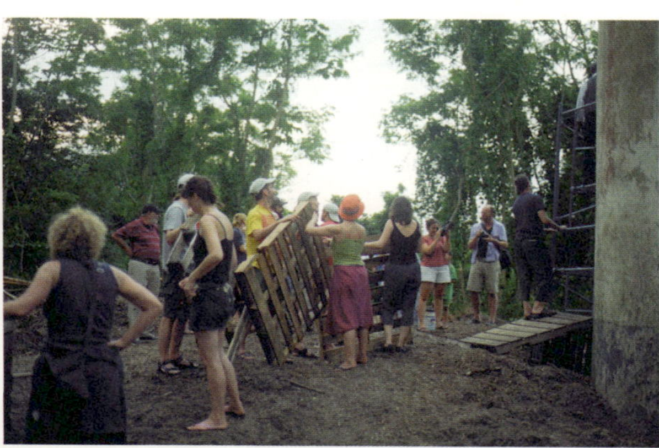

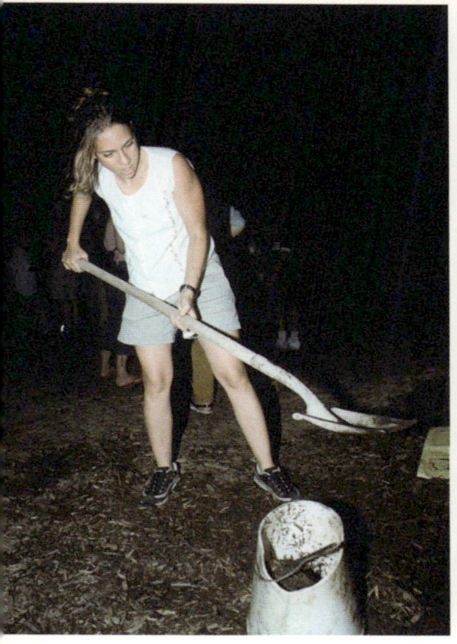

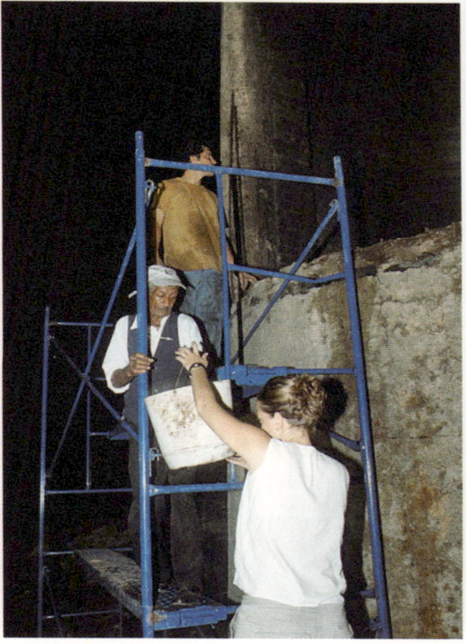

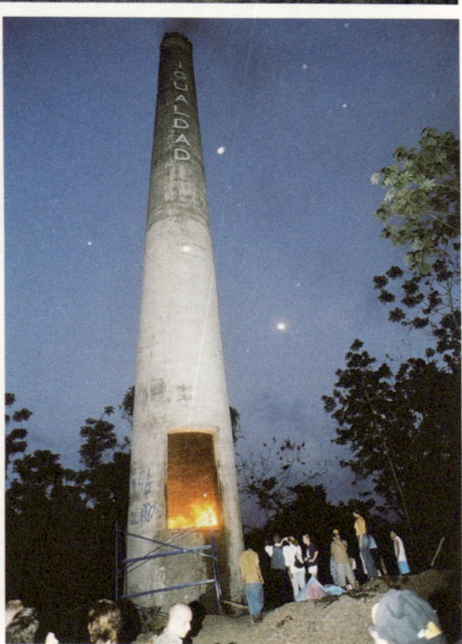


*Igualdad*, 2004, Rincón, Puerto Rico

Annex: A Dialogue Between Julieta González and Jesús Bubu Negrón (San Juan, 11/2009)

*Julieta González —*

There seems to be a very clear connecting thread throughout your work, which involves giving visibility to that which we usually do not see, either because society chooses to ignore or exclude it, or because we simply prefer to look at things from only one perspective. Tell me more about this action of giving visibility.

*Jesús Bubu Negrón —*

There is a concern for the social engagement of the work, its relation to the public, and its reception. These are concerns that go beyond art; for me it is about saying something, just like public figures from the worlds of sports, politics, and entertainment do. In art I have found my vehicle, a platform that allows me to make certain things visible. I have always wanted my work to be accessible to different kinds of audiences, to people who don't necessarily know much about art. I like to be a mediator between the public and the art context.

*Julieta González —*

But, more than a mediator, you have a very active engagement with your subjects and audience. There seems to be a personal investment on your behalf—you eliminate a distance between yourself and your subjects, and create real bonds that are central to the production of the work.

*Jesús Bubu Negrón —*

Many of these projects stem from concerns that I have always had, even before becoming an artist. When I started to make art, I found it only natural to meet these people and communities that I felt were excluded, and to try to give them voices through my work.

*Julieta González —*

There are three projects that specifically interest me in regard to the issue addressed by this book. Let's talk about *Cruce Frontera*, which you made in 2006 during an artist residency in the settlement of Frontera Corozal in the Chiapas region of Mexico. You collaborated with the inhabitants to construct a pedestrian crossing in one of the intersections of the town, which only has dirt roads. With this "urbanizing" action, you attempted to consolidate the incipient city, creating a type of structure codified within the language of the modern city, where there are areas for vehicles and for pedestrians, and, in this way, you actively participated and engaged the community's inhabitants in the construction of a city.

*Jesús Bubu Negrón —*

I was very attracted by the desire for "progress" of these people—not only in a technological way, but also in the sense of improvement of their community, their surroundings, and their living conditions. This was an experience that opened my eyes to social crises that I was quite unaware of and that transcended the art experience to become a real education for me. As in all my projects, I tried to deal with these problems by referring to universal human necessities, and decided to do this "urban" intervention with the collaboration of the community.

*Julieta González —*

In *Igualdad* you worked with the inhabitants of a former sugar mill to organize the lighting of the mill's abandoned chimney for seven days. People from all around started coming to the abandoned site, where only a few still live, asking if the mill was working again, and in turn you mobilized the population to work on feeding the chimney scraps of wood to maintain the fire. And then, they decided to hold a festival commemorating the lighting of the chimney.

*Jesús Bubu Negrón —*

In Igualdad I found many similarities to my hometown of Barceloneta, which is also identified by the chimney of its former sugar mill. Puerto Rico's economy was fueled by the sugar industry well into the early twentieth century, and these abandoned mills have become reminders of that past and dot the rural landscape of the island. When I found the chimney of Igualdad and its almost-forgotten community, I decided to do something with the chimney as a monument in order to rescue them from oblivion. My proposal was met with a lot of enthusiasm from the community's inhabitants and this created a bond between us, and created my relationship to the history of this little town.

*Julieta González —*

Some of your projects do point to problematic issues and to very precise shortcomings of inept and corrupt governments, which unfortunately are the norm in many parts of the developing world. Not surprisingly, the police usually try to intervene in these projects or to explicitly cancel them. For the Sharjah Biennial you managed to address a very complex and compromising issue—class distinctions—in the rapidly modernizing cities of the United Arab Emirates, especially regarding guest workers, which is somewhat a taboo issue in the UAE. You decided to use cigarette butts picked up from the streets to make painterly works, and employed different guest workers (Muslim and non-Muslim) who work in the lower-end of the labor pyramid in Sharjah in the collection of cigarette butts, and later in the production of an "oriental" rug with this urban waste. As with many of your previous works, a labor-intensive object maps out a series of socioeconomic dynamics and tensions at play in a given context and inscribed in the formation of the work—literally in its fabric. Could you tell us more about this work?

*Jesús Bubu Negrón —*

Again, there is a very personal investment in this work. I myself have worked menial jobs for many years to support myself and my work as an artist. I have been a gardener and also a cleaner and sweeper, and still work those kinds of jobs to make a living. So for me, the common experience of the menial job became the link between me and these workers who did not speak my language, and who came from such different cultures. It became a sort of shared language between us through which we could communicate. So the work was divided into two phases. One phase was the collection of the cigarette butts, which became a sort of action in the public space, since I had to wear the uniform of the workers in order to perform that task with the Indian guest workers. The other phase was the making of the "oriental" rug with Pakistani workers, who were higher up in the socioeconomic ladder because of their religion (Islam). So this division of labor and class distinction was clearly illustrated in the process of fabricating this art object that also blurred the distinctions between art and craft. The aesthetic nature of the object foregrounded the ethnic tensions it portrayed and thus was not perceived as a politically challenging object by the local authorities.

## Talisman

For the 2008 São Paulo Art Biennial, Paul Ramírez Jonas plays off of the mysterious and symbolic aspects of a talisman. In it, members of the public were encouraged to engage with the piece *Talisman* by offering a key they own in exchange for a key to the front door of the Biennial venue—the historic and iconic Ciccillo Matarazzo Pavillion. In addition, they had to sign a contract that established an agreement between the participant, the curators, the artist, and the biennial foundation stating their respect for the Pavillion. Although they were allowed to use the key after hours, they had to agree to abide by normal rules of conduct that were expected during regular hours.

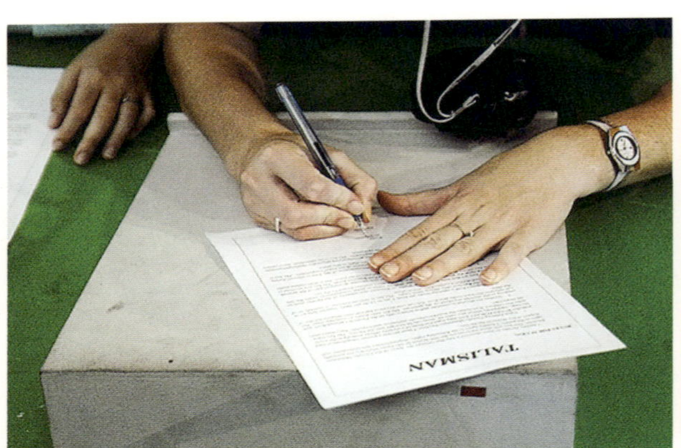


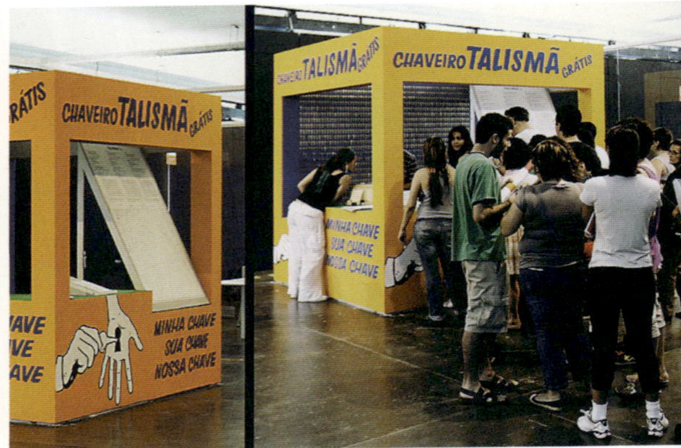


## Taylor Square

This is a permanent work of public art for Cambridge, MA. It has two doors that are always locked from the outside and unlocked from the inside. Five thousand keys were mailed to the homes nearest to the park. The keys came with the following text:

"Here is your key. It is one of 5,000 keys that opens to Taylor Square, Cambridge's newest park. The park and the keys are a work of public art that I made for you. The park has barely enough room for a bench and a flagpole; please accept this key as its monument. Add it to your key chain along with the keys that open your home, vehicle, or workplace. You now have a key to a space that has always been yours. Copy it and give it away to neighbors, friends, and visitors. Your sharing will keep the park truly open."

# Paul Ramírez Jonas

***Talisman***, 2008, São Paulo Art Biennial

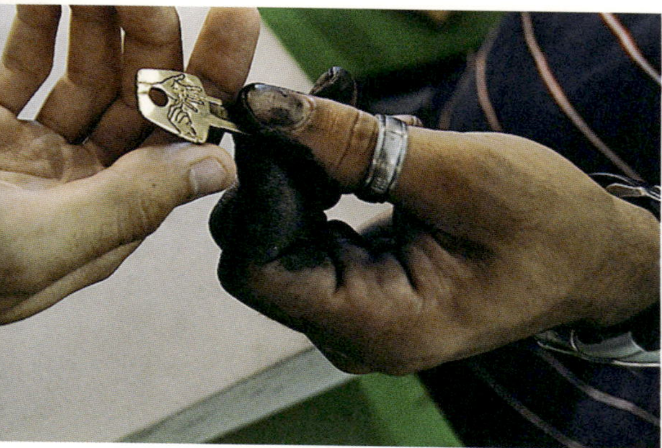

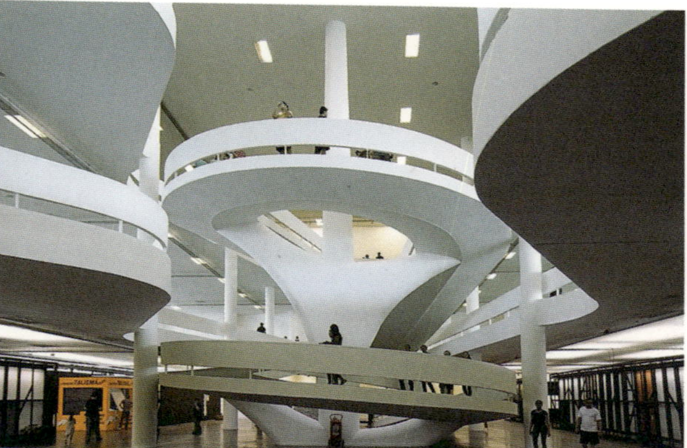

Julieta González
**Paul Ramírez Jonas**
Talisman / Taylor Square

Tinterillo

In Colombia, a *tinterillo* is a street scribe who provides literacy for the illiterate. In 2008, Ramirez Jonas hired a practicing *tinterillo* to transcribe memories dictated by the public. Through this interaction, voice becomes text and text occupies pages. At the end of the performance, the pages were bound into a storybook.

Annex: A Dialogue Between Julieta González and Paul Ramírez Jonas (San Juan/New York, 11/2009)

*Julieta González —*

Your work appears to be very heterogeneous in that it takes on radically different forms, but there is always a common thread that seems to point toward the negotiations that take place between the private and the public spheres, notions of trust and solidarity, and the very idea of utopia that is implied by works such as *A Better Yesterday* (1999), as well as toward the general reference to cooperative endeavor and forms of collective organization and memory present in many of your works. Could you elaborate on these "social" concerns in your work?

*Paul Ramírez Jonas —*

At some point I began to think of my works as monuments rather than as sculptures. This change of name, even if just to myself, was very helpful: a monument always addresses a public, the monument often seems without an author, and it addresses collective ideals, histories, and dreams rather than the individual expression of the artist. And monuments make every space public. Monuments have the capacity to commemorate super local events and persons (such as a local general or poet) as well as grand universalist ideas "Egalité, Fraternité, Supermarché." Monuments also strive to last forever, yet more often than not fail. The imperative to remind future generations of "something" seems full of anxiety and doomed to fail. Still, many monuments manage to last as surfaces for graffiti, as bird shelters, and as places to sit, smoke, and lean against.

*Julieta González —*

*Taylor Square*, *Mi Casa Su Casa*, and *Talisman* have all involved the exchange and circulation of keys. For this publication, I am specifically interested in *Taylor Square* and *Talisman* in terms of their particular approaches to public space and what they imply with regard to a certain behavior of the individual in that space. Could you comment more on these projects?

*Paul Ramírez Jonas —*

I have made three key projects to date and I am working on a fourth one. I like to say that every space in the world can be defined as open or closed—and that there is a key that allows you to enter or exit. This key can be a physical key, a passport, a password, the color of your skin, your education, language, a code, etc. *Taylor Square* and *Talisman* give individuals keys to a public space, but they do not expand access to the space. They simply remind you that both the space and the rules for the space have always been there. Here are some passages I wrote in the contract for *Talisman*:

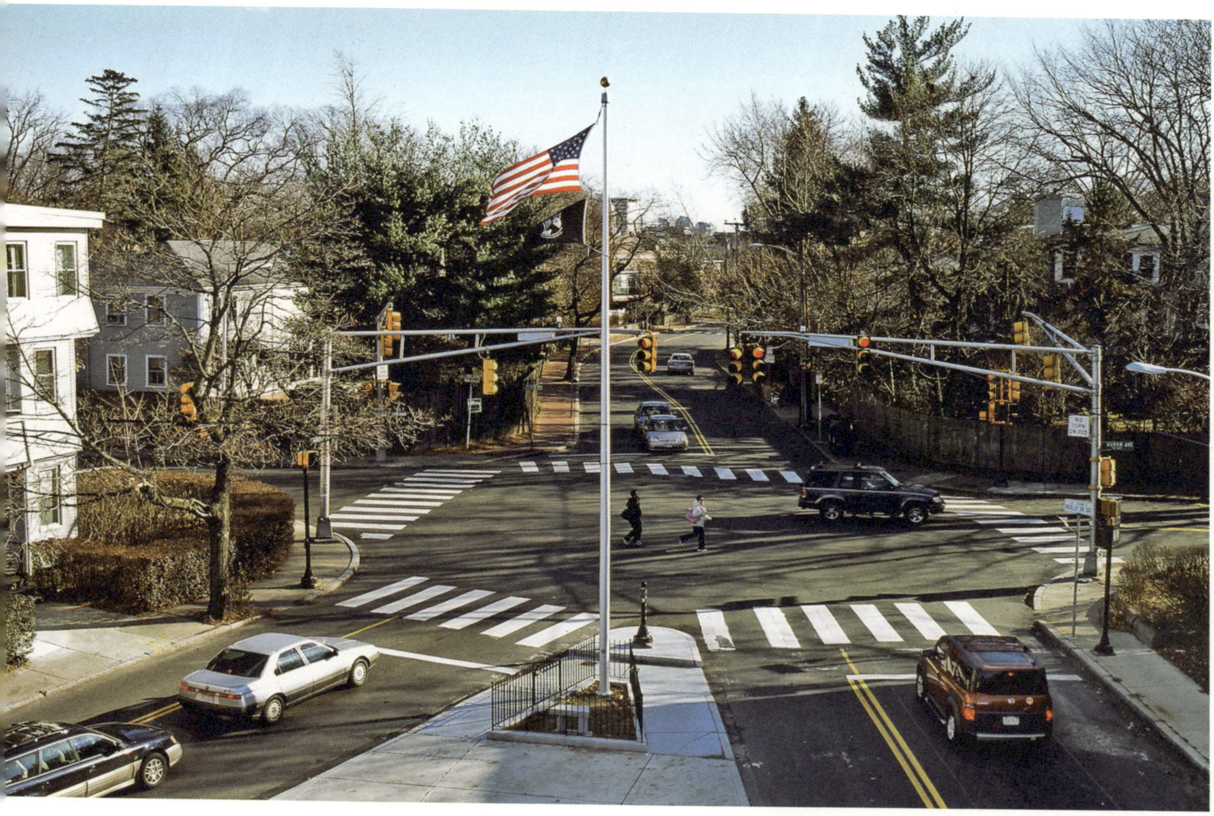

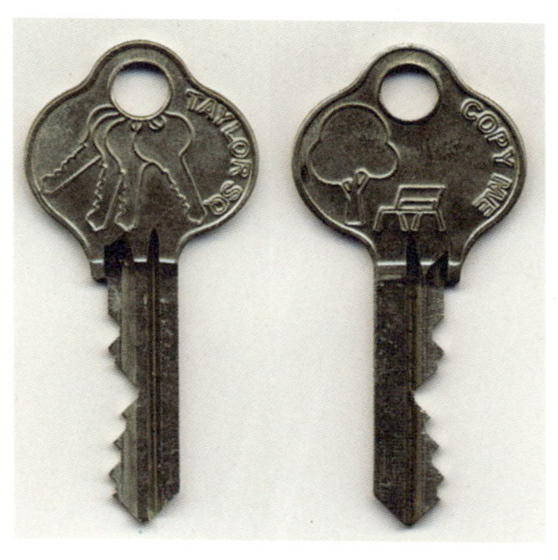


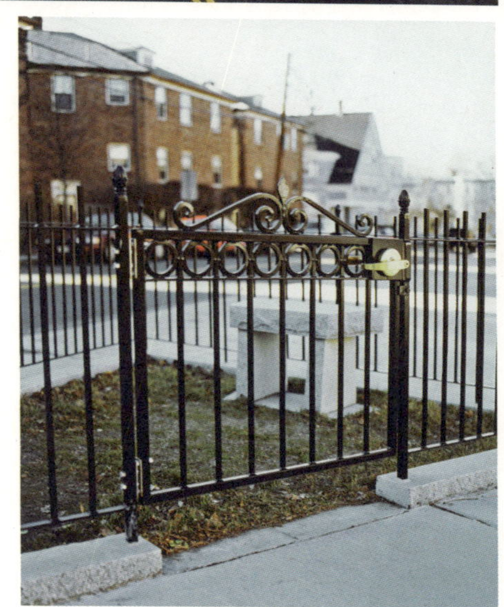

*Taylor Square*, 2005,
Cambridge, MA, USA

"The key represents this contract. It increases the trust between the institution and its public, but cannot undo all suspicions."

"The key only points to complete trust. You can rehearse this trust on the first floor. You can visit this piece but can only imagine the rest of the show."

"The key is only an exercise—it reminds us of greater freedoms but it cannot fully deliver them." "The key allows you access to this space, but the space remains bound by the law."

*Julieta González —*

Other works of yours involve the invocation of a collective memory and the construction of a fiction around this retrieved memory. *Tinterillo, I Create as I speak* (2008), and *Isnykimas* ("Missing") (2009), share similar strategies. What was the reaction of the public to these interventions in the public realm?

*Paul Ramírez Jonas —*

In *Tinterillo* the reaction was wonderful: about a hundred people sat down and dictated contributions in the form of memories or stories. Is that a lot? How many viewers are enough? One? Ten? One hundred? One thousand? Ten thousand? I don't know if anyone added bricks to the structure in *Isnykimas*, but my hope is that at least a few people saw the flyers around the city and then the piece in the museum. Some of my pieces expect a certain degree of apathy and passivity on the part of the viewer; my aim is that the public will imagine the participation in their mind. I also have an even more ambitious and uncertain hope, and that is that they might ask themselves why they did not participate. In general, this line between engagement and non-engagement is quite interesting to me. Thus, some pieces are very seductive, while others are for "arm chair participation."

Just this morning I was wondering: When did it happen that the image of a public became a group of people sitting down, in a grid, in semi-darkness? What a sign of the times.

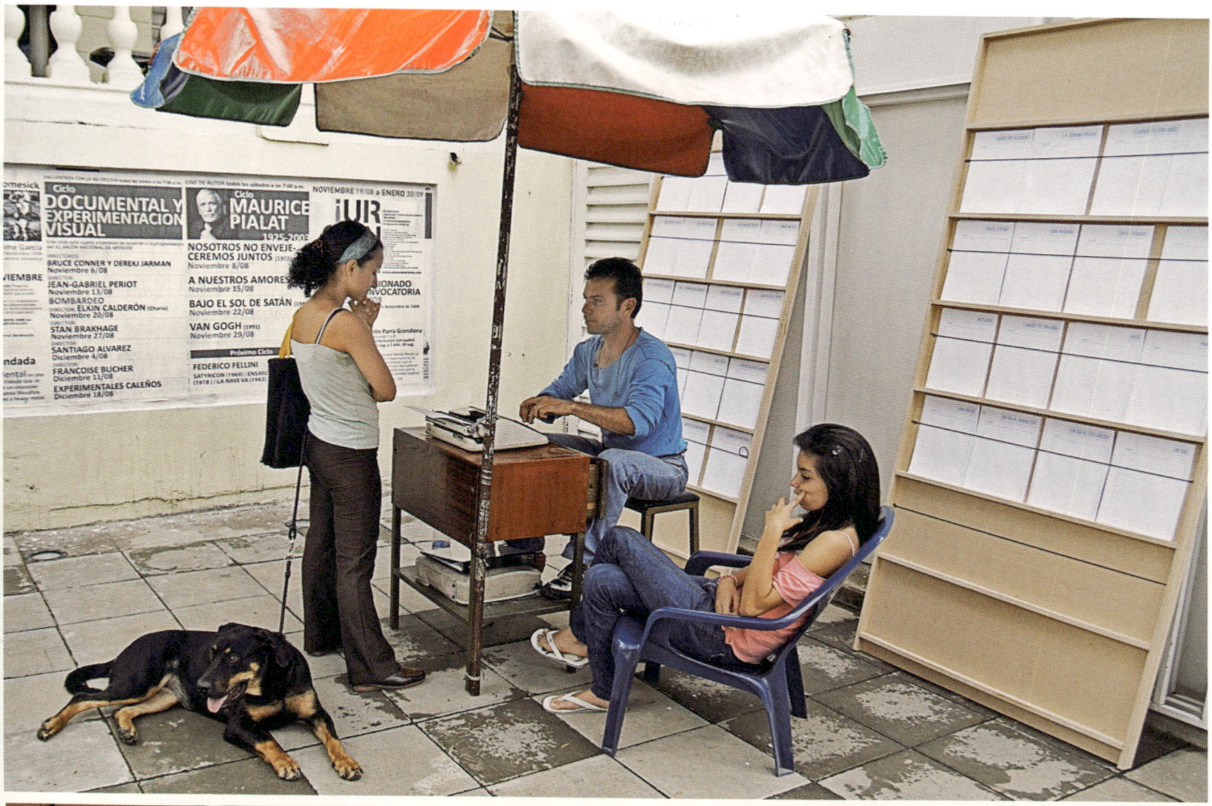

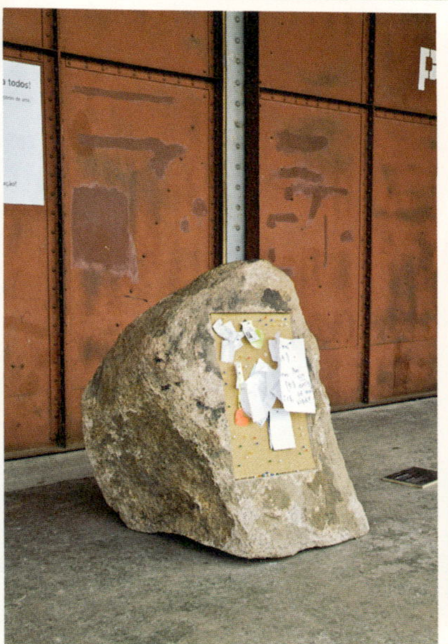

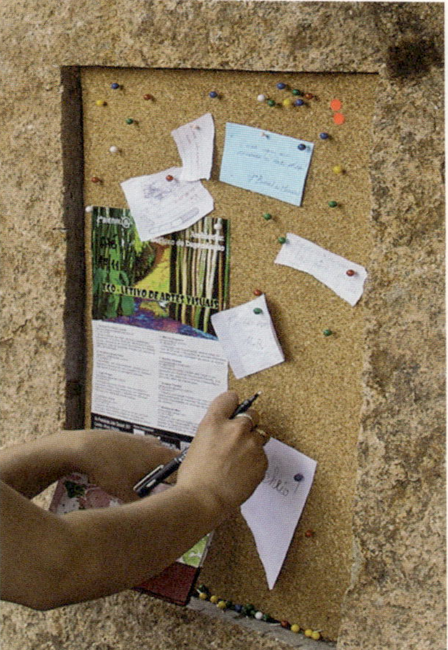

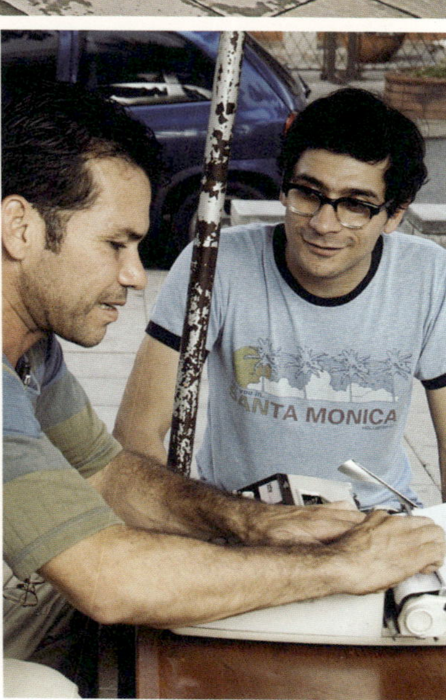

*Tinterillo*, 2008, Colomba

*One Flew Over the Void* was Javier Téllez's public intervention for Insite San Diego/Tijuana in 2005. In collaboration with patients of the Salud Mental del Estado de Baja California (CESAM) state psychiatric hospital near Mexicali, Mexico, the artist organized a public event that was evocative of a circus spectacle and that included a march by mental patients disguised as animals, different circus routines, poetry recitals, magic acts, etc. These framed the highlight of the event, a circus act by David Smith, human cannonball and Guinness world record holder in that discipline, in which he was propelled across the border, from Mexico to the USA.

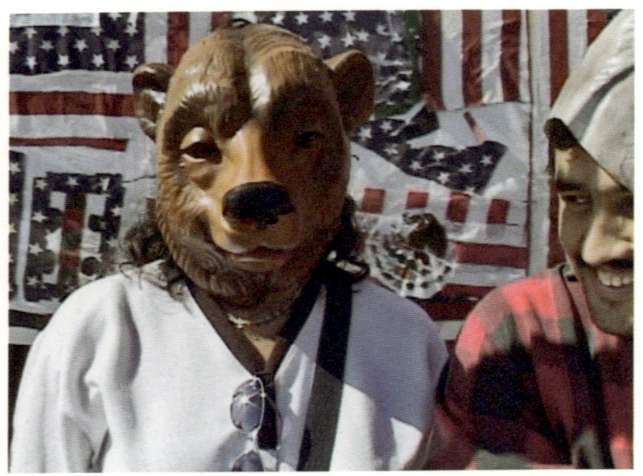

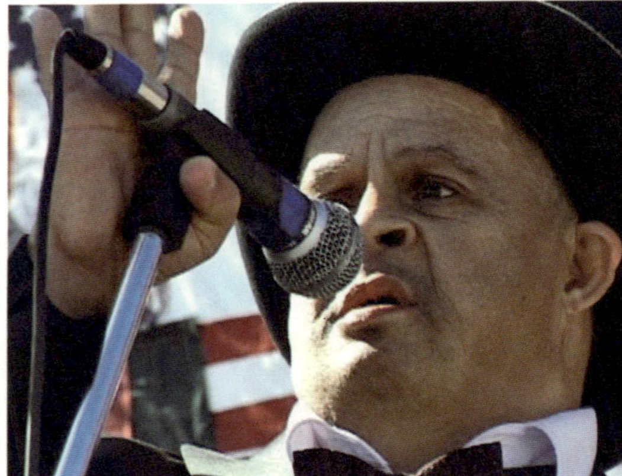

# Javier Téllez

***One Flew Over the Void*, 2005,**
Insite San Diego/Tijuana, still from video

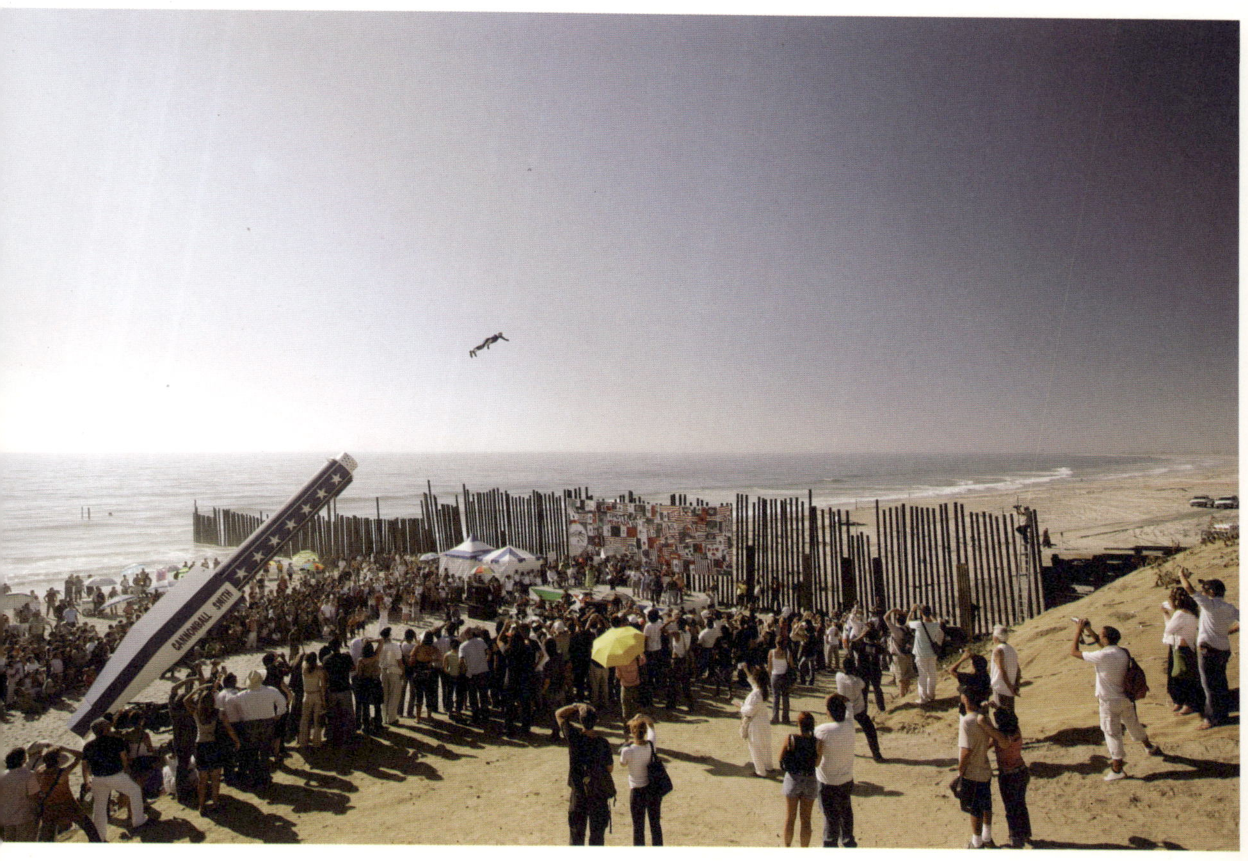


Julieta González
**Javier Téllez**
One Flew Over the Void

Annex: A Dialogue Between Julieta González and Javier Téllez (New York, 11/2009)

*Julieta González —*

Despite leaving a space for ambiguity and open interpretation, in your work you construct a very clear position in regard to the "other." Could you tell us more about this?

*Javier Téllez —*

Paul Klee's phrase "Art does not reproduce the visible; rather it makes visible" has always been an important motto for me. My work has been focused on giving visibility to the "canceled" language of madness and of other marginal discourses. The intention is to situate the discourse beyond the representations that society constructs around those who live on the margins of the systems of production and consumption characteristic of the production of capital, allowing those who are socially excluded to intervene in their own representation. Since I was a small child, I have been close to those who experiment around mental illness (my parents were both psychiatrists and their practice was transparent in our home) and it is thus natural for "madness" to have become one of the most recurring themes in my practice as an artist. In the representation of those who live with mental illness, the problem of "ethics" is fundamental. Emmanuel Levinas has conceived ethics as a devotion toward the "other": "I have to forget myself to access the other." Like Levinas, I also think that ethics must be understood as a responsibility toward difference. This responsibility is made manifest in my work by the inclusion of the "other" as an active participant in the process of production of events, videos, and films, in which not only are these patients the main actors, but they also work on the script, they choose props and costumes, they look at the footage and make comments that are later added to the material, etc. The idea is not to renounce my condition as "author," but to articulate the work upon the dialogue between my subjectivity and that of the "other."

*Julieta González —*

In *One Flew Over the Void*, there is a two-sided reflection on the idea of the border (also because it is the context in which this intervention in the public space was framed). On the one hand, there is a consideration of mental illness as a "borderline" condition and its mise-en-scène in a frontier that is overcharged with meaning such as the one between San Diego and Tijuana. Could you tell us more about your experience in Tijuana and your work with the patients of the Centro de Salud Mental del Estado de Baja California (CESAM) in Mexicali?

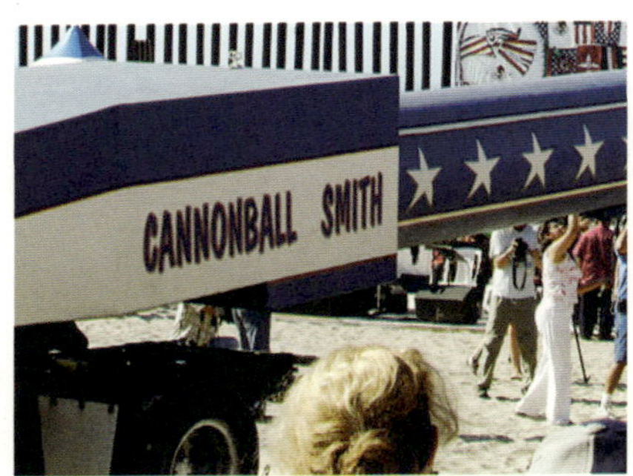


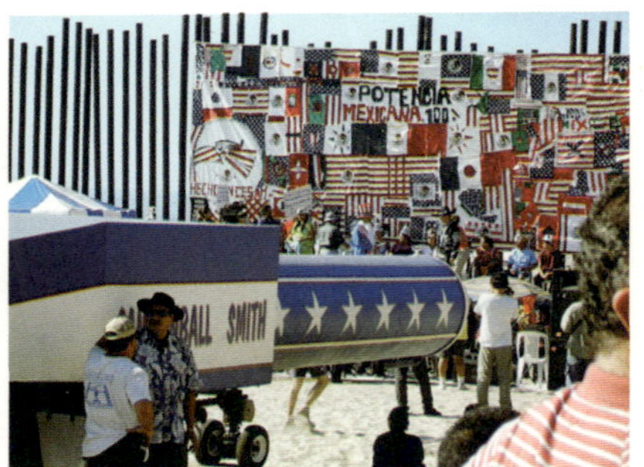


***One Flew Over the Void***, 2005, Insite San Diego/Tijuana, still from video

*Javier Téllez —*

As most of my work has consisted of specific projects made in collaboration with patients at psychiatric institutions in different cities such as Dublin, London, Tokyo, Mexico City, New York, Sydney, etc., I could say that I have symbolically tried to found a nation that goes beyond geopolitical borders: a global republic inhabited by the disenfranchised in their local contexts. The border has been a recurring theme in my work. For those who experience mental illness, the border is located in that liminal area formed by the definitions of normality and pathology. It is a mobile border that throughout history and geography is "embodied" today in the modern psychiatric institution. Martin Heidegger said, "A boundary is not that which something stops. The boundary is that from which something begins its presencing." I have always thought that the psychiatric hospital not only confines those who are enclosed within its architecture, but also those of us who inhabit the outside of it. My work is thus proposed as a bridge between both realities.

Whenever I visit a hospital in order to research a future collaboration with its patients, I propose an idea or an image in order to encourage dialogue. In the case of the work produced for "Insite 05," *One Flew Over the Void* ("Bala perdida"), 2005, the image I proposed to the patients at the CESAM, a psychiatric institution in Mexicali, was that of the human cannonball crossing the border between Mexico and the United States. For the patients of this institution, located precisely on the border with the US, "the border" is a fundamental presence in their lives; many have worked illegally in the US and have been deported. It was obvious that we would use the *border* as "locus" and metaphor in our project. After several conversations with the patients, we decided to stage an event that would frame the human cannonball crossing. The patients designed an advertising campaign that relied on the "perifoneo" (a car with a loudspeaker) and transmitted their messages throughout Tijuana promoting the event. They also filmed advertising spots that were broadcast on local TV and radio stations.

The patients saw the geopolitical border between the US and Mexico as a metaphor for another frontier: that which confined them in the mental institution. Because of the presence of the human cannonball, they embraced the idea of the circus, creating an animal parade, with the patients wearing animal masks and carrying signs that they wrote with sentences like: "Patients are also human beings" and "To live with drugs is not to live." This carnivalesque parade turned into a political demonstration that ended with a circus act in which the patients read speeches and performed a lion-tamer number. Under the question of choosing a flag to be hung on the *barda* ("fence") as a backdrop for the spectacle, they chose to create a new flag of fourteen meters of length made with cutouts of the Mexican and American flags—a new flag that embodies their desire to create a new nation constituted by those inside the mental hospital.

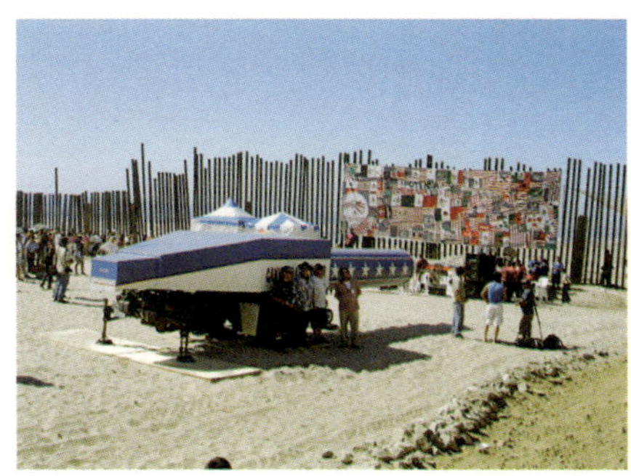

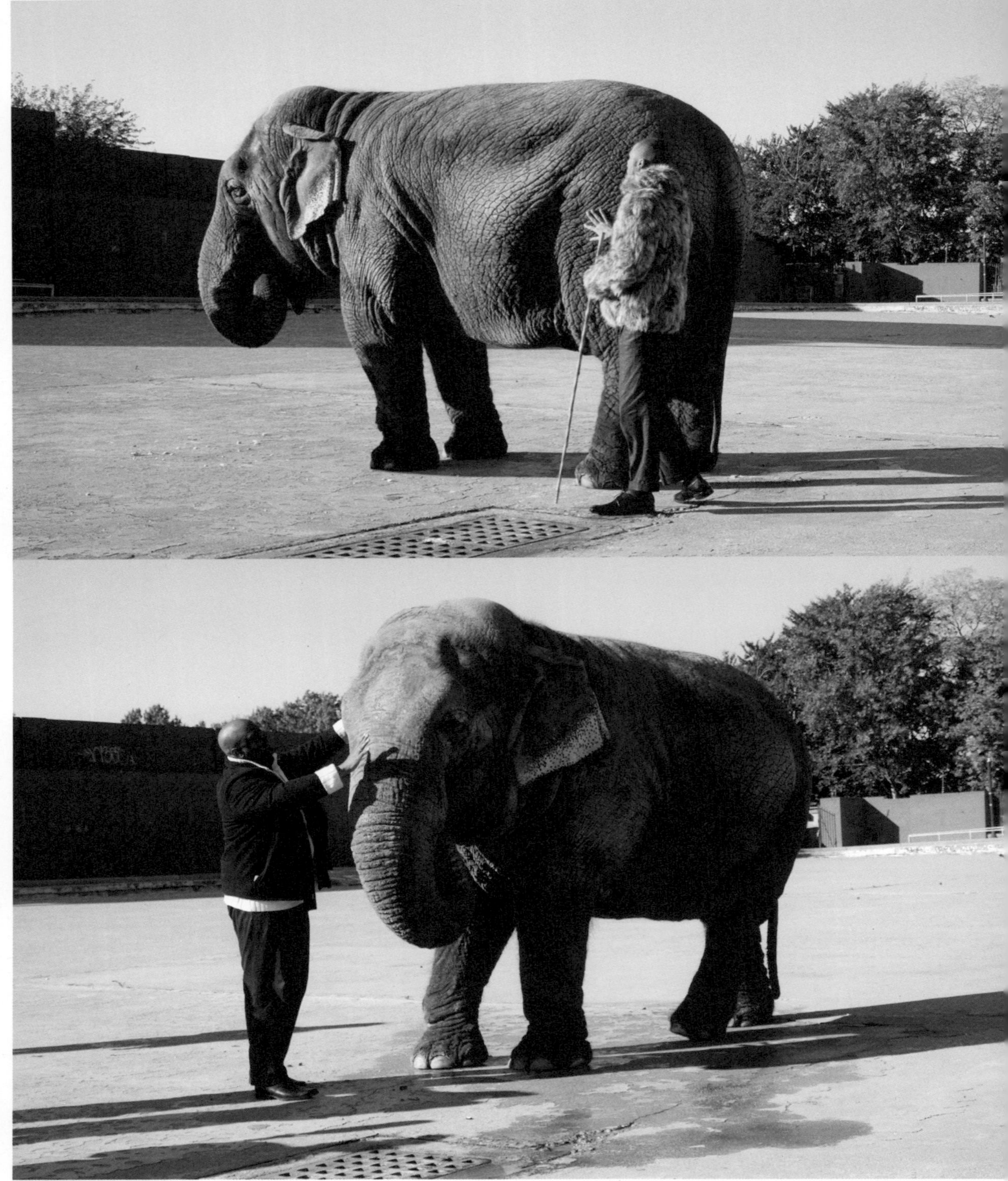

Javier Téllez' ***Letter on the Blind For the Use of Those Who See***, 2007, (still from high-definition video) draws from three sources: Diderot's homonymous *Lettre sur les aveugles à l'usage de ceux qui voient*, Plato's cave, and the Indian parable of the elephant and the six blind men, to further the reflection on otherness that is a constant in his work. Six blind men touch different parts of an elephant and attempt to identify it, and in the process they speak about their condition and the limitations and freedoms it implies. Blindness opens other windows of perception and imagination for them; a world that is defined in an utterly different way from ours, one that may provide other insights and knowledge for those who see.

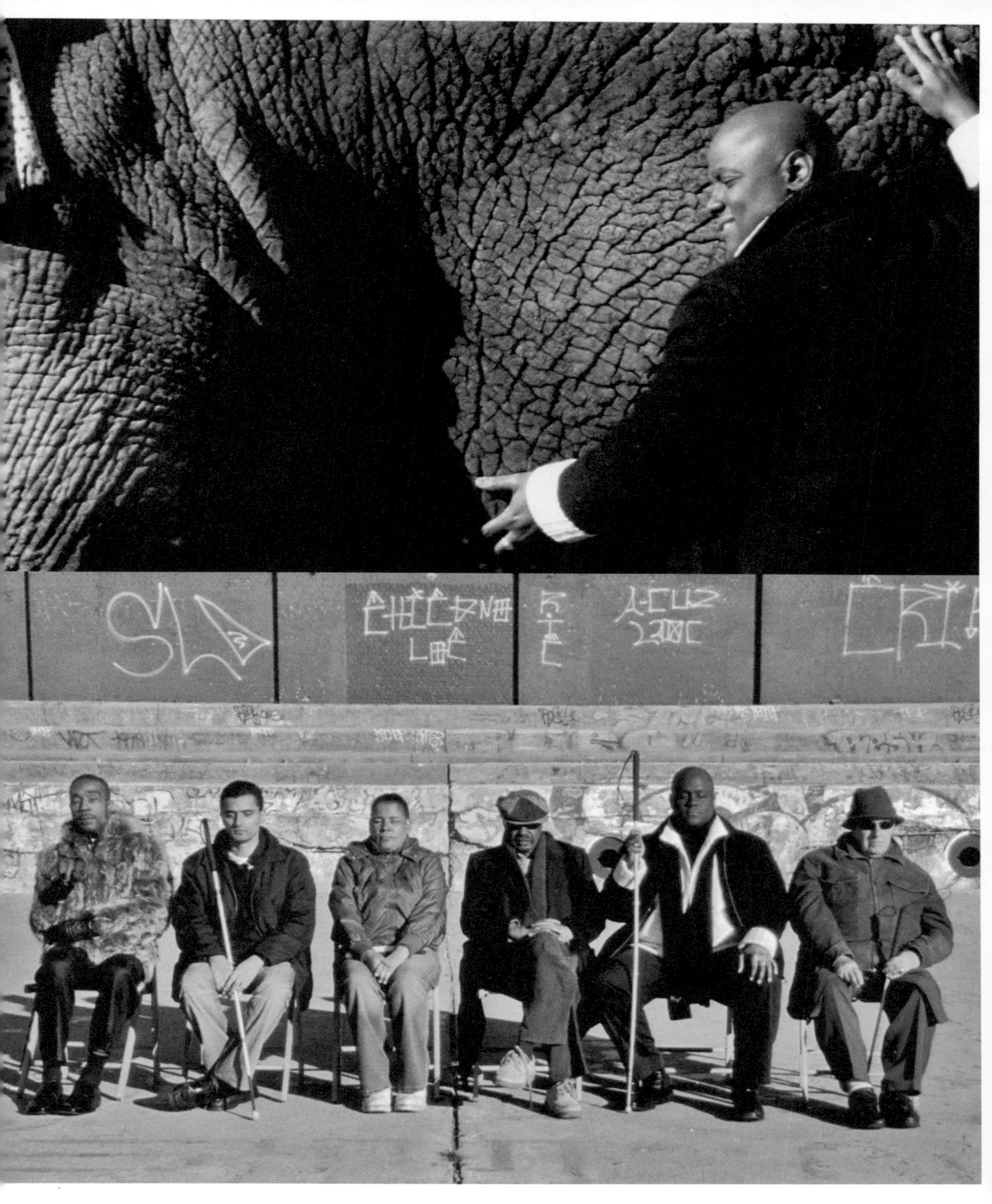

Julieta González
**Javier Téllez**
Letter on the Blind for the Use of Those Who See

### Vauxhall Pleasure

This project was a way of making ideas of the past, present, and future of Vauxhall Cross (London) collide through a performance event staged for a single day. Vauxhall Cross is on the site of the legendary Vauxhall Gardens pleasure gardens, which were renowned as a place combining pastoral beauty and fresh air with the musical entertainments, fountains, fireworks, and fun of eighteenth-century public urban culture. Anna Best worked with composer Paul Whitty, who rearranged music by Thomas Arne. Their aim was to explore the relationship between political protest and entertainment, traffic and pedestrians, and pollution, breathing, and song.

Fifty singers performed to the traffic, their singing conducted by the phases of the traffic lights, and in the evening recordings from the Vauxhall Cross performances were accompanied by a live chamber ensemble across the river in the Tate Britain. Alongside the singers, a research team from Imperial College measured the air pollution levels using a specially adapted bicycle.

### Occasional Sights

This work was conceived as a book that guides the reader to sites in London where fleeting and memorable things have been noticed but are no longer there. It is an anti-guidebook in the sense of guidebooks as memorials and palaces. Its footnotes guide the reader around its bibliography, which has been walked as meanderingly as the streets.

# Anna Best

***Vauxhall Pleasure***, 2004–2009,
Vauxhall Cross, London

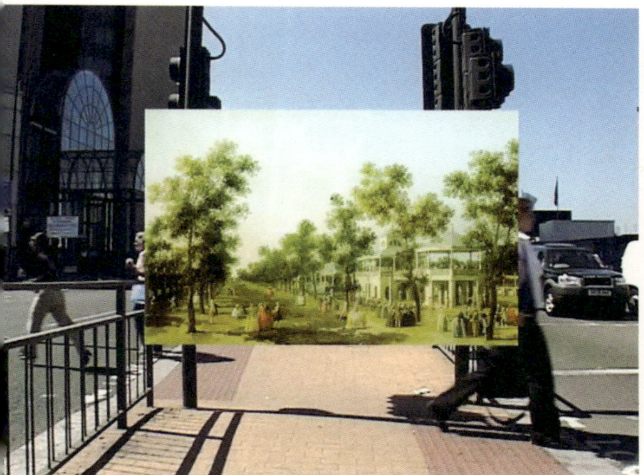

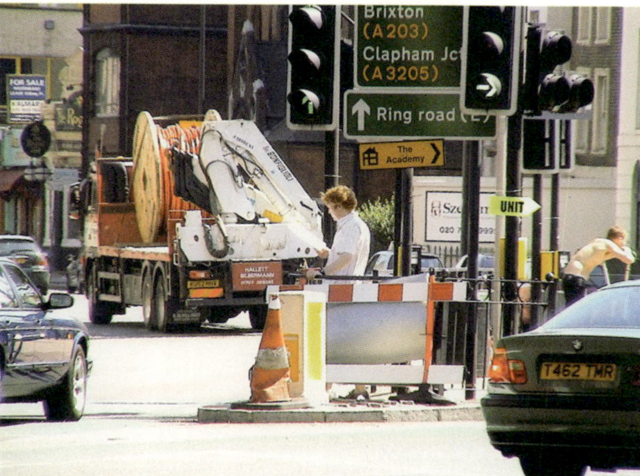


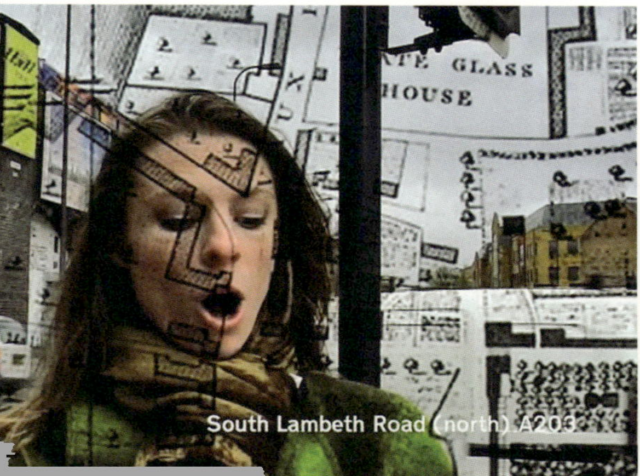


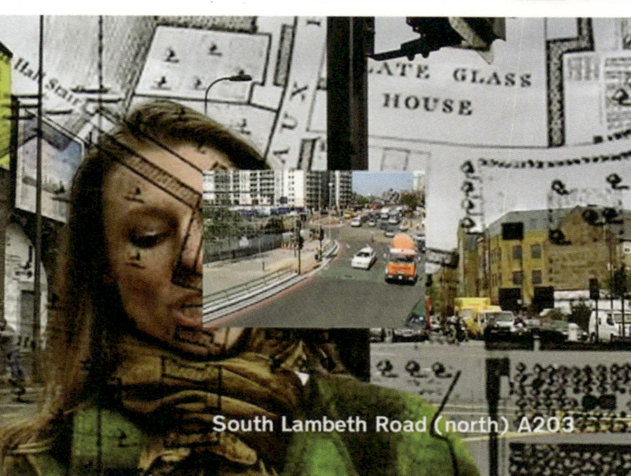

Annex: A Dialogue Between Julieta González and Anna Best (London, 11/2009)

*Julieta González —*

Unofficial and anecdotal histories, urban dynamics, and collaborative actions converge in your work in the most unexpected ways. Your works read sometimes as complex theatrical or cinematographic productions with lengthy casts of players and collaborators, as well as the active participation of the public. *Vauxhall Pleasure* is one such work, in which seemingly unrelated issues such as activism, leisure, local history, pedestrians, and conservation are addressed. Could you tell us more about the project?

*Anna Best —*

*Vauxhall Pleasure* is concerned with a seemingly diverse range of issues, as you say, but of course they are intricately bound together by capitalism's effects on the city, by the story of oil and the motor car. In fact, they sort of spiral out of these core issues in a similar manner to roads converging, overlaying, and racing on from the Vauxhall Cross transport interchange. At the heart of it is the place and the comparison between what we have chosen to do with our urban public space since Vauxhall Gardens pleasure garden's heyday in the eighteenth century and the past few decades. The gardens were an enormous meeting point of consumerism and live entertainment. They were a place where one strolled, socialized, heard music, watched theater, had sex, saw fireworks, etc., and a place that is now replaced by many tens of thousands of vehicle movements per day, which have been mapped by traffic engineers trying to enable the vehicles to move more quickly through the city. The project researches and records these existing lobbyists, a freeze-frame in time of people reacting and protesting. The local historical notes are full of clippings of complaints about the pleasure gardens. Residents are never satisfied, NIMBYism always rampant. But now the locality of Vauxhall Cross is just one example of a vast system that has more insidiously polluted and overridden humanity with its blatant disregard for anything in its way. *Vauxhall Pleasure* took place after the anticapitalist protests in London, in Seattle, at J18 (London), on May Day, etc. As a public art piece or as an action, it is reflective rather than active; I might call it emotional-political. Singing at traffic, the inhalations of polluted air. The space after a great action is often one of stillness—it takes time to know what's next. *Vauxhall Pleasure* tries to articulate this feeling. Is it a collective one? One of futility and undirected passion about the situation we find ourselves in?

*Julieta González —*

I am interested in your particular approach to art. Most of your works take place outside the exhibition space and engage in quite unusual dynamics that inscribe the absurd in the everyday. How do you relate to traditional modes of exhibition? Is there some sort of compromise in regard to museum and gallery-space conventions of display?

*Anna Best —*

With most projects, I have felt quite early on in the work that I am joining a history, joining a discourse with momentum, produced perhaps by activists, artists, and maybe citizens, who have been dealing with the issues and material for a long time. I find art history quite limiting—a specific compartment, like a form of autism—and much prefer the tangential nature of an "ordinary" conversation with many individuals. So, in a sense, my work is always collaborative as a research process, but differs greatly from one piece to another in how it is delivered to an audience. With regard to display in museums or gallery spaces, I have found that while conversation and social exchange have been the main tools of my work, it is unsuccessful to show this in a gallery on video. I am sorry to say I have tried it! And I have always been very interested in art that is unannounced, so that an audience is not prepared for it. Of course, the gallery has so many uses as an educational and public resource that I wish I could make use of this space better. There are questions around how one can judge some dialogic—social art as art—and this also interests me, the stripping of something from its context and the aspiration to pass judgment using generalized ideas. I do not believe in this, and like the fact that when something is related to a specific context it has its own frames of reference. I have appreciated gallery modes of display in the cases of being able to literally unpack an archive of historical material, to sell books, to show an artist's film and video, and simply to be used as a project space which is free to enter, warm and dry.

new relationship. It's more like saying to your friend – hold on a minute, I just want to close my eyes and think about something for a bit. The photographs I am making are artefacts from a process of making contact with people, of trying to encounter people. And they start to express how difficult that obviously is.

n

If the act of taking a photograph is an invitation to start speaking then, here, if he'd turned round and said – "Why did you take that picture?" – it would have turned into something completely different.

Another time when I met up with Sissu at Shoreditch Fire Station and we were taking photos of a fireman's boots, a fire engine drew up and all the fire fighters of Blue Watch got out of their fire truck and, precisely because we had a camera, stood in a row and posed for us. So you never know, if you just have a camera in your hand anything can happen...

n

Where's that photo then?

a

I don't know, maybe it's under 's' for Shoreditch.

How did the same stretch of road that spawned the citrus fruits on the railings also give us such an urgent graffiti to prospective homebuyers?

From Oval tube station on the Northern Line take a bus south towards Camberwell Green, a no.36 or a no.185

44_45

will do. The railings are on the right about halfway down and the graffiti was on the left but has long been replaced by a housing development.

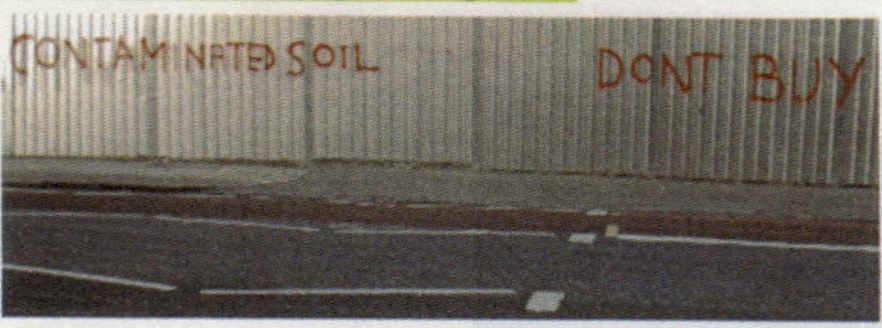


Adam, who sent me the Smart car photo, said he had been very encouraged to continue taking pictures like this knowing that I was also doing so. Over the phone he told me about a bus stop on Tower Bridge Road which had been misspelt on the tarmac road surface BUS STOB. He said he had cycled over it day after day, on the way to work, always promising himself to bring his camera with him. And then, one day, it had gone.

A similar thing happened to me with the orange on the railings. I saw a whole series of citrus fruits on them, but when eventually I returned with a camera, they'd disappeared.

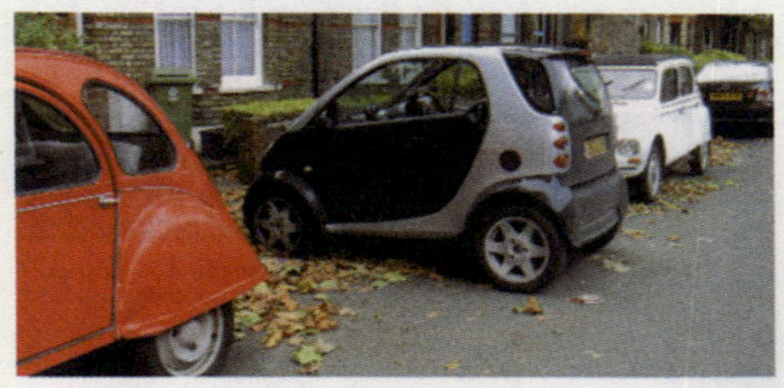

### Proyecto de escultura pública en la periferia urbana de Monterrey

*Proyecto de escultura pública en la periferia urbana de Monterrey* ("Project for a Public Sculpture on the Outskirts of Monterrey") in Mexico was part of a discussion on public places. What happens in a place that has no urban design? Tercerunquinto built a fifty-square-meter concrete platform, with half the platform on land that someone had invaded, and the other half on open land. The owner of the plot was in touch with religious groups that had sometimes held meetings there, and that was the starting-point, since the idea behind this project was for people in the community to conduct activities on the platform. People started using the piece as a forum and plaza, and the activities they did, such as having parties, distributing food and medicine, holding political and religious meetings, and conducting sports tournaments, were what defined the place.

### New Langton Arts

This project is an integral and structural analysis of New Langton Arts (San Francisco, CA): in particular of its characteristic as a non-profit organization with a thirty-year history, and more specifically of the "maximum capital"—its archive or what Tercerunquinto calls "documented historical memory"—of an institution like this. It examines New Langton Arts as a reference in recent art history—Vito Acconci, Nam June Paik, and Olafur Eliasson, among other artists, made projects and exhibited work there. *New Langton Arts' Archive For Sale: A Sacrificial Act* proposes that New Langton Arts capitalize on the sale of what it is that constitutes its maximum capital. For Tercerunquinto, the "real" site of Langton is not its building, but its archive. The building does not matter here; the institution is represented in a different way, not by its building but by its history.

### Muca Roma

For the intervention at MUCA Roma in Mexico City, Tercerunquinto addressed the issue of informal economy, proposing that the museum alter each of its small galleries with a door and a lock in order to make them available as storage spaces for the surrounding area's street vendors. The project involved a series of negotiations, first with the museum curators, who in turn had to negotiate with the General Direction of Cultural Diffusion, and then with the Law Department, who would ultimately give legal tenure to the project.

# Tercerunquinto

***Proyecto de escultura pública en la periferia urbana de Monterrey***, 2003, Mexico

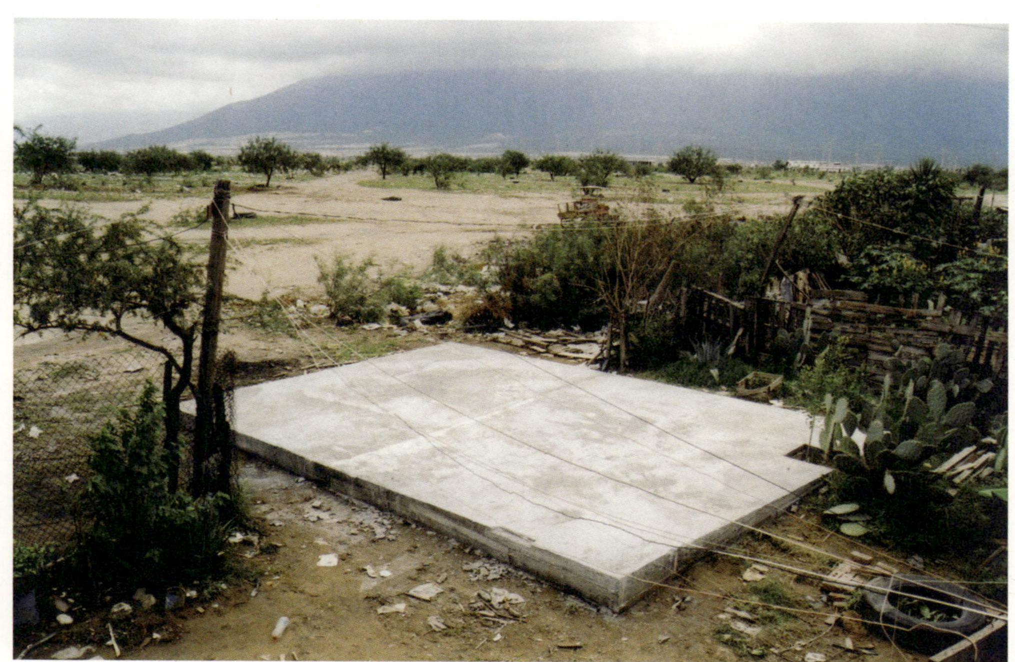

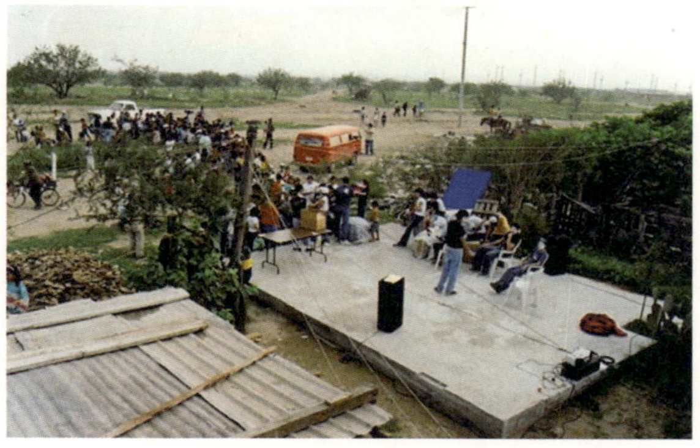

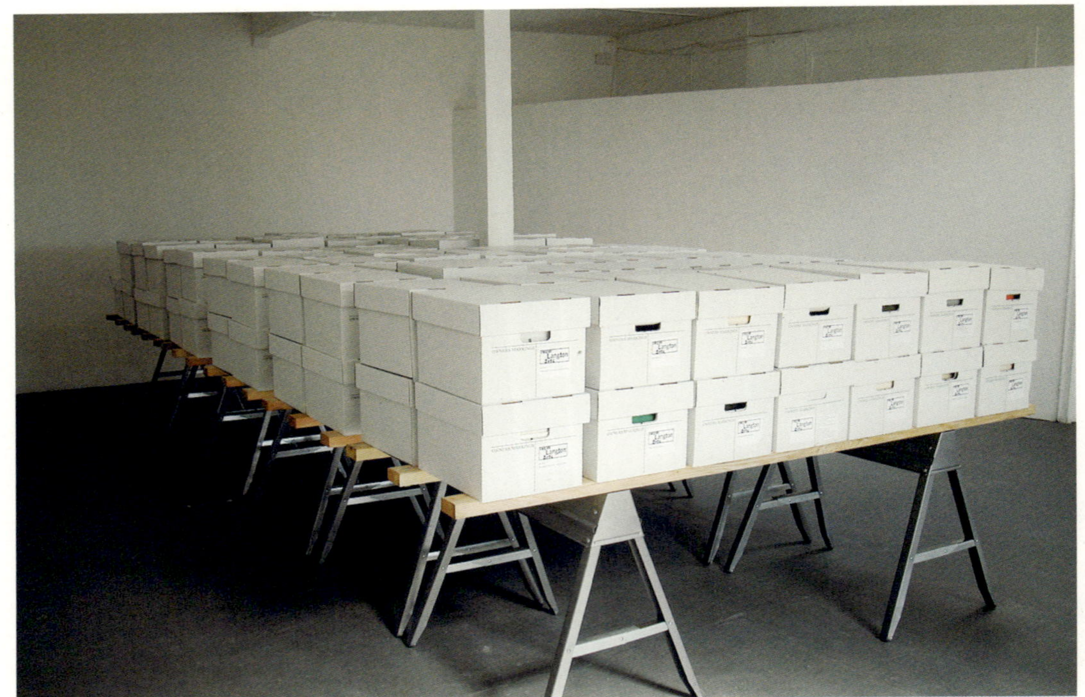

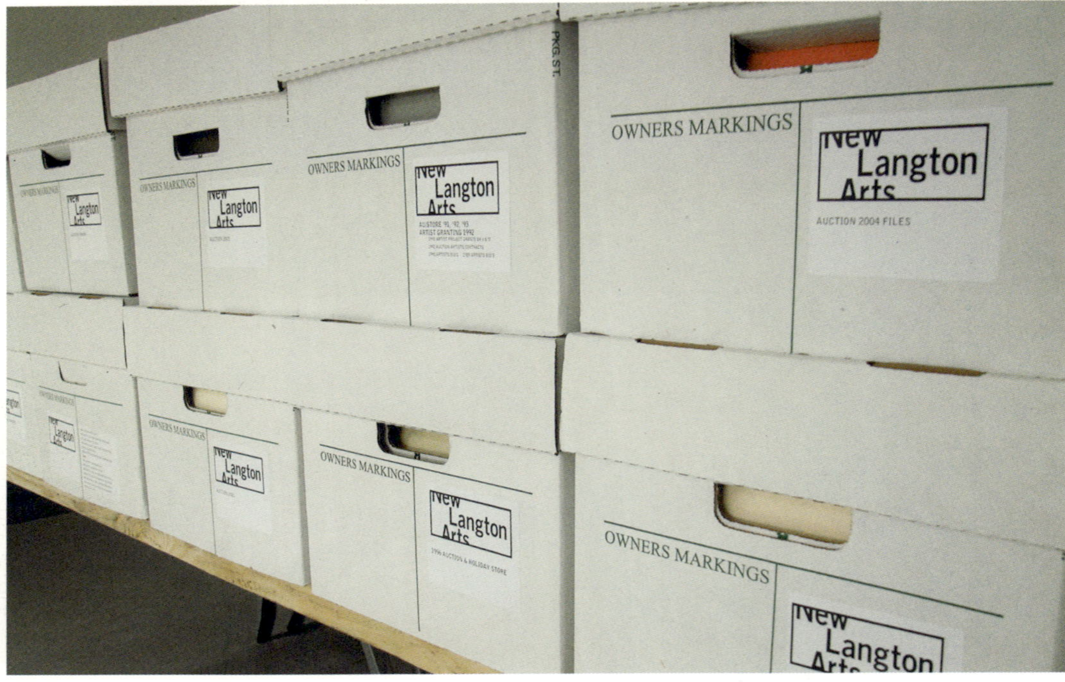


***New Langton Arts***, 2007,
San Francisco (CA)

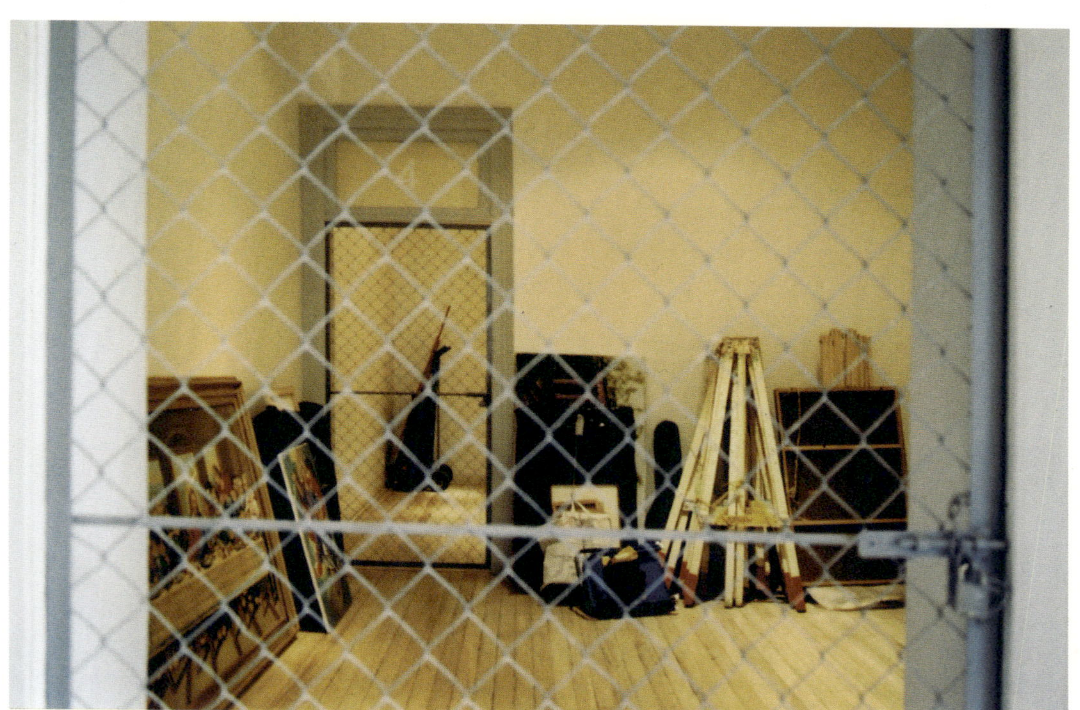

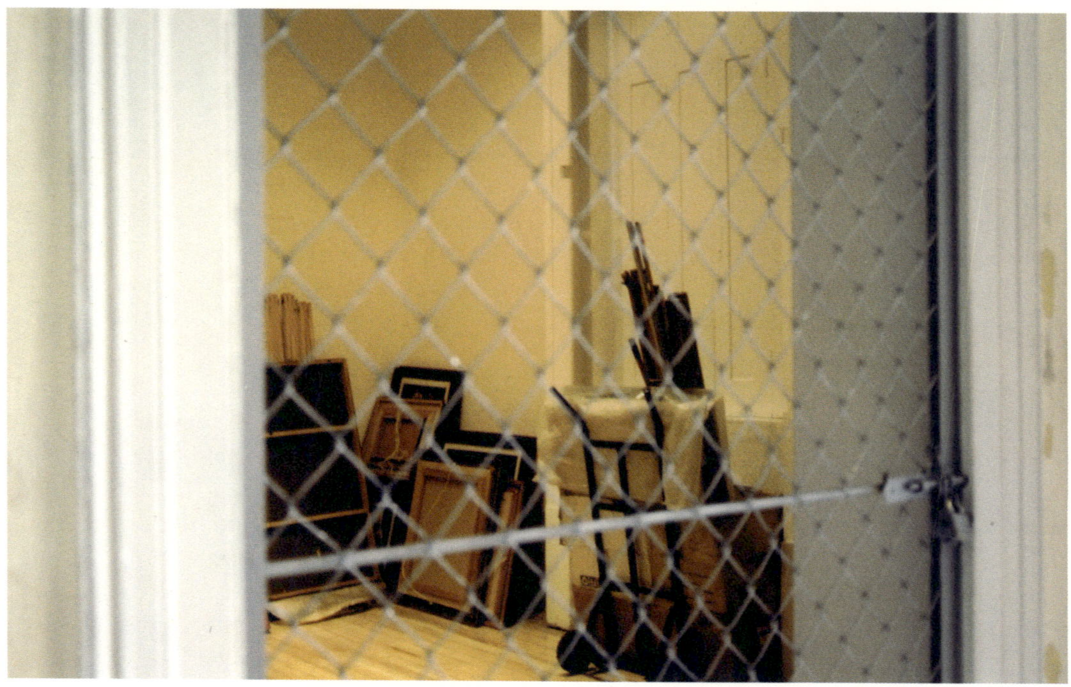

*Muca Roma*, 2007, Mexico City

Annex: A Dialogue Between Julieta González and Tercerunquinto (Mexico/San Juan, 11/2009)

*Julieta González —*

In my opinion, your *Escultura pública en la periferia urbana de Monterrey* (2003–2006) is very representative of your approach to architecture and urban design. On the other hand, the way it proposes the platform as a site of production and enunciation is very interesting; when you built that "platform" (literally and conceptually), the inhabitants of the place gave it the most diverse uses, but it also functioned as a critical element in the informal space of that neighborhood. Could you tell us more about this project and the way you address architecture and urban issues in your practice as artists?

*Tercerunquinto —*

The project was conceived as a reflection through which we could take critical positions in regard to a medium such as public sculpture. What we think is that public sculpture generally is very lax in terms of critical pertinence in the context in which it is inserted—it is ornamental, or in its monumental or statuary condition it celebrates supreme national values. Public sculpture crowns an urban or real-estate development; it is the "cherry on the cake," so to speak: frivolous and banal. What we wanted to do was to position sculpture in critical terms, working in a zone where the signs of urban development situate it in the periphery of a social and economic project. We decided to begin at the end, creating a sculpture that seemed to be waiting for signs of urban development, and development actually happened. Now the zone is in the process of being integrated to rest of the city. When we made this sculptural intervention, we decided to maintain a distance from any activity that was made on that site, and we only documented some of the activities that we had the opportunity to see.

*Julieta González —*

Recently you have focused on institutional dynamics and have made a series of projects in that direction. The projects for MUCA Roma (2004) and New Langton Arts (2007–2008), your exhibition earlier this year at the Museo Carrillo Gil, and your most recent show at Proyectos Monclova in Mexico are part of this body of work. I would like to know more about your interest in the institutional dynamics of the art world, and about how this transition from "architecture to institution" comes about in your work?

*Tercerunquinto —*

The relation with institutional spaces of art comes naturally for us. Obviously, in the beginning, our approach to a space, regardless of its nature, was very semantic, as we say. It was an attempt to understand a system (the architectural system in this case) by dismantling its constitutive elements. In this sense, we undertook a sort of exercise in which we tested the sculptural capacities of architecture and the architectural capacities of sculpture. With time, these reflections have become more complex and have exceeded the architectural space of the institution, widening our field of interest and leading to a reflection and a critique of other aspects of the institution. We must admit that there is an implicit self-critique here as well, since we are inside the institutional system of art, and in some of these projects we have engaged in this self-critique.

***Proyecto de escultura pública en la periferia urbana de Monterrey***, 2003, Mexico, collage

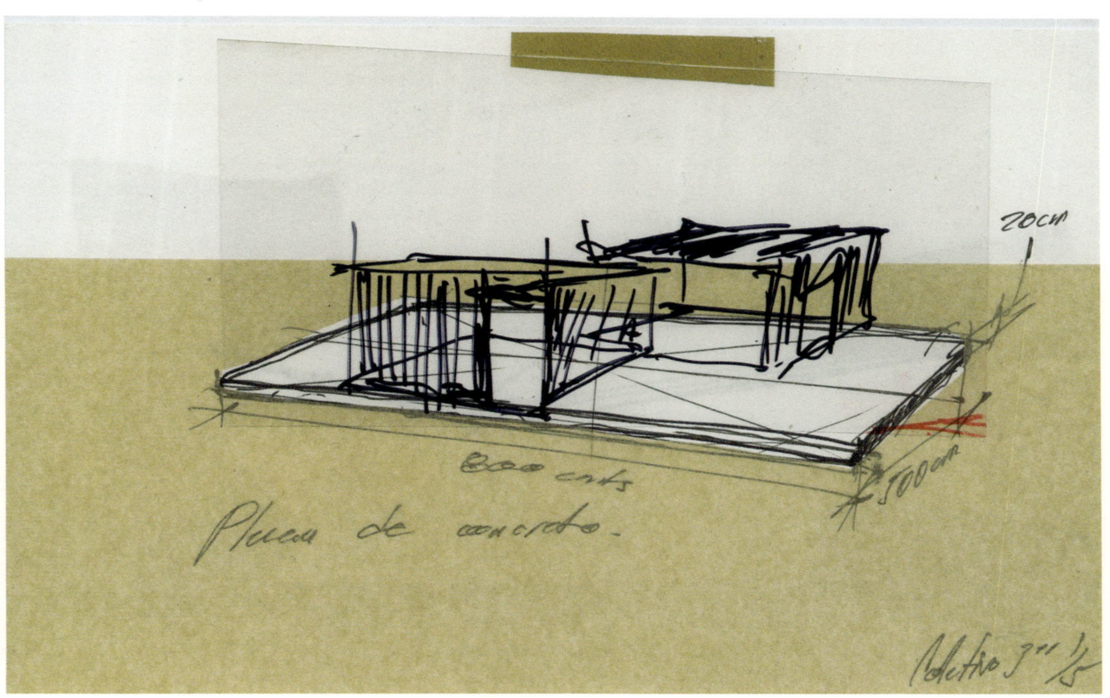

**Mihnea Mircan** (b. 1976) is an independent curator. At the National Museum of Contemporary Art in Bucharest, he curated exhibitions such as *Sean Snyder, Sublime Objects, Video Works: Jaan Toomik*, and the *Under Destruction* series of site-specific interventions. Other recent curatorial projects include: *History of Art, the* (David Roberts Art Foundation, London), *Since We Last Spoke about Monuments* (Stroom, The Hague), *Low-Budget Monuments* (Romanian Pavilion, 52nd Venice Biennale). He contributes frequently to monographs and international art magazines, having recently written on the work of artists Mona Vatamanu and Florin Tudor, Navid Nuur and Deimantas Narkevicius. He has recently edited the publication *The Impresent*.

**Ciprian Mureşan** (b. 1977) is an artist and an editor of IDEA art + society magazine in Cluj, Romania. His work was recently featured in exhibitions such as *The Generational: Younger Than Jesus* (New Museum, New York), *The Seductiveness of the Interval* (Romanian Pavilion, 53rd Venice Biennale), *Monument to Transformation* (Municipal Library, Prague, and Montehermoso Cultural Center, Victoria), *Like an Attali Report, But Different: On Fiction and Political Imagination* (Kadist Art Foundation, Paris). In 2010, he will have a solo presentation at NBK Berlin.

> petshopbeuys.blogspot.com

**Jill Magid** (b. 1973) is a visual artist and a writer. She received her Master of Science in Visual Studies at the Massachusetts Institute of Technology, Cambridge. Magid was an artist-in-residence at the Rijksakademie van Beeldende Kunsten, Amsterdam from 2000–2002. She has received various awards, including the Basis Stipendium from Fonds Voor Beeldende Kunsten in The Netherlands in 2006, and the Netherland-American Foundation Fellowship Fulbright Grant from 2001–2002. Magid showed *Authority to Remove* at the Tate Modern in London (2009) and has had solo shows in various institutions around the world, including Tate Liverpool (2004), the Stedelijk Museum Bureau Amsterdam, Sparwasser Berlin, Centre D'Arte Santa Monica (Barcelona), and Stroom (The Hague).

> www.jillmagid.net

**Jonas Staal** (b. 1981) has studied, monumental art in Enschede, The Netherlands and Boston, USA. His work includes interventions in public space, exhibitions, lectures, and publications, all of which emphatically relate to political subjects and developments. His recent shows include *Forty Years of Boredom 1968–2008* (Tent., Rotterdam, 2008) and *Democratism: An Introduction to Five Models of Civil Protest* (with Vincent van Gerven Oei, Tokyo Wonder Site, Tokyo, 2009). His essay *Post-Propaganda* (Fonds BKVB, 2009) was the theoretical basis for the manifestation *The People United Will Never Be Defeated!*, recently at Tent. and in the public space of Rotterdam.

> www.jonasstaal.nl

**Alon Levin** (b. 1975) studied in Amsterdam at the Gerrit Rietveld Academie and the Rijksakademie van beeldende kunsten. Recent exhibitions include *Art for Masses* at Ambach and Rice, Seattle; *Double Dutch* at HVCCA, Peekskill, New York; *Shifting Identities* at Kunsthalle Basel and CAC Vilnius; *Remodeling Systems* at CCS Bard, Annandale-on-Hudson, New York; and *Postponed Modernism* at KLEMM'S, Berlin. He recently published the artist book *Things Contemporary*.

> www.alonlevin.com

**Daniel McClean** (b. 1972) is an independent curator and art lawyer. He was previously a lawyer at Withers LLP, where he advised leading public and private art organizations, including Tate, the Arts Council of England, and Gagosian Gallery. His current clients include Seth Siegelaub's Stichting Egress Foundation, which he is advising on the construction of an advisory art law center. In addition to *Offer & Exchange*, he recently curated *False Twins* (SMAK, Gent) and a project with Superflex as part of the exhibition *Play Van Abbe* at the Van Abbemuseum (Eindhoven). He has commissioned and edited two pioneering publications on the relationship between art and law: *Dear Images: Art, Copyright and Culture* (2002) and *The Trials of Art* (2007).

> www.electra-productions.com

**Lisa Rosendahl** (b. 1974) has been the Director of the Baltic Art Center (BAC) in Visby, Sweden since 2008. She has been a visiting lecturer at the University College of Arts Crafts and Design in Stockholm, the Art Academy in Malmö, and the Valand Art Academy in Gothenburg. Lisa has published widely and had written catalogue texts for art institutions such as Magasin 3 (Stockholm), Centro Galego de Arte Contemporanea (Santiago de Compostela), and Musee d'Art Contemporain (Val-de-Marne). She is co-curator with Fredrik Liew and Gertrud Sandqvist of the next edition of the quadrennial of Swedish contemporary art held at Moderna Museet in Stockholm, opening in September 2010.

> www.electra-productions.com

**Robert Barry** (b. 1936) focuses on non-material explorations, encompassing installation, performance, and various forms of invisible media. He held a key place in the early conceptual movement with exhibitions such as *When Attitudes Become Form* (1969, Kunsthalle Bern, Bern), *Concept and Concept* (1970, Galleria San Fedele, Milan) and *Projections: Anti-Materialism* (1970, La Jolla Museum of Art, La Jolla). In 2008, his work has been shown in the exhibition … *5 Minutes Later* at Kunstwerke Institute for Contemporary Art, Berlin.

**Stefan Brüggemann** (b. 1975) has been exhibiting extensively both in Mexico and abroad since the mid-1990s. In recent years, he has received international recognition for his irreverent, radical, and often playful approaches to art production. Recent solo exhibitions were held at Yvon Lambert Gallery (Paris), FRAC Bourgogne (Dijon), Kunsthalle Bern, and at Sies & Hoeke Gallery (Düsseldorf).

> www.stefanbruggemann.com

**Santiago Sierra** (b. 1966) gained extensive international recognition in 2001, when he was invited to develop new projects by several major institutions worldwide, such as Kunstwerke Berlin and P.S.1 Contemporary Art Center in New York. In 2003, he represented Spain at the 50th Venice Biennale. Sierra has continued developing challenging new projects, including *House in Mud* (2005, Kestnergesellschaft, Hanover) and *245 m3* (2006, Stommeln Synagogue, Pulheim). Recent group exhibitions include *RAUM* (2007, Akademie der Kunste, Berlin) and *The Living Currency* (2008, Tate Modern, London).

> www.santiago-sierra.com

# An Image Instead of a Title

Consider two examples. For *Tree Mountain*, by Agnes Denes, 11,000 people planted as many trees on a hill in Ylojarvi, Finland. All planters received a certificate valid for 400 years: they can leave their trees to their heirs, celebrate or mourn by it, be buried under it, sell it, etc. While the forest is to remain intact, forms of ownership and use orchestrated around it can change, can mutate at the same speed as the forces traversing social space and reshaping its memosphere or notions of value. The forest is designed as a place at which to visualize the future, but also to withstand its possibly deleterious impact: to exhibit the future, as well as to exhibit itself as the impregnable past of that future. Changes in the articulation of ownership and individuality are to refract upon contact with Denes's work, their momentum decelerated by the contracts that stipulate the integrity of each tree in the forest. Thus *Tree Mountain* juxtaposes separate futures: it lays out its own future as 400 years of resisting obsolescence and the condition of ruin, in tandem with another future, that of the world around the work, its "ground." It introduces distance between these versions of the future—between their literalness and the allegories we use to prop up visions of our collective destination. It functions as a stage for the interpretive negotiations binding them.

The second example is a small, sketchy reproduction of the sculpture *Litanies*, accompanied by a notarized statement in which the artist Robert Morris withdraws "all aesthetic quality and content from the work." The *Statement of Aesthetic Withdrawal* pits authority against authorship, encodes authority legally to evacuate authorship from art history, into another historiographic territory where their disjunction can be resolved. The legalistic inversion operated here echoes one of the fundamental gestures of modern art, the designation of a urinal as a *Fountain* by Marcel Duchamp. It is probably not a coincidence that the *Litanies* themselves reproduce words from Duchamp's comments on the *Large Glass*, a work predated and prefaced by its explanation, submerged in the artist's own commentaries of it and in a sense preempting any subsequent interpretive effort as a commentary on the artist's commentary. Robert Morris's conceptual removal of artistic authorship situates *Litanies* right outside art history, and provides a vantage point from which to observe the mechanisms of naturalization and exclusion in the discipline.

I propose that one read *Tree Mountain* and the *Statement of Aesthetic Withdrawal* as extremities of a conceptual trajectory, interspersed with that of institutional critique, yet aimed at something markedly different from the exposure of white-cube ideologies. The institution engaged here is more venerable than the museum, and at least as successful in presenting its *capta* as *data*. Denes and Morris speak of the artist's participation in art history, in the historical inscription of the work—or in its "administration," to recuperate an important trope of institutional critique —and of the art historian's muted preoccupation with the future, the moment when art ceases to be and the archive comes together, complete. (While Agnes Denes adjourns this moment indefinitely, or complicates its emergence by pairing it up with a manifestation of the sublime, Robert Morris treats it as having already occurred, or assigns to it a condition of anteriority; one artist asks us for infinite patience, the other for infinite acumen.)

The project of institutional critique articulated its disempowerment of the institution with an empowerment of the participant. In fact, it invented the notion of participation, seeking to neutralize the complicity between art and other power systems: it formalized protest as a democratic counter-maneuver to the workings of the institutional. The revelation, or verdict, that ensued was almost theatrically staged for an audience invited to repossess the symbolic resources thus made available. The promise of institutional critique was that the power subtracted from the institution would be equal—and, later, commensurate—with the power it would grant the viewer-cum-participant. That power could indeed be reassigned within this triumvirate of dismantled institution, radical artist, and critical spectatorship. It was the task of the following decades to clarify whether this equation was correct, and whether arithmetic had anything to do with power. Art portrayed itself as in a condition of ghostly equivalence to power, and correspondences were, in vastly different ways, traced between the poetic and the political as equally legitimate modes of administrating the possible. Various strategies emerged from this tangle of synonymy, where each element manifested itself with all its political force or poetic dexterity to incarnate the other, and where transgression was forever matched by what was being transgressed. Yet institutional critique was confined to an attempt to localize or visualize power as a stable, definable interlocutor and to materialize a phantasmal transfer, or, conversely, confined to a protracted study into the capacity of power to mutate, relocate, put on masks, absorb shocks, never distribute, and never diminish.

As institutions made more space for the objections raised by artists, the striking perspectives opened up by the first assaults of this discourse on the relationships between art institutions and other configurations of power, on the assumptions and coercions of museological space and museological thinking, coalesced into a softer, nuanced stance, whereby art was supposed to pervade, meaningfully, society, while society was supposed to traverse, lastingly, the art institution. Institutions co-opted critique as rhetoric of a permanent self-sabotage; they internalized it in a pathology of self-definition, a syndrome of institutional anxiety that intensified as budgets and logistical capabilities grew. The eviscerated non-institution projected itself as a site of diaphanous bureaucracy, of unencumbered display and imponderable process. The institutional was supposed to be undone or made unrecognizable, reinvented as a set of tactics matched by counter-tactics that engendered not only an exhibition policy but also a system of monitoring it, ensuring that things are in flux and that the institution permanently extricates itself from the contexts it proposed. Eventually, this halfhearted self-contestation was matched in magnitude only by its contradiction (the inflationary wave of biennials and exorbitant prices), so that the art world progressively looked like a cancerous outgrowth on its own history.

If institutional critique dissolved into the institutional, a series of works and practices channeled its critical, transformative potential to other sites and modes of enunciation. Agnes Denes and Robert Morris posit the "elsewhere" as a rupture in the conditions and mediations that constitute and ensure both visibility and historical legibility of a work. The temporality of *Tree Mountain* overflows the capacity and relevance of institutional confines, elliptically rephrasing the ways in which art-historical past proceeds into an immaterial present, and toward a future anticipated as more, better art. Robert Morris's "outside"—the self-exclusion he institutes—is the discursive function of an absolute use of the instruments afforded by the "inside," of taking maximum advantage of one's position as an artist. The artists' comments on processes and protocols of historicization synchronize these two works with other ways of imagining past and future in contemporary art, and the political resonance these indirectly seek to attain. New modes of making and writing history, the communalities and political imaginaries these correspond to, our post-ideological condition or our ideological unrest—these are, of course, among the principal concerns of art today. But what futures can be imagined from art, or what futures can art imagine? What can be done and thought to extend an art-historical canon into a discoursing of our present, a present that does not adhere to the past as an inexorable condition or to a future as a necessity of confirmation? I believe the future available to art is neither futuristic nor futurological—not an allegory of technology or ecology—but rather is the future understanding of art, the extent to which works or practices partake in their interpretation, and script or construct it, inquiring what forms interpretation could take and what these could activate in interplay. A metonym of the future, then, rather than a metaphor; a hinge between a past that the work incorporates—consumes or makes its own, as opposed to illustrates—and the "how" or "what" of the art object's future significations.

The authority and disciplinary confidence of art history is today in dispute between three theoretically coextensive modes of enunciation. A default art history informs blockbuster exhibitions, is taught in some schools, and is popularized in "Great Masters" books and films. It concatenates artists, styles, and historiographic data in an epistemological vacuum; it has "flowed" since the times of Giorgio Vasari, and it demonstrates the course of history in the mirror of art. Another avatar of art history contends with both the first instance and the "end of history," with the disintegration of internal logic and self-sufficiency in the discipline. It tries to resituate art history after the putative halt of history—G.W.F Hegel after Arthur C. Danto—and to reconcile its complicated, messianic legacy with an incomplete evacuation of historicism. On this analytic stage, the critique of constructed symmetries and hegemonic exclusions in traditional art history engenders a series of prologues, antecedent to several histories that would—were they written—dispense with chronologic confabulation or mutations of style, non-histories both informed and incapacitated by strands of recent theoretical thought originating elsewhere in the humanities.

A third replica of the lost original, or another relationship to the object of historical desire, is mapped out in contemporary art's inordinate relation to what it sometimes perceives as its own adolescence, sometimes as a background against which to project its own legitimacy or prodigal anxieties, in its determination to have a history, even if premised on doubtful foundations and perfect malleability. A chronic historiographic compulsion is arguably the defining feature of today's art, with the inbuilt contradictions of a particular understanding of

Modernism as the prime locus of scrutiny: the past this art portrays reads like a series of quirks and blips of historiographic time, against a background of grand narratives relentlessly manifesting themselves. In this case, art history is both the site of futures unrealized—unjust or captive to political winners—*and* the lineage from which contemporary art would like to portray itself as descending. From these interrelated perspectives, art history operates today in the growing chasm between the contemporary—with its fatigue, diversities, and archeological disposition—and an unfamiliar, if not impervious, past. Or it could be said to operate in a former disciplinary topography, half excavated and turned into a museum for the fragments of a discursive apparatus: instruments of connoisseurship, iconography, or social history, absented categories, and the totems of the founding fathers. In a vacant site of declamation, where the angel of art history zigzags.

The selection of works that follows is only partly concerned with the institutional mechanisms and operations of validation through which contemporary artworks, at various points during their production, exhibition, or collection, enter art history. Instead, it focuses on the ambiguities and responsibilities of historical situatedness, on art history as an imperfectly configured network of possibility and influence and counteraction, but also as a discourse to be invoked: instituted, or awakened through the strategies of the works themselves. In some cases, the domain of art history intermingles with other spheres of symbolic operation, whereby the historicity of the object is to be extricated via an ampler set of negotiations, or imagined across distinct systems of control and exchange, inflecting and opening both to novel ways of being. Other works indicate how a database would be compressed and re-structured, disrupted by units of ambiguity or divested from a condition of pervasive correspondence. And I would argue that in yet other cases the production of history is located in the work, in objects defining themselves as historical and conceived so as to interlock with the configuration of imminent or distant historical interrogation. These create potential reciprocities between the object's conceptual protrusions and extensions, between deregulations of the interpretive script and modes of historiographic engagement—sets of operations that might look like indispensable genealogies when seen from the future.

In continuity with the argument that informs the selection, two projects—as opposed to one—have been chosen from among four artists and a curatorial duo. This is meant to put each work into each of the other's perspective, and to ask what their semantic reliance on each other (or their inseparability inside the same practice) might signify. Each work can be construed as the other's appendix or vanishing point, or perhaps as an index that figures and grafts the other into an archive where images and artworks organize themselves. One archival model that art history employed was an epistemology for articulating congruities between subjects and their object-worlds, as among objects and their subjects—a technique conceived to maintain modern identities, and the political entities these identities supported and justified. Contemporary art has purposefully ramified that epistemological script, made to include that which dispossesses it of its certainties. At the other end of the spectrum lies an Alexandrian model of the archive, where conservation and historical inquiry coincide with destruction. As the Library is synonymous with its real or imagined conflagration, each gesture of inscription in such an archive activates a vertiginous movement of self-abolition or erasure. A model of homogenous, pervasive correspondence between objects and subjects is made void even while laboriously rehearsed. The future archive of art history registers perhaps the movement via which an artwork entrusts itself to historiographic scrutiny, and lends itself to time. An index of images—of relations between images and the rules of legibility they institute—would serve at least to measure their divergence from art-historical equivocation, their fundamental resistance to interpretive terms not their own.

A young man lies, crushed, on the pavement, in a setting similar to that of Yves Klein's *Jump into the Void*. Shrek, the congenial animated ogre, slashes the eye of his companion in precisely the same way as that made famous in Luis Buñuel and Salvador Dali's *Un chien andalou*, while significant scenes from Andrei Tarkovski's *Andrei Rubliov*—scenes in some sort of metaphysical adjacency to the film's focus on sturdily 2-D icons—have been reproduced in 3-D animation, and are thus entrusted to the care of the generation whose habits of cultural consumption virtually exclude an encounter with the Russian filmmaker. In a recent drawing, the anamorphotic skull in Hans Holbein's *Ambassadors* is presented frontally, and we can assume that anamorphosis is relocated as a smudge of color, on the bodies of the Ambassadors themselves.

Ciprian Mureşan has a particular, disquieting relationship with appropriation. What his inversions of climactic moments from art past articulate is not a euphoric apology of the simulacral condition of the contemporary, and certainly not an ironic permutation, but a comment on cultural unbelonging. The manipulated, emptied, dislocated original is finally neither ours nor theirs (that of our precursors), neither to be understood in its own inaccessible terms nor perfectly translatable in ours. Original and corrupted copy dispossess each other of their capacities to illustrate a period or a paradigm; they are bound with each other in in-between-ness, which we should probably understand as the historical time separating two moments folded upon themselves and marked as the space of representation. In *Un chien andalou*, the artist seamlessly extends two types of filmic space into each other, and creates an elaborate Rorschach test for the postmodern intellectual. The work cannot be purged of its duck-rabbit directionality: writing the unlimited possibilities of animation into the original appears here as an infinitely delicate act which conflates destruction, preservation, and translation.

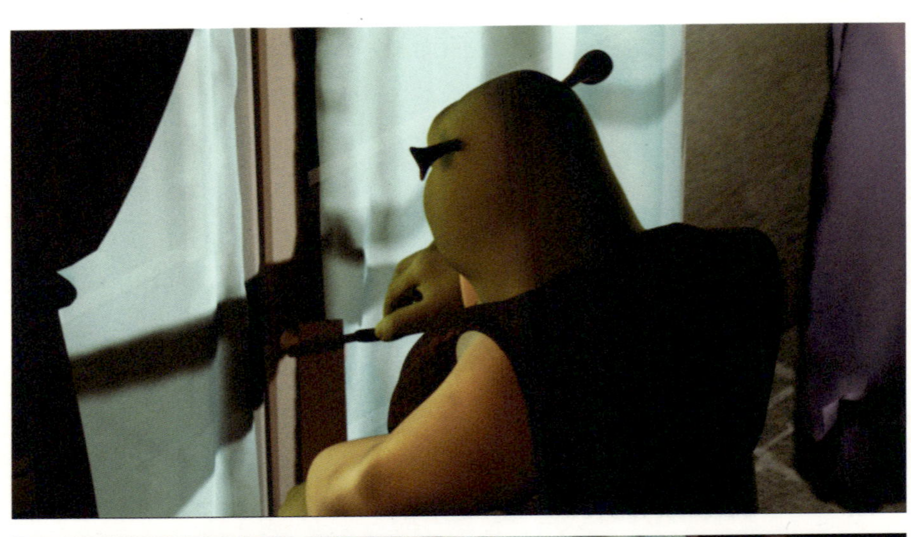
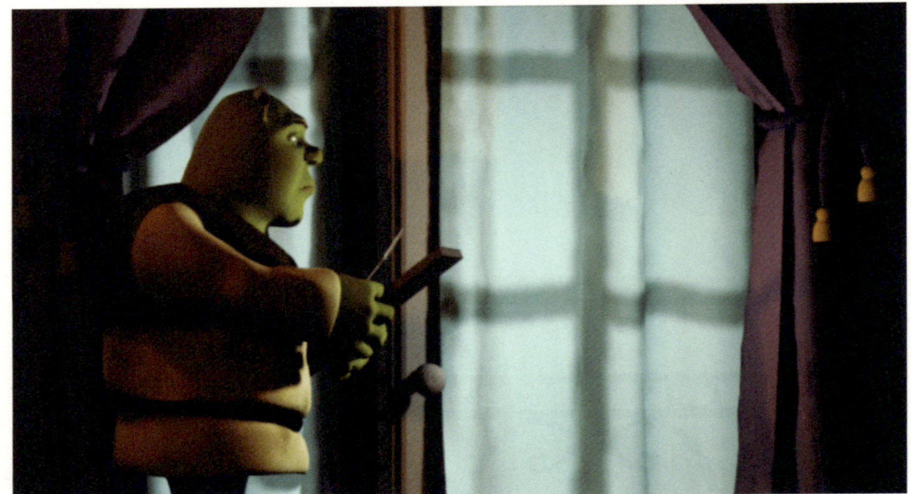

***Un chien andalou***, 2004, 3-D animation, 1 minute, courtesy Plan B Cluj (Berlin) and Prometeo Gallery (Milan), animation by Radu Constatinescu and Mihaela Sucala

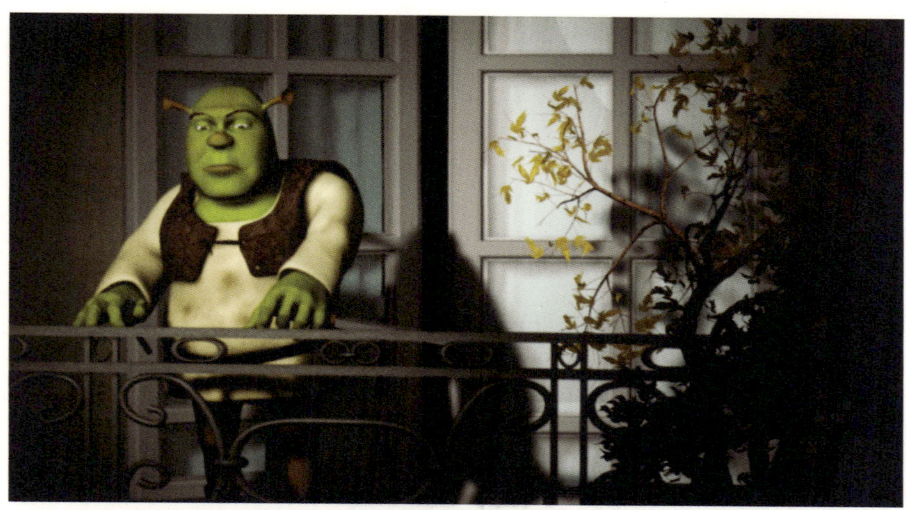

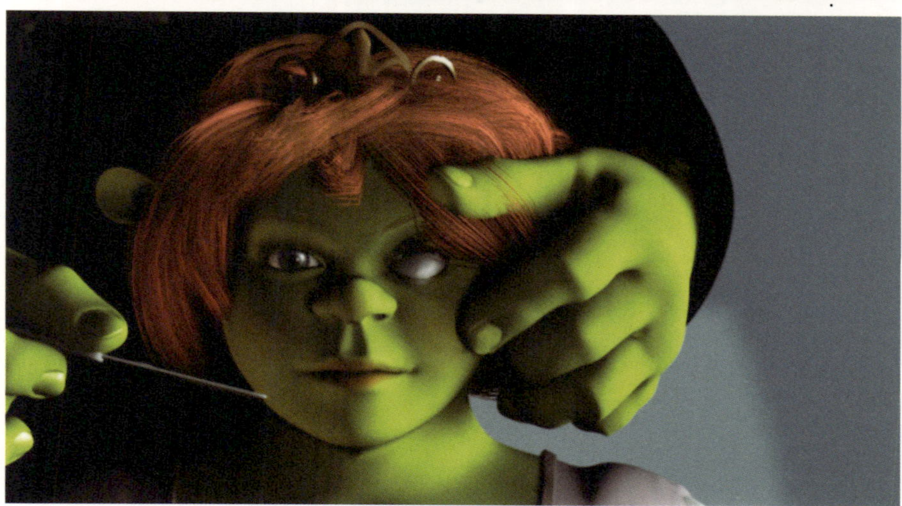

Belonging to another, connected strand in the artist's work, the abrupt *Communism Never Happened*, cut from communist propaganda records, could headline a political agenda or announce the inauguration of a gigantic shopping center. It is pure, implacable revisionism—one without an ideology—or a complex anachronism, indicating the ways in which post-communism and globalization endlessly complicate each other. Bound up with the certainty that communism happened, it signals the emergence of a generation of Eastern European artists that no longer reflect on trauma and analyze geographical or historical marginality as if it were one of Zeno's paradoxes. It is a slogan that bypasses political disputes about the left and personal histories: if more people agree that "communism never happened," the possibility of a community discreetly arises.

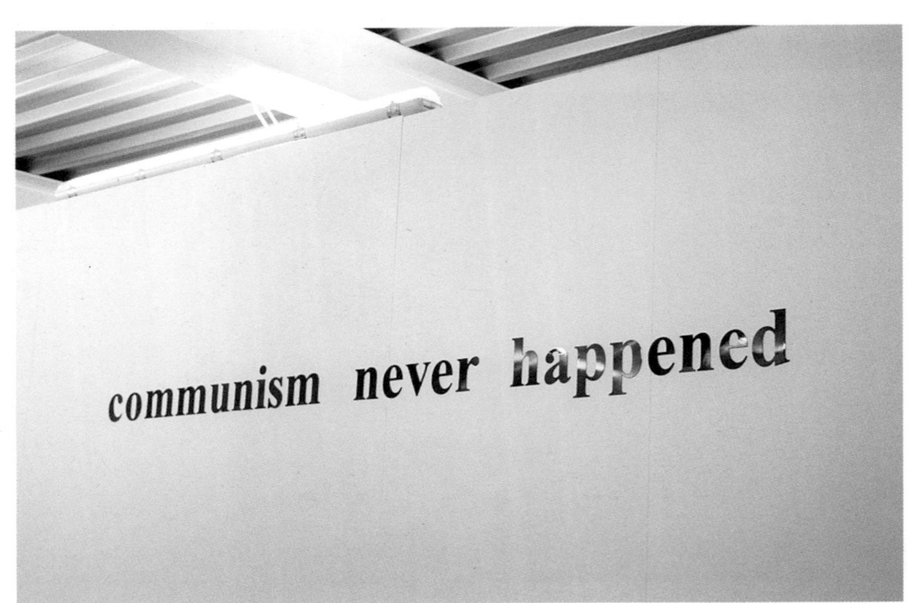

■□
***Communism Never Happened***, 2006, text, vinyl from propaganda records, photos by Bartha Lorand, courtesy Plan B Cluj (Berlin)

□■
***Leap Into the Void—After 3 Seconds***, 2004, courtesy of Nicodim Gallery (Los Angeles), Plan B Cluj (Berlin)

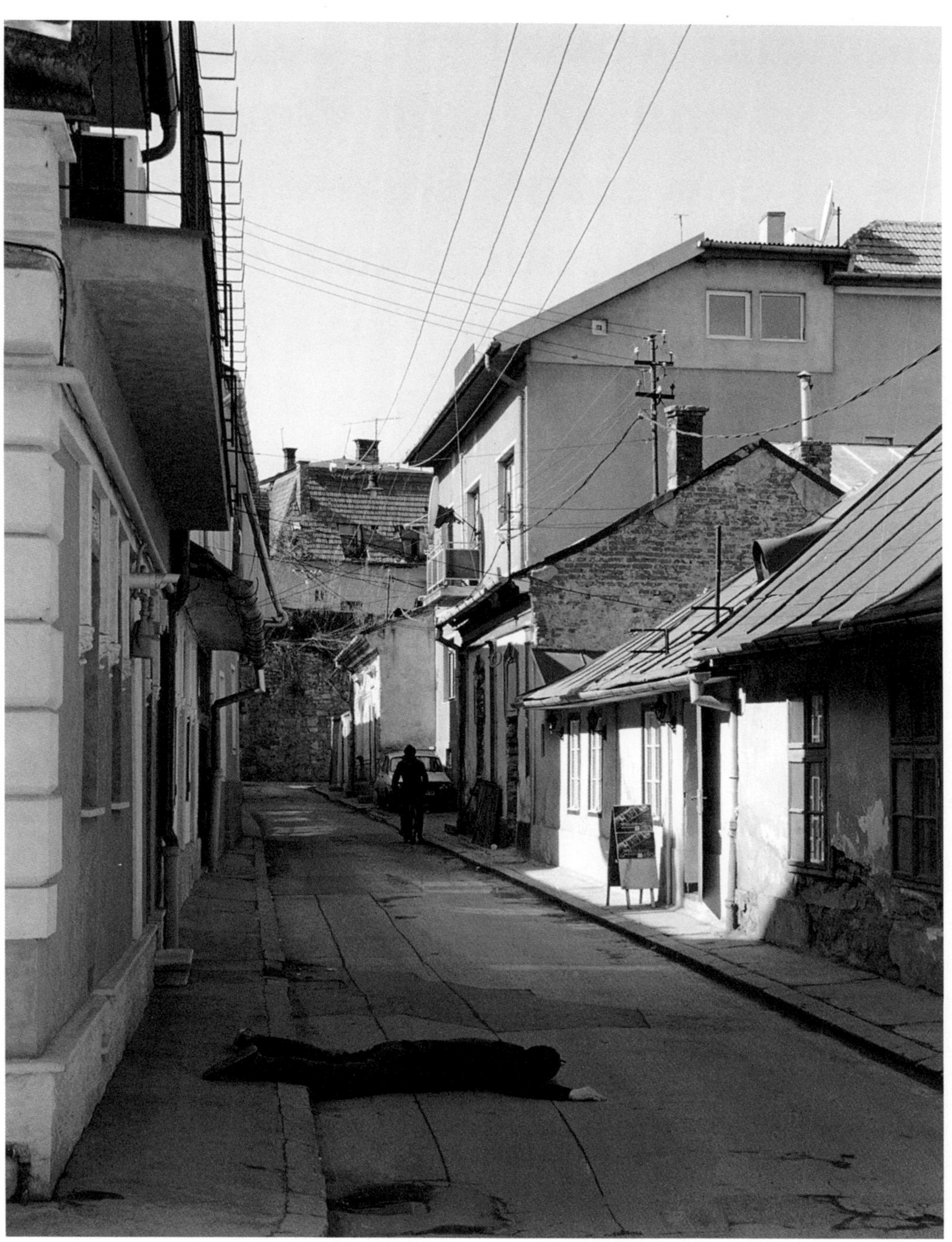

**"Dear Lifegem, Make me a diamond when I die. Cut me round and brilliant. Weigh me at one carat. Ensure that I am real. I understand that to make my diamond, you will use carbon collected from my remains. [...] Inspect me. Grade me. Deliver me. My beneficiary is waiting."**

A contract signed by Jill Magid and Lifegem to turn the artist's cremated remains into a one-carat diamond, in addition to an empty ring setting and a beneficiary contract, together constitute, for now, the work *Auto Portrait Pending*. The beneficiary contract hinges between the life of the artist and the post-mortem crystallization of her body in a mutually contaminative way. Jill Magid is expelled of her body to the same extent that the beneficiary of the diamond-to-come is separated from the object of desire. The love-letter tone of the preamble quoted above transfers the impossible possession of both body and diamond, into an inverted quasi-custody of both.

# Jill Magid

***Auto Portrait Pending***, 2005, gold ring with empty setting, ring box; photographer unknown; copyright Jill Magid, courtesy of the artist and Yvon Lambert, Paris, New York

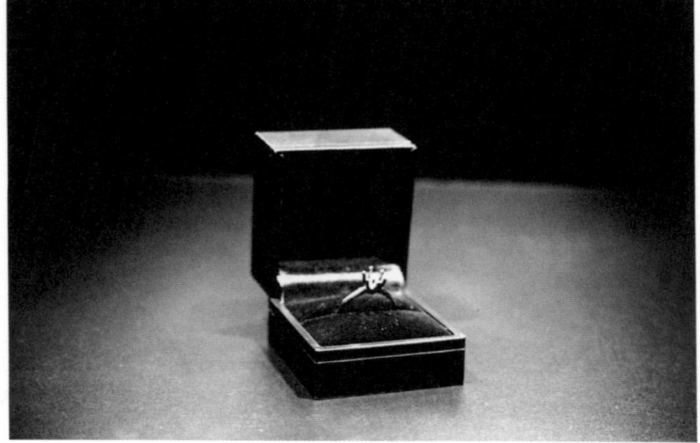

The somber literalness of possession, gesticulating awkwardly toward its object, engulfs a work that belongs to no one, whose operation is to resist ownership. While the collector buys the simultaneity of non-body and non-diamond, the possibility of ownership and its interruption, the art historian is given an ellipsis of all tropes of inspired artistry, legally disarticulated and recreated, concomitant with the rest of the artist's practice: between them, congruence will need to be written, or confabulated.

*Article 12* pursues Jill Magid's preoccupation with surveillance and seduction, with situations where the Panopticon materializes as a body behind the gaze, as an entity ready to negotiate the extensions, deregulations, reversals, or violations of that gaze. In *Article 12*, the Dutch Intelligence Agency has a status of coauthorship, its censorship of transcripts of the conversations between Jill Magid and secret agents functioning as gradual activation of the complexity of the project. Commissioned to find the "human face" of the organization, the artist gathered personal data about the agents by playing around professional jargon and the professional reflex of secrecy, and around the assumed or legally coded limits of the sayable. The experience translates into installations that bind up secrecy and privacy, or pit forms of trespassing against a progressively nebulous and distant object. Almost half of the book elaborating upon the conversations with agents was edited out by the agency, engendering a process whereby artwork takes shape by being extricated from incompatible sites of production, as dispute between disjunctive rules that, in interplay, threaten the work with nonexistence.

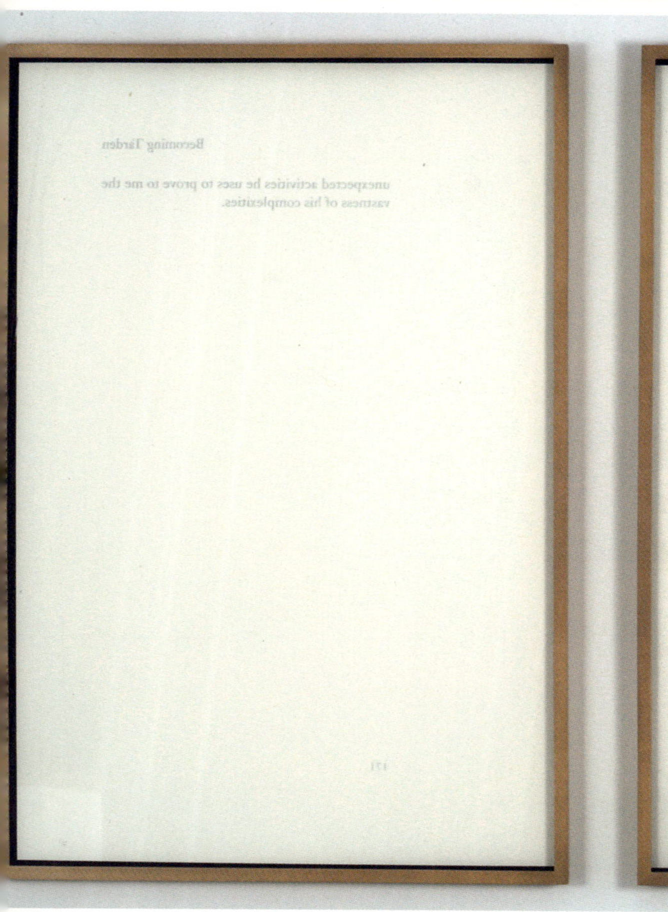

Epilogue

I title the exhibition for my commission "Article 12." The artworks have been lifted from my notebooks. Excerpts from *Cockpit* are hung along a wall that pierces through the gallery. My list of directives scrolls down from the ceiling and onto the floor. Eighteen prints describe my sources' faces. A red neon installation warns that I can burn them. My notebooks are closed and locked under glass. They will be surrendered.

The day before the opening, The Organization sends a group of agents to the gallery to review and approve my work. There are four of them: my Committee Head, an older woman whose position I do not know, a senior spokesman from the communications department, and the head of buildings and security. I take them on a tour of the exhibition and present the works within it. The spokesman reads aloud every neon word as well as those in the prints, as if he were performing them.

Before they leave, I give my Committee Head a rough copy of my report, my interviews with my sources,

173

***Epilogue***, 2009, silkscreen on paper

***The Live Drop***, 2009, black and white c-print (both images © Jill Magid, Courtesy of the artist and Yvon Lambert, Paris, New York)

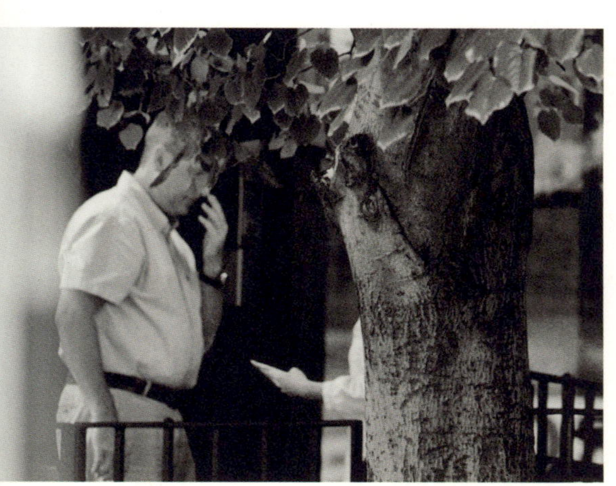

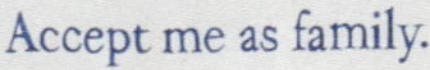

Accept me as family.

Take me into your warm bath.

PERMIT ME IN YOUR BUILDING, beyond the second façade.

I will build a cover; you will make it legal.

Teach me to believe in belief, after proving it's constructed.

Analyze my vulnerability.

Spot my connections. Trace my transactions.

Teach me not to stress.

Protect me from agent loving.

PUT ME IN THE FIELD.

Cultivate my trust.

Replace me when I come too close.

VET ME. Mine my data. Remove the proper nouns.

Train me to enter a premise, remove an object,
and return it within three days.

Give me a three-day limit.

DOCUMENT ME; be sure I am retrievable.

Stimulate my behavior.

CHOOSE A WALL and fill it with my artifacts.

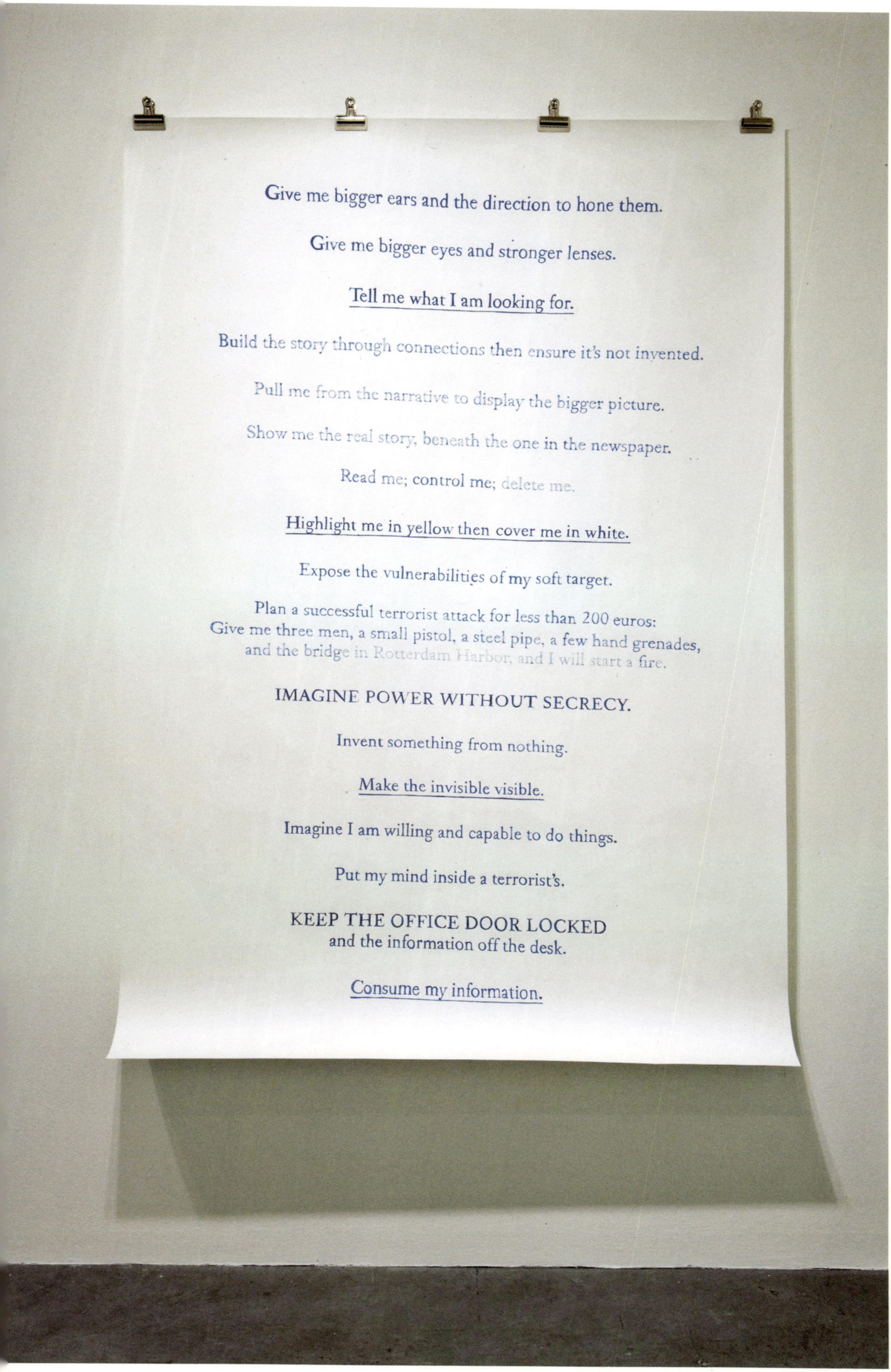

Give me bigger ears and the direction to hone them.

Give me bigger eyes and stronger lenses.

Tell me what I am looking for.

Build the story through connections then ensure it's not invented.

Pull me from the narrative to display the bigger picture.

Show me the real story, beneath the one in the newspaper.

Read me; control me; delete me.

Highlight me in yellow then cover me in white.

Expose the vulnerabilities of my soft target.

Plan a successful terrorist attack for less than 200 euros:
Give me three men, a small pistol, a steel pipe, a few hand grenades,
and the bridge in Rotterdam Harbor, and I will start a fire.

IMAGINE POWER WITHOUT SECRECY.

Invent something from nothing.

Make the invisible visible.

Imagine I am willing and capable to do things.

Put my mind inside a terrorist's.

KEEP THE OFFICE DOOR LOCKED
and the information off the desk.

Consume my information.

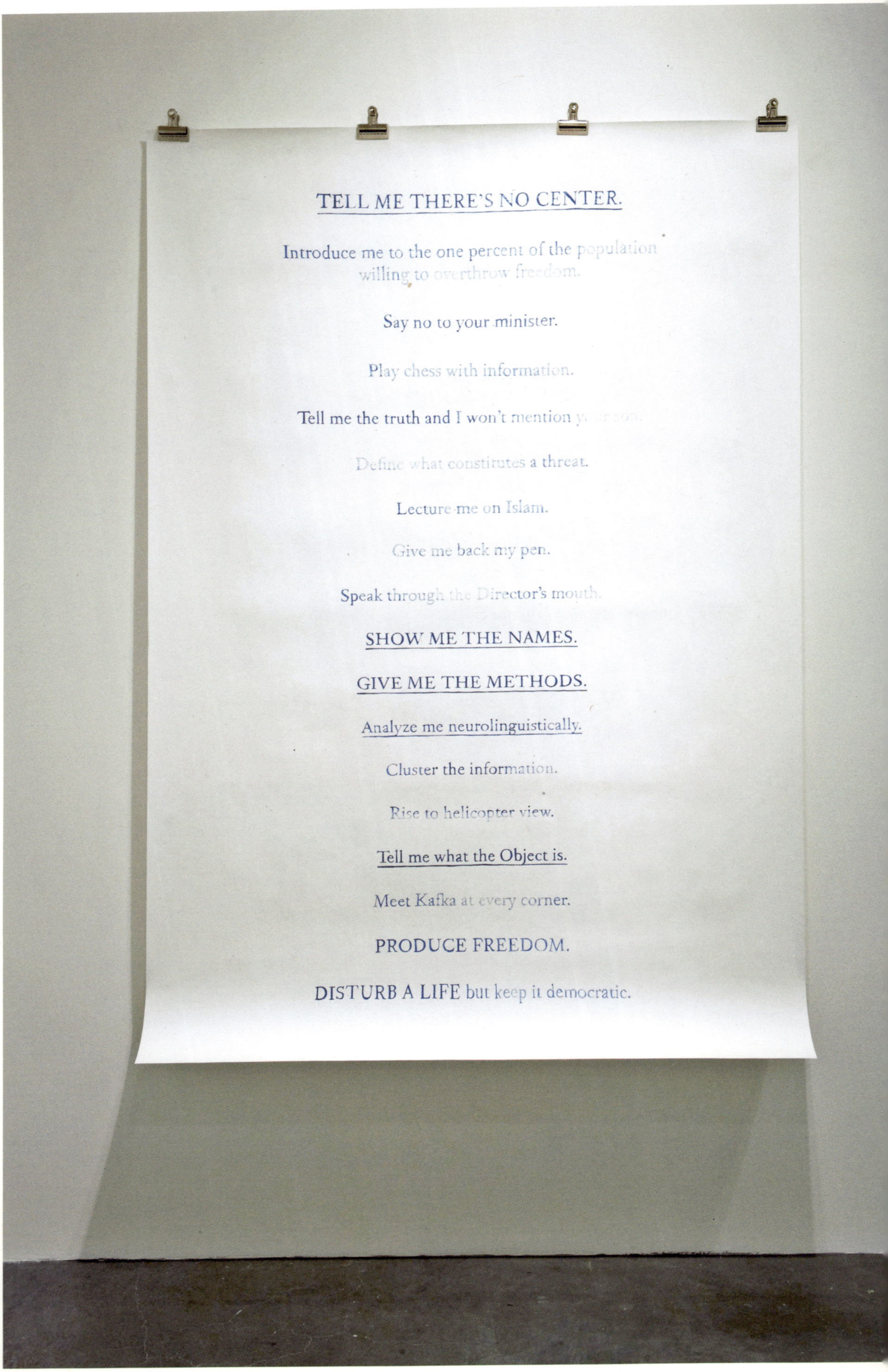

TELL ME THERE'S NO CENTER.

Introduce me to the one percent of the population
willing to overthrow freedom.

Say no to your minister.

Play chess with information.

Tell me the truth and I won't mention your son.

Define what constitutes a threat.

Lecture me on Islam.

Give me back my pen.

Speak through the Director's mouth.

SHOW ME THE NAMES.

GIVE ME THE METHODS.

Analyze me neurolinguistically.

Cluster the information.

Rise to helicopter view.

Tell me what the Object is.

Meet Kafka at every corner.

PRODUCE FREEDOM.

DISTURB A LIFE but keep it democratic.

*page 354–356*

***The Directives***, page 2 + page 3 + page 6, 2009, ball point pen on paper, Installation image from exhibition *Authority to Remove*, September 10, 2009–January 3, 2010 at Tate Modern, London; all images: photo credit Tate photography, copyright Jill Magid, courtesy of the artist and Yvon Lambert, Paris, New York

The cornerstone of Jonas Staal's prominent, complicated position in the Dutch art scene is a series of informal memorials that the artist installed over the course of a few nights throughout Rotterdam and The Hague. In a wry, fearless inversion of monumental conventions, these commemorated, with the common instruments of popular piety, the sadly departed politician Geert Wilders. Geert Wilders—alive, well, and vociferous—is the leader of the Freedom Party, self-anointed inheritor of Pim Fortuyn's legacy, and famous for pronouncements such as: "If Muslims wish to stay in The Netherlands, they have to tear out half of the Koran and throw it away" (an injunction which Staal dutifully carried out in another performance). Following the reactions of baffled passersby and the rumors the memorials triggered, Wilders took legal action against the artist and lost, while the trial was treated with all the ritual gestures of an exhibition opening. A few other works, most of which approximate the difficult contours of a contemporary monument, consolidated the artist's radical stance, immersed in the particular condition of Dutch politics. For example, when the Livable Rotterdam party reacted violently to a municipal initiative to build a monument to the guest workers that helped restore The Netherlands after the Second World War, and claimed that if a monument was due, then it should function as compensation to the real Rotterdamers who have been expropriated of their city by immigration, Jonas Staal proposed to this political party a vaguely Stalinist, muscular, and excessive image of a "real Rotterdam" family fleeing in horror a city that is no longer theirs. It "materialized" the description proffered, in full rhetorical exercise, by party leader Ronald Sørensen, and it was enthusiastically embraced.

Jonas Staal's take on the intellectual and political possibility of a new monumentality accretes in more subdued forms, but which are no less contentious in their capacity to invoke institutional critique precepts and to inquire whether these mutate into a devious discourse of "post-propaganda," whereby art becomes a collective, spectral recreation area, encouraged by governments precisely because it fuels their projections of pluralist tolerance.

# Jonas Staal

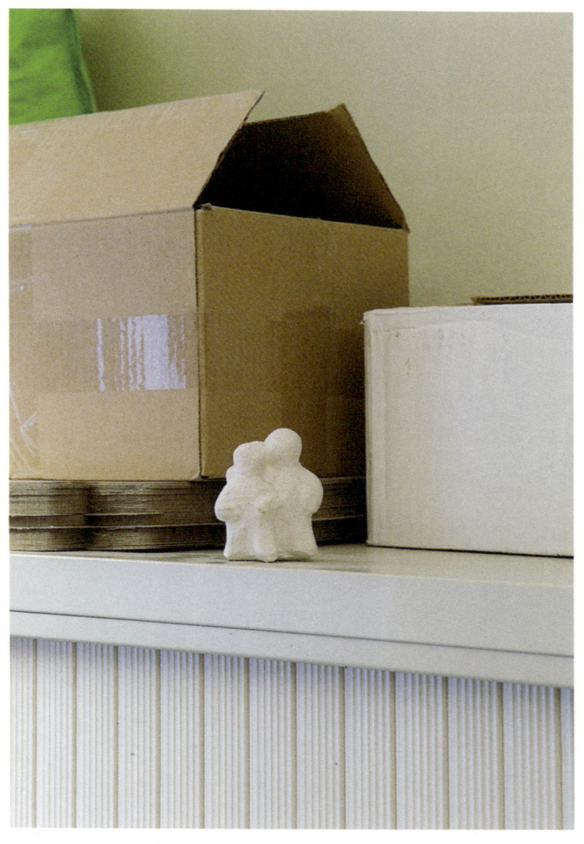

**■**

***Art, Property of Politics,*** Work from: Christian Democratic Appeal (CDA) Collection, title unknown, artist unknown, Date unknown (photo by Lotte Stekelenburg)

Clay statue bought by a party representative during a vacation in Turkey. The statue represents the importance of family values, the core business of the CDA party. The two figures, both with their head tilted upwards, seem to stare into a yet unknown future in which their bond, and their bond with God, will be their main certainty and comfort.

*Against Irony*, in collaboration with writer Vincent van Gerven Oei, is a series of four stones engraved with a counter-manifesto: a denunciation of—and a tombstone for—irony. Staal's preference for a mode of engagement that pursues the ultimate, most troubling and impure consequences of its own embeddedness, resurfaces in *Art, Property of Politics*, in which the artist curates works from the collections of seven Dutch political parties. This reverses the classic institutional critique scenario, and engages the complicity between art and politics at the other end, by treating the political party as an art institution. The investigation inquires into the correspondences between the art collected and the ideological self-perception of the collector, and asks how this art will figure against the unfolding of our political future.

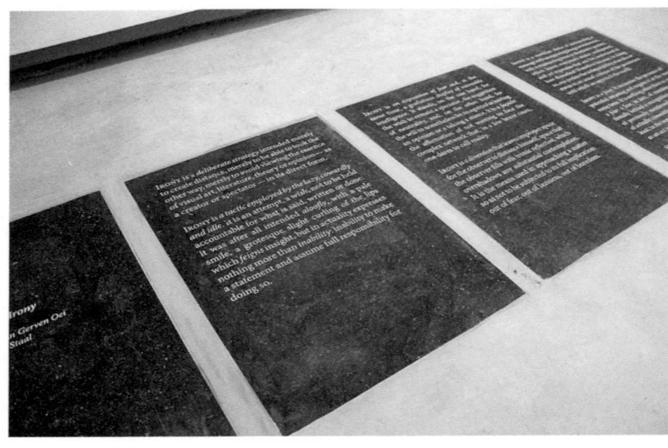


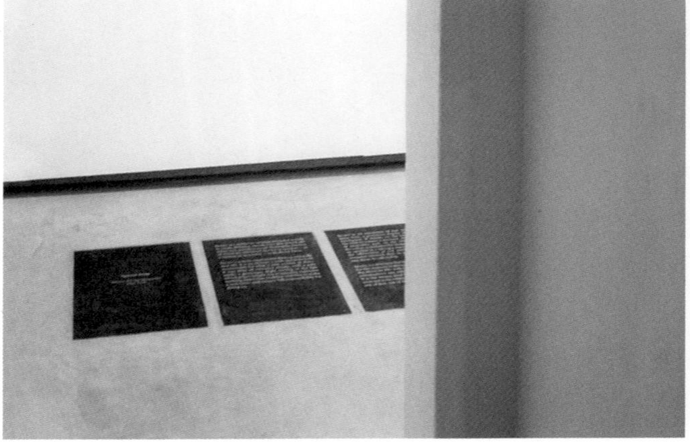

**Against Irony**, Jonas Staal and Vincent van Gerven Oei, 2008, engraved stones, on permanent loan to Stroom, The Hague

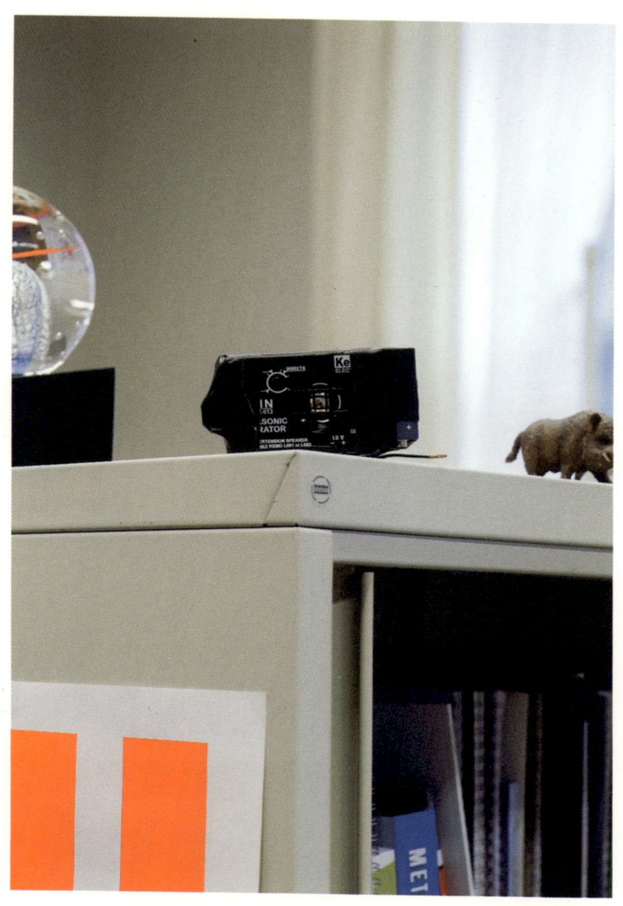

■

***Art, Property of Politics,*** Work from: Socialist Party (SP) Collection, Two Minutes of Silence for the Mosquito, Theo Coşkun and Kevin Levie, 2009 (photo by Lotte Stekelenburg)

The so-called "Mosquito" is a device that produces a high-frequency sound that can only be heard by those below the age of twenty-five. The device is used to clear streets of so-called "hanging youth" in problematic urban areas. The Socialist Party is against the use of this machine, and produced a Mosquito themselves that makes the same sound hearable for adults. During a gathering of the city council, SP-party leader Theo Coşkun asked for "Two minutes of silence for the Mosquito" and had the machine make its disturbing noise through his microphone, while stating his views against the use of the device. He could therefore not be heard by the audience.

*Art, Property of Politics,* Work from: Green Party (GroenLinks) Collection, Freedom, Nelis Oosterwijk, 2004, Edition 4/20, (photo by Lotte Stekelenburg)

This print was bought by party leader Anneke Verwijs during an auction in support of the Palestine struggle. The artist Oosterhuis was also active as a Green Party representative and was the founder of the Palestine Committee that organized the auction. The print shows a seemingly victimized boy and the release of the famous swallow, known as the logo of the Swedish Uddevalla Tändsticksfabrik. After having been "trapped" on the matchbox since 1874, the swallow sets its own course for the first time, thereby being a metaphor for the suppression of the Palestine people and the necessity of their liberation.

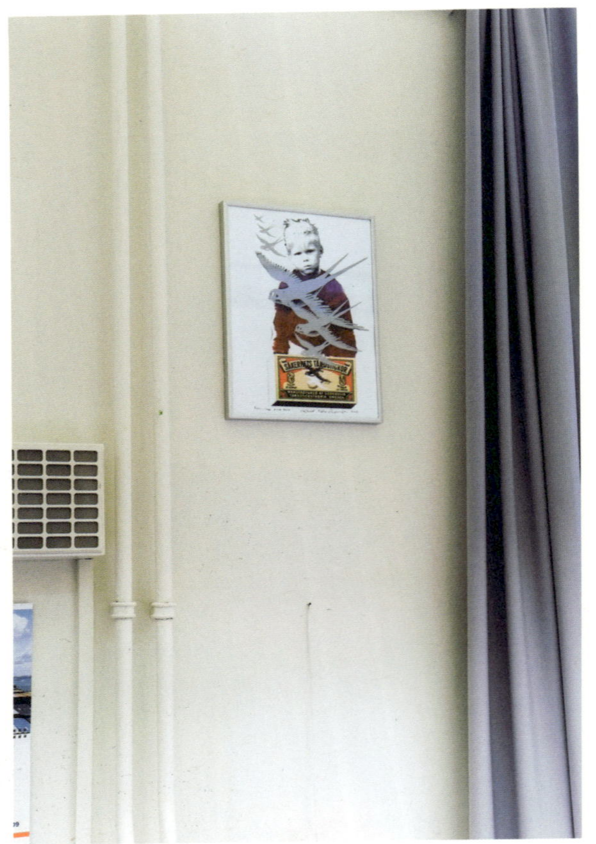

*Art, Property of Politics,* Work from: Labor Party (PvdA) Collection, Untitled, Arcadis Heidemij, Date unknown, (photo by Lotte Stekelenburg)

This sculpture was handed out to party representatives during a visit to a company that designs a new type of asphalt, more endurable under very high or low temperatures. Asphalt has an important symbolic meaning for the PvdA as it connotes providing jobs and freedom of movement for the working class. The most prominent Dutch socialist leader, Joop den Uyl, became famous and heavily criticized for his proposal to partly destroy the ring of canals in Amsterdam, to replace them with asphalt so to create more parking spots and roads in the city.

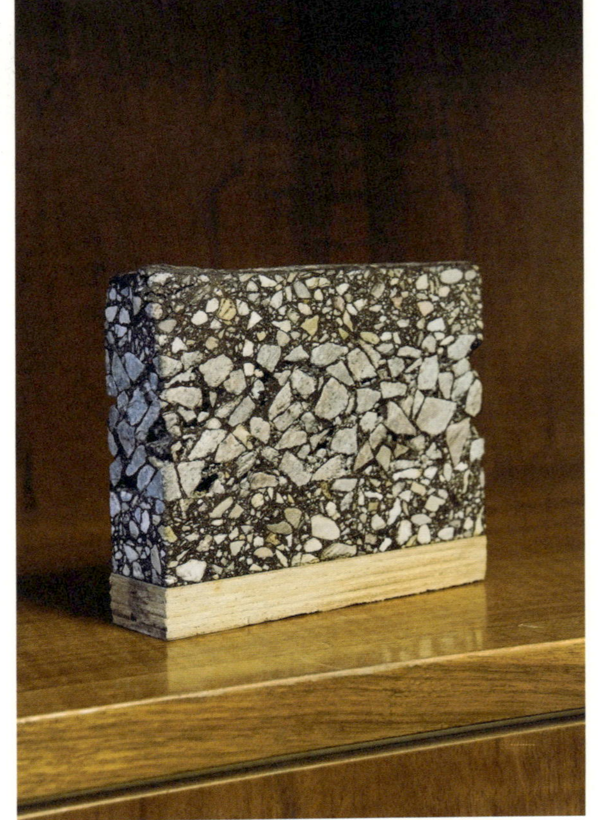

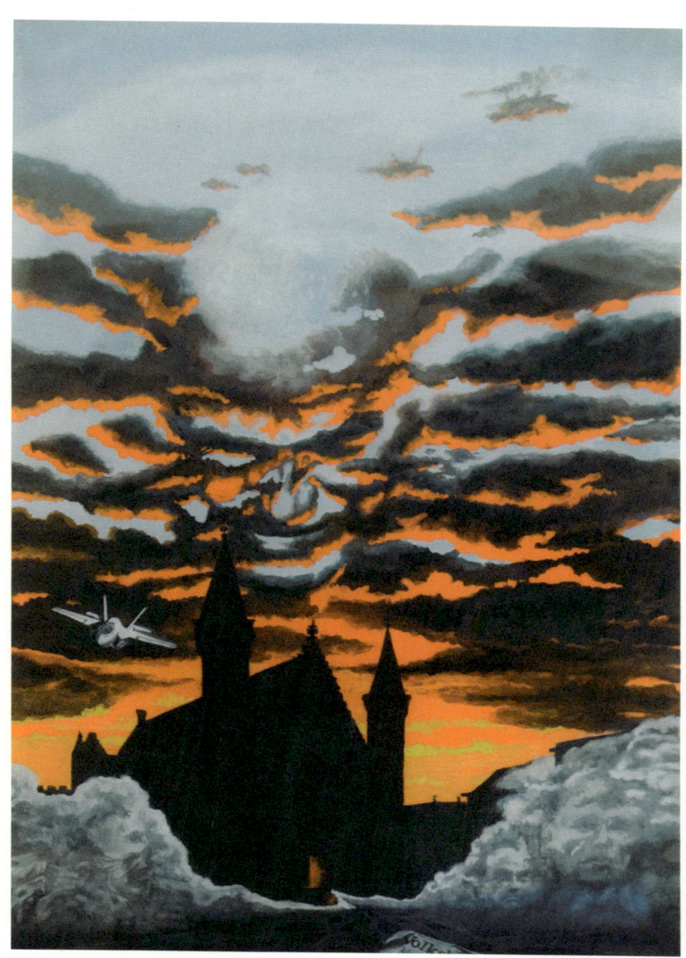

■

***Art, Property of Politics,*** Work from: Leefbaar Rotterdam Collection, 12,000,000,000, Ysher, 2003, Edition 2/10, (photo by Lotte Stekelenburg)

This print was realized by a supporter of the right-wing populist party Leefbaar Rotterdam, previously lead by politician Pim Fortuyn, who was murdered by an animal rights activist in 2002. The print shows the "Binnenhof": the political center of The Netherlands in The Hague. In the clouds above the main building the face of Fortuyn is recognizable, while apocalyptically looking down on a group of figures that appear in the mist beneath him, among which are his political opponents and murderer. The plane that flies beneath him is the Joint Strike Fighter (JSF): a new American fighting plane model that Fortuyn was against purchasing. Yet after his death his party agreed to the acquisition. This cost the government 12,000,000,000 Euro, which explains the title of this piece.

The installations of Alon Levin function often as abstract panoramas, as "history made visible" in the absence of protagonists and extras. The constructions recall or embody an archetypal disaccord at the core of history, the rattle of ideological machines, the very mutability of Order, negotiated between the unfolding of Progress, the liberating potential of the obsolete, and the entities that try to impersonate transcendence in the collective imaginary of the last centuries, and that fill out its structural place. The installations archive traces, echoes, part-objects, object-worlds, flags and insignia of identity, ruins and the promises of the new, chaos vanquished or chaos formalized, collapse and recalibration.

In works such as the series *The Fake, the Future and the Finite*, the artist prodigiously compresses and structures the suggestions of "everything"—ideas of organization, measurement and the immeasurable—into a view of how time passes through cultural constructs, and infiltrates, disrupts, and refashions the very discursive armature that was designed to insulate these against time. From a standpoint outside the totalizing ambitions of each new technological regime, and yet enmeshed in history, Levin observes the oscillation between vulnerability and ambition, acceleration and deferral of an ideal order—dominating, powerless, strenuous, never admitting to be the temporary armistice of orders—that traverses European culture. He refers to the ensemble of these processes as postponed Modernism: Modernism as perpetually unfulfilled promise, as geometry of destruction, visualized via abstruse calculations and permutations that thematize structure and disintegration.

# Alon Levin

***The Fake, the Future and the Finite (a Commemoration of the Absolute in the 21st Century) Part 2: Spiral, Tower, Donkey, Carrot,*** 2007, Installation view at de Appel, *Prix de Rome*, Amsterdam, NL

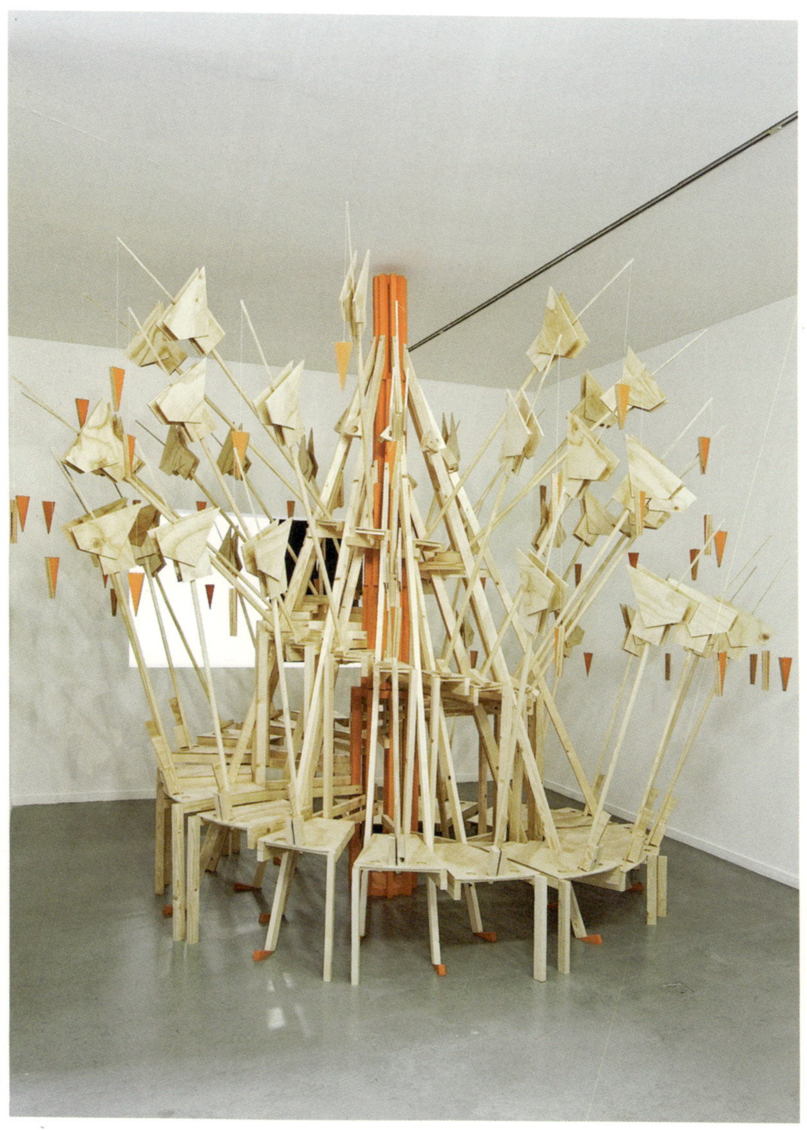

*A History of Economic Thought or the Execution of Progress* could be said to monumentalize error, or surplus, or the relationship thereof, like a disparity at the very heart of economic advancement. In imaginary tandem with Vladimir Tatlin's *Monument to the Third International*, the work could be said to perform the upward thrust of economic utopia, a drive that propagates its own scale and re charts the world in its own, improper system. The world must adapt—the gallery must be rebuilt, again and again, around a work that specifies its site by piercing, in its modular growth, the ceiling of the exhibition space. *A History of Economic Thought or the Execution of Progress* appears thus as structural disproportion, as a built celebration of its own logic. Its destructive escalation and permanent instability allow for a pairing with the disastrous circularity of the financial metaphor, its self-reproduction in a purely metaphoric territory, which has painfully entered public consciousness at the time of the recent economic crisis.

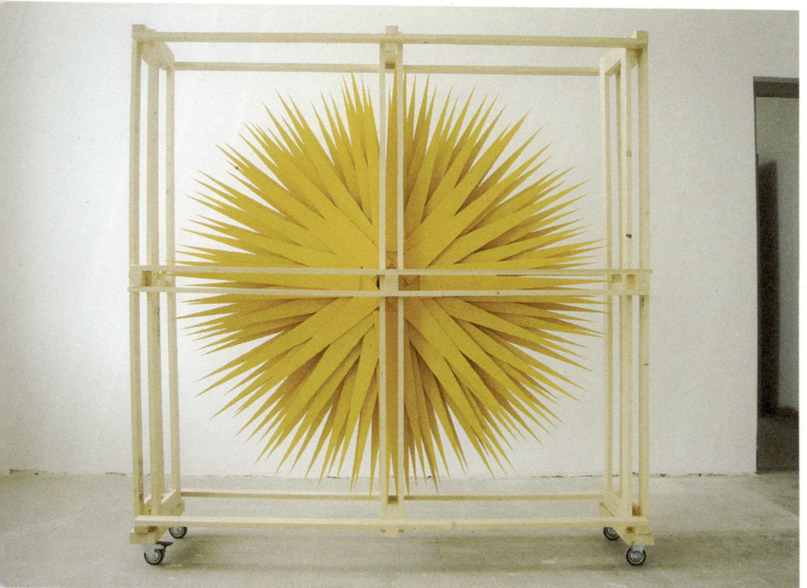

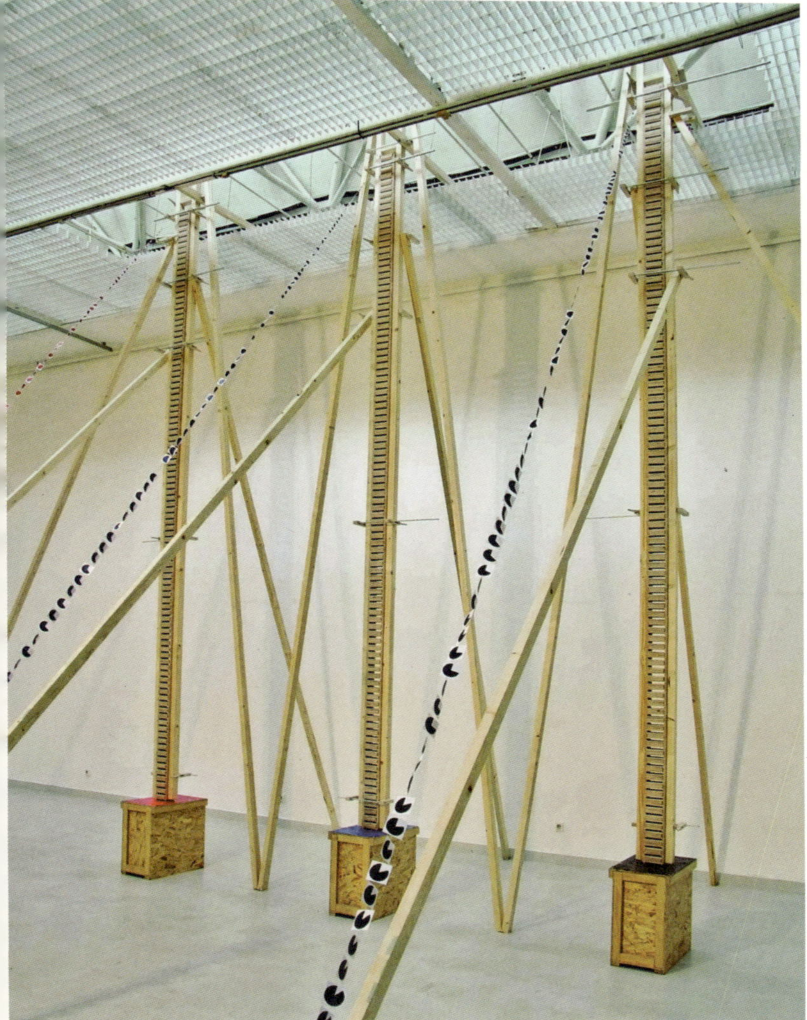

***The Fake, the Future and the Finite (a Commemoration of the Absolute in the 21st Century) Part 1: Sun, Rainbow, Arch (reinvented),*** 2007, Installation view at Smart Project Space, *The Stability of Truth*, Amsterdam

***A History of Economic Thought or the Execution of Progress,*** 2005/2008, Installation view from the exhibition *Shifting Identities—(Swiss) Art Now*, CAC Vilnius

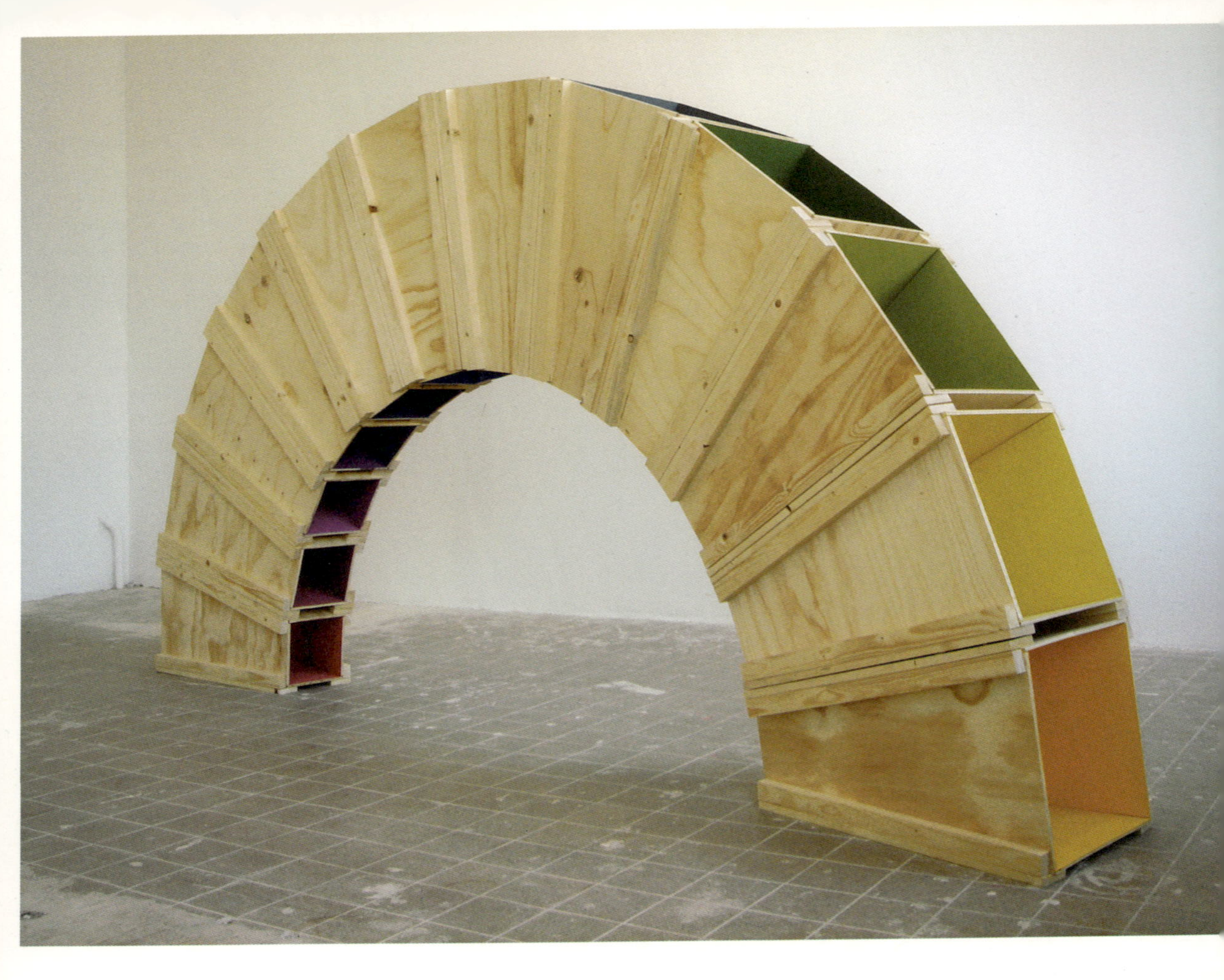

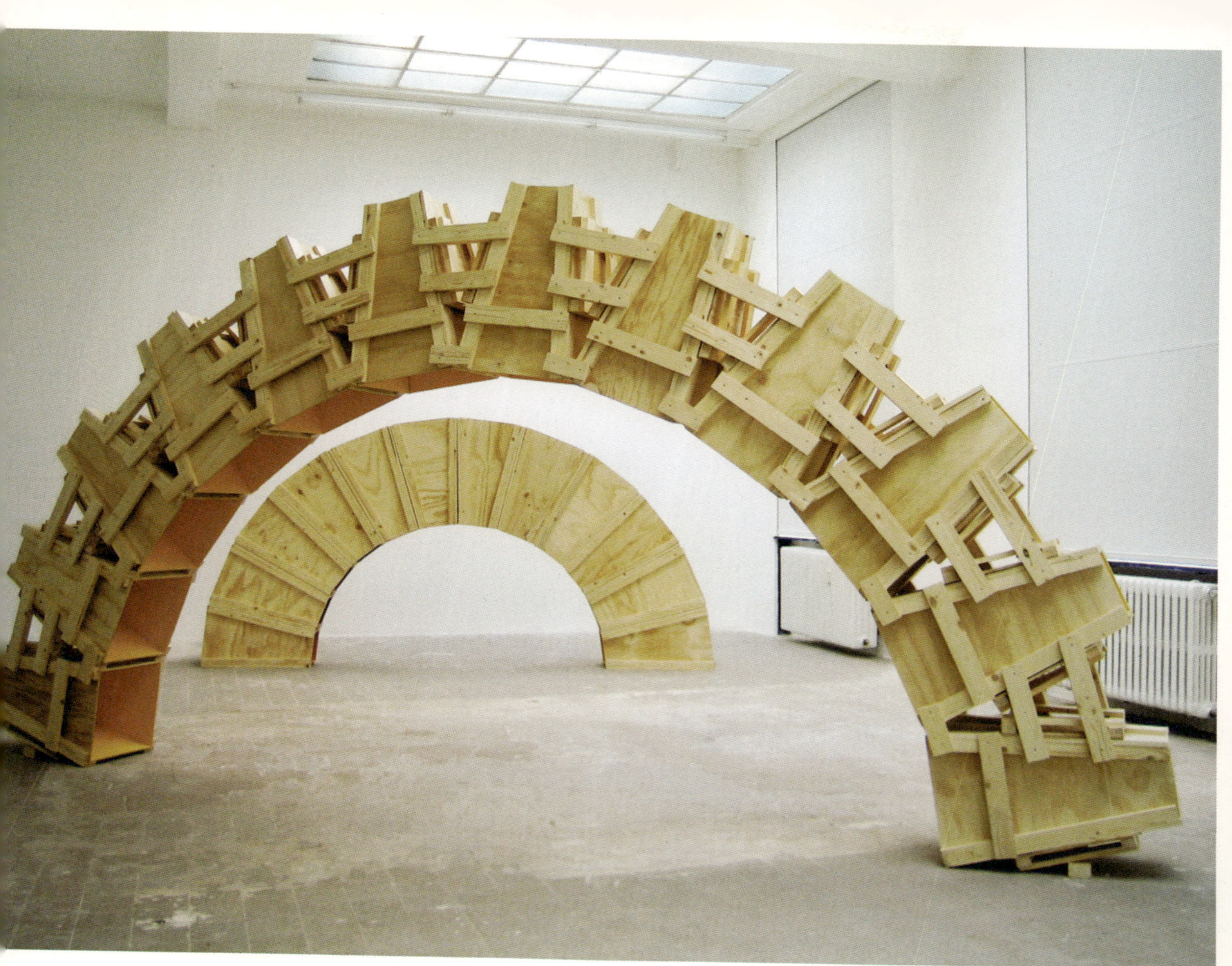

***The Fake, the Future and the Finite (a Commemoration of the Absolute in the 21st Century) Part 1: Sun, Rainbow, Arch (reinvented),*** 2007, installation view from the exhibition *The Stability of Truth*, Smart Project Space, Amsterdam

*Offer & Exchange: Sites of Negotiation in Contemporary Art*, commissioned by Electra (London), is a series of site-specific commissions using legal contracts as artistic frameworks. The curators Daniel McClean and Lisa Rosendahl conceive the commissions in relation to a typology of sites where art is exhibited, publicized, sold, or collected—sites of mediation understood to be equipped with specific constraints that vie with the work's own conditions for becoming work and becoming visible. The contracts created through processes of negotiation between the artists and curators at each site tease out tacit and conflicting assumptions: the relations that constitute the art world are translated into legal language and negotiated between various value-producing entities.

Stefan Brüggemann's SHIFT, for instance, made for the Frieze Art Fair, is an exchange of the authorship function between Stefan Brüggemann and Robert Barry, whereby two works transfer attribution every five years. As opposed to the more hazy operations of relational aesthetics, the undefined and politically agnostic forms of togetherness these proffer, *Offer & Exchange* seems to insist on the clarity of relations afforded by legal terms.

# Offer & Exchange

*SHIFT*, Stefan Brüggemann, 2009, contract between Robert Barry and Stefan Brüggemann

**Shift 1 (2009)**

**Medium: Acrylic, enamel and graphite on prepared paper**
**Dimensions: 67.6 x 101.6 cm**

**Certificate of Authenticity**

This document certifies that Shift 1 as described above is an original artwork defined by the rules of authorship agreed between Robert Barry and Stefan Brüggemann (the 'Artists') and contained herein. The Artists agree that:

1. Authorship of Shift 1 is currently attributed to Robert Barry, but that authorship of Shift 1 will transfer automatically from Robert Barry to Stefan Brüggemann at the end of a period of five years from 15 October 2009 (the 'First Transfer').

2. Authorship of Shift 1 will transfer automatically back from Robert Barry to Stefan Brüggemann at the end of a further period of five years from the date of the First Transfer ('the Second Transfer').

3. Authorship of Shift 1 will transfer alternately between the Artists in five-year intervals in accordance with the rules contained in clauses 1 and 2 above: this process being continued indefinitely so long as Shift 1 exists.

4. Shift 1 must always be exhibited and sold in accordance with the rules set out above and that authorship of Shift 1 must always be attributed to the Artist to whom authorship has been transferred at that time.

5. This certificate must always be attached to the back of the frame containing Shift 1 including when the artwork is transferred and sold.

Robert Barry...R. BARRY...

Date 15 SEPT 2009

Stefan Brüggemann... Brüggemann

Date..15/SEPT/2009

Another commission consists of an exchange between artist Santiago Sierra and Hiscox Insurers and Art Collection: the exchange of a sculpture and a life-insurance contract. *DEATH COUNTER*, by Santiago Sierra, was installed between January 1, 2009 and January 1, 2010 on the façade of the London headquarters of Hiscox Insurers. The LED sign registered the annual number of human deaths worldwide, currently estimated by the United States Census International Data Base at approximately fifty-five million deaths per year, at a resulting rate of nearly two deaths per second. The sculpture was loaned to Hiscox in exchange for an insurance policy of 150,000 Euros, payable in the event of the artist's death and valid for the duration of the one-year exhibition. *DEATH COUNTER* exists not simply as a sculpture, but also as a legally binding contract between Hiscox and the artist. It explores the transiency of life and capital, the mutual consolidation of value and risk. As is the case with most projects by Santiago Sierra, a tortuous equation is drawn between forms of social obliteration and their valorization when transcribed into images within the confines of the art world. Here, the value of the insurance policy has been set in relation to the value of the artwork. *DEATH COUNTER* places two systems of value speculation in relation to each other, and dramatizes the equivalence between "work" and "worth" by placing precise economical transactions, and their partially muted emotional resonance, in a visual context.

***DEATH COUNTER***, Santiago Sierra, 2009, LED counter

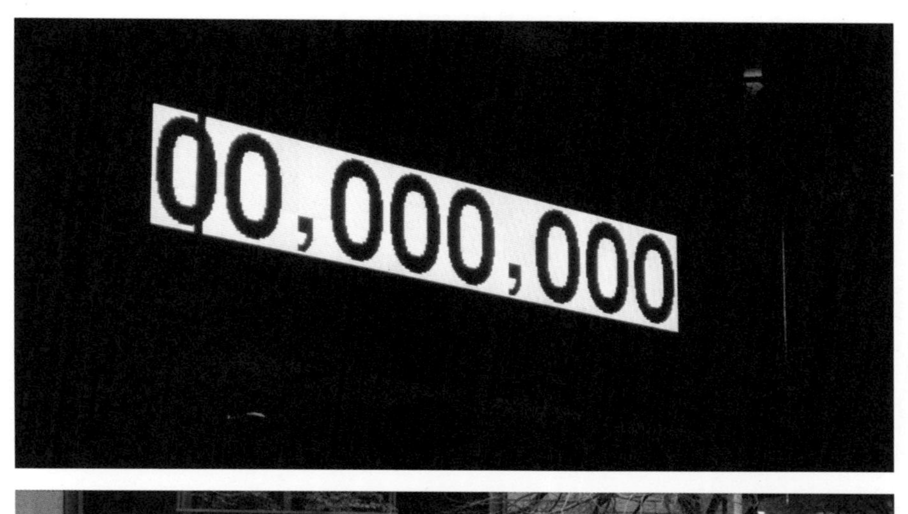


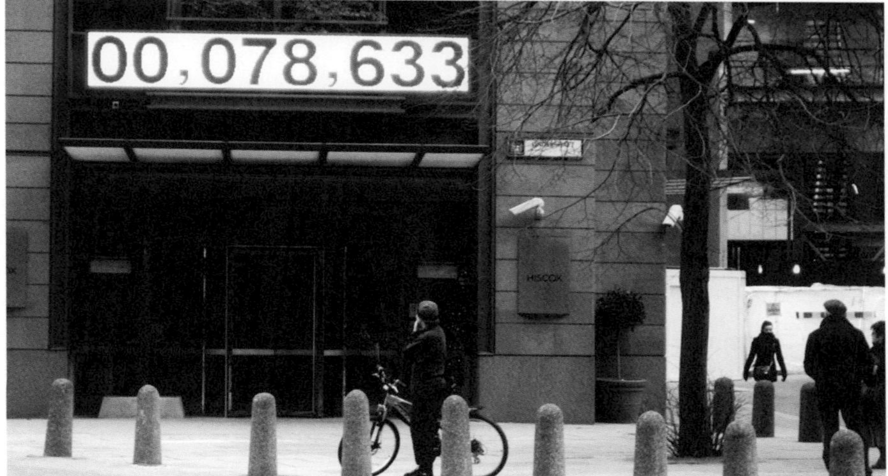


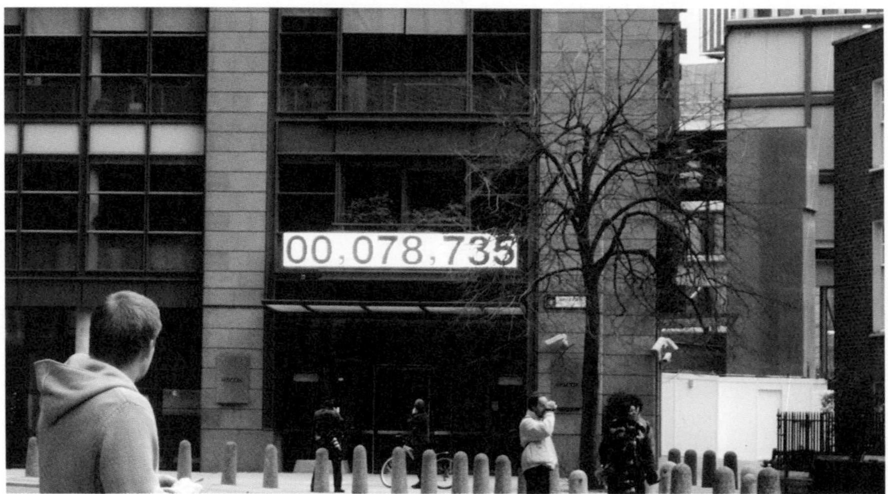

**SCHEDULE**

**Policy Number:**

**Insured:** Santiago SIERRA

**Insured person(s):** Santiago SIERRA

**Address for correspondence:**

SANTIAGO SIERRA
VIA SANTA GIUSTINA 29
55100 LUCCA
ITALY

**Telephone No:** Not applicable

**Facsimile No:** Not applicable

**Period of insurance:**

**From:** 00.00 GMT 1st January 2009

**To:** 00.00 GMT 1st January 2010

| **Benefits:** | **Amount Insured** | **Beneficiary** |
| --- | --- | --- |
| Accidental Death only: | EUR 150,000 | LUCIA SIERRA DAVID |

Hiscox
1 Great St Helen's
London EC3A 6HX

T +44 (0)20 7448 6000
F +44 (0)20 7448 6900
E enquiry@hiscox.com
www.hiscox.com

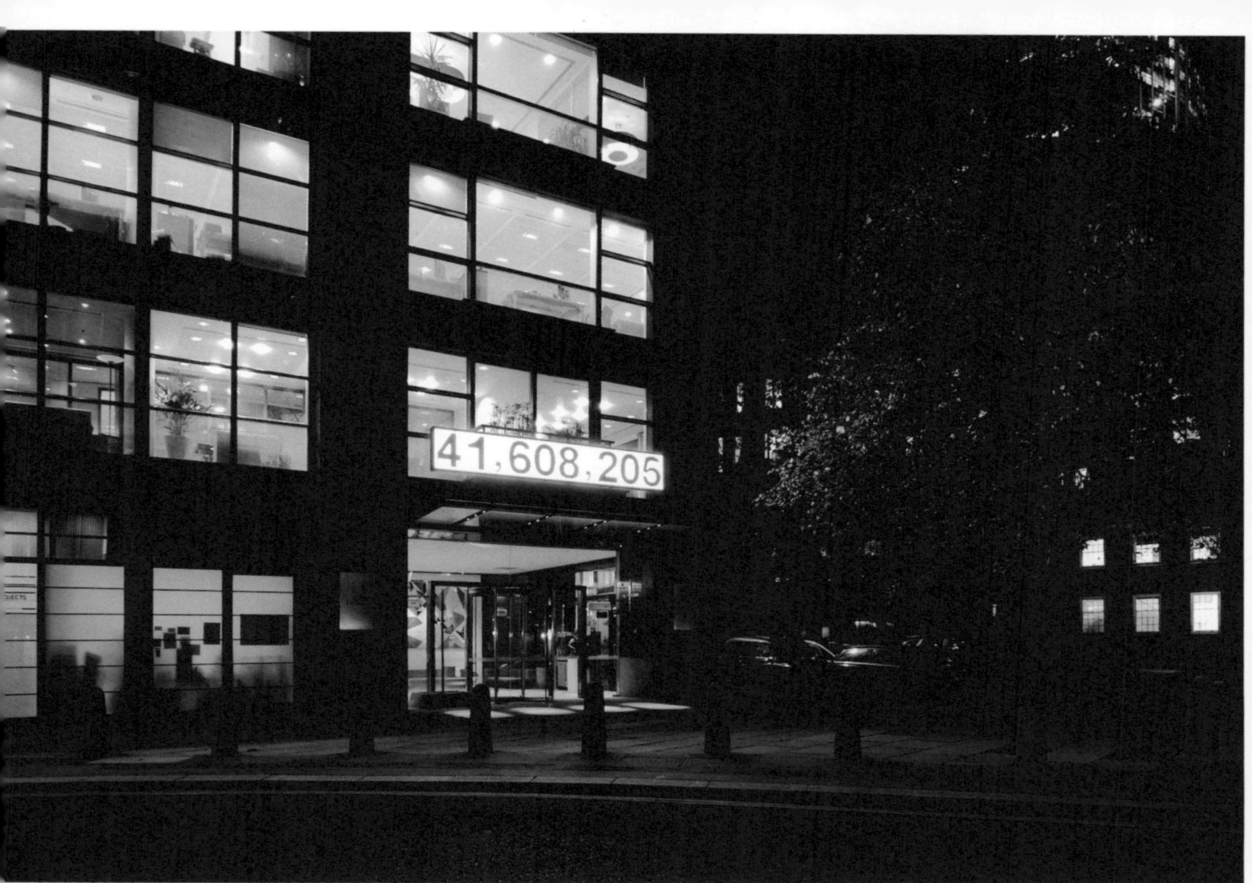


■□
***DEATH COUNTER***, Santiago Sierra, 2009, LED counter, contract between Santiago Sierra and Hiscox Insurers

□■
***DEATH COUNTER***, Santiago Sierra, 2009, LED counter, installation, Photos: Santiago Sierra/Thierry Bal, courtesy of the artist and Electra

# Cittadellarte–Fondazione Pistoletto

Cittadellarte was established in 1998 as the concrete implementation of the *Progetto Arte Manifesto* ("Art Project Manifesto"), through which Michelangelo Pistoletto proposes a new role for the artist, as activator of dynamics, projects, and creative ideas to stimulate responsible change in the various areas of society. Cittadellarte is a new form of artistic and cultural institution that places art in direct interaction with the various sectors of society. A place for the convergence of creative ideas and projects that combine creativity and enterprise, education and production, ecology and architecture, politics and spirituality. An organism aimed at producing civilization, activating a responsible social transformation necessary and urgent at a local and global level. The fundamental theme of Cittadellarte's activities is the relationship between the freedom of art and the ethics of social responsibility. Cittadellarte is indeed structured into thematic offices—operation centers called *Uffizi*, each dedicated to developing research and experimental practises with the prospect of relating artistic creativity with the shared construction of the "common good." Cittadellarte is a socially non-profit organization, chartered in 1998 and endorsed by the Region of Piedmont. Cittadellarte is located in Biella, in a former (nineteenth-century) wool mill, an historic building complex registered with the Italian Ministry of Cultural.

**Michelangelo Pistoletto**
**The *Progetto Arte Manifesto*, 1994**

*Progetto Arte* is based on the idea that art is the most sensitive and complete expression of human thought, and that the time has come for artists to take on the responsibility of establishing ties among all other human activities— from economics to politics, science to religion, education to behavior—in a word, among the threads that make up the fabric of society. A basic tenet of the project is the conviction that a civilization can no longer be understood in terms of clearly defined territories, an that an outlook that will stimulate the expression of a "global civilization" is necessary. One motto, in this sense, might be: "Eliminate distances while preserving differences." On this foundation, a workshop will be constructed with the intent of forming a "hot core" of energy that will radiate on a broad scale, and not just in a limited field—in other words, to gather together those creative urges that seek to unite the innumerable potentials that exist unexpressed, and to create, as a consequence, the channels of interaction that will form the spherical framework of human society on the planet. *Progetto Arte* is the visible sign of a possible principle—that of the joining of opposites—which can be applied to all social contexts, in terms both ideal and practical. Past and future are two opposites that join in the present. Consequently, to plan the future, one must look contemporaneously to the past. The project assigns a fundamental role to the encounter between art and architecture, in the belief that artist and architect acted as one person in imagining and formulating the great civilizations of the past, and that their action was made possible by a sense of commitment on the part of those invested with public power, with whom they engaged in the pursuit of common goals. Today, global power is managed by the so-called economic system—a system in which there is no place for thought offered free of charge and hence no room for the "opposite" of the rule of profit. It follows that there cannot be an initiative that proposes to formulate a complete configuration of civilization. Nevertheless, one cannot help but acknowledge that the economic system, which is responsible for creating and maintaining world imbalance, is the principal interlocutor of the artist-architect, and that the new course must lead to a reestablishment of the ancient connection between art and power. Another motto of *Progetto Arte* might be: "The artist as a sponsor of thought"—it expresses the intention to effect an exchange of roles, as well as a reversal of the traditional conception of remuneration. Due account must be taken also of the fact that the principles which define and divide religions probably contain the most potent seeds of the aesthetic and moral conflict. The harshness of dogmatic methods no longer corresponds to today's interpretative needs, which must reconcile the particular differences of cultures with the idea of universal concepts. Hence, I distrust all those positions that define their own view as the only positive one, perpetrating the primitive notion by which the negative sign is assigned to a frontal enemy who must be combated. In the history of great civilizations, the temples, too, were designed by artist and architects acting in syntony with mythical and religious thought. Hence, art must again take on the responsibility of establishing a spiritual connection between past and future—tempered by the awareness that the "churches" are also, anachronistically, the cause of a disastrous social imbalance; that they continue to provide the economic system with the support of the ancient cult of sacrifice; and that this cult is an inevitable accomplice of the modern machinery of war, which is profitable to the highest degree. Another slogan of *Progetto Arte* might be: "Love differences"—which means, to avoid thinking not of rigid rules of uniformity and equality, but instead to think of the extensive articulation of differences. Indeed, the project is not a preestablished and formalized design; it is a free, dynamic, fluid, supple sign that fits between the old trenches to form a capillary connection in the flesh of a new, complex, self-designing body.

# Continuing to Think That There Is a "Who"

by Anna Zegna, president of the Fondazione Zegna, and Andrea Zegna, head of the Fondazione Zegna's Art Projects

Long before Fondazione Zegna was set up in 2000, it was our grandfather Ermenegildo Zegna who taught us by his example that it is necessary to "take care"—not just of the quality of the fabric that comes out of the factory, but also of the quality of life of the surrounding community. Grandpa Gildo built many welfare and recreation buildings, and naturalistic and environmental works, such as the Panoramica, and he transformed the bare slopes of Monte Rubello into a green oasis by planting over half a million conifers, rhododendrons, and hydrangeas. In Jean Giono's *The Man Who Planted Trees*, the shepherd who manages to create a wood where previously there had been just a desert approaches his work with the very greatest care: he spends hours every evening checking that the hundred acorns he puts aside for planting are always absolutely perfect. He is convinced that it is important to act concretely, personally, and to do everything possible to work well.
This has also become the philosophy of the Zegna Foundation, which has decided to work in the social sphere and in that of scientific research, and of the environment and culture, both in its own territory (via the organizations FAI and Oceana) and in developing lands (via Amref in Africa, Care and Share in India, and WWF in China). It is both a family and an entrepreneurial vision—not a strategic decision—and it is based on the conviction that it is the responsibility of us all to build positively for the future.

Ethics and aesthetics are not two conflicting worlds; on the contrary, we believe it is important to establish a new dialectic between them. With its in-depth, polyphonic considerations in diverse cultures and geographical areas, the *visible* project works on a range of artistic actions that face reality outside of the protective context of art institutions. It is the most recent chapter in the decade-long journey of Fondazione Zegna. It is period in which we have often worked with Cittadellarte, ever since the Green Mind award, through to the UNIDEE campus and the creation of a work like *Woollen—La Mela reintegrata*, which symbolizes reconciliation between nature and artifice: a new possible equilibrium between human beings, the world of manufacturing, and the environment. It is what Michelangelo Pistoletto has referred to as the "Third Paradise."

In 2008, the Foundation also started up ALL'APERTO, a "public art" project curated by Andrea and Barbara Casavecchia, in which the artists Daniel Buren and Alberto Garutti were commissioned to make site-specific works for the Trivero area and for its inhabitants. In these operations, art helps us look with different eyes at what may even be a familiar place. Buren turned the roof of a factory into a green-and-blue rainbow of flags, celebrating the wind and the changing of the seasons. With the help of parents and children from elementary schools, Garutti made a singular "map" of the local territory. He placed realistic sculptures of dogs on a dozen concrete benches in various parts of the town, with captions that read: "The dog represented here belongs to one of the families in Trivero. This work is dedicated to them and to the people who talk about them as they sit here."

In his essay "The Ethics of Quality," which forms the introduction to the book we have published to celebrate the centenary of Ermenegildo Zegna Group, James Hillman writes: "When we look more closely into the word 'quality,' we discover that its Latin root *quales*, 'of what kind,' derives from a base, *qui*, *quis*, meaning 'who.' To ask for the specific whichness or whatness of any person or thing, to determine its specific essential quality, searches out the 'who.'" We believe the most important challenge is precisely this: continuing to think that there is a "who"—a person—an individual or collective recipient behind every project.